THE GREAT
BRITISH
RECORDING
STUDIOS

THE GREAT BRITISH RECORDING STUDIOS

HOWARD MASSEY

Hal Leonard Books
An Imprint of Hal Leonard Corporation

Published in 2015 by Hal Leonard Books
An Imprint of Hal Leonard Corporation
7777 West Bluemound Road
Milwaukee, WI 53213

Trade Book Division Editorial Offices
33 Plymouth St., Montclair, NJ 07042

Quotations from *Please Please Me* by Gordon Thompson (2008) used by permission of Oxford University Press, USA. http://www.oup.com.

Quotations from *Studio Sound* used by permission of New Bay Media.

Quotations from *MIX* magazine and *Sound on Sound* magazine used by permission of those publications.

While every reasonable effort has been made to contact copyright holders and secure permission for all materials reproduced in this work, we offer apologies for any instances in which this was not possible and for any inadvertent omissions.

Printed in the United States of America

Book design by John J. Flannery

Illustrations by James Husted are on pages 27, 45 (bottom), 46 (bottom), 53, 62, 65, 75, 90 (both), 109, 110, 121, 153, 199 (all), 200 (bottom), and 240.

Additional illustrations by Josh McKible are on pages 18 (all), 22, and 34.

Library of Congress Cataloging-in-Publication Data

Massey, Howard, author.
The great British recording studios / Howard Massey.
   pages cm
Includes bibliographical references and index.
ISBN 978-1-4584-2197-5
1. Sound studios–Great Britain–History–20th century. 2. Sound–Recording and reproducing–Great Britain–History–20th century. 3. Sound recordings–Production and direction--Great Britain--History–20th century. 4. Sound recording industry–Great Britain–History–20th century. 5. Popular music–Great Britain–1961-1970–History and criticism. I. Title.
ML3790.M3525 2015
781.490941'09046–dc23
                                              2015029972
www.halleonardbooks.com

Dedicated to Keith Grant
1941–2012

CONTENTS

Foreword by Sir George Martin • ix

Preface • xi

Acknowledgments • xiii

Introduction: The British Sound • 1

Chapter 1: Abbey Road (EMI Studios) • 15

Chapter 2: The Big Three • 41
   Decca • 41
   Philips • 69
   Pye • 75

Chapter 3: The Early Independents • 87
   IBC • 88
   Lansdowne • 99
   Advision • 107
   CTS / The Music Centre • 118

Chapter 4: 304 Holloway Road • 133

Chapter 5: Olympic • 149

Chapter 6: Trident • 177

Chapter 7: AIR • 195

Chapter 8: Other Important Studios of the Era • 221
   Levy's / CBS / Whitfield Street • 221
   Star Sound / Audio International • 226
   De Lane Lea / Kingsway • 230
   Ryemuse/Mayfair • 236
   Marquee • 238
   Sound Techniques • 241
   Wessex • 245
   Morgan • 248
   Chappell • 251
   Chalk Farm • 254
   Apple • 256

Island / Basing Street • 261
Pathway • 266
The Manor • 268
Scorpio Sound • 272
Chipping Norton • 275
Ramport • 277
Sarm • 278
Sawmills • 280
Roundhouse • 282
RAK • 285
Utopia • 289
Good Earth • 290
Matrix • 292
Townhouse • 294
Ridge Farm • 298
Odyssey • 300

Chapter 9: Mobiles • 303
The Rolling Stones Mobile • 307
The Pye Mobile • 314
Ronnie Lane Mobile • 316
The Manor Mobiles • 318
The Island Mobile • 322
The RAK Mobile • 325
Maison Rouge Mobile • 327

Glossary • 329

Bibliography • 339

Index • 341

FOREWORD

Sir George Martin. *(Photo by Robert Essel, courtesy C A Management)*

AFTER THE SECOND WORLD WAR, England was a battered nation with the hopes of its people at a low ebb. True, no enemy had landed on our shores, but the standard of living and morale were low. Everyone was weary, yearning for a sign of relief from the misery that war had brought. The heavy bombing of major cities like London and Coventry had done more damage to the spirit of the people than any material destruction of their homes and property.

But then, with the coming of the '50s, music began to lighten the scene. Records gave the young hope, and teenagers bought and swopped records from the USA as well as the homegrown ones. In a pretelevision age, sound was king. And the United States seemed to be the best place in the world for rock 'n' roll music.

So Britain woke up. Suddenly, good sounds were being made in good studios. Not just from the big boys like EMI and Decca, but also in little independent studios that gave free rein to their clients. We demanded and received better recording facilities. Tables were turned, and our records became the envy of other European nations.

And happily, I was there.

George Martin
November 2014

PREFACE

WHY WOULD AN AMERICAN be writing a book about the British recording studios of the 1960s and 1970s?

Well, basically, because I was asked. When APRS (Association of Professional Recording Services) chairman Malcolm Atkin first approached me with the idea of preserving the legacy of the iconic UK studios of the era in book form, I was flattered and also a little bit intimidated. There were, after all, so many great facilities back in those golden days when tape machines walked the earth and digital recording had not yet begun its fearsome conquest of the planet, and so many great recordings that had come out of those hallowed halls. And then there was the daunting challenge of rounding up information about the studios, most of which had gone out of business decades before. Many of the principal staffers were retired; some, I knew, were already sadly gone. What's more, to my amazement, nobody had ever written a book like this before, so there were precious few research materials available to me, other than the APRS archives to which Malcolm so kindly offered to provide access.

But the more I thought about it, the more the idea intrigued me, not least because it would give me the opportunity to return to my own roots. Despairing of the disco scene which was plaguing America at the time and being a longtime aficionado of British records, I had moved to England in the 1970s. There, I spent several years as a touring musician before landing a publishing deal and settling into the London studio scene, cutting my own demos when I wasn't playing on those of other aspiring songwriters. Knowing of my interest in the recording process—I had a TEAC and a Revox at home and even knew how to splice tape—I would sometimes be asked to help out in the control room when the teaboy was otherwise engaged (often, in fact, making tea). In 1979 I landed my first gig as a recording engineer, at a slightly shabby yet surprisingly good-sounding studio in North London called Pathway; incredibly, the very first session I did there was a mix for a single that went straight into the Top 20 on the British charts—despite me, not because of me, I can assure you.

After that, I was hooked. The thrill of selecting and setting up the microphones, plugging in the patch cords, and then moving the faders and twiddling the knobs until this joyous noise came leaping out of a pair of studio-grade speakers was indescribable. I loved my job! Everything about it was a blast—helping baby bands find their sound, getting to watch master musicians hone their craft, the buzz of witnessing a once-in-a-lifetime performance when an artist "nails it," the dry humor, the practical jokes, the greasy döner kebabs (the joint around the corner was the only place that delivered), even the long, long hours. (After a few months, the neighborhood bobbies got to know me on a first-name basis: I was, after all, the only "bloody Yank" driving a rickety '56 Morris Minor through the empty Islington streets on my way home at four in the morning.) You never knew the characters you'd meet when you turned up for work, or the kind of music you'd be listening to, but you always knew you'd be having fun.

Some of the recordings I made at Pathway ended up in the trashbin of history, but others helped artists secure major record deals, and a few of them even made the charts. As my reputation began to spread, I started getting opportunities to engineer and produce records at other studios in and around London, including a long stint at Trident, where I marveled at being able to sit behind the same Bechstein grand piano that Paul McCartney had played on "Hey Jude." I even had the chance to attend a couple of mastering sessions at Abbey Road, tingling with excitement as I walked through those famous front doors and strolled down the same corridors that the four Beatles and Sir George Martin had once frequented.

I left England in the 1980s and made a career shift toward writing about music instead of helping create it, but England never left me—something I suspect the canny Mr. Atkin knew when he approached me that fateful day.

It took me five long years to research and write this opus and it cost me more than a few sleepless nights, not to mention a right hip (long story). The truth of the matter is that it may have sometimes been a labor, but it always was a labor of love, and I am honored to have been entrusted with such an important project.

This book is my way of thanking the country that gave me so much, and all the good friends I have made during my travels there.

Howard Massey
New York
May 2015

ACKNOWLEDGMENTS

A PROJECT OF THIS LENGTH AND COMPLEXITY cannot be realized without the help of a great many people.

First and foremost I would like to express my heartfelt appreciation to Dave Harries, without whom this book could not have been written. Dave's unwavering support and perseverance opened up many doors that might have otherwise remained closed, and his unerring advice, technical skills, and keen eye for detail improved the book tremendously from first draft to final copy.

I only had the privilege of knowing Keith Grant, to whom this book is dedicated, for a very short period of time before he passed, but he threw himself into this endeavor with characteristic enthusiasm and good cheer, making personal introductions to many of the Olympic staff and offering me guidance even from his hospital bed. I'd like to think he would have approved of the final result!

I would also like to express my gratitude to Geoff Emerick, not only for his longstanding friendship, but also for his input and feedback as this project unfolded, not to mention all the wonderful stories from his days working with The Beatles and other major artists of the era at Abbey Road, Apple, and AIR.

Special thanks to Sir George Martin for his thoughtful foreword; to Malcolm Atkin, Peter Filleul, Francesca Smith, Trisha Wegg, Dennis Weinreich, Mike Banks, Andy Munro, Wes Maebe, Nick Dimes, Mike Brown, and everyone at the APRS for their endorsement and for their cooperation and assistance in bringing this work to fruition; to Tony Harris and Phil Burns of philsbook.com for laying the groundwork; to Matt Frost for conducting and transcribing many of the interviews included in this book; to Eddie Veale for technical drawings and the crash course in acoustic design; to Phill Brown for his unfailing courtesy and for the numerous lyrical passages from his book *Are We Still Rolling?* reproduced in these pages; to Chris and Justin Sheffield for their kind permission to use photographs and extensive quotes from Norman Sheffield's memoir *Life on Two Legs;* to Joe Meek biographers Barry Cleveland, John Repsch, and Mark Irwin for their thorough research and for allowing me to include excerpts from their work, as well as to Rob Bradford, Rob Humphreys, and Mark Newson of the Joe Meek Society for putting me in touch with several of the legendary producer's contemporaries and clients; and to John Cerullo and Jessica Burr at Hal Leonard Books for skillfully guiding this project from inception to completion.

I am especially indebted to those key studio staff from the era who gave of their time and expertise to proof various sections of the manuscript prior to publication, including Ken Townsend MBE, Brian Gibson, Peter Vince, John Kurlander, Alan Parsons, John Leckie, Derek Varnals, Bill Price, Jack Clegg, Roger Wake, Ron Godwyn, Philip Newell, Alan Florence, Brian Humphries, Howard Barrow, John Timms MBE, Richard Goldblatt, Sean Davies, Peter Smith, Denis Blackham, Peter Fautley, Adrian Kerridge, Terry Brown, Roger Cameron, Eric Tomlinson, John Richards, Kenny Denton, Tony Bridge, Robert Zimbler, Louis Elman, Ted Fletcher, Tony Kent, Malcolm Lenny, Phil Chapman, George Chkiantz, Chris Kimsey, Clive Green, Mick Mckenna, Malcolm Toft, Tony Visconti, David Hentschel, Neil Kernon, Mike Ross-Trevor, Geoff Frost, Richard Millard, Simon White, Gery Collins, Steve Holroyd, Roger Pharo, Phil Harding, Mick Glossop, Robin Black, Chris Tsangarides, John Iles, Vic Keary, Claude Harper, Frank Owen, Tony Platt, Steve Parker, Dave Grinsted, Richard Vernon, Gary Langan, Jerry Boys, Peter Gallen, John Mackswith, Jules Standen, and Barry Sage.

And of course, sincere thanks to all those who contributed technical or historical information, anecdotes, drawings, and/or photographs to *The Great British Recording Studios*: David Allen, Tom Allom, Louis Austin,

Colette Barber, Mike Batt, Joe Boyd, Tom Bullen, Bob Butterworth, Gerald Chevin, Dave Clark, Gus Coral, Neville Crozier, Jackie Da Costa, Michael Daly, Chris Darrow, Malcolm Davies, Debi Doss, Rod Duggan, Peter Duncan, Richard Elen, Morgan Fisher, Bill Foster, David Fromberg ("Smudger"), Vic Gamm, Mark Garrison, Doug Gleave, David Hamilton-Smith, James Harpham, Alan Harris, Peter Harris, Simon Heyworth, John Holbrook, Chris Hollebone, Mike Howlett, Robb Huxley, Lawrence Impey, Gregg Jackman, Arian Jansen, Chris Johnson, John Jones, Guy Katsav, Martin Keating, Peter Kelsey, Dan Labrie, Donovan Leitch, Martin Levan, Richard Lush, Gered Mankowitz, Abbey Masciarotte, George Massenburg, Sylvia Massy, Gwyn Mathias, Anton Matthews, Rafe McKenna, Anna Menzies, Norman Mighell, Mark Millar, Peter Miller, Nigel Mills, Adam Moseley, Marc Myers, Rupert Neve, Steve Nye, Alan O'Duffy, Frank Oglethorpe, Hugh Padgham, Chris Pearsall, George Peckham, Alan Perkins, David Peters, Ray Prickett, John Punter, Maggie Rodford, Walter Samuel, Adam Sharp, Norman Sheffield, Peter Silver, Keith Smart, John Smith, Allen Stagg, Mike Stavrou, Tim Summerhayes, Martin Theophilus, Chris Thomas, Josh Thomas, Mike Vernon, Phil Wainman, Mark Wallis, Rik Walton, Dr. Chris Williams, Pip Williams, John Wood, and John Woram. I apologize if I have inadvertently failed to acknowledge anyone who participated.

On a personal note, I would like to express my love and gratitude to Deborah Gremito for her patience and for standing by me through thick and thin, as well as for her editorial input and impressive proofreading skills! Also special thanks to Mike Finesilver, Wally Brill, and Jill Clayden for giving me my start at Pathway, and to Dave Taylor and Chris Stone for taking me under their wing at Trident; to Steve Parr and Tim Sanders for a friendship that has stood the test of both time and distance; to Drs. David Asprinio, Mathias Bostrom, and Mark Bodack, whose considerable skills, along with that of physical therapists Beata Wojcik and Tim Chamberlain, literally got me on my feet again after my encounters with a lunatic in the Edgware Road and the worst doctor in the world in a hospital not far from there; to Scott Goodman, Eric Battin, Erich Barto, and Micah Eberman of Zoom North America for their forbearance while I healed and completed the researching and writing of this book; to Craig Taylor, Marvin and Carole Tolkin, Mike and Betty Lospinuso, and Ken Pilgrim; and to my adopted family in the wilds of Wantagh: Kathy, Brian, Matt, Mike, and Connor Games.

INTRODUCTION

THE BRITISH SOUND

"Most music recorded today is created by performers—or operators—sitting beside the engineer; it passes directly on to a hard disk rather than reverberating in the air to be captured by microphones . . . In the quest for the perfect track, each part is added separately so that any mistakes can be easily corrected; inflexible rhythms are generated by a machine. [But] musicians in the '60s were still recording a large part of each track playing together in the same room at the same time, maintaining at least some of the excitement of a live performance, with vocals and solos usually added later. Rhythm sections breathed with the other musicians, accenting and retarding the beat as mood dictated. The acoustics of different studios varied widely, as did the styles of engineering and production. Computers theoretically let musicians and producers choose from an endless palette of varied sounds, but modern digital recordings are far more monochromatically similar to each other than were older analogue tracks."

—producer Joe Boyd, from his book *White Bicycles*

In 1877, the year Thomas Alva Edison invented the phonograph, our lives changed forever.

For the first time, great performances could be permanently captured on media and thus enjoyed by millions. The technological innovations that followed—new equipment and techniques for manipulating and altering sound—led to the creation of specialized studio environments optimized for recording. Eventually, recorded music would evolve into a new art form altogether, one which would lead to a mammoth cultural shift in the 1960s, spearheaded by artists like The Beatles and their innovative producer, Sir George Martin.

The four musicians who comprised The Beatles were, of course, all born and bred in Great Britain. What's more, apart from a single session in Paris in early 1964, the band recorded every note of their music in British recording studios. In their wake followed numerous other English musical artists of consequence, among them the Rolling Stones, The Who, Pink Floyd, David Bowie, Queen, Cream, Led Zeppelin, Genesis, Yes, The Police, the Sex Pistols, and The Clash. Though many of these artists recorded in studios in America and other countries at some point in their careers, their breakthrough singles and albums were almost invariably made on British soil, under the musical direction of British producers, with British engineers overseeing the technical aspects.

One of the more curious byproducts of the global economy that arose in the late 20th century was the homogeneity of recorded sound. Suddenly, even the most advanced recording products were available worldwide, at a more or less consistent price regardless of the country of origin. Moreover, technological advances allowed hit records to be made in home studios situated in garages, bedrooms, and other unlikely places, using computer-based equipment that was far more sophisticated (though arguably not as good-sounding) than the very best that the top studios in the world could offer only a couple of decades previously. Today, as Joe Boyd points out, it is nearly impossible to divine where a record was made, or even if it was created in a professional studio at all, as opposed to a home environment.

But back in the "golden era" of pop music—roughly from the mid-1950s, when rock 'n' roll made its noisy entrance on the scene, until the late 1970s, when the first digital audio devices such as drum machines began the inexorable march toward the dehumanization of music—there was a distinct "British sound" that characterized the records being made in Great Britain and distinguished them from those being created in America. Anyone who doubts this need only play any Beatles hit, followed immediately by a Motown hit of the same era, or, conversely, any Beach Boys single, then a Who single recorded the same year. In some cases the sonic disparities are striking, in others subtle, but there is little question that the records coming out of the studios in Great Britain (most of them located in London) sounded objectively different from those emerging from A&R in New York, or RCA Studio B in Nashville, or the Capitol Tower in Hollywood.

CULTURAL CONSIDERATIONS

Why then did a "British sound" (as distinct from an "American sound") evolve during that crucial time period? The reasons may be as much sociological as they are technical. England and America have sometimes been described as two countries separated by a common language. Despite a political and military alliance that has lasted for two centuries, the cultural differences between the nations are often vast: one a defiant republic, the other a benign monarchy; one based on capitalism, the other with distinct socialist leanings; one a society proud of wearing its emotions on its collective sleeve, the other steeped in the tradition of keeping a "stiff upper lip."

The popular musical traditions of the two countries are similarly delineated, despite the crossover of the occasional transatlantic hit record. Jazz, for example, is a uniquely American idiom, though co-opted in a modified form in the "trad jazz" that was performed in the Soho nightclubs of London. Blues originated in the cotton fields of the American South, sung by the children and grandchildren of onetime African slaves; when it evolved into the raucous rock 'n' roll of the 1950s, Great Britain's taste-makers, possibly alarmed at the deleterious effect it was having on the nation's youth, came up with a more placid (and considerably less threatening) version termed "skiffle."

Of course, the pendulum swings both ways. There is no direct American equivalent to the British pub "sing-song," nor was there ever a West Indies–influenced "ska" fad in the U.S. There was, to be sure, a so-called "punk" movement in both countries in the late 1970s, but one could easily make the case that, with the possible exception of the Ramones, the American version of punk was far more toned down than the dole-driven anger and aggressiveness that defined British punk.

So while The Beatles and the Rolling Stones could claim that their primary influence was American music (imported rock 'n' roll and country records in the case of the former; hard-edged rhythm and blues in the case of the latter), there is also no question that John Lennon, Paul McCartney, Mick Jagger, and Keith Richards all grew up listening to very different music than did Elvis Presley, Brian Wilson, Bob Dylan, and Paul Simon. Similarly, British producers like George Martin, Andrew Loog Oldham, and Mickie Most were steeped in musical traditions that were radically different from those of Phil Spector, Berry Gordy, and Phil Ramone. The same can undoubtedly be said of the recording engineers on both sides of the Atlantic, their aesthetic tastes having been shaped from sharply divergent backgrounds.

British engineer Bob Butterworth, who started his career at Lansdowne, recalls how the studio's clients were constantly asking the staff to deliver an "American drum sound"—something he found impossible to achieve because, in his words, "all the drummers who were coming in to do these sessions were English; most of them had a jazz background, and many of them had learned their craft in the military, which gave them a certain kind of precise feel." Then one day, an American drummer by the name of Andy Newmark walked in, sat down, and tuned up a hired drum kit—not even his own drums. "There it was," Butterworth reports incredulously. "Instant American drum sound! I wasn't doing a thing different—same room, same mics, same placements, same EQ, same everything. That session proved to me that the sound comes from the musician, not the control room."

Famed producer/engineer Glyn Johns had a similar experience early in his career at IBC, where he recalls constantly being challenged to re-create American sounds. "This proved particularly difficult," he writes in his 2014 memoir *Sound Man*, "because American musicians were creating a very different sound and feel to the English guys, something I was to have illustrated in triplicate when we had the privilege of prerecording the music for a TV show with Dusty Springfield called *The Sounds of Motown*. They flew the band in from Motown and set up straight off the plane. We turned the mics on and instantly there it was. Just like the records we had been listening to."

Another factor was that people were not nearly as well-traveled in those days as they are now: Up until the 1950s, the only practical way of getting between London and New York was taking a long ship voyage; flying was unreliable and extremely expensive. It wasn't until the mid-1970s that affordable flights were even available between the two cities; thus, there was relatively little cultural cross-pollination between the two countries other than that which was offered by the mass media of the day—primitive by today's standards. Even Glyn Johns, the first engineer in the U.K. to turn independent (as opposed to being a salaried member of studio staff), did not travel to America until 1969, some six years after going freelance. In addition, recording studios were spread all across the vast United States, making for greater cultural diversity from studio to studio, while almost all of the British recording facilities were concentrated within the 600 or so square miles of Greater London.

The relentless bombing by the Luftwaffe during the dark hours of World War II did more than just damage the British infrastructure and economy: In many ways, it caused injury to the psyche of the nation. During the painfully slow postwar recovery, with rationing still in effect, some English citizens came to admire, even envy, the American way of life, in part because of the economic boom being enjoyed by their wartime ally. "America used to be the big youth place in everybody's imagination," recalled John Lennon in an interview republished in *The Beatles Anthology*. "America had teenagers and everywhere else just had people . . . every movie we ever saw as children, whether it was Disneyland or Doris Day,

Rock Hudson, James Dean or Marilyn. Everything was American: Coca-Cola, Heinz ketchup—I thought Heinz ketchup was English before I went to America."

To Lennon's way of thinking, American records were superior as well. "I think the first English record that was anywhere near anything was 'Move It' by Cliff Richard, and before that there'd been nothing," he once stated. In his 2006 memoir *Here, There and Everywhere*, future Beatles engineer Geoff Emerick remembers one American hit record in particular as being a seminal influence. "The big breakthrough for me . . . came when Bill Haley and The Comets exploded onto the scene. Their rough, driving sound made an impact on me that was almost indescribable. When 'Rock Around the Clock' would come on [the radio] I could feel my pulse quicken, and my feet would start to move to the beat, as if they had a mind of their own. It was a visceral, emotional response—one that was different from what I felt when I listened to more 'serious' music, but no less compelling."

Gordon Thompson, in his authoritative 2008 study of '60s British pop *Please Please Me*, makes the case that these perceptions of American music being better than the homegrown variety permeated the English record industry. "Through all of the fifties and much of the sixties," he writes, "British studios and producers (and the artists they produced) sought to duplicate the recordings they heard coming out of New York, Nashville, Detroit, Chicago, Memphis, and Los Angeles. When they failed, they resorted to a time-honored solution: they sought their own sound."

Of course, those English musicians who could afford the time and expense to do so would take every opportunity to record in America itself. In June 1964, the Rolling Stones interrupted their American tour for two days of sessions at the famed Chess Studios in Chicago. There, they recorded the hit single "It's All Over Now," as well as material for their next EP. In November of that same year, they entered RCA Studios in Hollywood, where they recorded four tracks, including "Heart of Stone." Of those sessions, drummer Charlie Watts would later say, "The biggest advantage of recording strong rhythm and blues in Chicago was that the engineers were a lot more used to that sort of music. I don't think anyone anywhere could record this type of music as effectively as they did in Chicago."

"The methods of recording in England and America were completely different," added bassist Bill Wyman. "When we recorded at the Chess Studios in Chicago, we had Ron [Malo], the guy who engineered all the Chuck Berry, Bo Diddley, and Howlin' Wolf records. He knew exactly what we wanted, and he got it almost instantly."

"Nobody [in England] could record or had recorded the sound we were trying to get," agreed Keith Richards. "People weren't used to that kind of roughness. . . . No one could get a really good funky American sound, which is what *we* were after. The best move we could possibly do was get to America as quickly as possible and record there."

Despite their avowed preference for working at EMI's Abbey Road studios (particularly in the mid-sized Studio Two, where most of their hits were recorded, despite occasional forays to Trident, Olympic, and other U.K. studios), even The Beatles considered making a record in the States at one point. Under the exuberant headline "New Single Sensation!!!" the April 1966 issue of *The Beatles Monthly Book* excitedly proclaimed that "The boys may fly to Memphis on April 11 to record their new single. The reason for this is that they've heard so much about the American technicians and sound engineers—so they want to see for themselves whether it makes any difference. George Martin will be accompanying them, and they will rehearse their material at EMI Studios prior to their visit."

This long-rumored story was later confirmed by a recently unearthed letter written by George Harrison, as well as sources at Stax Studios. A 2008 posting on the WNEW Radio website elaborates:

> In 1966, the Beatles' manager, Brian Epstein, traveled to Memphis to inquire about the possibility of the Beatles recording at Stax Studios . . . By 1966, Stax was gaining an international reputation for its unique R&B sound—Booker T. and the MGs, Rufus and Carla Thomas, Sam and Dave, and Otis Redding had already scored hits by 1966, with more to come.

Epstein's visit with the Stax higher-ups was very hush-hush, but as Stax historian Rob Bowman relates, it took less than one day to leak out to the rest of the staff. It's easy to imagine the flurry of activity—and the dreaming—that resulted. Songwriters mobilized to develop songs the Beatles might choose to record; house musicians imagined sitting in with them; producer/guitarist Steve Cropper hoped to have the chance to engineer or even produce.

According to Deanie Parker, the former Stax publicist who now manages the Stax Museum, a week-long session was actually booked for April. A former Stax songwriter, Johnny Keyes, says that Elvis Presley offered to put the band up at Graceland. At that point, local reporters had gotten hold of the story, and Epstein, citing security concerns, decided that a Beatles session at Stax was simply unworkable. Epstein's Plan B was for the Beatles to record at Atlantic Studios in New York with Stax musicians. That didn't happen either. When the Beatles played Memphis in August, a reporter asked them about recording at Stax. George and Paul said that the Beatles were considering recording there, although the plan had been entirely called off by then.

If the April sessions had happened, the Beatles would have recorded tracks for *Revolver* at Stax. As Cropper put it, "*Taxman* could have been *Staxman*."

One can only wonder how the sound of "Tomorrow Never Knows" or "Yellow Submarine" might have differed if either had been recorded in an American studio without the benefit of EMI's unique acoustic echo chambers or extensive sound effects library. Funkier, perhaps, but almost certainly not the same.

By the late 1960s, it was not unusual for successful British artists to record in American studios, and vice versa. In May 1967, Cream entered Atlantic Studios in New York to record their second album, *Disraeli Gears*, with legendary engineer Tom Dowd; five years later, Black Sabbath recorded *Vol. 4* at the Record Plant in

Los Angeles. On the other side of the coin, the eponymous debut album from the American country-rock group the Eagles was recorded at Olympic Studios in London, where even seminal blues singer Howlin' Wolf would pay a weeklong visit to record his 1971 album *The London Howlin' Wolf Sessions* with Eric Clapton and various Beatles and Stones.

The rise of the British recording industry in the 1960s, and the cultural upheaval that led to that rapid expansion, is perhaps best summarized by Thompson in *Please Please Me*: "On 9 February 1964, as millions watched The Beatles on CBS's *The Ed Sullivan Show*, rock 'n' roll ceased to be an exclusively American art form. By the end of the decade, having overcome considerable political, economic, and technological hurdles, British performers and production teams were fixtures in an internationalized pop music industry. Indeed, London's pop music recording industry came from being a colony of distinctly American idiom to a major creative center in its own right in a few short years. . . . Lacking the economic and technological advances of their American counterparts, British studios succeeded in the sixties partly through skill, hard work and determination, and partly through luck."

TECHNICAL CONSIDERATIONS

To be sure, there were at least as many technical reasons why a distinct "British sound" evolved in the 1960s. For one thing, British recording studios were generally outfitted with very different equipment from their American counterparts. Large media corporations in the U.S., enjoying the benefits of a postwar economic boom, had encouraged companies like Ampex and RCA to allocate resources toward the development of recording technology, and the products that were created in response were quickly purchased in large quantities by American studios. In contrast, Britain's sustained financial difficulties in the postwar years resulted in government currency restrictions that impeded the importation of foreign (and particularly American) equipment. As a result, up until the mid-1960s, when professional console manufacturers such as Neve, Helios, Trident, and Cadac came into existence, almost every British studio used mixing boards that had been custom-built by their own technical engineers. Engineer/producer Hugh Padgham recalls that many English studios of the '60s and '70s had desks that only their staff knew how to operate: "When I was coming up, you used to worry about going into another studio because you weren't sure you would be able to work the console." In fact, there was a long period of time when many English facilities wouldn't even allow outside engineers in. As a result, in the words of Roger Cameron, who started as a recording engineer at Advision in 1960 and rose through the ranks to become studio manager, "you could often tell when listening to records produced during that era where they were done, because each English studio had so much of an individual sound at that time."

It wasn't just mixing consoles, either: The same was true of the instruments, amplifiers, microphones, and tape machines being used in British recording studios. The first electric guitar had been introduced by the American-based Rickenbacker company in 1931, followed in 1936 by popular models from Gibson. However, such instruments remained rare in Britain until nearly 1960, due partly to war shortages and partly to economic sanctions against importation. With American musical equipment so difficult to obtain, British musicians often turned to European instruments of lesser quality, such as those made by the German companies Höfner and Framus. There was a double whammy when it came to American-made amplifiers, since they ran on 110 volts, incompatible with the English 230-volt standard. As a result, a number of innovative British manufacturers such as Vox and Marshall solved the problem by creating their own amplifiers, some of which would eventually achieve an almost mystical reputation among musicians on both sides of the Atlantic.

Tony Visconti, an American-born producer who established his reputation working with David Bowie and T. Rex in London, made the observation in the author's 2000 book *Behind the Glass: Top Record Producers Tell How They Craft the Hits*, that British studios offered more condenser microphones than their American counterparts, resulting in more high end, due to the improved transient response. "I used to record in America in the early '70s, and I wouldn't see an awful lot of condenser mics," he recalled. "I'd see a lot of dynamic mics and RCA mics and things that we wouldn't normally have in Britain. A [Shure] SM57 was a vocal mic for stage [use] in Britain, but in America it was a studio mic, like other dynamics." He attributed this disparity to England's geographic proximity to Germany, speculating that "it probably [was] cheaper to buy a German microphone there than it would be in America. Telefunken and Schoeps mics—there's loads of them in England. I'd say the percentage of condenser mics to dynamic mics is greater in England than I've seen in American studios."

Similarly, most English studios, at least throughout the '60s, would tend to have British-made EMI or Swiss-made Studer tape decks,

A Tannoy/Lockwood cabinet circa 1960s.
(Courtesy of Tannoy)

as opposed to American-made Ampex and Scully machines (although a few facilities, such as Advision, Olympic, and Trident, were the exception to the rule). Even the monitoring was often different, with English studios having a distinct propensity for Tannoy speakers mounted in Lockwood cabinets, usually powered by British-made Radford or Quad amplifiers, as opposed to the Altec or JBL monitors and Crown amplifiers favored by most American studios of the era. U.S. engineer George Massenburg, who spent a great deal of time traveling between American and British studios in the '60s and '70s, recalls that the Tannoy/Lockwood combination yielded a "huge low end," in stark contrast to the Altec 604s commonly found in U.S. control rooms (especially in the New York studios), where they tended to be, in Massenburg's words, "hung from the ceiling on chains in utility enclosures, which gave them almost no low end whatsoever."

In the mid-1950s, fledgling Parlophone label chief (and future Beatles producer) George Martin, along with EMI engineer Peter Bown, was sent on a mission to try to identify the reasons why the records being made at Abbey Road in London were sonically inferior to those being made at Capitol Studios in Los Angeles. (Capitol was EMI's affiliate in the U.S.) "I'd had a minor hit with [producer Ron Goodwin] in the States called 'Swinging Sweetheart' and we took the opportunity to go to Capitol and see what they were doing," he explained in a 1999 interview conducted for *Behind the Glass*. "They were recording on Ampex 3-track half-inch [tape]; we were recording on mono quarter-inch, though our classical people were using stereo quarter-inch. We never used stereo in the pop world—stereo pop records didn't exist in England at the time. . . . This 3-track Ampex meant that you could record the band in stereo on the outside tracks, put the voice in the center track, and you had the freedom to balance them afterwards, after everybody had gone home. . . . It was also my first experience with the Fairchild limiter, which we still use to this day. We didn't have them at Abbey Road, we had nothing like that, so we weren't able to make records that were so dynamic. I came back from America telling everybody in England, 'We've got to do something about this, we've got to re-equip the studio, because without it, we're not going to make any good records, ever.' And that was a kind of turning point; Abbey Road started getting its act together."

A decade later, former Levy's chief engineer Geoff Frost paid a visit to Nashville on a similar mission, doing preparatory reconnaissance as he and partner John Wood prepared to launch their own London-based studio, Sound Techniques. "The sound coming out of America, particularly from Bradley's, really impressed me personally," he explained in a 2008 interview with *Sound on Sound* magazine. "[It was] just the kind of studio that John and I wanted to build. It wasn't full of deadening materials like English studios were—with English studios, the idea was to make everything as dead as possible, but Bradley's had a very minimal acoustic treatment with a very high ceiling. They also had very minimal equipment. In order to make the English sound more and more American, English studios were buying up more and more equipment. But Bradley's had a very simple desk . . . and they had outboard [Langevin] EQs . . . [all] locked in at [the] 3k 8 dB boost position and left there!"

Engineer Bill Price, who started at Decca in 1962, recalled that the studio's engineers were actively encouraged to get American sounds. "In the '60s a lot of British pop hits were straight copies of American records," he explained, "the originals of which at that stage, nobody was releasing in this country. Decca would employ a musical director who would listen to a Stax, Coral, or RCA single and 'transcribe it for orchestra,' so to speak, and give it to a bunch of London session musicians to play. The engineer would listen to the record and attempt to copy the latest Tamla Motown sound or what have you, which was incredibly difficult, though at times we could achieve a modicum of success. It was based on the principle 'We don't know what's good about it, but it's sold millions in America, so we just want to copy it as closely as possible.'"

And so at one point, Decca too sent a producer over to the States to try to discover the secrets to the American sound. Their emissary was apparently not someone who was especially technically savvy, but he nonetheless duly returned with a list of the model numbers he'd seen in use in the studios there, which he believed would give the Decca engineers extra ammunition in the war to capture "American" sonics within the confines of their studio. "Overnight we got a huge bank of Fairchild compressors and Pultec equalizers, the stock-in-trade of American studios," remembers Price.

Beatles engineer Geoff Emerick, in *Here, There and Everywhere*, spoke of frequent conversations he would have with Paul McCartney, always the Beatle most concerned with sonics and production values. "Paul had long been complaining that the bass on Beatles records wasn't as loud or as full as the American records he so loved to listen to. He and I would often get together in the mastering room to listen intently to the low end of some new import he had gotten from the States, most often a Motown track." Emerick, who had done a year-long apprenticeship as a mastering engineer at EMI, commented that disc cutting "was especially demanding when Tamla Motown material came in. I was always striving to match their full, bass-rich sound, but I found that I couldn't ever do it successfully, which was quite frustrating. It took me a long while to realize that the reasons had to do with the equipment we had at EMI, and not because of any limitations in my ability."

Emerick also recalled that McCartney, who had been heavily influenced by the Beach Boys' *Pet Sounds* (recorded at multiple studios in Los Angeles), specifically requested a "really clean American sound" when it came time to record "Penny Lane" at Abbey Road in late 1966. "I'd spent a lot of time mastering American records, and I was convinced that the best way to give Paul what he wanted was to record each instrument totally on its own so that there would be no leakage." Emerick was commenting on the accepted practice in America of recording each instrument separately on its own track so as to have maximum control during the mix process—something allowed by the luxury of having 8- and 16-track tape machines (which American studios had in abundance, long before British studios). Remarks Visconti in *Behind the Glass*, "By the time 8-track came along, Americans were superstitiously printing stuff to tape with no effects and waiting until the mix to do it all, whereas the British way was completely the opposite—if you had a great effect going, you printed it. . . . When Hugh Padgham came up with the gated Phil Collins drum sound [on the song "In the Air Tonight," recorded at Townhouse Studio 2—the famous "Stone Room"—in London in 1979], that was printed to tape—that wasn't a mix thing. You won't find Americans doing a thing like that; that could have only been invented in Britain. Nowadays you could simulate it, but that's a physical sound that Hugh Padgham had the foresight to think, 'I'd better print this.' That's really British thinking."

That willingness to make decisions on the spot and print (record) sound with effects meant that there was often less time spent on mixing in British studios. Visconti feels that was an absolute benefit to working in England, saying, "David Bowie and I have discussed this many times, that [having] less options in mixing is a positive thing. For instance, the snare drum on *Low* and "Heroes," which is that harmonized dropped-off thing—I would always print that to tape, albeit on another track; it wouldn't be on the snare track. But every time we put the multitrack up, it would be there. And it would keep us going in that direction—we wouldn't deviate from that sound. We'd want the album to sound that way, ultimately. A lot of people wait till the mix to do those things; they have no idea what the texture of their album is until they get into the mixing room, and then they'll sometimes spend months mixing to find the album's sonic personality. Whereas in England, we used to just go for it. When I made a T. Rex record, I did certain things like print a lot of slapback to tape—it was a T. Rex characteristic—and sometimes it would be on the guitar track itself, so it could not be removed. Because it would always be there, that dictated the direction of the subsequent overdubs—we'd always tailor the new overdubs to the old sound. Of course, it was only 16-track, but I could probably mix as many as three songs in one day. We'd just book a week to mix the album, and that would be indulgent."

Craig Leon is another American-born producer who spent a lot of time in London's studios in the 1960s and 1970s. In *Behind the Glass*, he states his opinion that another aspect to the evolution of the "British sound" may have been the somewhat unorthodox design of many English control rooms: "There's a different approach and a different mentality [in British studios versus American ones]. I think it's because the control rooms in England are drawn up more by the seat of their pants. You're working on speakers that are extraordinary, but they're not positioned using any kind of scientific method; they're placed according to what sounds good to the people that are working in the room, so it's done by ear. Whereas in America, I think it's done a little bit more technically by the book, and that creates a different sound.

"I find that I actually push myself a little more in English studios, because the environments are a bit unnatural. One of my favorite rooms to work in was

the old AIR Studios. The control room had big floor-to-ceiling windows overlooking Oxford Street. That was how the room was designed, yet George Martin would sit there and get the most incredible sounding things out of there, and I got really good results as well. All of which proves that the sound doesn't come from the equipment, but from the way you hear things in the room."

There also seems to have been more of a willingness in British studios—at least some of them—to break "the rules," whatever they were, even if it meant letting the lunatics take over the asylum at times. Paul McCartney recalled in *The Beatles Anthology* that "originally George Martin was the Supreme Producer In The Sky and we wouldn't even dare ask to go into the control room. But, as things loosened up, we got invited in and George gave us a bit of the control of the tools; he let us have a go."

In that same book, Martin himself said, "[The Beatles] would want us to do radical things . . . [for example,] they'd shove in high EQ on mixing, and for the brass they'd want to have a really 'toppy' sound and cut out all the bass. The engineers would sometimes wonder whether there should be that much EQ. We would go through the complete range of EQ [on the desk] . . . and if that wasn't enough we'd put it through another range of EQ again, multiplied, and we'd get the most weird sound, which The Beatles liked and which obviously worked . . . Geoff Emerick used to do things for The Beatles and be scared that the people above would find out. Engineers then weren't supposed to play about with microphones and things like that. But he used to do really weird things that were slightly illegitimate, with our support and approval."

That same spirit of experimentation was present in The Beatles' first recording engineer, Norman Smith, too, despite the fact that he was significantly older than Emerick (possibly even older than George Martin) and definitely of the old school. Thompson describes Smith's development of the "Mersey sound" (a subset of the "British sound" exemplified in the earliest Beatles recordings) as follows:

[Smith:] "I used microphones not right up close to things. And I relied quite a bit, to get in the right sort of balance and the right proportion, on splash-back off the walls, so one had kind of a natural reverberation. And that's how, in my view at any rate, the Mersey sound was born: placing the microphones further away or equidistant, shall we say, from their instrument and the wall, or the splash-back. In other words, not that great separation on each microphone."

Smith's . . . own experience as a performer (which he continued while working at EMI in order to supplement his income) led him to believe that musicians played better when they were in close proximity to one another. With The Beatles, he felt that "with this sound the boys were producing—their songs—that they wanted to be close together. And so I set them up virtually as they would be set up on stage." Consequently, he remembers, studio managers sometimes reprimanded him. . . .

The sound engineers at EMI "wanted 100 percent separation recording between each microphone and no spillover. If you opened up the bass mic, you didn't want to hear any drums on it. I never could understand that. I used the position whereby I could get the right kind of spillover to get this kind of reverb. That made it sound more natural, like a live performance."

But possibly the most important technical factor was the late adoption of multitrack recording technology by English studios, despite the fact that the modern tape recorder was invented in Germany.

THE RISE OF THE MULTITRACK RECORDER

Interestingly, it was American crooner Bing Crosby who was largely responsible for this seeming anomaly, and it came via an audio engineer by the name of Jack Mullin, who had been a member of the U.S. Army Signal Corps during World War II. Mullin's unit was assigned to investigate German radio and electronics activities, and in the course of his duties, he acquired two Magnetophon recorders and 50 reels of recording tape from a German radio station near Frankfurt. After having them shipped home, he spent the next two years having the machines adapted for commercial use, hoping to interest the Hollywood film studios in

using magnetic tape for movie soundtrack recording. Mullin gave a demonstration of his recorders at MGM Studios in Hollywood in 1947, which led to a meeting with Crosby, who subsequently invested $50,000 in a local electronics company, Ampex, to enable Mullin to develop a commercial production model. With Mullin as his chief engineer, Crosby became the first American performer to regularly prerecord his radio programs on tape. Ampex and Mullin subsequently developed a number of commercial stereo and multitrack audio models (initially 3- and 4-track, followed eventually by 8- and 16-track models), which were rapidly adopted by studios throughout the United States as the recording machines of choice.

Two-track recording became widely used for contemporary music in the U.S. in the 1950s because it enabled stereophonic recordings to be made and edited conveniently. (The first stereo recordings, on discs, had actually been made in the 1930s, but were never issued commercially.) Although many pop music and jazz recordings continued to be issued in mono through the mid-1960s, stereo gradually became the norm, in America, anyway—the format would not be fully adopted by British consumers until several years later. Yet, despite currency and trade restrictions, a few American-made Ampex 2-track recorders found their way into a number of English studios, including Decca, in the early 1960s. EMI, despite building their own stereo BTR/2 (BTR stood for "British Tape Recorder"), also purchased a number of 2-track machines from the Swiss company Studer.

Much of the credit for the development of multitrack (i.e., more than 2-track) recording must go to American guitarist Les Paul, who also helped design the famous electric guitar that bears his name. His experiments with tapes and recorders in the early 1950s led him to order an early custom-built 8-track machine from Ampex, and his pioneering recordings with his then wife, singer Mary Ford, were the first to make use of the technique of multitracking to record separate elements of a musical piece asynchronously. Paul's technique enabled him to listen to the tracks he had already taped and record new parts in time alongside them.

Long before they were able to produce a commercial version of the 8-track recorder, however, Ampex issued a series of 3-track machines. These remained in widespread use until the mid-1960s, and numerous famous American recordings—including many of Phil Spector's so-called "Wall of Sound" productions and early Motown hits—were taped on Ampex 3-track recorders. The next important development was 4-track recording, which gave engineers and musicians vastly greater flexibility. American engineer Tom Dowd was among the first to utilize 4-track recording for popular music production while working for Atlantic Records during the 1950s. EMI Studios in London installed Studer 4-track machines in 1959 and 1960, but their star act, The Beatles, would not have access to them until late 1963; all their recordings prior to the group's "I Want to Hold Your Hand" single were made on 2-track machines. The EMI engineers would become particularly adept at creating "reduction mixes" (known as "bouncing down" in the United States), in which multiple tracks were recorded onto a 4-track machine and then mixed together and transferred to one track of a second 4-track machine. In this way, it was possible to record literally dozens of separate tracks and combine them into finished recordings of great complexity. There were limitations to this technique, however, largely due to the buildup of noise during the reduction process.

Tape recorders with four or more tracks were restricted mainly to American recording studios until the mid-to-late 1960s, mostly because of import restrictions and the high cost of the technology. The first prototype Ampex 8-track recorder used 1" (25 mm) recording tape, the widest tape available at the time, and that soon became the standard. Atlantic Records' New York studio was the first commercial facility to offer 8-track recording.

By 1967, most American studios were using 8-track recorders; in contrast, most studios in England were still restricted to four tracks. 1968 saw the introduction of the first commercially available 16-track recorders (from both Ampex and competitors like Scully and Studer), followed two years later by various 24-track models (all of which still used 2" tape, thus resulting in reduced signal-to-noise ratio). Twenty-four-track analog tape recording would be the de facto standard in both American and British

recording studios until the 1990s, when the technology was mostly replaced, first with digital tape machines, and then with computer systems using hard drives instead of tape.

There is some dispute about who installed the first 8-track recorder in the U.K., though there is general agreement about the year it was introduced: 1968. Early that year, London's Advision (a studio used primarily for jingles) purchased an American-made Scully model. At around the same time, Trident Studios—a brand-new facility that had recently opened its doors—installed an Ampex 8-track, something which became a major selling point and which would ultimately attract The Beatles, whose first 8-track recording—a little ditty titled "Hey Jude"—would become a massive international hit single.

EMI's Abbey Road Studios was a bit slower off the mark, despite numerous complaints from The Beatles that the studio was behind the times. Abbey Road finally took possession of the first of three 8-track recorders in May 1968, though studio rules dictated that they had to first be disassembled and thoroughly inspected by the maintenance department. It was decided that modifications were required, and so the machine was not put into use until August of that year, when it was "liberated" by technical engineer Dave Harries from one of the studio's upstairs maintenance offices for use by The Beatles. Although a number of the songs recorded for the group's *White Album* received overdubs on the 8-track machine, it was not used for an entire Beatles album until their *Abbey Road* release, recorded during the summer of 1969. Of those sessions, engineer Geoff Emerick recalls, "One of the benefits of working in 8-track was that we were able to record Ringo's [drum] solo [in the song "The End"] in stereo, spread over two tracks, allowing the listener to hear different tom-toms and cymbals in each speaker. That was very unusual for a Beatles song: drums were almost always recorded in mono, even after we made the move to 8-track. The new mixing console also provided many more inputs than the old one, so I was able to put a dozen mics or so on Ringo's kit, as opposed to the three or four that I had used previously."

Trident was the first U.K. studio to install a 16-track machine (a 3M M56), in late 1969. By the end of 1971, there were some two dozen studios in London offering 16-track capability, leading to extensive creative experimentation by artists such as David Bowie, Pink Floyd, and Queen. In a few short years, even 16-track would become a largely obsolete format as most British studios made the transition to 24-track recording.

NAB VERSUS CCIR/IEC

When asked in *Behind the Glass* if he thought there was a qualitative difference between the sound of the records being made in English studios versus those being made in American ones, Tony Visconti vehemently replied, "There had to be, because, first of all, they didn't use the NAB equalization curve—they used the European [CCIR/IEC] curve, which always seemed to me to be brighter."

To understand this, one needs to understand the concept of *pre-emphasis* and *de-emphasis* (sometimes called *post-emphasis*), as used in recording to analog tape.* Glenn D. White's *The Audio Dictionary* defines pre-emphasis as "a type of high frequency boost applied to signals about to be recorded on tape [in order] to reduce the apparent noise level." De-emphasis is defined as "the complementary equalization which follows pre-emphasis."

The reason pre-emphasis and de-emphasis are needed is due to the inherent self-noise of the tape medium, which can be audibly apparent when reproducing signals of very low level; in extreme cases, it can even obliterate low-level signal altogether. A considerable amount of equalization is therefore required to maintain a flat input-to-output relationship when recording to tape. By boosting high-frequency signals being recorded, the ambient noise floor of the tape is reduced to minimal level. To restore the output signal to a flat response, an exactly opposite equalization must be applied during playback.

* Not to be confused with the pre-emphasis and de-emphasis used in some digital recording systems and by analog noise reduction technologies such as Dolby and dbx.

Unfortunately, there were two different "standard" equalization curves in use in the 1960s and 1970s: one for American-built machines, and the other for European-manufactured machines. In 1954, the American National Association of Broadcasters (NAB) established a standard pre-emphasis/de-emphasis curve (known as a "reproducing characteristic") for use in professional tape recorders operating at 15 inches per second (ips). The graph below shows the NAB de-emphasis curve:

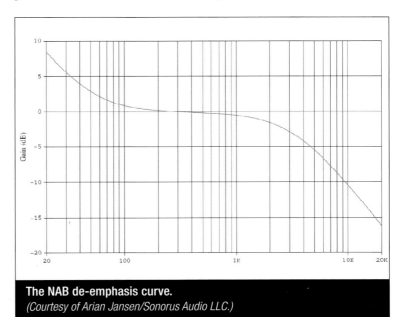

The NAB de-emphasis curve.
(Courtesy of Arian Jansen/Sonorus Audio LLC.)

As is evident, in addition to the high-frequency rolloff (above 3,150 Hz) required to compensate for the equivalent boost during recording, there is also a low-frequency boost. This is because the NAB pre-emphasis curve rolls off low frequencies (below 400 Hz) in an effort to improve hum rejection during playback.

The NAB equalization curve was quickly adopted as a standard by all American tape recorder manufacturers, and continues to be in use today. However, in the 1960s the European Comité Consultatif International pour la Radio (CCIR) developed a *different* standard (known as a "recording characteristic"), later adopted by the International Electrotechnical Commission (IEC) and used by all European manufacturers of tape recorders. The CCIR/IEC pre-emphasis curve rolls off high frequencies above 4,500 Hz but leaves the low frequencies completely untouched. The graph below shows the CCIR/IEC de-emphasis curve:

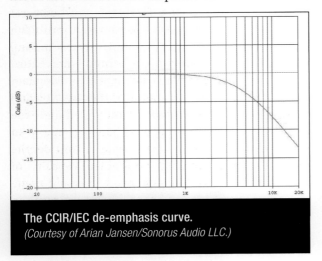

The CCIR/IEC de-emphasis curve.
(Courtesy of Arian Jansen/Sonorus Audio LLC.)

At least in theory, there is no problem if a tape recorded on an NAB machine is played back on a correctly calibrated NAB machine, or if a tape recorded on a CCIR/IEC machine is played back on a correctly calibrated CCIR/IEC machine, although many producers and engineers (Visconti among them) believe that the overall sound is somewhat smoother or brighter when the latter curve is used (some describe the sound as more "velvety")—another, if rather more subjective, component to the "British sound." The real problem occurs when an IEC/CCIR tape is played back on an NAB machine, or vice versa, as shown in the graphic at right.

As author John Woram explains in his 1989 *Sound Recording Handbook*, "If an IEC tape (with flat low-frequency response) is played back on an NAB system, it will exhibit a low-frequency rolloff and a +3 dB high frequency shelving response. The opposite condition is noted if an NAB tape is reproduced on an IEC playback system." In other words, tapes recorded in British studios will sound noticeably thinner (less low end) and brighter (more high end) when played back on American tape machines, while tapes recorded in Amer-

ican studios will sound much bassier and more muffled when played back on European tape machines.

This may account, at least in part, for the increased tape hiss heard on The Beatles' songs "Martha My Dear" and "Honey Pie" (from the likely boost in high end applied during mastering), both of which were mixed on Trident's Ampex 2-track machines (set to an NAB curve) but later played back on CCIR machines at Abbey Road—the only kind available at EMI at the time—so they could be sequenced into the *White Album*. (The same was true of the Animals' massive hit single "House of the Rising Sun," which was recorded at De Lane Lea Studios on an NAB machine but cut at Abbey Road by mastering engineer Tony Bridge, using a CCIR playback machine.) It also may explain the extended low end that Paul McCartney and Geoff Emerick claimed to have heard on American recordings when played back at Abbey Road.

Lest one believe that such technical inaccuracies (such as playback of an NAB tape on a CCIR machine, or vice versa) could not occur within the confines of a professional recording studio, one need only be reminded of the many well-known technical gaffes of the era, most famously Capitol Records' U.S. release of The Beatles' *Rubber Soul* album in twin-track (as opposed to mono) format, resulting ludicrously in isolated vocals coming from one speaker and all the instruments coming from the other.

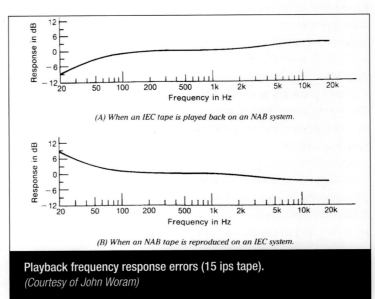

(A) When an IEC tape is played back on an NAB system.

(B) When an NAB tape is reproduced on an IEC system.

Playback frequency response errors (15 ips tape).
(Courtesy of John Woram)

Another hilarious (or, depending upon your point of view, tragic) anecdote describing technical ineptness is related by Geoff Emerick in his memoir: "Whenever assistants weren't working on sessions [at Abbey Road], one of [their] jobs was to put white leader tape in-between tracks of tape copies of albums sent over from Capitol in the United States, because most of their pop records were re-mastered in England—which made the recordings second-generation, with the resultant additional tape hiss. . . . For some reason, the Capitol executives [also] deemed it too time-consuming to make tape copies of singles (though they did make copies of albums), so instead they'd just stick a record in a bag and send it to us. Our mastering engineers would then literally make a copy onto tape, cut out any bad clicks, and recut it back on vinyl."

BRITISH INNOVATION

They say that necessity is the mother of invention, and perhaps nowhere was that more true than in the British recording studios of the 1960s and 1970s. In fact, the amount of innovation that came from English studios during that era is positively staggering, as is detailed in the pages of this book.

For one thing, the sheer degree of difficulty in converting old buildings—sometimes hundreds of years old—into modern recording facilities led to groundbreaking work in acoustic design, such as Ken Shearer's efforts at AIR Oxford Circus and his famed domed reflectors, first deployed at the Albert Hall, and later adopted for use in studios such as Advision. This was a legacy that would be carried forward by a whole generation of British acoustic designers and architects, from Sandy Brown (Lansdowne, Philips, Trident, Audio International, Chappell) to Keith Grant and his father, Robertson Grant (Olympic); from Eddie Veale (Marquee, Island, Sarm, Roundhouse) to Philip Newell, who, with engineer Mick Glossop, designed the famous, and totally unorthodox, "Stone Room" at Townhouse Studios. The same pioneering spirit applied to the development of dedicated mobile recording units such as the Rolling Stones Mobile—the first fully equipped control room on wheels (as opposed to trucks that simply transported portable recording equipment to remote venues).

Innovation, too, was the order of the day when it came to recording techniques. From Alan Blumlein's early experiments in binaural audio and stereo that led to the Blumlein Pair to Decca's classical department's breakthrough Decca Tree; from Glyn Johns' elegantly simple three-mic drum miking technique to the gated snare drum "shot heard around the world" developed by Hugh Padgham that came to define the sound of the late '70s and beyond, these have all evolved into tried-and-true methods of capturing and enhancing audio in studios and concert halls everywhere. And despite the power and seemingly unlimited capacity of today's digital recording systems, few would argue that any manipulation of bits and bytes can result in a sound quite the same as the original ADT (Artificial Double Tracking) invented by Ken Townsend at Abbey Road in the mid-1960s, or George Chkiantz's complex (but enormously effective) means of generating phasing, developed at Olympic just a few years later—interestingly enough, out of a desire to try to recreate ADT.

And then there are the products! From the legendary all-tube REDD consoles designed and built by EMI's technicians at Hayes to the famed "wraparound" boards made by Dick Swettenham for Keith Grant at Olympic (the precursors to the equally renowned Helios line); from the work done by Clive Green and Adrian Kerridge at Lansdowne that led to the formation of Cadac to Malcolm Toft's Trident A-Range and TSM mixers; from the sonically unique Sound Techniques boards crafted by Geoff Frost and John Wood to the creative collaboration between AIR Studios and Rupert Neve that led to the AIR Montserrat Neve console, vintage British mixing desks are quite properly revered today for their punch, clarity, and sonic excellence. Equally important are the innovations that came out of the maintenance workshops in the British studios of the '60s and '70s: From the DI (Direct Inject) boxes that Townsend designed for Abbey Road to the film synchronizers and cue mixers developed by Dave Harries and Malcolm Atkin for AIR; from Joe Meek's home-brewed "black boxes"—often built into tobacco tins and held together with little more than cellophane tape—to

An original Joe Meek compressor.
(Photo courtesy of Adrian Kerridge)

recording industry responded successfully because of the many different kinds of people engaged in solving the problem of creating a hit: "Production crews working in clearly differentiated roles brought a wide range of skills and orientations to London's recording sessions."

The Beatles, in collaboration with George Martin and the engineers at EMI, led the way, unceasingly pushing the envelope as they crafted recordings that constantly challenged the limits of what their audience would accept. Other English artists of the era followed, incorporating new elements into their music as they constantly tested and stretched the limits of the production tools at hand. By the mid-1960s, the best British recordings were as good as, or better than, any being made in America, or anywhere else in the world, for that matter.

Decca and Pye's studio-branded compressors and limiters; from EMI's ATOC (Automatic Transient Overload Control) look-ahead disc cutting system to their famed "Curvebender" equalizer, these were the products that helped shape the unique sounds that came out of the U.K.'s mixing and mastering rooms of the era, and would serve to influence the recordings made around the world for decades to come.

As author Gordon Thompson so correctly states in *Please Please Me*, "The challenges that British engineers and musicians faced . . . demanded that they become adept at improvising and experimenting with instruments, amplifiers, and sound recording. Invariably, they worked with technology that was several years behind America." Yet, he argues, the British

Essentially, then, the "British sound" was derived from a fortuitous combination of the right people being in the right place at the right time, having (or lacking) the right equipment at hand to realize their creative vision, and the ability to somehow overcome the convolution of a bewildering series of dueling technical "standards"—all this, along with a healthy dose of serendipity and misadventure.

A story, in other words, worth telling.

1

ABBEY ROAD

(EMI STUDIOS)

The world was a very different place in the 1920s. The Industrial Revolution was nearly complete, and with it came the introduction of mass production and mass marketing. Weary of a Great War that had lingered for years and cost the lives of millions of soldiers, the public was ready for a new form of entertainment. The answer came in not one, but two types of media: radio ("wireless" in England) and the phonograph ("gramophone") record. Both allowed people to enjoy music from the comfort of their homes, and at minimal cost. By 1922, the BBC was firmly established in Great Britain, and by the end of the decade, weekly sales of gramophone records in F. W. Woolworth's alone were exceeding a quarter of a million copies.

None of this escaped the attention of one Trevor Osmond Williams, chairman of the aptly named Gramophone Company, England's largest manufacturer of records. The Company, as it was known, had long been making original recordings at two small studios in its Hayes headquarters as well as in large venues such as Queen's Hall near Oxford Circus and Kingsway Hall in the City of London (using a mobile unit called the Lancia), but it soon became obvious that, while these places offered spectacular acoustics, their facilities were inadequate for the needs of the Company's artists. Sometime in the mid-1920s, Williams gave the financial approval for a suitable location to be found in London, with a Mr. F. H. Dart of the technical recording department placed in charge of the project.

Thus was born EMI Studios—later to be known simply as Abbey Road.

The purchase of a large plot of land at Number 3 Abbey Road, in north London's fashionable St. John's Wood district (followed shortly thereafter by the neighboring lot at Number 5) was only the first step. Dart's team of architects and builders faced a daunting series of technical problems as they did extensive renovations to the stately residence that stood on the property, compounded by the fact that no one had ever undertaken such an enterprise before. Construction took nearly two years, but on November 12, 1931, the three-studio facility finally opened, celebrated by a recording session for the London Symphony Orchestra, conducted by Sir Edward Elgar.

By then, The Gramophone Company had merged with its archrival, Columbia, to form Electric and Musical Industries, Limited—better known as EMI. For the next three decades, the studio forged a name for itself as one of the premier recording spaces for classical music and opera, as well as hosting many popular artists of the era, including Glenn Miller, Fred Astaire, Marlene Dietrich, Dame Vera Lynn, Alma Cogan, and Judy Garland, plus various members of a radio comedy team known as The Goons, featuring an up-and-coming star by the name of Peter Sellers.

Then, one day in June of 1962, four irreverent young men from Liverpool walked into Number 3 Abbey Road for a recording test with producer George Martin. They were to spend most of the rest of their careers recording at EMI, and, seven years later, when they decided to pose for their last album cover by strolling across the zebra crossing directly outside the studio, the legacy of Abbey Road was forever established.

English composer Sir Edward Elgar with conductor Sir Adrian Boult at the inaugural recording session in Abbey Road Studio One, November 1931.
(Photo by Hudson/Getty Images)

It didn't end with The Beatles, either. Throughout the '60s and '70s and beyond, EMI Studios continued to be popular with a wide range of artists in all genres of music, including Cliff Richard and the Shadows, The Hollies, Cilla Black, Gerry and the Pacemakers, the Zombies, Badfinger, Pink Floyd, and The Alan Parsons Project; in more recent years, artists like Radiohead, Oasis, and Kanye West have recorded there. Happily, despite numerous threats of closure in recent years, the Abbey Road facility remains open and fully operational at the time of this writing.

KEY PERSONNEL

"Pop" balance engineers: Stuart Eltham, Peter Bown, Malcolm Addey, Norman Smith, Peter Vince, Geoff Emerick, Tony Clark, Ken Scott, Phil McDonald, Richard Lush, Alan Parsons, Peter Mew, John Leckie

"Classical" balance engineers: Chris Parker, Neville Boyling, Douglas Larter, Bob Gooch, Mike Gray, John Kurlander

Maintenance Engineers*: Gus Cook, Arthur Pook, George Barnett, Ken Townsend, Keith Slaughter, Dave Frost, Jim Johnstone, Dave Harries, Martin Benge, Brian Gibson

* In the EMI parlance of the era, the members of the technical staff who had received extensive training at Hayes and were qualified to do location recording were given the title "recording engineers," rather than "maintenance engineers" or "technical engineers." The individuals who would be known today as "recording engineers" were termed "balance engineers."

PHYSICAL FACILITIES

The Abbey Road facility comprises three full-size recording studios as well as numerous mixing, mastering, and copying rooms, in addition to administrative office space and a tape library.

The largest of the three is Studio One, originally designed to replicate a concert hall (complete with a tiered stage at one end) and capable of housing a full 100-piece symphony orchestra. Located on the lowest level of the building, Studio One has 40' ceilings and provides over 5,300 square feet of space—more than enough for even the largest sessions. The smallish control room alongside offers one very unusual feature: an outside-facing window that let in natural light. Unusually, there was no direct access

from Studio One to its control room in the '60s and '70s: Artists had to take a long and circuitous route down the hallway to visit their producer and balance engineer! (The same was the case with Studio Three, prior to a 1974 redesign.)

Studio Two is best known as the room where the vast majority of Beatles recordings were done. Though not nearly as large as the cavernous Studio One, it is still quite spacious: over 2,200 square feet, with 28' ceilings. Perhaps the most recognizable feature of Studio Two is its famous wooden staircase leading up from the studio area. "That was where the grown-ups lived," Paul McCartney once said, speaking of the control room at the top of the stairs, where the producer, balance engineer, and assistant

Abbey Road studios circa 1960s.
(© Abbey Road Studios)

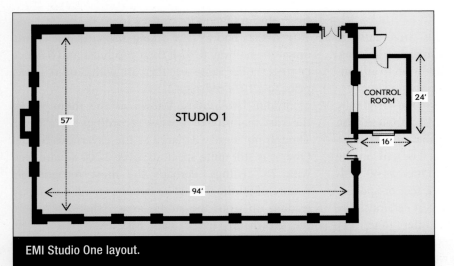

EMI Studio One layout.

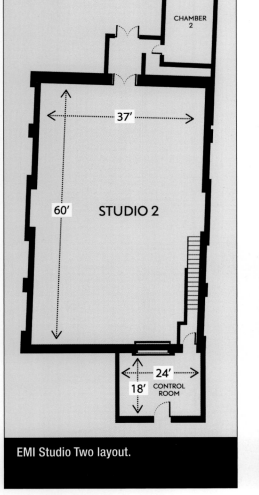

EMI Studio Two layout.

engineer / tape operator (better known at Abbey Road as the "button-pusher") wove their magic while the artists below played their hearts out. Beneath the steps lay an equally famous storage closet where EMI's vast collection of percussion instruments and various noisemakers were kept—many of which found their way onto not only Beatles recordings, but also those of many other pop and spoken-word artists who used the facility. The Studio Two control room has an unusually large double-paned window that provides a panoramic view of the proceedings going on down below.

Although only one-tenth the volume of Studio One, Abbey Road's nearly 1,300-square-foot Studio Three is nonetheless spacious enough to accommodate small chamber groups and/or pop bands; it is also used extensively for the recording of solo piano and for vocal overdubs. The Studio Three control room, like that of Studio One, features exterior windows that overlook the adjacent residences and workshops.

Acoustic Treatments

The acoustic treatment in the various Abbey Road studios and control rooms was actually fairly minimal in the 1960s. Bass traps

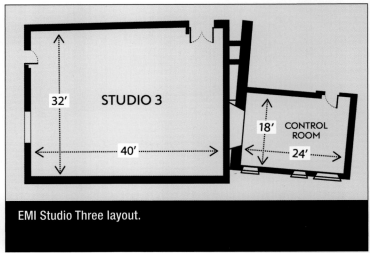

EMI Studio Three layout.

The Beatles in Studio One rehearsing for the "All You Need Is Love" broadcast, June 1967.
(© Abbey Road Studios)

were installed (most notably in Studio Two) to reduce low-frequency buildup, and screens, rostra, and large Indian rugs strategically placed on the hardwood floors were employed to create relatively "dead" areas with less reflected sound—areas that were generally used for piano and vocal overdubs—while brass and string instruments were typically recorded in the less treated "live" areas of the rooms.

Perhaps the most unusual aspect of the acoustic treatment were the long panels of quilted fabric that hung on the walls of all three studios, stuffed with a material similar to seaweed. In the days before fiberglass, this fabric (called Cabot's Quilt) was often used as an insulating material, but at Abbey Road the panels served to reduce sound reflections.

Studio Two was also the beneficiary of two pairs of large screens that were mounted on hinges on the wall and could be swung out as needed. These were covered with slotted hardboard and filled with a dense material, similar to the fiberglass and rockwall used in gobos (movable acoustic isolation panels). When deployed, these acted to temporarily reduce the size of the room and thus the amount of reflected sound.

Probably the studio that received the most attention in this regard was the cavernous Studio One, with its long reflection times. For example, sheeting and other fabrics were hung high in the rafters in the late 1960s in an effort to absorb frequencies at around 3.5 kHz, but this experiment was deemed a

"Let's make it sound like we're actually in a submarine"

NEARLY A WEEK after beginning "Yellow Submarine" in the spring of 1966, the four Beatles reconvened in Abbey Road Studio Two to complete the recording. The song had been conceived as a sing-along, and so a few of the band's friends and significant others had been invited along for the session, including Mick Jagger and Brian Jones of the Rolling Stones, along with Jagger's girlfriend Marianne Faithfull and George Harrison's wife, Pattie. There was a distinct party atmosphere, so balance engineer Geoff Emerick had his assistant Phil McDonald put a few ambient microphones around the studio and also rigged up a number of handheld mics on long leads so the group and their assembled guests could move around freely.

"We had the entire EMI collection of percussion instruments and sound-effects boxes strewn all over the place, with people grabbing bells and whistles and ocarinas at random," Emerick recalls. "At some point, somebody said, 'Let's make it sound like we're actually in a submarine,' so that got me thinking about how claustrophobic it was inside Chamber Two. Maybe instead of feeding sound electrically into the chamber, we should try actually putting people in there! John Lennon was especially excited about the idea; I remember him running in as soon as I went to open the door. He immediately began doing his 'Captain, Captain, drop the cable, cut the cable' bit, which had everyone in hysterics, and then a number of the others followed him inside. They immediately began looning about, shaking chains and all that.

"The ambience really was perfect, because of the concrete walls and the glazed sewer pipes laying around—the chamber was designed to be super 'live,' of course. But, in the end, only a handful of the effects on 'Yellow Submarine' actually came from Lennon and the others in the echo chamber, because they quickly got bored of it—plus, with the damp and all, it really wasn't very nice in there. All the party sounds—the clinking of the wineglasses, Pattie Harrison's shriek of laughter, Mal Evans beating on a big marching bass drum—those were all done inside Studio Two. Afterwards, Phil McDonald and I raided the sound effects tape library, which is where we found Stuart Eltham's recording of the Abbey Road power plant noises, many of which we ended up using—the steam hissing, the valves opening, things like that. I'm not sure they made for the most convincing submarine sounds, but it certainly was a laugh!"

failure by many of the balance engineers. Fortunately, Studio One underwent a complete redesign in 1971 under the direction of studio manager Ken Townsend.

Room Dimensions

Studio One: 94' x 57' (29 x 17 meters)
    Ceiling height: 40' (12 meters)
Studio One control room: 24' x 16' (7 x 5 meters)
    Ceiling height: 10' (3 meters)

Studio Two: 60' x 37' (18 x 11 meters)
    Ceiling height: 28' (9 meters)
Studio Two control room: 24' x 18' (7 x 5.5 meters)
    Ceiling height: 10' (3 meters)

Studio Three: 40' x 32' (12 x 8 meters)
    Ceiling height: 16' (5 meters)
Studio Three control room: 24' x 18' (7 x 5.5 meters)
    Ceiling height: 12' (4 meters)

Echo Chambers

Originally developed by American recording studios in the 1940s, echo chambers were simply small "live" rooms that housed a loudspeaker into which selected signal was routed, along with one or more microphones to pick up the resultant reverberant ("wet") sound, which was then returned to the mixing console to be added to the original "dry" signal. By the 1960s, most recording studios in the U.S. and the U.K. offered one or more echo chambers—sometimes specially constructed, other times little more than a spare storage closet or bathroom. No matter how plain or fancy, they were often touted as providing a sound unique to that studio.

The EMI studio complex at Abbey Road was no exception: In fact, by 1957 it offered three custom-constructed echo chambers. Each of the three was numbered, and although any studio could access any chamber via the central patch bay, they were not necessarily constructed to operate with the studio of the same number. For example, Chamber One was built for use with Studio Three, which, as the smallest of the facility's recording studios, was therefore the one most in need of ambient

The Beatles in Abbey Road Studio Two during the recording session for "She Loves You," 1963.
(Photo by Terry O'Neill/Getty Images)

enhancement. Conversely, Chamber Three (the last to be built, and the only one of the three situated on the roof) was specifically designed for use with Abbey Road's massive Studio One.

Chamber Two, which was situated directly outside Studio Two and designed for use with that room, would become the most famous of the Abbey Road echo chambers, its sound an intrinsic part of virtually every Beatles recording. Roughly 21' by 12', the chamber was characterized by low ceilings—there was barely room to stand up—and excess moisture, due to its lack of a "damp course" (an impermeable layer of material designed to keep water out, near-obligatory in humid environments like London, yet somehow overlooked during the chamber's construction). As a result, some staffers recall that condensation would occasionally run down the ceiling and walls. As damaging as this could be to the two Neumann KM53 omnidirectional tube (valve) microphones and Tannoy Gold speaker cabinet placed inside, an even bigger problem was the way the sound of the chamber changed on rainy days, when, according to balance engineer Peter Vince, the sound would become more dull.

But the most unique feature of Chamber Two was the eight glazed earthenware sewer pipes carefully positioned throughout the room—the idea of balance engineer Stuart Eltham. Five of them were approximately a foot and a half in diameter and six feet high (capped on top with flat paving stones to reduce resonance); the other three were smaller, each approximately a foot in diameter and three feet high. The curved surfaces of these pipes allowed extreme dispersion of the sound waves generated by the chamber's monitor speaker,

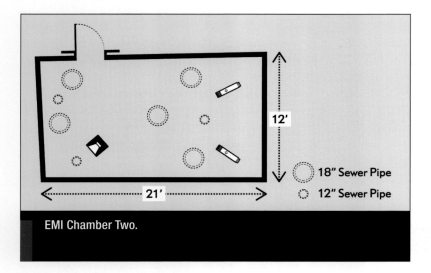

12'

18" Sewer Pipe

12" Sewer Pipe

21'

EMI Chamber Two.

which was angled slightly upward and faced a corner of the room (with a single short sewer pipe directly in front), as shown in the illustration above.

The positioning of Chamber Two's speaker cabinet, as well as the two microphones—indeed, the sewer pipes themselves—was not the least bit haphazard. In fact, their placement was arrived at only after much experimentation by Abbey Road's cadre of technical and balance engineers in the late 1950s. Once it was determined that the optimum sound had been achieved, the setup was carefully noted and pretty much left that way from then on. Most employees, in fact, were prohibited from going inside any of the echo chambers . . . although exceptions were sometimes made.

KEY EQUIPMENT
Mixing Consoles

REDD.37 and REDD.51 (valve)—There were undoubtedly several factors that went into the distinctive sound of recordings made at Abbey Road in the 1960s and 1970s. Chief among them was the skill of the engineering staff (both balance and maintenance), as well as the acoustic properties of the studios and associated echo chambers. But it can also be argued that much of it came from the installed equipment, most notably the facility's mixing consoles, all designed and custom-built by EMI technicians at the company's Record Engineering Development Department (REDD)

in Hayes, originally set up in 1955 to develop stereo recording, primarily of classical music. (Pop recording in the U.K. was pretty much all mono until the mid-1960s.)

The first of these mixers appeared at Abbey Road in 1956 (the 2-track REDD.17, developed in conjunction with EMI's German division Electrola), but at the very end of the decade, two advanced 4-track models, designated the REDD.37, were installed in Studios One and Two. In 1963, Studio Three received an updated model—the REDD.51, which differed from its predecessor only in the type of mic amplifiers it housed—and, in 1964, a second REDD.51 was brought in to replace the older model in Studio Two. (Studio One retained its REDD.37 until the end of the 1960s.)

Both REDD models were essentially 8 x 4 mixers, with eight main channel inputs and four outputs, but each channel had dual inputs, and two of those channels allowed both inputs to be used simultaneously, albeit with the same equalization. In addition, there were two "auxiliary" line-level channels, which, although they offered no EQ or mic amplifiers, essentially increased the number of inputs to 12.

Given their lush sonic footprint, many people are astonished at how rudimentary the EQ controls were on the REDD mixers. There were only two bands on offer: treble and bass, with cut or boost of +/-10 dB, in stepped 2 dB increments and the low frequency fixed at 100 Hz. The high frequency was also fixed and was determined by which of two physical modules—either "Classic" or "Pop"—was plugged into each pair of adjacent channels (that is, 1/2, 3/4, 5/6, and 7/8). These differed in that the Pop module utilized a peaking (as opposed to shelving) curve, centered around 5 kHz, similar to the characteristics of the classic Pultec equalizer used extensively in American studios of the era, while the Classic module utilized a shelving curve centered around 10 kHz. In a 2012 interview with *Sound on Sound* magazine, ex-EMI engineer

Ken Scott recalls how The Beatles had "got into the habit of saying, 'OK, we want full bass and full treble on everything.' So, we'd just turn the EQ full up on every track. . . . If you were to put a full [high-end] boost and full low-end boost on one of today's modern desks it would be unbearable. Back then, however, we could do it on every track and they still sounded good, which just goes to show how smooth the EQ was on those [REDD] boards."

Equally surprising, given the dearth of stereo in England in the 1960s, is the fact that the REDD mixers provided comprehensive stereo panning options, including a unique "Spreader" control that allowed the engineer to alter the width of the stereo image through the use of sum and difference transformers. Another interesting feature was called "Delta-Mono"; this enabled the recording of both a stereo signal and a summed (fold-down) mono signal simultaneously.

The REDD consoles also offered two echo sends, four echo returns, and a full-featured monitoring section that allowed the engineer to quickly and easily apply echo to the monitors only or to the tape returns as needed. There was also a quasi-soloing function, called "check circuit," which allowed selected signals to be monitored without interrupting signal flow to the tape recorders.

TG12345 (solid state)—In late 1968, the REDD.51 desk in Abbey Road Studio Two was replaced by the all-transistor TG12345, also designed and

The Studio Two control room circa 1960s, with the REDD.51 console front and center. Note the view through the window into the studio below, showing a pair of "White Elephant" speakers.
(© Abbey Road Studios)

custom-built by EMI technicians. Extremely large for its time (though dwarfed by the massive consoles of the late '70s and beyond), the TG was a 24 x 8 console that boasted no fewer than 479 knobs and controls, along with 37 meters!

The TG12345 provided four discrete echo sends, as well as subgrouping and two separate cue/foldback circuits. In addition, it offered compression/limiting for every mic channel and subgroup—decades before such a feature became standard on the digital consoles of the 1980s and beyond. Although its channel equalization was as basic as that of the REDD (treble and bass only, at fixed frequencies of 10 kHz and 50 Hz), there were selectable Presence controls on all subgroup and main outputs, enabling an additional 10 dB

of boost or cut at any of eight preset midrange frequencies (.5 kHz, .8 kHz, 1.2 kHz, 1.8 kHz, 2.8 kHz, 4.2 kHz, 6.8 kHz, and 10 kHz). Also carried over from the REDD design were an extensive monitoring system and a stereo "spreader" for each adjacent pair of microphone channels (which could be ganged together in stereo as needed).

Despite its many new bells and whistles and ultra-clean sound (especially on the top end), not every EMI engineer was a fan of the TG. "Personally, I preferred the punchier sound we had gotten out of the [REDD.51]," says Geoff Emerick. "It's subtle, but I'm convinced that the sound of that new console and tape machine [the 3M M23; see *Tape Machines* below] overtly influenced the performance and the music on [The Beatles']

Studio Two circa 1960s. Note the famous staircase leading from the studio floor up to the control room overhead. "That was where the grown-ups lived," Paul McCartney once said.
(© Abbey Road Studios)

Abbey Road. With the luxury of eight tracks, each song was built up with layered overdubs, so the tonal quality of the backing track directly affected the sound we would craft for each overdub. Because the rhythm tracks were coming back off tape with a little less edge, the overdubs—vocals, solos and the like—were performed with less attitude. The end result was a kinder, gentler-sounding record—one which is sonically different from every other Beatles album."

By 1974, the control rooms for both Studio One and Studio Two were outfitted with 44 x 16 EMI-built TG desks. However, with the ever-increasing number of tracks required by pop producers and musicians, the recording consoles grew in size to the point where it was felt that the TG design was simply too large for Studio Three. As a result, an order was placed with Neve for six custom 36 x 24 consoles, designed in consultation with EMI engineers. Five of those desks went to EMI studios overseas, while the sixth was installed in Studio Three in 1975 or 1976.

Monitors

Altec 605A—These coaxial ("duplex") speakers pairing a mid-treble horn with a 15" woofer were installed in the Studio Two control room (and possibly also that of Studio Three) in the 1960s as a direct response to the rise of pop music. Previously, all three Abbey Road control rooms had been outfitted with Tannoy speakers, but these proved to be woefully inadequate in handling the high monitoring levels demanded by the pop artists of the era. The 605As were characterized by their strong bass response (though they were incapable of reproducing subsonic frequencies), as well as a noticeable rolloff of high frequencies above approximately 10 kHz. Though not overly accurate, they provided EMI's balance engineers with the challenge of making the audio sound good despite the monitor's deficiencies. "If you got a decent sound on [the 605As], it did sound good on the radio, because you've got a little bit of extra top," observes maintenance engineer Dave Harries.

Tannoy Gold ("Lockwoods")—In 1968, newly appointed Abbey Road studio manager Allen Stagg made the controversial decision to replace all control room monitors with Tannoy Gold speakers mounted in Lockwood cabinets. The speakers used a "dual concentric" design in which a high-frequency driver was mounted in the center of a 15" woofer, allowing the composite signal to be emitted in phase, thus improving detail and imaging. However, the new speakers were so radically different in response from the Altec 605As they were supplanting that they met with an almost mutinous reaction from EMI's cadre of balance engineers. Dave Harries recalls that the Tannoys "tended to glorify the sound a bit. They were very bright. And, of course, no one liked them because suddenly you've got full frequency response. They were a bit peaky and the bass was a bit woofy. And, depending on where you'd put them, they would sound completely different."

EMI RS143 ("Dr. Dutton" speaker)—Visually similar to the Altec 605As favored by Abbey Road's pop engineers, the EMI-manufactured RS143 speakers (usually called "Dr. Duttons," after the designer of the speaker, Dr. Gilbert Dutton) were embraced by the studio's classical engineers. Installed in the Studio One control room (as well as various tape copying rooms throughout the complex), the RS143 featured a 15" Wharfedale woofer and dual GEC 3" tweeters. They were said to have delivered an extraordinary level of detail and boasted an extended low- and high-frequency response, though the studio's pop engineers considered them overall sonically inferior to the 605As.

EMI RLS 10 ("White Elephant")—These EMI-designed powered monitors were used for studio playback throughout the Abbey Road complex in the 1960s. The cabinets stood nearly five feet tall, and were painted white—hence their nickname. Inside was housed a 15" Wharfedale woofer, dual midrange drivers, and multiple GEC tweeters, along with a Leak TL25 amplifier. The only knob was a stepped input control. Because headphone monitoring did not become commonplace at EMI until 1966, many early recordings done at Abbey Road contain traces of speaker leakage. To minimize this, balance engineers often used microphones set in figure-of-eight polar pattern, with the speaker positioned off to one side of the performer.

By 1977, monitoring in all three studios was provided by JBL speakers (exact models unknown), though the Studio One control room also offered the option of Tannoy Lancasters.

Tape Machines

EMI BTR2 (mono)—The BTR2 tape recorder was a monster, both literally and figuratively: It weighed more than 600 pounds and was roughly the size of a washing machine. It was also one of the few EMI-manufactured audio products that was made available for commercial sale, and it quickly found use in several other British studios of the era, including Decca, and at the BBC. (See Chapter 2 for more information.) Used extensively for both monophonic recording and mixdown in all three Abbey Road studios, the BTR2, with its heavy-duty power supply, transformers, and valve amplifiers, offered extended headroom and was both rugged and reliable. Front-panel controls included a switchable VU meter (which could read line in, record head in, or line out) and both recording level and monitor gain knobs. One unusual control (and an extremely handy one) was an A/B Test switch, which allowed the operator to quickly check between the incoming signal and the signal coming off tape. The BTR2 (and its later sibling, the BTR3—see below) also provided adjustable speed spooling (both rewind and fast-forward), allowing the tape to be shuttled as slowly or quickly as was deemed necessary by the tape operator. Both machines used quarter-inch tape.

There were actually two different models of the BTR2, one of which offered tape speeds of 7.5 and 15 ips (inches per second), and another that provided 15 and 30 ips speeds (though 30 ips recording was rarely done at Abbey Road in the '60s and '70s). Another unique feature, called Auto-Follow, allowed one BTR to start recording or playback automatically when the end of the tape was reached by another connected BTR.

(Metal "contact strips" placed on the tape itself signaled when this circuit was to be activated.) This was particularly useful in classical sessions, where a lengthy performance might exceed the amount of available tape on any given machine.

EMI BTR3 (2-track)—Unlike the BTR2, the BTR3 was built strictly for use in EMI facilities. It offered fewer front-panel controls than its monophonic cousin (although the electronics inside had been extensively redesigned) and was employed in all three Abbey Road studios for both stereo and twin-track (dual mono) recording, as well as for stereo mixdown.

Telefunken T9u/M10 (4-track)—These 4-track tape recorders (the M10 was a later model) both used 1" tape and offered overdubbing capabilities, although this was rarely done in classical sessions, where the orchestra would typically be recorded over two tracks and one or two soloists recorded on the remaining tracks, thus allowing the balance engineer control over the relative levels. Like the later-model Studer J37 (see below), the Telefunkens provided separate tube (valve) output amps for both the record (sync) and playback heads; however, the output from the sync head was severely compromised, with a distinct lack of top end above 10 kHz.

Studer J37 (4-track)—A number of these precision-made Swiss 4-track recorders were purchased by Abbey Road in 1965, and their advanced design and sound quality soon made them the multi-track recorder of choice for both classical and pop sessions. Like their Telefunken predecessors (see above), they used 1" tape and provided separate tube amplifiers for both the sync and repro heads; however, the J37 sync head playback was vastly improved sonically, making the development of ADT (Artificial Double Tracking) possible. (See *ADT* below.) One of its most useful features was the provision of a front-panel mixer that allowed the tape operator to set the relative playback levels of the four tracks. This not only enabled the creation of a custom mix for the musicians during overdubbing—whether fed to "White Elephant" studio playback speakers (prior to 1966) or headphones (post-1966)—it also allowed the tape operator to

IT WAS THE SONG "US AND THEM" that probably required the most involved manipulation on Pink Floyd's 1973 album *Dark Side of the Moon*, according to engineer Alan Parsons. In the stereo version, the first word of almost every line sung by David Gilmour (the intentionally ironic exception being the word "without") is repeated by means of a long tape echo that moves from left to right on each successive repeat. In the quad (four-channel) version, each repeat was returned to a different channel, which entailed using a different tape system for each rather than recycling one signal back through the same system, as one would for a normal tape echo or digital loop. This was accomplished as shown in this illustration; the machine used was an EMI-modified 3M M23 8-track recorder.

Note that each repeat involves two record-replay stages. This was necessary to attain the length of delay needed for the tempo of the piece; in fact, to increase the delay further still, the tape speed of the

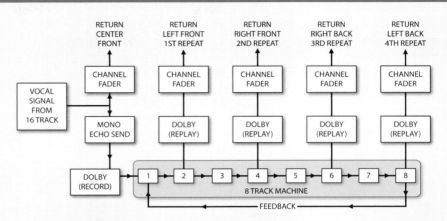

Configuration for "Us and Them" tape delays. *(Courtesy of Alan Parsons)*

machine was lowered. By the time the fourth repeat had arrived—about four seconds after the original signal—it had passed through eight stages of tape, so machine and Dolby lineup were extremely critical. This caused problems: Initially, the record/replay equalization was accurately set, as usual, but even the relatively slight speed reduction caused a noticeable elevation of the top end, and so the

M23 had to be realigned at the slower speed. In addition, the repeat from Track 8 is fed back into the record stage of Track 1 so that a further cycle takes place. Thus, in the quad mix, the fifth repeat returns left front; sixth, right front; and so on. The result is a round-and-round-the-room effect. The system is operated below unity gain, however, and so the sixth and seventh repeats are barely audible.

send varying amounts of signal to the ADT machine during mixing. Tape speed was selectable between 7.5 ips and 15 ips, and could be varied through the use of an external oscillator. "The varispeed on the Studers became very important for the Beatles," said engineer Ken Scott in a 2014 interview for *Record Collector* magazine. "They loved changing the timbre of instruments. George Martin was the first one to do that, recording a half speed piano on 'In My Life' on *Rubber Soul*. They learned from that how it changed the sound." Interestingly, although the stock J37 could be switched between the European CCIR and American NAB curves with the use of relays, EMI technicians disabled the latter option by literally soldering the relay in place!

3M M23 (8-track)—By the late 1960s, most American studios—and even some British ones, such as Trident—had moved on from 4-track recording to 8-track. Abbey Road, sadly, lagged behind, though its ingenious maintenance engineers had designed an ad hoc system that allowed multiple 4-track machines to be synced together, although, since there was no way to automatically start and stop the machines at precisely the same time, the results were sometimes iffy.

In mid-1968, studio management finally capitulated and purchased several M23 8-track recorders, manufactured by the American company 3M. However, with the exception of some Beatles *White Album* sessions, these were

Studio Three circa 1960s.
(© Abbey Road Studios)

not generally put to use for many months because a number of modifications needed to be made first. For one thing, the stock M23 came with only one set of playback amplifier cards, which meant that the signal could only be monitored from either the sync head *or* the playback head; EMI maintenance engineers installed a second set of cards, allowing monitoring from both. (This also allowed the M23 to feed an ADT machine.) Secondly, a small 8-track mixer (with dedicated master volume control and meter) was installed on the front panel, in simulation of the 4-track mixer provided by the Studer J37. Thirdly, a capstan input control was added to allow for varispeed recording (with the use of an external oscillator). In addition, a tape counter was installed.

One unique feature of the M23 was its "closed-loop" path (termed "Isoloop") for the 1" tape used by the machine. This served to minimize wow and flutter, but the design also placed an unusually long gap between the record (sync) and playback heads, making drop-ins (punch-ins) problematic. As a byproduct, this also allowed the machine to produce unusually long tape delays—something used to great effect by EMI engineer Alan Parsons on Pink Floyd's multiplatinum *Dark Side of the Moon* album, as described on the preceding page.

Studer A80—Produced from 1970 until 1988, the Studer A80 was perhaps the most ubiquitous tape machine in the history of recording, not just because of its excellent sound quality but also because of its versatility. Studer A80s could be ordered in any tape width configuration, from 1/8" to 2", and for any track count, from 2-track to 24-track, although the most popular were the 1/4" and 1/2" 2-track models, the 1" 8-track model, and the 2" 16-track and 24-track models. By 1972, Studer A80 2" 16-track machines were installed in all three control rooms at Abbey Road; by 1976, these were supplemented with two 2" 24-track models, which presumably went to the more pop-oriented Studios Two and Three.

All told, by 1976, the Abbey Road facility housed two 24-track machines, three 16-track machines, sixteen 8-track machines, eight 4-track machines, and a staggering fifty-six 2-track machines!

Main Microphones

Neumann U47/U48—The "workhorse" of Abbey Road, these large-diaphragm tube (valve) condenser mics were used extensively on everything from vocals to guitar (both acoustic and electric) to piano to strings. The two models are similar, except that the U47 offered a choice of cardioid or omni polar pattern, while the U48 offered cardioid or figure-of-eight.

Neumann U67—Another large-diaphragm tube condenser, this was the Abbey Road engineers' mic of choice for grand piano and electric guitar, especially when musicians began to turn their amps up loud in the late 1960s. (The U67's 10 dB pad and bass rolloff switches allowed it to handle the increased SPL loads without distorting.) The U67 was also used extensively for recording acoustic guitar and strings.

Neumann U87—This had the distinction of being the first solid-state microphone purchased by Abbey Road, in early 1969. Delivering a similar sound to the tube U67 (see above), the U87 offered additional robustness, and by the time the shift from tube to solid-state components began to take hold in the mid-1970s, U87s began to see increasing use in the studio's pop recordings.

Neumann KM53/KM54/KM56—These small-diaphragm tube condenser mics found a variety of applications within the Abbey Road complex, although the omni-only KM53 was generally used only in the studio's three echo chambers (see *Echo Chambers* above). The cardioid-only KM54 and the newer model KM56 (which provided three

switchable polar patterns: omni, cardioid, and figure-of-eight) were used frequently on electric guitar and occasionally on vocals, as well as on drums—most usually under the snare drum, but sometimes over the snare or even as an overhead or bass drum mic.

Neumann M49/M50—A staple of classical recording at both Abbey Road and Decca, these large-diaphragm condenser valve microphones were originally designed for German radio, and so had a degree of high-frequency lift. They were only rarely used on pop sessions at Abbey Road, though an M49 was sometimes used to record grand piano. Both were notable for producing clear, natural sound; the two models differed in that the M50 was omnidirectional only, while the more versatile M49 offered a variety of continuously variable polar patterns, which could be silently changed by remote control, even in the middle of a take.

STC 4038—Originally designed for broadcast use by the BBC, this bidirectional ribbon microphone was marketed to English recording studios by a company named STC (Standard Telephone and Cable). It was used extensively for recording brass instruments (particularly French horn) and was frequently used to capture the sound of rotating Leslie speakers. Beatles engineer Norman Smith—and his successor, Geoff Emerick—often used the STC 4038 as a drum overhead mic, although its fixed figure-of-eight polar pattern inevitably admitted a good deal of room leakage as well.

STC 4033-A—This unusual microphone (which was functionally identical to the Altec / Western Electric 639A) provided both dynamic and ribbon elements and offered three different polar patterns: omni, cardioid, and figure-of-eight. It was used to mic both bass amplifier and bass drum on many early Beatles recordings.

AKG D19c—This dynamic cardioid was considered by many of the Abbey Road engineers to be of the "cheap and cheerful" variety, yet it was used remarkably often, on everything from drum overhead to piano—at times, it even served as a control room talkback mic. The distinctive sound

Orchestral miking at EMI

THE LATE STUART ELTHAM, who joined EMI in 1950, was widely acknowledged by his peers as a master in mic placement. Although he was primarily categorized as a "pop" engineer, he nonetheless frequently recorded orchestras in those pre-synthesizer (and pre-sampling) days, both at Abbey Road Studio One and on location at concert halls around the U.K., using EMI's array of mobile equipment. "Stuart was absolutely brilliant," says Dave Harries, who frequently did pre-session mic setups for Eltham at Abbey Road, "and he always got good results wherever he recorded."

Ex-EMI classical music engineer John Kurlander recalls Eltham's signature Studio One orchestral microphone setup in great detail. "He would set four Neumann U67s (or, later, U87s) to cardioid; these would serve as his main mics. They would be placed on boom stands, with one positioned over the first violins, one over the second violins, the third over the violas, and the fourth over the celli, then raised ten feet above the violins and violas, and nine and a half feet above the celli, carefully arranged so that if the conductor looked up, he would see a semicircle of microphones overhead. In addition, a pair of unidirectional M50 mics would be used to provide ambience; these would be placed on boom stands ten feet behind the conductor, raised approximately eleven feet high.

"The main mics were supplemented by a number of spot mics: a U87 covering the horns; two KM86s left and right over the woodwinds; a FET U47 on piano; a KM84 for the basses; and one to four KM84s covering the harp, celeste, percussion, and timpani. No spot mics were generally required to cover the trumpets, trombones, and tuba, as they would normally come through loud and clear on the main mics."

When recording in 8-track, the four main mics would be panned in a stereo spread and routed to Tracks 1 and 2, along with the harp, piano, celeste, and horns (panned at 15-degree intervals between the two tracks). Woodwinds would be assigned to Track 3; the bass spot mic to Track 4; percussion to Track 5; timpani to Track 6; and the ambient mics to Tracks 7 and 8, in stereo. Normally, the only EQ applied would be a slight cut at 100 Hz and 10 kHz for the KM84 covering the timpani; the ambient mics might also receive a slight cut at 100 Hz.

of the "Lady Madonna" piano started life with a D19c placed deep in the bowels of an upright piano (near its sound hole) before being heavily compressed and limited by various Altec and Fairchild devices.

AKG D20—This robust dynamic with the recognizable square shape was used at Abbey Road mostly as a bass drum mic because of its ability to handle high SPLs, although it was originally designed for use for speech. (Hence the bass cut switch offering -7 or -12 dB of attenuation at 50 Hz.)

AKG C12—This was an unusually sensitive tube condenser mic that offered nine different polar patterns (omni, figure-of-eight, and seven cardioid patterns with varying degrees of side and rear rejection) via an external box that plugged into the power supply. At Abbey Road, they were used frequently on orchestral sessions, and the C12 also became Geoff Emerick's mic of choice when recording Paul McCartney's bass overdubs. ("I'd put it about six or eight feet away from the speaker cabinet and set it on figure-of-eight," Emerick recalls.) Vintage C12s are among the most sought-after microphones today.

RCA 44-BX—Dating back to the 1930s, this iconic ribbon microphone was used at Abbey Road primarily to record brass instruments such as trumpet or trombone, although the always contrarian John Lennon demanded that it be used to capture his vocal on the notably lo-fi song "Yer Blues."

Outboard Signal Processors

EMI RS124 (Altec) compressor—A heavily modified version of the monophonic Altec 436B valve compressor, the Abbey Road engineers of the 1960s generally referred to this device simply as "The Altec." Offering both input and output attenuators as well as a seven-position "Recovery" switch (which featured a "Hold" setting, unusual for the time), the RS124 was notable for its very slow attack time (which preserved transients). It also had a distinctive sonic signature—marked attenuation of low frequencies and harsh upper mids, combined with a subtle increase in low mids—which made it especially useful when applied to electric and acoustic guitar. The Altec was frequently used as a bus compressor during mixing, and Beatles engineer Norman Smith often applied it to a submix of the band's entire rhythm section—bass guitar and drums—to help "glue" the two sounds together.

EMI RS114 limiter—First introduced in 1954, this monophonic valve limiter had precise stepped knobs for both input and output, as well as a choice of slow or fast attack, and a six-position Recovery switch. The RS114 also boasted a unique Weighting control that changed overall response according to the high-frequency content of the input signal. Though used frequently by Norman Smith on vocals and guitars, it was not favored by many other Abbey Road engineers due to its instability and the resulting audio artifacts it sometimes imposed. In a 1978 article for *Studio Sound* magazine, ex-EMI engineer Malcolm Addey remembered the RS114 as being "a real thumper," adding that "equalising and limiting at the time of mastering to disc was the order of the day [at EMI]. In fact, the first time I wanted to use a limiter on vocal only in the studio, a memo was shown to me, expressly forbidding such a thing and I had to have that order waived at managerial level just to get it patched in!"

Fairchild 660 limiter—One of the most sought-after (and therefore most expensive) pieces of vintage audio gear, the Fairchild 660 monophonic valve limiter has legions of fans. Originally purchased by Abbey Road management as a replacement for the EMI RS114 (see above), the Fairchild 660 was quickly put to good use as a vocal limiter as well as for guitar and piano (due to its fast attack time, it was less suitable for bass). Though it offered just three control knobs (for input gain, threshold, and "time constant"—a combined attack/release control), the 660 was characterized by its extreme response, yielding a highly distinctive "squashed" sound, especially when overloaded. Beatles engineer Geoff Emerick used the device to great effect on the group's recordings, making a practice of sending a submix of the entire drum kit into the 660. "Because most of Ringo's drum patterns started with a bass drum hit, it often made the cymbals sound as though they were going backwards," he recalls. "That's because the bass drum hit was triggering the [660], shutting the cymbals down, and then when the bass drum released, the cymbals were coming back up in volume." Important EMI modifications to the original 660 included the addition of a sidechain input (for applications such as de-essing) and a stereo linking system that allowed one unit to mirror the dynamic response of a second connected unit.

Fairchild 666 compressor—This hybrid tube/solid-state monophonic compressor saw limited use at Abbey Road (certainly far less than its more famous 660 cousin), but nonetheless offered two unique controls: an "Auto Ten" (automatic attenuation) threshold knob, designed to reduce audible pumping or breathing in soft passages, and frequency-sensitive compression in the 3 to 4 kHz range, which allowed the unit to act as a de facto de-esser.

EMI RS56 Universal Tone Control ("Curvebender")—Introduced in 1951 and originally designed as a mastering tool (though eventually used by pop artists such as The Beatles for recording and mixing), this three-band tube equalizer was essentially a precursor to modern parametric equalizers—decades before they existed. Controls were provided for frequency (32, 64, 128, and 256 Hz for bass; 512, 1024, 2,048, and 4,096 Hz for treble [mid frequencies]; and 5,800, 8,192, 11,600 and 16,400 Hz for "top"), width ("Low end," "Blunt," "Med blunt," "Med sharp," "Sharp" and "High end"—with "Low end" and "High end" providing shelving filters), and gain (+/-10 dB, in fixed increments of 2 dB). Although this piece of outboard gear has achieved an almost mystical status over the years, not everyone at EMI was impressed at the time. "As was the case with so much equipment at Abbey Road, the Curvebender seemed to be designed more with classical recording in mind," wrote Malcolm Addey in a 1978 article for *Studio Sound* magazine. "From all accounts, though, it was the envy of our British competitors but what strange frequencies of operation. . . . They were mounted in the cutting room racks and I remember [mastering engineer] Malcolm Davies complaining bitterly that the Curvebender wasn't much use when trying to match the sound of an American pressing for release in the U.K. It was pretty useless to us in the studio also."

EMT 140 plate reverbs—EMI's three custom-constructed echo chambers (see *Echo Chambers* above) allowed its engineers to apply exceptionally good-quality reverberation to their recordings. However, each chamber had its own distinctive sound, which was literally set in stone, since it was the surrounding concrete that largely provided the acoustic profile. (As previously mentioned, staff were prohibited from tinkering with the positioning of the microphones and speakers contained within each chamber.)

For this reason—and because of the need for additional sources of reverberation—four German-designed EMT 140 units were installed in one of Abbey Road's machine rooms in the late 1950s. These were large (8' long, 4' tall, 1' wide) metal plates suspended vertically from springs so that they could freely resonate in response to an incoming signal applied by a speaker-like driver. Each came equipped with a remote-controlled mechanical damper system that allowed adjustable delay times of up to six seconds. (Remotes were installed in all three Abbey Road control rooms as well as all mixing and copying rooms, allowing any room to access any or all of the plates.) In addition, a pair of "delay drums" (see *Ambiophony* below) enabled engineers to apply pre-delays to the echo sends. Each 140 provided a mono input and a stereo output; two of them utilized tube amplifiers, while the other two were equipped with EMI custom-built solid-state amps. By 1976, three additional EMT 140s were added, giving the Abbey Road complex seven in total.

It is worth noting that EMT plates were largely viewed by many of EMI's engineers as supplemental sources of reverberation; they yielded a warm, dense sound that was pleasing but not considered quite as natural as that coming from the acoustic echo chambers.

KEY TECHNICAL INNOVATIONS
Blumlein Pair

Alan Blumlein was a pioneering design engineer at EMI's research facility in Hayes who had been with the company since its inception in 1931. One of the most significant inventors of his era, he received an astonishing 128 patents during his lifetime.

Though he perished while testing a secret radar system during World War II, much of his work was audio-related. For instance, Blumlein played a key role in the development of binaural audio, which later evolved into stereo. In addition to inventing the means for reproducing stereo sound from vinyl (with the use of a cutting head that stored the information for two channels of audio in a single groove), he also came up with an innovative way of capturing audio in stereo: a technique that uses two closely spaced matched bidirectional (figure-of-eight) microphones positioned at right angles to one another in an X-Y configuration—something that ultimately came to be known as the "Blumlein Pair."

Both ribbon and condenser microphones can successfully be used in a Blumlein configuration, and the resulting soundstage is generally strikingly realistic, although the ultimate quality of the recording is largely dependent upon the acoustic characteristics of the room.

Classical recording engineer John Kurlander (who started work at Abbey Road in 1967, when he was just 16, and remained there for nearly three decades) recalls, "In the '60s, there was a very strong philosophy at EMI to use the Blumlein Pair. But around the time when I started, Chris Parker, who was the chief classical engineer, expanded things a little bit and allowed staff to try out the Decca Tree (see Chapter 2 for more information), and so in the mid-'70s there was a bit of to'ing-and-fro'ing. A lot of the EMI engineers still stuck with the Blumlein Pair, but some others started using the Decca Tree, which works best in resonant and reverberant rooms, as opposed to spaces that are very dead. Abbey Road's Studio One was such a good room after it was rebuilt in the early 1970s under Ken Townsend's direction, you could use either technique. I'm not sure it was quite so friendly in earlier years, before the room was redesigned."

Kurlander continues: "It's important to remember that the hierarchies at EMI and Decca were very different, inasmuch as the producers and recording engineers at Decca were on equal status in terms of rank, whereas the producer at EMI was the boss, and [the person who] hired the engineer. So when Decca invented their Tree system, their engineers would say, 'Look, this system works really great [only] in certain acoustics and certain halls, so if you want to plan a recording in a hall where we don't think the Tree will work, let's not go there—let's just record in the halls where we know it will work really well,' and the Decca producers had to accept that. But the EMI producers would simply say, 'We're going to record such-and-such on this date in this place,' and if the engineers weren't too keen on that venue, it was just too bad: They'd have to find a way to make it work."

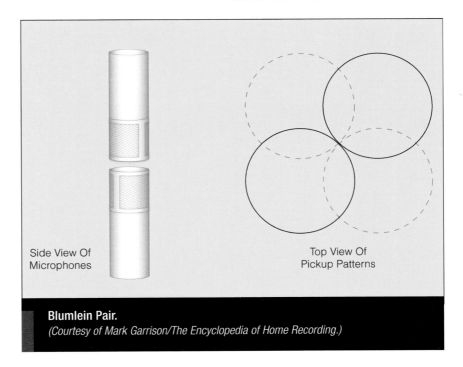

Blumlein Pair.
(Courtesy of Mark Garrison/The Encyclopedia of Home Recording.)

Side View Of Microphones

Top View Of Pickup Patterns

ADT

John Lennon insisted on calling it "Ken's flanging," though it was officially christened Artificial Double Tracking (ADT for short) by its inventor, Abbey Road extraordinaire Ken Townsend, who first started working at the studio in 1954 and was present at The Beatles' artist audition in June of 1962.

"ADT came out of a genuine need," Lennon once said. "We had got so fed up with spending so much time adding voice after voice that Ken and I used to talk about it continually until one day he went off and invented it."

"The idea came to me of using the sync head of the 4-track machine, with a suitable time delay, to add to the replay head signal on remix," recalled Ken Townsend some years later. "After all, the signal coming from the replay head had already traversed the sync head about 100 milliseconds earlier in the case of a J37. . . . We had already wired out the

synchronous motor of some BTR tape machines for variable speed operation, and had built a rather cumbersome trolley with power amplifiers to drive it for previous Beatles effects."

Essentially, ADT was an ingenious use of tape delay—a recording technique that had been in use at studios worldwide for more than a decade (many attribute the first use of the resultant "slapback" echo to Sam Phillips at Sun Studios in Memphis). This is accomplished by taking an incoming signal and splitting it, with one of the resulting two signals routed directly to the mixing console and the other sent to a tape machine, where it is instantaneously recorded, played back, and routed to a second input on the mixing console. The delay between the two signals occurs because of the physical distance between the machine's recording head and its playback head. The slower the tape speed, the longer the delay, and vice versa.

The problem Townsend faced was that even when playing the machine at top speed, the delay was still not short enough to create the illusion of double-tracking; instead, when played back with the original, it sounded like two discrete signals, one an echo of the other.

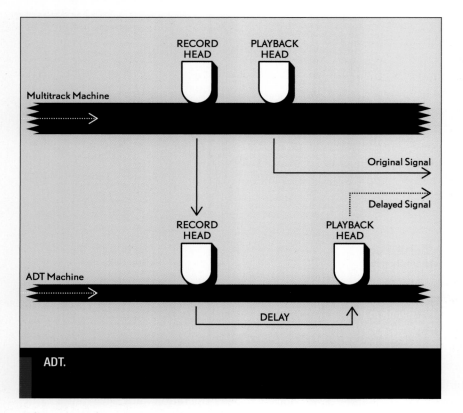

The answer lay in the design of the Studer J37 4-track machines in use at EMI during the 1960s. Unlike most tape recorders of the era, which only allowed playback from the playback head *or* the record ("sync") head (playback from the record head was necessary for overdubbing purposes), the J37 allowed both simultaneously, by virtue of being outfitted with two separate output amplifiers per track.

Thus, the delayed "half" of the signal could originate at the record/sync head instead of the playback head, as shown in the illustration above. When routed to an EMI BTR2 mono tape deck running at twice the speed of the J37, the delayed signal arrived back at the mixing console at almost the same time (since the heads of the BTR2 were twice as far apart as those on the J37). Even more serendipitously, due to slight and unavoidable drift caused by mechanical considerations, they did not arrive at *exactly* the same time, which could have resulted in comb filtering and phase cancellation problems. This same drift also introduced minute variations in pitch that helped further strengthen the illusion of two voices

singing instead of one. What's more, the quality of the signal coming off the J37 record/sync head was not severely compromised, as it was in most other tape recorders of the era—it was actually nearly as good as that of the playback head.

"The effect was startling," said Townsend, "and by use of a crystal oscillator on the BTR2 tape machine, the second voice could be spaced at any required time interval either side of the original"— even *ahead* of the originally recorded signal! This is one of the key features of the ADT developed at Abbey Road, and one that was not easily duplicated by other studios of the era; it would not be until the coming of digital recording decades later that pre-delay of any kind could be easily accomplished.

Delays (or pre-delays) of approximately 40 milliseconds applied to vocals were deemed to yield the best "double-tracking" results—that is, the sound of the two combined signals (the original and the delayed one) panned together sounded uncannily like someone singing the same part twice, albeit with a slightly artificial quality that was itself sonically appealing. Interestingly, panning the two signals to *different* areas of the soundstage (e.g., one hard left and the other hard right) yielded more natural effects and resulted in a lush stereo image.

The ability to freely alter the speed of the BTR2 gave the Abbey Road engineers unprecedented control over the sonic quality of the effect, and it wasn't long before The Beatles and other artists began applying ADT (by this time sometimes referred to as "Automatic" Double Tracking) to all kinds of signal— not just vocals. This in turn would lead to creative applications far beyond what even Lennon and Townsend originally conceived, as illustrated in the Story from the Studio on page 36.

DI (Direct Injection)

A little-known fact about Abbey Road was that the modern DI (Direct Inject) box was born there—specifically from the mind of Ken Townsend, the very same man responsible for ADT. "One of the most difficult instruments to record was the bass guitar," Townsend says. "The problem was that no matter which type of high-quality microphone we placed in front of the bass speaker, it never sounded back in the control room as good as [it had] in the studio."

The solution Townsend came up with was to design a box that contained a transformer that would convert the high-impedance unbalanced signal coming from an electric bass (or guitar) into a low-impedance balanced signal that could be connected directly to the mixing console via a patch bay. As a bonus, the DI box's output signal could travel over very long cable runs without losing fidelity (and with any external interference electronically canceled), thus allowing a bass player (or guitarist) to remain in the studio with his bandmates during recording, with everyone able to hear the sound of the instrument over headphones—and without any leakage into the studio microphones.

By the end of the 1960s, DI boxes—manufactured by many different companies, though all still using Townsend's basic design—had become a staple of recording studios the world over. "Ten out of ten for ingenuity," Ken has remarked, reflecting upon his singular achievement, "but no rise in salary!"

STEED

An acronym for "Single Tape Echo / Echo Delay," STEED was an echo chamber pre-delay system developed by Abbey Road engineers in the late 1950s and used extensively in the recordings of the 1960s and 1970s. Each control room had a dedicated "STEED machine"—actually just an EMI BTR2 monophonic tape machine—into which signal could be fed for recording and instantaneous playback before being routed on to that studio's echo

"I had no idea Ken had invented a completely different method of obtaining a similar effect"

SUCH WAS THE LEVEL of creative thinking at EMI that a form of ADT was invented even *before* John Lennon made his famous request of Ken Townsend.

"It came out of a conversation I had with George Martin sometime in 1965," recalls then–junior maintenance engineer Dave Harries, who had joined the studio only a year previously. "I was listening to this Percy Faith record and was really impressed with the way they had thickened some of the instruments. I described the sound to George and he asked me if I could come up with a way to duplicate the effect with our equipment."

Harries realized that the sound he was hearing was a particular kind of echo—a delay resulting from signal being fed to an external tape machine—and that it was something that could really simplify the process of overdubbing. "It was more like a doubling effect than an echo, actually," Harries recalls. "And it was much faster than the standard 'slapback' echo you heard on a lot of American records of the era, which meant that the tape had to have been playing back at an extremely high speed." The problem was that the 2-track EMI BTR machines in use at Abbey Road could only run at a maximum speed of 30 ips, which wasn't quite fast enough to achieve the desired effect.

Harries enlisted EMI technicians Jock Boland and Bernard Speight in the effort. They began by altering the head blocks of one of the BTR machines, moving the record head much closer to the playback head, thus shortening the delay time. This still wasn't sufficient, though, so Boland made a further adjustment by fashioning an oversize capstan sleeve (made of nonmagnetic brass). The increased diameter of the capstan, combined with the altered head block, did the trick.

"We first used it on an orchestral overdub for Billy J. Kramer's cover of [Burt Bacharach and Hal David's] 'Trains and Boats and Planes,'" Harries remembers, "and George was thrilled with the results. Unfortunately," he adds with a laugh, "a few days later I was sent on an outside recording job and was away for two weeks. When I came back, the very first session I was on, the producer asked for ADT and so I began making the connections to our specially modified machine. 'No, no,' the producer said. 'This is the way we get it,' and he described Ken's setup. I had no idea Ken had devised a completely different method of obtaining a similar effect, and in my absence it had become the EMI standard way of doing ADT!"

"I would literally be following the music with the ADT"

BY THE TIME RICHARD LUSH joined EMI in 1965, The Beatles were already the biggest recording artists in the world. Little did he dream that he would end up playing a key role in their most famous album of all—*Sgt. Pepper's Lonely Hearts Club Band*—as Geoff Emerick's assistant engineer.

"One of the benefits of working with The Beatles," Lush remembers, "was that, unlike other artists, they had the luxury of time. As a result, we'd spend hour after hour recording them, which would give Geoff and I the opportunity to work out exactly what sounded good and what didn't. Same for mixing—we were able to rehearse our moves over and over again and get them just right.

"The Beatles loved the ADT effect, and Geoff and I used to love adding it to their tracks, not only because it sounded good but also because it helped relieve the boredom. The particular oscillator that we used to control the BTR2 lived on a cart on wheels, which I'd set up right next to the tape machines in the control room, within arm's reach. In the mid-

dle of the oscillator was a large black knob with a plastic pointer. There were various settings, centered around 50 Hz, in small increments. Depending on the setting, you could get anything from flanging to double-tracking to audible delay when you listened to the two signals together. But when you'd change the oscillator speed manually as the tape was playing, the signal would go all wobbly—like we did on the 'Roll up . . .' backing vocals to 'Magical Mystery Tour,' which were flanged almost beyond belief. Sometimes I'd wobble the oscillator speed so much, the tape would nearly lift off the capstan! And, of course, the more you did it, the more silly it sounded . . . and the more encouragement I'd get from Geoff and the four Beatles.

"The nice thing about the oscillator knob was that you could set it precisely, so if you tried something on a particular note—say, a specific word on a vocal, or a bent note on a guitar solo—you could reproduce it every time. So if you'd hear something and think, 'Oh, that's quite good,' you could pretty much wob-

ble it the same way on every pass. I'd literally be following the music with the ADT and whenever I'd get an effect I liked, I would remember it and try to do the same wobble every time. It was just a matter of repeating the things that sounded good.

"ADT really was one of the unique sounds that you could only get in Abbey Road—other engineers [in other studios] would hear it and think, 'I wonder what that is?' It was only possible because we used that particular mix of Studer and EMI tape machines, which nobody else had. It was kind of like tape echo, where the specific sound you got depended upon the brand of machine and the distance between the tape heads.

"Another thing people [at other studios] didn't necessarily realize is that ADT could only ever be used on a mix session; you couldn't get it during tracking or overdubbing. That's because you could only derive signal from the sync head from something that had already been recorded— not signal that's coming in live. You could only apply it after the fact."

chamber. The application of this kind of pre-delay was a standard recording technique at the time, since separating the echo from the original signal yielded increased clarity. What made the STEED system unique was that it allowed for an internal feedback loop, whereby controlled amounts of the delayed signal could be fed back into the BTR2's record head, thus creating multiple echoes and thereby diffusing the chamber signal further still. The end result was a pleasing "thickening" of the sound coming back from the echo chamber. Even though this was a subtle effect, Alan Parsons recalls that "distinctive echoed delays could be achieved by overdriving the STEED feedback."

Compansion

One of the many things that set Abbey Road apart from other studios of the era was its formidable and forward-thinking cadre of design engineers working out of EMI's research lab in Hayes, Middlesex. The company was, after all, involved in every manner of advanced technology, including radio, television, and military devices such as radar. The various record labels owned by EMI—Columbia and Parlophone among them—as well as the studios located at Number 3 Abbey Road, were for a very long time little more than an afterthought to the parent company . . . at least before The Beatles burst upon the scene and began generating huge profits!

There was also tremendous pride within EMI, a belief that they could build products in-house that were as good as, if not better than, those of their competitors—and much of the time they were right. The proof lay in the sonically impeccable REDD and TG mixing consoles installed in Abbey Road's studios, as well as the EMI mono and 2-track BTR machines used throughout the facility and elsewhere. The same principle applied to outboard signal processors such as the Curvebender (see page 31).

So when a problem was encountered by an Abbey Road balance or maintenance engineer, the Hayes technicians would be brought in to solve it. The results were sometimes spot-on, sometimes spotty, but never anything less than innovative. A case in point was the TG12321 Compansion Unit,

designed to solve the tricky problem of audible tape hiss during quiet passages—an unwanted intrusion that plagued many operatic and classical recordings of the era. The EMI engineers' prescient solution was to apply dynamic range compression to the signal during recording and equivalent expansion during playback (hence the term "compansion")—a full three years before Ray Dolby founded Dolby Labs and began marketing a similar (though wildly commercially successful) product that would soon become an intrinsic tool in every recording studio worldwide.

The rising popularity of Dolby noise reduction soon relegated EMI's compansion device to the scrapheap of audio history, but let it be noted here that the Hayes engineers were the original pioneers in the war on tape hiss.

An orchestral session in the Studio One control room circa 1970s showing the massive 44 x 16 TG Mk IV mixing console.
(© Abbey Road Studios)

ATOC (Automatic Transient Overload Control)

The ATOC (short for "Automatic Transient Overload Control") was once described by Geoff Emerick as "a huge monstrosity which had blinking lights everywhere." Introduced into Abbey Road's mastering rooms in 1966, it was one of the most futuristic devices of its time, predating today's routine usage of look-ahead compression or limiting by more than 30 years.

A common problem in the era of vinyl records was that passages that were too loud or too bass-heavy could sometimes cause the needle of phonograph players (especially inexpensive ones) to literally jump out of the groove. The ingenious solution EMI's research lab came up with was to install an advance playback head in the tape machines used in the mastering rooms in order to detect such passages before they reached the cutting lathe. The signal from that head was then routed to the ATOC, which controlled the lathe and automatically increased the distance between the grooves ahead of time. In addition, it moved the lowest-frequency signals to the center of the soundstage and even reduced the overall bass content as necessary.

A cutting lathe in one of the Abbey Road mastering rooms.
(© Abbey Road Studios)

The ATOC did indeed allow records to be cut louder (it was used quite effectively on The Beatles' "Paperback Writer" / "Rain" single, where Paul McCartney's bass had been recorded with a speaker rigged up to act as a microphone), but at some sonic expense. When producer Mickie Most raised a strenuous objection to its use during a mastering session in 1970, the ATOC was quietly removed from Abbey Road's mastering rooms, never to be heard from again.

Ambiophony

It was the Grand Experiment that never quite worked.

In August 1965, Studio One received a massive face-lift, courtesy of Dr. Gilbert F. Dutton, head of EMI's research labs. Dutton had come up with an innovative scheme to artificially increase the room's relatively short reverb time (approximately two seconds), which was significantly less than that of most concert halls.

The premise was remarkably simple: Take the sounds picked up by the microphones in the room, delay them slightly (with semi-random variation), and then route them back into a series of speakers hung on the walls and ceiling, where they could be picked up once again by those very same microphones and recorded. The result, in theory, would be an apparent increase in reverb time, as determined by the length of the delays and the distance from the speakers to the mics.

In practice, however, the system was extremely problematic. For one thing, lots of speakers were required to diffuse the sound sufficiently: 96 of them, to be precise. For another, the technology of the day only allowed for a maximum of six discrete delays to be applied, and even this required the use of a bizarre device called a "delay drum" (as developed originally for the Binson Echorec). This was kind of like a cross between a turntable and a tape recorder: In its center was a heavy rotating platter of about 15 inches in diameter, the outer edge of which was coated with ferric oxide, the same material used to coat magnetic recording tape. Positioned around the spinning drum were seven heads: one for recording and six for play-back, spaced in an irregular fashion to simulate randomness. The idea was that incoming signal picked up by the microphones in the room would be routed to the record head, and then, as the platter spun around, would be reproduced by the playback heads, with the delay times determined by the drum's rotation speed and the distance to the various heads.

Each playback head routed signal to a discrete preamplifier, with dedi-cated volume and treble controls, and from there, it would be sent on to 16 of the speakers mounted in Studio One, where it would be picked up again by the microphones in the room. The whole system was essentially a large feedback loop, and therein lay the rub: It only functioned best when on the verge of howling, which made it largely uncontrollable. Worse yet, it didn't sound all that good. "It was too artificial," Townsend has said. "The results sounded a little phony."

Abbey Road's pioneering but fatally flawed Ambiophony system was used only a handful of times in 1966 and 1967 (most notably, an attempt was made to utilize it on the orchestral overdubs to The Beatles' "A Day in the Life" but it "did not fulfill expectations," according to notes made by Townsend during the session) and was scrapped altogether in 1971.

EMI technicians checking the Ambiophony system in Studio One.
(© Abbey Road Studios)

SELECTED DISCOGRAPHY

- Various classical recordings by Herbert von Karajan, Otto Klemperer, Maria Callas, Elisabeth Schwarzkopf, Jacqueline du Pré, Daniel Barenboim, Yehudi Menuhin, Itzhak Perlman, and many more
- Every Beatles album except *Let It Be*. (*Note: Various tracks from* Sgt. Pepper's Lonely Hearts Club Band *[1967] onward were recorded in other studios, but the vast majority of* Pepper, Magical Mystery Tour, *the* White Album, *and* Abbey Road *were recorded at Abbey Road.*)
- Every Beatles single except "Can't Buy Me Love," "Hey Jude," "Get Back," and "Let It Be." (*Note: The backing track for "All You Need Is Love" was recorded at Olympic Studios, but vocals, bass, guitar, and orchestral accompaniment were recorded, live [during the world's first satellite TV broadcast, no less], at Abbey Road.*)
- Pink Floyd: *Dark Side of the Moon, Wish You Were Here*
- Zombies: *Odessey and Oracle*, "Time of the Season" (single)
- Al Stewart: *Year of the Cat*
- Kate Bush: *Never for Ever*

2

THE BIG THREE

O nce upon a time, there were only four major record labels in Great Britain: EMI, Decca, Philips, and Pye. Some six years after EMI's Abbey Road recording complex opened in 1931, Decca countered with an ambitious multi-studio facility of its own, based in West Hampstead in North London. In 1956, Philips followed suit. Their entry into the recording arena was on a much more modest scale, though their studio had the advantage of being located in central London, near Marble Arch. Four years later, Pye would take over a nearby disused television studio and turn it into a multi-room recording facility.

And until the rise of independent studios in the wake of Beatlemania (which changed everything), these were pretty much the only places where British artists could make records. Here are the stories behind the studios owned and operated by the "Big Three" record labels—for many years, EMI's only serious source of competition.

DECCA

The Decca Gramophone Co. Ltd. was officially formed in 1928, but had its origins in musical instrument manufacturer and wholesaler Barnett Samuel and Son, established in 1832. Some time around the turn of the century, the company began producing a line of portable wind-up phonographs (or gramophones, as the English called them) which were designed for picnics but became popular with soldiers in the trenches of World War I.

Despite that success, the company ran into financial difficulty, and so Decca was sold to stockbroker Edward Lewis in early 1929. Following the dictum that the profits are to be made from the sale of the blades, not the razors, Lewis quickly decided that his new company should make records for the gramophones it was manufacturing. Accordingly, the Duophone Record factory in New Malden, South London, was purchased and became Decca Records' pressing plant. The first Decca session occurred in February 1929: The artist was Ambrose & His Orchestra, an early dance band, recorded in a venue in Chelsea. Over the next eight years, Decca would record and release some 10,000 sides of classical and other types of music, making it the second-largest record label in the U.K. (next to EMI).

Decca's history is inextricably tied in with the Crystalate Manufacturing Company, a plastics company that originally made billiard balls and poker chips. They had expanded into recording and manufacturing phonograph (gramophone) records in the 1920s, specializing in budget labels like Rex, Crown, Victory, and Eclipse Records—inexpensive "knockoffs" of hit recordings that were sold exclusively in discount shops such as Woolworths. In 1928, Crystalate moved its studio facility to North London and established premises at 165 Broadhurst Gardens, a building constructed in 1884 that had been used first as a factory, then, from 1915 onward, as the West Hampstead Town Hall. In March 1937, Decca bought Crystalate. Within a year, the Broadhurst Gardens facility, which at the time incorporated two studios, became the center of all Decca recording activity, although most orchestral recordings would continue to be done at outside venues such as Kingsway Hall, a former Methodist church renowned for its superb acoustics.

Two of Crystalate's key staffers at the time were Arthur Haddy and Kenneth Wilkinson, and they

Broadhurst Gardens in 1963, with the Decca studios on the right.
(Courtesy of Michael Daly, www.kevindaly.org.uk)

were quickly absorbed into the Decca fold, joining veteran Arthur Lilley. Haddy was a gifted inventor as well as recording engineer; in the late 1920s he'd built his own cutting amplifier and recording head, which was immediately put into use at Crystalate.

During the dark years of World War II, the Broadhurst Gardens facility would be used to record some 5,500 sides, with a staff of four or five. Reportedly, Studio 2, which was in the basement of the building, was used as much as possible because of the risk of bombing.

In 1949, Decca became the first British company to dub 78-rpm shellac records directly onto LP—quite an accomplishment in those pre-tape days. Accordingly, the Studio 2 control room was outfitted out with numerous 78-rpm players and a lathe. When tape was deemed reliable enough in the early 1950s, wax-cutting sessions ceased and several dedicated disc cutting rooms, tape libraries, and, later, tape copying rooms were added to the complex.

Throughout the '40s and '50s, Decca gradually expanded its property holdings in the area, buying up shops, garages, storage spaces, and even apartments (flats) to house some of its staff. In 1961, the company had the land immediately adjacent to 165 Broadhurst Gardens cleared and began building a third recording studio, deemed Studio 3. Likely modeled on EMI's Studio One at Abbey Road, this was an extremely large room designed to serve as a classical venue and spacious enough to accommodate a full symphony orchestra.

Decca continued to thrive throughout the 1960s, with newly signed popular artists (such as the Rolling Stones and The Moody Blues) and the classical division continuing to turn out highly regarded recordings, though the latter were mostly done at outside venues like Kingsway Hall instead of in Studio 3, which, to the dismay of everyone involved, was found to have substandard acoustics.

In early 1971, Decca acquired premises just west of Finsbury Park in North London to build a project studio (known as Studio 4) to take the overflow from its Broadhurst Gardens facility—a byproduct of artists of the era taking longer and longer to make albums. The building the company selected at 106 Tollington Park had been constructed in 1839 as one of nine late-Georgian villas and was completely renovated and converted by the Decca engineers.

The Tollington Park facility closed in 1979 and was purchased a short time later by Swedish brothers Hans and Anders Nordmark, who renamed it Jam Studios. After Jam closed in the late 1980s, the house became a Masonic hall, before falling into a state of disrepair and being uninhabited for six years. It was sold at auction in 1993 and is now a private residence.

Following the sale of Decca to Polygram in 1980, the Broadhurst Gardens facility too was closed and the building (renamed Lilian Baylis House) taken over by the English National Opera and repurposed as rehearsal space. The last-ever documented Decca Studios session was in Studio 3 on September 19, 1980, for the *Old Historic Music Series, Consort of Music*, pieces by William Byrd. The producer on the session was producer Peter Wadland, and the engineer, appropriately enough, was Arthur Lilley—one of Decca's longest-serving staffers.

KEY PERSONNEL

Pop recording engineers: Arthur Lilley, Arthur Bannister, Jack Clegg, Kevin Daly, Michael Goldman, Mike Savage, Terry Johnson, Gus Dudgeon, Vic Smith, Bill Price, Derek Varnals, Roy Thomas Baker, Martin Smith, David Grinsted, Peter Rynston, Adrian Martins, John Burns, John Punter, Iain Churches, Alan Leeming, Martin Haskell, Graham Meek

Classical recording engineers: Arthur Haddy, Kenneth Wilkinson, Gordon Parry, Jimmy Brown, Michael Mailes, Peter Van Biene, Jack Law, Peter Attwood, Alan Reeve, James Lock, Colin Moorfoot, Stanley Goodall, John Dunkerley, Simon Eadon, John Pellowe

STORIES FROM THE STUDIO
The Threshold story

WITH THE DEPARTURE of the Rolling Stones in 1970, The Moody Blues had become Decca's most successful pop band. Although splits in the group were beginning to appear, the five band members were in agreement on one important point: They were fed up with traveling into London to record, mainly because they all lived in Surrey, a leafy county south of the city. They'd made some tentative recordings in the studio at keyboardist Mike Pinder's house, but the results weren't overly impressive, according to engineer Derek Varnals.

In late 1972, the group's management began talks with Shepperton Film Studios, a facility much closer to their home base, exploring the possibility of opening two rooms there in a joint venture. The following spring, Varnals and Moody Blues producer Tony Clarke attended the AES (Audio Engineering Society) show in Los Angeles to scope out possible new equipment for the studio they hoped to open; it was there that they received their first exposure to the company Westlake Audio.

At around this time, talks with Shepperton appear to have broken down, so the group's management offered a deal to Decca chairman Sir Edward Lewis: If the band paid for new equipment and Decca paid for construction costs, the Moodys would take over Studio 1, a room already badly in need of refurbishment and heavily underutilized by staff producers and engineers, who much preferred working in Studio 2 or in Tollington Park.

Decca quickly agreed, as the deal meant not only saving on equipment expenditures but also keeping the label's top act reasonably happy (although the group members would still have to commute into North London to make records). The room they would build would become the first Tom Hidley–designed facility in Europe. Renovation was fairly minimal in the studio area (only a drum booth was added); the control room was, however, considerably expanded into what had been previously office and tape storage rooms in order to accommodate the Westlake acoustics. Under the terms of the deal, Studio 1 reopened in mid-1974, renamed Threshold Studios. From that point on, it essentially became The Moody Blues' private playground, although other artists were occasionally granted access when the group was on tour and the facilities otherwise unused.

Ironically, the 1981 release *Long Distance Voyager* would be the only Moody Blues album recorded in its entirety at Threshold before the studio was dismantled in the wake of Decca's sale to Polygram.

Of irregular shape with a floor area of
approximately 20′ ×20′
Part of the equipment comprises the follow
An ''Automated Processes'' Console with
input channels and 24 outputs, plus separa
Quad outputs suitable for the production o
Discrete Quad Tapes
One 24 track 3M Mincom Tape Machine usi
tape
Two 4 track 3M Mincom Tape Machines usi
tape
Two 2 track 3M Mincom Tape Machines usi
tape
32 DBX Noise Reduction Units.
10 Dolby Noise Reduction Units.
CCTV. 4 Monitors
2 API Quad Panners
4 UREI Limiter/Compressors
2 Eventide Phasers
2 EMT Stereo Reverberation Units
2 AKG Stereo Reverberation Units
Pandora Digital Delay Time line
Acoustic Delay—Cooper Time Cube
Echo facilities available
Control room designed and built by
Westlake Audio, Los Angeles

The revamped Studio 1 control room (now Threshold), circa mid-1970s.
(From studio brochure)

Maintenance engineers: Roy Wallace, Bob Goodman, Alan Reeve, Danny Gosling, Ken Thurlow, Noel Taylor, Wally Fisher, Bernie Davis, Mick Hinton, Dave Charles, Ron Godwyn

PHYSICAL FACILITIES

The inside of the Decca complex at Broadhurst Gardens was often described by ex-workers and visitors alike as being similar to that of a submarine: long corridors on several levels, with large pipes running along the walls. There were a myriad of doors opening into the facility's seven disc cutting rooms, six tape copying and editing rooms, and the three main studios themselves. Studio 1 was straight ahead as you entered the building, its control room high above the studio, accessible by a steep flight of stairs; Studio 2 was downstairs, and was the most intimate, and the most modern in feel. Studio 3 was a down a

long corridor toward the back of the building—the whole length of the Decca "submarine."

According to Derek Varnals, who joined Decca in 1963, Studio 1's raised control room was built on top of the roof of Studio 2. Above it was a so-called "listening room," used in the early days by record company executives, conductors, and the artist's management and entourage. This room, which overlooked the studio floor, had its own separate monitoring system, allowing visitors to hear the music being recorded without taking up valuable space in the control room below. A similar feature was later added to Studio 3, but was quickly "unplugged" from the studio and became a stand-alone listening room.

In 1963, the Studio 2 control room was moved to a new location and the old control room became a vocal booth and tape library. The larger space allowed the new solid-state mixing desk to be placed parallel to the window so that the engineer could see the musicians on the studio floor. Varnals describes the setup for a typical Studio 2 pop session of the era thusly: "We normally had the piano just by the control room window because it then left enough space between the end of the piano for the bassist and bass amp. Just in front of the piano we would normally have the acoustic rhythm guitarist. In front of the drum booth we'd have the electric guitarist and his amp. That allowed the backs of each microphone to be faced towards the other instruments to minimize leakage. It also allowed the musicians to see and hear each other, something that was important because headphones were quite rare in those days."

In Varnals' opinion, Studio 2—the rock 'n' roll studio down in the basement—was the best room in the Broadhurst Gardens complex. "Provided you didn't do anything mad, your recordings would come out really well," he says. "The sound in there was so controllable, you could get what you wanted. Plus it was so intimate: Sitting in the control room, you were literally only 12 feet from the drummer, with the bass player right against the window. You'd turn your head slightly and you could see the pianist and the conductor, as well as the backing vocalists and the leader of the strings. The only people you couldn't really see were the brass and wind players and the percussionists."

The massive Studio 3 and its associated control room was constructed in 1961; at the same time, a remix room (dubbed Remix 1), was also built on the new extension. In 1970, Decca added a second remix room (Remix 2) with a small vocal booth to the Broadhurst Gardens complex, constructed above the tape library. This was done to relieve the valuable studio time being "wasted" on small overdubs (mostly vocals) and remixing taking place in the control rooms for Studios 1 and 2.

Decca's spacious Studio 4 in Tollington Park was a preexisting extension built over what had been the back garden, described by Derek Varnals as being "kind of like a cross between Studio 1 and Studio 2, with a sound that was a little bit more open than Studio 2, but not as open as Studio 1."

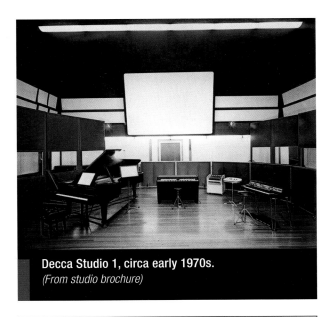

Decca Studio 1, circa early 1970s.
(From studio brochure)

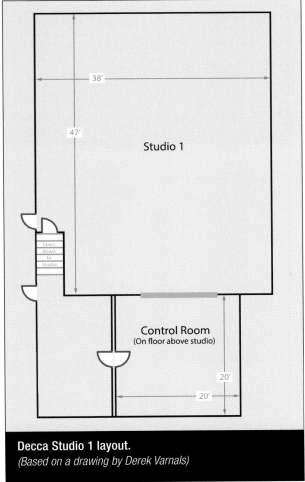

Decca Studio 1 layout.
(Based on a drawing by Derek Varnals)

STUDIO 2

Floor Area 21' × 38' (798 sq. ft.) } Approx.
Ceiling Height 16'
Orchestral Accommodation. Approx. 25 musicians

CONTROL ROOM 2

Floor Area 16' × 20'
NEVE Console with 24 input channels and 16 outputs
One 16 track 3M Mincom Tape Machine using 2" tape
One 8 track Scully Tape Machine using 1" tape
Two 2 track Scully Tape Machines using ¼" tape
20 Dolby Noise Reduction Units.
6 Limiter/Compressors.
Pandora Digital Delay Time Line
Echo facilities available

STUDIO 2

Decca Studio 2 and the Studio 2 control room. Note the "wave-like" ceiling fixture in the photo on the left.
(From studio brochure)

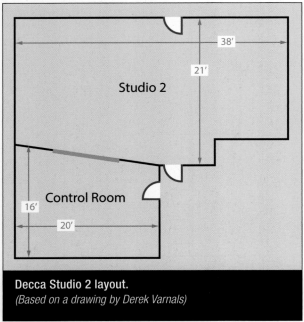

Decca Studio 2 layout.
(Based on a drawing by Derek Varnals)

Acoustic Treatments

The architectural acoustic design of Decca Studio 1 was rudimentary, according to Derek Varnals. "The room was big enough to make it sound spacious, and it allowed you to place loud instruments further away from the quiet ones. Nonetheless, it was a relatively difficult room to record in because it was quite live. It was an old-fashioned room with a wooden floor and very little deadening, and so it was quite challenging doing pop sessions in there. There were some curtains on the walls which could be drawn to deaden the sound a little bit and stop the drums pinging around. In addition, the ceiling was wavy—it wasn't flat; it had curves so the sound didn't come straight back down."

The Studio 1 recording area was slightly dampened acoustically during a 1966 refurbishment. "We put a bit more fixed carpet on the floor and added frames with fiberglass covered with slotted hardboard to the walls," recalls Varnals. "In addition, a number of large movable screens were added to allow the studio to be acoustically cut in half, though they proved to be ineffective, because, while one side was covered with classic peghole acoustic tiles, someone had decided to keep the other covered with slotted board to make the sound more lively for string sections. In addition, the long legs they were mounted on were too wide, and so they intruded on the studio space."

The original design of the Broadhurst Gardens facility presented some challenges during the Studio 1 conversion to Threshold Studios. "The shell of the building meant that we didn't quite have enough height in the Studio 1 control room, which was a problem because Westlake relied on the speakers firing directly and then not reflecting back from the back walls," Varnals says. "Ideally, the ceilings would have been much higher." Nonetheless, the control room received the typical Westlake treatment: heavy bass baffling in the ceiling, soffit-mounted speakers, and rock side walls and ceiling areas toward the rear. During the transition, Threshold's designers also installed heavier, thicker curtains on the studio walls.

In contrast, Studio 2 was reasonably dead, according to Varnals: "The dimensions were right, the monitoring in the control room was right." One of the room's most unusual acoustical treatments was a wave-like ceiling fixture that was installed specifically to help break up standing waves and minimize reflected sound. The floor was covered in carpeting, but the carpet was not tacked down, so engineers could create a live area if needed. As in Studio 1, there were curtains on the back walls that could be drawn to soften the sound; additionally, ceiling-mounted curtains could be drawn to reduce the apparent size of the room.

Studio 3 was, by all accounts, an acoustic disaster. "Everything in

there sounded very clattery and clanky," says Varnals. "When you walked across the wooden floor, it was like you were walking through an underpass. It was just all wrong, despite the fact that the designers had put in angled ceilings with semi-gabled ends so reflections would go up and bounce elsewhere. There were these panels in the walls that were put there to absorb low-frequency reflections, but everything was all a bit too hard. It was simply the wrong shape for its size because of the footprint of the site, surrounded as it was by Studio 2 and other properties."

A number of test sessions were run shortly after the room's opening in 1962, and it was quickly determined that it was simply unsuitable for recording classical orchestras. Instead, despite its massive size, the ill-fated Studio 3 would mostly be used to record light orchestral music, playing host to soloists and smaller lineups such as woodwind or string quartets. Even then, according to Varnals,

Future Police guitarist Andy Summers in Decca Studio 2, 1964.
(Photo by Jeremy Fletcher/Redferns)

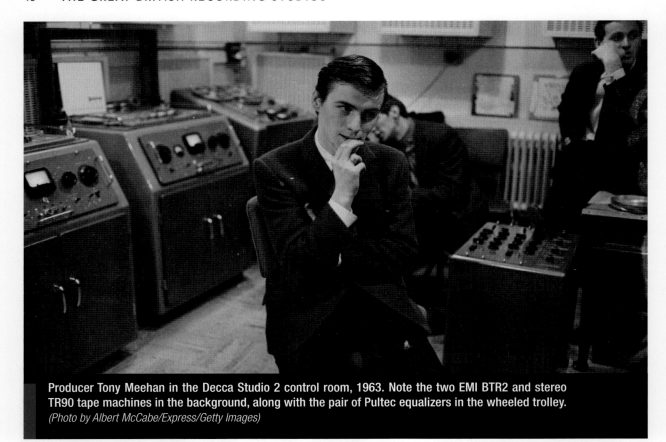

Producer Tony Meehan in the Decca Studio 2 control room, 1963. Note the two EMI BTR2 and stereo TR90 tape machines in the background, along with the pair of Pultec equalizers in the wheeled trolley.
(Photo by Albert McCabe/Express/Getty Images)

"whatever you did, the sound of the rhythm section would go all the way around the room and leak into every other microphone."

Said Bill Price, who would later become chief engineer at AIR Studios, "Studio 3 was very much like AIR Studio One, acoustically: not dead, but not pleasant either. The Decca classical engineers didn't like it; in fact, the only classical music I remember being recorded there was solo piano or solo violin."

Studio 4 at Tollington Park was said to have had a somewhat livelier sound than Studio 2 at Broadhurst Gardens. Contemporaneous photos disclose both carpeted and hardwood floor areas, and reveal that the 25-foot-high ceiling was gabled and baffled, with diffusers placed throughout both the ceiling and walls. As in Studio 2, ceiling-mounted curtains could be drawn to reduce the acoustic "size" of the room. The walls of the Studio 4 control room, like those of the Studio 2 and 3 control rooms, were paneled with slotted hardwood.

Room Dimensions

Studio 1: 47' x 38' (14 x 11.5 meters)
  Ceiling height: 22' (6.5 meters)
Studio 1 control room: 20' x 20' (6 x 6 meters)
  Ceiling height: 7' (2 meters)

Studio 2: 38' x 21' (11.5 x 6.5 meters)
  Ceiling height: 16' (5 meters)
Studio 2 control room: 20' x 16' (6 x 5 meters)
  Ceiling height: 8' (2.5 meters)

Studio 3: 82' x 50' (25 x 15 meters)
  Ceiling height: 36' (11 meters)
Studio 3 control room: 21' x 20' (6.5 x 6 meters)
  Ceiling height: 11' (3.5 meters)

Studio 4: 36' x 30' (11 x 9 meters)
  Ceiling height: 25' (7.5 meters)
Studio 4 control room: 24' x 13'6" (7.5 x 4 meters)
  Ceiling height: 8.5' (3 meters)

Echo Chambers

There were two brick-lined rectangular echo chambers on the roof of the Broadhurst Gardens building, added sometime prior to 1951. They were identical in shape and size, and each had a 12" speaker (probably a Tannoy) on a baffle board in one corner, with an AKG D19 dynamic mic in the other corner, facing the speaker diagonally. As in the EMI echo chambers, glazed sewer pipes were used to break up the direct sound.

Reportedly, Decca's engineers preferred using the studio's EMT reverb plates to the chambers because there was more work involved in tweaking sounds from the chamber.

KEY EQUIPMENT
Mixing Consoles

Like most studios of the era, Decca's mixing consoles were initially built in-house. Technical engineer Roy Wallace is widely credited as the lead designer of the studio's first stereo mixing desk, which offered five or six channel inputs and three outputs, so that engineers could record in both mono and stereo simultaneously. Wallace also built many of the portable mixers Decca engineers used for remote classical recording, such as the renowned Storm 64 model, which provided 24 mic inputs.

In 1962, remembers Bill Price, a ten-channel valve (tube) console with rotary pots for gain, treble, and bass was still in use in the Studio 1 control room. "By 1958, stereo was happening," explains Derek Varnals. "Decca needed a stereo desk, and the powers that be decided ten input channels would be enough for Studio 1." They were divided into two lots of three channels—1/2/3 and 4/5/6—which could only be routed left, center, or right, plus four additional channels, labeled A, B, C, and D, which were fully pannable.

Engineer Kevin Daly behind the console in the Studio 1 control room circa 1967, showing the new 20-input solid-state Decca console.
(Courtesy of Michael Daly, www.kevindaly.org.uk)

With the arrival of the first 4-track machines, the desk was converted to provide four outputs. "This desk offered various combinations of the input and output groups," Varnals says. "On pop sessions, I tended to want one mic routed to one track for the vocal, another mic routed to another track for, say, backing vocals, and all the other mics routed to the remaining two tracks; depending on the lineup, I might have routed six microphones to Track 3 and the remaining two mics to the fourth track. But you couldn't necessarily assign any channel to any track; it was all done in groups, so the order in which the mics appeared on the desk was not logical—you couldn't, for example, have the rhythm-section mics all in a row on the board. It was a bit of a nightmare!"

The explanation for this situation lay in the fact that the desk was really designed for classical use, according to Varnals. "On a pop 4-track session you weren't necessarily thinking in terms of two stereo pairs like the classical people did, where half the inputs were assigned to one pair of tracks and the other half were assigned to the other pair. Mostly, in pop sessions in those days, you were thinking in terms of mono and how you needed to re-balance what was coming from the studio floor, with maybe leaving a track for an overdub or a double-tracked vocal.

"In addition," he says, "if you wanted reverb, you had to consume a channel with the echo return. There were no dedicated echo returns, because classical people didn't use echo or reverb—mostly, they used the acoustics of the room." Ironically, very little classical recording was done on that desk, because Decca's engineers still preferred recording in outside venues like Kingsway Hall; in addition, at around

STORIES FROM THE STUDIO
"They were the people who'd been there at the very beginnings"

"I WAS LUCKY enough to work with some fantastic engineers [at Decca]," said Bill Price in a 1991 interview with *Studio Sound* magazine. "The chaps who were close to retirement in the recording engineering field at Decca [when Price started in 1962] were the people who'd [been there] at the very beginnings of the technology. They'd started recording on wax with one microphone and knew the techniques for recording a dance band with a single STC 'ball and biscuit' moving coil microphone. And they still had lots of the [same] equipment they had used in those days.

"The two main chaps I worked under in those days were Arthur Lilley and Arthur Bannister. They were an absolute fountain of information. Arthur Lilley recounted to me the absolute battles he'd had with the people who were responsible for building the recording equipment at Decca. [For instance,] he thought it would be a good idea . . . to have two microphones, one for the or-

chestra and one for the singer, because this would save putting off a singer who might be nervous about having to record by constantly shuffling backwards and forwards [to a single microphone] and hence worrying about the technical process. That is an excellent principle which easily translates into modern day recording [since] if you worry somebody with the technology when they're trying to give a good performance, that is the opposite of what a recording engineer is supposed to be doing.

"So good old Arthur was working along those lines many years ago and he finally persuaded Decca to build him something with two mic inputs. This was of such enormous benefit that they then made something you could plug *six* microphones into, which was rapidly extended with another four channels."

Martin Keating had the opportunity to frequently assist the redoubtable Mr. Lilley: "With Arthur, there

was nothing left to chance," he says. "If we had the London Symphony Orchestra coming in the next day, he'd have me go and set up for them the night before. He'd go home and leave me with this book that described exactly where the mics went. There was gaffer tape and markers all over the floors saying such-and-such mic needs to be here 20 feet in the air, because the studio had really high ceilings. Everything was really organized and everything was in the right place. My job was just to put [the mics] into place and then to check they were working, and then a half hour or so before the session he'd come in and we'd start recording immediately, straight to stereo. Obviously, with a 100-piece orchestra going straight to tape, there was no chance to experiment, so he just made sure everything was right beforehand. He recorded the same way every time."

Ex-Decca engineer Mike Mailes had equally strong memories of the time the desk was upgraded to 4-track, construction on Studio 3 had begun, with the intention that it would replace Studio 1 as the preferred room at Decca for orchestral recording.

In the book *Decca Studios and Klooks Kleek*, producer Tom Allom remembers walking into Decca Studios for the first time in 1964. His first impression of the mixing desk in the Studio 1 control room was more humorous than favorable: "There were these great big valves [tubes]—the size of milk bottles—in the back of the desk. . . . About every ten minutes the session came to a grinding halt and all these fellows in lab coats . . . came in with soldering irons. The console looked like it came out of a [WWII] Lancaster bomber—and it probably did!"

Engineer Jack Clegg, who worked at Decca from 1960 to 1963, is even more blunt. "The mixing console in Studio 1 was pretty bloody awful," he says. "There were ten channels, but if you wanted the bass on Track 1, you had to put the musician in a particular place in the studio. You actually had to physically move people around to get them on different tracks!"

In 1966, the desk was replaced with a solid-state 20-input model, designed by Decca electronics engineer Bob Goodman, who was in charge of the technical staff at the time.

This desk included the same EQ modules used in the Studio 2 console (which had been installed in 1962), supplemented with a Presence control that added a 3 or 4 dB boost at around 4 kHz. "It was a nod towards the pop people who wanted it," says Varnals, "but it was only useful on certain instruments and not very good on some voices."

classical engineer Kenneth Wilkinson's strict work habits. "Almost to the day of his retirement, if you did anything that was slightly different, you were considered to be not one of the real Decca people. It wasn't on. I remember Wilkie once walking through Studio 2, and I'd got the piano propped up on a little half-stick. He said, 'You can't record a piano like that.' I was quite young at the time, and so I brashly told him, 'Well, you come back at half past two when the session starts and I'll show you.' This was the only way we newer engineers could approach the fact that people wanted different sounds; you had to go about getting them in different ways."

In a 1987 *Studio Sound* interview, James Lock, who joined Decca in 1963 and became the head of the company's classical recording division seven years later, cited Wilkinson as being the main person who instructed him in what he calls "the Decca way of recording." "He taught me what a basic orchestra should sound like, and that a recording is only as good as the hall it's made in. . . . The [Decca] approach, as far as the actual recording goes, is basically to recreate, in an artistic way, all the nuances of a score, plus the embellishment of a nice ambient sound. This is where I part company with the purists who go to concerts every night of the week and then take a stance against certain recordings on the grounds that they don't sound like a performance in a concert hall. . . . Quite frankly, I don't intend my recordings to do so, and I don't think any of my colleagues [at Decca] would either.

"I know it should be up to the conductor to bring out the performance," he continues, "but you can't always rely on that. A good recording is a combination of the performance and the mix. It's necessary to use the technology to emphasize certain parts of the score, just as lighting is used to emphasize colors on film. With music, something needs to be added to replace the visual side of the performance that people obviously don't get on a record. . . . There is a distinction between making records and broadcasting, and for broadcasting there are stronger arguments for simply trying to recreate the sound in the concert hall. If you're sitting in your living room listening to a live broadcast, certainly you want to hear the sound of the hall in its raw, live state, and all the atmosphere just as it is; that's wonderful. But it doesn't work to apply that attitude to making records. You're selling entertainment. And that's a very important point."

Lock summarizes his philosophy as follows: "The criteria of a good record, in order of importance, are: 1, the musical work; 2, the performance; and 3, the technical quality. But it's very important to have all three, and Decca would never willingly compromise any one of them."

The massive Decca Studio 3.
(From studio brochure)

"Again, the classical people had most of the input for the new desk," Varnals continues. "It was a low-profile desk—very flat and very low so it didn't interfere with line of sight to the studio below. Other than that, it was pretty much the same kind of concept as the previous desk: four groups of five mic channels, although each input was fully pannable across a pair of tracks—and this time around you could choose the pair of tracks each of the four groups went to. The concept of the five channels came from the classical guys' typical orchestral and choir miking, where they'd have a Decca Tree with three mics panned left/center/right, plus two outrigger mics." (See *The Decca Tree* below for more information.) "The problem was that they were never going to record anything like that in Studio 1, but again it was the influence of the classical people. In the end, though, it turned out reasonably flexible in that we could have 15 microphones switchable between two tracks by the use of panpots, and then another five mics routed to the remaining two tracks. It was

a question of which group of mics you wanted in which position on the desk."

In 1968, coincident with the arrival of the first Scully 8-track machines at Decca, the board was upgraded to provide eight outputs. That desk would continue to be used until 1973, when Studio 1 was converted to Threshold Studios, at which time it was replaced by an API 32 x 24 console with separate quadraphonic outputs.

The Decca console installed in Studio 2 in 1962 also provided 20 input channels, but it had four outputs and provision for six subgroups, and was thus considerably more flexible. Among other things, it allowed for simultaneous 4-track and mono recording, which became the de facto way of making pop recordings at Decca for a while. (See *"The four tracks will look after themselves if we record the mono correctly"* sidebar on page 57.) However, according to Varnals, one major drawback of that desk is that it required two channels—one panned hard left and the other hard right—to create a center stereo image.

Interestingly, when the Studio 2 console was upgraded to accommodate the arrival of the new Scully 8-track machine in 1968, it only allowed the overdubbing of four tracks on top of an existing four tracks—there was no ability to record eight tracks at a time. This, according to Varnals, was a result of the desk's lack of modularity, in combination with Decca's reluctance to shut down such a busy studio even for a short period of time. "The label people understood that they couldn't just switch to 8-track without installing a whole load of new gear, and they didn't want to do that because they didn't want too much downtime. There were so many people making albums in Studio 2 by then! So if you wanted to record 8 tracks simultaneously, you had to use Studio 1 at that time."

In 1972, the Decca console in the Studio 2 control room was replaced with a Neve 24 x 16 desk—the same model as had been installed in Studio 4 at Tollington Park several months previously. As a result, there was an increasing interchange of overdub and mixing work between the two rooms.

Studio 3, which opened in 1962, was initially outfitted with a Decca 20 x 4 desk, similar to the one that would be installed in Studio 1 in 1966. "Again, this was designed with the classical people in mind," says Varnals. "You could either record all 20 channels to stereo, or you could record channels 1–10 on tracks 1 and 2, and channels 11–20 on tracks 3 and 4. And like other Decca consoles, you had to use channels for echo returns, which was a nuisance."

A 1972 trade listing indicated that the Studio 3 console offered five outputs; presumably, this odd configuration was adopted to allow engineers to record 4-track and mono simultaneously. In the mid-1970s, the Studio 3 control room was upgraded to 16-track and outfitted with a new 30-input, 16-output mixing console, which would prove to be the last-ever Decca-built desk—sporting, to the very end, the "ghastly green colour" (in the words of Derek Varnals) that characterized every piece of homebuilt

equipment to come out of the Decca workshop in the '70s. (Previously, their gear had been gray, which some felt was easier on the eyes.)

The two remix rooms at Broadhurst Gardens were both outfitted with Decca consoles as well: in the case of Remix 1, a 10-input / 2-output model (replaced by a Neve desk at around the time Studio 3 was upgraded); in the case of Remix 2, a 12 x 2 desk.

Monitors

Until the conversion of Studio 1 to Threshold in 1974 (when Westlake monitors with JBL components were installed in the control room), all monitoring at Broadhurst Gardens, in both the control rooms and remix rooms, was via Tannoy dual concentric speakers housed in Lockwood cabinets, powered by Quad amplifiers.

Prior to 1966, the Studio 1 and Studio 2 control rooms were outfitted with three sets of "three bank"

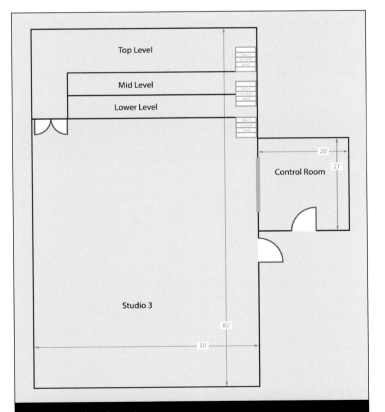

Decca Studio 3 layout.
(Based on a drawing by Derek Varnals)

cabinets described by Derek Varnals as being "open-backed boxes that contained three Tannoy 12" speakers wired in parallel, but with only one tweeter connected. The idea was to yield more bass, and they would go very loud." These were positioned left, right, and center, and could be used for both stereo and mono monitoring; if the engineer wanted to go *really* loud, he could use all three at once. In 1966, at the urging of pop engineer Terry Johnson, these were replaced with a conventional stereo pair of 15" Tannoys in Lockwood cabinets.

Although Studio 3 was equipped similarly, the monitoring in the control room was initially deemed a failure, according to Varnals. "Everything sounded very thin," he says. "The engineers working in there would say, 'We don't know where the bass went, but it didn't end up in the control room!' But it was on the tape. When I was about to do one of my first albums in there, I asked Arthur Lilley how much bass I should strive to be hearing. His answer was, simply, 'You'll just have to feel for it . . . and don't be tempted to turn up the bass knob too high!'"

In the mid-1970s, during the upgrade to 16-track, the monitoring in the Studio 3 control room was altered, with the glass partition between the control room and the tape machine room to the rear removed, making the control room bigger and more square, thus solving the "no bass" problem.

The Studio 4 control room at Tollington Park was also equipped with stereo Lockwood/Tannoys, but this was eventually supplemented with four JBL monitors (exact model unknown) for use during quadraphonic mixing.

Tape Machines

EMI BTR2 (mono)—Bill Price recalls that when he started at Decca in 1962, recording was primarily done to a 1/4" mono machine running at 15 ips, with tape-to-tape transfers done if extra tracks were needed. Derek Varnals concurs, stating that the machine in question would have probably been an EMI BTR2, since the Studio 1 control room housed two of them: one capable of operating at 7.5/15 ips and the other at 15/30 ips. (See Chapter 1 for more information.)

EMI TR90 (2-track)—Introduced in the late 1950s, these were "portable" versions of the EMI BTR machines, although they were still quite heavy and built like battleships.

STORIES FROM THE STUDIO
"Guitar groups are on the way out."

ON NEW YEAR'S DAY 1962, a scruffy, untested band from the north of England rolled up at 165 Broadhurst Gardens in a beat-up old van and were directed to Studio 2, down in the basement. There, to the annoyance of their waiting manager, an impeccably dressed businessman by the name of Epstein, they were informed by engineer Mike Savage that the Decca producer assigned to the session—Mike Smith—wasn't even there yet, having been delayed by the snowy weather and/or the ravages of a hangover from a party the night before.

The band, of course, was The Beatles, who just two short years later would find themselves on the brink

of unparalleled international stardom. But on this frigid morning they were just four young men riddled with nerves and winter colds, trying their best to pass an audition that had been set up by their equally inexperienced manager after frustrating months of pounding the London pavements in search of a way into what was then a very cloistered entertainment industry.

It was their first experience in a professional recording studio, and they failed miserably. In John Lennon's words, the group was "terrible . . . we were terrified, nervous." Drummer Pete Best was placed behind an isolation screen, making his unsteady drumming even more off-kilter, as

well as making it difficult for the others to hear him, and both Lennon and Paul McCartney delivered uncharacteristically timid performances, playing flubbed notes on their instruments and singing off-key. Only lead guitarist George Harrison turned in a decent performance, but it wasn't enough. The group's repertoire at that point in their development consisted mostly of cover songs, with some odd choices ("Besame Mucho," "Till There Was You," "To Know Her Is to Love Her") that made them sound dated and old-fashioned, and their original songs (tracks like "Like Dreamers Do," "Hello Little Girl," and "Love of the Loved") were unsophisticated and unpolished.

Ampex 354 (2-track)—Studio 3 was initially equipped with two of these tube (valve) 1/4" stereo machines, first introduced in 1960. The Model 354 came in either a 3.75/7.5 ips configuration or a 7.5/15 ips configuration (presumably Decca had the latter) and offered front-panel metering and, interestingly, dual headphone jacks.

Studer C37 (2-track)—First introduced in 1960, the C37 was an all-tube 1/4" 2-track tape machine and is widely considered to be the first real Studer master recorder. It incorporated modular electronics, with independent dual-mono record and playback boards. In 1966, a pair of Studer C37 2-tracks replaced the Ampex 354 machines in Studios 1 and 2.

Scully 280 (2-track)—By 1972, Studio 2 was equipped with two of these 1/4" 2-track machines. (See *Advision* in Chapter 3 for more information.)

Studer A80 (4-track and 2-track)—A 1" 4-track A80 and two 1/4" 2-track A80s were added to the Studio 3 control room sometime in the early 1970s, the latter possibly replacing the Ampex A354s that were initially installed. (See Chapter 1 for more information.)

Ampex A300 (4-track)—First introduced in 1949, the Ampex A300 was adopted as the standard tape recorder by most of the major studios in America in the 1950s, though it was rarely found in British studios. A pair of these 1/2" 4-track machines were installed in Studios 1 and 2 some time in 1961; later, a pair were also installed in Studio 3. Derek Varnals recalls that some of these were vertically mounted in racks instead of being housed in a chassis, thus saving Decca some money on the purchase.

Studer J37 (4-track)—In 1966, Studios 1 and 3 were equipped with Studer J37 4-track tape machines. (See Chapter 1 for more information.)

Scully 284-8 (8-track)—The 284-8 featured a beefed up version of the Scully 280 transport, with 12" reel capacity, automatic tape lifters, and motion sensing. Scully also offered a remote control that allowed switching of track safe/sync/repro and transport start/stop/pause at the engineer position. (Ampex offered no equivalent remote until the introduction of its MM1000 in 1968; see *Pye* later in this chapter for more information.) By 1972, both Studio 1 and Studio 2 were outfitted

---

The 15 tracks laid down that day were all recorded straight to mono, and most were first takes, although there were a handful of rehearsal run-throughs to establish balance. The group was never invited into the control room—what few playbacks they were offered occurred on the studio floor through less than adequate monitoring. They left somewhat dejected, though their manager, Brian Epstein, remained hopeful that his strong contacts at Decca—he owned a large record store up in Liverpool and was one of the label's biggest customers—would be sufficient to earn them a recording contract.

It was not to be. Some weeks later, Epstein was summoned to London to have lunch with Decca's executives, only to be told by A&R man Dick Rowe that the group was being rejected. Rowe's stinging comment, according to Epstein, was "We don't like your boys' sound. Groups of guitarists are on their way out." Rowe himself would go to his grave denying he said those words, but the fact remains that Decca missed a golden opportunity to land The Beatles, instead proffering a contract to London group Brian Poole and the Tremeloes, who enjoyed a modestly successful career, though one which paled in comparison to that of the Fab Four once they signed with George Martin's Parlophone Records

and began minting money for label owner EMI.

"For the longest time, The Beatles' audition tape was just sitting out in the tape store room," recalls ex-Decca engineer Bill Price. "In fact, I played it several times. It wasn't very good! It had lots of cover songs that bands did in pubs at the time. It did have a couple of original Beatles songs on it, but it wasn't any of the ones that became famous. One day somebody went in there to play the tape, and it had disappeared"—only to resurface on a series of bootleg vinyl records and, later, on CD. Five of the tracks recorded that day would also eventually be included in Volume One of the official *Beatles Anthology*, released in 1995.

Floor Area 21' x 20'
Decca Console with 30 input channels and 16 outputs
Suitable for the production of Discrete Quad Tapes
One 16 track 3M Mincom Tape Machine using 2" Tape
One 8 track Scully Tape Machine using 1" Tape
One 4 track Studer Tape Machine using 1" Tape
Two 2 track Studer Tape Machines using ½" Tape
6 API Quad Panners
36 Dolby Noise Reduction Units
CCTV, One Monitor
4 Decca Limiter/Compressors
Echo facilities available

The Studio 3 control room.
(From studio brochure)

with Scully 1" 8-track machines. Several years later, a third Scully 8-track was purchased by Decca and installed in Studio 3.

3M M56 (16-track)—First unveiled at the 1968 AES convention, the M56 was touted in the company's advertising as being "the first two inch recorder/reproducer that is as small as a normal four track machine." Like other 3M multitrack machines, it was characterized by a closed-loop ("Isoloop") tape path to minimize wow and flutter. Decca's Studio 2 was outfitted with one of these 1" 16-track machines sometime prior to 1972; a few years later, following a control room renovation, Studio 3 would receive an M56 as well.

3M M79 (24-track)—First introduced in in 1972, the M79 was the last analog machine manufactured by 3M. It incorporated 3M's patented Isoloop tape drive system and boasted variable internal speed control and improved timing accuracy as a result

of a redesigned capstan DC motor drive. By the late 1970s, the Threshold control room (formerly the Studio 1 control room) boasted an M79 2" 24-track machine, supplemented by two 3M 1/2" 4-track machines and two 3M 1/4" 2-track machines (exact models unknown). Studio 4 in Tollington Park would also receive an M79, albeit a 16-track model, sometime in the late 1970s, replacing the Scully 16-track machine that had been installed initially.

Remix 1 was initially equipped with two EMI TR90s, two EMI BTR2s, and a rack-mounted Ampex A300 4-track machine. At around the time Studio 3 was upgraded to 16-track, Remix 1 received a second 4-track machine, a Studer J37.

Remix 2 was equipped with 8-track and 2-track Scullys, plus a Studer J37 4-track and two Philips 1/4" 2-track machines (exact models unknown).

Studio 4 (Tollington Park) was initially outfitted with a 2" 16-track Scully, later replaced by a 2" 16-track 3M M79. In addition, the control room housed a Scully 1" 8-track and a Scully 1" 4-track, plus two Philips 1/4" 2-track machines (exact models unknown).

Main Microphones

Decca's approach to microphones was unusual in two respects. First of all, unlike other multi-room facilities, each studio had its own microphone cabinet. "All the mics at Broadhurst Gardens were color-coded for a while," says Varnals: red for Studio 1, yellow for Studio 2, and blue for Studio 3; in addition, the classical engineers added black bands to the particular mics they liked to use. Ostensibly, this color-coding scheme was employed to help the technical engineers so that they would know where to send mics back after routine maintenance. According to Varnals, things began to loosen up in the early 1960s: "Because the desk and the acoustic treatments in Studio 1 were not suitable for smaller lineups, many of the Studio 1 microphones began to find their way down to Studio 2," he says. "If all else failed, you could usually do a deal with the engineers in the other studios and borrow the microphones you needed and they didn't need. It all got quite blurred in the end."

Secondly, Decca's maintenance engineers were renowned for constantly tinkering with the studio's microphones in an effort to improve them. "There was always something done to make it better—to make it Decca; to put the Decca imprint on it," researcher Mike Gray told Tom Flint in *The Polymath Perspective* magazine. "That was, I think, the genius of Decca: the people doing the mixing were also telling the maintenance guys what they needed. That was Arthur Haddy's work. Haddy was an engineer to his boots and [he] wanted everything to be just right and that's what they got."

As a result, "everything was tweaked by the backroom guys," says Gray. "They might

"The four tracks will look after themselves if we record the mono correctly"

IN THE EARLY 1960S, pop artists at Decca Studios were normally recorded simultaneously on both 4-track and mono machines—something that was seen as both a time- and money-saver: If the balance on the mono machine was deemed acceptable, it removed the need for a separate mixdown session.

That approach was exemplified one Sunday afternoon in July 1964 when Derek Varnals was assigned to assist engineer Terry Johnson on an audition session for a then unknown Belfast band named Them. "Terry said to me, 'Apparently, it's quite an important session because Mervyn Solomon is coming over.' Mervyn Solomon owned a distribution company in Northern Ireland and was a manager of artists, a big fish in the relatively small Irish musical world. The Solomon family were also well-connected with Dick Rowe, head of A&R at Decca.

"I was told that we'd be recording everything live, including lead and backing vocals, and that the band was going to be supplemented with two session players: keyboardist Arthur Greenslade and drummer Bobby Graham. Bobby gave me a quid [a pound, or about $23 in today's money] to set up his drums, which is more than I would earn for the whole day! At Terry's instruction, I put his kit by the side of the vocal booth.

"We recorded the lead vocal on one track, backing vocals on another, Bobby's drums on a third track, and the entire rest of the band on the fourth track. I remember Terry telling me, 'The four tracks will look after themselves if we record the mono correctly.'" Lead singer Van Morrison was placed in the vocal booth, with the rest of the musicians on the studio floor. The bass player and guitarist sang into a single microphone set on figure-of-eight, and Bobby Graham's kit was miked with a single overhead mic. "Because we didn't have any more dynamic mics left," recalls Varnals, "I ended up putting a condenser on his bass drum—an AKG C28 or something similar, positioned slightly off-center. That's why the bass drum sound works so well—because Bobby could really hit it hard, putting a lot of energy into this microphone.

"One of the tracks we did that day was 'Gloria,'" he remembers. "It was just an audition, but they played it so well, it ended up being the version released. If you listen to the stereo mix on the album (which was derived from the 4-track), you can hear Bobby Graham's drums to one side with the backing vocals, the whole rest of the band to the other side, and Van Morrison in the middle. But the single version was the straight mono tape, just as it was recorded live to the BTR2 that day." In fact, eventually all eight titles recorded that afternoon got released—pretty good for an audition!

Tollington Park, home of Decca Studio 4.
(Photo by Tony Harris)

replace a microphone's tube with a MOS-FET, or change some of the resistors to flatten it out, but the key point is that none of the equipment was stock." Alan Reeve, one of Decca's leading technical engineers, is fondly remembered as someone who routinely solid-stated the electronics in Neumann M49s and M50s for the classical department. Martin Keating recalls that classical recordings made by Arthur Lilley routinely used mostly modified Neumanns on orchestra, though he sometimes supplemented them with Sennheiser pencil mics [models unknown] on percussion.

Neumann M49 / M50—Broadhurst Gardens had a dozen of these, which were mainly used for outside classical recording sessions and occasionally in Studio 3, most often in a Decca Tree config-uration. (See *Key Technical Innovations* below.) (See Chapter 1 for more information.)

Neumann U87—Decca owned a number of these, all FET models. (See Chapter 1 for more information.)

Neumann U67—Decca owned eight or nine of these revered tube mics, with two or three allocated to each Broadhurst Gardens studio. (See Chapter 1 for more information.)

Neumann U47—Decca owned two of these, which were purchased on a trip to America by one of the label's A&R men. "He was trying to find the key to the great Nashville and New York sounds, and bizarrely thought it was just down to the micro-phones being used," says Varnals. (See Chapter 1 for more information.)

Neumann KM53/KM56—Decca owned quite a few KM56s; in addition, each studio had one or two KM53s. "They were good for classical recording," says Varnals. "We'd use them for woodwinds or as overheads on harp or solo violin." In pop sessions, KM56s were often used by Decca engineers on piano and acoustic guitars, and sometimes also as drum overheads. (See Chapter 1 for more information.)

Neumann KM64—This small diaphragm cardioid tube condenser was a transition model of the mid 1960s between its predecessor, the KM54 (which had a nickel capsule and an A701 tube), and its successor, the KM84 (which had a Mylar capsule and a solid-state FET amp). (See Chapter 1 and Chapter 5 for more information.)

AKG C12—One of these was also purchased in America following the U.S. field trip. (See *U47* above and Chapter 1 for more information.)

AKG C28—These cardioid small-diaphragm condenser mics were electronically similar to the C12 and were introduced by AKG in the 1950s. Each studio at Broadhurst Gardens had two or three C28s.

RCA Type 77DX—First introduced by the RCA Corporation in 1954, these so-called "poly-directional" ribbon microphones were unique in that their directionality was continually variable. A rotating backshutter on the acoustic labyrinth, controlled by a screwdriver-operated slot at the rear of the microphone, allowed the engineer to vary the microphone's pattern from omnidirectional in the fully closed position, to cardioid, to figure-of-eight (bidirectional) in the fully open position. The 77DX was widely used as a vocal mic by artists like Frank Sinatra, Johnny Cash, and Elvis Presley. Little wonder, then, that two of these mics were purchased during the U.S. field trip in the A&R department's apparently unending quest

STORIES FROM THE STUDIO
Quad: Ahead of its time, or just a bad idea?

IF TWO CHANNELS ARE GOOD, wouldn't four be better?

That was the thinking behind the development of quadraphonic ("quad") recording technology in the 1960s. The concept was simple enough: Record (or mix) audio onto four discrete tracks instead of two, so that independent signals could be routed to four speakers—the traditional two stereo speakers in front of the listener, and an additional two behind (rear left and rear right), arranged in a square pattern.

In 1971, the Japanese company JVC introduced the first commercial quadraphonic product: the "CD-4" disc (not to be confused with the current compact disc), playable only by its new line of CD-4-compatible turntables. Over the next several years, companies like Electrovoice, Sansui, and Sony introduced competing products—all with competing formats and competing names (Quadraphonic, Quadriphonic, Quadrophonic, Quadrisonic, Quadrasonic, and Tetrasonic among them).

Confused? So were consumers of the era. Yet the professional audio industry was excited by the potential of the new format—so excited, in fact, that many recording studios in the U.K. and U.S. began converting their monitoring systems to accommodate the new technology.

Mixing and listening back in four channels was a relatively simple (though often expensive) upgrade for the studios, but creating quadraphonic records was a challenging and complex process for the manufacturers. Quad was at its essence a matrix system, but several different implementations were used—all totally incompatible with one another, of course. Some recorded all four signals in one, or sometimes two grooves; others recorded the rear channels as ultrasonic signals, using analog decoders for the conversion back to audio-range signals. Still others utilized 90-degree phase-shift circuitry. But all the different processes required specialized turntables and cartridges, and, worse yet, they all caused a significant loss of fidelity, with poor front left/right separation (around 12 dB) and even worse rear left/right separation (around 2 dB).

Even though new integrated circuits introduced by Motorola in the mid-'70s helped lower the cost of quad systems, it was not enough to save the technology. By 1975, those record companies that were offering four-channel discs began dropping them from their catalogs, and retailers began selling off their inventories of both the discs and the players.

Yet the technology lived on for a while, both in movie theaters, where it was renamed "Sensurround," and in home theaters when videos and laser discs began to be released in Dolby's encoded matrix Pro Logic four-channel format. Quad was also, of course, the precursor to the 5.1 surround sound systems widely in use today, the major differences being the modern usage of digital encoding/decoding and the addition of center and subwoofer channels.

So was it an idea ahead of its time, or simply a bad idea? You be the judge.

STUDIO 4 TOLLINGTON PARK
Floor Area 30' x36' (1080 sq. ft.) } Approx.
Ceiling Height 25'
Orchestral Accommodation. Approx. 40 musicians

CONTROL ROOM
Floor area 24' x13½'
NEVE Console with 24 input channels and 16 outputs
Suitable for the production of Discrete Quad Tapes
One 16 track 3M Mincom Tape Machine using 2" Tape
One 8 track Scully Tape Machine using 1" Tape
One 4 track Scully Tape Machine using 1" Tape
Two 2 track Philips Tape Machines using ½" Tape
20 Dolby Noise Reduction Units
6 Limiter/Compressors
Echo facilities available

Studio 4 at Tollington Park.
(From studio brochure)

to capture the "Nashville sound." (See *Neumann U47* above for more information.)

AKG D19—There were one or two D19s in each studio at Broadhurst Gardens. (See Chapter 1 for more information.)

STC 4038—Decca had two of these, sometimes used as drum overhead mics. (See Chapter 1 for more information.)

Telefunken ELA M251—These general-purpose large-diaphragm tube condenser microphones are described on Telefunken's own website as being "U47-esque." They offered both cardioid and omnidirectional polar patterns, as well as a figure-of-eight configuration. Fewer than 3,700 total original ELA M systems were built from 1960 to 1965, when Telefunken discontinued production. Modern re-creations of these classic vintage microphones have, however, reappeared from time to time and are widely available today. An ELA M251—also a result of the American field trip—was in the Broadhurst Gardens mic locker. (See *Neumann U47* above for more information.)

Derek Varnals recalls that Decca also built a handful of its own microphones "based on the old Neumann CMV 3 prewar bottle type used by the classical guys." Although they were used in the first FFRR recordings (see *The Development of Stereo* on page 67), they had largely fallen out of favor when the Neumann M49 and M50 mics arrived in the early 1950s. In addition, he remembers there being about a dozen RCA BK 6B miniature dynamic "neck" [lavalier-style] mics, which some of the engineers used as a "Decca thing," described by Varnals thusly: "Each violinist would be wearing one of these little neck mics, which yielded a close, bright signal with very little rhythm section leakage. Six would be wired together into a single channel, supplemented by overheads, which supplied the quality. We'd put a little reverb on the neck mics to smooth them out and blend them with the overheads, which were relatively dry. It used to make the strings sound quite nice. I think we were the only studio that did it, unless the idea was nicked from America."

Varnals also reports that the Studio 4 mic cabinet in Tollington Park consisted of all "reliable FET mics and AKG dynamics," though the exact models are unknown. Although mics would regularly be swapped between the three studios at Broadhurst Gardens (after the color-coding scheme was abandoned), there was a strict ban on "to-ing and fro-ing" between the two facilities.

Outboard Signal Processors

EMT 140 plate reverbs—The Broadhurst Gardens complex had a dozen of these, housed in a separate room under the Studio 1 floor, accessed via audio tielines from all three control rooms and the two remix rooms. "Interestingly enough," says Derek Varnals, "the EMT plates were located right under where we normally put the drums, but nobody ever complained about the sounds leaking into anybody else's EMT plate in another studio, which was remarkable. They were obviously well insulated." Martin Keating disagrees, stating that the separation between the units was less than optimum. "If we were using one of the plates in the reverb room, we had to tell the other studios not to use them because we'd pick them up on our mix or recording," he says. Moody Blues producer Tony Clarke recalls another pair of EMT plates being installed for Remix Room 2. Tollington Park also had four EMT plates, located in a room above the control room. (See Chapter 1 for more information.)

Decca Compressor/Limiter—These hand-built dual-channel dynamics processors were all-tube (valve) and used multiple transformers to "thicken" the tone. Said to sound somewhat similar to the Teletronix LA-2A, they offered per-channel controls for gain, threshold, and recovery time, as well as metering, stereo link, and overall gain and balance controls. Only a couple dozen of these venerated units, which were designed for in-house use only and were never commercially sold, are believed to still be in existence. Every control room and stereo cutting room at Broadhurst Gardens was equipped with Decca

(See Chapter 1 for more information.)

STORIES FROM THE STUDIO
The best-laid plans . . .

HUMOR (OR HUMOUR, as the Brits spell it) has long been an intrinsic part of recording studio culture, though at times it has been carried to an extreme. "I was present at one thoroughly ridiculous Decca session in 1967," producer Tom Allom remembers, "where they were doing a stereo demonstration record called 'How to Give Yourself a Stereo Checkup.' Arthur Bannister, who was in charge of the session, wanted to get the sound effect of a piano breaking up when it fell from a great height, thinking that it would make this amazing sort of 'boing-boing' crash with the strings breaking and the wood smashing.

"They decided to do it early one morning when the streets were quiet, and I made a point of being there to witness the event. By the time I arrived, everything was set: They'd put mics all up and down the mews at the back of Broadhurst Gardens, and they had an upright piano hoisted up onto the roof. The assistant engineer rolled tape and someone pushed the piano off the roof and it landed on the sidewalk . . . but it

just went THUD, with no cacophony whatsoever—not even a single string popping. Yes, it made quite a loud noise, but there wasn't the slightest bit of reverberation. Disappointing, of course, but everyone fell about laughing at the absurdity of it all." Fortunately, the piano movers had a spare one on the van due for disposal, so a second take was attempted . . . albeit with the same unsatisfactory result.

Bill Price, who would later serve as chief engineer at AIR, was an assistant at Decca at the time. "All the staff were asked to come in to help out that morning, so I was there, too. We had discussed the logistics beforehand, and one big question was, 'Well, how loud is it going to be?' There was quite a lot of argument about that, so we decided to set up several pairs of microphones with each routed to different tape machines, and we set the gain of each pair at something like 10 dB different. So we thought, OK, we've got that covered, and then whoever was responsible for pushing the piano off the roof went up there

and someone else—a very junior person, probably, because we all wanted to actually see it happen—was responsible for putting the tape machines into record.

"Eventually, the piano got pushed off the roof, and the sound was indeed way less than spectacular, but we thought, well, at least we've got it on tape. But when we went back to the various tape machines and played back the first recording, it was horribly distorted. OK, on to the next one . . . and it, too, was hopelessly overmodulated. Finally, the last one, which was set for 20 or 30 dB less gain than the first one . . . and again, meters pinned, completely useless. So for all that, we got nothing.

"Nonetheless, [engineer] Gus [Dudgeon] was unflappable. He said, 'Right, we'll soon get that sorted.' He had us start the tape machines up again, and he went out there and got a stick, and he started hitting the strings of the piano with it, and eventually we got something vaguely useful out of it. But it was a lot of work for very little reward.'"

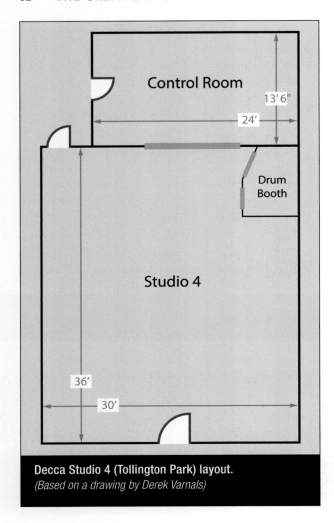

Decca Studio 4 (Tollington Park) layout.
(Based on a drawing by Derek Varnals)

compressor/limiters—four in Studios 1 and 3, eight in Studio 2, and two in each cutting room.

Fairchild 660—According to Bill Price, a significant number of these tube compressors were added to the Decca stockpile of outboard gear after staff producers made a trip to the U.S. to ascertain the equipment being used in American studios. Two were installed the Studio 1 control rooms, with others put to use in the cutting rooms. (See Chapter 1 for more information.)

Pultec EQP-1A3—These classic equalizers were unique in that they offered "no-loss" passive electronics, which meant that the signal level going in was reduced (insertion loss around 16 dB) and then restored by an onboard amplifier. As a result, there was no change in signal level when equalization was switched in or out; the amplifier stage remains in circuit when the EQ is bypassed and adds character to sounds passing through it, largely due to the tubes driving the amp. In addition, there is another special feature: the ability to boost and cut the selected low frequency simultaneously—a trick that works because the respective frequencies at which the boost and attenuation shelves are centered are not exactly the same. This makes the EQP-1A especially well suited for carving out frequencies from instrumental backing tracks, creating space for vocals to sit nicely in the mix. Because they add warmth to the lower registers without clogging up the critical mid band, Pultecs are also widely used on bass, acoustic guitar, and male vocals. The EQP-1A3 was the two-rackspace version of the EQP-1A tube equalizer. A number of these were added to Decca's control rooms following the field trip to American studios, says Bill Price.

Pandora Time Line—This digital delay line was a popular piece of semi-pro gear in the 1970s. It employed modular construction, allowing the main unit, which offered five outputs and a whopping (for the era) 4.49 milliseconds of delay, to be expanded so as to provide longer delays. Delay times were variable in 1-millisecond steps via front-panel patching or internal "strapping." Broadhurst Gardens had one of these installed in the Studio 2 control room, and a second one was added to the Studio 1 control room after the changeover to Threshold; a third unit may have been installed at the Tollington Park location as well.

AKG BX20—These spring reverb units came with a remote that allowed the decay time to be adjusted from 2 to 4.5 milliseconds. Although it had a distinctly "darker" sound than EMT plates or Gold Foil, the BX20 nonetheless provided a fairly natural and smooth-sounding reverb, with little of the "boing" effect typically associated with spring devices. The Threshold (Studio 1) control room offered two BX20s, although Derek Varnals recalls them as being "bought on a whim, and not very good—the reverb time just wasn't long enough."

UREI 1176—This enormously popular American-made solid-state peak limiter was first introduced in 1967. It was common to use the 1176 in "all-button mode" (sometimes known as "British mode"), where all four of the ratio buttons were depressed simultaneously, yielding a ratio somewhere between 12:1 and 20:1, with the bias points changing at various points throughout the circuit— an effect that was particularly marked in the program-dependent 1176. The resultant change in attack and release times, as well as compression curve, yielded a trademark overdriven tonality, with a noticeable lag time to the transient content—a sound that has sometimes been described as "reverse look-ahead" limiting. The outboard rack in the Threshold (Studio 1) control room had four of these.

Eventide Instant Phaser—First introduced in 1975, the mono in / stereo out Eventide Clockworks Instant Phaser was made popular by Led Zeppelin guitarist Jimmy Page, who used it extensively onstage. An Oscillator control set the speed of the LFO, and a Depth control allowed the user to determine the mix of phased and direct signal, in conjunction with a Phase Change knob that set the position of the effect when the LFO was in the center position or was switched off. The Instant Phaser could also be used as an automatic envelope follower, with separate Threshold and Release controls (phase decay time could be set between 0.01 and 10 seconds). The Threshold (Studio 1) control room offered two of these units.

UREI Cooper Time Cube—Co-designed by Dr. Duane H. Cooper of the University of Illinois and famed engineer Bill Putnam, the Cooper Time Cube was one of the most unique delay lines ever made, in that it was completely mechanical, as opposed to electronic or digital,

Inside the Cooper Time Cube.
(Photo by Sylvia Massy/Chris Johnson)

in nature. It literally used a length of garden hose with a driver at one end and a pickup at the other to achieve a few milliseconds of delay coupled

Brings new meaning to the term "mixing in the box"

IN APRIL 1971, Moody Blues producer Tony Clarke and engineer Derek Varnals were in Decca Studio 1 recording keyboardist Mike Pinder's contribution to the band's album *Every Good Boy Deserves Favour*, a major opus called simply "My Song."

Like much of the group's material, it featured a lengthy instrumental section and had a philosophical bent, with references to the earth being a single living entity. Accordingly, Pinder wanted to give the impression of the singer in the song being outside the world, looking down on it.

"As if you were on a spacewalk in your space suit?" asked Varnals. "Exactly," came Pinder's answer. "Do it so you can hear me breathing, but make it sound really close and claustrophobic."

Assistant engineer Dave Baker came up with the idea of putting a large carton on Pinder's head, into which Varnals carefully placed a small microphone, making sure it didn't touch either the box or the singer. "I then filtered the signal to make it sound like a transmission from space," says Varnals. "We were trying to create something serious, but everyone was laughing hysterically—everyone except Mike, who was the only person who couldn't see what we were seeing: a quite Monty Python–like image of someone standing perfectly still with a box covering his head. It eventually ended up sounding a bit like Darth Vader, but this was several years before *Star Wars* was made."

STORIES FROM THE STUDIO
The sound of space, emptiness, and eternity

A FEW DAYS BEFORE The Moody Blues came into Decca to start recording their 1969 album *On the Threshold of a Dream*, engineer Derek Varnals took a call from producer Tony Clarke, who said that he had heard one or two of the new songs about to be laid down, and felt there was a particularly spiritual quality about them. "He wanted me to create a certain kind of mood to open the album," reports Varnals with a smile. "Specifically, he wanted the sound of space, emptiness, and eternity."

Fortunately, this was the kind of abstract request the Moodys and their producer had often made in the past, and so Varnals was quick to grasp the concept. "I thought about it for a moment and asked him, 'Do you mean something like the sound of the background radiation from the Big Bang?' 'Yes,' came the reply. 'That's exactly what I want, but have it going on forever.'

"Later that evening, my assistant Adrian Martins and I went to the maintenance lab and borrowed their frequency generator, which also was able to generate white noise, which I knew from experience could easily be filtered into narrow bands of sound to create pink noise. We laid down about five minutes' worth of this noise, with echo, centered on about 500 Hz, on two tracks of the 8-track machine. We then added another two tracks centered at 60 Hz, and 10 kHz, but slightly different to avoid them combining, and to keep them 'stereo.'

"A few days later we played it to Tony, who was delighted. It became the basis for the opening track 'In the Beginning,' on top of which we eventually overdubbed voices and Mellotrons. When we mixed the album, in order to give the effect of eternity we had the sound reappearing at the end of the album with the intention of having it right throughout the runout groove into the locking groove, as per *Sgt. Pepper*."

Another passage in *On the Threshold of a Dream* that tested Varnals' ingenuity was creating the sound of "The Great Computer" in the opening track. "In those days, computers, like watches, were mostly mechanical," he explains. "The ticking and clicking sounds on that section of the song came from all the watches we could lay our hands on, underneath a metal megaphone on a tray. A C28 was poked down the mouthpiece, and out came this vast sound of whirling and clicking gears; I remember one watch being rejected for being too loud and drowning out the others! We also overdubbed two layers of the sound of the drive mechanism of the Mellotron, which wasn't exactly quiet, but quite rhythmic."

with an unusual spatial reverb effect. There were just three settings (14, 16, or 30 milliseconds), making it suitable for short delays and doubling only, yet the resulting signal was said to have had an uncanny ability to sit perfectly in the mix. A Cooper Time Cube was installed in the Threshold control room.

According to Derek Varnals, the Studio 2 control room also received a monophonic "IBC limiter," as it was called, in 1964. This was actually a breadboard prototype built by Decca at the request of staff engineer Terry Johnson and based upon a circuit diagram of an IBC unit (Johnson had previously worked at IBC). "Terry loved it on piano and vocals and occasionally even overall on a mix," Varnals remembers. "It was a bit of a sledgehammer, but it could make things sound quite punchy if you understood about input and output and thresholds and you didn't overcook it; it was ever so easy to overuse. There was an uncalibrated fluorescent linear moving-line kind of thing on the front panel which showed when it was limiting." In 1968, again at Johnson's request, Decca replaced this with a stereo unit.

The Threshold (Studio 1) control room also included several dbx compressor/limiters (exact models unknown), which Varnals describes as being "really good for vocals because they offered infinitely variable attack times, release times, and thresholds. You could have one set to a gentle compression before the fader to generally reduce the dynamics, and then patch another one after the fader so if you over-pot it, it holds the signal back and does a brick wall thing. That was a great technique to use on unreliable singers who were very peaky and dynamic."

In addition, the Threshold outboard rack included a Master Room spring reverb and, interestingly, 32 channels of dbx noise reduction, as well as ten channels of Dolby.

All the cutting rooms at Broadhurst Gardens were eventually equipped with Neumann lathes and cutting heads coupled with Decca-built correction and drive amplifiers, as well as Decca equalizers and compressor/limiters. (The latter were also installed in the tape copying rooms.)

KEY TECHNICAL INNOVATIONS
The Decca Tree

The Decca Tree is a spaced microphone array for orchestral recording developed by maintenance engineer Roy Wallace in the early 1950s. It was first commercially used in 1954 by Arthur Haddy, Kenneth Wilkinson, and other Decca classical recording engineers. Correctly employed, it provides a strong stereo image while maintaining a sharp central focus.

A Decca Tree setup consists of three omnidirectional microphones mounted on a "T" bar of approximately six feet in length, fitted on a tall boom and suspended high up in the air, roughly above the conductor, with the shorter center stem (approximately three feet in length) facing the signal source. One microphone is mounted on each end of the "T," as shown in the illustration to the right.

The signal from the two side microphones is routed hard left and right, with the center microphone sent to both left and right channels. The level of the center microphone has to be set sufficiently high to sonically fill in the "hole" left by the widely spaced outer microphones, but is not so high as to cause the recording to become overly monophonic. Though most often used to capture large orchestral or choir performances, the Decca Tree can also be used as a room miking technique, although it works better in large environments than it does in smaller rooms.

Initially, the Decca Tree used three Neumann M50 small-diaphragm tube condenser omnidirectional microphones. These microphones, which were designed for German radio, are not truly omnidirectional at the higher frequencies, but exhibit some high-frequency lift and directionality—something which is said to positively affect the stereo imaging. Decca engineers later experimented with using Neumann KM53, KM56, and Schoeps M201 microphones (the latter is a unidirectional mic) with varying degrees of success.

"The original trees back in '54, '55, used Neumann M50s with a variety of baffles," researcher Mike Gray told Tom Flint in *The Polymath Perspective*. "The microphones were positioned close together so baffles were used to isolate the mics and thereby avoid spillage from one to another. The M50 was omnidirectional so the fear was losing that precise

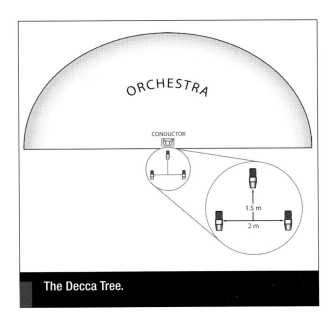
The Decca Tree.

center image. They later discovered that it wasn't necessary to baffle or have the microphones close together," particularly when using KM56 mics.

Interestingly, the standard representation of a Decca Tree is just one of many arrangements tried out by Decca over the years, according to Gray. "It's not

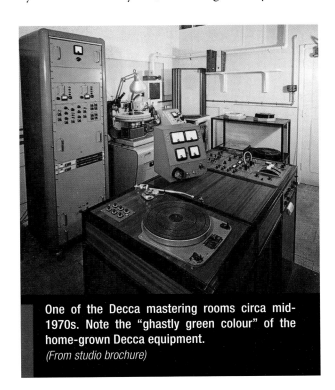
One of the Decca mastering rooms circa mid-1970s. Note the "ghastly green colour" of the home-grown Decca equipment.
(From studio brochure)

well known," he said, "but there were at least seven or eight different tree formations with a variety of microphone types, and there were two philosophies of using a tree. One was the Roy Wallace philosophy, which was the tree by itself, which produced a wonderful three-dimensional image; the second came from Kenneth Wilkinson, who . . . decided that the tree needed help from outriggers [spot mics] focusing on violins on the left, cellos on the right. Eventually their techniques blended."

Elaborated James Lock in a 1987 interview with *Studio Sound* magazine: "The tree is generally between 10' and 11' above the ground. Then, on either side, in line with the tree, are two more M50s facing diagonally across the orchestra, to open the sound out more. For the soloists I use individual cardioid mics, and simply position them according to how strong their voices are. I see the mics very much like lenses in photography, and what I'm trying to do is to focus them so as to get a clear image but with the right width and depth of field. . . . In a nutshell, the most important points with a recording are the balance between direct and reverberant sound, and a good stereo image. . . . I know of no other system that can consistently work as well as the Decca Tree."

It was a technique that was not just used by Decca engineers in concert hall location recording; Bill Price remembers also using the Decca Tree exclusively when recording classical music at Broadhurst Gardens. "It was really nothing more than two bits of Dexion angle iron," he says with a laugh. "We used it mainly because

STORIES FROM THE STUDIO
The Decca/EMI rivalry

FOR MUCH OF THE '60S and '70s, EMI and Decca were the two largest record labels in the U.K. Virtually all of the classical and operatic recordings in Europe were being created and/or distributed by the two; each boasted pop artists who were earning huge profits (The Beatles and Pink Floyd in the case of EMI; the Rolling Stones and The Moody Blues in the case of Decca); and each owned a large multi-studio complex. Little wonder, then, that each developed its own way of working, as closely guarded as any corporate "secret formula" . . . and little wonder, too, that, as a consequence, a sometimes fierce rivalry sprung up between the two companies.

In a 1997 interview for *Studio Sound* magazine, EMI's Ken Townsend recalled that by the time he joined Abbey Road studios in early 1954, "there was apparently a pact between the studio managers of Decca and EMI that no staff would be given a job at either of the other ones. In fact, there was probably some sort of unwritten law [since] nobody did move be-

tween those two two companies." In fact, according to Townsend, EMI and Decca staffers weren't even allowed to speak to one another at the time, "because you had your own recording techniques and they were absolutely dead secret."

As Decca researcher Mike Gray observes, "In those days [recording techniques were] a closely guarded secret and, in fact, there was a 'no poaching' agreement between EMI and Decca. It was an informal agreement which said that when a Decca or EMI technician was let go the other company would not hire them, because they had their own little secrets. That continued well into the '70s and '80s even though their studios were located within a mile of each other! For instance, in Kingsway Hall the microphone connectors for Decca were wired one way . . . whereas EMI's were the opposite. So even though they both had facilities there until the hall closed in '84, they were entirely separate."

Says Tom Flint in the *Polymath Perspective*, "Having interviewed many of

the Decca engineers who were working during the 1950s and '60s, Mike [Gray] believes that, in general, their methods were a little less formal [than at EMI] and that the technicians had more say in what went on during a session. . . . At Decca it was, 'OK, let's get together and try something,' so it was much looser and more independent."

However, Gray is quick to add, "It really depended on the setup. The orchestra was in a certain place in Abbey Road and it was in a certain place in Kingsway. It was also a certain size and had percussion here, horns there; and so you really had to adapt your microphone setup to what the orchestra was doing."

Bill Price, who started at Decca in 1962 when he was just 18 years old, agrees, commenting that "Decca Studios operated slightly differently from that of Abbey Road; there was less hierarchy, and the technical department was very small, so everybody who worked in the studio was expected to be able to repair and maintain the equipment as they

we didn't have enough big booms, really. We only ever had three big booms, so the Tree was useful because you could get three microphones on one boom."

The Development of Stereo

Decca was very much in the forefront of the early development of stereo in the U.K., in contrast to its main rival, EMI, which seem to have initially viewed stereo largely as a novelty, as evidenced by their relatively late adoption of the format.

The origins lay in the company's 1943 invention of the Decca Navigator, a location finder system that employed multiple land-based transmitters broadcasting radio signals to aircraft and ships. In response to a request from the British government, Arthur Haddy and the technical team at Broadhurst Gardens also developed a high-fidelity low-frequency range hydrophone capable of detecting individual German submarines by the signature engine noise of each. After the war, the technology was used to produce better-sounding records that Decca labeled "FFRR," short for "Full Frequency Range Recording." The frequency range of FFRR records was 60 Hz to 15 kHz, with a signal-to-noise ratio of 60 dB. While Decca's early FFRR releases on 78-rpm discs had some noticeable surface noise that diminished the effects of the high-fidelity sound, the company nonetheless set an industry standard that was quickly imitated by its competitors. Their release of the Ernest Ansermet recording of Stravinsky's *Petrushka* was key in alerting the listening public to the potential of high fidelity in 1946.

went along. Mostly you'd just pull out a module and shove another one in, though, and the recording engineers would line up their own tape machines. It was only when something totally failed that you'd take it upstairs to the chaps in the workshop, and there weren't very many of them." In a 2000 interview for *MIX* magazine, he added, "In the '60s, the ethos of Decca Studios was very much that engineers were expected to be just that—engineers. The maintenance department was always very much of the nine-to-five, bring-it-up-to-the-workshop-if-it's-not-working variety. It was quite normal for the engineer to be groveling in the back of a valve desk, changing [tubes], while 25 valve [tube] mics were frying gently over a 60-piece orchestra."

But there was probably no one event that encapsulated the rivalry between the two studios—which by the mid-1960s had become a little more friendly—than the Christmas Eve Incident of 1967. Some time that afternoon, a large packing crate, roughly the size of a phone booth, arrived at Decca Studios. Inside was a toilet with a cast-iron cistern at the top, inscribed "The Original Burlington." (Burlington was the name of a Decca publishing subsidiary at the time, as well as a famous manufacturer of Edwardian bathroom fixtures.) The bowl contained the label of a Rolling Stones 45 single scrunched up at the bottom. Tucked behind the drainpipe was an envelope with a Christmas card inside, boasting a hand-written verse that read:

> *You're loyal, it's true,*
> *   but it's evident*
> *That Jagger and Co. are*
> *   just sediment;*
> *Your miserable load*
> *Should use Abbey Road,*
> *'Cause our folks really are*
> *   EMI-nent!*

In response, Arthur Haddy instructed one of the assistant engineers to buy four large plastic beetles, which were then nailed to a board and sent back to Abbey Road with Christmas greetings in turn. "The toilet episode was revenge for a prior Christmas Eve hoax when a number of Decca staff turned up at EMI in a hired minibus and pretended to be a Welsh choir," says Derek Varnals. "No such session was in the diary and panic ensued."

Years later, it was revealed in an Internet posting on iorr.org that the EMI team charged with making the actual delivery "had worked out all sorts of plausible excuses for getting the crate accepted in case they were challenged, and had armed themselves with walkie-talkies, which in those days were both rare and rather heavy." But they had reckoned without Decca's almost total lack of concern for security in that long-gone era. "When they arrived at Broadhurst Gardens," the post continues, "they found the front doors unlocked and no one there to stop them, as was the case most of the time, and so they simply lifted the crate up the steps and left it in the middle of the main entrance hall."

Decca was also quick to adopt the 33-rpm long-playing (LP) record, first launched in America by Columbia Records in 1948. This new format enabled recordings to play for up to half an hour without a break, compared with the three-to-five minute playing time of 78s. In addition, they were made of vinyl (as opposed to 78s, which were made of brittle shellac), which enabled FFRR recordings to be easily transferred to disc. Decca LPs first appeared in 1950, in contrast to EMI, who stayed with the older format until 1952. (Both companies would continue to issue 78s until early 1960, in recognition of the fact that so many 78-rpm gramophones had been sold in the U.K.)

Little surprise, then, that Decca would lead the way when it came to stereo. The first Decca recordings were made in May 1954, at Victoria Hall in Geneva. Decca thus became the first European record company to use stereo technology, only two months after RCA Victor began stereophonic recording in the U.S., in March 1954.

Stereo FFRR recordings made with the usage of the Decca Tree (see *The Decca Tree* above) were labeled "FFSS," short for "Full Frequency Stereophonic Sound." Even after stereo became standard and well into the 1970s, Decca recordings boasted a particular sonic quality characterized by aggressive use of the highest and lowest frequencies to convey a sense of spaciousness and ambience, enhanced by considerable and frequent re-balancing of specific orchestral voices, known as "spotlighting."

In the early 1960s, Decca developed a process called "Phase 4," in which arrangers and orchestrators would be asked to rescore the music in order to place individual instruments where they were deemed musically most desirable at any particular moment in time, making use of directionality and movement. Scores for Phase 4 recording sessions actually included instructions for the engineers, telling them where each particular instrument and/or voice was to be placed in the stereo field, and whether the instrument should be recorded on one or two tracks of the tape machine (so it could be panned). These recordings quickly became known for their characteristic bright yet rich sound, and Phase 4 albums (mostly recorded and mixed in Studio 3 at Broadhurst Gardens) would continue to be released all the way up until the late 1970s.

Digital Recording and Mastering

In late 1978, the technical engineers at Decca began developing digital audio recorders for in-house recording, mixing, editing, and mastering albums. Each unit consisted of a modified IVC (International Video Corporation) Model 826P open-reel 1" VTR and outboard DAC and ADC converters, connected to a custom codec mainframe with time-code capability (using a proprietary time code developed by Decca). The codec initially recorded audio to tape in 18 bits, although later versions of the system used 20 bits. With the exception of the VTRs (which were modified to Decca's specifications by IVC's U.K. division in Reading), all the electronics for these systems were developed and manufactured in-house by Decca. These digital systems were used for mastering most of Decca's classical music releases to both LP and CD well into the late 1990s.

SELECTED DISCOGRAPHY

- Various classical recordings by the London Symphony Orchestra, Vienna Philharmonic, L'Orchestre De La Suisse Romande, the Concertgebouw Orchestra of Amsterdam, Benjamin Britten, Ernest Ansermet, Karl Richter, and many more
- Moody Blues: "Nights in White Satin" (single), *Days of Future Passed*, *In Search of the Lost Chord*, *On the Threshold of a Dream*, *To Our Children's Children's Children*, *A Question of Balance*, *Every Good Boy Deserves Favour*, *Seventh Sojourn*
- Tom Jones: "It's Not Unusual" (single)
- David Bowie: *David Bowie*
- John Mayall: *Bluesbreakers with Eric Clapton*, *A Hard Road*, *Crusade*, *Bare Wires*, *Blues from Laurel Canyon*
- Ten Years After: *Ten Years After*, *Stonedhenge*
- Thin Lizzy: *Vagabonds of the Western World*

PHILIPS

Singer Dusty Springfield in the Philips control room, 1962.
(Photo by Harry Hammond/V&A Images/Getty Images)

Philips Records, a company that initially simply pressed records for Decca's outlet in Amsterdam, was founded by the Dutch electronics giant Philips in 1946. In 1950, the label began issuing its own recordings of classical artists from Germany, France, and the Netherlands on 10" 78-rpm discs, with LPs following in 1954; Philips would also become the U.K. and European distributor for the American label Columbia Records. The first British Number 1 hit single on the Philips label was Frankie Laine's "I Believe," released in April 1953.

Many of the early Philips recordings were produced by Norman Newell (later to join EMI) and A&R chief John Franz.

In August 1956, the label opened its own single-room recording facility, Philips Studio, located in Stanhope House at Number 2-4 Stanhope Place, an elegant early-19th-century mansion near Marble Arch in central London. Staff engineers would, however, continue to make classical recordings in larger outside venues such as Walthamstow Town Hall in East London.

Over the coming 26 years, Philips Studio would be used for the recording of everything from pop, folk, and jazz to light orchestral music, as well as film music and jingles—even Shakespearean plays. The studio's client list was equally eclectic and would include Cleo Laine, Sandy Shaw, Vicky Carr, Sir John Gielgud, Benny Goodman, Kenny Ball, Humphrey Lyttelton, Rod McKuen, Dusty Springfield, Jose Feliciano, Chuck Berry, Manfred Mann, the Walker Brothers, The Move, ELO, Status Quo, and Ultravox.

Following its acquisition of Chappell Studios in 1968 (see *Chappell* in Chapter 8 for more information), Philips turned its attention more to the growing MOR ("Middle of the Road") market, signing artists like Lena Zavaroni, Peters and Lee, Nana Mouskouri, and Demis Roussos, all of whom recorded almost exclusively in the Marble Arch facility. In 1972, Philips, along with Fontana, Mercury Records, and the newly formed Vertigo Records, was amalgamated into a new company called Phonogram Records; shortly thereafter, Philips Studio would be renamed Phonogram Studio. In late 1979, Phonogram signed Dire Straits; the band would later be chosen to help launch the CD format, which was developed jointly by Philips and Sony.

In 1980, Phonogram and Polydor Records merged to become PolyGram Records. Three years later, Phonogram Studio was put on the market for sale. It was bought by Jam guitarist/singer/songwriter Paul Weller, who changed the name to Solid Bond Studios. Weller closed the facility in 1990.

KEY PERSONNEL

Recording engineers: Bill Street, Peter Oliff, David Voyde, Roger Wake, Chris Harding, Steve Brown, Steve Lillywhite, Richard Ashley

Maintenance engineers: Ron Godwyn, Mick Moriarty

PHYSICAL FACILITIES

Due to its basement entrance, visitors to Philips Studio at Stanhope House often likened the experience to going backstage. Entering the facility required first going down a stairwell on the street and in through a kind of stage door on the side of the building, then turning left and heading up a stairway back to the ground-floor level, where the studio and control room were located directly next to one another (though the control room was raised two or three feet higher than the studio). Even though Philips operated just a single recording studio, staff nonetheless referred to it, perhaps somewhat sardonically, as "Studio One."

A typical session setup would place strings at one end, with the drums and other instruments, including guitars and bass, at the other end; horns and brass would be placed in the middle. Despite its somewhat modest size, 32-piece orchestras were routinely booked in to do sessions at Philips.

In addition to the main studio and control room, the Stanhope House facility included various offices, maintenance workshops, and a small "reduction" (tape copying) room. (A second copying room was added in the 1970s.) There was also a separate machine room off to one side of the control room that housed the studio's tape recorders and editing equipment. Communication between the two was via a talkback system and a small glass window.

The Philips control room circa 1966, showing the newly installed Neve solid-state console.
(Photo courtesy of Ron Godwyn)

Acoustic Treatments

Little information about the acoustic treatment in Philips prior to 1966 is available. However, that year, the studio received a makeover supervised by renowned acoustician Sandy Brown, which was said to have "improved greatly on the original treatment and decor." One byproduct was the alteration of the studio's and control room's acoustics in response to the rising popularity of pop recordings: Reportedly, the reverberation time in the studio was reduced to 0.3 seconds, and, in the control room, to 0.15 seconds. (Presumably, both rooms were considerably more live initially.) Contemporaneous photographs of the studio show a ceiling covered in slotted wood diffusors and walls lined with curtains and wood-framed panels that presumably contained acoustically absorbent material; also employed were a number of movable acoustic screens designed by Brown. Given that a faint rumble could reportedly be felt whenever the Tube train (subway) passed below, the facility probably did not have floating floors.

Ironically, the small size of the Philips recording area seemed to have worked in its favor, at least in the early days, when producers the world over were looking to emulate Phil Spector's fabled—and hugely successful—"Wall of Sound." Certainly many of the records coming out of Philips' modest facilities (such as Dusty Springfield's "You Don't Have to Say You Love Me") sounded massive; this may well have been the result of placing large numbers of musicians in a cramped space, similar to the conditions Spector and his engineers worked under at Gold Star Recording in Los Angeles. (In the case of this particular record, there was another factor: As authors Penny Valentine and Vicki Wickham report in the book *Dancing with Demons: The Authorized Biography of Dusty Springfield*, "The sound engineer Peter Oliff went to the basement to sort out the sound on Dusty's echo chamber. He noticed how good the sound was coming back up the stairwell. Dusty, who had always hated what she heard in the 'dead' sound of the studio in Stanhope Place . . . went out there and sang into a mic suspended over the stairwell and the sound was perfect.")

In 1977, Phonogram Records (Philips Records' parent company) moved its offices to another building, but decided to continue operating the studio at Stanhope House. This decision necessitated adding extra sound isolation so that the new tenants would not be disturbed by sessions going on in the basement. At the same time, it was decided to alter the acoustics substantially once again.

Accordingly, the studio was stripped back to its bare walls and rebuilt by Tom Hidley of Eastlake; a year later, the control room received the same treatment. But this was to be no typical Hidley treatment; indeed, as a 1977 article in *Music Week* proclaimed, "The completed studio only has a little of the well-known air of an Eastlake opus. Under firm, polite pressure from [technical director Ron] Godwyn and Peter Oliff, deputy studio manager and chief engineer, the characteristic Hidley deep acoustic trapping along walls was taken out of the design, so that floor space would not be reduced. With 23 feet of ceiling height available, Hidley was persuaded to put most of his trapping up there."

A 1978 *Studio Sound* article elaborated: "As soon as the internal isolating structure was completed—including two new concrete floors—the acoustic treatment geometry and finishes were added. The resultant room has a 'live shell,' intended for strings, with marble floor, natural elm timber walls and ceiling, and a giant mirror. This gives good first reflections and a warm string sound. The opposite end of the room [the area closest to the control room] has a drum booth and a generally lower ceiling. . . . One entire wall of the studio is constructed from quarried York stone blocks, which . . . gives good dispersion of sound. The wall directly opposite is a sound trap covered from floor to ceiling with drapes. The heavy shag pile carpet and the sloping fabric covered ceiling complete the picture."

The article includes a boast from an unnamed source at Phonogram that the acoustics of the redesigned studio were "uncanny," with "none of that dead 'cotton wool' feel" found in many studios of comparable size. However, many clients and staff reportedly disliked the resulting dead sound, and so the rooms were said to have been repeatedly altered over the following years in an attempt to make them sound more live.

STORIES FROM THE STUDIO
Rupert Neve and the Neve console

RUPERT NEVE is considered one of the founding fathers of the modern mixing console, but he was clearly also something of a child prodigy. Neve began designing audio amplifiers and radio receivers in 1939, when he was just 13 years old. Four years later, he converted a retired U.S. Army ambulance into a mobile studio, recording local choirs, music festivals, and public events on 78-rpm lacquer discs.

In the 1950s, Neve began working for Rediffusion, an early cable TV provider in the U.K., and soon thereafter formed his own company, CQ Audio, which built hand-wired hi-fi speaker systems. In the early 1960s,

he designed and built a mixing console for an Irish composer named Desmond Leslie; a year later he formed Neve Electronics.

By 1964, Neve had developed high-performance transistor equipment that replaced traditional tube designs. His first client for one of the new mixers was Philips Studio, which quickly led to orders from other recording studios. With the rapid expansion of the British recording industry in the wake of The Beatles' worldwide success, Neve Electronics began developing and manufacturing an entire line of mixing consoles and signal processors renowned for their

clarity of sound and extraordinary workmanship.

In the mid- and late 1970s, Rupert Neve collaborated with engineers from George Martin's AIR studios to develop the famed AIR Montserrat consoles, widely considered to be among the most sophisticated analog mixers ever built. (See Chapter 7 for more information.) During this period Neve also introduced NECAM, the first computer-controlled moving fader mix automation system. Neve continues an active involvement in the professional audio industry to this day, through his U.S.-based company Rupert Neve Designs.

Room Dimensions
Studio: 40' x 22' (12 x 6.5 meters)
   Ceiling height: 20' (6 meters)
Control room: 18'6" x 11' (5.5 x 3.5 meters)
   Ceiling height: 14' (4 meters)

Echo Chambers
Philips had one acoustic echo chamber, located down a flight of steps at the rear of the building, though according to both engineer Roger Wake and former technical director Ron Godwyn, it was rarely used from the 1960s onward. The room was covered in white tiles with no parallel walls. At one end was a Leslie cabinet permanently wired in; at the other, an antique humidifier, presumably (and curiously, given London's usual damp weather) used to help keep the environment moist. Whether this was for sonic purposes is unknown, but it certainly would have had a deleterious effect on the Leslie speakers and electronics!

KEY EQUIPMENT
Mixing Consoles
Initially, a monophonic 12-input Neumann tube (valve) console was installed in the Philips control room. In

1958, the board was rebuilt for stereo, and subsequently for four-track recording. The Neumann was replaced in 1966 with one of the first Neve solid-state consoles, which provided 16 input channels and four outputs and employed germanium transistors. In 1968, when the studio went 8-track, the desk was upgraded to a Neve 20 x 8 model.

The relationship between Philips and Neve dated back to 1959, when the company contracted Rupert Neve to build a portable mixer for transporting to outside venues; this was a hand-built ten-input, three-output console, augmented by a six-channel sidecar (which could be used independently of the main console if necessary), with two-band EQ and high-pass filtering on every channel, all with selectable frequencies. (See *Rupert Neve and the Neve console* above.)

In 1972, a custom L-shaped 32 x 16 desk built by parent company Phonogram in Holland (with design input from Philips engineers Roger Wake, Ron Godwyn, and Mick Moriarty) replaced the studio's Neve. "Particular attention was paid to flexibility, logical layout and simplicity of operation, especially the latter, as ergonomics, colour coding etc. were aimed at single operator control of the vast array of facilities," said studio manager Tom Stephenson in a 1973 *Studio Sound* article. "The layout is an important feature," added Ron Godwyn in that same article. "For example, the engineers want to see the text in low-lighting conditions, and they need the rows of controls distinctly colour-coded and positioned in order of priority." Clearly, those goals were accomplished, as the desk was reportedly installed and placed in service in just one week's time, without even the benefit of test sessions.

The new Phonogram console offered several unique features. One was its use of special thin-film Class B op amps throughout each channel. These were only 18 by 21 millimeters in size and were described at the time as being "a major breakthrough in circuit design." Their compact dimensions allowed each of the 32 mic channels to be only 40 millimeters wide—an important space-saving innovation, particularly in a control room as small as the one at Philips. Another was the inclusion of so-called "Unipots," which could serve as either stereo or quad panners. In addition, the console provided phase reversal, pre/post insertion switches, and four echo sends, plus four foldback sends on each channel. In a nod to the future (mix automation was already on the horizon), external inputs to each channel's voltage controlled amplifier (VCA) were wired to the patch panel. Last but not least was the cassette recorder mounted in the desk and hardwired into the monitoring system—a true relic of the '70s.

In the late 1970s, the original Phonogram mixing desk was replaced by a newer 24-output Phonogram console that had originally been designed for use in Chappell Studios. Possibly this change in destination was due to the imminent merger between the Polydor and Phonogram labels, which ultimately resulted in Chappell closing its doors permanently. (See *Chappell* in

Chapter 8 for more information.) This board would remain in use at Stanhope House until 1985, even after the changeover to Solid Bond Studios.

Monitors

Monitoring in the Philips control room was initially via Tannoy speakers powered by Radford amplifiers (models unknown). By 1977, Tannoy HPDs in custom-built enclosures were used for monitoring, with each cabinet containing two speakers.

Tape Machines

Philips Pro 75 (4-track) and Pro 50 (2-track and mono)—First introduced in the 1950s, these all-tube three-motor tape machines were part of the Philips "Pro" line that included two consumer models (the Pro 20 and Pro 25). They offered plug-in head assemblies and operated at speeds of 15 and 7.5 ips, with automatic tape tensioning. Philips Pro machines also featured an analog minutes/seconds indicator, with provision for a remote control.

There were also a number of Philips EL3501 2-track machines in the control room and/or reduction room, and engineer Roger Wake (who began working at the facility in 1965) also recalls there being several Philips 3-track machines (models unknown).

In 1968, when Philips went 8-track, the studio added an Ampex 8-track machine; later, Ampex MM1100 16-track/24-track machines were installed as well. (See *Pye* in this chapter for more information.) By the late 1970s, most if not all of the Ampex

The portable mixer hand-built by Rupert Neve for Philips circa 1959.
(Photo courtesy of Ron Godwyn)

The Phonogram Magnetic Audio Delay Wheel.
(Photo courtesy of Ron Godwyn)

with envelope follower; and, most unusually, a Phonogram "Magnetic Audio Delay Wheel." The latter was similar to the "delay drum" employed at EMI as part of their experimental Ambiophony system (see *Ambiophony* in Chapter 1 for more information), although the Phonogram units provided four independent tracks and had movable heads that enabled continuously variable delay time between 10 and 880 milliseconds. This odd contraption was most often used at Philips to delay the sends to reverb devices. (See *Chappell* in Chapter 8 for more information.)

Another listing from 1979 states that Philips was offering four "electronic" echo chambers; one or more of these were certainly EMT plates, but at least one of them may have been what one source calls an "enormous in-house spring reverb," which would indicate that it was a homebuilt unit.

An unusual feature of the Philips control room post-1972 (when the first Phonogram mixing console was installed) was its patch bay, which used five-pole Tuchel connectors, thus providing both input and output on a single elastic patch cord.

tape machines were replaced by or supplemented with Studer A80 24-track, 8-track, and 2-track models. (See Chapter 1 for more information.)

Main Microphones

The Philips mic locker featured microphones from AKG, Beyer, Philips, and Neumann. A 1991 inventory following the sale of the studio listed the following models: AKG C414, C451, C535, D12, D20, D24, D25, D190, D190E, D224E; Beyer M66, M67, M201, M260; and Neumann KM64, KM86, KM84, SM69, U64D, U87. Roger Wake also recalls the studio owning several Neumann U67 microphones.

Outboard Signal Processors

A 1977 studio listing indicated that the outboard gear at Philips included Phonogram "compact" limiters and compressors; ADR (Audio & Design Recording) limiter/compressors; an Eventide digital delay line and Harmonizer; a Phonogram analog delay line

SELECTED DISCOGRAPHY

- The High Numbers (The Who): "I'm the Face" (single)
- Dusty Springfield: *Ev'rything's Coming Up Dusty*, "You Don't Have to Say You Love Me" (single)
- Electric Light Orchestra: *Electric Light Orchestra*
- The Move: *Do Ya*, "Tonight," "China Town" (singles)
- The Walker Brothers: *The Sun Ain't Gonna Shine Anymore*, "Make It Easy on Yourself" (single)

PYE

The Pye Company was a scientific instrument manufacturer founded in the late 1800s and originally based in Cambridge, England. In the 1930s, Pye became one of the first U.K. companies to manufacture televisions; it also built TV cameras for the BBC. During World War II, the company branched out into military wireless communication devices.

Pye entered the record business when it bought Nixa Records in 1953. Two years later, it acquired Polygon Records, one of the first British independent record labels. This was later merged with Nixa Records to form Pye Nixa Records. In 1959, Pye Nixa became Pye Records, with television broadcast company ATV acquiring 50 percent of the label; ATV would go on to purchase the other half in 1966.

In 1956 Pye opened a modest in-house recording studio in a mansion house in London's Marylebone district. Four years later, the studio would move to ATV House, a sizable building in Great Cumberland Place, just north of Marble Arch in central London.

Pye Studios would become renowned as the place where most of The Kinks' hits were recorded—the exception being their first big single, "You Really Got Me," which was done at IBC Studios following an early, failed attempt at Pye. (See *IBC* in Chapter 3 for more information.) In the '70s it became the recording facility of choice for the British rockers Status Quo.

When the rights to the name Pye expired in 1980, both the label and the studio changed their name to PRT, short for Precision Records and Tapes. PRT ceased operations in 1989 and the studio was sold shortly thereafter. The site of the former ATV House is now a casino.

KEY PERSONNEL

Recording engineers: Bob Auger, Alan McKenzie, Barry Ainsworth, Alan Florence, Brian Humphries, Ray Prickett, Dave Hunt, Mike Brown, Eddie Kramer, Vic Maile, Alan O'Duffy, Howard Barrow, Terry Evennett, Geoff Calver, Kenny Denton, Larry Bartlett, Kim Maxwell, Alan Perkins

Maintenance engineers: Ken Atwood, Noel Jesuadian, John Timms, Philip Newell, Peter Duncan, Ian Sylvester

PHYSICAL FACILITIES

ATV House was a large building that occupied nearly a full city block and sat like an island just north of the Marble Arch tube (subway) station, in the heart of central London. It was originally intended to serve as the London headquarters for Associated Television, the independent broadcast company owned by Lew Grade, a prominent show business agent and budding media tycoon of the era, who had his offices there.

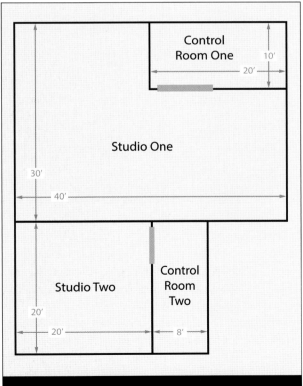

Pye Studios layout.

FOREWORD

This booklet describes the comprehensive sound recording facilities operated by Pye Records Ltd which are now available for custom working.

The facilities offered from the recording studios to the factory producing final disc pressings are some of the most modern in the country and the staff are highly skilled in the most up-to-date sound recording techniques.

Whether your requirement is for a simple audition disc for immediate playback or for a full orchestral long playing gramophone record for distribution to the trade, you may rest assured that the services offered herein are the best available to suit your needs.

Finally, the studios and dubbing suites are conveniently sited in the Marble Arch area which allows busy artistes to travel quickly to and from other engagements in the West End of London.

Robert Auger,
Technical Manager,
Pye Records.

STUDIO 1

Three studios are available, the two largest being equipped for multi-track tape recording and the smallest specially fitted for speech recording with ancillary facilities.

This studio is one of the very few recording studios which has been designed and built for the specific purpose of making the highest quality sound recordings. The great majority of studios are adapted from already existing premises. The acoustic treatment which has been extensively tested is of the very latest design and affords comfortable playing conditions for artistes as well as allowing the balance engineer complete control over separation problems.

A 9 ft. Bluthner concert grand piano is always available in the studio.

The control room is fitted with a most comprehensive mixing console with a formidable array of facilities including equalisers, limiters, artificial reverberation plates and chambers etc. This equipment is the latest available from Great Britain, the United States and Europe and is exclusive in Britain to Pye Records.

Monaural or Multi-track recording with separate or combined monitoring is at the client's disposal.

Studio 1 — Control Room

A Pye Studios brochure circa 1963 showing the Studio One control room with view into the studio area below.
(From studio brochure)

Although most of ATV's programming was produced in its large Elstree studios in Hertfordshire, north of London, in the late 1950s the company began building a small television studio in the basement of ATV House, with the idea of it serving as a London-based continuity suite. (A continuity suite is the place where between-program announcements, messages, and graphics originate.) However, management eventually discovered that, under the rules of the day, the entire building would have to be unionized if the studio became operational—something ATV most definitely did not want.

As a result, construction was abandoned midway through the project. In 1959, when ATV acquired 50 percent ownership of Pye Records, the decision was made to consolidate the two companies by moving the label into ATV House, with the abandoned television continuity suite converted into a large recording studio and other audio facilities added.

The Pye Studios complex eventually included two recording studios with control rooms, a separate small vocal booth for voice-over work (this was termed "Studio Three" in an early Pye brochure), two remix rooms, three disc cutting rooms, two tape copying rooms, and, in the 1970s, a room for making masters for 8-track cartridges—all housed in a huge basement area that ex–maintenance engineer John Timms described as "very subterranean, like living in catacombs."

Entrance to Pye Studios was gained via Bryanston Street, around the corner from the building's main entrance, and then down a flight of stairs into what ex-engineer Alan Florence termed "quite a rambling underground rabbit warren." At the bottom of the main staircase was the reception area and, to the left, the entrance to the control room for Studio One. In the style of the era, the control room looked down onto the studio floor; hence, there was an extra set of steps to go down into the large Studio One floor below. Various corridors beyond the reception area led to a smaller Studio Two and its control room, as well as to the remix, cutting, and copying rooms, the maintenance workshop, the echo plate room, and three acoustic echo chambers.

Every type of music was recorded at Pye Studios—not just pop and rock, but big band and jazz, too; even some classical. Studio Two quickly became the facility's "rock 'n' roll" room, where most of the early Kinks records and other pop hits were crafted, while the larger Studio One was mostly used for other genres, although on some classical recordings, the musicians had to be split into both rooms because Studio One was not quite big enough to house a full orchestra. In those pre-video days, this was no easy process, since communication between the two control rooms was strictly via talkback mics and headphone feeds.

Acoustic Treatments

The job of converting the basement of ATV House into a multiroom recording facility fell to Pye's chief technical engineer, Bob Auger, who had recorded Duke Ellington, Sammy Davis Jr., and other prominent stars of the '50s and '60s. His first decision was to repurpose the abandoned continuity suite as the large recording area that became known as Studio One.

It was no easy task, according to ex–mastering engineer Bill Foster. "Because it was originally designed as a television studio with lighting gantries, Studio One had very high ceilings," he says. "There were still big lighting looms up where the overhead

Feedback and the Village Green Preservation Society

"**THEY HAD TO KNOW** their sonics, those guys," Kinks front man Ray Davies said of the recording staff at Pye Studios in a 2010 interview with writer Matt Frost for *Sound on Sound* magazine. "I had good engineers: Bob Auger, Alan McKenzie, Alan O'Duffy, Ray Prickett, all employees at Pye, all really good solid studio guys. I learnt a lot from those people. It was a new music and they were using a lot of old equipment, and there was a BBC kind of feeling about the rules still, but The Kinks came in and broke the rules.

"I remember the first time there was feedback on a [Kinks] record, on 'I Need You.' It was a mistake, but as I was doing the count-in, Dave's guitar went off. [*Ray's brother Dave Davies was the lead guitarist in the group.*] Bob Auger was engineering it, and this man with all his experience just knew what to do and that was the take. It was a combination of new, young musicians like The Kinks coming through with radical ideas, and then very knowledgeable, experienced people who knew how to record it. There's a real debt owed to a lot of those engineers working with us."

Perhaps the best-loved Kinks album recorded at Pye was, not coincidentally, also the first to be solely credited as a Ray Davies production: *The Kinks Are the Village Green Preservation Society*—a quintessentially English album celebrating traditional country life.

"*Village Green* was a reaction to a lot of the culture that was around at that time, because it was a very warlike culture," he explained. "Pete [Townshend] was smashing up his guitars with the Who and Jimi [Hendrix] was setting fire to his guitar. I wanted to react in a more peaceful way, and I saw that album as a sort of . . . reaction to what was happening in the world at that time. . . . It was a very paranoid time, and I saw *Village Green* as a peaceful antidote."

Davies took an equally unorthodox approach to the record's production. "I actually asked them [the Pye engineers], 'Can you turn the mic? Can someone knock the mic off to one side so the electric guitar sounds like it's not miked up properly?' They didn't understand that at all, to tell you the truth, and I wouldn't if I were in their position, but I wanted guitars sounding like they [were] being played in another room. . . . It's an underachieving sound; I wasn't going for direct guitar sounds. I wanted them to be off-mic and more like a recording environment instead of a studio."

All-Star copycats

LIKE DECCA, Pye owned numerous subsidiary labels that specialized in issuing inexpensive "copycat" recordings of the hit records of the day. Ex–studio manager Howard Barrow recalls with fondness the many future stars who would hang around the studio every Thursday or Friday, after the charts came out, hoping for work.

"With Pye being so close to Marble Arch, we were central to everywhere, and so everyone would turn up," he says. "Singers—even famous ones—used to come by in the hope that one of the tracks would suit their voice. And the players? Unbelievable! Reg Dwight [*later Elton John*], Jimmy Page, Jack Bruce, Steve Marriott, John McLaughlin, Clem Cattini, Big Jim Sullivan, Vic Flick—sometimes even Ginger Baker, if he could be bothered!"

lights would have been, with hundreds of cables just hanging there. As a result, there was always lots of fill [leakage] going across the ceiling. You almost didn't need drum mics, especially if you had a session in with strings. You'd hang a [Neumann] U47 over the strings on a big boom, and the drums would be on everything, so really all you had to do was open up the mic and you had most of the total sound even before you even opened the drum mics."

And even though Studio One retained the original linoleum flooring over concrete along with wooden slats on the wall ("a TV design, not a sound acoustic design," says Alan Florence), it somehow worked. "It became the famous Pye sound—so-called 'strings with echo'—but that was because the drums [were being] picked up on the string mics, so you had this distinctive ambience on everything," Florence comments. "I didn't realize it at the time, but when you listen to old Pye records, they have a lovely live presence, and that was just a fluke of the room."

Eventually, at Florence's instigation, management installed some angled curtains that absorbed excess low and high frequencies. Along with the use of tall acoustical screens, this allowed Studio One to be partitioned, allowing engineers to isolate percussion instruments and to place strings on one side and brass on the other.

Ex-Pye engineer Ray Prickett says that Studio One was "a very good room even though there was really not much done to it the years I was there [1962–1978]. I think it had a reverb time of about 1.8 seconds, which actually made it a good room for musicians to play in. Most of the recordings I did there were done live." There was, however, apparently limited acoustic isolation in the building itself. John Timms recalls that "if you had an open mic in Studio One, you could sometimes actually hear the 'Mind the gap' announcements coming from the tube [subway] station underneath the studio."

Studio Two, which may have had its initial acoustic treatments done by Robertson Grant (father of Olympic Studios designer/engineer Keith Grant), was equally successful, even though it sported the same linoleum-over-concrete-floor and television-style slotted wooden paneling on the walls as was found in Studio One. Ex-Pye engineer Kenny Denton describes Studio Two as having been a "dingy, dark, untidy, and old-fashioned place." Nonetheless, he marvels, "it was phenomenal how many hits kept coming out of there."

In 1977, Studio Two underwent a complete acoustic remake, courtesy of Tom Hidley and Eastlake Audio. At that time, it received the typical Eastlake/Westlake design that was popular in the era, with the control room walls variously coated in brown cork, hardwood paneling, and areas of volcanic rock said to have been specially imported from Hawaii.

Room Dimensions

Studio One: 40' x 30' (12 x 9 meters)
    Ceiling height: 18' (5.5 meters)
Studio One control room: 20' x 10' (6 x 3 meters)
    Ceiling height: 10' (3 meters)

Studio Two: 20' x 20' (6 x 6 meters)
    Ceiling height: 18' (5.5 meters)
Studio Two control room: 20' x 8' (6 x 2.5 meters)
    Ceiling height: 10' (3 meters)

Echo Chambers

Pye had three small custom-built acoustic echo chambers located near the maintenance department at the rear of the building. All had plaster walls, and

This studio is eminently suitable for recording plays for broadcast purposes or small musical groups etc. The studio was also specially constructed for its function and similar facilities are available as for Studio 1.

This is a small studio specifically designed and fitted for speech recording. Gramophone decks with 'spin-in' facilities are available together with artificial reverberation effects etc.

Any combination of the three studios can be connected together at a moment's notice thereby allowing superimposition of one studio over another on a monaural recording or allowing the three studios to be recording simultaneously on separate tracks on one multi-track recording.

The range of facilities thus offered are virtually unlimited.

Our staff are most widely experienced in all manner of mobile recordings on location. No job is too large or too small and we should be happy to discuss client's requirements.

DISC CUTTING

We are able to undertake the work of transferring sound from tape to disc. The most up-to-date equipment is available for this purpose and discs for immediate playback or master discs for factory processing can be cut as required.

TAPE EDITING AND DUBBING

Editing and Dubbing can be handled in the Dubbing Suite which has been equipped for the purpose or if the client desires in one of the studio control rooms. Either reduction dubbing or multi-track to multi-track work can be undertaken.

American Star Bobby Rydell at a recent session

Studio 2

More from the Pye Studios brochure circa 1963 showing two views of Studio Two.
(From studio brochure)

all were equipped with "ball and biscuit" STC Coles 4021 microphones and KEF monitors (exact model unknown but probably Slimlines; see *Monitors* below). "They had an amazing sound," says ex-Pye engineer Richard Goldblatt of the acoustic echo chambers. "It was completely different than what you got from the EMT plates; in fact, I think a lot of the pop records that came out of Pye Studios used the chambers more than they used the EMTs."

KEY EQUIPMENT
Mixing Consoles

Studio One at Pye was originally outfitted with an all-tube (valve) Neumann desk. "It had been cobbled together from components that Pye used on their early mobiles," says Ray Prickett. "It was a typical German board in that it was built like a battleship. The mic preamps were the famous Telefunken V72s. It worked fairly well; I think for its time it was probably a good desk." Eddie Kramer, who began as an assistant engineer at Pye in 1962, recalled that "the preamps were down on the floor, and my job was to run down and move the attenuator 10 dB, 20 dB."

The board had 12 main channels and three outputs, plus two additional auxiliary-type channels, but it only had equalizers for eight channels. As a result, says Alan Florence, "you had to decide beforehand what were the least important channels, the

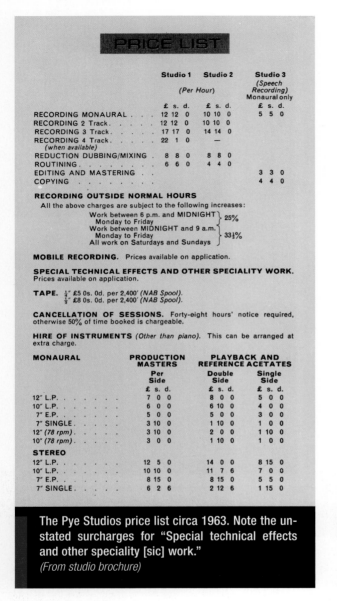

PRICE LIST

	Studio 1	Studio 2	Studio 3 (Speech Recording) Monaural only
	(Per Hour)		
	£ s. d.	£ s. d.	£ s. d.
RECORDING MONAURAL . . .	12 12 0	10 10 0	5 5 0
RECORDING 2 Track	12 12 0	10 10 0	
RECORDING 3 Track	17 17 0	14 14 0	
RECORDING 4 Track	22 1 0	—	
(when available)			
REDUCTION DUBBING/MIXING .	8 8 0	8 8 0	
ROUTINING	6 6 0	4 4 0	
EDITING AND MASTERING . .			3 3 0
COPYING			4 4 0

RECORDING OUTSIDE NORMAL HOURS
All the above charges are subject to the following increases:

Work between 6 p.m. and MIDNIGHT Monday to Friday — 25%
Work between MIDNIGHT and 9 a.m. Monday to Friday — 33⅓%
All work on Saturdays and Sundays

MOBILE RECORDING. Prices available on application.

SPECIAL TECHNICAL EFFECTS AND OTHER SPECIALITY WORK.
Prices available on application.

TAPE. ¼" £5 0s. 0d. per 2,400' (NAB Spool).
½" £8 0s. 0d. per 2,400' (NAB Spool).

CANCELLATION OF SESSIONS. Forty-eight hours' notice required, otherwise 50% of time booked is chargeable.

HIRE OF INSTRUMENTS (Other than piano). This can be arranged at extra charge.

MONAURAL	PRODUCTION MASTERS Per Side	PLAYBACK AND REFERENCE ACETATES	
		Double Side	Single Side
	£ s. d.	£ s. d.	£ s. d.
12" L.P.	7 0 0	8 0 0	5 0 0
10" L.P.	6 0 0	6 10 0	4 0 0
7" E.P.	5 0 0	5 0 0	3 0 0
7" SINGLE	3 10 0	1 10 0	1 0 0
12" (78 rpm)	3 10 0	2 0 0	1 10 0
10" (78 rpm)	3 0 0	1 10 0	1 0 0
STEREO			
12" L.P.	12 5 0	14 0 0	8 15 0
10" L.P.	10 10 0	11 7 6	7 0 0
7" E.P.	8 15 0	8 15 0	5 5 0
7" SINGLE	6 2 6	2 12 6	1 15 0

The Pye Studios price list circa 1963. Note the unstated surcharges for "Special technical effects and other speciality [sic] work."

(From studio brochure)

ones you didn't need to EQ." Nonetheless, he has fond memories of the sound of the Neumann. "It yielded a warmth and a fatness we could never reproduce with the Neve desk that replaced it [in 1968, when the studio went 8-track]. I never thought the Neve had the balls or the oomph that the old desk had, but everybody else seemed to love it."

Ray Prickett—who was apparently one of the few engineers at Pye consulted—remembers the story behind the design of Studio One's new Neve 24 x 8 console, which, like the Neve board installed

at Philips, employed germanium transistors. "Neve came down to see us and they said, 'What do you want?' I said, 'Well, I don't want anything that's shiny and black, for one thing.' All the desks they'd made up to then were shiny and black, and I felt that was not a color to have in a control room. So we spent a day down at their factory to talk things over, and they said, 'What color would you like it?' They gave me a sheath of about 40 different pieces of metal with different colors, and they said, 'Pick your color out of that.' I picked the one that most of the desks use even today—sort of a gray-blue with a matte finish. The other thing I asked them to do was color-coding. I think it was the first desk they built where all the reverb sends were one color, all the foldbacks another, etc. It's a standard thing they do even today. But more importantly, the sound of the desk was brilliant." By the mid-1970s, when Pye went 24-track, this was replaced with a Neve board that offered 24 outputs.

But probably the most famous recording console at Pye—the one used to record most of The Kinks' early hits—was installed in the Studio Two control room. This all-tube (valve) board, designed and built in-house by chief maintenance engineer Ken Atwood and chief mastering engineer Derek Sticklen, offered 12 input channels and four outputs. It featured Paignton quadrant faders and just rudimentary EQ—bass and treble only—on rotary Bakelite controls, with VU metering. The Pye console had a distinctively punchy sound that proved to be perfect for the pop recordings of the era. By the late 1960s, however, it became clear that more inputs and outputs were required, and so the beloved Studio Two mixing board was replaced by one of the first Neve Series 80 desks—a 24 x 8 model.

In 1977, the first Cadac automated CARE system anywhere in the world was installed in the Studio Two control room. The console was equipped with 32 mic/line input channels and 32 monitor/output channels, plus four echo sends with EQ, and eight echo returns (also with EQ) that could double as extra mic/line inputs if required.

Remix Room 1 at Pye was outfitted with a 12 x 2 Neve Series 80 desk. Remix Room 2, which rarely was used, was built in the late '60s to enable rough 8-track mixes to be run without tying up a control room. Like Studio Two, it was equipped with a homemade

Pye desk, built by Atwood out of the remains of the original Neumann desk, complete with ten Langevin passive equalizers built right into the console: eight miniature two-band EQ251-As and two EQ252 seven-band graphic EQs.

Monitors

Monitoring in all Pye control rooms, remix rooms, cutting rooms, and copying rooms was initially done via Tannoy speakers. These were originally driven by Pamphonic amps, later replaced in Studio One by Radford MA25 amplifiers and in Studio Two, by Leak TL12s; by 1972 the amplifiers in the Pye control rooms were all Quads, exact models unknown. According to ex–maintenance engineer Philip Newell, the speakers were almost all 15" dual concentric Tannoy Reds housed in stand-alone Lockwood cabinets, although some of the smaller rooms were equipped with Tannoy Lancaster hi-fi cabinets. (See Chapter 4 for more information.)

Alan Florence recalls that the control room for Studio One, which initially was 3-track, had three speakers side by side above the control room window—one for each track—and that a fourth was added when the studio went 4-track. This configu-ration remained for quite some time—even after the studio went 8-track—because the Neve console that replaced the original Neumann had a push-button switch matrix for monitor panning, with four buttons for each group allowing routing to any indi-vidual loudspeaker or any pair of loudspeakers. "By pressing the inner or outer pairs," says Newell, "you could get a phantom center."

Following a major redesign in 1977, the Studio Two control was made quadraphonic-ready and was fitted with four Eastlake TM-3 monitors recessed into the control room walls, driven by Amcron DC300A amplifiers.

KEF Slimline—These were the likely models of speaker in the three Pye acoustic echo chambers. First introduced in 1961, the Slimline was the first loudspeaker product from the British manufac-turer KEF (short for Kent Engineering & Foundry). As its name suggests, it was a compact monitor designed for use where space was a premium (such as in an echo chamber). It was a three-way floor-standing system, housed in an enclosure less than five inches deep, and capable of handling maximum input power of 25W rms, 50W peak.

STORIES FROM THE STUDIO
The Savage

THERE IS PERHAPS no more fond-ly remembered device from the early days at Pye than a gigantic machine known by the staff as "The Savage." (The name came from the company that manufactured the unit.) It consisted of four shelves of Pamphonic 25-watt valve am-plifiers, each driven from a sine-wave oscillator, and each fed into a single transformer, with one large knob controlling the entire appa-ratus. By removing a dummy plug, the Savage could be connected to any of the studio's Ampex or Scully tape recorders, at which point the machine's capstan motor would be driven from the oscillator instead of

from the mains. "You needed a rack this big to vary the speed of just one tape recorder," explains Philip Newell, "because the capstans were driven by 100-watt synchronous motors."

Richard Goldblatt, who recalled using the Savage frequently when assisting for engineer Alan Florence, elaborates: "In the days before you could easily put a speed control on your tape machine, it changed the electricity from 50 cycles [Hz] to anywhere between 40 and 60 cy-cles. That's how Alan did the phas-ing on [the Status Quo record] 'Pic-tures of Matchstick Men,' although George Chkiantz had done it first at

Olympic." (See *Phasing* in Chapter 5 for more information.)

"The knob had to be moved slow-ly so that one machine operated at between 48 and 52 cycles, while the master machine continued playing back at 50 cycles," explains Florence. "It was the slight variation in speed between the two machines that caused the sound to phase. By ex-perimenting, I found that adding EQ at certain frequencies to the track playing back at the varied speed created a deeper phasing effect. It was trial and error until you got it sounding good. Then you'd mix both signals to a third mastering machine, and voilà! Instant phasing."

A Triumph TR4 in the summertime

HOWARD BARROW was the engineer for Mungo Jerry's smash 1970 hit "In the Summertime"—one of the best-selling singles of all time—recorded both in and around Pye Studio Two, as he explains.

"If you listen to the record," says Barrow, "the song is essentially the same thing repeated twice, with a few bits added on the second half." The original recording was actually a lot shorter—approximately half the length, in fact—but it got extended as a result of a casual remark made by producer Barry Murray, who, according to singer-songwriter Ray Dorset, pointed out that if the track were made a bit longer, the group would receive double the performance royalty every time it was played on the radio.

"That's when Ray got the idea about overdubbing on the sound of a motorcycle," Barrow recalls. "We tried getting it from some sound effects records we had on hand, but there was nothing that really worked. This happened to be an evening session, and so I'd parked my [Triumph] TR4 outside the studio door. Barry, who'd remembered seeing my car there, suddenly got an inspiration, saying, 'What we want is *that* revving up!' So I got a dynamic microphone, an AKG D224, probably—there was no power upstairs so I couldn't use one of the old Neumanns, because they had a power pack on them the size of a lunchbox—and trailed the cable up the steps. With Barry holding the microphone four or five feet away from the back of the car, I started it up and revved the engine for a couple of minutes while my assistant recorded the signal on a piece of 2-track tape.

"When I went back inside, I copied the song onto another 8-track machine, edited the copy onto the original, leaving a small gap in the middle, and then laid the revving engine in between. Then we mixed the track and panned the engine noise from left to right for a stereo effect. That's all it took!"

Tape Machines

Pye's Studio One and Studio Two control rooms were initially outfitted with tube (valve) Ampex A300, 350, and 351 mono tape machines. Some time after the complex was opened, a 3-track Ampex 350 was added to a separate machine room, which could be accessed from either control room. In early 1963, this was replaced with an Ampex 350 4-track, and by the end of the year, a second 4-track was added to the machine room, making 4-to-4 reductions possible, although there was as yet no way of synchronizing the two machines. Also added to the control rooms and Remix Room One in subsequent years were Ampex tube 354 and MR-70 models, as well as AG-350 transistorized machines, followed soon after by AG-440s. Remix Room Two, built some time later, was equipped with an EMI TR90 stereo recorder.

According to Bill Foster, all the Ampex machines at Pye were American 110-volt models, due to the fact that they were considerably less expensive than the equivalent 230-volt versions produced for the British market. "There was an entire room with big transformers, wired for 110, which was highly unusual," said Kramer in a 2003 interview with *MIX* magazine.

"Next to every 13-amp mains socket was an American socket," adds Foster, "and all the Ampex machines were plugged into that." The reason, according to Eddie Kramer, was that Bob Auger "thought the machines performed better at 110."

Peter Duncan, who joined Pye's maintenance staff in 1968 and would eventually become the studio's chief engineer, adds that, incredibly, the machines were also without grounding (or, in the English vernacular, "earthing"). "To minimize hum," he explains, "the installers had disconnected the mains earth, and so the earthing went through the audio cables—which was great for the sound, but if you got a cross between two points, it could be quite interesting with the little recharge you could get. You certainly couldn't get away with something like that these days! Health and safety was minimal at the time."

Scully 284-8 (8-track)—In 1968, Pye installed a 284-8 in Studio One. (See *Decca* earlier in this chapter for more information.)

Ampex MM1000 (16-track)—First introduced in 1967, the MM1000 was a quick "fix" Ampex released in response to the higher track-count demands of the era. Multitrack MM1000s were available in several different configurations: a 1" 8-track, a 2" 16-track, or, eventually (special ordered) as a 2" 24-track; the latter two were the first-ever mass-produced 24-track machines. The 8-track model was especially attractive to cash-strapped (or penurious) customers, because it could later be converted to a 2" 16-track at relatively low cost. The MM1000 used discrete class A electronics, and was equipped with transformers on the inputs and outputs of every channel. Its tape transport was adapted from Ampex's video recording division; the capstan was a synchronous motor type, although later, a 24-volt DC capstan was offered. By 1970, the Studio Two control room at Pye was equipped with an Ampex MM1000 16-track machine, although the Studio One control room still offered only 8-track recording.

Studer A80 (24-track, 16-track, 4-track, 2-track)—By 1977, most of the tape recorders at Pye were Studer A80s. A studio listing from that year indicates that Studio One was equipped with 24-, 16-, and 4-track models, plus two 2-track machines; Studio Two was outfitted similarly, though it boasted three 2-track machines. (See Chapter 1 for more information.)

Main Microphones

The Pye mic locker was unusually expansive and offered a wide variety of microphones, including:

Neumann U87 and U67—Neumann U87s and U67s were the main workhorse mics at Pye; 87s used mostly for vocals, strings and piano; 67s often used on guitars. (See Chapter 1 for more information.)

Neumann U77—The U77 is considered to be the first solid-state microphone built by Neumann with a transformerless output. It was a large-diaphragm condenser that was manufactured for only four years in the late 1960s and designed to run on 12-volt T-power instead of 48-volt phantom power, thus requiring its own power supply. The sound of the U77 is said to be a cross between a U67 and a U87, with a distinctive clarity and an unusually strong signal; it also had an extremely quiet noise floor. The U77 was a particular favorite of Ray Prickett at Pye.

Neumann U47/U48—A pair of U47s were frequently used a as drum overheads at Pye. (See Chapter 1 for more information.)

Neumann M49—(See Chapter 1 for more information.)

Neumann KM56—(See Chapter 1 for more information.)

AKG 414—First introduced in 1971, this large-diaphragm condenser microphone provided four selectable polar patterns—cardioid, hypercardioid, omnidirectional, and figure-of-eight—and an unusually wide dynamic range said to exceed 126 dB. It offered two-stage preattenuation pads (of -10 and -20 dB) and a bass cut filter, and was capable of handling very high SPLs, up to 160 dB. 414s quickly gained favor with engineers in recording studios everywhere and were widely used for vocal, piano, percussion instruments, and, most popularly, as drum overheads.

AKG D224—The D224 was a dynamic microphone that offered a pair of coaxially mounted diaphragms connected together via an electronic combining network. Since the diaphragms could withstand high SPLs yet were optimized for extended frequency ranges, the D224 was advertised as being able to "bring the sound of a condenser microphone to a dynamic." According to Philip Newell, there was an "abundance" of these at Pye.

Engineer Alan Florence behind the Pye console in the Studio Two control room.
(Courtesy of Alan Florence)

BBC-Marconi Type AXBT—This ribbon microphone was produced by the BBC and the Marconi Company between 1934 and 1959 and was designed to emulate RCA's popular model 44-BX. (See Chapter 1 for more information.) Its double-sided design accepted sound from front and back but not from the sides, making it particularly suited to vocal duo recording and broadcasting. This design also gave the microphone its characteristic shape, which has entered popular culture as the icon for audio in nearly all modern-day computer software. The original "Type A" model used a thick aluminum ribbon that produced a harsh resonance. This was soon replaced with a thinner ribbon, and was named Type AX. In 1943, the AXB model was launched, featuring balanced wiring. A year later, the microphone was renamed the AXBT, with the addition of a Ticonal magnet to increase sensitivity by 6 dB. The AXBT had a figure-of-eight polar pattern and weighed a massive 9.25 pounds; Howard Barrow recalled using it frequently (hopefully on a sturdy boom stand!) to record brass instruments at Pye.

Beyer M88—First introduced in 1962, the M88 was a high-output dynamic microphone designed for both live and recording applications. It had a hyper-cardioid polar pattern, a built-in humbucking coil, and an unusually wide frequency response of 30 Hz–20 kHz.

Beyer M160—First introduced in 1957 and still on the market today, the M160 is unusual in that it is a ribbon microphone with a hypercardioid pickup pattern. It utilizes two ribbons, mounted back-to-front just 0.5 millimeters apart, with the second said to increase sensitivity.

Electrovoice RE20—This large, heavy dynamic cardioid microphone—a staple of radio broadcast studios—was originally conceived as a "condenser killer." First introduced in 1969, it is still manufactured today, essentially unchanged from the original design. The RE20 uses EV's patented "Variable D" design to minimize proximity effect and features an internal pop filter for close-in voice work, along with an internal element shock-mount to reduce vibration-induced noise.

RCA Type 77DX—These were sometimes used at Pye on brass instruments. (See *Decca* earlier in this chapter for more information.)

Sennheiser MD421—This large-diaphragm dynamic cardioid debuted in the 1960s and continues to be popular today, not just for recording but also in the broadcast industry and in live performance, where it sometimes does double duty as a vocal mic. Its high sensitivity and slight "bump" in high-

---

STORIES FROM THE STUDIO
The answer is blowin' in the wind

JOHN TIMMS RECALLS spending a memorable couple of days at Pye with famed producer (and ex-EMI engineer) Alan Parsons, working on a track that had some unusual requirements.

"Alan wanted to create a virtual instrument which would consist of various wind instruments playing long looped notes," Timms explains. "He then wanted each note to come up on a different fader so he could play the console like a Mellotron."

The problem, of course, was that human players would need to take a breath every once in a while, which would spoil the flow of what Parsons envisioned as being *extremely* long held notes. After a short period of figuratively "bashing my head against a brick wall," Timms came up with an ingenious solution.

"I went into one of the disc cutting rooms and cannibalized the vacuum unit that was used to suck up the swarf [excess material] as the groove was being cut; I reversed the motor so that instead of vacuuming it was blowing air out instead. I then brought it into Studio One and used an air line to hook it up to one of the wind instruments so it effectively acted like a pair of lips. Then we gaffer-taped over the appropriate finger holes to get it to play different notes and miked the instrument up. It was a nightmare figuring out ways to get the air flow just right and to find something suitable to attach the air hose to the instrument! But in the end I think we accomplished what Alan wanted, although I don't know if what we created was ever used on any of the Alan Parsons Project records." (*Note: A similar effect, albeit with vocal loops instead of wind instruments, was used on 10cc's 1975 hit record "I'm Not in Love."*)

frequency response give it an unusually bright sound for a dynamic mic. At Pye, 421s were often used to record bass guitar and bass drum.

Shure SM58—This dynamic cardioid mic was first introduced in 1966, a year after the SM57. It offers an unusually rugged construction and minimal handling noise, and is often used for vocals in live performance. SM58s were mostly used at Pye to record snare drum and tom-toms. (See *CTS / The Music Centre* in Chapter 3 for more information about the SM57.)

STC Coles 4021—This dynamic mic, frequently referred to as a "ball-and-biscuit" microphone because of its distinctive shape, was first introduced in the mid-1930s for radio broadcast. Some early recording studios repurposed it as a talkback mic because of its largely omnidirectional characteristics and limited frequency response. Three of these were employed in the Pye acoustic echo chambers.

STC 4038—(See Chapter 1 for more information.)

Outboard Signal Processors

Pye compressors—According to Philip Newell, these tube (valve) compressors manufactured by the Pye Company in Cambridge (as opposed to Pye Studios) were held in quite low regard by the Pye staff. "Everyone hated them," he says bluntly. "You were always having to align the things to try to minimize the thumps. They were noisy, too, plus each one was huge—five units high or something like that!"

Westrex 32532 compressors—These tube film-based compressors were said to be the "mainstays" of the Pye engineers, and were frequently used on piano and vocals.

Neve 2254—First released in 1969, the 2254 was a mono limiter/compressor that incorporated discrete Class A electronics and transformer-coupled circuits in the input stage, and innovative bridge-driver design in the sidechain and output stages. The 2254 is revered to this day for its distinctive sound and smooth compression characteristics. Several of these five-inch-square units were fitted to the meter bridges of the Neve consoles added to the Pye control rooms in the late 1960s. Although a great admirer of these units, which he reports as being far superior to the studio's Pye compressors

(see above), Philip Newell remembers having to send them back to Neve for modification shortly after they arrived. "Our engineers wanted Neve to add gain makeup pots to them—something which later became standard—because as you turned the compression up, there was a tendency for the overall gain to go down. With this modification, they were able to leave the faders where they were and wind up the gain to bring it back up to the right level in the mix." (See Chapter 7 for more information.)

Teletronix LA-2A—These so-called "leveling amplifiers," first introduced in the early 1960s, were in fact tube-based optical compressors. The early models were completely hand-wired and employed an electroluminescent panel together with a cadmium-sulfide light-dependent resistor to provide gain reduction. The properties of this so-called "T4 cell" gave the LA-2A a unique sonic signature due to the response being entirely program-dependent. Attack time was fixed at 10 milliseconds, and the release time was approximately 60 milliseconds for 50 percent release and 0.5 to 5 seconds for full release, depending on the previous program material. The front-panel controls were simple and straightforward: A Peak Reduction knob controlled the gain of the side-chain circuit (and therefore, the gain reduction), and a Gain control allowed the user to set makeup gain; plus a VU meter that could be switched to show either gain reduction or output level.

UREI 1176—(See *Decca* earlier in this chapter for more information.)

Pultec EQP-1A/MEQ-5 equalizers—Pye owned numerous Pultec EQP-1A and MEQ-5 equalizers, although they were mainly used in the disc cutting rooms. The tube (valve) MEQ-5 focuses on the "power" midrange frequencies from 200 Hz to 7 kHz, with separate narrow-range boost and cut bands for low mid and high mid. (See *Decca* earlier in this chapter for more information.)

ITI ME-230—Said to be the first commercially available parametric equalizer, the ME-230 was co-invented by recording engineers Burgess Macneal and a young George Massenburg, based on a design by Massenburg's college friend Bob Meushaw. First introduced at the 1971 AES show, it offered three bands of equalization (10–800 Hz, 100 Hz–8 kHz, and 400 Hz–25.6 kHz), with continuously variable control over bandwidth ("Q"), from 4 to 14 dB/octave, and boost and cut of up to 12 dB for each band. Due to its purposeful lack of inductor circuitry, ringing on transients was said to be virtually nonexistent. Pye was one of the first studios in the U.K. to install an ME-230.

Klein & Hummel UE400—This German-built two-channel equalizer provided three identical full-range parametric EQ sections covering the full audible bandwidth, from 15 Hz to 20 kHz, with variable Q from broad to sharp, plus both low- and high-frequency shelving. Two of these were installed at Pye, at the urging of chief engineer John Timms.

EMT 140 reverb plates—Pye had at least six and possibly as many as eight EMT 140 stereo plates in a small room near the maintenance workshop. The sends to these plates were typically delayed by tape running at 7.5 ips. (See Chapter 1 for more information.)

In addition, Pye also offered a number of tube (valve) Marconi limiter/compressors. A 1977 directory listed both Dolby and dbx noise reduction, as well as flangers and digital delays (exact models unknown), with the disc cutting rooms outfitted with Neumann lathes.

SELECTED DISCOGRAPHY

- The Searchers: "Needles and Pins" (single)
- Petula Clark: "Downtown" (single)
- Donovan: "Catch the Wind" (single)
- The Kinks: *Kinda Kinks, The Kink Kontroversy, Face to Face, Something Else, The Kinks Are the Village Green Preservation Society, Arthur (Or the Decline and Fall of the British Empire)*, "All Day and All of the Night," "A Well Respected Man," "Sunny Afternoon," "Waterloo Sunset" (singles)
- Mungo Jerry: *Mungo Jerry*, "In the Summertime" (single)
- Status Quo: *Picturesque Matchstickable Messages from the Status Quo, Spare Parts, Ma Kelly's Greasy Spoon, Dog of Two Head*

THE EARLY INDEPENDENTS

"It was a bit like the Civil Service in the British record industry in [the early] days. . . . The majors had a stranglehold—they had their own studios, factories, you could not get records manufactured unless you went to a major company. Decca, EMI, Pye, all came out of large electronics groups; Philips the same. So the record division was just one division of a large corporate entity. The top management of these companies thought of the record industry as 'just another division,' like television manufacturing, records and radio. But it was creative, you needed creative people. But it didn't have creative people, it had civil servants. . . . All that changed [when] the independent producer suddenly came along. There was a huge revolution: Independents became a significant part of the UK record industry."

—former EMI managing director Dave Hunt

For nearly three decades, from the time of the opening of Abbey Road in 1931 through to the late 1950s, almost all the recording studios in England were owned by one of the country's four major record labels: EMI, Decca, Philips, and Pye. Each studio had been constructed within existing buildings rather than designed from the ground up, and each recorded only its label's signed artists, using equipment almost exclusively designed, built, and maintained by its own technical staff.

In other words, each operated not just in competition, but in virtual isolation from one another.

As a result, engineers at these early facilities developed techniques based largely on the particular equipment they were using—techniques that might or might not translate elsewhere. These were considered to be highly guarded company "secrets," and for an engineer to jump ship to a rival and take those secrets with him (for in those days this was strictly a male-dominated profession) was considered taboo—something that was "simply not done," to use the vernacular.

Yet there was change in the air. IBC Studios, a facility created for the production of radio programming, had been in operation since the early 1930s and, thanks to the excellence of its equipment and staff, was beginning to attract those producers and artists who had sufficient clout to tell their record label that they wanted to record there instead. Ditto for CTS, a studio initially designed strictly for film scoring work, and Advision, originally intended specifically for voice-over and television ad production. Eventually Denis Preston, an independent producer who was one of IBC's main clients, entered into a partner-ship with IBC staff engineer (and future impresario) Joe Meek to found Lansdowne Studios, conceived from the get-go as a music recording facility.

By the mid-1960s, there were more than a dozen major independent recording studios in England supplementing the four label-owned facilities. For the first time, staff engineers and producers were moving from facility to facility (not only taking their "secrets" with them, but also evolving their techniques to a new level as they encountered new environments and new equipment), and artists had nearly complete freedom of choice as to where they wanted to record. Some of the label-owned studios were even taking on work from their fiercest competitors. (The EMI mastering rooms, for instance, sometimes cut discs for Decca.)

James Lock, who joined IBC in 1955 before moving on to Decca some years later, said in a 1987 interview for *Studio Sound* magazine, "As far as the level and quality of the productions we handled [at IBC], it was on a par with the [studios owned by the] major record companies. . . . The major difference . . . was that with record company studios, all the costs were absorbed by the label and so there was no great pressure [regarding] studio time. Our clients, on the other hand, were very often paying for everything themselves, and so they wanted it done quickly. Hence, there was quite a lot of pressure to work quickly, and if you were slow, you simply weren't chosen for the next session. All the engineers were great friends . . . but it was highly competitive."

"The early '60s was a time when the majority of studios in London had a reputation for being stuffy and oppressive, manned and administered by scientists in brown lab coats who had little interest in the 'nasty' guitar music that had so rudely thrust itself upon them," summarized writer Matt Frost in a 2008 article for *Sound on Sound* magazine. "But by the middle of the decade, these studios' dominance was being eroded by a handful of hip new young independents, bristling with young, enthusiastic engineers and producers with as much passion for popular music as the musicians they were recording."

Here now is the story of four of the most important independent recording studios that rose to prominence in the U.K. during that heady period.

IBC

Leonard Plugge was a British businessman who happened to be a radio enthusiast. He was also someone who was prone to taking long motoring holidays on mainland Europe, where he made a habit of visiting local radio stations. Soon the two hobbies would converge fortuitously.

Long considered the father of commercial English radio, Plugge (pronounced "Plooje," in recognition of his Dutch ancestry) became the first person to seriously challenge the autonomy of the government-owned BBC (British Broadcasting Corporation), which did not allow commercials on the airwaves. In 1930, he came up with a simple but ingenious way of getting around the ban: He would form a new company—IBC (an acronym for the International Broadcasting Company)—and then purchase time on continental European radio stations, many of whom had strong enough transmitters to allow their

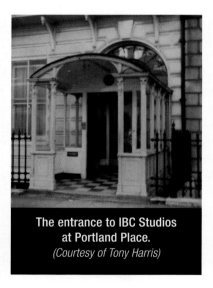

The entrance to IBC Studios at Portland Place.
(Courtesy of Tony Harris)

signal to be picked up in the U.K. The time would then be resold to British companies who could use it for advertising purposes. Eventually, this expanded to the production of entire radio programs for rebroadcast overseas—something that required specialized recording studios and cutting rooms, duly constructed within IBC's new headquarters at 35 Portland Place, an expansive town house nestled among numerous governmental embassies, located around the corner from the company's original facility on Hallam Street and just down the road from the BBC's Broadcast House.

By the end of the '30s, IBC had become the hub of a veritable empire of interconnected radio stations, most famously Radio Normandy; there were even plans being floated for the development of an independent television station. Then came World War II, and everything had to be put on hold—and not just because of wartime shortages of manpower and other resources. In fact, IBC was secretly being used by the government as a special weapons research unit—something that was only revealed in the 1960s.

After the war ended, the studios at Portland Place continued to function as an independent production house, making programs for competitor Radio Luxembourg, among others. At the same time, the staff was expanded and a mobile unit assembled to record classical performances at nearby Conway Hall (where IBC maintained a small monophonic control room) and other London venues. At around this time the company began transitioning from radio production to music recording. Its studio's impressive collection of homegrown equipment had attracted the attention of Pye and Philips, the only two major English labels that did not yet have studios of their own. (Philips would open a recording studio in 1956, and Pye in 1958; see Chapter 2 for more information.) Soon most of their artists (and some of Decca's as well) were recording at IBC under the direction of producers like Denis Preston, who would go on to poach some key IBC staffers when he founded Lansdowne Studios. (See *Lansdowne* below.)

Following Plugge's sale of the studios to BBC orchestra leader Eric Robinson and musician George Clouston in 1962, the shift from radio production to music production would accelerate. By the late '60s, with The Who as one of its main clients (many of the band's early hit singles and much of *Tommy* was recorded there), IBC was considered one of the top recording studios in London.

In July 1978, IBC Studios was bought by former Animals bass player (and former Jimi Hendrix manager) Chas Chandler and renamed Portland Recording Studios. The facility was later purchased by manager Don Arden (father of Sharon Osbourne) for use by his Jet Records label. In 1985 the building was sold and converted into offices.

KEY PERSONNEL

Recording engineers: Allen Stagg, Eric Tomlinson, Joe Meek, Adrian Kerridge, Jack Clegg, Keith Grant, James Lock, David Price, Ray Prickett, Terry Johnson, John Timperley, Glyn Johns, Alan Florence, Mike

---

STORIES FROM THE STUDIO
Generation gap

IN EARLY 1963, a fledgling band making waves in the local London R&B club scene was brought into IBC by then–senior engineer Glyn Johns to record a demo tape. Their name? The Rolling Stones.

"I had an arrangement [with IBC owners Eric Robinson and George Clouston] that I could bring in any musician or band that I liked in my free time to record, the stipulation being that the tapes would remain their property," Johns later explained. Unfortunately, Robinson and Clouston were, in Johns' words, "approaching middle age at the time and not particularly clued up about the pop scene." As a result, they took the tapes "to all the wrong people . . . even the classical guy at Decca." No matter. The Stones would soon secure a record deal with Decca after their new manager, Andrew Loog Oldham, approached the *right* people at the label, who were anxious to redeem themselves after famously rejecting The Beatles a year earlier.

The Stones would go on to do many more recording sessions with Glyn Johns, but unfortunately not at IBC—by then the famous engineer had gone independent (the first engineer to do so in the U.K.) and had made Olympic his new base of operations. (See Chapter 5 for more information.)

Claydon, Damon Lyon-Shaw, Mike Weighell, John Pantry, Peter Robinson, Bryan Stott, Andy Knight

Maintenance engineers: Bernie Marsden, Ian Levine, Peter Harris, Peter Smith, Dennis King, Peter Fautley, Sean Davies, Dave Angel

PHYSICAL FACILITIES

In describing the IBC facilities of the 1950s, James Lock pointed out that "the studio wasn't purpose-built, as such, and its layout was simply a result of how the original rooms were. So although it didn't have to accommodate much equipment, the control room was huge and had a large open fireplace in it as the sole source of heating. I always found it terribly amusing that there we were trying to judge sound with this deafening crackling and snapping going on in the background. But it was always considered more

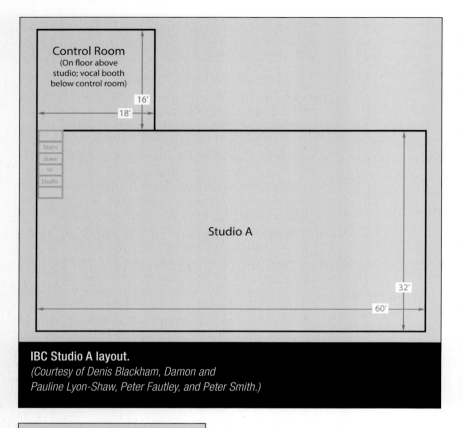

IBC Studio A layout.
(Courtesy of Denis Blackham, Damon and Pauline Lyon-Shaw, Peter Fautley, and Peter Smith.)

IBC Studio B layout.
(Courtesy of Denis Blackham, Damon and Pauline Lyon-Shaw, Peter Fautley, and Peter Smith.)

important to keep everyone reasonably warm, and in fact one of our most pressing duties in cold spells was to keep the fire fed! It was more like a rather palatial living room than a high-tech studio atmosphere."

Studio A, which Lock is describing, was more or less two large rooms of the original house knocked through. A small remix room with vocal booth, called Studio B, was added some time later. There was also a small "assembly room" overlooking the Studio A control room. This contained various tape machines and a small mixer, and was used for tape copying as well as assembling and editing radio shows. Like Studio Two at EMI (and, later, Studio One at Olympic in Barnes, designed by ex-IBC engineer Keith Grant), the control room for Studio A was located above, and looking down at, the studio floor.

Former IBC maintenance and mastering engineer Sean Davies provides the following guided tour: "You went through the door of 35 Portland Place, and there was the lady on the switchboard and then there was a lift [elevator]. If you went on down the corridor and turned slightly left at the corner, you came to [studio manager] Allen Stagg's office, with a men's toilet beyond. There was a small outdoors area with a plastic roof which led to a back building, where the cutting rooms were located.

"If you went up the stairs or took the lift to the first floor [*Note: This is the equivalent to the second floor in American parlance*], you came to Studio A; you could then walk up the stairs to the mezzanine floor and the Studio A control room. Studio B was on the floor above that, and the top floor was all offices. In the basement, there was this rabbit warren of rooms where you could easily get lost. Among these was the workshop [maintenance area] and the echo chamber, as well as the EMT plate room."

Acoustic Treatments

Former engineer and studio manager Allen Stagg joined IBC from Radio Luxembourg in 1950. "At the time, IBC was recording mostly radio shows," he says, "and there was only one studio." According to

Stagg, his first assignment at IBC was to redesign the room (known as "Studio A") and to oversee the construction of a second studio being built to accommodate small groups; this room would be designated "Studio B."

Studio A's control room, which overlooked the studio floor, was originally almost the same size as the studio, according to Stagg. Following the redesign, the control room was reduced considerably in size, although its acoustic treatment (and that of the

STORIES FROM THE STUDIO
The making of "You Really Got Me"

IN A 2009 INTERVIEW with *Sound on Sound* magazine, producer Shel Talmy sang the praises of IBC, which, in his words, "had the deserved reputation of being the progenitor of most of England's best engineers [and] was probably my favourite studio there. The live area had very good acoustics and great natural echo chambers, while the upstairs control room had IBC's own 24-input board, an Ampex 3-track machine, and an Ampex mono machine."

These were the reasons why, on July 12, 1964, Talmy brought in a group named The Kinks, recently signed to Pye. The band had already attempted to record the song "You Really Got Me" once before, at Pye Studios, but with disappointing results. "After it was done, I said it was overproduced and I didn't want to put it out," composer/singer Ray Davies later remarked. "[I thought] we should do it on 1-track and get the raw sound we wanted." In the end, the remake was done to 3-track, but it was at the faster tempo that Davies wanted—the Pye version was quite a bit slower, with a bluesy feel—and with considerably less echo than the original.

At IBC, Davies and his bandmates were once again joined by session drummer Bobby Graham, but this time keyboardist and future Deep Purple co-founder Jon Lord was brought in to supplement the sound. One critical component that was retained from the original Pye recording was lead guitarist Dave Davies' signature distortion, achieved by

playing his Harmony Meteor guitar through an Elpico amp slaved to a Vox AC30, with the speaker cone of the Elpico—affectionately referred to as the "fart box"—having been sliced by a razor and punctured with knitting needles.

It was with that setup that Dave played the song's instantly identifiable riff—one that, according to Ray Davies, had evolved while working out the chords to "Louie Louie." "The shitty little amplifier made it raunchier . . . and I enhanced it by using a couple of mics and pushing [the level] on the board," said Talmy. "I brought it up on a couple of faders and limited one like crazy while keeping its level just under the one that wasn't limited."

Talmy remembers engineer Glyn Johns using quite a few microphones on Graham's drum kit. Though unable to identify exactly which models were used, Talmy recalls Johns placing one inside the kick drum, and one about three inches from the top of the snare, with another underneath, plus individual mics on each of the toms, hi-hat, and ride cymbal, supplemented with two overheads—all recorded onto a single track, requiring careful balancing.

Despite the complicated setup, the session, by all accounts, was speedy and efficient. "Nobody messed around," reported Talmy. "In those days, if you spent a lot of time in a studio, it meant you were a really shitty band and couldn't play very well." According to Ray Davies'

autobiography, *X-Ray*, there were exactly two takes of "You Really Got Me." The second one kicked off with a fortuitous bout of amnesia. "When Dave played the opening chords," Davies wrote, "Bobby Graham forgot the complicated introduction he had planned and just thumped one beat on the snare drum with as much power as he could muster, as if to say, 'OK, wimp—take that!'"

At the start of the guitar solo, Ray shouted words of encouragement at Dave, something that "spoiled his concentration momentarily. He looked over at me, as if he had done something wrong." Then, realizing that he hadn't in fact misplayed anything, "his face broke into that arrogant sideways smile that I had learned to love and hate over the years. The little runt hadn't even heard me shout."

The second take was the keeper, to which three or four lead vocal overdubs were added, the best of which was double-tracked while copying the recording onto another machine—a loss of a generation deemed worthwhile for the powerful vocal effect it yielded.

"You Really Got Me" would of course become a massive hit when it was released a few weeks later—the first of many The Kinks would enjoy over their long career. Apparently at least one member of the group knew it immediately. "When I left the studio I felt great," Ray Davies later wrote. "It may sound conceited, but I knew it was a great record."

A session in IBC Studio B, circa mid-1950s.
(Photo by A.G.K. Ware, courtesy of Denis Blackham)

newly built Studio B and its control room) remained minimal—a few acoustic panels on the wall, and not much else, as photos of the era attest.

Room Dimensions

Studio A: 60' x 32' (18 x 10 meters)
    Ceiling height: 20' (8.5 meters)
Studio A control room: 18' x 16' (5.5 x 5 meters)
    Ceiling height: 7' (2 meters)

Studio B: 25' x 17' (7.5 x 5 meters)
    Ceiling height: 12' (3.5 meters)
Studio B vocal booth: 16' x 10' (5 x 3 meters)
    Ceiling height: 9' (3 meters)

Echo Chambers

IBC had a large and often-used acoustic echo chamber located in the Portland Place basement. It was equipped with a microphone (model unknown) and a Voight corner horn speaker, which eventually

fell apart because of the damp conditions that caused the plywood to separate.

James Lock recalled that remote classical recordings done at Conway Hall were often piped in via standard telephone lines so that ambience from the echo chamber could be added during recording and broadcast. "The frequency response must have been terrible," he reflected many years later, "but we were more interested in an overall warm sound in those days, as opposed to . . . technical perfection."

KEY EQUIPMENT
Mixing Consoles

Like most British recording studios of the era, the mixing consoles at IBC were all custom-designed and built by the maintenance staff. Unusually, however, IBC continued to use these boards well into the 1970s, even after the sale to Chas Chandler and renaming to Portland Place Studios, despite the fact that multiple third-party companies such as Neve, Cadac, and Helios were manufacturing consoles by then.

Unfortunately, most of the known IBC mixing boards have since been dismantled and so many of the details about them have been lost to the mists of time. Former engineer Jack Clegg recalls that the original mixer in Studio B had only six input channels, with its single output routed directly to an EMI BTR1 mono machine. "If you anticipated the need of *the* (Pultec) equalizer or *the* limiter," he adds, emphasizing the fact that IBC apparently had only one of each at the time, "you had to arrange to borrow them in advance from the disc cutting facility, which was two floors below in the mews at the back of the building. Each unit was about the size of a small suitcase." Clegg would later go on to record much of the music for the American TV series *Gunsmoke* in IBC's larger Studio A.

Presumably the early Studio A consoles were mono only, but by the late 1950s they were replaced by models equipped for stereo. Ex–maintenance engineer Sean Davies recalls helping install a 10-input tube (valve) desk with individually replaceable mic preamps. By the early 1960s, Studio A was equipped with a new console that offered 24 inputs and at least three outputs; this was replaced by a 32 x 16 console in 1971 when IBC went 16-track. One notable feature of the latter was that it offered continuously variable midrange equalization, as opposed to the fixed frequencies provided by most consoles of the era. Studio B was refitted with a 20 x 4 console some time in the early 1960s and would continue to use that mixing board at least until the facility's sale in 1978.

Adrian Kerridge, who started his career as an assistant engineer at IBC, notes that the mixing boards built by IBC in the 1950s and 1960s were fully transistorized, although he recalls that they were outfitted with rotary carbon pots, which were problematic. "They used to go noisy and the maintenance staff would have to keep taking them out and changing them," he says. Another unusual feature of the IBC consoles, according to Kerridge, was that they were outfitted with small BBC-type peak-reading (PPM) meters, as opposed to the VU meters in common use at the time. This may have been where Keith Grant (who worked at IBC for a time) received

his first exposure to this type of metering, which he later insisted had to be included on all mixing desks built by Dick Swettenham for Olympic Studios. (See Chapter 5 for more information.)

In the mid-1970s, the boffins in the IBC basement workshop designed and manufactured one of the first quadraphonic mixing desks, under the direction of technical director Dennis King. This desk was still in operation in the late '80s, and most often used for mixing soundtracks for large events. (See *Quad: Ahead of its time, or just a bad idea?* on page 59 for more information.)

Monitors

Monitoring for both control rooms at IBC was initially provided by 15" dual concentric Tannoy Reds in Lockwood cabinets, powered by Radford STA25 25-watt power amplifiers. According to former maintenance

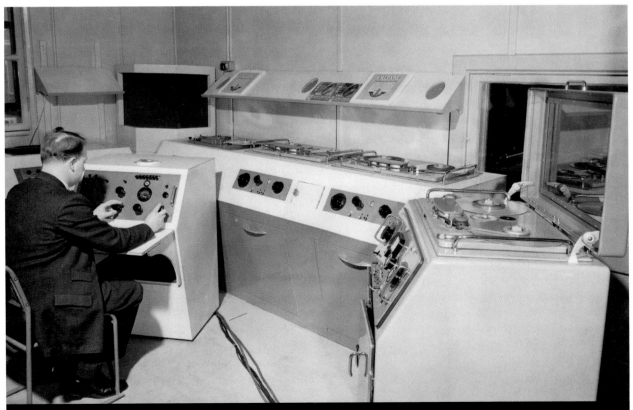

The IBC Assembly Room, circa mid-1950s.
(Photo by A.G.K. Ware, courtesy of Denis Blackham)

Joe Meek behind the lathe in one of the IBC cutting rooms, mid-1950s.
(Photo by A.G.K. Ware, courtesy of Denis Blackham)

engineer Peter Fautley, as monitoring level requirements increased (along with coil burnout), the Tannoy Reds were later replaced by Tannoy Golds driven by Radford STA100 100-watt amps, even though "everybody said they did not sound as good as the Reds." (See Chapter 1 and Chapter 4 for more information.)

Stereo, 1950s-style

IN A 1997 INTERVIEW for *Studio Sound* magazine, Eric Tomlinson recalled the first-ever stereo session at IBC, with Adrian Kerridge engineering. "It was for an American [record] company, I believe," he said. "These Americans came over and they brought with them a brown plastic attaché case in which was one of the portable Ampexes. It was a shiny brown leathery-type hard case and [when] you opened [it] up, [it] broke in half and the top half was the deck, and the bottom part the amplifiers, and then two speakers popped out. We were very short of mics, but we managed to find Adrian a couple. We had the Ted Heath Band there, and he put one mic at one end and one at the other, and we were all outside in the corridor listening to this fantastic stereo. It took the wind out of my sails a little bit but nevertheless it really was quite good, considering he just had two microphones up."

Tape Machines

Contemporaneous photos show that the IBC "assembly room" at Portland Place was outfitted in the 1950s with EMI BTR1 full-track and BTR2 mono machines, which by 1958 were replaced with Ampex AG350 and "portable" AG300 models. The two control rooms were also equipped with Ampex machines, probably the same models. According to former IBC mastering engineer Denis Blackham, there were also one or two 1/2" 3-track Ampex machines housed in a small side room next to Studio A, remotely controlled from the control room; these were used mostly for tape delay and phasing. (See Chapter 1 and Chapter 5 for more information.) Some time prior to 1963, the 3-track Ampexes were replaced with 4-track models.

By the mid-1970s, both control rooms at IBC were equipped with a full cadre of Ampex machines: 16-track, 8-track, 4-track, stereo, and mono. The 8-track and at least one of the 2-tracks were AG-440 models; in addition, there were one or more ATR-102 2-track machines. By the end of the 1970s, these were supplemented with Ampex MM1200 24-track machines and Studer A80 2-track machines. (See Chapter 1 for more information about the A80 and Chapter 6 for more information about the AG-440.)

Main Microphones

Neumann U87—According to Peter Fautley, the IBC mic locker may also have included some U87i models. (See Chapter 1 for more information.)

Neumann U67—There were a significant number of these tube mics at IBC, used on everything from guitar amps to orchestra. (See Chapter 1 for more information.)

Neumann U47—IBC had several of these, both tube and FET models. (See Chapter 1 for more information.)

Neumann KM84—(See Chapter 5 for more information.)

Neumann M49—Sean Davies recalls that one of his first jobs at IBC was to replace the studio's sole M49 MSC2 tube with an AC701. (See Chapter 1 for more information.)

AKG C24—One of the first microphones purposely designed for stereo recording, the C24 is often viewed as simply being a stereo C12, but there are subtle differences between it and the C12 in both electrical design and sound quality. Although both use the same 12AY7 tube, the improved transient response of the C24 yields a sound that has been variously described as "dryer" and "harder" than that of the C12. In addition, the C24 boasts a number of unique features, including nine remotely controllable polar patterns for each of its two "systems" (capsules) and a rotatable upper capsule (up to 180 degrees), allowing its use for X-Y and MS (Mid-Side) recording.

BBC AXBT—IBC owned one or two of these old-fashioned ribbon mics, although, according to Sean Davies, they were not often used at IBC Studios. (See *Pye* in Chapter 2 for more information.)

STC 4033-A—IBC owned several of these. (See Chapter 1 for more information.)

STC Coles 4021—IBC owned several of these "ball-and-biscuit" microphones. (See *Pye* in Chapter 2 for more information.)

Telefunken ELA M251—IBC owned four of these. (See *Decca* in Chapter 2 for more information.)

A 1972 studio listing indicated that IBC's mic cabinet also included Beyer dynamic mics (models unknown). By 1979, Portland Recording Studios had added one or more AKG C28s and C414s, as well as some unknown Sennheiser models.

Outboard Signal Processors

Jack Clegg states that IBC initially owned only one limiter, which lived in the cutting room in the outbuilding at the rear of the facility and had to be lugged

upstairs when needed by one of the recording engineers. Later, there were two limiters in use, both located in the "assembly room," as opposed to the control rooms. One of these, according to Allen Stagg, was an American-made Fairchild; the other was a custom limiter built by IBC technical director Dennis King. According to Sean Davies, the latter was based on a BBC design, with Woden transformers. In addition, IBC owned one or more Pultec equalizers, and sometime in the 1960s at least one EMT 140 plate reverb was installed in the basement, near the workshop.

A 1979 listing for Portland Recording Studios indicated that an ADR Scamp rack had been added to the outboard gear, as well as an MXR digital delay and a Klark Teknik DN34 "analog time processor" delay line.

In 1958, IBC became the first studio in London to purchase a Lyrec stereo cutting lathe with an Ortofon cutting head. John Holbrook, who worked in the IBC cutting room from 1968 to 1969 (mastering, among other iconic records, The Who's *Tommy* and

Singer Petula Clark in the IBC Studio B control room, 1957.
(Photo by Popperfoto/Getty Images)

STORIES FROM THE STUDIO
Tweakers delight

ONE CHRONIC PROBLEM at IBC during the years that Joe Meek worked there (1954–1957) was that he was an inveterate tweaker. Worse yet, he developed the infuriating habit of changing gear drastically—sometimes totally off-spec—during a session and then just leaving it that way for whoever came after. "That was a nightmare," said mastering engineer Ray Prickett in Barry Cleveland's book *Joe Meek's Bold Techniques*. "If you had a session you used to have to find out if Joe had been in there before you, because if he had you made sure you had an extra half-hour, and got the workshop up to check everything out. There was no guarantee that everything was going to be working at a basic standard."

In particular, Meek would often adjust the tape recorders, especially their high-frequency response. "He'd pile as much level as he could on the tape," says Adrian Kerridge, "and he would take specific precautions to either increase the level going onto it, or take it down, as the case may be. It would be either avoid distortion or increase it."

Exacerbating the problem, according to Prickett, were Meek's technical limitations, which sometimes had him getting a bit ahead of himself. "On some occasions," Prickett explains, "[Meek would] alter the record EQ to get an effect. Then he'd tweak the replay EQ curve to make it play back differently, until he got what he wanted. But then that particular tape might not play back right in every machine, if the tape's being sent to another place [to be mastered or copied]. What it boiled down to was that if he'd produced a tape that way, for it to be played back properly the EQs on those machines would have to be set the same way."

Jimi Hendrix's *Electric Ladyland*) recalls that the tape playback machine in the mastering suite was equally advanced. "It had track-mounted sliding preview heads which would adjust for the various combinations of tape speed and disc format," he says—though there was apparently a price to be paid for being at the cutting edge (pardon the pun) of technology. "From time to time the string (!) that operated these heads would break and the tension spring would fling the heads violently against the end of the track, requiring care and attention from the technical department."

From the mid-'70s onward, the IBC cutting room in the back building served as a home for ex-Apple mastering engineer George Peckham, joining IBC staffer Brian Carroll.

KEY TECHNICAL INNOVATIONS
The Inimitable Joe Meek

Joe Meek, who would later open the first home studio in the U.K. (see Chapter 4 for more information), began his career as an IBC engineer. Even in those early days, Meek stood out, as much for his outside-the-box thinking as his obsessive nature and other personal quirks (such as a proclivity for foot-stamping temper tantrums).

Adrian Kerridge, who worked closely with Meek at both IBC and later at Lansdowne, said of the famed producer, "He used to think he was technical, and he wasn't really technical, not *technical* technical. He'd say, 'We're gonna do this.' He wouldn't really know why. He couldn't give a technical explanation why, but he'd do it, and it would work . . . and the results were, for those days, enormously progressive."

Producer Arthur Frewin had this to say about Meek: "Very often in the studio after a run-through you'd say, 'That's great, Joe.' And he'd say, 'Look, I've just had an idea—can we have another run-through?' All of a sudden something would click in his mind and he'd get, say, 20 strings sounding like 60 strings. And he'd come up with ideas that nobody else had at the time—[he was] well ahead of his time. He'd have all sorts of ideas, like throwing echo in—but he knew how to control echo and make it work for him." James Lock recalls Meek building a spring reverb at home and bringing it into the studio, housed in one of his infamous "black box" chassis (so that no one could see inside and steal his ideas).

Frewin also claims that Meek was the first engineer to discover phasing. "It came off on some of his pop records way back in '57 and '58, and people wondered how the hell he did it," he says. "During the 'live' take he'd play back the previous take into the studio with a microphone by the speaker, and blend the two [signals]. He worked that out himself. He was the first in many, many things. He distorted brass by making [the musicians] play against a wall; this hit the next sound coming out, breaking the sound up."

Adds Kerridge, "Joe Meek was the first to use two microphones on four trumpets, and two feet away; the sound was like a trumpet in your ear. One day he had a big session with four trumpets. We used to use these old STC pencil microphones, and Joe said, 'I'm not gonna put four trumpets and a mic up there. I want two microphones, and they're gonna be that far away, two feet away from the bells of the trumpets. I'm gonna put two in parallel, into one mic socket.' That was unheard of, really, and it was a tremendous trumpet sound."

Kerridge identifies another Meek innovation at IBC, one he claims began as early as 1955. "Joe and producer Michael Barclay would work what they called 'composites'—another word for pre-mixing, made track by track. Instead of the recording being laid down all at once on one track, they'd make a rhythm track—the first composite—add something else to it, and then something else, and finally put the voice on top, so it would end up three or four generations removed from the original. What they were effectively doing was multitrack recording. No one else to my knowledge in England was recording music that way." (*Note: What Kerridge is describing here is track bouncing, which was already being done in America by the pioneering Les Paul; this was a technique that would also, of course, later be used to great effect by The Beatles at EMI Studios.*)

Studio Workshops

Shortly after joining IBC in 1950, Allen Stagg—always one for doing things "by the book"—instituted a program of formal training for fledgling engineers, probably the first in the U.K. In those days, even staid studios like EMI and Decca had no formal apprenticeship program; new staffers were expected to "learn the ropes" simply from observation and by asking questions.

The approach Stagg took was to set up regular "studio workshops," at which bands, orchestras, and groups would be invited to come in and be recorded by a trainee, under Stagg's supervision. The artist would get a free recording, and the IBC staffer would get free practice time. "The aim," Stagg explains, "was to give trainees experience and a place where they could make mistakes with no consequences."

But as in the simulator training that NASA astronauts would later receive, Stagg made a point of throwing a monkey wrench into the works wherever and whenever possible. "I would ask the engineer to devise a setup and then we'd discuss it," he says. "Then I'd tell them something like, 'Well, today we've got a great shortage of mics and we haven't got any limiters and we haven't got any compressors.' I wanted them to find the solution for recording in the most straightforward, basic way possible.

Pete Townshend in IBC Studio A recording "The Seeker," 1970.
(Photo by Chris Morphet/Redferns)

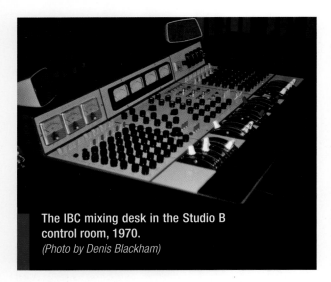

The IBC mixing desk in the Studio B control room, 1970.
(Photo by Denis Blackham)

"So if there was a jazz group coming in with piano, bass, drums, sax, and trombone, I'd say, 'OK, well, let's have a look at your setup. Fifteen mics? We can't afford 15 mics. Have another think about it.' In the end, we would cut the setup down to about three mics. Now, you can't go very much lower than that, but that also allowed for overlapping, so a single mic would maybe be picking up all the drums or whatever. I would then sit with them on the session, and they'd say, 'God, I didn't think we could do that with such a small amount of equipment!' Keith Grant later told me he learned more from those sessions than anything else. What he learned was how not to use a lot of equipment!"

SELECTED DISCOGRAPHY

- The Kinks: "You Really Got Me" (single)
- The Who: "My Generation," "Anyhow Anyway Anywhere" (singles), tracks for *Tommy*
- Thunderclap Newman: "Something in the Air" (single)
- The Small Faces: "All or Nothing" (single)
- Cream: "Badge" (single)
- The Bee Gees: "To Love Somebody" (single)
- Status Quo: *Piledriver, Hello!*

STORIES FROM THE STUDIO
The Mellotron: reliably unreliable

THE VARISPEED SERVO DESIGN was poor. The tapes would stick inside their frames and refuse to rewind. If the environment was too smoky, too hot, or too humid, the damn thing wouldn't work at all. Large and unwieldy and reliably unreliable, the Mellotron nonetheless became an integral part of the sound of popular music in the '60s and '70s (think Moody Blues; think "Strawberry Fields Forever").

What exactly was a Mellotron? Basically, it was a set of tapes that played when you hit a note on its keyboard. It looked like a bulky harpsichord, but beneath each key was a playback head and one or more prerecorded monophonic tape loops—recordings of real instruments (most famously, flute and violin). Each loop had a playing time of only eight seconds or so, after which the tape came

to a dead stop and rewound to the start position, which meant that if you were playing a chord, you had to release different notes in sequence—a process some compared to a spider crawling across a keyboard.

Originally developed in the U.S., the Mellotron found its way to England's shores in 1962, marketed initially mostly to cocktail lounges as a futuristic kind of organ (some of the tapes were cheesy rhythm accompaniments). Eventually, a subsidiary company named Mellotronics was formed and set up shop in IBC Studios—an ideal location for the recording of new sounds. Maintenance engineer Dennis King built a customized 9-into-3 recording desk for just that purpose, and so began the process of recording tape loops for the instrument, using session musicians conducted by bandleader

(and IBC co-owner) Eric Robinson. Unfortunately, according to veteran IBC engineer Sean Davies, it was a nightmare for those assigned to the sessions, to the point where nearly the entire staff were ready to go out on strike. The reason? Sheer tedium.

Davies explains: "Let's say, for example, you were making loops of an alto sax in the key of G. Each note on the instrument had to recorded separately, then cut to exactly the right length, with leader tape spliced at each end, and the leader tape had to be exactly the right length and this then had to be made up onto a NAB spool . . . and that's just alto sax, in the key of G. Every instrument was recorded like that, and the process took absolutely forever." Anyone who ever recorded a sample for one of the early 1980s digital sampling keyboards can no doubt relate!

LANSDOWNE

By 1957 Joe Meek had had it.

Ridiculed by many of his fellow engineers at IBC for his somewhat sloppy work habits and personal eccentricities, reined in by overly controlling management, who disapproved of his unorthodox methods, and already beginning to show traces of the mental illness and paranoia that would ultimately lead to his untimely demise, Meek desperately needed a fresh start.

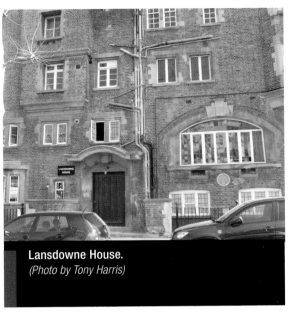

Lansdowne House.
(Photo by Tony Harris)

That start would be provided by independent producer Dennis Preston, who had supervised numerous important British jazz recordings in the 1950s at IBC, with Joe behind the board. In the course of conversation, the two men discovered that Preston was equally "fed up" with IBC, and they decided to go into business together. Preston's role would be to provide the funding and clientele, while Meek was tasked with finding suitable premises where he could design and build a new studio to compete with IBC, revenge having apparently been a major motivating factor.

It didn't take Meek long before he found just what he was looking for. Lansdowne House, in London's fashionable Holland Park district, was erected in 1902 by William Flodthart, a benevolent South African diamond millionaire and patron of the arts who wanted to provide a place where struggling painters could work. As a result, the ceilings were unusually high and the sub-basement squash court spacious— perfect, in fact, for a recording studio.

Some time previously, assistant engineer Adrian Kerridge—who knew Joe Meek and Denis Preston from his time at IBC—had gone off to do his compulsory two-year National Service (the equivalent to the American draft), during which he received an assignment at a military radio station. At some point toward the end of Kerridge's tour of duty, Preston was asked to help the Army produce some jazz broadcasts, and when he arrived at the radio station he found his former colleague there. Preston excitedly described the new facility he and Meek were planning, and invited Kerridge to join them and help with the design and construction of the studio.

Renovation took nearly a year, and Lansdowne Studios, as it was named, opened its doors in 1958. There was no shortage of clients, thanks to Denis Preston; many of the artists he had crafted hit records for at IBC followed him to Lansdowne. Most of them were jazz artists, but there were some major pop stars, too. It didn't take long before the studio became so renowned for the clarity of its recordings that the engineers at IBC started referring to it, perhaps somewhat sardonically, as "The House of Shattering Glass."

The first control room at Lansdowne was exceedingly small and equipped for mono only, but luckily Kerridge and maintenance engineer Peter Hitchcock had the foresight to allocate space immediately on the floor above it for the construction of a much larger stereo control room, which was operational by 1962. Like EMI Studio Two and IBC's Studio A, this control room was upstairs, looking down over the studio floor.

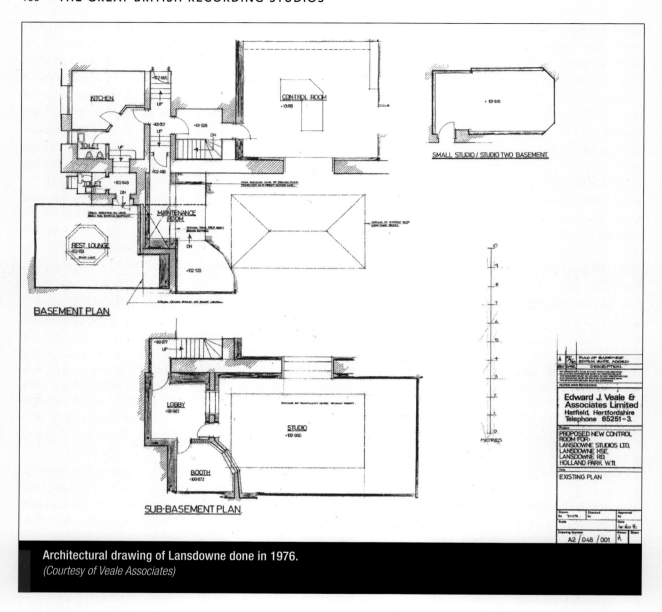

Architectural drawing of Lansdowne done in 1976.
(Courtesy of Veale Associates)

Unfortunately, by that time Meek was gone. In January 1960, after a dispute with Preston, he left Lansdowne to found Triumph Records; from there, he would start his own studio and compete with *both* of his former employers. (See Chapter 4 for more information.)

In 1970, an office just outside the studio area was converted to a modern, spacious control room, at which time the two old control rooms were repurposed as isolation booths, with the larger of the two—the one that had previously been the stereo control room—used primarily for drums.

In the early 1980s, studio management made the decision to refocus from music recording to sound for picture; accordingly, the small Studio Two (really just a tape copying room) was converted into a telecine transfer suite. For the next two decades Lansdowne flourished as a postproduction facility despite fierce competition in that arena and the concurrent rise of home recording. Eventually, however, the studio had no choice but to bow to the inevitable. Lansdowne closed its doors in September 2006.

KEY PERSONNEL

Recording engineers: Joe Meek, Adrian Kerridge, Terry Brown, Vic Keary, David Heelis, John Mackswith, Bob Butterworth, Chris Dibble, Hugh Padgham, Nick Patrick, Peter Gallen

Maintenance engineers: Adrian Kerridge, Peter Hitchcock

PHYSICAL FACILITIES

Lansdowne consisted of a single large sub-basement studio, with, initially, a tiny monophonic control room on the same level. In 1962, a larger control room, equipped for stereo, was opened on the floor above, alongside the maintenance workshop; this would be expanded greatly in 1970 when the studio upgraded to 16-track. At some point in the early 1960s, a kitchen and a small tape copying room, called "Studio Two" (even though it didn't have a mixing console), were added to the basement level.

Acoustic Treatments

Though little specific information about the original acoustic treatment at Lansdowne is available, it is known that it was overseen by jazz clarinetist

---

STORIES FROM THE STUDIO
Two trains colliding

BARRY CLEVELAND, author of *Joe Meek's Bold Techniques*, describes Joe Meek and Denis Preston as "two trains racing towards each other on a single track." There were numerous reasons why. For one thing, Preston had rewarded Meek by granting him virtual producer status on many sessions, something that inevitably led to power struggles. In addition, Meek had begun writing songs and lobbying hard for them to be recorded by the acts Preston was producing—another source of friction.

"Denis Preston, who had lots of experience dealing with quirky and temperamental jazz artists, was temporarily able to keep Meek at least partially pacified by allowing him considerably greater creative freedom than other engineers typically enjoyed, and by bankrolling his gear craving," writes Cleveland. At one point Meek was even given a company automobile, but he took no more interest in it than he did anything else unrelated to recording. Said Adrian Kerridge, "From the day that he had it until the day he left, he never put a drop of oil in it, and he never had it serviced. The tools that came with the car, he brought them into the studio, and they were used in the studio and never on the car. He used to get in, and if it didn't start, he'd leave it."

Cleveland's analysis is that Meek's "ambitions began to outgrow his position, and he became increasingly disinterested in simply being an engineer, albeit a highly appreciated and nearly unrestricted one. For one thing, he felt that he had more to do with Preston's successful records than Preston himself. For another, he felt that he knew more about how to make hit records than most of the A&R men that he had to serve and answer to as an employee of the studio. He could do all of their jobs and probably some others too: scouting out new artists, choosing their repertory, producing and engineering their records—maybe even writing the songs." For his part, Preston was growing increasingly disenchanted with the engineer who he once described as being "in a sense a split personality. When things were going well, [Meek] was the most marvelous person to work with. But if there was a crisis, he'd blow up and [become] impossible."

And so a parting of the ways was inevitable. It occurred on the morning of November 4, 1959, when the two protagonists were struggling with a difficult mix in Lansdowne's hot, cramped control room (there was no air-conditioning in those days). Meek made the mistake of choosing precisely that moment to begin pestering Preston about a new song he'd written.

"Joe, for Christ's sake, if you want to talk about songs, talk about them later," snapped the beleaguered producer. "We're trying to make a record."

At which point Meek labeled Preston with his favorite epithet ("rotten pig") and walked out. The next day Meek received a phone call telling him not to bother coming back. In the weeks that followed, Adrian Kerridge was promoted to full engineer, then studio manager (he would eventually become a director and co-owner of the facility), and life at Lansdowne went on, albeit a little less contentiously. Denis Preston would continue to quietly make records until his passing in 1979; Meek would do the same, but in a typically more boisterous fashion, until his suicide in 1967.

Joe Meek behind the custom-built EMI mixing console at Lansdowne, 1959.
(Photo by Dr. Chris Williams, courtesy of John Repsch)

and former BBC technician Sandy Brown, who owned one of the few acoustic design companies in London at the time.

Room Dimensions

Studio: 45' x 25' (13.5 x 7.5 meters)
    Ceiling height: 15' (4.5 meters)
Control room*: 25' x 22' (7.5 x 7 meters)
    Ceiling height: 12' (3.5 meters)
The stereo control room, post-1962.

Echo Chambers

Lansdowne had a basement echo chamber, one that was by all accounts especially good-sounding. "It was a small room with a hard brick surface, a 'ball and biscuit' [STC Coles 4021] microphone in one end, and a speaker [model unknown] in the other," says Kerridge. The room's stone walls, ceiling, and floor were all coated with high-gloss paint to improve reflectivity.

In addition to the purpose-built echo chamber, Lansdowne Hall had another feature that was sometimes used for that purpose: the open elevator shaft that ran all the way up to the roof. "On some sessions," Kerridge reports with a grin, "we'd put a speaker way up top and use the shaft as another reverberation chamber, mostly for guitar and Hammond organ. The

[building's] residents hated it, of course, and they'd complain like hell, especially if it was late at night. But it was a different sound from our acoustic echo chamber, and you can't always rely on just one reverb; sometimes you've got to use several to get the right effect."

KEY EQUIPMENT
Mixing Consoles

The original Lansdowne mixing console was a custom 12 x 2 tube (valve) desk built by EMI to Joe Meek's precise specifications, including, in true flamboyant Meek style, a maroon finish with gold trim. The cost was reported to have been £4,500, or some $120,000 in today's dollars. According to Adrian Kerridge, Denis Preston was not at all happy with the expenditure. "He used to say, 'This console? I could have bought a Mercedes for that!'"

The board featured Painton quadrant (semiround) faders, which had to be cleaned frequently because of their tendency to audibly "tick" when dirt got inside. There was a single PPM meter in the center that was said to be unusually responsive, and EQ on every channel. "It was simple, but it was a very clean desk, apart from the fact that we had measurable phase problems with it," Kerridge says. "Things could have sounded a lot crisper; the bandwidth of the desk wasn't that high—it only went up to perhaps 25 or 30 kHz. Because it had small transformers, the phase shift, especially in the top end, was quite substantial. It was almost 180 degrees, and the lag in the bass end was significant as well." In 1961, Kerridge began modifying the circuitry to address those issues until he achieved a reasonably flat response. "After that, of course, all the sounds changed completely," he reports. "That's when we got this tremendous reputation for our string sound, our rhythm sound and our bass sound, because it was a very clean signal path, with minimal electronics."

In 1967, Adrian Kerridge recruited ex-Olympic maintenance engineer Clive Green to begin the process of replacing all the tube components of the EMI desk with transistor circuitry, as well as modifying the desk for 8-track recording. They quickly discovered a shared passion for console design and began plans to create a new desk altogether. A year later, ex-Lansdowne engineer Terry Brown, now helping Barry Morgan set up his new Morgan studios (see *Morgan* in Chapter 8 for more information) asked to buy the designs for the new desk. Green suggested instead that they build the desk for him, and recruited technicians David Bott and Charles Billet to aid in the endeavor.

And so the manufacturing company formed by Clive, Adrian, David and Charles—or the acronym Cadac—was born. In June 1970, a 28 x 24 Cadac console was installed in Lansdowne's new control room off to the side of the studio. The original frame would be used for the next 20 years, though many of the modules would be upgraded and replaced over time.

"Clive and I worked quite closely together on that desk," says Kerridge. "I told him, 'We really should make it an L-shape.' People used to complain, 'It's back-to-front,' but eventually they accepted it, even though it was difficult to get the point across. It was completely different. It was a radical change."

"The mic transformers in our console were huge octal base," Kerridge adds, "and the switching for track selection and internal selection was via gold-plated relays. We had found that ordinary palladium-type relays affected the high frequencies when you put a signal through them; with gold-plated relays, you didn't have that problem. They were very expensive, but it's the sound that counts."

The equalization circuit in the Cadac board was designed so that it was brought in from each coil only when needed; when the EQ was out, it was a virtual straight-through signal path from beginning to end, with high-frequency response in excess of 75 kHz. "People asked us, 'Why did you need to go that high?'" Kerridge remembers. "My answer was that if you start to bend the harmonic structure, you get phase problems and it doesn't sound right. My contention was, if it's right higher up, it's going to be right lower down."

The console was also designed to have a significant headroom. "The output was very important to us," says Kerridge. "The first Cadac desks had unbalanced outputs so you had to be extremely careful with the earthing (grounding); otherwise you'd get all sorts of hum loops and other problems. The inputs were always balanced, but the outputs also eventually became balanced transformerless as well."

The board was also carefully set up for mono/stereo compatibility, something that was of particular importance in those transitional days. "Unlike some other consoles of the era, when you switched between stereo and mono, you didn't get any change in level," reports Kerridge.

Another Kerridge request was that the Lansdowne console be modified so that he could apply four compressors to the mix bus. "I'd use two stereo pairs of linked 1176 limiters, feeding the rhythm section through one pair and the brass and the strings through the other," he explains. "I'd then set the levels carefully and bring them both back to one stereo pair, with the summation of the two signals coming up to full zero VU. In those days, if you compressed an instrument and the rhythm section played a bit heavier, it would drag the front line down. But with this technique, you wouldn't even know that we were using compression even though it would make things sound loud."

STORIES FROM THE STUDIO
"Young man, don't point that thing at me!"

DIVAS ARE TIMELESS, as this story from engineer John Mackswith amply demonstrates.

"We were recording a jazz album with Denis Preston at Lansdowne, and Denis was very much in vogue for producing jazz at the time," he recalls. "He'd decided that he was going to have Dame Edith Evans give the narration of the story and plot throughout this record, so, in the vocal booth, I'd set up a table and a microphone for her. She sat down very, very delicately, but as I adjusted the microphone in front of her for the narration she suddenly exclaimed, 'Young man, don't point that thing at me! Take it away!'

"I went back to Denis Preston and said, 'Dame Edith doesn't want a microphone. She feels it's an intrusion.' He didn't say anything, so I had to come up with a solution, fast. I decided to have my tape op stand next to Dame Edith, ostensibly to turn the pages of the script for her. But I instructed him to make sure he put his elbow on her chair the whole time because he had a KM54 stuffed up his sleeve. This way, he could keep it pointed directly at her without her ever knowing, and the session continued without a hitch."

The Dave Clark Five in Lansdowne Studio, with vocalist Mike Smith second from left.
(Courtesy of Dave Clark)

In 1977, when Lansdowne went 24-track, additional modules were added to the original Cadac frame to give it 36 x 24 capability. This modified desk initially used the coil EQ modules from the previous console, although Kerridge later decided to change them over to transistorized circuitry. At around that time he also requested that Clive Green develop an automation system for the board. Cadac's solution was to provide motorized faders with dual sliders—one that was operational and the other one showing the previous level, with LEDs to indicate when the two were in balance.

Monitors

The original control rooms at Lansdowne (both the downstairs mono room and upstairs stereo room) were outfitted with Altec monitors, exact models unknown, although they were likely 605As. (See Chapter 1 for more information.)

For the new control room, opened in 1970, Adrian Kerridge designed a custom Cadac monitoring system, which he described as being "huge, in both size and sound. The cabinets were sand-filled, weighed over a ton each, and were braced inside." Each of these behemoths housed two 18" low-frequency speakers (make and model unknown), paired with an Altec Lansing HF unit with the horn removed. The monitors were biamped, driven by Crown DC300 amplifiers.

Tape Machines

EMI TR50 and TR51 (2-track and mono)—These were monophonic "portable" tape recorders (each weighed 59 pounds) designed for location use. Though mechanically similar, they differed in that the TR50 was only a two-head machine (erase and record/play), while the TR51 offered three heads (erase, record, and play). They delivered good sound quality, but apparently needed constant tweaking to keep them in spec. Another drawback was that their 8.25" spool capacity allowed for only 20 minutes of recording when running at 15 ips. Both the TR50 and TR51 could be operated at 7.5 or 3.75 ips, with different EQ settings automatically applied as the speed selector control was changed.

EMI TR90 (2-track and mono)—At least two TR90s were added to the Lansdowne arsenal in the early 1960s. (See *Decca* in Chapter 2 for more information.)

Telefunken M15 (2-track and mono)—These large, bulky machines were preferred by Adrian Kerridge to the various EMI models at Lansdowne, despite the fact that they offered no onboard metering.

Ampex A300 (4-track)—Lansdowne added this classic 4-track half-inch recorder in 1963, and it would serve as the studio's main multitrack until the major renovation that occurred in 1970. (See *Decca* in Chapter 2 for more information.)

Scully 284-8 (8-track)—This machine was installed at Lansdowne in late 1967, after Adrian Kerridge and Clive Green had completed the refurbishment of the studio's custom EMI console. (See *Decca* in Chapter 2 and *Advision* below for more information.)

Studer A80 (16-track)—One of these was installed at Lansdowne in 1972. (See Chapter 1 for more information.)

Main Microphones

Neumann U87—(See Chapter 1 for more information.)

Neumann U67—All the U67s at Lansdowne had tube (valve) electronics. (See Chapter 1 for more information.)

Neumann U47—There may have been both tube and FET U47s at Lansdowne, since Adrian Kerridge recalled that singer Mike Smith of the Dave Clark Five preferred using a tube model for his vocals. (See Chapter 1 for more information.)

Neumann KM54—These were often used at Lansdowne to record acoustic bass and accordion . . . and, at least on one occasion, as the Story from the Studio on page 103 illustrates, for a surreptitious vocal. (See Chapter 1 for more information.)

Neumann M49—At Lansdowne, these were used primarily on brass instruments. (See Chapter 1 for more information.)

AKG D12—A large-diaphragm dynamic microphone first introduced in 1953, the D12 was said to be the world's first dynamic cardioid mic. It was based on new developments in microphone technology at the time, which eliminated much of the characteristic shrillness in earlier microphones and extended the low-frequency response, thanks to a special "bass chamber" that boosted the frequencies in the 60–120 Hz range. Though originally designed for vocals and for use on brass instruments, D12s were often used at Lansdowne as bass drum mics.

BBC AXBT—There were a pair of these venerable broadcast mics at Lansdowne. (See *Pye* in Chapter 2 for more information.)

STC Coles 4021—At Lansdowne, a 4021 "ball and biscuit" mic was employed in the acoustic echo chamber. (See *Pye* in Chapter 2 for more information.)

STC 4038—(See Chapter 1 for more information.)

STORIES FROM THE STUDIO
A candle in the wind (shield)

"MIKE SMITH [of the Dave Clark Five] was a good singer," recalls engineer Adrian Kerridge, "and his voice matched well with Lansdowne's valve [tube] U47, but he used to pop like mad.

"But I didn't want to put a pop shield on the mic because I didn't want to kill the top end. So after some thought I put a candle between his lips and the microphone, and if he blew it out, he knew he was popping! He learned very quickly how to modulate his voice to prevent that from happening, and soon he was able to sing close up to the microphone without a single pop. After that, his vocals got very, very punchy and right on the nose."

Asked how he was able to come up with that particular trick, Kerridge's answer is self-effacing. "It was just instinct, I guess. I know I didn't learn that from anybody. I just invented it on the spot, I suppose, just as we invented lots of sounds in those days."

STORIES FROM THE STUDIO
On no account do this!

BOB BUTTERWORTH STARTED at Lansdowne in 1971 as a teaboy; by 1973, he was a full engineer, having learned his craft from Adrian Kerridge and John Mackswith.

One of the studio's biggest clients at the time was Weinbergers Music Library. One might expect that recording sound effects wouldn't be nearly as exciting as making hit records with a famous group, but Butterworth felt differently. "I loved doing sessions for Weinbergers," he says, "in large part because their main producer was this chap named George Barker. Like [studio owner] Denis Preston, he was into experimentation. If we got a new piece of gear in, he'd tell me to go straight to the owner's manual and find out where it said, 'On no account do this'—and then go straight ahead and do it! In my experience, that's actually how most innovative sounds are created—either by deliberately disregarding the 'proper' way of doing things, or by making a mistake. Somebody somewhere along the line must have accidentally phased something, because who would ever think of doing that?

Outboard Signal Processors

UREI 1176—There were several of these tube limiters at Lansdowne, many of which had been outfitted with modified transformers. (See *Decca* in Chapter 2 for more information.)

Fairchild 670—With its unusually fast attack time of 50 microseconds, the 670 was an advanced version of the 660, available in both stereo and single-channel versions and designed primarily for use in broadcast and for mastering. In the mid-1960s, Adrian Kerridge persuaded Lansdowne's directors to import one from the U.S. at a cost of just under £600. "Now, that was a lot of money at the time," he says with a laugh, "but we eventually sold it to a studio in the States who were working on some Beatles material and we got £16,000 for it!" (See Chapter 1 for more information about the Fairchild 660.)

EMT 140 plate reverbs—Two of these were installed in the Lansdowne subbasement, probably during the 1963 redesign. Engineer Bob Butterworth recalled that "we couldn't actually use the plates much at night because the room wasn't soundproofed, so it would make the other residents in the building very unhappy." (See Chapter 1 for more information.)

EMT 240 Gold Foil—Essentially a scaled-down EMT 140, the 240 used a 12-inch-square piece of ultra-thin gold foil instead of a massive steel plate to produce echo effects, resulting in a sound that was somewhat thinner and more subtle, thus making it more suitable when long reverb times were desired. According to advertising of the era, it had "double the resonant density" of a 140, with "three times the delay of the first reflection." Adrian Kerridge recalls that Lansdowne installed an EMT 240 during the 1970 renovation. Apparently, it was viewed as a replacement for the studio's acoustic echo chamber, which fell into disuse shortly thereafter.

According to Kerridge, Lansdowne also possessed a Marconi compressor/limiter (purchased new in 1961) as well as several Altec compressors (exact models unknown) and at least two custom units made by Joe Meek: a tube EQ unit similar to a Pultec, and one of his "black box" limiter/compressors.

In addition, a 1977 advertisement indicated that Lansdowne was offering at that time an Eventide Digital Delay and Eventide Phaser/Flanger, as well as MXR phasers and flangers, dbx limiters and compressors, and ADR Vocal Stressors. By 1978, an Eventide Harmonizer and Klark Teknik graphic equalizer had been added to the complement of outboard gear.

SELECTED DISCOGRAPHY

- Lonnie Donegan: "Cumberland Gap" (single)
- Dave Clark Five: "Glad All Over," "Do You Love Me," "Bits and Pieces," "Over and Over" (singles)
- Donovan: "Mellow Yellow" (single)
- The Animals: *Animalism*
- Marianne Faithfull: *Marianne Faithfull*
- The Strawbs: *Grave New World*
- Graham Parker: *Squeezing Out Sparks*

ADVISION

The origins of Advision are rather more shrouded in mystery than those of some other English studios of the era. Their original location at 83 New Bond Street, in London's upper-class Mayfair district, had been the site of a small independent recording facility called Guy de Bere Studios, taken over in 1956 by Guy Whetstone and Stephen Appleby, who renamed it Advision. As the name implied, their concept was to specialize in the recording of voice-overs and jingles for cinema and television ads—a timely endeavor given the formation of Independent Television a year previously. ITV, as it would become known, was England's first commercial television network—one which, unlike the austere government-owned BBC, actually allowed advertisements on its airwaves.

A few years later, Advision was sold to Kevin Hibberd, a producer of TV commercials. His intention was to turn the company into the U.K.'s leading servicing facility for television ads, but things didn't quite work out that way. Instead, Advision began gaining popularity as a music recording studio.

By the mid-1960s, Advision had developed into one of the top London studios for rock and pop music, turning out hit records for The Who, the Yardbirds, and The Move. In early 1968, Advision became one of the first studios in the U.K. to offer 8-track recording. (The studio's Scully multitrack machine may or may not have been installed a short time before rival studio Trident's Ampex; see Chapter 6 for more information.)

The Advision control room in New Bond Street circa 1965.
(Photo by Roger Cameron)

In 1969, Advision moved to much larger premises at 23 Gosfield Street in London's Marylebone district, not far from IBC and BBC Broadcast House. There, a custom-designed studio complex was built, with the main studio spacious enough to house a 60-piece orchestra, complete with two good-sized isolation booths and a 35mm projection screen to accommodate film scoring work. A second, smaller studio for remix work was constructed in the basement, and a large voice-dubbing theater added upstairs, with tielines linking all the rooms to a centralized Westrex recording system. During the move, Advision updated to 16-track as well—again, one of the first studios in London to do so.

By the early 1970s, Advision had become home away from home for progressive rock groups such as Yes, Gentle Giant, and Emerson, Lake & Palmer. "It was a really good studio, and the equipment was first-rate," said staffer Eddy Offord, who engineered and/or coproduced records for many of those artists. "It was a comfortable place to work."

Advision continued to flourish throughout the 1980s, although it began to repurpose itself primarily as a film-dubbing facility. Ultimately, though, the studio had to bow to economic realities and closed its doors in the early 1990s. The Gosfield Street location has been occupied since 1993 by a postproduction facility called The Sound Company.

Engineer Gerald Chevin behind the custom console at Advision circa 1966. Note the proximity of the four (!) Tannoy Lockwood speakers.
(Photo by Roger Cameron)

KEY PERSONNEL

Recording engineers: Roger Cameron, Gerald Chevin, John Mackswith, Eddie Kramer, Eddy Offord, Martin Rushent, Hugh Padgham, Geoff Young

Maintenance engineers: Andy Whetstone, Dag Fellner, Eddie Veale, Dave Deardon

STORIES FROM THE STUDIO

Rube Goldberg / Heath Robinson would have loved this

AIR-CONDITIONING IN ENGLAND was pretty much nonexistent in the early 1960s. Engineer (and later studio manager) Roger Cameron recalls that Advision's method of cooling the New Bond Street control room at the time utilized a technique that Rube Goldberg himself (or his British counterpart, Heath Robinson) would have loved.

"At the end of the room, we had a large panel with a big door in it that led to an outside stairwell," Cameron relates, "and connected to the door was this old Garrard 301 turntable with a cranked arm. There was a switch on the console that, via a couple of relays, would set this turntable turning, which would pull on the arm and open the door. That was our air-conditioning in those days."

According to another Advision engineer who wished to remain anonymous, it served a secondary purpose, too. "Whenever the musicians would start moaning that the studio was getting too hot," he said, "Roger would push the button on the console and close the door so he couldn't hear them complaining."

PHYSICAL FACILITIES

At New Bond Street, Advision consisted of a single mid-sized studio in the basement, alongside of which was a small control room, plus a disc cutting room and a small film-dubbing theater at the other end of the building, about 100 yards away. Audio tielines enabled access to the console preamps, which were located in a cupboard behind the control room, as well as the studio's sole source of limiting: the Westrex camera in the film-dubbing theater. Audio tielines enabled interconnection among the different rooms.

The Gosfield Street complex consisted of two studios: the very large Studio One, with a spacious control room and 18' ceilings, and a second, mid-sized remix room (Studio Two) in the basement, which included a small isolation booth. In addition, there was a dubbing theater on the upstairs level.

Acoustic Treatments

"In terms of acoustic treatment, all the studios at that time were extremely primitive," says Roger Cameron. "When we were in New Bond Street, the studio was located in a basement underneath a shopping parade, and there were just a few acoustic tiles on the walls and ceiling, so I used to have massive sonic problems."

The new facility at Gosfield Street, however, received professional treatment courtesy of a Swedish acoustician by the name of Stellan Dahlstedt. Later, the decision was made to install large domed deflectors in the ceiling of Studio One; reportedly these came from the same mold used for those at the Royal Albert Hall. In addition, the studio floor was floated and constructed with triple walls, primarily to minimize the vibrations coming from the tube (subway) trains running underneath.

Good as the new facility may have sounded, it wasn't always to everyone's taste. "I found the acoustics in the recording room to be a little dead for my liking," said Eddy Offord, who often put up sheets of plywood to liven the sound up. Nonetheless, the soundproofing at Gosfield Street must have been more than adequate, since they only ever had one problem with a neighbor, despite the fact that the studios were often in use 24 hours a day, seven days a week at the height of their popularity. "It was this little old lady named Pauline," remembered Roger Cameron, "who came in and complained that we were keeping her awake at night." His solution was to hire her as the studio's tea lady. "That solved that problem!" says Cameron with a laugh.

Room Dimensions

New Bond Street:
Studio: 30' x 14' (9 x 4 meters)
    Ceiling height: 9' (3 meters)
Control room: 14' x 12' (4 x 3.5 meters)
    Ceiling height: 9' (3 meters)

Gosfield Street:
Studio One: 40' x 30' (12 x 9 meters)
    Ceiling height: 18' (5.5 meters)
Studio One control room: 24' x 14' (7.5 x 4 meters)
    Ceiling height: 12' (3.5 meters)

Studio Two: 20' x 12' (6 x 3.5 meters)
    Ceiling height: 9' (3 meters)
Dubbing theater: 30' x 20' (9 x 6 meters)
    Ceiling height: 13' (4 meters)

Echo Chambers

At New Bond Street, Advision used the cellar as an acoustic echo chamber. It was outfitted with a "ball and biscuit" (STC Coles 4021) microphone at one end, and a speaker (model unknown, but probably a Tannoy) at the other.

"Of course, since it was under a busy street, with a promenade overhead, it wasn't exactly the quietest of environments," says Roger Cameron of the echo chamber. "I remember one very funny occasion—

though it wasn't funny at the time—where I was recording a 30-piece orchestra for a film score. We would run the picture in the studio from a projector so the conductor could follow the action, and the sound would then be recorded onto 35mm magnetic stock. Our studio was quite small, so I had to rely on echo to a large extent to make it sound big. On that particular day, I turned up the echo send, but there was no echo whatsoever, and nothing I tried worked. There were 30 musicians sitting around getting paid for their time, so there was no question of my saying, 'Can you hang around for an hour or two while I get something sorted out?' So I went out and had a look in the chamber, and the cone of the speaker had been eaten away by the mice! The shreds were just dangling there."

There were no acoustic echo chambers at the Gosfield Street facility.

KEY EQUIPMENT
Mixing Consoles

The mixing console at New Bond Street was custom-built by Advision technical director Andy Whetstone. It was all-tube, and had a total of nine inputs—all with wide quadrant (semi-round) Painton faders—plus one master gain control. The only facility apart from the input faders were simple treble and bass controls and a single echo send control for each channel. Initially, it offered one mono output only; however, shortly after the studio purchased its first Ampex A300 4-track tape recorder, the board was revamped to provide what Roger Cameron termed a "quasi-stereo" output.

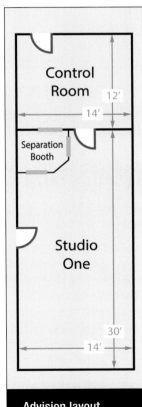

Advision layout (New Bond Street).
(Based on drawing by Roger Cameron)

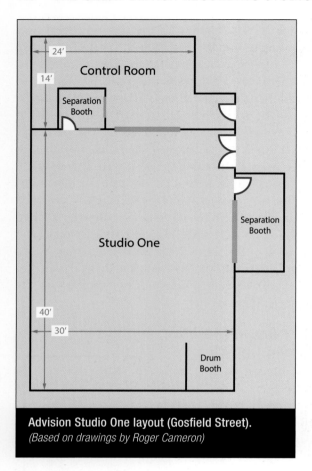

Advision Studio One layout (Gosfield Street).
(Based on drawings by Roger Cameron)

At the center of the console was a large routing section. To provide foldback to musicians in the studio, for example, the engineer would have to take a channel output from the console and patch it into a splitter amplifier, which would feed a set of external transformers. The signal would then have to be patched back into the studio, with individual level controls provided by each splitter amplifier. Despite the convoluted patching, Cameron feels there was a hidden benefit: "Because it was so primitive, because you had to actually construct everything you wanted to do, it actually taught you the structure of how consoles worked and what was actually required to get what you needed."

Interestingly, the mic and line input amplifiers were external to the console—three 19" rackmount units, housed in a cupboard outside the studio. Bizarrely, the line/mic input switches were *inside* the amplifiers, so to make this simple change, the engineer would literally have to leave the control room and go around the back of the cupboard, where the racking system was located, then blindly feel around inside—with all the tubes and rectifiers powered on, of course; apparently it never occurred to anyone to put the switch on the front panel! According to Gerald Chevin, half the time this dangerous operation would result in the engineer receiving "a massive hair-standing-on-end electric shock," no matter how careful he was.

STORIES FROM THE STUDIO
Sweet revenge

"DIRECTLY ABOVE the basement studio at New Bond Street was this very high-class menswear shop," remembers engineer Gerald Chevin. "One afternoon, we had The Who in, and to say that they played loudly was an understatement!

"The studio was properly soundproofed and there had never been any complaints before, but The Who started playing, and immediately the posh manager from the menswear shop came down into the control room and said to me, 'This is ridiculous! We can't sell any of our clothes because of the noise levels.' I offered him some concert tickets to go and see the group, and that shut him up instantly, but after he left, I went out into the studio anyway and asked the band if they could play just a little bit quieter. You can imagine what their two-word response was—the last word was 'off.'

"Anyway, we got the backing track done and then it was time to do the overdubs. I put Pete Townshend and Roger Daltrey in the little vocal booth to record their vocals and started to play the backing track. I could see them singing but I couldn't hear anything, so I checked everything in the control room twice—the mixing desk, the patch bay, but there was nothing amiss.

"Now I was getting a bit confused, so I went into the booth and checked the microphones. Again, nothing. They looked at me a bit quizzically and I told them, 'I can't understand it. I can't hear you.' After another five minutes of me pulling out my hair, I was certain there was no technical reason why the equipment wasn't working.

"Then finally they let me in on their little game. It turned out I was right. They were miming, the bastards, just to get back at me!"

In the year leading up to the move to Gosfield Street, Whetstone's successor, new technical director Dag Fellner, had begun building an 8-track desk in anticipation of making a deal with Scully to bring the first of their new 8-track machines into the U.K. and get Advision set up as Scully's English distributor. At around that time, the studio hired Eddie Veale, who would eventually become one of Britain's top recording studio designers and acoustic consultants. "My job was to complete the console [even though] I had never seen the inside of a studio console before," Veale later related. "Dag had actually designed [it] and started the project off, but was now more tied up with Scully and didn't have time to do that as well as finish the project. It had been going on for about a year, and [owner] Kevin Hibberd was getting frustrated because the job wasn't getting completed. . . . [It] took about six months to complete, by which time Dag had got the Scully and was busy trying to impress the rest of the industry with it so he could sell them. With the assistance of Roger Cameron, we installed the desk and the machines and got the studio running."

The new console was solid-state and had 22 inputs and eight outputs, with sophisticated equalization circuitry and four aux channels. It was later moved to Studio One at Gosfield Street, where it would be used for many successful recordings of the early '70s, including hits for Yes, Emerson, Lake & Palmer, and Shirley Bassey. Studio Two, in the meantime, was outfitted with a Neve 20 x 16, while the new dubbing theater received a 14 x 4 custom console. In 1972, when Advision went fully 16-track, the console in Studio One was upgraded to provide 16 outputs.

By 1974 Advision was ready for a major overhaul, in the opinion of studio manager Roger Cameron. "I was quite convinced that mix automation was the way to go," says Cameron, "and the only two companies that were making automated consoles

Roger Cameron behind Dag Fellner's new 8-track console circa 1967.
(Courtesy of Roger Cameron)

were Quad Eight in America and Neve, although they hadn't yet gotten their NECAM console off the ground. Quad Eight were the only company that were prepared to build a custom console for me; Neve only offered their stock console range, and it really wasn't what I wanted."

Advision's new Quad Eight, installed in Studio Two, was equipped for quadraphonic mixing and was the U.K.'s first computer-aided console. (See *Quad: Ahead of its time, or just a bad idea?* on page 59 for more information.) Unfortunately, it was not without problems. "At first there was a lot of difficulty with the data noise bleeding through, so we had to be very careful how we used it in automation situations," remarks Cameron. "But we got around that

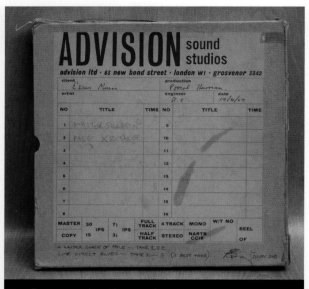

Tape box detailing a historic 1967 session at Advision: Procol Harum's first attempt at recording "A Whiter Shade of Pale," with engineer Roger Cameron at the helm. The version that become an iconic symbol of the '60s was a later rerecording done by Keith Grant at Olympic.
(Courtesy of Gerald Chevin)

eventually, and it really was a very good desk, very flexible, and we kept it for quite a long time." A year later, a second Quad Eight console was installed in Studio One, though this one was not computerized because it was not anticipated that it would be used

STORIES FROM THE STUDIO
Coo Coo Ga Joob

"WHEN ADVISION WAS LOCATED in New Bond Street," Roger Cameron recalls, "there were a bunch of pigeons that used to nest above the acoustic tiles in the studio ceiling. We used to do a lot of jingles early in the morning because that was the only time the top session players were free for an hour's work, and of course it was at that time of day when the pigeons would be most active. There were plenty of mornings when I would put the mics up and raise the faders, and all I could hear were these bloody pigeons cooing!

"At those times," he says with a grin, "I would turn the monitors down and begin a long conversation with everyone in the control room so that they would tend to be listening to me rather than what was coming out of the speakers."

for mixing. By 1977, when Advision had gone fully 24-track (and more; see *Technical Innovations* below), Studio One was outfitted with a Quad Eight 56 x 24 (non-automated) and Studio Two with a Quad Eight 32 x 4 automated console.

Monitors

At New Bond Street, monitoring was provided by 15" dual concentric Tannoy Golds in Lockwood cabinets, driven by Quad amplifiers. (See Chapter 1 for more information.)

Following the move to Gosfield Street, monitoring in all three rooms (the two control rooms and the dubbing theater) was provided by custom-made speakers using JBL components. "They actually weren't that good in reproducing the low end," commented Eddy Offord, "and so that had to be taken in to account as we mixed." These were driven by Crown and Radford amps.

A 1977 directory listing indicated that the monitors in both control rooms had been replaced by JBL 4350s. (See Chapter 7 for more information.)

Tape Machines

Ampex A300 (4-track)—Advision acquired a 4-track tube A300 in the mid-1960s, while still located at New Bond Street. (See *Decca* in Chapter 2 for more information.)

In addition, there were at least two Lyrec TR4 mono mastering machines and at least one Philips stereo machine at New Bond Street. Eddie Kramer also had a recollection of there being a mono Telefunken machine, which had a tendency to send sparks flying whenever the Stop button was hit. (Who said being a tape operator was not a dangerous job?)

Scully 284-8—This 1" 8-track machine was delivered to Advision some time in late 1967, well before the move to Gosfield Street, although it may not have become operational until shortly before—or shortly after—Trident installed its Ampex AG-440 8-track (thus the controversy about which studio offered 8-track recording first). Interestingly, the

The Scully story

"MORE THAN MOST other English studios, Advision always seemed to aspire to deliver an American sound." So says famed producer Hugh Padgham, who began his career as a teaboy (the British equivalent to today's runner) at Advision in 1974. Roger Cameron concurs. "We always admired the records that were coming out of America, though we never could emulate the American sound, like the stuff Phil Spector was doing," he says. "Interestingly, I had heard that American engineers were admiring the records coming out of England but could not duplicate *our* sound. The problem, in my view, really stemmed from a lack of communication. But I spent a lot of time in the States touring American studios, to see what they looked like and how they operated, and to see if I could somehow capture that feel and import it back into the U.K. Of course, they were doing the same with us, in reverse! And I have to admit that I was thinking that if I got some American gear into Advision, we might get closer to emulating the American sound."

Nowhere, perhaps was this commitment more apparent than in Advision's decision to form a strategic alliance with the American company Scully.

Scully Recording Instruments was a manufacturer of professional tape recorders and other audio devices based in Bridgeport, Connecticut. Larry Scully, who founded the company, was a gifted machinist and designer who built the original acclaimed Scully cutting lathe. However, when Neumann lathes arrived in the U.S., he opted to enter the tape recorder market rather than to compete directly. Their first tape machine was the Scully 270, a long-play 1/4" stereo unit with 14" reel capacity and auto-reverse. It was primarily used for playback of background music at automated radio stations.

The 270 enjoyed limited success, but Scully had overbought parts for it, so Dan Cronin, chief engineer at Bell Sound (and designer of the playback amp that had been used in the Scully 270), was contracted to create a new machine, with a mandate to use up the excess Scully 270 parts. The result of his efforts, the Scully 280, was introduced in 1965. It boasted a newly developed transport that had several innovative features. Instead of the gate cover / tape lifter used on Ampex machines, the 280 had a handle that actuated the tape lifter and retracted the playback head shield. The shield could also be locked in the retracted position—something that appealed enormously to engineers who frequently edited tape.

By the mid-1960s many recording studios in both the U.S. and U.K. were looking to upgrade to 1" 8-track. Although Ampex had invented Sel-Sync and built the first 1" 8-track (Les Paul's "Octopus") and several other machines as special orders, the company failed to dominate the industry, at least initially. Seeing an opening, Scully positioned itself to gain this market and entered it aggressively in June of 1966.

"We'd heard of this American company called Scully who were making an 8-track machine," remembers Roger Cameron, "so I called Larry Scully, the owner of the company, and I went over to New York with Dag Fellner, who at that time was working with us as a technical engineer. We met Larry and [U.S. distributor] Ham Brosius, and with the Scully people we went to New Jersey to see the 8-track recorder Ampex had made specially for Les Paul and Mary Ford. Afterwards, we decided to buy the Scully machine for Advision and to assume the company's exclusive U.K. distributorship. In light of the success we had with Scully, we later became the distributor for a number of American audio companies, including JBL monitors."

By the end of 1967, Scully was a major player in the studio market, introducing both 1" 12-track and 2" 16-track machines. Nonetheless, the company's 1/4" 2-track and 1" 8-track models remained Scully's best sellers, due in part to stiff competition from 3M, which introduced its M56 16-track machine in 1969.

In 1971, the Scully 100 2" 16-track machine was introduced with a list price of under $11,000—some $4,000 less than competing models. However, corners had been cut: By eliminating the repro head and using one high-quality narrow-gap head for both record and repro, the expense of repro/sync switching circuits was eliminated. As a result, the machine had only limited success. Scully backed out of the multitrack market before 2" 24-track caught on and concentrated on the broadcast market instead, developing an updated 8-track machine, the 280B. Though an excellent machine that built on the reliability of the 280 transport with new low-noise electronics, the 280B entered a market that now included the MCI JH-110, Ampex AG-440, 3M M79, and Studer B67, in addition to early entries from Tascam and Otari.

Sales never took off, and after several changes of ownership, Scully closed down in the mid-1980s.

(*Excerpted from the Museum of Magnetic Sound Recording website: http://museumofmagneticsoundrecording.org/ ManufacturersScully.html.*)

Producer Tony Visconti and engineer Gerald Chevin in the Advision control room circa 1968. Note the 8-track Scully tape machine in the background. *(Courtesy of Tony Visconti)*

Advision technical staff encountered much the same problem with their newly installed 284-8 as Trident's staff did with their 440. "As you might imagine, the whole industry was watching us with bated breath, wondering what was going to happen," recalls Roger Cameron. "I did the first session with our new 8-track Scully, and of course halfway through, the tape machine seized up and caught on fire! The problem was that, being an

American-built machine, it had a 60-cycle motor, whereas in England we use 50 cycles. Somehow nobody had thought of that—they just slapped a 60-cycle motor in there and of course the damn thing just burnt out." (See *Decca* in Chapter 2 and Chapter 6 for more information.)

Studer A80 (4-track and 2-track)—A 1977 listing indicated that Advision was equipped with two 2-track A80s (one in each studio) as well as a 4-track model, housed in Studio Two. (See Chapter 1 for more information.)

MCI JH-16 (24-track and 16-track)—MCI (an acronym for Music Center Incorporated) was an American manufacturer of mixing consoles and tape machines founded by a technician named Grover "Jeep" Harned in the mid-1950s. Starting in the 1970s, all MCI professional audio products carried a "JH" prefix in honor of the owner's initials. The company's tape machines offered several advanced features, including constant tension reel servos, wrap and azimuth adjustable heads, long-wearing ceramic capstans, and one-button punch-in and punch-out. The JH-16 was a 2" 16-track model that was subsequently made available with a 24-track head block. (MCI would later manufacture a dedicated 24-track machine, the JH-24.) JH-16s were equipped with input and output transformers on each control card, plus a head coupling transformer on the reproduce card. By 1977, Advision had acquired at least four JH-16s: a 16-track and two 24-tracks, housed

STORIES FROM THE STUDIO
Pseudo Dolby . . . in 1960

ENGINEER and eventual studio manager Roger Cameron (who would be immortalized by the Yardbirds on their *Roger the Engineer* album) first joined Advision in 1960, while the studio was still located in New Bond Street.

"Everything was mono at that time, of course," he remembers. "We had no facility for stereo at all, or even 2-track recording. I would generally record the rhythm section onto quarter-inch tape, and I would then play that back to the musicians in the studio whilst recording voice-overs or backing vocals, together with the original signal, onto a second tape recorder. Then we'd repeat the process a third time to add the lead vocals, so that the original rhythm track was now three generations removed from the original.

"Unfortunately," he adds, "each time you went through that pro-

cess, you lost some signal, so I had to resort to all sorts of tricks to try to maintain the quality as much as possible. Often I would increase the treble on the original recording so that when I subsequently rolled it off, the noise would be reduced a little bit—kind of like a manual Dolby effect. Plus, of course, with each generation you would lose a little treble anyway, so it was helpful to stick on a little extra."

STORIES FROM THE STUDIO
"Arder, Pete, 'arder!"

IT WASN'T LONG after Hugh Padgham started working at Advision that veteran glam-rock band Mott the Hoople—a group with an apparently well-deserved reputation for being, shall we say, boisterous—turned up to record their seventh album, *The Hoople*. "It was during the making of that album that I experienced one of the craziest sessions ever," Padgham recalls. "Specifically, I was called upon to mic someone's head."

Someone's head? "On this particular evening," he explains with a grin, "everyone had had a few too many ciders. We were working on this song that had a long decrescendo and they wanted it to end with a big crash, but they didn't want it to just be something ordinary like a cymbal crash. Now, Advision had this lovely lady who used to make the tea, and she used to bring it in on these tin trays. So someone had the idea of using one of those trays for the sound, which seemed reasonable enough. They started out by hitting it with their fist, but the result wasn't spectacular enough to suit them."

"'Well, why doesn't somebody go out into the room and they can kneel down and then we'll smash the tea tray on their head?' one of the band members asked. So I had to go and mic up [guitarist] Ariel Bender's head with a [Neumann] U87 while [bassist] Pete 'Overend' Watts smashed him in the head with the tray. I'll never forget Ariel lying there on the ground going, "arder, Pete, 'arder!'"

in Studio One (the 24-tracks could be locked together via API MagLink to provide 48-track recording; see *Technical Innovations* below), and another 24-track JH-16 in Studio Two.

Main Microphones

Neumann U87—(See Chapter 1 for more information.)

Neumann U67—(See Chapter 1 for more information.)

Neumann U64—This was a small-diaphragm cardioid condenser microphone that was produced in very limited quantities between 1964 and 1971. It had an extended high-frequency response and was characterized by what Neumann termed an "independence of the directional characteristic from frequency," meaning that tonal quality remained consistent even during the level change that would result when moving around the microphone, as an actor might do.

AKG C28—Eddy Offord frequently used these on guitar at Advision. (See *Decca* in Chapter 2 for more information.)

RCA 44-BX—(See Chapter 1 for more information.)

STC Coles 4021—At Advision, as at Lansdowne, a 4021 was employed in the acoustic echo chamber. (See *Pye* in Chapter 2 for more information.)

There were also a number of small-diaphragm Altec condenser microphones used at Advision, exact models unknown.

Outboard Signal Processors

Roger Cameron states that the sole source of dynamics processing at New Bond Street was the limiter built into the Westrex film camera located in the film-dubbing theater. "When I needed to access it in the studio, I had to patch through to it via various tielines, which ran a good hundred yards, and I'd have to speak to the engineer in the dubbing room by telephone to get him to change various parameters as I was monitoring in the control room!"

EMT 140 reverb plate—Three of these were installed at the Gosfield Street facility, which had no acoustic echo chambers. (See Chapter 1 for more information.)

A 1977 directory listing indicated that Advision's arsenal of outboard equipment then included Pye compressors (see *Pye* in Chapter 2 for more information), various graphic equalizers and noise gates (exact models unknown), Spectrasonics, UA and ADR compressors, and Eventide digital delays, flangers, and harmonizers.

Yes recording their album *Fragile* in Advision Studio One (Gosfield Street), 1971.
(Photo by Michael Putland/Getty Images)

Advision's disc cutting room lathe had a tube (valve) cutting amplifier and a Grampion cutting head; according to Roger Cameron, the groove pitch meter was actually a converted aircraft altimeter. This system was later replaced with a Lyrec-Ortofon cutting lathe.

Film Equipment

Even at New Bond Street, Advision offered basic film-dubbing facilities, including various Westrex 35mm recorders.

A 1972 trade listing indicated that the move to Gosfield Street had resulted in an expansion of the

STORIES FROM THE STUDIO

Fire . . . I bring you fire

"I AM THE GOD OF HELLFIRE!"

This is the solemn proclamation that begins The Crazy World of Arthur Brown's hit single "Fire," which topped the U.K. charts in 1968—their only chart success, as it turned out. The record was characterized by Brown's manic vocals and ended with the sound of what he and producer Kit Lambert envisioned as being as a "wind from hell." The job of achieving that particular sonic

goal fell to Advision engineer Gerald Chevin.

"It was fairly easy to get," he chuckles, "because every piece of valve gear in those days—even if it wasn't supposed to—would generate more noise than it should. Instead of a signal-to-noise ratio, we used to call it a noise-to-signal ratio!

"So I just recorded some white noise from something sputtering

away, then I used the old-fashioned method of phasing it by putting it on two machines at once while varying the speed of one of them. [See *Pye* in Chapter 2 and *Phasing* in Chapter 5 for more information.] When I got it to what I thought was right, I said to Arthur, 'What do you think of this?' 'Amazing! Absolutely amazing!' was his reply. And that's what we used. It was just a matter of being a little bit inventive."

STORIES FROM THE STUDIO
The making of *The Yes Album*

IN THE AUTUMN OF 1970, a mid-level prog-rock band with the affirmatively positive name Yes entered Advision studios to record their third album. It truly was make-or-break time for the group, whose previous records had been released to the sound of one hand clapping. Atlantic Records had been patient with them up until now, but the band knew all too well that a third failure could well result in the label dropping them.

So this time they were going to do things differently. Gone were the cover songs and string arrangements that marked their previous efforts. And in was a new guitarist by the name of Steve Howe. More significantly, this time around they were determined to produce themselves, though they hedged their bets by offering Advision's young staff engineer Eddy Offord (who had worked with them on their first two albums) co-producer status.

"We spent at least two months working on the album," Offord later said in an online interview for the *Notes from the Edge* website. "They were extremely anxious to get every bar of music really perfect, plus some of the music wasn't prewrit-ten. It was developed in the studio. Songs could be quite long, but they would be recorded in 30-second sections so that each section was really right on the money. Any time there was a change in the music—when it would go from one feeling to another—they would then make that an edit. I would record the first section, and then I'd do a little quick mix of that to 2-track. I'd feed them the section that they'd just recorded into their headphones so they'd get the tempo matched up, then they'd just count it in and record the next section. After it was all spliced together, the keyboard and guitar overdubs would smooth out the edits.

"It wasn't until the whole song was finished, recorded, and mixed that they would then go and learn how to play it live," he added. "It was a very experimental kind of thing. We'd spend hours coming up with new sounds, doing all kinds of stupid things."

Asked what a typical day in the studio was like during the making of the record, Offord replied, "They were very long sessions. The basic tracks were pretty much just drums and bass, maybe with a guide guitar track and probably no keyboards. [Bassist] Chris [Squire] was extremely precise and would want every kick drum and bass note to be locked in, time-wise. I think eventually that drove [drummer] Bill [Bruford] crazy! He wanted a little more freedom. But getting a minute of music might take several hours of experimentation. So the basic tracks were long, long sessions; they might start at two in the afternoon and go until two or three in the morning."

The album would come to be called simply *The Yes Album*, and it did indeed provide the breakthrough the band so desperately needed, yielding the hit single "Your Move," along with fan favorites like "Perpetual Change" (which featured two totally different rhythm sections playing at the same time, one in each channel—no easy thing to accomplish when you have just 16 tracks at your disposal), "Starship Trooper," and "Yours Is No Disgrace," all of which quickly became concert showpieces.

"There were times when making the album was a little frustrating," Offord says in what may be classic understatement, given the group's reputation for perfectionism, "but overall it was a lot of fun."

range of film equipment on offer, which now included Magna-Tech 35mm 3-track, Albrecht 16mm and 35mm 1-track, and Ampex 35mm 1-track machines, in addition to the Westrex recorders. The Pink Floyd soundtrack contributions to the 1970 film *Zabriskie Point* were recorded at Gosfield Street.

KEY TECHNICAL INNOVATIONS

With their installation of a first Quad Eight console in the mid-1970s, Advision was one of the first U.K. studios to provide mix automation. In addition, it was the first studio in England—and possibly one of the first in the world—to offer 46-track recording by successfully locking up two 24-track machines. (One track from each machine was used for time code.) "It was not the most reliable of systems," says Roger Cameron, commenting on the API MagLink synchronizer Advision used at the time, "and so it required a great deal of engineering ingenuity to get it to work."

Roger Cameron behind the automated Quad Eight console in Advision Studio Two, circa 1974.
(Courtesy of Roger Cameron)

One of the first 46-track recordings done at Advision was the 1978 hit concept album *Jeff Wayne's Musical Version of The War of the Worlds*, engineered by Geoff Young. Wayne was a composer and conductor who had used the studio almost exclusively since the mid-'60s, mainly for advertising jingles and film scores; he'd also produced records for a number of artists there, including David Essex.

But *War of the Worlds* was to be an album (in fact, a double album) unlike any that had come before: It featured a full orchestra, exotic instruments like *santoor* and *tar*, a cast of thousands (slight exaggeration), and no less a personage than Shakespearean actor and film legend Richard Burton providing the narration, though he was reportedly three weeks late for his session. All in all, an epic project that took nearly three years to complete . . . including, presumably, three weeks of waiting around for Burton.

SELECTED DISCOGRAPHY

- The Who: "Magic Bus" (single)
- The Crazy World of Arthur Brown: "Fire" (single)
- The Yardbirds: *Roger the Engineer*
- Yes: *Time and a Word, The Yes Album, Fragile,* "Roundabout" (single)
- Emerson, Lake & Palmer: *Tarkus*
- Mott the Hoople: *The Hoople*
- Jeff Wayne: *Jeff Wayne's Musical Version of The War of the Worlds*

CTS / THE MUSIC CENTRE

Cine-Tele Sound (CTS) Studios Ltd. was launched in 1956 by a consortium that included Peter Kay, John Elliott, and celebrated jingle writer Johnny Johnston. The original location was 49-53 Kensington Gardens Square in London's fashionable Bayswater district, a building that had previously been owned by retail magnate William Whitely. The studio itself was housed in a converted banqueting hall known as the Whiteley's Gentleman's Dining Club—a large room with an ornate molded ceiling that had also sometimes been used for fashion shows. Chief main-

tenance engineer Peter Harris remembered that "the drawback we had there was that underneath the studio were the storage cellars of the furniture company next door (Frederick Lawrence & Co.), so at crucial times you'd hear these steel-wheeled trolleys being trundled around downstairs. One had to rush round and beg the gentleman who controlled the loading bay to get these guys to lay off for a little while."

The intention of the three owners was to specialize in music for picture—both film scoring and television advertising—and the well-equipped studio enjoyed immediate success. With many of the British film sound stages of the day still using prewar equipment, CTS was able to attract top film composers like Burt Bacharach, Jerry Goldsmith, John Barry, Ron Goodwin, Henry Mancini, and Quincy Jones and achieve a near-monopoly of the early commercial TV jingle market. Internationally renowned artists like Frank Sinatra, Sammy Davis Jr., Bing Crosby, Fred Astaire, and Shirley Bassey all made records there, as were most of the soundtracks to the early James Bond movies.

By 1972, CTS had evolved into a 16-track facility, with upgraded mixing consoles and tape machines. However, toward the end of that year, studio management were informed that a property development company had acquired the Bayswater building with the intention of repurposing it. A search was immediately begun for suitable new premises.

It was no easy task. As if finding a large enough location in London wasn't difficult enough, the city was undergoing a housing boom, and rents were sky-high. The solution came in the form of a fortuitous merger between CTS and De Lane Lea Music.

William De Lane Lea was a French intelligence attaché for the British government during World War II. In 1947, he founded a company called De Lane Lea Processes Ltd.—an enterprise initially dedicated to one sole purpose: dubbing English films into French. At first, the company operated out of a laboratory in Soho, but soon began to expand its business interests into voice-overs and mixing for film, television, and advertising, then into full-fledged orchestral scoring work and popular music recording. For a time, they rented various spaces around London, but eventually opened De Lane Lea Studios in Kingsway, in London's central Holborn district—a facility that quickly attracted artists such as The Beatles, the Rolling Stones, and Jimi Hendrix; the Animals' smash hit single "House of the Rising Sun" was also recorded there. (See *De Lane Lea / Kingsway* in Chapter 8 for more information.)

Despite the Kingsway studio being enormously profitable, De Lane Lea was forced to relinquish the space in the late 1960s. Fortunately, its parent company, BET, owned Wembley Stadium and some adjacent land that had been used as a parking garage.

The decision was made to construct a multi-room studio complex there, directly above what had once been an ornamental boating lake.

De Lane Lea Music Centre—or The Music Centre, as it came to be known—was conceptualized and designed by Kingsway studio manager Dave Siddle, whose dream, according to former De Lane Lea engineer and director Louis Elman, was to build a single facility housing a number of studios to cater for all aspects of music recording, all under one roof. The end result was the first purpose-built multi-room recording complex in the U.K. consisting of three studios, the largest of which was sizable enough to accommodate even the largest orchestras. Construction took two years, and in 1971 The Music Centre was formally opened by Princess Margaret.

It quickly became the talk of the industry, and the first artists to record there included Deep Purple, Thin Lizzy, and Fleetwood Mac. Unfortunately, several serious problems soon became apparent. Siddle was nothing if not forward-thinking, but his ideas were perhaps a little too advanced for the time and the equipment he installed too untried and untested. For example, he contracted with Sound Techniques, a London recording studio that was transitioning into a commercial manufacturer of audio products, to build the mixing consoles for the new facility. (See *De Lane Lea / Kingsway* and *Sound Techniques* in Chapter 8 for more information.) But the desks that were delivered to The Music Centre had numerous glitches and a troubling tendency to reconfigure themselves randomly during sessions. The custom tape machines Siddle designed for the Wembley facility experienced similar, if not more severe problems. "If the playback matched what you heard on line-in, you felt lucky and relieved," commented engineer Alan Florence. "Then again, most times it didn't!"

Word quickly got around, and it wasn't long before The Music Centre was bereft of clients. It was a beautiful, spacious, brand-spanking-new facility with three recording rooms, but it was being horrendously underutilized, run by a company that had little reputation for film work. CTS, on the other hand, had a sterling reputation in that field but was about to lose its premises. In 1973 the two companies concluded

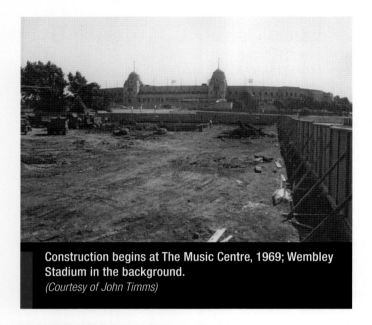

Construction begins at The Music Centre, 1969; Wembley Stadium in the background.
(Courtesy of John Timms)

Studio 1 being constructed circa 1970.
(Courtesy of John Timms)

rience in recording music for picture. Each had their own way of working and their own equipment preferences, with little common ground. By 1973, in the words of engineer Richard Goldblatt, "the atmosphere was dire. Basically the [two factions] didn't understand each other or the music that they recorded . . . the terminology, the working methods, and the music were worlds apart." Kenny Denton, who joined The Music Centre in 1971, recalls that it took a good six months for the politics to get resolved.

Ultimately it would be the lucrative film work that would win out, leading to Siddle's ignominious departure. When the dust settled, The Music Centre had essentially become CTS Studios Redux, in all but name. (This was rectified in 1982, when the name of the facility was officially changed to CTS Studio Ltd., better known as CTS Wembley.)

And, as it turned out, the supposedly imminent demolition of the original CTS location in Kensington Gardens never happened. The space was taken over by Marcus Studios in late 1980, with a focus on television rather than film work, though popular artists like Leo Sayer and Gary Numan made records there as well. The site was later redeveloped into a residential block of flats.

Lansdowne engineer/studio manager/owner Adrian Kerridge and business partner Johnny Pearson acquired CTS in 1987 and began doing business under the name CTS-Lansdowne Ltd. Under the new ownership, the Wembley complex continued to thrive. Studio 2 was not only rebuilt and redesigned from the ground up, it also went totally digital, with its disc cutting facilities evolved into a digital editing suite. Throughout this period, CTS continued to attract major film scoring projects, including Oscar-winning pictures such as *Four Weddings and a Funeral* and *Shakespeare in Love*. In June 2000 the complex closed after being sold to make way for the redevelopment of Wembley Stadium and its surrounding area. In 2002, the facility reopened briefly under the name Phoenix Sound; however, just two years later, the building was demolished and replaced by a parking garage.

a complicated series of negotiations and CTS was purchased by De Lane Lea and relocated to Wembley.

It was—at least on paper—a match made in heaven.

Unfortunately, it didn't work out that way. There was an immediate clash of cultures between the CTS people, who were classically oriented and trained to do film work, and the De Lane Lea staffers, who were, by and large, into rock music and had little or no expe-

KEY PERSONNEL

Recording engineers: Eric Tomlinson, John Richards, Jack Clegg, Dick Lewzey, Paul Carr, Norman Waring, Louis Elman, Dave Hunt, Dick Plant, John Acock, Alan Florence, Martin Birch, Louis Austin, Terry Johnson, Rafe McKenna, Tony Duggen, Andy Chapman, George Sloan, Desmond Magicadomi, Mike Thorn, Kenny Denton, David Strickland, Keith Dickens, Paul Hume, Richard Goldblatt, Robert Zimbler, Tony Gibber, Howard Sommers, Pete Wandless, Mike Pela, Mark Philips

Maintenance engineers: John Elliott, Peter Harris, Dave Siddle, John Timms, Terry Yeadon, Peter Duncan, Ken Attwood, Roger Peyton, Clive Kavan, Tim Hunt, Ian Davison, Antony Connor

PHYSICAL FACILITIES

According to engineer John Richards, the CTS studio at Bayswater was set up in a "classic rectangular 'shoe box' configuration. The control room was set at one end and on the same level as the studio, with the console at 90 degrees to the studio. One had to look left through a large rectangular sound lock window to observe the musicians. The studio [which was enormous—quite possibly the largest recording area of any studio in the U.K.] could comfortably accommodate 60 to 70 musicians, which at that time was considered to be a good-size orchestra."

The Music Centre at Wembley consisted of three studios, two remix rooms, two cutting rooms, two telecine rooms, a sound camera room, and a film projection room. The studio complex footprint was horseshoe-shaped and on three levels. Studio 1 formed the center of the horseshoe and was at basement level. Access for percussion and heavy instruments was via a side ramp down to the rear of the studio. The Studio 1 control room was at ground level (looking down at the studio floor) and to the front and center of the building, with stairway access down to the studio floor. This layout gave an uninterrupted line of sight to the enormous (30' by 13') projection screen on the studio's back wall, but not to the musicians below, something that was rectified by installing a remote video camera that could be operated from controls next to the mixing console.

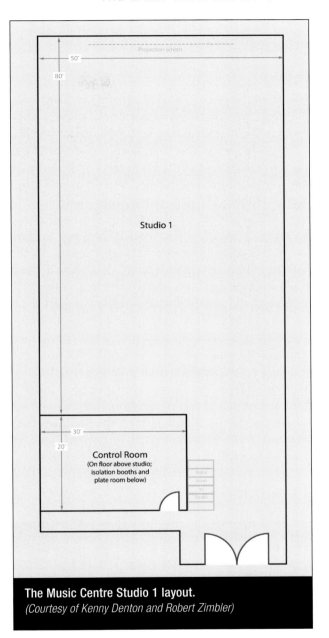

The Music Centre Studio 1 layout.
(Courtesy of Kenny Denton and Robert Zimbler)

One arm of the horseshoe at the ground-floor level housed Studios 2 and 3. The other led to a small remix room with an isolation booth (later converted to separate rooms and renamed Studio 4), as well as the tape copying rooms, disc cutting rooms, tape library, and maintenance department. The second-floor level (called the "first floor" in English vernacular) was accessed via stairs from the front entrance foyer, and was home to the 35mm projection and sound camera rooms directly above the Studio 1 control room. A conference room and various offices were located in one leg of this level; farther down the corridor were special "telecine rooms" that allowed film to be projected into TV cameras and linked to the other studios for scoring, as well as the studio's restaurant and lounge area, complete with a full bar.

An isolation booth—used mostly for drums—was situated at one end of Studio 1, directly underneath the control room, and to its side was a small vocal booth. Oddly, the room that housed the complex's ten EMT echo plates (shared by all the studios and accessed by audio tielines) was in-between the two iso booths and apparently not well isolated. In the words of former engineer Richard Goldblatt, "If there was a drummer in there, watch out for your reverb!"

One of the strangest quirks of the Wembley location was the natural spring running underneath Studio 1—no surprise, since the studio floor was constructed directly over what had once been a lake. According to former chief engineer Peter Duncan, pumps had to be kept running continuously to keep water out, and that the air was quite damp as a result. John Timms even recalls one memorable day when the Studio 1 floor was covered knee-deep in water because the foundations had sprung a leak.

Session musician Mike Slea remembers being impressed by the row of clocks arrayed on the wall behind the reception area. "The clocks showed the time all round the world where sessions were held: London, Los Angeles, New York, Paris, Amsterdam, and Tokyo. [The message was that] this was a place that the whole world came to—the film music world, that is." Nonetheless, despite its imposing size and these attempts at elegance, the reception area was, in the words of one frequent visitor, "a bit austere and impersonal, like the lobby of a five-star hotel." Former studio manager Robert Zimbler agrees: "Bands didn't like coming to CTS because it was very clinical, like Abbey Road. Even the reception area and bar were clinical. Wembley always felt like a big factory."

Zimbler feels that Studio 3 became the de facto "rock studio" at CTS (as opposed to Studio 1, which was almost always used for orchestral recording) largely because of its location down the end of the corridor. "People could hide away there and not bump into anyone else, which made it a nicer, calmer place." Studio 2 was described, in his words, as being "the halfway house—sometimes used for MOR [middle of the road] sessions, or for TV commercials, with the occasional pop or rock band."

Though its distance from central London was a distinct disadvantage for CTS Wembley, this was somewhat offset by the ease of parking, something that most competing studios could not offer. "Some session players found coming here annoying to begin with because it was far away from all the other studios," says Alan Florence, "but they eventually got used to it."

Acoustic Treatments

Eric Tomlinson joined CTS in 1959 and was the chief recording engineer at Bayswater. "The space worked well," he reports. "It was a fairly dry room [one source states that it had a natural reverberation time of 0.8 seconds] and, although close-miking was generally done there, I brought in a Schoeps stereo microphone which gave me a large [ambient] sound, reinforced by close microphones."

The three studios at the Wembley location, in particular Studio 1, exhibited a markedly different acoustic, at least initially, thanks to Siddle's radical approach. "Dave was

---

STORIES FROM THE STUDIO
Bringing the house down

ENGINEER RICHARD GOLDBLATT recalls one memorable occasion in which he was almost responsible for the collapse of the Wembley roof. "It was a very hot summer day, and for some reason that completely escapes me now, I brought in a load of balloons and a great number of us went up to the roof of the building to water-bomb arriving musicians and staff, running back and forth on the roof and aiming as best we could. This went on for an hour or more.

"Later that night," he continues, "[engineer] Kenny Denton was recording vocals in the newly constructed Studio 4, and at some point in time, the wires fixed into the concrete roof holding the suspended ceiling collapsed, possibly as a result of the large footfall activity earlier in the day. Somewhere there exists a vocal track with the sound of crashing ceilings!"

trying to create a completely 'dead' space that could be transformed with the aid of EMT echo plates into whatever acoustic the engineer wanted," explains mastering engineer Tony Bridge, who recalls spending "many weekends firing starting pistols into the space of the newly built studios, measuring decay times and adjusting acoustic tiles to obtain Dave's optimal measurements."

According to engineer Rafe McKenna, the end result was that the rooms were "dry and dead-sounding, with very little reflection. The material on the walls had these boxes that absorbed everything and they were full of rockwool, with acoustic tiles everywhere

The completed Studio 1, showing the isolation booth (straight ahead, on the studio floor level), window to the control room (one level up), and windows to the projection and telecine rooms (two levels up).
(Courtesy of John Timms)

and carpet on the floor." Richard Goldblatt is even more blunt: "The acoustics [in Studio 1] were absolutely shit! There was no live environment in there at all. Carpet on the floor, everything was dead . . . there was no natural sound like there was at studios like Abbey Road. All the studios [at Wembley] had the same nonexistent acoustics. Everything had to be manufactured through echo plates."

Worse yet, reports Goldblatt, Studio 3 was built on top of the air-conditioning plant, "which imparted a wonderful low-level hum to everything you recorded there." Engineer Louis Austin adds that Studio 3 "was probably OK if you wanted to record a triangle, but everything else had this haunting rumble on it. No problem, though, because the monitoring was so rubbish, you could not hear it until you played your tracks back somewhere better—say the 8-track [cartridge] player in your car!" Austin states flatly that he "absolutely hated Studio 3. It was like recording in a cardboard box stuffed with pillows. It was so dead that you had that awful feeling of dread when the door shut behind you." In addition, there was poor acoustic separation between Studio 3 and Studio 1,

leading to extensive bleed-through when there was an orchestra in Studio 1 and a band in Studio 3.

Many of the CTS engineers spent a good deal of time trying to rectify the situation on their own. "I used to get in big planks of wood and put them on the floor," recalls Rafe McKenna. "We'd put a couple of them out, and you could fit six or eight cello players on [one of] them. I [then] started to use them for recording drums and stuff like that just to get some reflection into the room."

According to maintenance engineer Peter Duncan, acoustic problems were not confined strictly to the recording areas at Wembley, either. "The control rooms were basically over-square," he says, "which made for a lot of standing waves." As a result, significant time and effort were spent trying to adjust the rooms' acoustics by increasing their size and installing traps behind the walls to soak up some of the errant frequencies.

In a major refurbishment undertaken in the spring of 1984, the acoustic treatment at The Music Centre underwent radical modification, with the carpeting torn up and parquet flooring laid down in its place, thus livening the sound considerably.

Room Dimensions

Bayswater:
Studio: 120' x 40' (36.5 x 12 meters)
   Ceiling height: 30' (9 meters)
Control room: 18' x 30' (5.5 x 9 meters)
   Ceiling height: 18' (5.5 meters)

Wembley:
Studio 1: 80' x 50' (24 x 15 meters)
   Ceiling height: 30' (9 meters)
Studio 1 control room: 30' x 20' (9 x 6 meters)
   Ceiling height: 10' (3 meters)

Studio 2: 44' x 30' (13 x 9 meters)
   Ceiling height: 18' (5.5 meters)
Studio 2 control room: 25' x 20' (4.5 x 6 meters)
   Ceiling height: 10' (3 meters)

Studio 3: 30' x 28' (9 x 8.5 meters)
   Ceiling height: 16' (5 meters)
Studio 3 control room: 26' x 14' (8 x 4 meters)
   Ceiling height: 14' (4 meters)

Studio 4: 14' x 10' (4 x 3 meters)
   Ceiling height: 10' (3 meters)

Echo Chambers

There were no acoustic echo chambers at either the Bayswater or Wembley locations, but Kenny Denton recalls that much of the building directly adjacent to The Music Centre was vacant and therefore sometimes used an ad hoc—albeit very sizable—echo chamber.

KEY EQUIPMENT
Mixing Consoles

For many years, the CTS staff at Bayswater enjoyed the reliability of their 12-input gray Telefunken mixing desk, which offered three sets of EQ on rotary potentiometers and flexible outputs that could be grouped to left, center, right, or "spare." By 1968, the console was upgraded to 17 channel inputs. In 1969, this was replaced by a 26-input / 11-output custom-built Neve desk.

In stark contrast, what awaited them at Wembley was, by all accounts, an unmitigated disaster.

Designer Dave Siddle had asked Geoff Frost, CEO of Sound Techniques, to construct custom mixing consoles for the new facility, all essentially identical but with varying numbers of channel inputs. On the face of it, it was a sensible decision: The Sound Techniques board Siddle had used during his time as studio manager at Kingsway Studios had been reliable, and it sounded great. But this time he was asking for logic control and intelligent switching that would largely eliminate the need for patch bays—two requirements that were very much on the bleeding edge of technology in the early 1970s.

Writes Frost on the Sound Techniques website: "The Wembley contract was a massive challenge. . . I felt that the actual circuit design was beyond me. [The] guy who [made] our printed circuit boards . . . appeared to have an in-depth [knowledge] of digital logic design . . . but the logic circuits were a disaster. Some of the blame was mine. I had insisted that he used a particular method of switching, and this started the problems."

"The logic system controlled your monitoring," Frost explained in a later interview. "The idea was, instead of having to patch your inputs and outputs, you could do it by pushing buttons. There was a central unit with illuminated buttons on the desk that was about four inches wide. You had to decide what function you wanted the desk to perform and you'd press that button. Ninety-five percent of the time it worked, but unfortunately it did occasionally crash and it would take five minutes to reset, which wasn't good at all if there was a famous band or artist in the studio. It was a problem we never could quite fix."

Kenny Denton agrees with Frost's assessment that the consoles (a 30 x 16 model in Studio 1; a 24 x 16 model in Studio 2; a 20 x 16 in Studio 3; and a 20 x 4 in Studio 4) did indeed work correctly most of the time. "There were lights at the top of the desk that would light whenever there was an error. Ninety-five percent of the time there was no error, but it didn't make the engineer feel very comfortable. Worse yet, it was a source of major worry for the client."

Elaborates John Timms, "The Sound Techniques desks at Wembley were the very first to be semi-automated. You had to ask the console permission to go into Sync, Ready or Record. The console would then

The view from the Studio 1 control room during an orchestral session.
(From studio brochure)

allow you to switch your Dolbys and do the necessary routing, but there were times when the power supply on the console, the +5 volt rail, would go very slightly out of range and the row of error lights on the console would start lighting up. So our engineers always prayed when they hit the Record button that everything was going to happen right on the take. Maintenance was a nightmare, too, because you had to lay on your back underneath the console and undo panels and tweak trimpots with a voltmeter attached while the client was topside watching all this go down!"

In addition, according to Richard Goldblatt, there was significant bleed-through between all the channels—something that was thoroughly unacceptable even though the overall sound of the desks was said to be quite good, with exceptionally clean equalization circuitry.

Shortly after CTS moved into Wembley, Music Centre technical director Peter Harris decided the Sound Techniques consoles had to go. Unfortunately, the original CTS desks had already been sold. Instead, a new custom Neve 30-input / 16-output console was ordered for Studio 1 and installed in 1973. This was moved to Studio 2 when an upgraded Neve 30 x 24 was delivered a year later. Thus began a long period of rotating consoles at Wembley; whenever a new Neve would arrive for Studio 1, the old console would be shunted to Studio 2, and Studio 2's console moved to the smaller Studio 3, and so on. The 30 x 24 desk in Studio 1 was upgraded in 1979 to a 36 x 24 model; that same year, the 26 x 24 desk residing in Studio 2 was upgraded to a 32 x 24 model. Studio 3—the main remix room at the complex—became the recipient of a 20 x 16 model

Gregory Peck looks down on a film scoring session in Studio 1.
(From studio brochure)

with NECAM automation in 1977; this too was upgraded a year later to an automated 30 x 24 Neve. The small Studio 4 was initially equipped with a modest 20 x 16 Neve, upgraded in 1979 to a 26 x 24 board.

Says Rafe McKenna, "The Neve consoles we had at first were pretty basic. You had a mic input control which was studded; if you wanted to attenuate the microphone, you could step it down. EQ consisted of a top control which was basically a very broad sort of 10k shelving type of EQ and then you had midrange and low-frequency controls, each of which had four or five bands, plus a high-pass filter. There were 16 or 24 routing buses and maybe four sends per channel." By the late '70s, the Neve consoles installed at Wembley offered slightly more in the way of equalization control, particularly in terms of low-

frequency selection. Not only did the engineering staff at Wembley love the sound of the Neves, they all agreed that the new desks were far more reliable than the experimental Sound Techniques consoles they had replaced. At long last, sessions could be run without the fear of error lights going off and things resetting themselves!

Monitors

At Bayswater, the CTS control room offered Tannoy speakers in Lockwood cabinets, driven by HH amplifiers.

Monitoring for the four studios at Wembley were by Tannoy Reds in Lockwood cabinets, driven by Crown D150s. Their sound was described by Rafe McKenna as being "quite boomy in low end, [but] very flattering in the high end." They were later replaced by Tannoy

Golds, and ubiquitous small Auratone speakers were added for near-field monitoring. (See Chapter 1 and Chapter 4 for more information.)

Tape Machines

In the early 1960s, CTS Bayswater was equipped with mono, stereo, and 3-track Philips tape machines capable of running at 7½, 15 and 30 ips. By 1968, these were replaced by a series of Ampex machines, including a 1" 8-track as well as a number of 4-track, 2-track, and mono models.

As with the mixing consoles, the tape machine situation immediately following the move to Wembley was dire, thanks to another disastrous decision by Dave Siddle.

"I had sold Dave [on] the idea that we should design and build the tape amplifiers," writes Geoff Frost on the Sound Techniques website—something that, in his words, became "the straw that broke the proverbial camel's back."

Frost continues: "Dave and I had found a new British manufacturer of tape transports called Unitrack. When we first met them, they had just finished their prototype transport. I liked the use of printed circuit motors, and their use of digital logic (again—you say!) for control of the transport's functions. They had yet to design and build any amplifiers. Ideal. We would supply these. Our first 8-track transport arrived. It frequently screwed up the tape. This they diagnosed as faulty logic design. Then I left for a holiday in the Canaries [Canary Islands]; the next day, I received a telegram saying Unitrack had gone broke. Within a couple of days, we had agreed to use 3M transports [instead] for the multitracks. They were about the same price and very fashionable. They were also readily available. Ampex were selected for the quarter-inch decks.

"It was a very complex situation," he says, in what seems like understatement in retrospect. "I designed the electronics . . . [but] there must have been something wrong with my design. I very much regret agreeing to build the tape machine electronics. I think it was too much for us at the time. I should have just agreed to do the desks."

In the end, Siddle decided to forgo both 3M and Ampex transports, and to use Scully ones instead.

These presented their own set of problems. In fact, in the words of John Timms, they were a "bloody nightmare."

"You couldn't leave the machines switched on with tape in the tape path," he explains, "because the capstan was rough enough to keep niggling away at the tape. We came back from a coffee break during one particular session to find that the master had been wrapped round the capstan and had wound into a two-inch ball!" Adds Robert Zimbler, "the Sound Techniques tape machines were absolutely useless. They were noisy, and they would regularly break down." As if that weren't bad enough, according to Kenny Denton, "the minute you dropped in, you got a massive click on the tape. I eventually worked out that what you had to do was pull the little arm off near the tape heads half a second or so before you dropped in, so that the tape was not in contact with the heads. That way, there was no click, but it wasn't something we should have had to do, either."

By 1973, everyone at the studio was so completely fed up with the Scully/Sound Techniques machines that they were replaced en masse with a battery of 16-track and 8-track Studer A80s, supplemented in the mid-'70s by 2" 24-track models. In the late '70s, an Audiokinetics box was installed to enable the synchronization of dual 24-track machines for 48-track recording.

Studer A80 (24-track, 16-track, 8-track)—(See Chapter 1 for more information.)
Studer B62 (2-track, mono)—The B62 was the successor to Studer's popular A62 transistorized 1/4" 2-track machine. There were seven B62s at Wembley—six stereo and one mono. (See Chapter 7 for more information about the A62.)

Main Microphones

The original CTS mic locker included a number of AKG, Neumann, and STC microphones (probably some of the same models listed below). It is worth noting that, while the original Bayswater studio was acoustically tuned correctly and therefore allowed the sound of even a full orchestra to be captured successfully with just a few mics set at appropriate distances away, the compromised acoustics of the Wembley

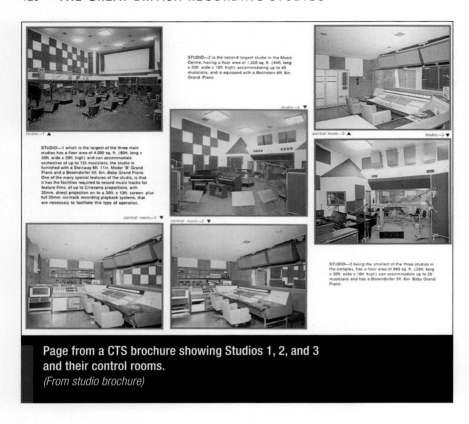

STUDIO—1 which is the largest of the three main studios has a floor area of 4,000 sq. ft. (80ft. long x 50ft. wide x 30ft. high) and can accommodate orchestras of up to 135 musicians, the studio is furnished with a Steinway 6ft. 11in. Model 'B' Grand Piano and a Bosendorfer 5ft. 6in. Baby Grand Piano. One of the many special features of the studio, is that it has the facilities required to record music tracks for feature films, of up to Cinerama proportions, with 35mm. direct projection on to a 30ft. x 13ft. screen, plus full 35mm. six-track recording playback systems, that are necessary to facilitate this type of operation.

STUDIO—2 is the second largest studio in the Music Centre, having a floor area of 1,320 sq. ft. (44ft. long x 30ft. wide x 18ft. high) accommodating up to 40 musicians, and is equipped with a Bechstein 6ft. 6in. Grand Piano.

STUDIO—3 being the smallest of the three studios in the complex, has a floor area of 840 sq. ft. (28ft. long x 30ft. wide x 16ft. high) can accommodate up to 20 musicians and has a Bosendorfer 5ft. 6in. Baby Grand Piano.

Page from a CTS brochure showing Studios 1, 2, and 3 and their control rooms.
(From studio brochure)

location necessitated close-miking and the use of considerably more microphones—something which in turn required an unusually expansive mic locker.

The main microphones used at Wembley included:

Neumann U87—The standard "workhorse" microphone at CTS, in common with most other studios of the era. At Wembley, Alan Florence recalls that studio manager Dave Siddle wanted an extra circuit added to the facility's Neumann microphones to change their response—leading him to ask the rhetorical question, "Why change Neumanns?" (See Chapter 1 for more information.)

Neumann U67—(See Chapter 1 for more information.)

Neumann U47—Rafe McKenna recalled occasionally using one of these—set a good distance away—for kick drum at CTS. "I'd set up two small stands on either side of the kick drum to build a tunnel and cover it with a blanket, then put something like a U47 further out for a distant sound." (See Chapter 1 for more information.)

Neumann KM53/KM54—(See Chapter 1 for more information.)

Neumann KM64—(See *Decca* in Chapter 2 for more information.)

Neumann KM84—(See Chapter 5 for more information.)

Neumann KM86—First introduced in 1968, the KM86 was essentially a phantom-powered FET version of the Neumann KM66 tube mic; both models featured a switch on the body that allowed selection of cardioid, omnidirectional, or figure-of-eight polar patterns. Unlike large-diaphragm multipattern mics, which create switchable polar patterns by combining the output of two sides of a dual-diaphragm capsule in a variety of ways, the KM86 utilizes twin single-sided capsules (the same ones found in the KM84), mounted back-to-back, with one centimeter of space between the diaphragms. Because the figure-of-eight performance of most dual-diaphragm capsules suffers in the low frequencies, the KM86 and related microphones offer superior low-frequency reproduction. KM86s were occasionally used as snare drum mics at CTS; Rafe McKenna recalls that they were also "particularly good on acoustic guitar."

Neumann KM88—This small-diaphragm "pencil" mic was essentially a solid-state version of the KM56. It was designed with a slight boost in the high-frequency range and offered the user a choice of three polar patterns: cardioid, figure-of-eight, and omnidirectional. (See Chapter 1 for more information.)

Neumann M49—(See Chapter 1 for more information.)

AKG C12/C12A—(See Chapter 1 and Chapter 5 for more information.)

AKG C414 B-ULS—This was an advanced version of the AKG C414. (See *Pye* in Chapter 2 for more information.)

AKG D12—As with many other studios of the era, this was the kick drum mic of choice at CTS. (See *Lansdowne* above for more information.)

Sennheiser MD421—Often used as tom-tom mics at CTS, also sometimes on kick drum. (See *Pye* in Chapter 2 for more information.)

Electrovoice RE20—CTS engineers occasionally used this as a kick drum mic. (See *Decca* in Chapter 2 for more information.)

Shure SM57/SM58—First introduced in 1965, the SM57 is an inexpensive unidirectional dynamic that is one of the best-selling microphones in the world to this day. It is widely used in both live sound reinforcement and in recording studios, most often employed as a snare drum mic or guitar amp mic due to its small size, sturdy construction, sound rejection characteristics, and ability to withstand large sound pressure levels without distortion. SM57s and SM58s were often used as snare drum mics at CTS. (See *Pye* in Chapter 2 for more information about the SM58.)

Outboard Signal Processors

For such a large and busy facility, CTS Wembley had, by all accounts, a limited selection of outboard equipment (other than the ten—count 'em, ten—EMT plates). "There was simply not enough outboard gear to go around the four studios," says Kenny Denton, "so you had to make sure you booked popular items like Eventide Harmonizers well before your session."

More bass, mon

MASTERING ENGINEER TONY BRIDGE recalls that CTS was the cutting room of choice for many U.K.-based reggae producers, as well as a number of Jamaican producers, during the time he worked there. "They used to turn up with a suitcase full of unboxed tapes and have a seven-hour session having us cutting everything willy-nilly," he says. "Often, they would bring in a pile of 7" records, and we would cut straight from the disc onto lacquer, with a heavy compressor on everything. There was certainly a lot of recreational intake! I can still picture Lee Perry with the hugest spliff I've ever seen, disappearing behind a cloud of smoke, saying, 'More bass, mon, more bass . . . more top, more top . . . more middle, more middle . . . BOOST AT ALL FREQUENCIES!!!'"

EMT 140 reverb plate—By 1968, three EMT 140 plates were installed at CTS Bayswater. Perhaps as a byproduct of its overly dead acoustic design, the Wembley facility had ten of them, shared by all four studios via audio tielines. The trademark

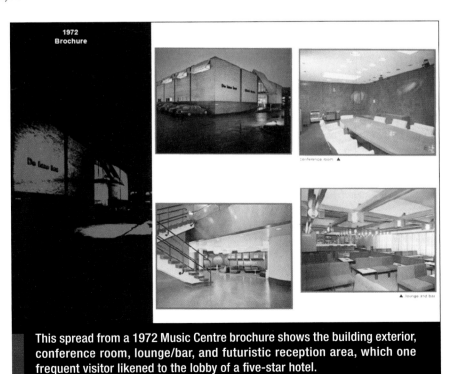

This spread from a 1972 Music Centre brochure shows the building exterior, conference room, lounge/bar, and futuristic reception area, which one frequent visitor likened to the lobby of a five-star hotel.
(From studio brochure)

Very, very sucky

IN HIS 1979 BOOK *All You Need Is Ears*, producer George Martin writes about recording the orchestral soundtrack to the animated movie *Yellow Submarine* at CTS. "One sequence shows a enormous monster without arms, but with two long legs with wellington boots on each and a huge trunk with a head sticking on top of it . . . but in place of a nose there is a kind of long trumpet, which it uses to suck up other little monsters as it wanders around on the sea floor. Eventually it sucks up not only all the other monsters but the yellow submarine itself with the cartoon Beatles inside—at which point it gets ahold of the corner of the screen and sucks that up too!"

Obviously this required a special "sucky" sound, but Martin's dilemma was how to achieve that with a symphony orchestra. The solution he came up with was to record the orchestra playing backwards. (Reverse recording was a trick that he and the real Beatles had used repeatedly, and with great success, on the group's 1966 *Revolver* album.) He duly came up with a 45-second music cue that would fit the picture when played backwards, and CTS engineer Jack Clegg arranged to have the film projected in reverse during the actual recording so that the cue would play backwards when the film was shown running forwards.

At the end of the take, however, Martin was surprised to hear Clegg's voice on tape speaking in some weird Japanese-type language. "I had no idea what was going on," he wrote, "until the time came to play the film back. At the start of the take you could hear Jack's voice saying something like 'Myellah summarin, teek tree.' While we had been recording, he had carefully worked out what his announcement should be if he spoke it backwards, so that when it was played forwards it would sound roughly English! It was a very difficult thing to do, and we all fell about—laughing, amazed, but also full of congratulation—when we heard it."

Jack Clegg elaborates: "It's standard practice when recording music cues for film to audibly identify each cue immediately before the music starts in a very precise formulation. For example: The announcement '3M2, take three' would mean: 'Reel number 3, music cue number 2, third take.' ('1M1' is almost always the main title music, for obvious reasons.) Without this standardized formality, absolute chaos would ensue in the later editing process, with dozens of similar-sounding but unidentified little cues lying about, so it's very important. The only way I could adhere to this procedure on this very unusual occasion—since we were recording the music backwards—was to reverse the normal procedure by recording my spoken ident at the end, rather than the beginning of the music, and speaking it in reverse. I wasn't just fooling around; I was just trying to be practical—in highly unusual circumstances—to avoid confusion for others in later editing and dubbing. It's just something I happened to be able to do without much effort, and it was useful at the time—not particularly clever, just pragmatic.

"So," he concludes with a laugh, "you see, even the most pointless of talents can sometimes be useful."

CTS Wembley slapback echo was created by a 140 coupled with a delay (of around 167 milliseconds) achieved via the physical gap between the record and reproduce heads on analog tape machines running at 15 ips. (See Chapter 1 for more information.)

UREI 1176—Rafe McKenna recalls that there were eight of these limiters at Wembley. (See *Decca* in Chapter 2 for more information.)

Neve 2254—There were three of these compressors built into each Neve console at CTS. (See *Pye* in Chapter 2 for more information.)

Eventide H910 Harmonizer—First introduced in 1974, the H910 offered pitch shifting (±1 octave), delay (up to 112.5 milliseconds), and feedback regeneration. It was used extensively on vocals and guitars to thicken them and to spread mono sounds into stereo. Interestingly, the 910 was named after a Beatles tune (the model number refers to the "One After 909").

Other Music Centre outboard equipment on offer in the '60s and '70s included Pultec tube (valve) equalizers and Klark-Teknik graphic equalizers, as well as various digital delays, phasers, noise gates, and de-essers (exact models unknown). Kenny Denton also recalls a half dozen or so small rack-mounted modules that added fuzz, wah-wah, tremolo, and other guitar effects at line level, as opposed to "stompbox" style units. (Manufacturer unknown, although they were apparently not made by Sound Techniques.)

Film Equipment

A 1964 studio directory listing indicated that CTS Bayswater offered substantial film equipment, including RCA magnetic 35mm triple- and single-track recorders and RCA optical 35mm recorders with provision for ten tracks. There were also two Westar projectors (one 16mm and the other 35mm) with cloverleaf facilities. By 1968, RCA magnetic 35mm quad, triple-, and single-track recorders were also available; with the move to Wembley, 6-track and 4-track recorders were added to the studio's arsenal.

It is worth noting that in the early 1960s, most film work was recorded either direct to mono or to 3-track, in groupings that would permit re-balance during dubbing. Three-track orchestral recordings were generally allocated as follows: strings, woodwinds, and harp on Track 1; rhythm, percussion, and keyboards on Track 2; brass and horns on Track 3.

KEY TECHNICAL INNOVATIONS

The Music Centre had the distinction of being the first major purpose-built recording studio in the U.K.—all the other studios that had come before had been retrofitted into existing buildings. And once the difficult merger between the CTS staff and the De Lane Lea staff was complete and all the acoustics and equipment problems overcome (essentially by virtue of ripping out everything and starting afresh), CTS would enjoy a prolonged period of immense success, becoming one of the best-known and busiest studios in Great Britain—in fact, in the world—for orchestral and film soundtrack recording, while at the same time continuing to attract contemporary music artists like The Who, Fleetwood Mac, Slade, and Roy Wood.

In 1985, Studio 1 enjoyed a further distinction when it became the world's first comprehensive all-digital professional recording studio with the successful recording of Maurice Jarre's score for *The Bride*.

He did it from scratch, and he did it on a piece of swampland

DAVE SIDDLE, DESIGNER OF THE MUSIC CENTRE, with its overly dead acoustics, barely functioning tape machines, and mixing consoles that unexpectedly reconfigured themselves at the worst possible moments, took a lot of flak from a lot of people shortly after the studio complex first opened, but he has at least one defender: ex–De Lane Lea engineer Kenny Denton. "Dave may have done a lot of things wrong, but he had vision," Denton says vehemently. "Just the idea of building that kind of studio complex at Wembley was phenomenal: three studios, a remix room, projection facilities, cutting rooms, connecting tielines everywhere, a car park, lounges for visiting artists, even a full restaurant and bar. I remember walking in there for the first time and it just took my breath away. The room spaces were fantastic, and this was at a time when a lot of other studios were like dungeons. The concept of this amazing building was genius, and it was all down to Dave Siddle.

"He had a blank checkbook and a load of ideas, and he went on this journey, and he built his dream," Denton continues. "When I hear people badmouth him, I say, 'Look, that's really not fair.' Dave's concept was to build a studio like no other, and he was ahead of his time in many ways. People need to remember that he worked on the design for 18 long months. It's easy to look at it today and say, 'Oh yeah, well, it had a bad start,' but Dave tried his best and his initial idea was fantastic. It did have teething problems, but he couldn't get everything right.

"And what was his frame of reference? There was none. He created it from scratch, and he did it on a piece of swampland! He may have got some things wrong, but we shouldn't forget that he got a lot of it right, too. And without his vision, a lot of the success that followed would have never happened."

SELECTED DISCOGRAPHY

- Soundtracks for most early James Bond films, including *Dr. No*, *From Russia with Love*, *Goldfinger*, *Thunderball*, *Casino Royale*, and *You Only Live Twice*
- Soundtrack for *The Mission* (composer: Ennio Morricone)
- Soundtrack for *Murder on the Orient Express*
- Soundtrack for *The Omen*
- Fleetwood Mac: *Bare Trees*
- Renaissance: *Turn of the Cards*
- Harry Nilsson: *A Little Touch of Schmilsson in the Night*

4
304 HOLLOWAY ROAD

t was the original home studio.

After run-ins with management at IBC and Lansdowne, Joe Meek came to the only conclusion possible: There was no one he could work for except himself.

At the time, it had never been done, at least not in Britain. No one had ever opened a recording studio without the backing of a record label, broadcasting corporation, or major producer. Undaunted, Meek turned to a business acquaintance with the improbable name of Major Wilfred Alonzo Banks, and a deal was struck whereby Meek would receive the necessary funding—and a modest salary—in exchange for his services as an independent producer. Probably what appealed to him most was his freedom to choose the artists he wanted to record.

Only one problem remained, and that was to secure a location for the studio. As it happened, Banks had offices on Holloway Road in north London, and Meek soon found a three-floor unit for rent just blocks away. It seemed like an unlikely place for a recording studio—the space was situated in a run-down building above a leather goods store, plus the road outside was congested with noisy, heavy traffic. Worse yet, there was no elevator, meaning that musicians would have to lug heavy equipment up two flights of stairs, but the lure of a long-term lease convinced Meek that he could make it work. With the help of one of his artists—Dave Adams, who also happened to be a skilled carpenter—the space was transformed over a three-month period into a workable, if somewhat shambolic recording environment. The studio at 304 Holloway Road (it was never given a proper name, although Meek's company was called RGM Sound) opened its doors for business in September 1960.

Meek songwriting partner (and arranger) Geoff Goddard remembers it thusly: "It wasn't really a studio—it was [just] some rooms above a shop. The [recording area] was a double bedroom, and the control room was the bedroom across the landing. The wires ran over the floor, so you had to be careful where you walked, and there was always the danger of electric shocks there. It was all very primitive—bits of old wires stuck together and old tape machines." Peter Miller, the guitarist for Meek artist Peter Jay and the Jaywalkers, adds, "People lived next door, and [so] we always had to stop recording at six o'clock because of the neighbors; he could not have a session after six at night. We'd have three hours to do two sides, and very often we'd do four or five sides in those three hours. There was always a pile of masters all over the place—[Meek] was a messy bastard. And he wasn't big on plugs; he would twist all the wires together,

[so] when you went into the room he'd say, 'Don't step there, don't step there.' I stood in this mess many times, doing a guitar overdub or something, because he didn't have speakers in the studio. He had headphones, but he never had any speakers out there."

Yet despite the haphazard nature of the setup, hits began pouring out of Meek's homebuilt studio, the biggest one being the Tornados' recording of his composition, the iconic 1962 instrumental "Telstar"— a relentlessly hooky melody layered over an unearthly pastiche of electronic sounds. It was a record that would eventually top the charts in both Britain and the United States, a rare occurrence in those pre-Beatles days. And while Meek's life was a troubled one—he was a closeted homosexual in an era when it was illegal in Britain, and he suffered from various mental disorders, including a severe streak of paranoia—he was, in his own strange way, a master of his craft. By

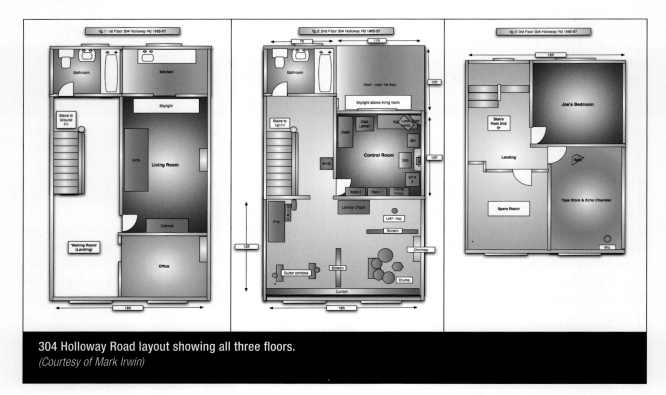

304 Holloway Road layout showing all three floors.
(Courtesy of Mark Irwin)

the time of Meek's death in 1967—a combination homicide/suicide in which he murdered his landlady before turning the shotgun on himself—he had left a legacy of quirky yet powerfully compelling recordings behind. More importantly, he proved—a quarter of a century before the advent of digital recording—that hit records could indeed be made in a bedroom . . . provided there's a genius at the helm.

KEY PERSONNEL
Producer/engineer: Joe Meek

PHYSICAL FACILITIES
The main recording area of the 304 Holloway Road studio was at the front of the building, on the third floor ("second floor" in British parlance), with two large windows overlooking the busy street below. Entrance was gained through a single, non-sound-proofed door opening into a narrow hall leading to the control room, a stairwell, and a bathroom. Access to the control room was via a door opening from the corner closest to the entrance of the studio, but not affording a direct view of it. Interestingly, there was

no window between the control room and the studio, presumably a conscious decision made by Meek, perhaps in line with his penchant for secrecy.

Acoustic Treatments
Carpenter/musician Dave Adams, who did most of the construction work at 304 Holloway Road, reports in Barry Cleveland's book *Joe Meek's Bold Techniques* that "the studio windows were insulated, and then boards were nailed over them and acoustic tile and drapes [were placed] over the boards." Packabeats lead guitarist Malcolm Lenny remembers that "there were various carpets spread all over the floor to act as sound absorbers." During the session for "Evening in Paris," he recalls that the band's drummer was placed just in front of one of the boarded-up windows. "Behind him was a mattress or two to deaden the sound, and just a Chinese screen separated him from the rest of the room." Yet despite the noisy road outside—a main artery bringing heavy trucks from the north of England into London's docks and markets—and the minimalist acoustic treatments, Adams insists "we heard very little outside sound."

Room Dimensions

Studio: 18' x 13' (5.5 x 4 meters)
   Ceiling height: 8' (2 meters)
Control room: 12' x 11' (3.5 x 3 meters)
   Ceiling height: 8' (2 meters)

Echo Chambers

There is some controversy as to whether or not the 304 Holloway Studio actually had a dedicated echo chamber, despite Joe Meek's own statement that there was indeed one "above the control room" (see *Meek on Meek* below)—which would seem to indicate that the smaller of the two bedrooms on the third floor had been converted for that purpose, perhaps doubling as a tape library. Peter Miller concurs, stating that there was a room upstairs that was used as an ambient acoustic echo chamber. "From time to time the vocalist would get sent up there," he recalls. "Certain vocalists that couldn't sing in tune too well, [anyway]—to sing from within the echo chamber, to try and help them. Joe had a speaker and a mic up there. It was a live room with nothing in it. He would pump the sound up there . . . and it was great, better than any electronic device."

Yet Dave Adams—the man who did the actual renovation work—insists that there was no actual echo chamber, despite his sister Joy remembering a room painted completely black, which would indicate such a usage.

The confusion may stem from the apocryphal story that Meek frequently recorded singers or instrumentalists in the upstairs toilet in order to take advantage of the room's acoustic reflectivity. (Bathroom tiles, unlike acoustic tiles, reflect sound rather than absorbing it.) According to *Joe Meek's Bold Techniques*, "at least one of Meek's artists, Screaming Lord Sutch, confessed to being 'sent to the loo' in order to echo-up his voice, and it is quite likely that he was not the only one to suffer that indignity."

Guy Fletcher, a backing vocalist who appeared on many Meek recordings, agrees, saying that "Joe used the tiled bathroom in his flat as an echo chamber, with a speaker at one end and a mic at the other. Although it never seemed to bother him, the yip of the neighbor's dog could often be heard on the echo return!"

Nonetheless, it's entirely possible that Meek may have been bluffing about the room upstairs being converted into an actual echo chamber, just as he publicly denied having ever recorded anyone in his bathroom; paranoid as he was, he made a career out of trying to mislead the competition, whom he increasingly viewed as mortal enemies.

It's quite a mystery. Nonetheless, the fact remains that many of the recordings done at 304 Holloway

---

STORIES FROM THE STUDIO
Meek on Meek

THERE WAS, of course, no one better qualified to describe the studio at 304 Holloway Road than Joe Meek himself. In November 1962, Meek sat down and recorded an off-the-cuff "guided tour" of the facility for the now-defunct magazine *Audio-Record Review*. Though the story was never published, here is a description of the studio in Meek's own words:

"The studio itself [is] . . . the size of an average bedroom—no larger. I've covered all the walls with acoustic tiles—except one, which is covered with a thick curtain. This has a very good absorbing power, and the studio is extremely dead. The floor is carpeted, and the ceiling is completely covered in tiles. And only the one wall has some tiles missing, and this gives me a certain amount of brightness, but basically it's completely dead. I have no playback speaker in the studio and no cue lights. I have a piano which I've put drawing pins in the pads and it produces a more metallic sound which is much better to record, and is much more suitable for pop records.

"My control room . . . is about the size of a small bedroom. It was actually used as a small bedroom, I should imagine. In this control room I have a desk with the equipment piled on it and I have a table and a rack.

"Above my control room, I have a room which I've made into an echo chamber. It's quite remarkable for the size of it. It really gives me a very, very good echo sound, which is on all my records. Also I use electronic echo and this is used quite a lot on my records too, especially on guitars and percussive sounds."

Road do seem to feature the sound of an acoustic echo chamber. The logical conclusion is that either the third-floor bedroom or second-floor bathroom—or possibly both—was probably used for that purpose, at least on occasion.

KEY EQUIPMENT
Mixing Consoles

For the first two years of its operation, the sole mixing console in use at 304 Holloway Road was a homemade four-channel rack-mounted unit designed and hand-built by Joe Meek himself, augmented by several additional small preamplifiers (see below) that he used to sum line-level feeds from various sources. The only equalization offered by Meek's mixer was a variable "top lift" (high-frequency boost) on each of the four channels.

By September of 1962, Meek had added a Vortexion 4/15/M four-channel tube (valve) mixer, which he described as [doing] "a pretty good, solid job," despite it offering no equalization whatsoever. The company's products were, however, known for their reliability and were widely used in the recording and broadcast industries at the time, as well as in the military.

<hr />

STORIES FROM THE STUDIO
Evening in Holloway Road

"JOE MEEK WAS VERY, VERY IMPORTANT to what is going on today. He was one of those flawed geniuses." So says former Packabeats lead guitarist Malcolm Lenny, whose band recorded their hit single "Evening in Paris" at 304 Holloway Road under the watchful eye of the fabled producer in 1962.

"Joe had sent us a demo played by either himself or Geoff Goddard on piano," Lenny recalls, "along with probably some of his house band, The Outlaws. The tune was all played on the black notes, but it was quite a nice melody. We had made an arrangement which we thought was OK, and thankfully Joe liked it, too, as he was notorious for losing his temper with all sorts of people over almost nothing at all. Yet by the time we had finished the session, everything sounded fantastic! How the hell Joe got such great sounds out of his setup, I'll never know."

According to a Vortexion ad of the time, 20,000 ohms was the standard output impedance for that model, "but the noise pick-up on the output lines is equivalent to approximately 2,000 ohms due to the large amount of negative feedback used." Inputs were balanced line-level via three-point jack sockets mounted on the front of the compact tabletop unit. By using the Vortexion in conjunction with his homemade mixer, Meek had access to a total of eight high-quality channels—four with EQ—which could be combined in various ways.

In addition, the studio had several preamplifiers with multiple inputs that Meek could use to combine several signals before they ever reached a mixer. He called the one he relied on most his "cooker"—in reality, an RCA Orthophonic hi-fi preamplifier/filter unit that provided three inputs and simple tone controls: bass, top, and middle "lift" (boost). Because it could be easily overdriven into a smooth and very musical distortion, it soon became a key component of the Joe Meek sound.

As Peter Miller described the unit in *Joe Meek's Bold Techniques*, "Essentially it was something like you'd use [in] a fancy home system. It was a mono unit, with volume, middle, treble, bass, slope, and a couple of filters. For its day it was quite a comprehensive little equalization device. It had five or six tubes in it, and you could overload the crap out of it to get some really cool sounds." Meek himself termed the unit "quite handy" in that it allowed him to "mix without having to walk about the control room too much." The "cooker" was most often used on vocals and other "front-line" instruments.

Other preamplifiers in the 304 Holloway Studio arsenal included an RCA LM1/322 15A, and an American Dyna PAS/2 stereo model, both of which were used to provide additional inputs or tone coloration as needed.

Some sources state that in July of 1964, Meek added a six-channel stereo mixer to the studio, but little is known about this mystery device, or even if it existed at all. What is clear, however, is that the primary mixers in use at 304 Holloway Road were Meek's hand-built model, along with the Vortexion 4/15/M and the RCA Orthophonic "cooker."

The Tornados rehearsing at 304 Holloway Road.
(Photo by Hulton Archive/Getty Images)

Monitors

Tannoy Red—These speakers, which had a frequency response of 23 Hz to 20 kHz (extraordinary for the time) and an active crossover fixed at 1 kHz, were in common use in most major recording and broadcast studios throughout Britain and Europe at the time, and so had become the de facto reference standard. The main monitor in the 304 Holloway Road control room was a 15" dual concentric (center-mounted high-frequency driver) Tannoy Red built into a Lockwood enclosure measuring 44 by 24 by 17.5 inches. (A second, identical Tannoy Lockwood speaker was downstairs in the lounge, where Meek generally played back acetate test discs; there were no speakers in the studio itself). Peter Miller felt that "they were the best speakers I ever heard—so sweet." Adds Malcolm Lenny, "We never quite got over Joe's playback speaker cabinet, which stood in front of the fireplace. It was a monster, the size of a double wardrobe, [and] it made playback so exciting that your ears nearly bled. No wonder his landlady used to complain about the noise!"

The Tannoys at 304 Holloway Road were driven by Quad AC88 amplifiers and matched Quad 22 preamplifiers, the latter of which provided dual EQ switches to match the frequency response of standard 45- and 78-rpm records. The studio also owned several other power amplifiers, including a stereo Sagatone, a pair of Dyna models, and a pair of RCA Model LM1/322s, any or all of which might have been called into use as the need arose.

In addition, Meek had a Tannoy "corner" speaker in the control room, driven by, as Ted Fletcher recalls, a Leak TL50 power amplifier "fed from a bunch of nasty little valve mixers in various states of undress. But the sound was quite magnificent, probably enhanced by the second order distortion from the overdriven valves." Interestingly, Meek mainly used this speaker to monitor just the vocal channel, although, according to one interview he did, he was less than satisfied with the quality, describing its sound as "rather metallic." He went on to explain, "I only use it at low levels. I can't really balance [mix] on it, although I've tried. It seems to have an artificial top lift that rather misleads you."

Tape Machines

Lyrec TR16-S—The stereo version of the Lyrec TR16, this was Joe Meek's "go-to" tape machine. It ran at 7.5, 15, and 30 ips and utilized individual high-speed motors for rewind and fast-forward. One unusual feature was a switch that allowed the right and left channels of the stereo head to be collapsed into mono and played back through a single amplifier in order to check phase relationships. While the stock TR16-S did not have the ability to monitor playback of one recorded track while recording a second track in sync with it (often referred to as "sel-sync"), Meek modified the 304 Holloway Road machine for that purpose.

Vortexion WVB—Vortexion tape machines were built around the tape deck transport originally developed for Ferrograph, but used their own preamplifiers. Unlike the Ferrographs, they had low-impedance (30-ohm) mic inputs, which allowed for long cable runs, and a rear-panel

STORIES FROM THE STUDIO
Ping-ponging, Joe Meek–style

IN HIS BOOK *The Legendary Joe Meek*, biographer John Repsch states that "layering one sound on top of another—sometimes up to half a dozen times—allowed [Meek] to concentrate on one section of the recording at a time, getting the performance he liked best and giving him the chance to change his mind as he went along. The finished recording would end up on two tracks—the backing on one track and the voice on the other.

"First of all he would deal with the backing," Repsch continues. "The rhythm section would go into the studio and play while the singer sang along as a guide, unrecorded behind an old screen. While this performance was going on, he would be recording it onto one track of the [EMI] TR51 [mono recorder]. He might record 20 takes before deciding which one he wanted and moving on to the

first overdub. This might [be] an extra drum sound, so he would choose the take he liked best and relay it out into the studio for the drummer to play along to. The two sounds combined would be channeled onto one track of the Lyrec [twin-track recorder]. When he again had a take that satisfied him, he would perhaps overdub a guitar and do exactly the same again, playing the last recording out and collecting both sounds together on the [remaining] track of the Lyrec.

"Depending on the sound he was after, he would gradually add more and more instruments, spinning spools [of tape] back and forth until his backing track was done. When all the backing was happily on one track of the Lyrec, he would have the vocalist sing along to it. The only difference this time was that he liked to keep the singing separate, so he would give the singer headphones

and play the backing track through them instead. Then eventually, after messing around on his own adding sound effects and so on, he had the two finished tracks on his Lyrec."

In the 1962 recording he made for a never-published *Audio-Record Review* article, Meek described the process this way: "The main recording machine is a Lyrec twin-track. I usually record the voice on one track and the backing on the other. The other recorder is a TR51, and this I use for dubbing. The [singer] has his microphone, a U47, in the corner of the studio, screened off from the rest of the musicians. He can sing his heart out, without anyone taking notice of him. He's going on a separate track [of the Lyrec]. The bass is fed in direct, the guitars have microphones in front of their amplifiers, and the drum kit has two or three microphones placed around it. Each musician has

rheostat on the for adjusting the erase bias. Unfortunately, the meters on the WVB were quite erratic and therefore difficult to use with any precision. (See *Overcompression, Distortion . . . and an Abundance of Echo* on page 144.) Meek used his Vortexion tape recorder almost exclusively for delay and echo; however, the studio may or may not have also been equipped at some point with a Binson Echo unit—a device that recorded onto a metal disc rather than magnetic tape.

EMI TR50/51—(See *Lansdowne* in Chapter 3 for more information.)

EMI BTR2—Added to the 304 Holloway Road studio in February of 1963. (See Chapter 1 for more information.)

Ampex 300—Although most Model 300s were twin-track, the machine installed at 304 Holloway Road in March of 1963 was mono. It operated at both 7.5 and 15 ips but employed an indirect capstan drive, which made absolute speed accuracy difficult to attain; in addition, increased flutter was noted with wear. (See *Decca* in Chapter 2 for more information.)

Ampex 351—This was a sturdy, roadworthy 1/4" tape recorder first introduced by Ampex in 1958. It operated at both 15 ips and 7.5 ips, and was available with either a full-track (mono) or half-track headblock. Purchasers of the latter option could choose between "2-track" models and "stereo" models; the latter offered separate erase heads for each track. Ampex also offered a wired remote control for relay operation of Start, Stop, Rewind, Fast-Forward, and Record. The 351 employed printed circuit boards instead of point-to-point wiring, used miniature tubes, and had an internal power supply. Its electronics were connected to the transport via a six-pin Jones plug.

Ampex PR10—This was a small portable tape recorder that incorporated Ampex Model 354 electronics, but with a different faceplate. As with most portable machines of the era, it could only

been given the chord sequence for a song, or has been listening to a record downstairs on my player, and dotted down the chords. Then we go ahead and we record until I have a very good track. I'm not worried if the artist [singer] is in tune, or phrasing properly—I want a good rhythm track for the A-side. We do the same for the B-side, and then [that's] all for the backing group. Off they go, and then I dub the artist's voice on again. I listen to the tracks we've already got . . . sometimes they're good enough, but as a rule, he wears headphones and the track's played back to him, and it's dubbed onto my TR51. So we have voice and rhythm tracks . . . sometimes [we overdub] four strings—never any more—four violins, say, a French horn, and a harp. Sometimes [also] a choir, say three girls. After I've finished, I've ended up dubbing from my TR51 onto [one track on] the Lyrec. [After recording the orchestra on the second track of the Lyrec] I have the extra orchestra on one side, and the voice and the [rhythm] track on the other. And that's all I do at my premises. I then edit out the best takes, and go along to IBC and [master] them."

In *Joe Meek's Bold Techniques*, Peter Miller described a varied approach after Meek purchased an EMI BTR2 in 1963, saying that the producer would "very often get the band recorded onto the Lyrec, which was usually his first machine. He would put the band on one track and the vocal on the second track. The vocal track would also include maybe a guitar track or solo sax or something else—whatever lead instrument wasn't playing at the same time as the vocal. And then he would mix that onto his EMI BTR2, mono, one track. At the [same] time, he would add on anything else that he wanted, either another track, or effects processing."

Ted Fletcher offers a slightly different recollection: "The technique he used most of the time while I was there was to lay down the backing track on the full track of the BTR2 so that the recording occupied the full quarter-inch in mono. He would then remove the tape and put it on to the Lyrec machine where he would erase one half. There would still be the original backing track on the one half of the tape and he would add to that either the lead voice or backing vocal on the other half of the track. He would then mix the backing track and the vocal track together live while he was recording another part and send the three elements back to the BTR2, live in mono on full track. If he had everything he wanted by then, he would do a final mixdown with additional compression and EQ."

Joe Meek in the 304 Holloway Road studio.
(Photo by David Peters)

accommodate seven-inch reels, thus minimizing effective recording times. (See *Decca* in Chapter 2 for more information.)

It is worth noting that there is no direct evidence that there was ever a multitrack tape recorder in use at 304 Holloway Road, although a somewhat mysterious bill of sale from Ampex UK dated January 10, 1966, surfaced in the Meek archives after his death. Ted Fletcher is adamant that this was indeed a multitrack but that the machine was destroyed after Meek threw it down the stairs in a fit of pique.

Main Microphones

Neumann U47—Meek described these ubiquitous valve (tube) large-diaphragm condenser microphones as being the studio's "main microphones,"

adding his opinion: "I think this is a wonderful microphone, and I use it for all my vocalists. It has a very good characteristic for close work—that is, for instruments you need a lot of presence on. To help this, I use a small piece of foam plastic on it—this stops pops and bangs when a vocalist is working close to it." Ted Fletcher adds, "The U47 [at 304 Holloway Road] was suspended on a huge, great industrial mic stand, and it was always fixed in the same place. It was also swathed in foam rubber [pop shields], until the head of the mic was actually as big as a football [soccer ball]. The approved method was to sing so that your nose was just about touching the pop shield. You get a very close, present sound, and that's how Meek did it." Other sources indicate that Meek sometimes used a U47 as a drum overhead mic. (See Chapter 1 for more information.)

AKG D19—These small dynamic microphones (which Meek described in 1962 as being of the "types that are very popular today") were mainly used at Holloway Road on drums (snare and overhead) and for guitar amp miking. According to Ted Fletcher, Meek not only close-miked guitar amps with an AKG "rammed up against the front," but would also toss a large blanket over the whole thing, presumably in an effort to gain some separation in the small studio area. (See Chapter 1 for more information.)

Reslosound Ribbon—A pair of these inexpensive ribbon microphones were added to the Holloway Road studio mic cabinet in 1962. One unusual characteristic of these microphones is that the ribbon itself is positioned to the rear and the shells surrounding it are removable, allowing various acoustic filter pads to be fitted that modify both frequency and polar response to a degree.

Reslosounds were used extensively by Meek not only for vocals, but, surprisingly, also on bass drum. Though the exact model is unknown, Ted Fletcher recalls that the studio owned the type that was used for PA applications, "like for factory announcements. It was so heavily padded," he adds, "that there was no way that you could have damaged the ribbon by putting it in front of a bass drum. It was a type of Reslo that was almost indestructible."

Taking advantage of the figure-of-eight polar pattern normally employed by ribbon microphones, Meek often used the Reslos for backing vocals, having the singers work both sides of it so that they could see one another. "Really the [Reslos] aren't all that expensive," Meek said in a 1962 interview, "but they're very efficient, and being such a small studio, they're used pretty close to the instruments."

Other microphones in use at various times at 304 Holloway Road included:

An RCA variable impedance dynamic mic (model unknown)
An RCA dynamic mic (model unknown)
An HMV 235CH ribbon mic—a large, classic, radio presenter-style microphone, complete with "Nipper" badge
A Western Electric ribbon cardioid, which one source says was probably an Altec 639A or 639B
A Neumann SM2—a stereo condenser mic based on the KM56
A Telefunken NSH condenser
A Telefunken ELA M250 condenser
A Telefunken ELA M251 condenser—a neutral/ bright-sounding mic with an AKG-made C12-type capsule
An AKG D60 hypercardioid dynamic
Beyer M61 and M23 dynamics
Two Micro Kit Omni Capacitor tube microphones made by Meek, sometimes used on drums

Outboard Signal Processors

Paranoid as he was, it should come as no surprise that the most famous pieces of outboard gear at 304 Holloway Road were the homemade "black boxes" that Joe Meek himself built over the years. These included a spring reverb and two compressor/limiters.

"Black Box" spring reverb—According to Adrian Kerridge, Meek built the first iteration of his "black box" spring reverb as early as 1957. "Joe used to carry it around with him in a case, taped-up," Kerridge commented in

Joe Meek's Bold Techniques before revealing that the mysterious device was in fact an old fan heater!

"These [HMV-built devices] were used then at Lansdowne to heat various offices," Kerridge said. "[They] were made from fairly tightly coiled suspended wire that twanged when you moved them. Joe got hold of a broken one and made [it into] a spring echo unit, using transducers—I can't remember which [ones he used]. It worked very well and . . . produced a very twangy sound that he used to great effect on many of his recordings."

Dave Adams adds that the unit was an ongoing experiment, stating that it "went through various transformations and springs. The spring itself was wired at both ends. I always assumed that the sound actually traveled down the spring, but it's anybody's guess."

In addition, the studio owned a Fairchild 658 Reverbertron, a rack-mounted unit based around three spring tanks and an optical attenuator, and possibly also a Grampian 636—a fairly advanced device for its time that provided dual mic inputs (one balanced and one unbalanced), as well as two aux line inputs and a remote switch.

"Black Box" compressor/limiters—There were two such homebuilt "black box" dynamics processors that Meek favored and used on almost all of

---

STORIES FROM THE STUDIO
The Joe Meek drum miking technique

IN *JOE MEEK'S BOLD TECHNIQUES*, Peter Miller states that Meek would "often use a Reslo on the bass drum, which now I realize . . . how did he get away with that? A ribbon mic? Maybe he just put new ribbons in every morning when he had his coffee.

"He always used that Reslo on the bass drum, and he used an AKG on the snare, and an AKG on the overhead. Or occasionally maybe a U47 on the overs. But he never used more than three mics on the drums. And this was new— I'd never seen any other engineer do this—he would put a big blanket right across the front of the drums, draped actually on the drums, and tape it to the tom-toms, with the mic between the blanket and the drum."

Joe Meek at work in the cluttered control room, 1963.
(Photo by John Pratt/Keystone Features/Getty Images)

his recordings at 304 Holloway Road, and both were all-tube. One of these was a modified BBC limiter that Meek described at the time as being "30 years old" (which would have made it vintage 1936) and a second unit (possibly in the style of a Langevin compressor/limiter) that may have been similar to a unit he made while at Lansdowne in 1958.

The always circumspect Meek described his two homemade dynamics processors in only the vaguest of terms. "I have some bits of gear that you don't usually find with the keen recordist," he said in one interview. "These include an old BBC

limiter which I use on the voice track. It is very ancient, as it has the old large pin type valves. This is very efficient and isn't all that noticeable in its operation. Then I have a compressor that I built myself. I found the design in one of the magazines."

Ted Fletcher recalls that both these units were tube devices that contained "various modified bits of Fairchild photoelectric compressors, often fixed in tobacco tins with Sellotape [Scotch tape]," one of which "had no covers on it, exposed valves, and a bit of chassis." That particular device, he says, was called into play constantly. "[Meek] bunged everything through it [put every signal through it] as a matter of course, so that everything was compressed every time it went through it, which was generally between three and four times."

In addition, the studio owned two Altec tube leveling amplifiers and a variety of Fairchild dynamics processors (mostly inexpensive models), as described below. Of these, Meek was said to have favored the Altec units, which he modified to decrease the attack and release times in order to get heavy "pumping" effects out of them. Ted Fletcher recalls that most of the Fairchilds in the 304 Holloway Road control room (presumably with the exception of the coveted 660, which had become an integral part of Beatles recordings) were "very simple things with one or two knobs on the front and a vertical edgewise meter. They sounded not very good, actually."

Altec 438A—A tube leveling amplifier designed primarily for PA applications, though it was often found in radio and TV broadcast studios as well. The 438A had dual mic-level inputs and a built-in mic preamp. It provided up to 30 dB of gain reduction with a fixed attack time of 50 milliseconds and a fixed "recovery" (release) time of one second. It sported a small front-panel meter that displayed the degree of compression; however, the only control was a Volume (input level) knob.

Altec 436B—(See Chapter 1.)

Fairchild 660—(See Chapter 1.)

Fairchild 661 AUTO TEN—The compact Fairchild 661 was an optical noise gate that shared a nearly identical schematic with the 663 compressor (see below). Attack time was fixed at 40 milliseconds, but front-panel controls were provided for threshold and release time (variable from three to seven seconds). The built-in "Auto Ten" (automatic attenuation) circuitry was designed to reduce audible pumping in soft passages. (See Chapter 1 for more information.)

Fairchild 663—This inexpensive miniature compressor measured only 1½ by 7 by 4½ inches and provided up to 20 dB of gain reduction. Attack time was fixed at 40 milliseconds, but front-panel controls were provided for threshold and release time (variable from three to seven seconds).

Fairchild 670—(See *Lansdowne* in Chapter 3 for more information.)

Fairchild 673 Dynaliser—Meek owned a pair of these passive dynamics processors, which have been described as "reverse de-essers." They acted as an automatic loudness controls, but applied a Fletcher Munson loudness curve-like equalization to boost highs and lows as levels dropped. The 673 used the same optical system as the Fairchild 661 and 663.

Like the reverbs and dynamics processors, the selection of outboard equalizers at 304 Holloway Road was a mishmash of professional and homemade units. It includes a vaguely named "tone control unit" and an equally mysterious "mid lift control," as well as two EMI passive equalizers (models 843 and 844). In addition, there were an Astrosonic "response control unit" (a consumer-grade phonograph equalizer) and an IBC CU-3H, which was probably an in-house item dating from Meek's days at IBC. According to Ted Fletcher, some of Meek's EQs were, like his other black boxes, simply "things in tobacco tins, with little inductors and capacitors soldered together," although at least one of them was based on the classic Pultec design.

Meek once described how he used one of his homegrown equalizers; typically, he failed to mention exactly which one he was talking about. Here's what he had to say: "I feed [the electric bass] through an equalizer unit. On this unit I have experimented and I feed the output back. I believe it's positive feedback, but when carefully done and through a choke, it gives you the effect of the string being plucked; you get a sort of metallic pluck of the string itself and this is quite effective on recordings." By "choke" it is probably safe to assume that he was referring to the process of manually dampening a note to shorten it by stopping the string vibration, since the application of feedback he described would tend to make a sound brighter by accentuating the high harmonics through the creation of a resonant harmonic peak and a short "ring."

Other outboard devices used prominently at 304 Holloway Road included at least three disc cutters, including models from MSS, Simon Sound Services, and Ferranti, which he used for making test acetates prior to bringing tapes to outside studios (most often IBC) for proper mastering.

In addition, there was a wide range of maintenance equipment such as meters, oscilloscopes, and test oscillators (at least a few of which found their way onto his recordings). "I service my own gear," Meek once explained. "I have an Advance oscillator and a small oscilloscope. . . . The oscillator is very important. I quite often use it on sound effects on some of my records."

"Three of his main pieces of equipment were his sine wave generator, his oscilloscope, and his soldering iron," adds Peter Miller. "Without those three, Joe would never have been the man he was. He used them for adjusting and modifying his equipment, because he messed with everything. As soon as he got it, it came out of the box—he wanted to see what was in there and how he could make it different." Ted Fletcher maintains that Meek's control room "literally looked like a workshop because nothing had its cover on. He never had the tops screwed on to anything; everything was in chassis form, with the sides or the top off. Even the old EMI BTR2 machine was always operating with the amplifiers half pulled out. Always it looked like a collection of skeletons."

But perhaps the weirdest device of all at 304 Holloway Road was an intriguing guitar-like instrument (complete with onboard effects) called the WEM Fifth Man—a collaboration between Meek and fabled amplifier and instrument designer Charlie Watkins. According to *Joe Meek's Bold Techniques* author Barry Cleveland, "it may have been the earliest attempt at creating a guitar synthesizer." Pioneering though it may have been, the Fifth Man apparently performed poorly and consequently never went into production. (See the Story from the Studio below.)

KEY TECHNICAL INNOVATIONS
Overcompression, Distortion . . . and an Abundance of Echo

Joe Meek was considered a master of compression—or, perhaps better stated, overcompression. Meek biographer John Repsch explains that "he had to watch out for loss of quality [because] each time he transferred from one track to the other, a little of the original sound was lost. So he had to use limiters and compressors which gave him a

ROBB HUXLEY, vocalist and guitarist with the Saxons, remembers that "Joe's influence upon us was mainly in an instrumental vein, which was probably due to his desire to create another 'Telstar.' After we had played the song 'Sun God' to Joe, he got quite excited and suggested that [guitarist] Pete [Holder] play an organ guitar that he was developing together with the Watkins electronic people. So after we had finished the basic backing track, Joe brought out this weird little guitar that looked like it could have been homemade and plugged it into Pete's amp. Immediately, all kinds of crackling and sizzling sounds emanated from the instrument—I almost expected to see sparks flying and smoke pouring out! Joe did not seem to be bothered by this at all and proceeded to fiddle about with some wires and controls on the guitar. We all stood around, wondering what was going to happen next, afraid that the whole contraption would suddenly explode. Pete had a look of amazement on his face. On one hand, he was feeling very honored that he was to use this great new invention that Joe had been working on, and on the other hand he looked concerned that he might get electrocuted at any moment!

"Still, Pete was able to get most of the lead melody down after a few takes," Huxley continues. "Sometimes the guitar gave out a sputter or two here and there, but we finally got one down, although right at the very end of the song, the last extended note burst into a crackle. Joe, seeing that we were disappointed by this, told us that it was nothing and everything would be all right. I believe that had we ever got round to finishing that track, Joe would have probably disguised that crackle with some effect that would make it sound like something strange and would not be seen as a mistake on the recording. The whole thing probably would have turned out to be beneficial to the song—just another spark of genius from Joe Meek."

louder signal. They could also give him the sound of pumping. This he would often use to add to the overall excitement, [playing] an integral part in his unique sound." In the words of Jaywalkers guitarist Peter Miller (see *Not so much the song as the sound* on the next page), "Joe's use of extreme compression—squashing signals through his Fairchild 670 compressor—was his magic wand."

In today's digital world, distortion is anathema. Yet in the pioneering days of analog recording it was often a powerful tool, especially in the hands of someone as inventive as Joe Meek. As Ray Prickett, who worked with Meek at IBC, commented in *Joe Meek's Bold Techniques*, "Joe's mind was on the creative side, not on the technical aspects. . . . His recordings often tended to be a little bit distorted, but that was what he was trying to achieve. Sometimes to get the sound he wanted during the actual recording session, he'd alter the recording equalization. Then if he still wasn't happy with it, he'd tweak the replay equalizers to make it play back differently till he got the effect he wanted. But unless [the mastering engineers] knew exactly how he'd tweaked them, nobody would ever achieve that effect again."

By staying late and working with the mercurial producer after hours, Miller eventually discovered that the recognizable Joe Meek sound could be simulated by "overloading the valve preamps of certain tape recorders, hence saturating the tape." Geoff Goddard observed that "the indicator [on his tape recorder] was often right in the red, indicating that the level was too high, but he would be deliberately over-recording it to get a particular sound. Nothing like that," he added, "would have happened in a respectable recording studio."

Adds Ted Fletcher, "The levels on the tape were always 6 dB above what anybody else would dare to do and [so] they were distorted. The mastering engineers at the time would criticize him and he wasn't very happy being criticized. He was a one-off professional and he had been around; he had done a lot of work for Radio Luxembourg and he knew what he was doing. He knew how [to do it] when it came to getting the sound 'out there.' They certainly never refused to master his records . . . but there was

Joe relaxing in the lounge.
(Photo by David Peters)

a lot of ill feeling. Engineers didn't like mastering his stuff. They thought that professionally it was just not good, not done, in the same sort of way engineers used to like the faders up the other way [where moving them back increased the volume, as in some older mixing consoles] and wear lab coats."

Denis Preston, founder of Lansdowne, once credited Meek with being "the first man to utilize distortion." While that might have been a bit of a stretch, there's no question that intentional distortion played an important role in many of his records, to the point where it became an indelible part of the fabled Meek "sound."

Another factor, of course, was the abundance of echo that permeated Meek's recordings. Fellow engineer Adrian Kerridge, who worked closely with Meek at both IBC and Lansdowne, comments that "Joe was an echo man. He used a lot of echo because it sounded commercial. In those days pop recordings didn't have a tight sound with artificial reverberation; they had a room sound with some echo. But Joe's approach was very tight, punchy, forward sounds with lots of echo and compression and limiting."

Meek himself, in a 1962 interview, explained that adding selective amounts of echo to different channels yielded "what I feel is a more commercial sound than to get the instruments to balance themselves in the studio." But Meek biographer John Repsch, perhaps used to taking the quirky producer's public pronouncements with a grain of salt, takes a slightly different view, saying, "In an effort to get a different kind of sound he would sometimes have a recording take place all over the house with perhaps the rhythm section in the studio, the singer in the living room, the choir in the bathroom, the brass in the bedroom and the strings on the landing and up the stairs, presumably in an effort to capture different natural room sounds on each." Singer John Leyton experienced this firsthand during the recording of his hit single "Johnny, Remember Me." "I was in the sitting room behind a little screen," he says, "[and] the rhythm section was in the room with me. [But] the violin section was on the stairs, the backing singers were practically in the loo, and the brass section was underneath, on another floor altogether, and there was Joe next door, playing his machine like another musical instrument."

Close-Miking

According to Ted Fletcher, Joe Meek was "fanatical" about separation. And the main way he dealt with the challenges of trying to achieve that while recording in a cramped space with minimal acoustic treatment could be summed up in two words: close-miking. In fact, according to Adrian Kerridge, Meek was solely responsible for introducing the technique in the U.K., although there are probably some engineers from the period who might take issue with that.

Nonetheless, it's fair to say he was one of the first to use close-miking on *all* the instruments being recorded, if for no other reason than that there really was no other option in the tiny 304 Holloway Road studio.

Yet even in Meek's IBC days, where he did have a decent-sized room to record in, Kerridge remembers Meek as embracing close-miking. "[Other] engineers would use one microphone suspended one and a half meters [approximately five feet] above the kit," Kerridge says. "[But] Joe would say, 'No! Right on the snare drum, right on the cymbals.' Other engineers would be frightened to do this." Adds fellow engineer Arthur Frewin, "[Meek] was the first man to take the front off the drums and put the mic inside the drums to get a drum sound so you get the impact on the skin the whole time. The drummers didn't like it because it meant them having to do some work."

Not so much the song as the sound

"JOE REALLY HAD AN EAR and a notion for the exact sound he wanted," says Jaywalkers lead guitarist Peter Miller, who remembers buying "every Lonnie Donegan record that was released" during the height of the skiffle craze, although it wasn't until many years later that he realized that it was Meek who had engineered some of the best Donegan records. "It was not so much the song as the sound, the tones, the groove," Meek once said of those recordings. "Of course I didn't know what producers really did at the time," Miller adds, "but later on I realized that they could imprint a certain identifiable sonic footprint."

The Jaywalkers' first experience with Meek was recording the song "Can Can 62" at Decca Studios with Meek producing, but, as Miller recalls, "Joe didn't get along with the Decca engineers because he couldn't get the sounds he wanted. [They] would not allow him to push the equipment beyond the limits into the distorting red zones, which was one of the secret ingredients to his unique sound." After that difficult session, Meek announced that he was only going to record the group in his own studio from then on.

"Our second single was 'Totem Pole,'" Miller says, "which we did in Joe's Holloway Road studio, but he didn't like the B-side that we'd prepared and decided that he wanted to do something else. So he sent the boys down to the pub and asked me if I would stay and write the B-side with him. I was fiddling around with the guitar coming up with lines, and a tune came together which we called 'Jaywalker.' It only took about 20 minutes or so. I remember at the time I was kind of surprised that he would let me get away with some of the bits I was playing—there were things on there which a Decca producer would probably have not accepted."

A studio as small as his could not be expected to accommodate more than a few musicians at a time, yet Meek routinely brought in string and brass quartets, as well as vocal "choirs" consisting of as many as four singers. "When I first started recording here," he said in one interview, "I used to get a lot of leg-pulls from the musicians, who are top musicians, often playing in, say, Mantovani's orchestra, and classical orchestras—really the cream of the musicians. They used to come in, look around, and say, 'Where do you want me? Am I supposed to be in the bathroom?' But after they've heard a playback, I don't usually get any more criticism. They realize what presence there is on their instruments, and that they've really got to be on form or it'll show up in the recording.

"The method I use for recording strings," he went on to explain, "is to have a microphone pretty close to them. The four of them sit two opposite each other, and then I delay the signal with the . . . Vortexion [tape recorder]. I feed this back in again which adds a reflection that gives you eight strings. On this, I put my echo chamber sound and also some of my electronic echo—this way I seem to get a very big string sound. The other instruments are recorded pretty ordinarily. I do add quite a lot of top to the harp, and a lot of echo on the French horn."

Other factors in Meek's never-ending pursuit of separation included the amount of damping and screening he used (mainly wooden screens and old army blankets), along with, in the case of bass and sometimes guitar, the use of direct inputs. The piano at Holloway Road was a player piano from which Meek had removed the roller mechanism, leaving plenty of space for a close microphone, so he probably would have just placed a microphone into the top of the body above the hammers and then closed the lid.

Creative Tape Editing

One of the most important tools in Joe Meek's production arsenal was the razor blade. Like many engineers

---

STORIES FROM THE STUDIO
Smile and the whole world smiles with you

ELICITING A GOOD PERFORMANCE from an artist is one of the biggest challenges facing any producer. In *Joe Meek's Bold Techniques*, musician Dave Adams—who also did the renovation work at the 304 Holloway Road studio—recalled something that Meek had his singers do: "[He would] insist that they smile while singing. It didn't matter if the song was the most miserable [one] you ever heard, the smile had to be there. Joe would know from the control room, without seeing the singer, whether they were in fact smiling or not.

"In retrospect," Adams continues, "I see that it was a way of getting the singer to articulate. Try mumbling with a smile on your face!"

---

of the era, he did a good deal of tape editing in the course of a day's work, but Meek came up with many creative uses beyond simply trying to patch together an acceptable track or splicing in short sections that had an abundance of overdubs (and consequent generational loss) so as to not reduce the overall sonic quality of the entire recording. For example, he would often record individual sections of a song (such as an introduction or a bridge) separately, so that he could apply dramatically different processing to each, and then join them together later—an eerie precursor to the way many songs are constructed in digital audio workstations today.

Meek was also heavily into tape loops. He'd splice together short sections of sound or musical phrases and then add them as effects. Ted Fletcher remembers that the pegboard in the 304 Holloway Road control room often sported "30 or 40 tape loops hung on nails, five or six loops per nail—all unlabeled." Another favorite trick of Meek's was to wrap splicing tape around the capstan of the tape recorders being used for delay echo in order to introduce "flutter" modulation.

SELECTED DISCOGRAPHY

- The Tornados: "Telstar" (single)
- The Honeycombs: "Have I the Right" (single)
- John Leyton: "Johnny Remember Me" (single)
- Mike Berry with The Outlaws: "Tribute to Buddy Holly" (single)
- The Packabeats: "Evening in Paris" (single)

5

OLYMPIC

The story of Olympic is truly a tale of two studios, one having its origins in a French sanctuary turned synagogue, and the other in a movie theater turned television production facility.

The story begins in 1957, when a nearly blind 24-year-old business impresario by the name of Angus McKenzie took a lease on an 18th-century West End house of worship known as Carton Hall, situated in Carton Street, near London's Marble Arch. Some years previously, McKenzie had purchased a modest "cut-your-own-disc" enterprise named Olympia Studios, based in Fulham, South London. But McKenzie had much bigger ambitions, and, with the aid of partner and electronics wizard Dick Swettenham, he planned to convert the much larger Carton Hall into a professional recording studio—in the process, changing the last letter in Olympia from an "a" to a "c," for a more majestic name: Olympic.

At around the same time, a student by the name of Keith Grant had decided to leave school and pursue his passion for music. Grant was dyslexic—an affliction about which little was known at the time—and his grades suffered as a result, though he was in fact brilliant and inventive, having already designed and built several pieces of audio gear while still a teenager. On his 16th birthday, he landed his first job, at the small Regent Sound Studios in London's Denmark Street, home to many of England's music publishers. (See *The Tin Pan Alley studios* in Chapter 8 for more information.) His employer quickly recognized the young boy's talents, and he was soon tasked with rebuilding the studio from the ground up, in terms of both equipment and acoustic treatment.

Word of his abilities quickly spread, and within a year Grant was poached by IBC Studios—London's most successful independent recording facility at the time. Under the tutelage of mentor Eric Tomlinson, he rapidly became one of IBC's top audio engineers, which in turn brought him to the attention of McKenzie and Swettenham, who were looking for just such an individual to attract clients to their newly opened Carton Street studio.

Within two years, Grant had been appointed manager of Olympic Studios and business began booming as artists and producers started flocking to the facility, which offered spaciousness (it could house a full symphony orchestra), superior acoustics (after being tweaked by Grant, that is), skilled engineers (including Grant himself, as well as Glyn Johns; even a young Gus Dudgeon worked there for a time as a "teaboy" before moving on to Decca and eventual fame as Elton John's longtime producer), and

advanced electronics, courtesy of Swettenham. The Carton Street facility was also equipped with a 35mm film projector, enabling it to take on jingle and television work as well as conventional music recording.

But in 1964, things took a drastic turn when McKenzie was informed that the Carton Hall lease would not be renewed—the landlords had decided to knock the historic building down to make way for an underground parking lot. It was Keith Grant who was given the job of finding a suitable premises for the second iteration of Olympic, and so begins the tale of the second studio.

The sedate but fashionable West London suburb of Barnes had long been a hub for artists, writers and entertainers. One of its most prominent buildings was Byfeld Hall, an Edwardian music hall built in 1906, situated in Church Road, just a stone's throw from the historic Bull's Head pub—one of the first and most important jazz venues in Britain. In the

Engineers Frank Owen (behind console) and Terry Brown at Olympic Studios in Carton Street, 1963.
(Photo by Phill Brown)

1930s, Byfeld Hall had become a movie theater, and in the late 1950s it was purchased by Guild TV and converted into a television/film studio.

By the time Grant paid his first visit to the facility, it had long fallen into disrepair. "When we found it, it would have made you cry if you'd seen what the inside of it was like," Keith told writer Matt Frost in a 2012 interview for *Sound on Sound* magazine. "You could see out of the roof! The floor was all up and the water had gone right through to the basement." But even through the dust and grime, Grant could see the potential in Byfeld Hall and duly made his recommendation to McKenzie that it serve as Olympic's new home.

However, disheartened by his failing sight, McKenzie had already made the decision to leave the audio industry, and in 1965 he sold his share of the business to Grant and bandleader/singer Cliff Adams. Following an extensive period of renovation, the new Olympic Sound Studios, now located in Barnes, opened its doors in late 1966. It became an immediate success, with rock royalty of the era—everyone from the Rolling Stones (who recorded there almost exclusively until 1971) to Jimi Hendrix, Led Zeppelin, the Eagles, even The Beatles—flocking to the facility. By 1969, a smaller second studio and a remix room had been added and an extraordinarily talented staff assembled, including soon-to-be-famous engineers Eddie Kramer, Andy Johns (Glyn's younger brother), George Chkiantz, Phill Brown, Chris Kimsey, Phil Chapman, and others. Olympic's status as one of the world's leading recording studios was sealed.

But, as they say, all good things must come to an end. In 1988 the business was sold to the Virgin Group—the same company (run by multimillionaire Richard Branson) that already owned competing studios The Manor and Townhouse. Shortly thereafter, Virgin management made an ill-fated decision to rebuild and redesign Olympic. In an ironic example of things coming full circle, Olympic Sound Studios was converted back to a cinema after its doors finally shut in January 2009.

KEY PERSONNEL

Recording engineers: John Timperley, Frank Owen, Roger Savage, Keith Grant, Terry Brown, Glyn Johns, Eddie Kramer, Vic Smith, George Chkiantz, Phill Brown, Andy Johns, Steve Vaughan, Alan O'Duffy, Keith Harwood, Chris Kimsey, Anton Matthews, Phil Chapman, Doug Bennett, Rod Thear, Jon Astley, David Hamilton-Smith, Nigel Brooke-Hart, Laurence Burrage, Toby Alington

Maintenance engineers: Dick Swettenham, Terry Allen, Jo Yu, Clive Green, Roger Mayer, Mick Mckenna, Les Harris, Hugh Tennent, Jim McBride, Dave Fromberg ("Smudger"), Jim Dowler, Clive Kavan

PHYSICAL FACILITIES

In his 2010 memoir *Are We Still Rolling?*, engineer Phill Brown recalls a 1964 visit to the original Olympic Studios, where his older brother Terry had been working for several months. He describes it as being housed in a "narrow, three-storey, bizarre-looking building . . . in a mews off Carton Street." (Terry Brown remembers that the mews was "lined with small apartments which in fact were converted garages or originally horse stables. Rumour had it that [the Duke of] Wellington stabled his team in that very spot.") After entering the main building via a small reception area on the ground-floor level, the two brothers headed for Studio One, which ran "the whole width of the building." (A 1965 industry listing gave the dimensions of the Carton Street studio as 40' by 40'.)

"The walls, ceiling and isolation screens," Phill Brown goes on to say, "were all covered in cream-coloured acoustic pegboard tiles," yielding what he termed "dead" acoustics. "In one corner," he continues, "there was a grand piano, a Hammond organ and a large collection of mic stands, cables and headphones.

"Down in the basement I was taken through a series of small rooms, including ones used for maintenance, tape copying and tape storage. All these rooms had un-plastered brick walls, painted white. Fixed to them (but not concealed) were all the audio, telephone, [and] electricity cables and air conditioning ducts for the offices and studio. It was an untidy and dirty area.

"On the first floor was the control room. This was set parallel to the studio and looked down into it. [*Note: In the U.K., "first floor" refers to the floor above ground level, equivalent to the second floor in the U.S.*] Like the studio itself, the walls were covered in off-white acoustic tiles. There were four large loudspeaker cabinets standing on the floor. . . . Immediately in front of [them] was the sound desk. . . . Cables and wires oozed from the back of the desk and disappeared into either the wall or boxes lying on the floor. To the left of the desk was a small window giving a restricted view down into the studio room. To the right was a small seating area for about three or four people. On the remaining wall and floor space were the large 4-track tape machine and a couple of 1-track mono machines, all housed in metal cabinets. Wires ran from these, connecting to a patch bay, amps and meters in metal cabinets on the wall. It all looked very dirty, with lighter patches on the wall where equipment had once been but was now removed, and there were badly worn areas of carpet, especially directly behind the desk."

"There was a reasonably sized control room at Carton Street," confirms former Olympic maintenance engineer Clive Green, who would go on to fame as one of the principal founders and designers of Cadac consoles. "It was upstairs looking down on the studio floor—a long room with a couch down one side and four loudspeakers on the other side of the desk. In a separate building across the mews was Studio Two,

The Rolling Stones in Studio One recording tracks for *Their Satanic Majesties Request*, 1967.
(Photo by Gered Mankowitz © Bowstir Ltd. 2015/Mankowitz.com)

where there was basic equipment for jingles and voice-overs, plus tape copying and editing features."

"The upstairs control room [at Carton Street] was a real pain," recalled Keith Grant. "It had all valve [tube] equipment, and because of noise problems, we had to have everything insulated heavily, so it was like a permanent sauna up there. There were probably 200 valves or more in the room, and bodies, and you couldn't even put a fan through to the outside world because it would let sound out. You didn't keep cool up there!"

Of his initial visit to the dilapidated former television studio in Barnes, Keith Grant would say, "All the walls were like a thick wodge of a mineral wool, which had chicken wire all over it and it was just nailed on the wall, and had been on there forever and ever and ever. It was thick with dust, and I mean, thick, thick dust! . . . Around the edge of [the room] was a gantry welded to

the wall, which was wide enough to get a camera and dolly to ride all the way round the studio."

But Grant's long-standing motto was that "nothing should ever get in the way of the music," and the long, difficult, and expensive renovation that was undertaken at Barnes was proof positive of his commitment to that principle. Staff engineer Eddie Kramer (in a 1994 interview with *Studio Sound* magazine) stated flatly that the reborn Olympic "was the finest studio in the whole of the world."

Engineer Phil Chapman, who joined Olympic in 1970, provides a vivid description of the layout of the Barnes facility. "As you came in, on one side was the reception area and accounts office," he recalls, "and on the other was a door to the basement. Directly ahead was a stone staircase, initially leading to a half landing from which you could continue forward to cross underneath Studio One to the other side of the

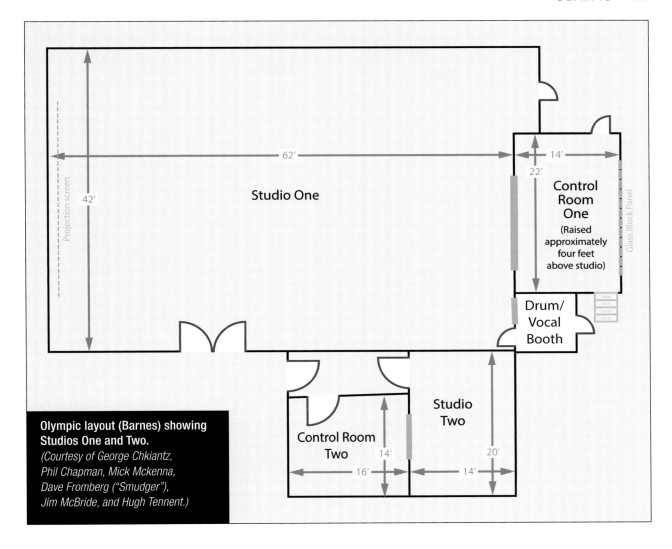

Olympic layout (Barnes) showing Studios One and Two.
(Courtesy of George Chkiantz, Phil Chapman, Mick Mckenna, Dave Fromberg ("Smudger"), Jim McBride, and Hugh Tennent.)

building, though you'd have to take care not to run or tread heavily if there was an orchestral session in progress. The staircase continued up to a stone landing where the large double doors to Studio One faced you. The canteen and Keith Grant's office was to the left, and a door leading up to [owner] Cliff Adams' office was to the right.

"The Studio One control room was raised approximately four feet above the studio floor; you could access it from the studio or gain direct access from the other side of the building, where Studio Three, known as the 'reduction room,' was located. Below that was the copy room, a room containing the echo plates, and the maintenance room, as well as another set of stone steps—great for recording drums—

leading up to the projection room situated above the Studio One control room."

Acoustic Treatments

Keith Grant once described the Carton Street studio as being "like a biscuit tin," adding that "it shouldn't have worked as well as it did. I was involved in the changing of the acoustics—it was a bit clattery when I got there," he said. "We had half-meter, triangular, square-based cones stuck all over the wall, full of mineral wool, and perforated fiberboard in lots of places. It was a very nice room and a lot of . . . records were made with no screens. You'd have strings, bass, choir, drums and everything in there at the same time, and they stood up acoustically. They didn't sound like a mess:

Burn, baby, burn

THE ROLLING STONES ENTERED Olympic Studio One in March of 1968 to begin recording their *Beggars Banquet* album—the last to feature founding member Brian Jones. It was reportedly a grueling process, made more difficult by the constant presence of a film crew. Yet under the steady hand of producer Jimmy Miller and engineer Glyn Johns, the all-night sessions were productive if somewhat chaotic. Assistant engineer Phill Brown recalls the room as having been "crowded [with] maybe 20 or 30 people at a time. There would be mountains of coffee cups, Coke bottles, roaches, and dog ends [cigarette butts], all of which had to be removed from the studio floor each morning when recording was done.

"We tried out every possibility when recording songs," he says. "'Street Fighting Man' was transferred [to multitrack] from a basic cassette demo of [guitarist Keith Richards']. Because of the limited selection of studio effects then available, sounds had to be created at the source, so we tried different guitars, amps, microphones, and various unusual locations in the studio building, including having [drummer] Charlie [Watts] play an African tom-tom in the stairwell."

"It was quite amusing sitting in the control room, looking down on the Stones sitting in a circle on a carpet playing their instruments, with this Philips 3302 cassette machine and its little plastic mic in the middle, Keith struggling with the rather fiddly joystick-like switch that controlled it," adds George Chkiantz, who assisted on some of the early *Beggars Banquet* sessions, with Eddie Kramer behind the board. "Once a take had been achieved," he continues, "the cassette recorder was taken into the vocal booth, put on top of a Lockwood extension speaker cabinet, and played back into a U67 positioned about a foot away. We'd EQ the signal from the mic a bit and record it on the 4-track. Unfortunately, on the final mix you can't hear much of this little mono 'starter' track, but all the real parts were added on top of it—something that was only possible, by the way, because Charlie Watts was one of the few drummers who could successfully overdub drums!"

On the evening of June 10, 1968, as Mick Jagger was recording the vocal to the song "Sympathy for the Devil," his then-girlfriend Marianne Faithfull was seen writing the words "Burn Baby Burn" in red lipstick on the control room window. It was a gesture that turned out to be strangely prophetic.

"Sometime later, in the middle of a take, there was a loud pop and I noticed Jagger look up to the ceiling and step to one side," Brown recalls. "Down floated a piece of burning paper, followed by some small pieces of debris."

Soon everyone in the studio was staring up at the ceiling, but it wasn't until flames began shooting out that the seriousness of the situation became apparent. "I began moving mics away from the area directly below the fire," says Brown, "while the Stones and their roadies and friends grabbed guitars and tried to remove amplifiers."

While Glyn Johns went down to the reception area and called the local fire brigade, producer Jimmy Miller remained in the control room spooling off the multitrack, with only one thing on his mind: preserving the precious tapes that contained nearly three months of hard work. Miller coolly instructed Brown to retrieve the other Stones tapes from the studio's tape library and to call him a cab. Within 15 minutes from the moment flames appeared, the producer was gone, with the tapes safely in his custody.

Once the building was evacuated, the young assistant stood across the road and watched the grim firemen battle the blaze. "There was a huge amount of smoke billowing into the air and a roaring sound that made conversation difficult," Brown remembers. "One of the fire engines was being used to spray water directly on to the roof." Olympic—part of a larger cluster of shops and flats— was now under direct threat from water damage as well as the fire.

When he was finally allowed to re-enter the building, Brown noted that the studio floor was covered in wet soot and dotted with fragments of charred debris. "More importantly," he says, "there was now a large hole in the roof through which the sky could clearly be seen." It was later determined that a lightbulb had set fire to the diffusing paper being used by the film crew, which had in turn set alight an acoustic panel and then the insulation in the ceiling.

The hole in the roof remained for the next week or two while the band put the finishing touches on the album, although Brown recalls that "we had to stop recording whenever a plane flew over." Eventually the tapes were taken to Sunset Sound Studios in Los Angeles for mixing, with the finished product released to critical acclaim and massive worldwide sales. Marianne Faithfull would, of course, go on to enjoy a long and successful career as a singer, though history does not record whether her abilities as a soothsayer were ever put to the test again.

A year later, the Stones return to Studio One to record *Beggars Banquet.*
(Photo by Keystone-France/Gamma-Keystone via Getty Images)

it worked and it all gelled very well together." Terry Brown, who engineered The Who single "Substitute" at Carton Street, concurred, stating that the room "had a great sound to it," though he adds that "miking Keith Moon's drum kit in particular was quite a challenge, because in those days we used three or four mics on a kit at most; so much of the sound was acoustically derived, as opposed to miking every individual drum."

Following the relocation to Barnes, Keith Grant recalled, "I totally got my own way with the studio, which was fantastic, and I brought in the people that I wanted to bring in, all of whom were amazing." One of those people was Grant's own father, renowned architect Robertson Grant. The acoustics for Studio One were designed by Keith and Russel Pettinger, and although it would ultimately come to be regarded as one of the best recording spaces in England, it

was not without its birthing problems, one of which involved the ceiling tiles.

"The tiles were meant to be 70 percent absorptive and 30 percent reflective," explained Grant, "but they went up the other way round [upside down]. When the roof was up,* we put this hard vinyl floor down, and when we tested the sound, we went, 'Oh, no!' but it was a bit too late to do anything. After about two or three weeks of trying to cope with how it sounded, which I hated, a dear friend of mine, Chris Hind, and I spent a whole weekend 20-odd feet off the ground in a sort of fireman's lift and we draped hessian cloth, which killed [the problem]." (*Note: George Chkiantz, who joined Olympic in 1966, does*

*The Barnes roof had to be filled with compressed straw to minimize the sounds of planes flying overhead, necessary since the studio was directly in the flight path leading to Heathrow airport, 11 miles away.

not recall there being draped hessian cloth; instead,
he states that an acoustic structure had been installed
in the ceiling that consisted of a 3 x 3 matrix of one-
meter cubes.)

The fire proved to have unintended consequences
in that the roof was later rebuilt with the tiles installed
correctly, not upside down. "It was a blessing in
disguise," said Keith Grant, "because we put the place
right and then it was just glorious."

There was, however, one other early error made
during the acoustic treatment of Studio One—a
problem that was quickly remedied by Grant and his
friend Chris Hind. "I believe a studio should have
no parallel surfaces, so if you've got two walls facing
each other, then you've got to make it so they aren't
parallel," Grant explained. "The way I did that in
Barnes was to use slats of wood, which should have all
been nailed in at different angles, but somehow that
hadn't been understood or taken on board. They were
all nailed flat, so you'd still got parallel surfaces. I was
doing so many other things at the time that I hadn't
noticed. So Chris and I went in one Sunday with a
crowbar and a hammer and just pulled them all out
on their nails and redid them. When [the studio] first
opened, I was very disappointed in the slap [echo]
because you could hear it in the orchestral stuff. I was
tearing my hair out. But once we fixed that, it was just
lovely. That was the end of the tweaking. The room
then worked with no secondary echo and just very
clean sounds throughout."

"It was quite an amazing space," Glyn Johns
wrote in his 2014 memoir *Sound Man,* referring
to Olympic Studio One. "Incredibly versatile. You
could record anything from a sixty-piece orchestra
to the loudest rock and roll band in there and
somehow it would adapt."

By 1968, a second studio (named Studio Two) had
been added to the complex at Barnes. Studio Three,
added in 1974, consisted of two separate, similar-sized
rooms (although the one that served as a control room
had slightly lower ceilings) connected by a corridor. It
was said to be a favorite of Pete Townshend, although
it was Studio Two that became unexpectedly popular
with rock bands after it was upgraded to 16-track—
so much so that its decor and furnishings ended up
being designed by none other than Mick Jagger.

According to George Chkiantz, Studio Two had
been purpose-built to accommodate rock groups, in
order to free up Studio One for orchestral and film
scoring work. However, in his 2012 interview with
Sound on Sound magazine, Keith Grant stated otherwise. "We never, for one second, imagined that the
groups would want to go in [Studio Two]," he said.
"It was opened for little jingles and things like [that]
. . . just generally quiet, sort of sedate, innocuous
sessions. But then the groups liked it and, of course,
that then presented no end of problems, like when
you've got 600 watts of guitar amp in Studio Two and
200 watts of orchestra in Studio One! We had to do
something about it, so we just bit the bullet and spent
the money."

Keith's father Robertson Grant once again came
to the rescue. "Dad saw the problem and went away
and thought about it and said, 'Oh, this is what we
do!'" said Grant. "He [redesigned] Studio Two as a
completely floating box, all on rubber pads, and the
steelwork [alone] weighed about 17 tons. When we
shut the door, you could put a rock band in there flat
out, and you wouldn't hear a thing outside. . . . The
new room was like a fridge on casters. It had its own
air-conditioning system and it worked—you really
couldn't hear anything next door. It was very impressive, particularly in those days, because that sort of
acoustic architecture hadn't really come into its own
in any way. People were lead-lining walls with the
hope of trying to stop some sound getting out of a
room, but Dad said, 'Oh no . . . we'll just float the
whole bloody lot!'"

Phil Chapman says that, while the problem
was largely ameliorated following the redesign,
"there were always separation issues between the
two [studios], especially if you had a big orchestral
thing going on in Studio One and the likes of Deep
Purple in Studio Two. We were occasionally asked
to turn down."

Eventually Keith Grant capitulated to popular
demand and decided to alter the sonics of Studio
Two so it could meet the needs of both rock bands
and jingle clients. Accordingly, he had his maintenance staff install rough sawn wooden slats—similar
to vertical blinds—which could be adjusted with the
pull of a cord to cover or reveal the sound-absorbing

panels behind, thus changing the acoustics of the room as needed. (According to George Chkiantz, the slats in Studio Two were an experiment, as the room was quite dead.) One corner of the studio floor was sectioned off with sliding doors to act as a drum/vocal booth.

The Studio Two control room also had its share of problems. According to Chkiantz, it "went through several phases as the geometry of the room kept on throwing up major acoustic problems. Finally, it was turned through 90 degrees and the desk lowered—it had been on a plinth and this had wreaked havoc with the bass end."

For all that, the acoustic treatment in the Studio Two control room remained minimal. "There was this purple pegboard everywhere," recalls Chapman, "but [no] baffles or bass traps. The space was configured according to how it best worked ergonomically. When they were redesigning the Studio Two control room, I noticed that there was a window behind one of the monitors and not the other. I remember George [Chkiantz] saying that the one that had the wall behind it used to reflect the bass better."

Room Dimensions

Barnes

Studio One: 62' x 42' (19 x 13 meters)
    Ceiling height: 28' (8.5 meters)*
Studio One control room: 22' x 14' (7 x 4 meters)
    Ceiling height: 8'6" (2.5 meters)
Studio One vocal/drum booth: 8' x 8' (2 x 2 meters)
    Booth height: 6.5' (2 meters)

Studio Two: 20' x 14' (6 x 4 meters)
    Ceiling height: 14' (4 meters)
Studio Two control room: 16' x 14' (5 x 4 meters)
    Ceiling height: 14' (4 meters)

Studio Three: 21' x 11'6" (6.5 x 3.5 meters)
    Ceiling height: 9' (3 meters)
Studio Three control room: 21' x 11'6"
        (6.5 x 3.5 meters)
    Ceiling height: 7' (2 meters)

*Maximum height of the pitched roof.

STORIES FROM THE STUDIO
Sometimes you just have to have Faith

WHEN ERIC CLAPTON, Ginger Baker, Stevie Winwood, and Ric Grech got together in early 1969 to form a new band called Blind Faith—dubbed the first "super-group," in recognition of the individual members' long pedigree on the rock scene—producer Jimmy Miller initially elected to record their debut album at Morgan Studios with engineer Andy Johns. However, by mid-spring, the project was moved to Olympic Studios, with Alan O'Duffy replacing Johns behind the board.

"We added a few more tracks [to the ones originally recorded at Morgan], and we did all the overdubs and mixing," O'Duffy recalls. "But one of the tracks [Winwood's 'Had to Cry Today'] was one of those nine-minute songs that's wrapped around a single riff. It wasn't exactly boring—there was some wonderful playing on it—but it was like a very long jazz record, so it did require some innovation in terms of the mix because it needed something to keep the interest going; it was just one of those tracks where you couldn't simply put the faders up.

"The question I was asking myself was: 'What can you do with what you have in order to make the mix as exciting as possible?' I was trying everything I could think of. I had already been using what [Pye engineer] Bob Auger called 'French echo,' where you put the sound of the voice out into the studio speakers and then record it on two mics in stereo, using the room ambience to add some space, and I was also playing with plate echo a bit, adding it in spots.

"But there was this point at around three or four in the morning where I had a mad idea, and it turned into something quite interesting. I got a handheld stage mic—a [Shure] SM58—and put it on a long cable, then I went out into the studio and used it to record the playback [of the entire track] from the speakers in mono, on a separate machine. And at a certain point in the song, as we got to the particular bit I wanted to get more exciting, I began spinning the microphone over my head, faster and faster. Then I went back into the control room and cut that section into the track." [*Note: This occurs between 6:41 and 6:51.*] The end result, as keen listeners will hear, went a long way toward adding to the sonic "vibe" of the track—proving yet again that necessity is often the mother of invention.

Echo Chambers

Keith Grant recalled that the Carton Street facility had "a basement with a vaulted cellar in it which we turned into an echo chamber." As was the fashion of the day, "we blocked it all up and put a speaker and a microphone in there."

There may have been one or two acoustic echo chambers at Barnes, although accounts differ. Keith Grant stated that one was "built into a disused stairwell approximately 1,400 cubic feet [in size]," with another one a "500 [cubic foot] unused oil tank with a speaker and two microphones, used for special effects."

George Chkiantz has no recollection of either, although, he is quick to add, "we used most of the stairwells and corridors at one time or another as 'echo chambers' and for other effects, mostly at night and under threat of disturbing the neighbors. There was talk of doing a proper conversion of one of the unused ones, but it was a fire escape route, and it also wasn't the best-sounding one," so apparently no such construction ever took place.

KEY EQUIPMENT
Mixing Consoles

Although the Carton Street studio was initially outfitted with the tube (valve) recording console from the original Olympia Studio in Fulham, by 1961 it boasted a transistorized desk custom-built by Dick Swettenham, who had joined Olympic as technical director upon its formation in 1958—a position he would hold for 11 years. That console—the first of a series of custom consoles specifically built for Olympic by its maintenance staff—is now widely considered to be the first professional solid-state mixing console in the U.K., and it would be used to craft hits for artists like Dusty Springfield, The Troggs, the Rolling Stones, the Yardbirds, and The Bee Gees. Clive Green, who would join Olympic's maintenance team in 1964, recalled that the Carton Street console was outfitted with germanium PNP resistors—mainly OC44s, according to George Chkiantz.

In *Are We Still Rolling?*, Phill Brown provides a description of the desk: "By today's standards," he observes, "[it] was extremely small and basic, with just 12 input channels. Each input had six large Bakelite knobs to control top, mid and bass EQ, feeds for the headphones and a track/record selector switch. In the centre of the desk were four round [PPM] meters and below these, four toggle switches to select monitors." Older brother Terry, who worked at Carton Street for more than a year, remembers it as being "an amazing-sounding console." Added Glyn Johns in a 1981 interview with *Studio Sound*, "There are some desks where, by pure fluke, it actually enhances the sound—Dick Swettenham's first desk at Olympic, for example."

In a 1982 interview, Dick Swettenham described the equalization circuitry in some detail: "Its character of sound, given mainly by the shape of the midrange curves arrived at empirically by listening tests, derived originally from the choice of particular inductors available. It could be switched to give a family of troughs in the midrange somewhat sharper than the peaks, thus enabling a few notes in the range of an instrument which stuck out too prominently to be reduced without sucking out too much of the midrange energy of the sound. The bass lift section, instead of the more usual shelf leveling continuing down to perhaps 40 Hz, was a broad peak boost, originally centered on 250 Hz, which fell back to a very small lift by 60 Hz so the hum and rumble were not exaggerated. Later versions [of the console] added a choice of bass peak frequencies."

The relocation to Barnes provided the impetus to create a new mixing console for Olympic, and this time, Swettenham was able to integrate the expertise of chief engineer Keith Grant. "Dick and I worked very well together," said Grant. "[His] wonderful attribute was that he would never be happy. He would make something and bring it to me to evaluate, and I'd listen to it and say, 'Make it just do a bit of this and a bit of that.' He'd take it away and he'd adjust it and he'd bring it back again and I'd go, 'Hey, that's really good, Dick. I like that!' But he'd take it away and adjust it again and you'd say, 'Now that's not as good,' and you'd have to force him to go back one stage. From the ears side, sometimes you can make things better, but they're worse technically, like third-harmonic distortion. He'd say, 'We can't have third-harmonic distortion!' and I'd say, 'But we love third-harmonic distortion, what are you talking about?'"

Beyond its extraordinary sound, the new desk installed in Studio One was the first to utilize a revolutionary "wraparound" design—something that was unequivocally Keith Grant's idea. "The problem with that first 'flat' Dick Swettenham desk, and the problem with most desks to this day," Grant explained, "is that if you want to do some things, you've got to stand up, go tweak, tweak, tweak, and then sit down again. I'm basically sedentary, which is a posh word for being lazy! But if you're adjusting an EQ, you want to adjust it from where you're sitting. You don't want to be standing up and moving four feet forward into the sound [field] while adjusting the EQ, because when you sit down it sounds different. So we designed the desk so everything was in your hands and you didn't have to move your head more than necessary."

This pioneering approach brought with it a welcome side effect, as Grant explained with a laugh: "The producer couldn't get on the desk! [He] couldn't get in your way and he couldn't get his hands on the board—although we did have a 'DFA' fader for the producer, at the very end [of the console]: 'That's yours, OK?' 'What's DFA?' 'That's yours, that'll work!'" ("DFA" is well-known British studio slang, an acronym for three words, the first of which is "does" and the last of which is "all." Readers may work out for themselves what the middle word is.)

Initially equipped with 16 input channels and four output channels, the Studio One console was upgraded to 24 x 8 in 1969 with the arrival of the studio's new 3M M23 8-track machine. The new desk offered direct outputs from each channel, patchable to the multitrack inputs, and a redesigned monitor section. Internally, the circuitry used Lustraphone transformers and germanium transistors—components that were the keys to the Olympic sound, according to maintenance engineer Jim Dowler.

It was an instant hit with both clients and with the engineers who sat behind the controls. Eddie Kramer would later claim it was "the best console in England, and possibly the world at the time." In another interview, he went on to say, "That console . . . was fantastic because it showed people what could be done with a very intelligently laid-out board. You could do panning and equalization and change levels all within a very small framework . . . right in front of

STORIES FROM THE STUDIO
Whole lotta drums

LED ZEPPELIN'S 1970 HIT "Whole Lotta Love" has long been revered by recording aficionados for its many pioneering aural effects, including pre-echoes, theremin-influenced guitar, primal vocals, and wild panning, courtesy of mix engineer Eddie Kramer. It also features an enormous drum sound, recorded by engineer George Chkiantz in Olympic Studio One.

"Management had installed our 16-track recorder in the small [studio, Studio Two] with hopes of luring rock bands in there and away from [Studio One], where we recorded mostly classical works and film scores," Chkiantz told the *Wall Street Journal* in a 2014 interview with journalist Marc Myers. "But

Jimmy [Page] chose the larger one [Studio One]—even though it only had an 8-track recorder. He wanted the extra space so the drums could be miked properly for stereo."

Added guitarist/producer Jimmy Page, "For the song to work as this panoramic audio experience, I needed Bonzo [drummer John Bonham] to really stand out, so that every stick stroke sounded clear and you could really feel them."

Chkiantz may have been a relative novice then, but he knew that what Page was asking for could not be accomplished using Olympic's traditional method of miking drums. So he simply invented a new way, as he explained to Myers: "I didn't mic the snare, since that would have re-

duced the size and space of the drum sound. Instead, I used a stereo mic on an 8' boom above the drums along with two distant side mics to give the tom-toms edge, and [an] AKG D30 positioned about two feet from the bass drum." Because the floor at Olympic was made of wood and not cement, Chkiantz also made the decision to place the drums on a platform about a foot and a half off the floor in order to minimize kit rumble transmission to the other microphones in the room, which had the added bonus of increasing the bottom end tremendously. The end result, courtesy of Messrs. Page, Chkiantz, and Kramer, is a studio masterpiece.

(*Reproduced by kind permission of the author.*)

British bluesman Alexis Korner in Olympic Studio One, Barnes. Note the raised control room window behind the piano.
(Photo by Estate of Keith Morris/Redferns)

you. You hardly had to move your hands further than nine inches to get anything done." George Chkiantz reports that he was able to adjust the two furthest-away knobs on the desk without moving from the central position, adding that Keith Grant would actually keep track of which knobs he had used and how often he had used them in designing the ergonomics of the desk.

Engineer Alan O'Duffy states that the console was "not a modular desk, although it was modular in construction . . . by the processing of the amps within it, it had a particular sound." Even rival EMI engineer Geoff Emerick complimented Swettenham's board after hearing Keith Grant's recording of the Beatles song "Baby You're a Rich Man" (done in Olympic Studio One), saying, "[It] was a totally different design than [EMI's consoles] and was capable of passing lower frequencies so there was quite a smooth bass sound." In the mid-1970s, after several refurbishments and upgrades, the original Studio One desk was replaced by a new in-house board, designed and built by maintenance engineers Jim McBride and Jim Dowler.

Studio Two was initially outfitted with the old 4-track mixing desk from Carton Street, revamped with sliding faders instead of the original quadrant faders. This was soon replaced by a new 24 x 4 mixing console hand-built by Dick Swettenham and his team in the basement workshop. It had two subgroups (effectively providing six outputs), plus two foldback and four post-fader echo sends. Monitoring was through four speakers fed by the tape tracks, and most patching was accomplished with ultraminiature pins instead of jacks. In the words of George Chkiantz, "It was just brilliant!"

Later, after Swettenham had left Olympic to form his own manufacturing company, Helios, Keith Grant duly commissioned him and his team to build a custom 18 x 16 desk for Studio Two—the first and only Helios console to be installed at Barnes. Jim Dowler points out that "the first generation of Helios consoles contained all silicon transistors," yielding a distinctively different sound from the germanium-transistor-equipped console in Studio One.

Nonetheless, the Helios became Phil Chapman's favorite desk at Olympic, in large part due to his discovery that increasing its mic gain could also increase line gain. He explains, "I was working with producers Tommy Boyce and Richard Hartley recording a doo-wop revival group named Darts. Tommy was a rather excitable American character who'd had success as a solo artist as well as co-writing and producing hits for The Monkees. We'd had hits with previous Darts recordings, featuring a heavy backbeat with a '50s-style treatment, but Tommy was becoming more demanding, wanting everything to sound louder than everything else. So during one of the rhythm track recording sessions, I added 10 dB to all the mic gains, but instead of outright distortion, the sound merely squared off and appeared to be much louder without any apparent increase in level—a peculiarity of that particular console. It was an effect not dissimilar to overdriving the leveling amplifiers used in cutting rooms. When the band came in for the playback, I turned up the monitors and watched with amusement the looks of disbelief. However, we used it, and from then on I was having to repeat the process. I even borrowed a rack of those modules to try in other studios!"

A 12 x 4 custom Swettenham-built desk (later updated to 24 x 4) was initially installed in Studio Three, the limited number of outputs presenting little problem since the room was used mostly for remixing. Also, in recognition of the fact that little or no recording ever took place in Studio Three, the desk had no mic amps. The EQs in the desk were similar to those in the Studio One console, but they offered greater frequency selection.

In the late 1970s, all the custom-built consoles at Olympic were replaced by Raindirk desks, though, according to former maintenance engineer Clive Kavan, the original Swettenham EQs were transplanted into Studio Three's Raindirk, where they continued to see good service for many years afterward.

Phil Chapman feels that one of the keys to Olympic's success was that "Keith Grant was always open to ideas, no matter how offbeat, hence everything was continually modified," including, of course, the studio's mixing consoles. For example, all of Olympic's custom-built desks were fitted with BBC-spec PPMs [Peak Program Meters] at a time when most other studios—even American ones—were still using VU meters. "Keith was adamant about having PPM metering," says George Chkiantz, "and with good reason. PPMs allowed the engineer to know how much he was pushing the tape in all circumstances, whereas VUs just sort of give you relative loudness. I would agree with Keith that that is what your ears are for."

"With things like percussion instruments," adds Chapman, "VU meters weren't fast enough to

register, so the tendency was that you would over-record them, but PPMs would register percussion accurately so you wouldn't overload."

Monitors

Tannoy Silver—The Carton Street facility monitoring was through a pair of 15" dual concentric Tannoys with 16-ohm voice coils. These units, later known as Tannoy Silvers, were extremely sensitive—some 3 dB/watt better than Tannoy Golds (which, according to Chkiantz, were given a trial at Olympic at one point but found to be lacking). They had their drive units specially angled to point at the engineer and were mounted in Lockwood cabinets. Following the move to Barnes, these monitors were installed in the Studio Two control room, initially hung on chains from the ceiling.

The exact make and model of the monitor amps used at Carton Street are lost to the mists of time, although they were certainly tube (valve). "I suspect at one time an old 30-watt/channel Westrex with meters on the front was used," says George Chkiantz, who also believes that the Avantics amplifiers initially installed in Studio One at Barnes may first have been used in Carton Street.

The Studio One control room originally had four Tannoy Silvers (later Reds, which were upgraded to Super Reds in the mid-1970s), arrayed across the top of the glass window overlooking the studio area and mounted in bass reflex custom-built cabinets, similar to Lockwoods. Interestingly, the four monitor outputs for the console in the Studio One control room were color-coded red, yellow, blue, and green: Red and green fed the left and right outside monitors (the main stereo pair), while yellow and blue fed the middle pair of monitors (used for film recording). It is not known whether each pair of monitors was identical or if there was any difference between the two pairs, other than their physical placement.

Studio Three was outfitted with a pair of Tannoy Golds in Lockwood Major cabinets, mounted on two-foot-high plinths. In Phil Chapman's opinion, Studio Three provided the most accurate monitoring

Studio Two control room, 1969.
(Courtesy of Phil Chapman)

of the all the rooms at Olympic. (For more information about the Tannoy Gold, see Chapter 1; for more information about the Tannoy Red, see Chapter 4.)

The amps powering the monitors in the Studio One control room initially were Avantic 30-watt models. In 1968, they were replaced by English-made Radfords. These were professional dual-channel 100-watt tube amplifiers first introduced commercially just a year previously, so they were state-of-the-art at the time. The Radfords were later modified to limit their output power because Keith Grant was worried that his engineering staff could have their hearing damaged by the rated power, in combination with the sensitivity of the speakers. (In George Chkiantz's opinion, Grant also wanted to reduce the chances of burning out speakers!)

Studio Two's control room went through a variety of power amps throughout the '60s and '70s. During

the period when the Carton Street desk was installed there, Quad II tube amps were employed, but they were deemed underpowered and so the Avantic amps from the Studio One control room were moved there once the Radfords arrived. Later, some "quite terrible" (in Chkiantz's words) homemade transistor amps were tried, along with a variety of other amps, including Quad 303s.

Studio Three started out with Quad 303s, later replaced by Leak TL50+ amps, which Chkiantz termed "excellent, though a tad underpowered for use in the studio."

Tape Machines

Ampex A350 (4-track)—"Keith [Grant] once told me that we used Ampex and other U.S.-made equipment so that American clients would feel as if they were in a familiar environment," George

Chkiantz reports. "Certainly he was after that trade." Accordingly, the Carton Street control room was outfitted with at least three Ampex A350 4-track 1/2" machines—cited by many as being the first 4-tracks in England. They were mounted in 19" equipment racks with the separate tube electronics underneath, complete with a big, yellowing VU meter in the middle—one per channel. The studio also owned 1/4" stereo and mono head blocks, as well as a 1/2" 3-track head block, each of which could be fitted to the A350s. The latter was used to play back 3-track tapes coming from other studios and to record classical music, using the American standard of the time, in which a left-center-right concept was used for recording before mixing to two-channel.

Other tape machines at Carton Street included two stereo Telefunkens (possibly M5s) and an EMI BTR2. (See Chapter 1 for more information.) The copy room was outfitted with Philips Pro 51 machines that could, in the words of George Chkiantz, "wind tapes so fast that you could get long static sparks jumping between the reels." Chkiantz also recalls a French-manufactured Tolana tape deck that had been used at Carton Street. "It had piped (!) oil lubrication from a central reservoir to the motor bearings," he says, "and it was made in the late 1940s. It freaked out [fellow assistant engineer] Andy Johns that it was older than he was and, as I often teased him, in somewhat better nick!"

Ampex AG330 (4-track)—Following the move to Barnes, the Studio One control room was initially equipped with an AG330 4-track—a machine described by George Chkiantz as a "slightly upgraded AG300 with transistor electronics"—four rack-mounted units above the horizontal deck. (The Studio Two control room inherited two of the Carton street AG300s, with the third one floating as a "portable" 4-to-4 reduction machine.)

3M M23 (8-track)—Just two short years after the relocation to Barnes, 8-track recording became the de facto standard in the U.K., and so the Ampex AG330 4-track in the Studio One control

room was replaced by a 3M M23 1" 8-track machine. According to George Chkiantz, this was purchased specifically because of Keith Grant's confidence that its "Isoloop" drive could keep the wider 1" tape flat on the heads, especially since those decks were derived from 3M's computer drives, which had given the company experience in dealing with wider tape. Chkiantz's recollection is that the M23 was never as solid as the Ampex machine it had replaced: "Every so often, the logic board would weld up its relays and the deck would try to go into rewind and fast-forward at the same time!"

Phill Brown remembered the M23 as being "a monster. It resembled a six-foot-high, floor-standing cooking stove on casters, with . . . large, illuminated transport switches in different colors. There were polished metal arms to prevent the tape from snagging, glistening rollers, a brass capstan, and a hum guard that closed over the tape heads. There were rows of switches marked Record, Playback and Sync, and pots marked Record Level, Playback Level and such. Most obvious of all were the eight backlit VU level meters with their needles jumping erratically as the tape was played." (See Chapter 1 for more information.)

3M M56 (16-track)—By the mid-1970s, all the studios at Olympic had gone 16-track. Scully dual-head 2" 16-track machines (possibly Model 100s) were initially installed, but they had their problems. "They had very tricky tape handling," recalls George Chkiantz, "but if you could get them to behave, they were probably the best-sounding machines we had." Nonetheless, the Scullys were soon replaced by 3M M56s. (See *Decca* in Chapter 2 for more information.)

3M M79 (24-track)—By the late 1970s, Olympic went fully 24-track and replaced its 16-track M56s with 24-track M79s. The new machines presented a number of challenges to the Olympic staff. "The relays that switched from record to play to sync had tiny pins on them, so they sometimes fell out when you switched modes," reports Chkiantz. "The transport logic was better than the M23, but still screwed up from time to time. Worst of all, the heads started to wear after six weeks or so. At £3,000 a head this was no joke!" (See *Decca* in Chapter 2 for more information.)

Ampex 351 (2-track and 1-track)—There were a number of these at Olympic, eventually supplanted by Philips EL3501 2-track and 1-track machines. (See Chapter 4 for more information.)

In addition, all three studios at the Barnes facility were outfitted with Revox A77s, used for delay and flutter echo effects (through the use of controlled feedback). The Revoxes were also supposed to be used to delay the sends to reverb plates, but according to George Chkiantz, the Ampex 351s were more usually utilized for that purpose because of their superior sound quality. The copy room was equipped with a pair of Studer B62s, eventually replaced by Studer B67s.

Main Microphones

Neumann U67/SM69—The Olympic mic cabinet boasted a large number of tube and FET (solid-state) U67s, as well as an SM69 (the stereo version of the U67, with the capsules mounted above one another; the top one could twist through 270 degrees, and both had adjustable patterns). Phil Chapman described the tube U67s in particular as being the studio's "main all-purpose mics," preferred sonically to other mics in the cabinet, although he recalls that "they would occasionally 'fry,' which would be troublesome to identify and replace on a large orchestral session." (See Chapter 1 for more information.)

Neumann U87—Olympic also had a number of FET U87s. According to Anton Matthews, they were "the standard fare that we used for almost everything . . . a stereo pair of U87s were usually placed above the orchestra to do film music." "As a general rule, they were always used for strings," adds Phil Chapman. (See Chapter 1 for more information.)

Neumann U47—(See Chapter 1 for more information.)

Telefunken ELA M250/M251—These were sometimes used at Olympic for vocals. (See *Decca* in Chapter 2 for more information.)

Neumann KM54 and KM84—Keith Grant stated that Olympic boasted a "vast collection" of these small-diaphragm condenser microphones (the KM54s were tube models). Both microphones were cardioid-only; according to a Neumann catalog of the era, the directional characteristic of the KM84 was "almost independent of frequency," so that "a sound source that moves in a three-quarters circle around the microphone will therefore be recorded with constant tone quality," making it a good choice for drum overheads and for miking musicians with a propensity to fidget a lot. (See Chapter 1 for more information.)

Neumann KM86—Olympic had four KM86s. Phil Chapman recalls using them on strings "for a smooth, slightly muted sound." George Chkiantz often used KM86s for backing vocals. (See *CTS / The Music Centre* in Chapter 3 for more information.)

Neumann M49—(See Chapter 1 for more information.)

AKG C12/C12A—Olympic had only one C12 but numerous C12As. Originally released in 1964, the C12A was a large-diaphragm condenser microphone widely recognized as being a cross between an iconic tube C12 and a standard AKG 414. It offered both omnidirectional and figure-of-eight polar patterns and incorporated a peculiar device known as a "Nuvistor." (First introduced in 1959, these precursors to solid-state electronics were actually small vacuum tubes—mostly triodes—encased in thimble-sized metal cases.) The C12A was advertised as having "exceptionally low distortion" as a result of the Nuvistor.

Nonetheless, George Chkiantz disliked the C12As specifically because of what he terms the "dread" Nuvistor. "The C12As would suddenly start to whistle, and you had to flick the casing of the mic to stop them," he explains. "You learned to avoid putting them on high booms! They also had the most maddening hinge arrangement, which meant that they would slowly droop from where you set them unless you could succeed in taping the lead to the stand to try and keep them pointing in the right direction." (See Chapter 1 for more information about the C12.)

Keith Grant behind the famous wraparound console in the Studio One control room, posing for a 1975 publicity still with the group Jigsaw and arranger Richard Hewson.
(Photo by GAB Archive/Redferns)

AKG C24—There were two of these at Olympic, which George Chkiantz describes as being "very warm and rich-sounding." (See *IBC* in Chapter 3 for more information.)

AKG C451—This cardioid small-diaphragm condenser microphone with a distinctively airy sound was AKG's first FET microphone. It was introduced in 1969, and an acoustically similar version continues to be marketed today, albeit with updated electronics. Switches on the mic body provide -10 and -20 dB pads, as well as a 12 dB/octave high-pass filter that can be set at either 75 or 150 Hz.

The 451 was actually part of a complete system of snap-on small-diaphragm condenser microphone capsules that could be interconnected with various preamps and accessories (such as a pop filter for use on vocals, which made it look like a small ball mic), making them extremely versatile. Available capsules included two different cardioid models (one with a "shaped" rising high-frequency response of +6 dB at 10 kHz), as well as hypercardioid, omnidirectional, and figure-of-eight polar patterns, plus both long and short shotgun designs. The C451 was extremely bright-sounding, but it also imparted a bit of warmth and had a tight, well-defined low end. It was typically used wherever good definition of high frequencies was desired, such as drum overheads, and on strings, piano, and acoustic guitar. However, because it tended to distort at higher sound levels, the C451 was unsuitable for close-miking drums and guitar amplifiers.

AKG D12—D12s were often used at Olympic as percussion mics and occasionally for kick drum if the more popular D30 was unavailable. (See *Lansdowne* in Chapter 3 for more information.)

AKG D20—These were sometimes used at Olympic for kick drum. (See Chapter 1 for more information.)

AKG D25—Acoustically identical to the AKG D20, this dynamic cardioid mic "looked like a D20 in a [shockmount] cradle," in the words of Phil

Roger's big scream

ANTON MATTHEWS, who frequently assisted Glyn Johns at Olympic, has a clear memory of recording [Who singer] Roger Daltrey's oft-copied-but-never-duplicated scream at the end of the band's seminal track "Won't Get Fooled Again"—and of how the momentous session began with just a casual conversation. "One morning Glyn said, 'I've got something else on today, but Roger's coming in, so could you just put a microphone up and get him to scream?'" Matthews recalls. And so the session began.

"It was amazing. I used a [Neumann] U87, not close-miked because I knew he was going to shout loud," Matthews explains, "and I remember that it was recorded in Studio One. It was an extraordinarily electric moment because Roger had psyched himself up so much for it, he didn't have to practice. He did two takes, both of which were used in the final mix...and then he went home hoarse. He literally couldn't speak after he'd done it!"

Chapman. It was generally the second choice of Olympic engineers for kick drum if the AKG D30 (see below) wasn't available.

AKG D30—Said to be the first multipattern dynamic microphone, the D30 was manufactured in limited quantities exclusively for the European market between 1958 and the early 1960s. Dual internal capsules allowed its use in omni, figure-of-eight, and both front and rear cardioid polar patterns, with a selectable bass rolloff at 50 Hz. At Olympic, D30s were used on tubas in orchestral sessions. A D30 was also reportedly the only kick drum mic ever used on Rolling Stones and Led Zeppelin recordings made at the studio; in fact, according to Phil Chapman, Glyn Johns would *always* insist on using a D30 for kick drum—and so, therefore, would most of the other engineers there!

AKG D224—These were widely used by Olympic engineer Keith Harwood as an "all-purpose" mic. (See *Pye* in Chapter 2 for more information.)

While one might expect that rugged dynamics such as the AKG "D" series would be the mics of choice for drums, apparently that was not the case at Olympic. George Chkiantz reports that he, as well as Keith Grant, Glyn Johns, and Eddie Kramer, "always or nearly always" used condenser microphones on drums, sometimes even on kick drum. "Using dynamics on drums would probably have been a good idea in theory," he says, "but they didn't have the sound we were after."

STC 4038—According to Phil Chapman, these ribbon mics were used at Olympic for French horns and "not much of anything else." George Chkiantz points out that they were somewhat eclipsed by a couple of prototype BBC ribbons at Olympic called PGDs (the precursors of the PGS/4038s). "These were wonderful oval brass devices we used for trumpets in orchestral settings but could be surprising in many other ways," he says. "You had to be careful, though, as the ribbons were very easily broken and difficult to replace." (See Chapter 1 for more information.)

Beyer M160—Olympic had several of these ribbon microphones, which were said to be favorites of Eddie Kramer. (See *Pye* in Chapter 2 for more information.)

Outboard Signal Processors

Reportedly, the Carton Hall facility was well stocked with outboard signal processors, most of which were retained and rehoused in Barnes. The specific models are unknown, although it is probably safe to assume that some of the older gear listed below (e.g., the Pye compressors and the Pultec equalizers) falls into that category.

The Barnes location, however, definitely offered the following in the way of outboard gear:

Moving the wraparound console out of Studio One in preparation for the installation of the new board, circa 1975. Left to right: Recording engineer Phil Chapman, maintenance engineer Jim Dowler, and maintenance engineer Jim McBride.
(Courtesy of Phil Chapman and Jim Dowler)

Pye compressors—According to George Chkiantz, these solid-state compressors "sliced up the waveform at high frequency and reduced the energy in the signal, a bit like a light dimmer. They worked well as long as the switching frequency didn't bleed through." (See *Pye* in Chapter 2 for more information.)

Pye limiters—Each control room at Barnes was equipped with one of these solid-state limiters. (See pages 252–253 for more information.)

ADR F600—Advertised as having "minimal" overshoot, these stereo limiters were aimed primarily at the broadcast market. They used a diode bridge gain-changing circuit and offered six fixed attack times and nine fixed release times, as well as continuously variable input and output attenuation. A year or two after the Barnes facility opened, four of these were added to each control room.

UREI 1176—There were several 1176s at Olympic. (See *Decca* in Chapter 2 for more information.)

Pultec equalizers—Olympic owned four of these classic tube equalizers: Two HLF-3Cs, which were mostly used for telephone effects or for removing unwanted subsonics, vocal "pops" or hiss; and two EQP-1As, which were revered at Olympic for their broadband low- and high-frequency boost (especially in the 60 Hz and 16 kHz ranges),

which exceeded the equalization capability of the Swettenham-built boards. (See *Decca* in Chapter 2 for more information.)

EMT 140 plate reverbs—There were either four or five of these (accounts differ) in the Olympic basement, meaning that if the echo needed changing, in Phil Chapman's words, "we had go on a trek down there to adjust the wheel manually," although Studio Two was equipped with a remote control, which made such a journey unnecessary. According to Chapman, most Olympic engineers would set their echo at around of three or four seconds, but he typically preferred shorter delay times, which would allow him to use more echo in the mix without muddying the sound. (See Chapter 1 for more information.)

EMT 240 Gold Foil—Olympic was one of the first English studios to install an EMT 240. (See *Lansdowne* in Chapter 3 for more information.)

AKG BX20—Olympic owned one of these spring reverb units. (See *Decca* in Chapter 2 for more information.)

STORIES FROM THE STUDIO
Birth of the Drawmer Gate

"THE KEPEX GATES we used at Olympic were great, but [even at their fastest release time setting] they always had an audible decay when they turned off," says Phil Chapman. It was something which the engineer always found a bit frustrating. "I used to physically switch the echo plate on and off to try and get this sound I heard in my head but could not accomplish with the Kepexes."

That changed in January 1980 when Chapman found himself recording a Sheffield band called The News with co-producer Jon Astley. "I got chatting with the keyboard player, who had this very strange-sounding and strange-looking organ. I said, 'Where did you get this?' and he said, 'Oh, I made it myself,' which really impressed me." The keyboardist's name was Ivor Drawmer and there was no doubt as to his technical skills. "Bit by bit, I got him to make me a gate," Chapman recalls. "I said, 'Look, the thing is, the Kepex keeps decaying. I just want it to turn off.' So he made one for me and, although Ivor was quite skeptical as to its usefulness, it was just what I needed to fuse the reverb into elements of the drum sound. I introduced him to our maintenance guy, Jim Dowler, who saw the potential of it, and that is literally how Ivor got started with his first product [the Drawmer DS201 Dual Noise Gate, released commercially in 1982]. He made one for me, and I was so pleased with it, I ended up using it on everything. He also put in a sidechain input so that I could control the frequencies that the gating was applied to."

"Without doing any research I [initially] built this thing that switched on, held for a certain amount of time and then just switched off," Drawmer writes on the company's website [http://www.drawmer.com]. "In practice of course it was no good at all, so I then spent some time going around studios looking at how gates were being used. What really surprised me was how long engineers spent fiddling with gates trying to get them optimally set up and I realised very quickly that a better design was needed." The DS201 effectively transformed the noise gate from what had previously been a simple "on/off" device to a powerful creative tool which even today—in both its vintage hardware and modern software plug-in configuration—plays a significant role in production. "It was the kind of unit that people discovered uses for and it immediately enabled engineers to do the things they'd always dreamed of with minimum fuss," says Drawmer. And it all came from a chance meeting between a young engineer at Olympic and an equally savvy keyboardist from Sheffield.

Altec 436C—First introduced in 1966, the 436C was capable of automatically reducing gain up to 30 dB. It offered 2:1 and 4:1 compression ratios, as well as variable input level and release times (from .3 to 1.3 seconds), with a fixed attack time of 50 milliseconds. Olympic owned several of these tube level-controlling amplifiers, frequently used on guitar. (See Chapter 1 for more information.)

Allison Research Kepex noise gates / expanders—Short for "Keyable Program Expander," Kepexes were widely used at Olympic to reduce noise, minimize leakage, tighten guitar and drum sounds, take the squeak out of bass drum pedals, remove excess cymbal ring, and increase overall dynamic range. They were renowned for their responsive (though fixed) attack time, which allowed them to impart a smooth sonic footprint without dulling the signal.

Another key, and unique, outboard signal processor at Olympic was Keith Grant's homemade Leslie speaker emulation. This was an eight-inch speaker in a box facing upward into a plywood deflector panel that rotated on a spindle driven by an electric motor and an elastic band. The speed could be varied by changing the drive pulley—a black Bakelite knob from the Olympic collection of useful bits and pieces. "Sadly, the bearings tended to squeak," comments George Chkiantz, though oil helped somewhat. "Eddie [Kramer] and I used it frequently on Hendrix and Traffic recordings; it worked especially well in the corridor under Studio One, though obviously this could only be done late at night." Grant's invention was retired when the studio purchased proper Leslies, which presumably had non-squeaking bearings.

Other outboard equipment in the Olympic arsenal included various Teletronix and Helios compressor/limiters, plus, in Phil

Chapman's words, "this funny square wave modulator that George [Chkiantz] sometimes inserted on vocal tracks to add grit and make them almost growl. I remember him using it to great effect on Noddy Holder [lead vocalist for the band Slade], giving him a kind of Robert Plant sound." Several engineers also recall using a Fairchild 660 compressor at Olympic, though it is uncertain whether it was owned by the studio or rented as needed.

Film Equipment

According to Clive Green, even the original Carton Street facility had film projection capabilities. "We had a 35mm projector and did a lot of commercials for television," he explains. "We didn't have a screen in the studio—there wasn't room—but Dick Swettenham designed an adapter so we could use a CCTV camera and TV monitor instead." Keith Grant described the projector at Carton Street as being "really beat-up, ex-army. . . . We had a full-time staff projectionist because we were doing so much jingle work. We also did no end of television work. The BBC used to use us a lot, and ITV used to use us a lot."

From those primitive beginnings came full-fledged film facilities once Olympic relocated to Barnes. As Keith Grant explained in a 2010 interview with journalist Mike Collins, "Olympic was one of the few major recording studios [that] treated film music seriously. . . . There were 2 x Gaumont Kalee 35 mm projectors in a specially constructed projection facility capable of projecting a 35' image in [the] room where the orchestra assembled. . . . The screen was used for recording music to film, live!" (There was a 32-foot-wide screen permanently installed on the wall of Studio One.) "Our film projection was excellent," says

Phil Chapman behind the new Studio One control room mixing console custom-built by maintenance engineers Jim McBride and Jim Dowler, 1977. *(Courtesy of Phil Chapman and James Harpham)*

STORIES FROM THE STUDIO
A little wah-bongo

PHIL CHAPMAN CREDITS fellow engineer George Chkiantz as instilling in him the philosophy that "you could modify things in an unorthodox method; that you didn't have to follow standard procedure."

Nowhere is this influence more apparent than on the 1972 recording of Wings' version of the traditional nursery rhyme "Mary Had a Little Lamb," with Phil Chapman assisting producer/engineer Glyn Johns. "Paul [McCartney] always entertained everybody's input during recording sessions, and for some ridiculous reason I suggested we put the bongos through a wah-wah pedal," Chapman remembers with a smile. "Paul just said, 'Oh, OK,' and Glyn [Johns] was fine about it, so we went ahead and did it, with me operating the pedal by hand in the control room. I'd put other things through a wah-wah pedal before, so I thought, 'Why not? Maybe it'll sound like one of those funky guitar things.' I remember being really pleased that one of my ideas, simple as it was, had found its way onto a Paul McCartney track!"

The Glyn Johns 3-mic drum recording technique.
(Courtesy of Kore Studios, www.kore-studios.com)

KEY TECHNICAL INNOVATIONS
The Glyn Johns Drum Miking Technique

Of his famously spartan approach to drum miking, engineer Glyn Johns once said, "The principle behind it is that it allows the drummer to express his own dynamics in what he's playing. At the same time, the idea is to capture the sound that's unique to him, as all great drummers tune their kits in their own particular way."

Chris Kimsey, who often assisted Johns on sessions at Olympic, describes the three-mic technique this way: "The two main mics were usually Neumann valve [tube] U67s set to a cardioid polar pattern. [*Note: According to Johns' 2014 memoir* Sound Man, *U47s or Telefunken 251s would sometimes be substituted.*] One would be directly over the drummer's head, about three feet high, looking down into the gap between the snare drum and the rack tom-tom. The second mic was placed on a smaller stand at the side of the floor tom, about three feet high, and it would be angled so that it was not only looking at the floor tom, but at the snare as well. The two mics would be roughly equidistant to the snare and would yield an extreme left-right image with the snare in the middle. The bass drum mic, panned in the center, was always an AKG D30, positioned about a foot away. The front skin of the bass drum was generally left on, but that depended on who the drummer was."

One byproduct, says Kimsey, was that "there was sometimes a phase problem between the two main microphones, which actually gave the sound something quite special, kind of like an increase in the

George Chkiantz, who remembers watching *Fantasia* there in stereo (after a hasty mod to the audio heads on the projectors). "We were equipped with two 4-track magnetic film recorders and several mono machines, all of which could be run in sync. This meant that we had a theoretical 8-track or more facility at Barnes right at the outset, although it was only really used in this way for film work, as overdubbing would have been problematic and expensive."

Notable film soundtracks recorded at Olympic in the '60s and '70s include *The Prime of Miss Jean Brodie* (1968), *The Italian Job* (1969), the movie version of *Jesus Christ Superstar* (1973) (the original cast album had also been recorded at Olympic four years previously), *The Rocky Horror Picture Show*, recorded in Studio Two in 1975, and *Monty Python's Life of Brian* in 1979.

width of the stereo image." (Johns normally panned the two main mics half-left and half-right.)

It was a technique that worked best with skilled drummers, according to Kimsey, "because the balance of the drums was determined by how the drummer would hit the drums, and by the balance between the cymbals and hi-hat, and especially that of the hi-hat and the snare drum."

One last point: In his memoir *Sound Man*, Glyn Johns is quick to correct a myth about this drum miking technique that has arisen over the years. "Contrary to popular belief, I have never used a tape measure," he writes. "It is not that precise, it is just a matter of using common sense and believing it will work, making small adjustments depending on the kit, the balance the drummer is giving you, and what he is playing."

Phasing

They say that most innovation arises from creative accidents, but phasing is one studio effect that came about through meticulous planning.

It was June 14, 1967, and The Beatles, along with producer George Martin, were in Olympic Studio One to record the backing track for the song "All You Need Is Love," which would be performed semi-live on television—the first global satellite broadcast ever—11 days later. The engineer assigned to the session was Eddie Kramer, assisted by a young tape op who had already developed quite a reputation as a technical wizard. His name? George Chkiantz.

"At some point that afternoon," Chkiantz recalls, "George Martin asked us to put an effect on John Lennon's voice which they had used at EMI—something called ADT. He described it to us, but we couldn't figure out how to do it with the equipment we had. He said not to worry, that they could always add it later when they went back to EMI [for the final mix], but I can tell you that learning that EMI had an effect that we didn't know how to do was something that did not go down at all well with us.

"At the time, I was interested in getting more interesting tape delay effects than just the usual 15 ips echo, so I had been mucking around with various combinations of tape recorders after hours to see what I could come up with. I realized that the reason we couldn't get ADT at Olympic was because we were using Ampex 4-track machines, not Studers. The Studer J37s they were using at EMI had separate amps for the sync [record] head, with an output that bears some resemblance to the actual input signal. Ampex machines didn't do that; for a variety of reasons—mostly good ones—their record heads made for very poor playback heads.

"In order to get past this problem, I had been feeding signal from the record heads into other Ampex machines we had, then using their playback head amps, which required moving machines around and doing a fair amount of rewiring. I was forever trying to get past the falling frequency response of the Ampex sync head, and I'm glad to say with some success, but I would spend a good hour lining the electronics up to get the best signal I could. Fortunately, all Ampex head blocks were standard head gap, to a relatively high precision, which meant that the delay between the record head and playback head on the two machines—that is, the offset between the signal playback on the delay machine versus the original machine—was pretty much exactly the same.

"We'd long been wanting a variable speed mechanism for our 4-track machines so we could adjust pitch and speed, so after the 'All You Need Is Love' session, I persuaded Dick Swettenham to pursue this, which he did. He got ahold of something that I think had been a disc cutting amp at one stage—it was a very old valve [tube] amplifier which looked like something out of a Frankenstein movie; it was built on a five-foot rack and had mercury vapor rectifiers. We put it in a tiny room off the tape copying room so no one would be in the vicinity when it was on, because of the amount of UV the mercury vapor was producing. In order to get varispeed, we had to use this laboratory signal generator which had a very slow, smooth vernier knob on it and then run this huge long mic lead down the corridor to go into this room with the amplifier, then loop the signal going there into a 'mains' feed coming back, from a 100-volt line transformer, like the kind they use in theaters to distribute sound to speakers. It was a monstrous setup [and] everyone knew when we were using it because there were these spooky flickering lights coming from around the door!

"Nonetheless, one of the things where we fell lucky—luckier than EMI, I think—was that the Ampex had quite a heavy flywheel which didn't respond to the varispeed very quickly, so there was a kind of inertia which smoothed out the speed changes. As a result, you'd have to anticipate the sweep a bit, and it was really quite tricky doing that."

One afternoon, Chkiantz finally achieved satisfaction. "I thought I'd come up with something that sounded absolutely brilliant, and as it happened, [engineer] Glyn [Johns] had come in early for a Small Faces session. I buttonholed him and said, 'Hey, you've got to hear this,' and he was suitably impressed. Later that day, we were mixing the song 'Itchycoo Park,' and all of a sudden Glyn turned around to the band and announced that I'd come up with this swooping kind of phasing effect and would they be interested in using it on the track. I sort of went numb because I'd figured out how to apply the effect after the fact, but I wasn't quite sure how to apply it during a live mix. I had tried it out once or twice and discovered that it was one thing applying the effect to a stereo master that's already been mixed; it was quite another thing to get it to work while some poor soul—in this case, Glyn—was trying to mix a track, because he wouldn't want to be hearing it a head-gap delay later. So I knew that getting the effect in real time would be difficult.

"But the Faces were up for anything, and they had heaps of roadies who were quite happy to move heavy machines around and Glyn said he'd manage, so we raided the studio next door and grabbed its 4-track. It was quite a lash-up, but it worked absolutely beautifully and we all went off happy.

"The next night, I was off but I heard that [Faces manager] Andrew Loog Oldham had come in to have a listen. He decided he loved the effect we'd put on 'Itchycoo Park' but hated the mix! He said to Glyn, 'Well, can't you remix it with the effect?' And Glyn—many thanks to him—said no. He said, 'I don't know how to do it, and even if I did I wouldn't tell you. So you can bloody well wait until George comes in tomorrow.' Glyn was always very good about things like that.

"Then of course the next major step was using the effect on the Jimi Hendrix track 'Bold As Love,' only this time instead of phasing in mono, we did it in stereo. In essence, this doubled or quadrupled our problems, in terms of having all that many extra machines to deal with. There were a lot of grim faces at Olympic that day—even Keith [Grant] was saying, 'Look, don't keep moving the machines all the time because sooner or later, you're going to break something'—many of the machines had valves in them. But nothing ever did break.

"Eventually we came up with much simpler solutions, and the advent of 8- and later 16-track machines made it easier if you had a spare track or two, and of course specialist boxes were developed by various manufacturers. After that, the effect took off like wildfire. However, there is still nothing that sounds quite like the original with the above setup. But I can't deny that phasing probably wouldn't have happened if it hadn't been for George Martin asking for ADT—that's what got things stirring. Mind you, it wasn't like they came in and told us what to do and we did it—it was us picking up on something they suggested and developing it into something quite different."

Compression Blending

The technique of blending a highly compressed signal in with an uncompressed one to precisely achieve the desired amount of dynamics processing has long been used in recording studios on both sides of the Atlantic. But according to engineer Terry Brown, it was an idea that originated with ever-inventive Olympic owner Keith Grant. "Keith was always coming up with great ideas," says Brown, "and I often assisted him, watching his every move. He was a wonderful teacher!

"The first time I saw that done was on a session with Keith at the original Olympic in Carton Street in 1964. Clive Green had invented these really cool little light-emitting diode-type compressors, and they worked really well—they had a huge sound to them. In those days, we were generally working in mono even though we had a stereo console, so we only needed the left side. Keith would strap this compressor of Clive's across the right side of the stereo bus and adjust the amount of compression by lifting that fader until he got the sound he was looking for. I thought that was a very clever usage of that technology—and it was a technique that we used often at Olympic, to great effect."

"I think we've got their hearts beating now!"

KEITH GRANT was as renowned for his eccentric dress sense and proclivity for practical jokes as he was for his formidable engineering skills and devotion to his craft. Engineer David Hamilton-Smith elaborates: "Keith loved to play jokes and was always up for a laugh on his sessions. Yet beneath his joker's exterior lay a consummate professional who cared deeply about how good something could sound. To judge Keith Grant by his clowning was to totally misunderstand the man. Physically he was big, with a shock of black curly hair and beard. When I first met him, he reminded me of Bluto from the Popeye cartoons—but this Bluto had a mind like a steel trap!"

Indeed, many of Grant's exploits have reverberated throughout the annals of session lore. One tale that is oft told is the saga of an argument he had with violinist Patrick Halling over the placement of a microphone during an orchestral session. In a fit of rage, Grant threw Halling's violin—well known to be a priceless Guarneri—to the floor and jumped on it, smashing it to bits, to the shock and horror of the other members of the orchestra. Of course, the instrument Grant destroyed was a cheap copy he had switched for the Guarneri, and Halling was in on the gag . . . but it had the desired effect of loosening up the stuffy musicians and leading to an inspired take.

Hamilton-Smith has an equally outrageous Keith Grant story to tell. "We often used to set up Studio One the night before a morning booking," he explains, "particularly if it was an orchestral session. In those days a great many bands wanted to emulate The Beatles and overdub orchestra or strings onto their tracks. [On this particular evening,] Keith asked me to set up for 16 strings.

"Normally, this would take up a small area of the studio, since Studio One was capable of accommodating a full 82-piece orchestra, rhythm section, and choir. "However," Hamilton-Smith recalls, "on this occasion Keith specified that he wanted every player in each 'desk' (two violinists who would usually be sitting side by side) to be at least six feet apart. This spread the 16 players all over the studio.

"We knew that Keith always had a good reason for doing what he did, and we never queried anything until we had a good idea of why he had done something—otherwise we would be sent away with a smile to 'work it out' [for ourselves]. Often only when we were getting close would he reveal the secret behind his methodology. So I set the studio up and went home, my mind racing.

"Could it be something spatial? Perhaps because the musicians were spread all over the studio, more of the wonderful Studio One room sound would get recorded. But I dismissed this theory.

"Could it create a bigger stereo image in the mix? Again, I felt I was reaching.

"Did this setup allow for more control over the levels and placement of each player in the recording? On and on, I struggled to find the technical answer. [By] the morning I was chomping at the bit to find out why Keith had ordered this peculiar configuration.

"It was a 9 a.m. start. I was there, as usual, an hour beforehand to double-check the microphones, the foldback for the players, the music stands, the ashtrays (yes, horror of horrors, most musicians smoked in the studios in those days!) and the conductor's rostrum, and to make sure that all the extension leads were taped to the floor so no one tripped over them. At about 8:30 a.m., the musicians began to turn up. By nine o'clock all the musicians were sitting, albeit a bit bemused, at least six feet apart, ready to play, and the conductor was looking at his watch in expectation.

"At that moment, the huge double doors to Studio One opened and in came the big man himself—on the smallest electric mini-motorbike you have ever seen! It was one of those kids' bikes that he had found in a skip [dumpster] and had rebuilt—something he enjoyed doing to player pianos, generators, mixing consoles, and anything mechanical or electrical. His mass of black curls wafting in the breeze he was creating, he proceeded to zoom up and down, in and out and all around the musicians, who were frantically trying to rescue their precious violins from becoming roadkill. Sheets of music and music stands went flying.

"Keith finally braked to a stop in front of the control room window and said to me, 'Close them up, David. I think we've got their hearts beating now!'

"So much for my technical conjecturing," Hamilton-Smith concludes. "It had simply been Keith's way of having some fun whilst at the same time injecting some energy into the session musicians so that they played with more gusto!"

Keith Grant to the rescue

"TO BE SURE, I saw the lighthearted side of Keith," says Chris Kimsey, who began his career at Olympic in 1967, "and how he could relate and help the artist-producer relationship, and he did teach me the Boy Scout method of being prepared for everything. But there was one wonderful moment where Keith really saved my bacon."

It occurred while the Rolling Stones were in Olympic recording their *Sticky Fingers* album. Kimsey had been assigned to assist engineer Glyn Johns, "maybe for the second or third time."

"Glyn and [producer] Jimmy Miller had been in with the band one evening," Kimsey recalls, "and at the end of the session, at around three o'clock in the morning, Glyn said, 'I need to make a safety copy of the "Wild Horses" multitrack.' I said, 'Fine, I'll do it now so it will be ready for you tomorrow.'

"So everybody left, and it was just me in the building. I set up the 8-track master tape in Studio One to play back, and I was going to record the copy in what was called the reduction room, at the other end of a corridor. There was quite a walk between the two rooms, so I had to run down to the reduction room, lace up the tape and start it up, then run back to Studio One and press play on the master machine, then run back down to the reduction room to listen to the copy as it was being made.

"I'm sitting there listening to the copy and everything is going fine, but then after a couple of minutes, the sound stopped and I heard this odd noise. I thought, 'That's weird; I wonder what's happening there.' So I went back to Studio One and found that because the take-up spool on the master machine was slightly bent, it had gotten stuck, and the tape had wound itself around and around the capstan motor until it couldn't wrap itself any more and stopped.

"There was a good two minutes of the song wrapped around those capstan motors; I thought I was go-ing to die. I started carefully peeling the tape off, and I was still at it at six in the morning, when Keith came in, because he had a very early jingle session that day. He saw me sitting on the floor with this distraught look on my face and this pile of creased tape all around me, and he said, 'What's happened here?'

"I explained, half-expecting to be given the sack [fired], but he said, 'Don't worry—there's an iron down-stairs and some tea towels. Just take the iron and set it to very low, put some tea towels between it and the tape, and iron it out, then play it through for a couple of hours and it will be fine.' I said, 'Really?' He said, 'Yeah.' And it was!

"That was Keith's whole attitude about everything: There's nothing you can't fix. If microphones went down or something went wrong during one of his sessions, he always found a way to circumvent it and keep the energy going. He was truly one of a kind."

Optical Compression

"Keith was an innovator," Clive Green said of Olympic's chief engineer and designer. "He used to love getting me to build odd bits of equipment, particularly compressors. He was always experimenting. Sometimes I'd say, 'How about it, Keith? How about this?' and he'd say, 'Well, that's a good idea, go and see what you can find and make it work!' He was always interested in different sounds and different ways of creating sounds.

"When Olympic was located in Carton Street," he continues, "the only commercial compressor on the market at the time was the Fairchild, but it used valve technology and was very expensive. VCAs [voltage-controlled amplifiers] didn't exist at all in those days, but you could buy something called a light-dependent resistor (LDR) and the cell had a particular resistance, and, if you shone a light on it, the resistance would go down. So if you used it in a piece of analog circuitry with a lightbulb whose intensity varied according to the audio going through it, you'd get a very effective compressor. And the advantage of using a compressor like that is that the beginning of the sound gets through before it starts to compress, so it produces a very nice sound, though you couldn't use it as a brick wall limiter because it was far too slow."

The optical compressor Green built for Keith Grant turned out to be the first of its kind devel-oped in the U.K. for studio use. "Initially, we used a small car sidelight as the light source and a small 10-watt transistor amplifier to drive the bulb. The big problem was that the filament was slow to act on the

LDR, and also the LDR was slow to change its resistance. This made for a slow attack time but allowed the initial transient to get through before compression started, something that was generally desirable. You could, however, improve that by bleeding current through the filament to keep it warm and thus make the response time faster. LEDs, which came along later, had a much faster response time, since you didn't have to wait for a filament heating up in a bulb." Materials played a role in the sonics as well. "The standard LDRs available at the time were made using cadmium sulfide," adds Green. "It was not until cadmium selenide became available that the response time become much faster."

According to George Chkiantz, Clive Green's optical compressor was used frequently right through the mid-1970s for a variety of effects. He also credits Green's invention as providing some of the "backwards" sounds in the Beatles song "Baby You're a Rich Man," recorded at Olympic in May 1967.

KEITH GRANT, VISIONARY, 1941–2012

As a designer, Keith Grant built one of the finest recording facilities in the world. As an engineer, he recorded nearly 120 Top 20 hits, including Procol Harum's "Whiter Shade of Pale," still one of the most widely played tracks on the radio. But it is Grant's legacy as a human being that will endure.

"One great thing about Olympic was that nobody kept secrets, particularly on the recording side," he once said. "If anybody found out how to do something, everybody was told. When George Chkiantz discovered how to do phasing on 'Itchycoo Park,' everybody knew about it the next day, everybody! And the same with miking an orchestra up, the way you set up the studio, EQ settings and echo settings. Everybody shared ideas and there were no secrets.

"The camaraderie there was of the highest. The way it worked was that if you weren't needed, you didn't have to work, and if you were needed, you did have to work. It was a straightforward deal. You might have to do a hundred hours this week but next week, you might go home and we'd pay you anyway! And

if you were needed to help somebody else, it wasn't a question of 'Oh, that's not my job.' We'd all get stuck in. I'd go and make the tea. It worked like that right across the board. . . . We all were equal and nobody was actually in charge. You knew what you had to do and you did it."

Phil Chapman states flatly that "what made Olympic unique was that the staff had complete freedom. We were free to try out any creative idea, no matter how harebrained. There was no such word as 'can't' in Keith's vocabulary." Adds George Chkiantz, "As Keith often said, nothing was allowed to get in the way of the music. I don't recall any session ever being canceled for a technical reason. We just kept on working, 24 hours a day, seven days a week."

Keith Grant left Olympic in 1987, shortly before it was purchased by Virgin, who would, to his considerable dismay, completely redesign and rebuild the entire Barnes facility. In his retirement, Grant worked closely with ex-Olympic maintenance engineer and close friend Jim Dowler in a venture to market the original modules from the original Studio One and Studio Three desks designed and built by Dick Swettenham, repackaged in a "lunchbox" format. He also set up one last studio, this one on the grounds of his home at Sunbury-on-Thames. In his last years he doted on his family and spent considerable time on the River Thames in his skiff *Boozer*.

And to the very end, the twinkle in his eyes never dimmed, not once.

SELECTED DISCOGRAPHY

- Rolling Stones: *Beggars Banquet*, *Let It Bleed*, *Sticky Fingers*
- The Beatles: "Baby You're a Rich Man" (single)
- Jimi Hendrix: *Axis: Bold As Love*, *Are You Experienced*, *Electric Ladyland*
- Led Zeppelin: *Led Zeppelin*, *Led Zeppelin II*, *Led Zeppelin III*, *Houses of the Holy*, *Physical Graffiti*
- Blind Faith: *Blind Faith*
- Emerson, Lake & Palmer: *Brain Salad Surgery*
- The Who: *Who's Next*

6

TRIDENT

rident was as much a philosophy as a recording facility. "I'd opened the studio thinking it could be something very different to the antiseptic, almost laboratory atmosphere of Abbey Road and the other big studios," wrote founder Norman Sheffield in his 2013 memoir *Life on Two Legs*. "People there wore white coats and behaved like boffins. It sucked the creative life out of artists. From the outset I'd wanted Trident to be a place where musicians could be free to express themselves. I wanted a different vibe."

It was Sheffield's background as a musician himself that shaped his unique (for the time) view. An ex-drummer who had enjoyed moderate chart success with the '50s and early-'60s instrumental band The Hunters, Norman had even played at one point with teen idol Cliff Richard, most notably during a live television performance at the London Palladium in 1958.

But with a family on the way, life on the road was no longer practical, and so, with his wife, Chris, Norman Sheffield opened a music and record shop in the north London suburb of Waltham Cross. Soon thereafter, he hired younger brother Barry, who had been developing technical skills as a television repairman, and they began getting involved in local music promotions, organizing various dance hall gigs and booking major artists such as The Who and The Animals. At around the same time, Sheffield began getting commissions to write music for television commercials.

In the process of gathering an inventory of records and musical instruments for sale, the shop had begun acquiring a rather impressive collection of secondhand recording equipment, and so Norman and Barry set up a makeshift control room in the upstairs office, with audio tielines running downstairs to the main showroom so that local musicians could come in and record during off-hours.

By 1966 it became apparent that the enterprise had outgrown its space, and so the Sheffield brothers began to cast their sights further afield. Initially they planned to stay local, but the ambitious Norman was drawn to the West End—particularly the Soho district, long considered the creative hub of London and home to many film postproduction facilities and editing suites, as well as famous music venues like the Marquee Club.

And so began a long search for suitable premises, one that eventually led to a disused engraving works located at 17 St. Anne's Court, an alleyway tucked away between Wardour Street and Dean Street, in the very heart of Soho.

It had to have been dispiriting at first. "The crumbling interior of the building was like something out of a Dickens novel. I half expected to find Oliver Twist and the Artful Dodger hiding in the shadows," Sheffield would recount some 35 years later. "The air was filled with the smell of damp and stale urine. It looked as if someone had ripped the place apart. There were bare walls and exposed floors, lead acid tanks, a furnace, and cables and trunking hanging down everywhere. . . . It was a bloody sorry sight.

"But," he is quick to add, "it was exactly what I was looking for. The more I looked at the building the more it felt artistically right. It was a place where—for a century or more—men had done intricate, creative work. That had to be a good sign, I told myself."

With brother Barry in agreement as to the building's potential—despite its rather shocking state of disrepair—a lease was obtained and renovation begun. The brothers' plan was to create a double-height facility, with the studio at basement level and the control room above it—something that necessi-

St. Anne's Court in London, with the Trident entrance on the right.
(Courtesy of Justin Sheffield)

I wanted to do the same thing [at Trident], create a situation where the artist and the producer weren't staring each other in the eye all the time. I knew from personal experience that this was intimidating, and restricting for performers. I wanted to give the artist more space, both literally and psychologically." Of course, this wasn't an entirely new design approach—there were similar setups at Abbey Road's Studio Two and Olympic's Studio One, among others, and the trend would continue in other British studios to come, but in this case it clearly was an extension of Norman Sheffield's core philosophy.

Construction of the 5,000-square-foot facility, including building an in-house film preview theater, took more than a year and required both Sheffield brothers to mortgage their homes and cede a controlling interest to an outside investor. Yet Norman Sheffield remained unfazed. "From the outset," he wrote, "I knew that two things were crucial if this venture was going to succeed. First, we had to go for broke and create something big. But I also knew that it had to be a place that encouraged musicians to be creative."

Trident Studios, which opened in March 1968, remained true to that vision and quickly became one of the most successful recording facilities in the U.K. Trident's fate was sealed on July 30, 1968, when The Beatles, reportedly unhappy with both the vibe at Abbey Road and the studio's inability to provide anything more advanced than 4-track recording, arrived at St. Anne's Court to lay down Paul McCartney's composition "Hey Jude," with Barry Sheffield behind the board. It was the group's first 8-track recording,

tated ripping up the entire ground floor. Amazingly, the landlords agreed—provided the floor was reinstated when the lease expired.

"The idea of having a setup where the control room was on a different level to the artists was already central to my thinking," wrote Sheffield. "It had worked at the shop—more by accident than design.

and one which would of course become a massive worldwide hit. The Fab Four would return to Trident in the coming months to record numerous songs that would appear on the *White Album*, including "Dear Prudence," "Honey Pie," "Savoy Truffle," and "Martha My Dear," as well as the backing track to John Lennon's emotionally cathartic "I Want You (She's So Heavy)," which would close side one of the group's *Abbey Road* album.

In the following year, mastering (disc cutting) and tape reproduction facilities were added, along with a separate remix room. Sheffield explained the thinking behind the latter this way: "I had begun to see the recording process as being similar to the film industry, where they shot the movie on location or in a studio and then edited it in a different building. I was trying to introduce the same principle, recording in the studio downstairs, [then] moving the tape facilities upstairs to a room with the same acoustics and equipment—with a small adjacent room [vocal booth] for adding extra instruments or vocals—as well as some new toys to complete the recording. This room would also allow us to double the studio's output and look after two clients at once."

Throughout the late '60s and 1970s many major artists would make Trident their home away from home, enjoying the creative freedom that the studio allowed. The star-studded list includes Elton John, David Bowie, Marc Bolan, James Taylor, Supertramp, Genesis, and Queen—a band managed by the Sheffields who were granted unlimited "downtime" to record their first two albums. Under Norman Sheffield, Trident's business interests expanded into console manufacturing (see *Mixing Consoles* below) and video production (see *Trilion Video* below).

In December 1981 Trident was sold to a consortium of ex-staffers and former clients, including drummer/DJ Rusty Egan. For several years afterward, the studio continued to operate under different names. In 1993, new owners made radical changes to the building at 17 St. Anne's Court, creating a larger double-height studio and control room (now both situated in the basement), with the original control room reduced in size. The facility remains open today under the name The Sound Studio, focusing primarily on film and video postproduction.

KEY PERSONNEL
Recording engineers: Barry Sheffield, Malcolm Toft, Ken Scott, Robin Cable, Roy Thomas Baker, David Hentschel, Mike Stone, Neil Kernon, Ted Sharp, Dennis Mackay, Peter Kelsey, Nick Bradford, John Brand, Stephen W. Tayler, Steven Short, Adam Moseley, Chris Stone

Maintenance engineers: Ron Goodwin, Barry Porter, Peter Booth, Henri Edwards, Barry Spencer, Bernie Spratt, Piers Plaskett

PHYSICAL FACILITIES
17 St. Anne's Court was a narrow six-story building tucked into an alleyway off Wardour Street. Visitors arriving at Trident passed through a heavy wood-paneled glass door into a lobby area, with the reception desk to the right and steps to the left, leading downstairs to the main studio and upstairs to the remix room, offices, and kitchen. Directly behind reception was a short staircase leading to the control room.

The entrance to the studio was at the narrow end, with Trident's celebrated Bechstein grand piano usually situated just beyond the door, though it was on wheels and so could be moved to other areas if desired. Beyond that and off to the left was the famous men's toilet (often used as an echo chamber), directly off the studio floor. Although there was a moderately dead drum booth underneath the control room, drums were sometimes set up in the far side of the room, in what was the most acoustically live area. Behind the drum booth was a mic cabinet and a room that housed the studio's two EMT reverb plates. Ambient mics were often placed on boom stands raised high up in the ceiling rafters, allowing engineers and producers to successfully capture the excellent room sound. "The studio at Trident was long and narrow," reported Chris Thomas, George Martin's assistant, who was present at the "Hey Jude" session. "When we did the orchestral overdub we had to put the trombones in the very front so that they didn't poke anyone in the back!"

Trident was unique, too, in that its tape machines were initially housed not in the control room itself, but in a separate machine room, controlled remotely—another Sheffield brothers

**John Lennon and Yoko Ono
in the Trident machine room, 1968.**
*(Photo by John Reader/The LIFE Images Collection/
Getty Images)*

control room, and so they were duly moved and the machine room was thereafter used for storage.

During the period when the tape recorders were housed in the machine room, the control room was spacious enough to accommodate full rock bands and their sometimes sizable entourages—another feature that drew popular artists to Trident. The 20 x 8 Sound Techniques mixing board originally installed in the control room was small enough to be positioned sideways, with the left edge facing the window looking out over the studio floor. The second Sound Techniques board and the later Trident A-Range were also installed at right angles to the window. In fact, one of the core design specifications of the original A-Range was that it had to fit into a five-foot space, because that was the maximum size that the Trident control room could accommodate. This necessitated a remote patch bay set into the wall. After the control room was extended in the late 1970s, its new TSM console, which was quite a bit larger than the A-Range, was installed lengthwise, parallel to the glass window.

The remix room, opened in 1969, was located on the second floor (in British parlance, the "first" floor). It was initially outfitted with the 20 x 8 Sound Techniques desk originally used in the control room downstairs, eventually replaced by an early 28 x 24 Trident TSM (see *Mixing Consoles* below). One unusual feature of the remix room were the overhead outboard racks mounted in a wooden frame directly above the console, and thus within easy reach of the engineer, who could access the collection of most-used outboard gear installed there without having to leave the sweet spot—a clever use of available space not dissimilar to the cockpit layout of a modern jet plane. Similar racks would eventually be built above the mixing board in the main control room as well.

innovation. "We had two trains of thought here," Norman explained. "First, we wanted to remove the distraction of the tape machines turning over while the musicians were playing, and secondly, we wanted to reduce the number of bodies in the [control room]." By the late '70s, however, it had become apparent that in the interest of improved communications (particularly during overdubbing and tape editing), greater efficiency could be achieved if the tape recorders were housed in the

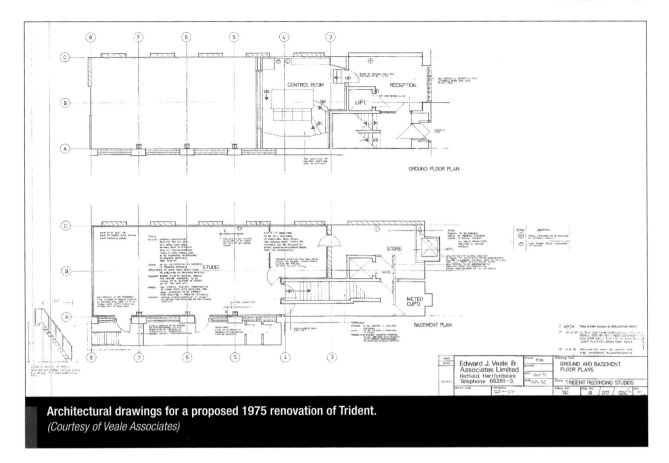

Architectural drawings for a proposed 1975 renovation of Trident.
(Courtesy of Veale Associates)

One additional bonus of the remix room was that its back window overlooked a number of small flats rented by the hour to neighborhood ladies of the night, complete with the obligatory red lights in the windows and curtains that were rarely drawn. Clients with a tendency to interfere in the early stages of a mix were often introduced to this window, where they might be treated to a show that would keep them distracted until the producer and mixing engineer were ready to receive input.

Acoustic Treatments

The acoustic treatments at Trident were created by Sandy Brown, who was the top acoustic designer at the BBC at the time. In consultation with the Sheffield brothers, he opted to have most of the studio carpeted to provide absorption, along with a smaller live end fitted with hardwood floors and polished cork tiles on the plastic-coated plasterboard walls.

Difficulties soon presented themselves in the form of next-door neighbors who operated rostrum cameras bolted to an adjoining wall, causing loud vibrations. This was dealt with by constructing a false wall two inches inside the original.

Like other recording facilities of the era, sound absorption and diffusion was largely accomplished by a large number of wooden strips nailed to the highly absorbent material that lined the walls of both the studio and control room. (See Chapter 5 for more information.)

"Even though it had fairly high ceilings," producer Tony Visconti recalls, "Trident was not an especially live room; it had a tight, controlled sound. All the studios of the era were like that; no one was interested in the artifacts of a room sound. Everything was dead and in your face—the close-miked snare drum with a tea towel over it. That was the philosophy of recording in those days."

"You could put your ear to that grille and know what the next George Harrison single was going to be"

TONY VISCONTI IS CANDID about his favorite recording trick at Trident. "It was the men's room," he says with a laugh. "Trident was unique in that, right off the studio floor—literally ten feet from where you would position a singer—there was a men's room. It didn't take long before I realized, 'Wow, this is a good acoustic space'—a real shortcut to a very live sound, and far superior to any echo plate setting. So instead of creating echo artificially, I'd literally have the artist record in the men's room. As a bonus, it was so conveniently located, the cables would easily reach in there.

"As early as 1968, I was recording T. Rex in the men's room. On 'Ride a White Swan'—the group's first hit single—the handclaps and tambourine were done there. Eventually we put Marc Bolan's guitar amp in there, miking it both up close and a short distance away, and when he would crank it up, the reverb was just glorious! Not only was it nice and short—under a second—but the tile and pipes and all those hard, reflective surfaces gave it a great sound, too. I can't tell you how many times we put musicians or amps in there. Sometimes we would just leave the door open and stick a mic in there so we could catch some drum ambience. It was a great alternative to the studio's two EMT plates, which were the only other source of echo available at Trident in those days."

The extensive use of the toilet as an alternate recording space did, however, lead to some difficulties with the local merchants, though it also provided a bonus to avid music fans wandering the Soho streets. Visconti elaborates: "Unfortunately, the men's room vented to a grille that led to the street. People walking by couldn't figure out where the sound was coming from, but at times it was pretty loud. The owner of the corner sandwich shop often used to complain about how we were chasing away his customers. This was actually a little surprising, given that the bathroom door was usually partially open and there was often loud drumming going on in the studio, which wasn't completely soundproofed anyway, so something was always going out into the street. You could put your ear to that grille and know what the next George Harrison single was going to be!"

Room Dimensions
Studio One: 30' x 18' (9 x 5.5 meters)
    Ceiling height: 20' (6 meters)
Studio One control room: 18' x 12' (5.5 x 3.5 meters
    Ceiling height: 8'6" (2.5 meters)

Studio Two: 20' x 16' (6 x 5 meters)
    Ceiling height: 8'6" (2.5 meters)

Echo Chambers
Although there was no dedicated acoustic echo chamber at Trident, the men's toilet was often used in that way. "It was a tiled room just off the studio [floor]," wrote Norman Sheffield, "and it gave us the perfect, almost metallic sound we wanted." In fact, the men's room was so frequently used for echo, by the late 1970s microphones were permanently installed there—sometimes to the chagrin of those who used the toilet for its intended purpose.

KEY EQUIPMENT
Mixing Consoles
From the very outset, the Sheffield brothers were determined to equip Trident with the best recording gear available, including, of course, a state-of-the-art mixing console. Through the grapevine they had heard of a company called Sound Techniques, which had a studio in Chelsea (see *Sound Techniques* in Chapter 8 for more information). Like many studios of the era, Sound Techniques built its own desks, but with a difference: The company's consoles were not just for use in its facility, but were made commercially available as well—even to rival studios in London.

The Sound Techniques desk initially installed in the Trident control room was a custom board with 20 inputs and eight outputs, considered quite advanced for the time. In common with other Sound Techniques consoles of the era, it incorporated transistorized mic and line amplifiers and used hand-wound transformers for both input and output. It was renowned for its clear sound and low distortion, as well as its smooth clipping even when overdriven.

However, shortly before it was delivered, Norman Sheffield discovered that the desk was housed in a steel-and-aluminum frame, something that raised his ire. "I hated it," he wrote. "It reminded me of the monstrous machines you find at the BBC or EMI. I wanted our studio to feel softer, warmer, and less robotic than that. So I asked Lockwood—the company that was making our [speaker cabinets] . . . to create a teak veneer outer casing for the desk." And so a trend was started, one that continues to this very day—housing mixing desks in custom-built wooden frames.

In preparation for the upcoming installation of a brand-new Ampex 16-track recorder (see *Tape Machines* below for more information) the original board was replaced in late 1969 by a larger Sound Techniques model that offered 16 outputs. (The original 20 x 8 desk was moved upstairs to Trident's newly opened remix room.) However, this board proved to be unreliable and by 1972, staff engineers had begun lobbying for new console. The problem was that the features they wanted were not offered by any of the mixing boards available from the manufacturers of the era. Enter engineer Malcolm Toft, newly promoted to the position of studio manager.

Norman and Barry Sheffield at Trident's opening night party.
(Courtesy of Justin Sheffield)

"I'd always been interested in what went on under the hood," said Toft in a 2009 interview with *MIX* magazine. "From my early teens, I'd built little consoles and messed around, always interested in putting stuff together. I always thought my career path would be that I'd end up some day owning my own studio. To do that, I had to get equipment, so I built my own.

"Around 1970 . . . we needed a new console for the move up to 24-track. We weren't happy with the second console from Sound Techniques . . . [so] we researched the market, and at that time there were three major players: Neve, Cadac and Helios. The Neve and the Cadac were way too big to fit in our control room, and we didn't like the ergonomics of the Helios.

"I'd been dabbling around and we had this tech at Trident named Barry Porter who had been helping me design a mixer. [Note: *This was a small 6' by 2' desk that was ultimately installed in the tape copy room.*] So I [told the Sheffields], 'We've got Barry on staff, I know all the systems and engineering, we've got good engineers; surely between all of us we could design a console.' After various meetings, they said to me, 'If you'll manage the project, we'll give you a year and room at Trident [to do it].'"

The result of their efforts was the first Trident A-Range. It was installed in late 1971, despite what Norman Sheffield later described as a "minor hiccup." The console had been built in a workshop on the top floor of St. Anne's Court; the idea was that it would be placed in the elevator and brought downstairs to the control room when it was complete. But on the day of the move, it was discovered that it wouldn't fit through the doors. Accordingly, a carpenter had to be summoned to remove the door frame and part of the wall.

Malcolm Toft behind the main control room
Sound Techniques mixing console, 1968.
(Courtesy of Malcolm Toft)

The Trident A-Range was also the first British console to offer equalization on the monitor circuit. According to Toft, this was because the studio frequently got tapes from the U.S. that used the NAB pre-emphasis/de-emphasis curve. (see pages 11–13 for details) "When we played them on our tape machines that were set to CCIR," he explains, "there was a difference in the top end and bottom end. So rather than re-EQing the machine, we used the treble and bass on the monitor circuit to equalize the difference in characteristic." It was also one of the first consoles to utilize a "split monitor" design, in which the monitor channels could be used as extra line inputs during mixdown, effectively doubling the number of channels available.

Unlike modern consoles, the original A-Range—one of only 13 ever built—had no built-in patch bay; instead, there was a separate bay mounted vertically in the control room wall. The patch bays at Trident in the '60s and '70s also used full-size TRS jacks, not the compact TT that are used in modern bays.

The original Trident A-Range was a 28-input, 24-bus "super-console," in Toft's words, with especially musical equalization and sonics that were said to be superior to many of the consoles of the era. "That sound was created through painstaking listening tests by the engineers at Trident; people like Ken Scott, Roy Thomas Baker, Barry Sheffield and myself would get together and literally change components until we got sounds we were happy with," said Toft. "It was something you couldn't possibly quantify technically and quite honestly if we'd been able to measure things accurately we probably would never have got those kind of results."

The A-Range and less expensive B-Range (released in 1973) were somewhat similar in terms of electronic structure. They used the same equalization circuitry as well as the same amp and preamp components; however, the B-Range mic gain controls offered fewer steps, and there were also fewer selectable frequencies in the EQ section—just one mid band, for example. The B-Range, which was the precursor to the later Series 80, also lacked output transformers and had a much simpler mechanical construction.

By the mid-1970s, the mixing board in the control room had been replaced by a 32 x 24 TSM, later upgraded to a 28 x 48 model. At around the same time, the remix room was outfitted with a 62 x 12 TSM, replaced in the late 1970s by an early Trident Series 80. (See *Trident Audio Developments* on page 192.)

As Malcolm Toft once said of Trident, "We were a rock-and-roll recording studio, and a rock-and-roll recording console company"—an opinion Tony Visconti shares. "All the Trident boards were made for rock 'n' roll," Visconti says. "The EQ frequencies they offered were perfect for bringing out presence in guitars and bass. Boosting at 800 or 300 Hz, just a little nudge, did something that would allow you to hear bass through a small speaker."

Both the TSM and the A-Range were unique in that they provided equalization control on faders, as opposed to knobs. Says Visconti, "It wasn't a sweep EQ—it had fixed frequencies—but the midrange and HF frequencies were close to one another, and so with the two faders you could come up with some interesting curves; you could pinpoint precisely what you wanted. It served as a kind of missing link between conventional fixed-frequency equalization and sweep EQ, or parametric control with selectable width, which came later.

"It was very innovative, and it was nice to be able to treat EQ like it was level, because it actually *is* changing level in a way. But instead of turning a knob like you do on most consoles, you were increasing and decreasing the level of EQ with a fader. Psychologically, that appealed to me."

Monitors

When it first opened, Trident was renowned for having the loudest control room in London, and rightfully so. Each of its four massive Lockwood cabinets—two per side—housed a 15" dual concentric Tannoy Red, powered by 60-watt Radford amps. It was a monitoring system that almost begged to be cranked up full, and many clients delighted in doing just that—a practice that sometimes chagrined the maintenance engineers charged with replacing blown drivers, but one that was not especially discouraged by the studio's cadre of young recording engineers, many of whom took just as much pleasure in having their

long hair blown back as did the paying customers. That, too, was in stark contrast to the more conservative monitoring levels favored by engineers at other facilities, and something that contributed greatly to the "hip" vibe of the studio. (See Chapter 4 for more information about the Tannoy Red.)

Lockwood-housed Tannoy Reds were also installed in the Trident remix room (also powered by 60-watt Radford amps), although these were later replaced by JBL speakers driven by HH amps (which were themselves replaced in the mid-1970s with Crown amps). The exact make and model of those speakers is unknown, though it was highly likely they were 4350s—the loudest monitors JBL had produced to date, capable of a sustained output of over 125 dB.

Tape Machines

Ampex AG-440 (8-track and 4-track)—A 4-track version of the Ampex AG-440—an all-discrete transistor tape machine with class A electronics and improved tape stability—debuted in 1967, the same year Trident opened. Norman Sheffield had already, in his words, "fallen in love" with the Ampex stereo tape recorder purchased from IBC and used at the Waltham Cross shop, years before opening Trident. And so it was with great enthusiasm that he and brother Barry visited the Ampex office in Reading (west of London) to begin equipment purchases for the new facility. They ordered two MR-70s (see below)—one mono, the other stereo, as well as an AG-440 4-track, then the most popular multitrack in American studios. But one of Norman's core beliefs was that Trident should always have the very best equipment available, and so they also ordered, sight unseen, a still-in-development AG-440 8-track, something they were particularly excited about since it would be the first such machine in Europe.

It arrived about six weeks after Trident's official opening, one of only three such machines in the world at that time. (Machine 1 was housed at Ampex headquarters in California, while Machine 2 had just been installed at Atlantic Studios in New York under the watchful eye of ace engineer Tom Dowd.) However, there was a problem: It had been shipped with the wrong motors and was set up to operate at

60 Hz (the American line voltage standard), instead of the 50 Hz used by the British electrical system. As a result, it ran too slowly—closer to 12 ips than 15 ips. An ex–World War II rheostat provided a temporary fix until the new motors eventually arrived, but the first few clients to use the 8-track at Trident had a nasty surprise in store when they attempted to play back their tapes elsewhere.

3M M56 (16-track)—Trident became the first operational 16-track studio in the U.K. when an M56 was installed in 1969. A second M56 was installed in the newly opened remix room a year later. (See *Decca* in Chapter 2 for more information.)

Ampex MR-70 (2-track and 1-track)—Rumored to have been specifically designed to dub EMI Beatles masters at Capitol Studios for the U.S. market, the MR-70 made its commercial debut in 1966. It was extremely expensive for its time—a 2-track 1/4" version cost $4,500, which translates to $28,000 in today's dollars—and so it never achieved the success of other Ampex machines, but it is renowned today for its tape handling capability. The MR-70's massive die-case frame was designed to tight tolerances, allowing the heads to be mounted for fixed azimuth. It used a viscous damped reel idler with a booster motor to bring it up to speed, and offered varispeed fast-wind and constant tension tape supply.

Studer B62 (2-track)—One of these was mounted in the wall of the Trident control room. Since hardly any mixing was done there (usually done in the remix room upstairs), the B62 was used mostly for tape echo, although it was sometimes pressed into service to receive reference monitor mixes . . . as long as no tape echo was required. (See *CTS / The Music Centre* in Chapter 3 for more information.)

STORIES FROM THE STUDIO
Sometimes you pay a price for innovation

TRIDENT MAY OR MAY NOT have been the first studio in the U.K. to offer 8-track recording (some sources attribute that distinction to Advision, whose new Scully 8-track may have been installed shortly beforehand; see *Advision* in Chapter 3 for more information), but they were certainly the first to offer 16-track recording. And there is also no question that the first session with their new 3M M56 machine was fraught with difficulty.

The artist was David Bowie; the producer, Tony Visconti. The track: "Wild Eyed Boy from Freecloud," which would appear on Bowie's 1969 album *Space Oddity*.

Visconti sets the scene: "The song was crying out for a symphony orchestra, and I convinced the label to let me hire 50 musicians to do the overdub. We were perfectly happy recording it to 8-track, but on the day we were scheduled to record, one of the Sheffield brothers came running in and announced that they had just installed their brand-new 2" 16-track machine and that we'd be using it on the session. We'd had problems when they installed their 8-track machine, so I was a bit dubious about this, but the 8-track had already been disconnected, so we had no choice."

Norman Sheffield picks up the story in *Life on Two Legs*: "In anticipation of trouble Tony made Barry and I promise that the 16-track was set up and working properly. . . . We assured him that it already was and that everything would be fine."

David Bowie had made the decision to sit in the middle of the orchestra and strum along on his 12-string guitar to act as timekeeper while Visconti conducted. "After about five rehearsals," Visconti reports, "I told [engineer] Malcolm Toft to record a take. But when I asked him for a playback, he told me something was wrong—and he was absolutely right: What they got on tape was a signal at about -100 dB; you could just barely hear the sound. It was full of hisses and crackles and snaps and pops, with a little bit of music in the background."

Maintenance engineer Ron Goodwin, who, along with Barry Sheffield, was sitting in, reassured the producer that the problem would be fixed shortly. "They said, 'Don't worry—we'll figure it out; just go back down to the studio and keep rehearsing,' reports Visconti. "So I went back downstairs and we rehearsed many, many times, and after about 20 more minutes I told the engineer to lay down another take. We go upstairs to have a listen . . . and it's still the same! The sound was all hiss, and very, very little program.

"I asked what the problem was and the maintenance guys sheepishly admitted that it was all their fault,

Studer C37 (2-track)—There were three C37s installed in the Trident remix room when it first opened; one received the mix, while the other two were used to make copies—in real time, if need be. (See *Decca* in Chapter 2 for more information about the C37.)

Studer A80 (24-track and 2-track)—By 1977, all the tape machines at Trident had been replaced by a battery of Studer A80s. (See Chapter 1 for more information.)

Main Microphones

Neumann U67—This was the main "go-to" mic at Trident, particularly since the studio had no U47s. U67s were frequently used for vocals and as piano mics; they sometimes also served as drum overheads. (See Chapter 1 for more information.)

Neumann KM54/KM56—These small-diaphragm condenser microphones were often used at Trident as snare and tom-tom mics. (See Chapter 1 for more information.)

Neumann KM84—(See Chapter 5 for more information.)

AKG C451—Trident engineers frequently used 451s as drum overheads. (See Chapter 5 for more information.)

AKG C12A—(See Chapter 1 and Chapter 5 for more information.)

AKG C28—These were mostly used at Trident for close-miking of tom-toms, and also for electric guitars. (See *Decca* in Chapter 2 for more information.)

AKG D12—Used at Trident, as in so many other recording studios around the world, primarily as a bass drum mic. (See *Lansdowne* in Chapter 3 for more information.)

---

that they had forgotten to order a 2" lineup tape; all they had was the 1" 8-track lineup tape. So at best, they could line up the bottom eight tracks.

"Now, again, we've got a studio full of very expensive orchestral musicians, plus David Bowie growing increasingly nervous, so the maintenance guys simply wildly tweaked based on their knowledge of the 8-track machine until they got something vaguely usable."

The orchestral players, of course, were union members, and they had been booked for a three-hour session, due to end at 1 p.m.—now just literally five minutes away. "The musicians were looking at us all with utter contempt," reported Norman Sheffield. "There was no way on earth they were going to give us any free time. And if we went into overtime, they were eligible to get double the fees—that was the way it worked with the Musician's Union then."

"I told Malcolm, 'This has got to be it,'" says Visconti, "and he said he thought they had fixed the problem. I was going out of my mind with aggravation! So we recorded it one last time and I looked up at the control room, and they said, 'We got it; it's OK,' and I thanked the musicians and sent them on their way. At least we had two hours and 50 minutes of rehearsal!"

"By the time [that last take] was done, we saw the musicians packing up their cases," says Sheffield. "David and I went upstairs for a playback," continues Visconti, "and, yes, they did get something on tape, but now it was maybe -20 dB or -15 dB, and God knows there was nothing like an NAB or CCIR curve. It was acceptable as long as you muted the instruments that weren't playing at any particular time, which I knew by looking at my score.

"A few days later, the maintenance guys finally got a lineup tape and

were able to line the machine up, so the subsequent overdubs—guitar, vocals, handclaps—were fine, even though the orchestra remained substantially under-recorded. It took five people manning the mute buttons and faders—including myself, David, Mick Ronson, and Malcolm Toft—to mix that track! The choreography was rehearsed for hours until we managed to get an almost noiseless mix."

Visconti leans back in his chair with a smile as he recalls the nerve-racking session. "Trident was like that—they always had to have the latest equipment as soon as it came out.

"I loved the fact that the Sheffields were innovative," he says, "and that they had the latest equipment and their own boards—the Trident consoles were very different from those being made by other manufacturers. But sometimes you paid a price for that innovation."

IN HIS BOOK *LIFE ON TWO LEGS,* Norman Sheffield described The Beatles' July 30, 1968, session at Trident (during which they recorded the backing track to "Hey Jude") as being "long and pretty intense."

But, like most recording sessions, it had its lighter moments, too—and this one also involved the famous Trident toilet located off the studio floor. Sheffield explains: "At one point they started another take of the song, with Paul playing the piano. It was a long lead-in to the moment when the rest of the band came in, and halfway through everyone noticed that Ringo wasn't there. It turned out he'd gone to the toilet.

"Paul was just getting to the point where the drums came in when Ringo appeared in the corner of the studio and started tiptoeing towards his kit. He crept past Paul's back and arrived on his stool almost at the exact beat when he needed to come in. He couldn't have timed it better. Everyone collapsed with laughter in the control room upstairs."

AKG D202—The legendary "Sound Rocket" (so named because of the distinctive shape of its windscreen, which caused the mic to resemble a heavy lift booster), this classic cardioid was originally developed for broadcast and live sound and was the first "Two Way" mic manufactured by AKG. "Two Way" was the company's name for its patented system that utilized twin dynamic capsules—one to sense high frequencies and the other to sense lows (with the LF entry point, unusually, at the base of the stem)—along with a built-in crossover network. The 202 was renowned for its smooth sound and lack of proximity effect, and was frequently used at Trident for percussion and to mic bass amplifiers.

AKG D224—This dynamic mic was sometimes used at Trident for hi-hat, primarily because of its directionality. (See *Pye* in Chapter 2 for more information.)

Electrovoice RE20—At Trident, RE20s were used mostly to mic kick drums and for electric guitar. (See *Decca* in Chapter 2 for more information.)

STC 4038—These ribbon mics were often used at Trident on horn sections and called into play as ambient mics. (See Chapter 1 and Chapter 5 for more information.)

Sennheiser MD441—This high-end super-cardioid dynamic mic had an unusually crisp tonal quality and offered a five-position low-frequency contour switch and a two-position high-frequency switch. First introduced in 1966, the MD441 was advertised as being "perfect for vocals," although it was most often used at Trident as a hi-hat mic.

Sony C38B—This all-purpose large-diaphragm condenser microphone made its debut in 1965. It had FET electronics and was designed to handle sound sources with high SPL, such as percussion and wind instruments. A mechanical switch allowed the polar pattern to be changed from cardioid to omni, and there was also an onboard low-cut filter and 8 dB pad. At Trident, C38Bs were used frequently for close-miking snare drums, and also as spot mics on oboes.

A trade listing from 1979 indicated that Trident's mic locker also included Beyer dynamic mics, although the exact models are unknown.

Outboard Signal Processors

One of the major attractions at Trident was the sheer quantity (as well as quality) of the signal processors that filled its outboard racks, which included the following:

Teletronix LA-2A—Trident owned at least two, and possibly three LA-2A optical compressors, and they reportedly saw frequent use both in the main control room and the remix room. (See *Pye* in Chapter 2 for more information.)

UREI 1176—Trident owned at least a half dozen of these popular peak limiters; judging from the punchy sounds of many recordings made there, it's probably safe to assume that "all-button" mode was used a lot of the time. (See *Decca* in Chapter 2 for more information.)

UREI LA-3A—The LA-3A debuted in 1969 and combined solid-state transformers from the UREI 1176 with the electro-optical attenuator of the Teletronix LA-2A. The result was a unique sonic signature with a distinctive punch, particularly in the lower-mids, which made it especially effective on guitar. Trident owned at least two LA-3As. (See *Decca* in Chapter 2 for more information about the 1176.)

Universal Audio 175B—Like Fairchild compressors, the Universal Audio 175 (and 176) was based around a variable-mu design, with gain controlled by a dual triode tube. (Variable-mu tubes have the ability to reduce their "mu"— that is, gain—as the input signal increases.) Said to be the smallest available compressor when it was first introduced in 1961, the original 175 still took up two rack spaces and weighed in at a hefty 15 pounds!

Although it was a compressor and not a limiter, the 175 had much in common with the 1176: Threshold was set with the Input control, and the Attack and Release controls were at their fastest when fully clockwise. Attack time was adjustable from 100 to 1,000 microseconds; release time was adjustable from 27 to 527 milliseconds. Unlike the 1176, the 175 had a fixed ratio of 12:1. The 175B model released in the mid-1960s added separate gain controls for input and output. Trident owned at least two 175Bs. (See *Decca* in Chapter 2 for more information about the 1176.)

Pultec EQP-1A—There were at least two of these passive tube equalizers in the Trident remix room, possibly more in the control room. (See *Decca* in Chapter 2 for more information.)

Astronics graphic equalizers—Engineer Neil Kernon, who worked at Trident from 1971 through 1975, recalls that "we had racks of Astronics equalizers back in the day. We used them all the time for doing extreme EQing." Most likely these were model A1671 nineband graphic equalizers, first introduced in the U.K. in the early 1960s. These solid-state devices employed germanium transistors and came with a remote—something that was quite unique for the era. Reportedly, their unusually fat bottom end was due to the large coils used in the circuitry.

"You could give him a shoe box and he'd get a good sound out of it"

"PEOPLE THINK THAT SESSION MUSICIANS get gigs because they're good musicians, but that's only half of it. They get the gigs because what they're really good at is knowing to play their instrument for the engineer," observes Malcolm Toft, Trident's first chief engineer and eventual studio manager.

"I remember doing a big orchestral session one morning with Clem Cattini booked to play drums," he says by way of illustration. "He came in and said, 'I'm having trouble parking—would you have a house kit I can use instead of my own?' Norman Sheffield, who owned Trident, was a drummer, and I knew he had a modest kit down in the drum locker, so I said, 'Well, yeah, you can use Norman's drums.' He said, 'OK, fine, I'll work with that.' I'd left the drums for last since there was so much going on, and so I was running out of mics. All I had left were a handful of them to put on the kit—the ubiquitous D12 on the kick drum, a KM54 on the snare, maybe a U67 as an overhead. In fact, I think I only had one track free to record the drums.

"With just moments to spare, I pushed up the faders, and it was all there—it sounded great! Even though there hadn't been time to tune the kit, Clem knew how to lay his stick on the snare to make it sound just right, and he hit it with the same force each time so you never lost one of the beats. You could give him a shoe box and he'd get a good sound out of it.

"Even more amazingly," Toft continues, "later that same afternoon [producer] Tony Visconti came in for a session and he saw the drums and he asked if he could use them as they were already set up. Well, we ended up putting ten mics on that kit and spending five hours to get a decent drum sound with exactly the same setup, but a different drummer. That's my point: The great thing about Clem and all the top session guys was that they knew exactly how their instruments needed to sound in a studio, which is completely different from how you might want it to sound at a live gig.

"Same with Herbie Flowers. It didn't matter whether he was playing acoustic bass or electric bass, or what mic you put in front of him—it always sounded great, with each note on each string sounding the same; he knew how to play certain notes on certain strings louder so as to make up for any deficiencies in the pickups or instrument setup. That's why, as an engineer, you always wanted him called in to play bass—not just because he was a great player, but because he gave you exactly what you wanted."

David Hentschel behind the Sound Techniques console in the Trident remix room, 1971.
(Photo by Steve Cahill)

Eventide FL201 Instant Flanger—First introduced in 1979, the FL201 offered time delay, not just phase delay, and so it was able to generate convincing Doppler effects as well as flanging. It came with a remote and allowed manual flange control, as well as providing an automatic envelope follower.

EMT 140 plate reverbs—Trident had two of these mounted in a small room off the studio floor. Tielines allowed accessibility to either from both the control room and remix room. (See Chapter 1 for more information.)

Other signal processing equipment included Trident CB9146 FET stereo compressors; Trident CB9066 single channel three-band parametric equalizers; Helios RE24 stereo four-band equalizers; and Orban graphic equalizers and de-essers. In the

late 1970s, AMS and Eventide digital delay units were added to the outboard racks.

In 1970, Trident became one of the first studios in the U.K. to offer Dolby noise reduction, with units installed in both the main control room and the remix room. "I remember the day they got their first Dolbys in," says Tony Visconti. "That was a good experience with new equipment—not hearing the tape hiss before the band came in. This time— unlike our initial experience with the 16-track machine (see *Sometimes you pay a price for innovation* on page 186)—they had obviously lined them up correctly!"

Film Equipment

At a very early stage in Trident's planning, the Sheffield brothers made the decision to include a preview theater along with the recording facilities at St. Anne's Court. "The logic here was simple," Norman Sheffield explained. "Long term we knew we'd want to work with sound and vision as a dubbing facility and perhaps making [promotional] films to accompany singles." In addition, with St. Anne's Court in the middle of the British film industry's backyard, they felt it would be easy to attract name directors to use the theater, particularly after they hired top film projectionist Dick Slade, a familiar name in the business.

The preview theater was actually the first room to be completed, and it opened shortly before the studio itself. Among the first clients was J. Lee Thompson, director of the film *Mackenna's Gold*, starring Gregory Peck and Omar Sharif.

KEY TECHNICAL INNOVATIONS
Trident Tape Services

Trident was not the first major recording studio in Britain to offer mastering services; Abbey Road had been doing that almost since their inception, as had Decca, IBC, and a few other studios. But they were probably the first to offer custom tape duplication services.

It stemmed from a decision made by Norman Sheffield in 1969 to get into the prerecorded tape business. At the time there were two competing formats—cassette and 8-track cartridge—and both were used widely in car audio systems as well as home stereos, which Sheffield saw as a golden opportunity. It was a complicated venture: Specialized equipment had to be imported from the U.S. and suitable manufacturing premises found. Trident Tape Services was eventually headquartered in an old handbag factory in north London—a facility that Ray Dolby himself would eventually use to develop the Dolby system for cassettes.

It helped, of course, that Sheffield had extensive industry connections, which led to several lucrative contracts, including the exclusive license to duplicate Elton John's early albums, not coincidentally recorded at Trident. The enterprise was successful, but fierce competition in the late 1970s led to shrinking profit margins, and so Trident Tape Services was sold off and eventually merged with another duplicating company.

Trident Audio Productions

Managers managed. Producers produced. Publishers published. From the earliest days of "show" business, that was simply the way things were.

But Norman Sheffield was determined to overturn the status quo wherever and whenever possible. Accordingly, in 1971 he and his brother Barry decided that Trident would be branching out into A&R (Artists and Repertoire), normally the province of record companies. The goal of their newly formed Trident Audio Productions venture was to find artists to manage and produce, as well as songs to publish.

The first two artists they signed were singers Eugene Wallace and Mark Ashton. They were, unfortunately, destined for the ash heap of obscurity.

STORIES FROM THE STUDIO
The Trident piano

TRIDENT'S HANDMADE BECHSTEIN grand piano was more than 100 years old and became a significant part of the studio's attraction. It was used by many prominent artists, including Paul McCartney (on "Hey Jude"), Elton John ("Your Song," "Levon," and "Candle in the Wind"), Carly Simon, Genesis, Supertramp and then-house pianist Rick Wakeman, who played it on the David Bowie tracks "Changes" and "Life on Mars."

The seven-octave piano (serial number 44064) was "concert-size" (most likely 7'6") and featured an ebonized metal frame with ivory naturals and ebony accidentals. Sometimes described as the "best rock 'n' roll piano ever," it had an unusually bright sound due, reportedly, to the hardening of the hammers, as well as the fact that its stiff action forced players to attack the keys with gusto. Trident purchased the piano in 1986 after having rented it for nearly 20 years.

Unsubstantiated reports indicate that the Trident Bechstein was resold several times in the next two decades, including, allegedly, on eBay in 2008 for more than $350,000. What is certain is that in May 2011, the piano went up for auction with a guide price of between £300,000 and £400,000 (approximately $500,000–$650,000 in today's money); neither the purchaser nor the final purchase price have been revealed publicly.

Not so the third act: an eclectic band with a cerebral lead guitarist and a flamboyant front man. Their name was Queen.

Under the terms of their management and production contract, Queen were given virtually unlimited access to studio downtime (i.e., unbooked hours) at Trident. The band—notorious perfectionists, all—began eating up the hours at a voracious rate, with staff engineer Roy Thomas Baker behind the board. Though the relationship between Queen and Trident would eventually end acrimoniously, there was no question that signing with the Sheffield brothers (who would steer the group's early career and land a distribution deal with EMI for the release of their first two albums) helped enormously in their rise to stardom.

Trident Audio Developments (TRIAD)

Even before the installation of the first Trident A-Range in the studio's control room, word had begun to spread. In early 1972 Malcolm Toft and Barry Porter were asked to build a scaled-down version for musician and producer John Congas—a console that would become known as the Trident B-Range. When a second order came in from Chipping Norton Studios (see *Chipping Norton* in Chapter 8 for more information), the Sheffield brothers officially formed Trident Audio Developments (TRIAD) as a manufacturing company.

TRIAD would continue under Toft's management until 1988, evolving a line of consoles that improved on the A-Range and B-Range. These included the TSM (Trident Sound Mixer), which primarily used ICs rather than discrete electronics in the signal chain; the Fleximix, the company's first live console; and the popular Series 80—a fully modular system that offered improved panpots. More innovations followed in the years ahead, and despite several changes in ownership, Trident Audio Developments remains in business today.

Trilion Video

The early success Trident studios enjoyed gave the Sheffield brothers the opportunity—and the resources—to expand their business further still. "The music business was changing fast," wrote Norman, "and I sensed that the next big thing was going to be video." Accordingly, in 1973 they purchased Lion Television, a video production company based at the renowned Shepperton Film studios, and, adding the first three letters from the name that had served them so well, rechristened it Trilion Video.

During the mid-1970s, the company's operations expanded greatly with the acquisition of several remote broadcast trucks and a telecine operation, along with early time-code editing equipment. Trilion eventually secured a lease on De Lane Lea Studios in Dean Street, Soho (see *De Lane Lea / Kingsway* in Chapter 8 for more information), and converted it into a shooting soundstage, complete with a full lighting rig. Handily, the rear entrance of the studio was just a few doors down from the back entrance of the famed Marquee Club, and so live acts were often filmed there.

The music business was, of course, the business the Sheffields knew best, and so Trilion specialized in music videos, with clients that included the Rolling Stones, Genesis, Thin Lizzy, 10cc, Leo Sayer, and Paul McCartney (for whom they shot the "Jet" promotional video). In 1975, despite the fact that Queen and Trident were in the midst of a rancorous and emotionally charged parting of the ways, Trilion was contracted to produce the video for the group's single "Bohemian Rhapsody," still regarded as one of the most compelling and effective music videos ever crafted.

By the late 1970s, Trilion was widely acclaimed as being one of the pioneers in the music video business. "We used our experience and expertise as a recording studio to revolutionize sound [for video]," wrote Norman Sheffield. "We used the same multitracking systems that we used in the Trident recording studio." As their success in that field grew, opportunities arose in other arenas. Soon Trilion was being contracted to film everything from West End plays to sporting events like boxing and football matches—even the Winter Olympics. Assignments from the BBC and the ITV Network followed, including live coverage of Prime Minister Margaret Thatcher's opening speech when she assumed office in 1979.

In 1981, Trilion Video was sold and floated publicly; the company continued to operate into the mid-1980s. Trilion SA, a South African affiliate, remains in business today.

NORMAN SHEFFIELD, 1939–2014

Norman Sheffield was a musician, an entrepreneur, and a rebel. With an unwavering vision and a keen sense of the importance of creative freedom, he and his brother Barry turned a derelict engraving works in Soho into one of the preeminent recording studios in the world.

He assembled a first-class team of recording engineers, founded a successful (to this day) console manufacturing company, launched the career of an internationally renowned band, and oversaw the filming of seminal music videos.

His career didn't end with the demise of Trident Studios, either. Far from it: Sheffield would go on to open one of the first Apple dealerships in the U.K., importing early computers from the U.S. and pairing them with power converters that allowed them to be used in England. Later, with his sons, he started a cutting-edge advertising agency that would garner numerous industry awards.

Norman Sheffield enjoyed his retirement years on the peaceful shores of Cornwall, where he would sometimes sit in and play drums with local musicians at his daughter's restaurant. He passed away on June 20, 2014, leaving his wife, Chris, four children, seven grandchildren, and an everlasting legacy.

Norman Sheffield.
(Courtesy of Justin Sheffield)

SELECTED DISCOGRAPHY

- The Beatles: "Hey Jude" (single)
- James Taylor: "Carolina in My Mind" (single)
- Free: "All Right Now" (single)
- George Harrison: "My Sweet Lord" (single)
- Carly Simon: "You're So Vain" (single)
- David Bowie: *Space Oddity*, *Hunky Dory*, *Ziggy Stardust*, *Aladdin Sane*
- Elton John: *Elton John*, *Tumbleweed Connection*, *Madman Across the Water*, "Candle in the Wind" (single)

7

AIR

By the end of 1963, George Martin was the most famous record producer in Great Britain. The recordings he'd crafted for The Beatles and other artists had occupied the Number One spot in the U.K. charts for 37 weeks and had earned his employer, EMI, 2.2 million pounds.

He was earning a salary of just over 3,000 pounds.

So he did what any self-respecting person would do: He quit. And a year later, he was the most famous record producer in the entire *world*.

The genesis of AIR lies in the failed negotiations between Martin and EMI throughout 1964 as the producer lobbied to receive fair compensation for his efforts. As Martin would write in his 1979 book *All You Need Is Ears*, "bitterness, anger and resentment . . . had come to be the unhappy ingredients of my feelings towards EMI." In August of 1965, he and fellow producers John Burgess, Ron Richards, and Peter Sullivan formed a company called Associated Independent Recording—AIR for short.

Even after the formation of AIR, Martin would of course frequently return to EMI's studios in Abbey Road, but this time on his own terms, receiving a share of the profits from his work. And now, no longer contractually obligated to EMI, he was able to record at other studios, too—something that was creatively freeing, but which made little financial sense. "The more work we [AIR] got," he said in *All You Need Is Ears*, "the more money was being spent on other people's studios. It didn't take a genius to work out that if we had our own studios the trend would be reversed—not only would that money not have to be paid out, but some might even start coming in. In addition, the company was enjoying an ever-increasing income from royalties, which was likely only to be fodder for the taxman. So it made sense for us to . . . plough back the money into our own company, quite legitimately, to finance the building of our own studios."

The first task was to find premises, with the goal of locating the studio centrally. "[That] choice was greatly affected by the fact that I wanted a multi-purpose studio," Martin explained, "one that could be used for dubbing films as well as making records. To make that pay we would have to attract the American trade. I wanted the best American film and record producers to use the studios. That indicated somewhere within easy distance of Claridges and the Connaught [hotels]."

A suitable location was finally identified, atop the Peter Robinson department store in Oxford Circus—the very heart of London. The entire fourth floor of the impressive building had been used as an enormous banquet hall, featuring, as Martin describes, "a high vaulted ceiling with neo-classical frescoes, marble columns, and kitchens at each end."

Lease signed and architects, contractors, and acoustics consultants duly engaged, renovation began in 1969 under the watchful eyes of technical engineers Keith Slaughter and George Barnett (both ex-EMI), joined shortly thereafter by technical engineer Dave Harries (another ex-EMI employee) and newly appointed chief recording engineer Bill Price (purloined from Decca). There were a number of problems to be tackled, not least of which was the rumble emanating from the underground Tube (subway) station directly underneath the building. This was dealt with by completely "floating" the entire facility two feet above the original floor, with the walls and ceilings suspended by acoustic mounts—a time-consuming and extremely expensive endeavor. There were

A.I.R. Studios have been designed and constructed by producers, for producers. My colleagues and I have put all of our experience in recording into the design of a Studio complex which approaches our ideal.

It is our aim to provide the world's finest recording facilities, right in the heart of London, and to provide producers with every aid to production that we ourselves have longed to have available when working in other studios.

The location of A.I.R. Studios, overlooking Oxford Circus, could hardly be more central, making it easily accessible by all forms of public transport, and with ample car parking facilities within easy reach.

With many of the most talented personalities in the sound recording business, and the most sophisticated equipment available, A.I.R. Studios will, we feel sure, meet every requirement of even the most demanding producer.

George Martin,
Chairman.

George Martin's description of the AIR Oxford Circus facility in a brochure issued shortly after the studio's opening in 1970.
(From studio brochure)

difficulties with air-conditioning, too; obviously, the road noise coming from Oxford Circus (one of the busiest road junctions in the world) precluded outside windows in the recording areas. In the end, construction took more than a year, at a cost of £136,000, plus another £200,000 for equipment (translating in today's money to some £3.6 million, or more than $6 million).

As work progressed, additional staff were hired, including ex-Decca recording engineers John Punter and Jack Clegg. (Clegg had also done a stint at CTS, where he gained invaluable film scoring experience.) EMI's Geoff Emerick, who had long worked side by side with Martin recording The Beatles, was also offered a job at AIR but initially declined, deciding instead to aid the band in the resurrection of their Apple Studios following a failed first effort by "Magic" Alex Madras (see *Apple* in Chapter 8 for more information); Emerick would leave Apple in 1973 and finally join the team at AIR.

The launch party, held in early October 1970, was by all accounts a night to remember; allegedly, some 450 bottles of the finest Bollinger champagne were consumed during the festivities. The first non-orchestral session followed days later, with the

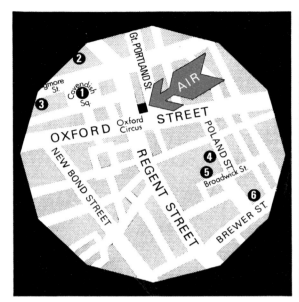

Situation & Parking facilities

The location of A.I.R. Studios, overlooking Oxford Circus, could hardly be more central, making it easily accessible by all forms of public transport, and with ample car parking facilities within easy reach.

1. Cavendish Square.
2. Harley Street Garage.
3. Debenham & Freebody, Wigmore Street.
4. Poland Street Garage, Poland Street.
5. National Car Parks, Dufours Place.
6. National Car Parks, Brewer Street.

Credits

The Architect : JACK PARSONS of
W. ROSSELL ORME & PARTNERS
The Acoustic Consultant : KENNETH SHEARER.
The Main Contractors : MARSHALL-ANDREW & CO. LTD.
The Electrical Consultant : W. O. 'BILL' HIGGINS.
The Electrical Contractors : T. CLARKE & CO. LTD.
The Air Conditioning Consultants :
KENNETH FOWLER & ASSOCIATES.
Plant Contractors : ELLIS (KENSINGTON) LTD.
Steel Work : A. E. BEER & PARTNERS
W. H. ARMFIELD LTD.
Fibrous Plaster and Acoustic Treatment :
B.C.L.
ALLAWAY ACOUSTIC PRODUCTS.

This page from the same 1970 brochure provides AIR's location details and an exterior photograph of the building housing the studio, as well as comprehensive credits for the outside contractors who played a role in constructing the Oxford Circus facility.
(From studio brochure)

Climax Blues Band recording tracks for their third album, *A Lot of Bottle*. (The CBB had actually done some test sessions at Oxford Circus back in August, before the official opening; interestingly, they were also the first band to record in AIR Montserrat when it opened nearly a decade later.)

Initially, the facility encompassed just a single large studio with a small projection room overhead, designed primarily for film scoring work. This was Studio One, sizable enough to accommodate nearly a full orchestra. The more modestly sized Studio Two, meant for use by pop artists and rock bands, opened its doors a month later. By the beginning of 1971, a third "dubbing theater," complete with an isolation booth and a raised projection room, was in operation. In 1972, all three were outfitted with 24-track Neve consoles and Studer tape machines, putting AIR at the cutting edge of new recording technology. A year later, a fourth overdub/mixing room (Studio Three) was added. It is worth noting that although originally conceived as a film scoring hub, the Oxford Circus facility never garnered much success in that field; instead, it morphed into an immensely popular music recording studio.

In 1975 AIR was sold to the Chrysalis Group, yielding a new infusion of cash, which allowed

Dave Harries and George Martin in AIR Studio 5, 1987.
(Photo by Jib Jones)

Opened in 1979 following two years of construction, AIR Montserrat comprised a single large, well-equipped studio (complete with an oversized control room housing a custom 46-channel console designed to Dave Harries' and Geoff Emerick's specifications by Rupert Neve himself) and a number of surrounding villas in which visiting artists could stay in comfort and style. For more than a decade, the facility played host to the elite in the rock world, including Paul McCartney, Elton John, Michael Jackson, Stevie Wonder, The Police, and Eric Clapton. Unfortunately, in 1989, disaster struck in the form of Hurricane Hugo—a monster storm that destroyed 90 percent of the island's structures, bringing an abrupt and permanent end to the studio's short saga.

With the lease on the Oxford Street premises about to expire, AIR Studios relocated in 1992 to Lyndhurst Hall, a converted Victorian church in the quiet northern London suburb of Hampstead. Though Sir George Martin (he was knighted in 1996) is no longer directly involved, AIR Lyndhurst continues to be active today under new ownership—a facility ironically best known for film scoring.

George Martin to realize another long-held dream. "The concept of a 'total environment' studio always appealed to me," he wrote in *All You Need Is Ears*. "I loved the creative freedom it gave." Accordingly, he began searching for a place to build a new, residential studio, one with all the technical advancements that the Oxford Circus facility offered, but with the peace, quiet, and isolation that could only come from an exotic location. His first inclination was to build it on a ship—a floating studio that could go anywhere in the world, preferably to warmer climes. Finally dissuaded of the idea by the reality of high running costs and the technical difficulties of both constructing and maintaining such a facility, Martin next set his sights on the Caribbean. He became drawn to the island of Montserrat, one of the few remaining British colonies, and a place that he described as a "luscious green tropical island with a . . . natural friendliness . . . [and] a fresh charm of its own." Accordingly, a 26-acre farm atop a hill overlooking the Caribbean Sea and surrounded by mango, citrus, and coconut groves was purchased, and the planning begun.

KEY PERSONNEL

Recording engineers: Bill Price, John Punter, Jack Clegg, Alan Harris, John Middleton, Steve Nye, Denny Bridges, Geoff Emerick, Mike Stavrou, Pete Henderson, Jon Kelly, Jon Jacobs, Nigel Walker, Steve Churchyard

Maintenance engineers: Keith Slaughter, George Barnett, Dave Harries, Danny Wise, Peter Jones, Paul Nunn, Malcolm Atkin, Tim Cuthbertson, Henry Dienn, Frank Oglethorpe

PHYSICAL FACILITIES
Oxford Circus
The Oxford Circus facility encompassed the entire fourth floor of the Peter Robinson department store

at 214 Oxford Street. "Previous to our moving in," says former technical director and studio manager Dave Harries, "it had just been a big open space, a marble banquet hall with painted frescoes of Italian operas on the ceiling. We stuck girders through the ceiling and ripped off the marble—sacrilege!"

The largest of the four studios at AIR Oxford Circus was Studio One, designed to comfortably accommodate in excess of 50 musicians. It had hardwood floors, with plaster walls and ceilings. A number of large custom-built acoustic screens were installed—they reached nearly to the ceiling and had reversible soft and hard surfaces so that the reflection characteristics of areas of the room could be varied. Two large isolation booths—one housing a nine-foot Bechstein grand piano (later replaced with a Bösendorfer after a vociferous complaint by none other than composer Karlheinz Stockhausen) and the other generally used for vocals—had removable carpeting above the hardwood floor

below. Studio One was also outfitted with a large film screen at one end, with a small projection room above the control room at the other end.

Former tape op Chris Michie described a typical AIR recording session in Studio One this way: "Depending on the engineer, bands would generally set up at the south, control room end of the studio, with the drummer in [the] roofed booth. . . . gobos would go between guitar and bass amps and the piano was usually baffled [with additional gobos] and covered in packing blankets, with microphones inserted under the lid, which was put down on the short stick or propped open with a two-by-four. . . . Organ parts might be done at the same time, in which case the Leslie cabinet would be baffled off with two mics on the top for stereo swirling noises and one or even two mics on the bottom speaker." Vocal overdubs, he states, were usually performed by placing the singer "in a three-sided temporary vocal booth made up from gobos."

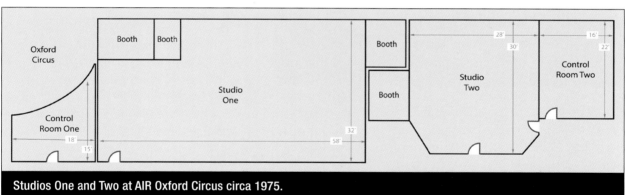

Studios One and Two at AIR Oxford Circus circa 1975.
(Based on a drawing by Malcolm Atkin)

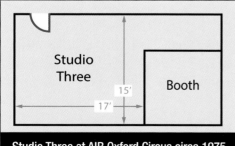

Studio Three at AIR Oxford Circus circa 1975.
(Based on a drawing by Malcolm Atkin)

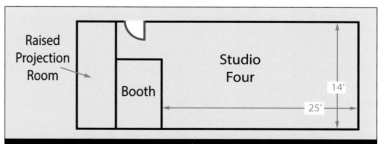

Studio Four (the "dubbing theater") at AIR Oxford Circus circa 1975.
(Based on a drawing by Malcolm Atkin)

MONTSERRAT

Recently refurbished control room now featuring 60 channel custom built console incorporating 48 channels by SSL with automation and TR and 12 fully integrated channels by Rupert Neve of Focusrite, two 32tk Mitsubishi X850 digital machines and 24tk Studer A800. Digital mixing on two Mitsubishi X86. Very comprehensive ancillary equipment list.
Contact: John Burgess 01-408-2355 in London or Yvonne Kelly 0101-809-491-5656 in Montserrat.

The AIR Montserrat facility and listing of installed equipment in 1988.
(From studio brochure)

AIR Montserrat layout circa 1979.
(Based on a drawing by Malcolm Atkin)

Though similarly constructed, Studio Two was considerably smaller than Studio One, though it was large enough to accommodate fair-sized string sections and full rock bands. It also incorporated an isolation booth, designed for drums. Though situated at the end of a long corridor and thus the furthest studio from the facility's main entrance / reception area, Studio Two was the closest to the upstairs canteen.

The control rooms for Studio One and Studio Two were at opposite ends of the building, on the outside corners of the building; the former overlooked Oxford Circus, while the latter looked out over Upper Regent Street. Both had low sofas for client comfort and raised platforms on which the console and engineer sat. This was done primarily to allow thick cabling to be installed in the floor beneath, but also served to improve visual communication with the studio floor.

Directly across the corridor from Studio Two was Studio Three, a small remix ("reduction") room with a good-sized isolation booth suitable for overdubs. Studio Four was a long, narrow room directly across from Studio One. Commonly referred to as the "dubbing theater" and built primarily for film applications, it included a screen and tiny isolation booth at the rear of the room and a raised projection room above the console. In the late 1970s, the iso booth in Studio Three was repurposed as a tape copy room (later a MIDI composition room) and renamed Studio Five.

Montserrat

Dave Harries and Malcolm Atkin did the bulk of the planning and supervision for the construction of AIR Montserrat over the course of 1977 and 1978, with significant input from Geoff Emerick (who had experience in studio design through his prior employment with Apple). Although the final result "sounded absolutely nothing like Studio One in Oxford Circus," in the words of Dave Harries, "given that they had completely different sizes and shapes and acoustics," there were, nonetheless, some similarities.

For one thing, the studio area was divided into a high-ceilinged "live end" and a low-ceiling "dead end," with the live end encompassing the bulk of the area—approximately 30 square feet. In *All You Need Is Ears*, George Martin explained the reason why. "[The Montserrat studio is] built for the kind of instruments a rock group uses . . . such as guitars, piano and drums. Therefore, since I like a moderately live drum sound as long as it doesn't affect the other instruments, we . . . still keep a live end in the studio."

The Montserrat studio included two isolation booths: a large drum booth (approximately ten feet square) with an independently sprung floor, and a unique piano booth that stuck out into the main room, enabling the player of the studio's 7'4" Bösendorfer to maintain visual contact with the rest of the band. Harries describes it thusly: "We had a corner of the studio made of blockwork and we had a wooden panel placed over the top, filled with about five feet of fiberglass. You could push the piano in there—it just fitted inside the gap, with only the keyboard sticking out. So it wasn't in its own room—it was just the sound-producing part of the piano that was in a kind of box. That enabled the engineer to place mics a reasonable distance away from the piano and get a really good sound with no leakage from other instruments, or you could easily overdub it afterwards since there was also no leakage coming from the piano when recording backing tracks. If the engineer wanted a more live, ambient piano sound, he could simply pull it out into the room.

"We also had a couple of guitar traps, similar to the Eastlake design," Harries continues. "They were like chimneys, with an open bottom end filled with hanging rockwall panels. When a guitar amp was placed inside one of the traps, you could actually play pretty loud without the sound spilling onto anything else."

Also worthy of note also was the unusually large size of the Montserrat control room, although Harries later described it as "really just a great big shoe box, with absorbers around the outsides and a big window that offered a spectacular view of the golf course below."

Acoustic Treatments
Oxford Circus
The acoustic treatment at the Oxford Circus facility was overseen by Ken Shearer (renowned for his innovative work at the Royal Albert Hall), in conjunction with AIR technical engineers Keith Slaughter and Dave Harries. It was a project that was challenging on several different fronts. For one thing, there was the problem of the rumble coming up through the building from the three different Tube (subway) lines running directly underneath the building. The solution was to construct the entire facility so that it was completely independent of the surrounding building. This was no simple floating floor, either; essentially, a huge box had to be built and acoustically isolated from the main structure, with the studios and control rooms mounted inside.

Complicating this daunting undertaking were severe restrictions on floor loading, which forced the builders to resort to using lightweight building materials (primarily plasterboard) and wide air voids [empty spaces] with springs in-between to ensure isolation. "The floor of Studio One was a big platform on springs," says Dave Harries. "It was about three feet

STORIES FROM THE STUDIO
Ground control

HUM IS THE ENEMY OF AUDIO, as every engineer knows, and studios are often only as good as their electrical ground. Creating one for a studio being constructed on a small Caribbean island with limited resources was unusually challenging, as maintenance engineer Malcolm Atkin recalls.

"The electrical ground at AIR Montserrat consisted of 1" by 1/8" copper tape formed into a ladder shape of one-foot squares," he says. "We made up about 45 feet of this and laid it into the drain line of the swimming pool, which was a trench about 12 feet down going out to the side of the hill.

"A lot of the locals used charcoal for cooking at that time, so it was readily available in large quantities. We lined the whole trench with charcoal and then laid in the copper 'ladder' with more charcoal on top. I seem to remember we got a reading of less than 0.5 ohms, which was pretty good! However, a few weeks later I met the chief engineer of Radio Antilles, which was broadcasting a quarter of a million watts medium-wave from Montserrat right across South America. When I proudly told him about the earth we'd created for the studio, he said that at the radio station, they towed half a mile of copper tape out into the ocean, giving them effectively a connection to earth of zero ohms. That shut me up!"

Roxy Music in the AIR Studio Two control room, 1972. Left to right: Andy Mackay, assistant engineer Denny Bridges, engineer Bill Price, Paul Thompson, Brian Eno, producer Chris Thomas, and singer Bryan Ferry (standing). *(Photo by Gijsbert Hanekroot/Redferns)*

above the actual floor, on springs filled with rockwall and fiberglass insulation, with a bit of wood-wool slab to beef it up. The walls were sitting on top and were made of fibrous plaster, bowed [half-rounded] in order to avoid parallel surfaces and the resultant standing waves. All those round surfaces made the room a little too live, though, so we had to deaden it down slightly, which we did by putting a bit of absorption between them. I put those in with Ken Shearer's blessing, but I covered them with a little bit of cling film [plastic wrap] to brighten it, to bring a bit of top back, so there was just a bit of midrange absorption going on.

"So you had that fibrous plaster shell and then a void and then some glass doors and then the glass outer windows—that's all the isolation there was on that side of the building! The void was quite wide, though—you could actually walk down it. In fact,

we put the echo plates in them, between the wall and the windows."

Comments Malcolm Atkin, "When AIR first opened its doors in 1970, Studio One was actually a very live room which had a very long reverb time. But all through the '70s we were damping it more and more. Mind you, during that time, studios everywhere became more and more dead-sounding; I suppose we were all trying to emulate the Steely Dan drum sound, which is completely in front of your nose. But at the end of the decade there was a change in flavor; suddenly everybody wanted live-sounding records. So we did a complete acoustic rebuild of Studio One in 1980. We took out all the acoustic damping, and the room instantly became extremely live—it was like night and day; we were blown away by how different the room sounded."

"When we went 24-track, a lot of overdubbing sessions would get booked into Studio One, where artists would use a big room for just one or two instruments," adds Harries. "You didn't have the problem that we had in the early days where you had a lot fewer tracks so you had to record many more instruments at once, and so you needed a bit of separation, hence the need for a lot of screens and a deader studio. Once you had more tracks available, you could go a bit more live, which suited the tastes of the time."

In the quest for livening up the sound of Studio One, another innovation was added during the rebuild. "We had this whopping great two-foot high, ten-foot by ten-foot square riser built," explains Atkin. "It actually consisted of two boxes, each made with a ten-foot by five-foot sheet of 3/4-inch plywood. You'd put drums on there and they would sound enormous!" Harries recalls that the drum riser was constructed at the request of a number of visiting American engineers. "Ron Nevison was one; he came in and wanted that, and when he put the kit on top of that riser, he got the biggest drum sound you ever heard."

The smaller Studio Two was built similarly to Studio One, although heavier plasterboard was used for the walls, with precisely constructed wooden boxes mounted on the surface for diffusion and absorption. George Martin elaborated on these in *All You Need Is Ears*: "We have around the walls [of Studio Two] a number of boxes, all of different shapes and dimensions; each has a little lead weight, fitted in the centre of the front of the box. The boxes are tuned so that their fronts vibrate in sympathy with the bass frequencies, absorbing the impact. It's rather like a boxer taking a punch. They don't resonate and make any noise themselves, but they do move, and in doing so absorb the sound."

Acoustic experimentation was unceasing at AIR, even if it meant pushing the limits of floor loading safety. At one point, says Atkin, "we went out and bought about ten square pieces of big, heavy, two-inch-thick concrete paving slabs and put them into Studio Two to try to liven the floor up. Placing drums on those really helped tighten up the bass end since, instead of playing on a loose wooden floor, you're playing on a solid surface."

Yet for all these elaborate efforts, Studio Two was "always a bit too dead," according to Harries. "It never really had a perfect acoustic; we never were able to figure out how to brighten that room up enough. Which was fine for the recordings that were being made in the '70s, but Studio One was the room that was really in demand."

Both Studio One and Studio Two were capable of adhering to the popular "live end / dead end" trend of the times. As George Martin explained in *All You Need Is Ears*, "We generally have a hard floor and a fairly reflective ceiling at the string end of the studios. We keep one end of the studio live, and the other, where I normally put the rhythm section, dead."

The construction of the control rooms at AIR Oxford Circus was equally well thought out. As Dave Harries told journalist Janet Angus in a 1988 *Studio Sound* interview, "the principle acoustic treatment in all four control rooms is in the ceiling. The walls perform midrange absorption, whilst the ceiling takes care of the bass end, comprising a series of tuned acoustic panel absorbers at varying frequencies."

STORIES FROM THE STUDIO
"That sounds nice, but . . ."

VETERAN ENGINEER JACK CLEGG was assigned to do the very first orchestral session at AIR Oxford Circus, with singer Cilla Black. Despite his many years of experience at CTS, he remembers having no small degree of trepidation. "I recall thinking it somewhat unwise to go in at the deep end with a large orchestra when there would almost inevitably be some teething problems in the early days of AIR's operation," he says.

To his considerable relief, the first take went off without a hitch, but when he played the track back to the singer, Black's response was, "That sounds nice, but could you take some of the echo off? It's too much."

With a laugh, Clegg says, "I had to tell her that there was no added echo at all, and what she was hearing was the natural acoustic of the studio!" The days that followed were busy ones indeed for Dave Harries and his maintenance crew as they scrambled to deaden up the acoustic response of the studio accordingly.

Montserrat

In a 1979 interview for *Studio Sound* magazine celebrating the upcoming opening of AIR Montserrat, Dave Harries explained that "at Oxford Circus, the soundproofing [was] to keep the sound out, but [Montserrat] is a quiet little island and [so the soundproofing there] is to keep the sound in; otherwise, we would keep everyone awake at night!" Accordingly, double-cavity construction was employed for sound isolation, with rockwall of differing depth separated by wide, empty air voids.

The interior design was a bit more difficult, since for the most part the builders had to use only those materials that were readily available on the island; shipping in large amounts of specialist materials would have been cost-prohibitive. For example, there was no shag carpeting on the walls (as was the trend at the time); instead, slotted hardboard covered with display felt was used.

A large bass absorber was also placed across the back wall of the control room, above the tape machines. "We tried to use the optimum acoustic ratios (lengths and heights and widths) to minimize standing waves," Harries says. "Then I got out my acoustics book and calculated all the absorbers to put in. We purposely over-absorbed everything, and then when we tuned the room, we just put a hammer through the front of the absorbers that we didn't need."

The Montserrat studio walls were also covered by curtains that could be pulled back for a more live sound; engineers found that by doing so to even just one wall of the studio, the acoustics would change significantly. "What you couldn't change, though, was the ceiling, and over the years that became too absorbent for people like [Police engineer] Hugh Padgham," says Harries with a laugh. "As a result we had to put wood paneling over the absorbers to liven the room up. It was all about changing fashion. We had to liven up AIR Montserrat because of Hugh Padgham!"

Room Dimensions

Oxford Circus:

Studio One: 55' x 29' (17 x 9 meters)
 Ceiling height: 20' (6 meters)
Studio One control room: 18' x 15' (5.5 x 4.5 meters)
 Ceiling height: 10' (3.5 meters)

Studio Two: 39' x 36' (12 x 11 meters)
 Ceiling height: 20' (6 meters)
Studio Two control room: 16' x 16' (5 x 5 meters)
 Ceiling height: 8' (2.5 meters)

Studio Three: 17' x 15' (5 x 4.5 meters)*
 Ceiling height: 9' (3 meters)

Studio Four ("dubbing theater"): 25' x 14'
 (7.5 x 4 meters)*
 Ceiling height: 10' (3.5 meters)
*Control room only.

Montserrat:

Studio: 30' x 30' (9 x 9 meters)
 Ceiling height: 16' (5 meters)
Control room: 25' x 20' (7.5 x 6 meters)
 Ceiling height: 11' (3.3 meters)

Echo Chambers

Oxford Circus

There was no custom-designed acoustic echo chamber at AIR Oxford Circus; however, there was an old bathroom next to the upstairs projection room that was sometimes used for that purpose—a room that had never been refurbished since the building's original construction in 1926. "It was completely tiled with no parallel surfaces at all," recalls Malcolm Atkin, "and, as it was wedged into a mansard roof, it had a superb flutter-free reverb." Tielines ran from the various control rooms to the bathroom, allowing the engineer to route signal to the installed Tannoy Lockwood speaker and from a microphone of the engineer's choice. The room was approximately 10' by 10', with just enough space for, as Atkin describes, "three stand-ups, two sit-downs, and two wash basins," and a ceiling height estimated to be 12' to 14'. This ad hoc echo chamber was used most famously during the mix of the 1984 Dire Straits *Alchemy Live* album, on which it was credited as "Walkers 'Power Toilet'" (named after AIR engineer Nigel Walker).

Engineers at AIR Oxford Circus also employed the main staircases on occasion to act as echo chambers, but as these were outside the studio premises, doing so often incurred the wrath of the building managers, so this usage was generally restricted to nighttime hours.

STORIES FROM THE STUDIO
Tree frogs in the machine

WHEN PRODUCER Hugh Padgham traveled to the Caribbean in early 1981 to begin work on what was to become The Police's multiplatinum album *Ghost in the Machine*, he encountered an immediate problem. "AIR Montserrat provided a great working environment, but I felt the studio area was just too dead to record drums in," he explains. "Having previously worked at the Townhouse, I was into using a natural acoustic for drums at the time—the Phil Collins thing, where you needed a lot of room reflections to achieve that sound."

His solution? Record Stewart Copeland's drums in the communal dining room in the residential villa. "The room had a gabled ceiling and a wooden floor," he says, "so it provided a suitable liveliness. I normally used a [Shure] SM57 on the snare, [Sennheiser] 421s on the toms, Coles 4038 ribbon mics for the overheads, and [Neumann] U87s as room mics, placed about ten to 15 feet away and compressed a little. Obviously we didn't use the room sound as much as we did for Phil, but it still worked.

"Unfortunately," Padgham recalls with a laugh, "it was also semi-outdoors, which meant we had to stop at nightfall every evening because the tree frogs started making a terrible racket, all of which was of course picked up by the mics!"

Montserrat

There was no echo chamber per se at AIR Montserrat. However, visiting engineers and producers often used the residential villa next door for that purpose—although, as the Story from the Studio above illustrates, neighbors of the amphibious type made this possible only during daytime hours.

KEY EQUIPMENT
Mixing Consoles
Oxford Circus

All throughout the 1970s, AIR Oxford Circus used Neve consoles exclusively, although new models were installed periodically to meet the demand for more input channels and increasingly large numbers of recording tracks. In 1972, for example, the consoles in Studios One, Two, and Three were all 24 x 16 (a model A27, A29 and A45, respectively), and the one in Studio Four was a very modest 12 x 4; these were all updated significantly in subsequent years. The "AIR Montserrat" A4792 console was a custom board built by Rupert Neve to Dave Harries and Geoff Emerick's precise specifications, duly installed in the Montserrat studio in 1979 (see *The AIR/Neve collaboration* on the following page for more information). A second, similar model was built at around the same time and was installed in Studio Two at Oxford Circus; a third was built at a later date and is still in use at AIR Lyndhurst today. "Malcolm Atkin designed the system of

that one so that it was like a free-grouping desk," says Dave Harries. "It wasn't in-line, but it could be set to off-tape monitoring or input."

In late 1976, Neve NECAM mix automation was added to the console in Studio Three. As it initially contained just 8k of memory (8 *kilo*bytes), Neve soon informed AIR that an additional 8-kilobyte chip was required to carry out advanced operations. The cost of the tiny chip? A very substantial £5,000—some £25,000 (or $42,000) in today's money!

Montserrat

The Neve A4792 custom-designed for Montserrat offered many advanced features, including 52 channel inputs—each with eight aux outputs (two of which were stereo, complete with panpot) that could be used for foldback or echo/reverb sends—plus six bus outputs. Most importantly, it had extraordinary sound quality, with an unusually wide frequency response of 10 Hz to 180 kHz.

Monitors

"When we opened AIR Oxford Circus in 1970," says Dave Harries, "there weren't many professional loudspeaker manufacturers; in fact, the only British one I can remember was Tannoy."

Accordingly, Tannoy Golds were installed in the Studio One and Two control rooms, fitted into cabinets custom-designed by Harries and driven by Quad amps (later replaced by Crown DC300s). "We actually had four Tannoys across the front of each control room, situated along the studio window," he remembers. "They were all right, although they wouldn't go really loud, which was a bit of a problem for us.

"We tried swapping over the Golds in Studio One to HPDs; then we tried JBL 4350s in both studios, which we ended up putting into Montserrat as well. After a while I got a bit fed up with the JBLs, though, because they relied on horns to get some level in the high frequencies, and I didn't care for that sound. I ended up trying lots of different makes of speakers, but sometime in the late 1970s, I was given a pair of Dynaudio beryllium ribbon tweeters, which were really just hi-fi components, but they were amazing: they went up to 125k! So I made a big cabinet and played around with a lot of different speakers, but in the end it came down to using the beryllium tweeter

STORIES FROM THE STUDIO
The AIR/Neve collaboration

"WE HAD THREE DESKS specially made for us by Rupert Neve," remembers Dave Harries. The reason, he recalls, was that engineer Geoff Emerick (who had recorded most of The Beatles' output at EMI from 1966 onward) had "gone off the sound of the Neve desks we'd installed at AIR; he said it was like listening from behind a net curtain."

Hard to believe today, with vintage Neve desks renowned for their clarity of sound, but Emerick confirms Harries' memory. "A few years after joining AIR [in 1973], I'd worked on various projects [including the band America and the *Sgt. Pepper's* film] in the States," he says. "Most of the studios there had API or MCI desks, which I'd grown to really like. When I returned to AIR Oxford Circus, I couldn't believe how lackluster their Neve desks sounded—they had no sparkle whatsoever—especially in comparison to both API and MCI, as well as other Neve desks I'd heard."

Accordingly, Emerick began lobbying strongly to have an MCI board installed in AIR Montserrat, which was in the planning stage at the time. It was a suggestion that was met with some resistance. "I didn't mind having MCI tape recorders," says Harries, who was charged with overseeing the design of the new facility on the Caribbean island, "but I didn't really want an MCI console in

there. So George Martin and Geoff and I got together with Rupert, and as a result Rupert did a series of now famous blind listening tests with Geoff, using different transformers in boxes as well as different tunings of transformers and straight wire. Geoff always picked the straight wire! He proved that you could hear the differences—and subsequent tests have proved it as well—and that you could perceive a tone as high as 50 kHz, or at least the way it affected frequencies in the audible range."

In a 1998 interview for *Audio Technology* magazine, Rupert Neve recalled both the tests and their effect on future development. "A 48-input console had been delivered to AIR, and Geoff Emerick was very unhappy [with] it. It was a new console, made not long after I had sold the Neve company in 1977. . . . So I went and spent time there, at George Martin's request, and Geoff finally managed to show me what it was that he could hear, and then I began to hear it, too. . . . And once I'd heard it, then I knew what he was talking about. We measured it and found that in three out of the 48 channels, the output transformers had not been correctly terminated and were producing a 3 dB rise at 54 kHz. People said, 'he can't possibly hear that,' but when we corrected that problem—and it was only one

capacitor that had to be added to each of those three channels—Geoff's face just lit up!"

"The frequency response of the standard Neve desk went up to about 70 or 80k, whatever the transformer allowed, and then it just died off," adds Harries. "And although both figures are beyond the range of human hearing, your ears can tell that something's not right. And Rupert's always said since that you need 100 kHz flat for your hearing not to be affected; it's to do with phase relationships."

"We did a lot of R&D and product testing for manufacturers in those days," explains Malcolm Atkin, "and we had an especially close relationship with Neve. For a long time, we were trying to push them on their understanding of what an audio engineer wanted; they were great at design and engineering, but they really didn't know how people were using their products."

According to Atkin, the biggest problem with the Neve consoles of the '70s was that they had too many transformers. "They were absolutely bulletproof—you never got an earth loop or anything like that—but there were a total of something like eight audio transformers between the mic inputs and the mix outputs. People revere transformers these days for their sound, but when you've got eight of them in a line, it slews

and Dynaudio soft-dome midrange, plus four 12" Dynaudio woofers in one big box, driven by HH V800 MOSFET amps. Eventually we installed those in the Studio Two control room."

Tannoy Gold—This 15" dual concentric speaker was the industry standard in the U.K. in the 1960s and early 1970s despite having a limited capacity to handle high volumes. Because Montserrat had an unusually large control room, the maintenance staff at one point experimented with putting two Tannoys in a single cabinet with just one of the tweeters wired up, in an attempt to get more level. The experiment was deemed unsuccessful, however, and so the control room's JBL 4350s remained in place. (See Chapter 1 for more information.)

Tannoy HPD—Released in 1974, these were similar to Tannoy Golds except for having a higher

[increases the slew rate] horribly. Worse yet, by the mid-'70s many of their consoles had a split design—we called them 'jukebox' mixers—where you had an input side and a separate monitor section for playing back off tape quickly, so you didn't have to re-patch. When it came time to do the mix, you sent the signal off tape to the input side of the board instead, where you had access to EQs and everything else. The monitor section had a very simple 24-into-2 mixer with maybe one auxiliary feed for a bit of echo or what have you.

"The trouble was that engineers on sessions sometimes spent weeks doing rough mixes off the monitor section and then, when they'd start to do the proper mix on the same board, the sound would be completely different! Sometimes it would be a complete nightmare, with producers asking why the board suddenly sounded horrible through the input side, while it had all this punch on the monitor mixer. We'd have to say, 'Yes, you're right'... and we were terribly frustrated that there wasn't a lot we could do about it."

One afternoon Atkin and Harries decided to quantify the problem. "We shot ten pulses at 10 kHz through the console with a tone burst generator," Atkin explains, "and we routed it to a storage scope, which allowed us to take photographs of the screen, which, at the time, was the only way we had of measuring transient response in a system. We discovered to our horror that there were only nine pulses coming out the other end! We did the same thing with a Cadac, and I think we got nine and a half; later I did the same experiment with an MCI from that era, and that was pretty good—that was getting nine and three-quarters on the output.

"So it was obvious that all these transformers were slewing the output; there was no transient response left. We sent the photographs to Rupert Neve and said, unless you do something about this we're not buying any more of your consoles, which is how the AIR Montserrat console was born; it was a complete innovation from top to bottom—completely redesigned electronics all the way through."

Perhaps the most important by-product of the redesign was that there were just two transformers per channel—a microphone transformer and an output transformer. In addition, says Harries, "the transformers in the Montserrat desk were toroidal, very low loss, very high frequency. The open circuit frequency response of those desks was flat to 180k!"

The Montserrat desk also had 32 bus outputs, as opposed to the more usual 24. "At that time," Harries explains, "MCI were looking at releasing a 3" 32-track machine running at 20 ips, so we specified 32-track monitoring on the Montserrat desk because we thought that's what would be in place by the time we opened the studio."

Rupert Neve initially built two versions of the Montserrat-specification desk: one had the producer/monitor section on the right-hand side and the other had the section on the left-hand side. The former went into AIR Oxford Circus Studio Two, because the exterior window in that control room was on the right-hand side, looking over the Oxford Street shops; the other one was installed at Montserrat. Enthuses Harries, "We angled the window of the control room there such that, when you were sitting at the desk, it perfectly framed the view to the Caribbean ocean"—true attention to detail.

Another unusual feature of the "AIR Montserrat" consoles, as they have come to be known, were their remote control mic preamps. "Rupert had a thing about mic leads being kept short," Harries says, "because he felt that long capacitive mic cables could compromise high-frequency response. As a result, the mic pres were out in the studio, remotely operated from the console. It was not a feature we asked for—it was something Rupert offered, one of his many innovations."

The famed AIR Montserrat console and view from the control room into the studio.
(Photo by Frank Oglethorpe)

power rating and ribbed strengthening on the woofer for reduced distortion; in addition, the low-frequency driver surround was made from plastic foam. The HPD came in 10", 12", and 15" sizes; it is believed that the ones installed at AIR Oxford Circus were 15 inches.

JBL 4350—The successor to the JBL 4311 (widely used in American recording studios during the 1970s), the 4350 was a large biamplified monitor that incorporated dual 15" low-frequency loudspeakers in a ported enclosure, along with a 12" midrange speaker, a 4" high-frequency compression driver, and an "ultra" high-frequency compression driver, with high-frequency output distributed via a horn/lens assembly. Stated frequency response was 30 Hz–20 kHz.

Tape Machines

AIR Oxford Circus was originally intended to be an 8-track facility, but planning and construction delays meant that the format was already obsolete by the time the studio's doors opened in 1970. Consequently, Studer 16-track machines were ordered, but the manufacturer failed to deliver them on time, and so four 3M M56 2" 16-track recorders were purchased and installed instead.

3M M56 (16-track)—This multitrack came with a somewhat primitive remote control (sans tape counter), prompting maintenance engineer Malcolm Atkin to hand-construct a number of sophisticated tape counter systems some years after the machine's arrival at AIR. (See *Decca* in Chapter 2 for more information.)

3M M79 (24-track)—M79s replaced the M56s at Oxford Circus a year or two after the facility opened. The M79 offered options for both transformer and transformerless input/output; it is believed that the AIR machines had transformers. (See *Decca* in Chapter 2 for more information.)

MCI JH-16 (24-track)—Two of these were installed at Montserrat, with an MCI synchronizer that allowed 46-track work. (One track on each machine was used to carry time code.) While 46 tracks for recording seems miserly by today's digital standards, going beyond 24 tracks was of particular importance in the analog era, since a tape might have typically gotten spooled a thousand times or more by the time overdubs were completed, with the resultant loss of fidelity. To get around this, the AIR Montserrat engineers often recorded the drums and rhythm section on one JH-16, then did a stereo reference mix onto two tracks of the other machine, thus allowing them to put the first tape away until needed for mixdown. (See *Advision* in Chapter 3 for more information.)

3M M23 (8-track)—(See Chapter 1 for more information.)

Studer J37 (4-track)—(See Chapter 1 for more information.)

Studer A62 (2-track and mono)—First introduced in 1965, this small and lightweight 1/4" machine was said to be the first fully transistorized professional tape recorder. Several of them were available at AIR Oxford Circus for mixdown and/or tape echo purposes. They offered interchangeable "butterfly" heads—a design attempt to use more of the tape than standard half-track heads, with a smaller-than-usual gap between the tracks in the middle, yielding slightly higher output and dynamics, though at the expense of slightly more crosstalk between channels.

Ferrograph Studio 8 (2-track and stereo)—The professional successor to the company's popular 1/4" Series 7 home tape recorder, the Studio 8 was designed for broadcast facilities, and was released in the early 1970s. It offered tape motion sensing and plug-in equalization boards (for NAB and IEC curves), as well as, oddly, interchangeable stereo and 2-track head blocks, which differed in that they covered slightly different tape widths (2.75 mm versus 2 mm). Several of these were purchased by AIR Oxford Circus, where they were used primarily for tape echo. According to Chris Michie, it was common practice at AIR to delay the signal a few milliseconds by passing it through a 2-track machine before sending it on to an echo chamber or EMT plate. "It was also common to have one or two 2-track machines running for tape echo or pre-echo delay, so the tape op would have to rewind and cue as many as four machines before every mix pass," Michie noted.

Studer A80R (2-track)—The A80R was a later version of the ubiquitous Studer A80, with an advanced

---

tape path and electronics. It was the "go-to" 1/4" 2-track mixdown machine at AIR Oxford Circus—several of them were purchased and were installed in all four studios, and several more were installed at AIR Montserrat. Jog and shuttle features made razor-blade editing a relatively simple process, and there was also a built-in monitor speaker and headphone jack that allowed the engineer or tape op to check input or output signal—helpful when troubleshooting patching or signal routing difficulties. (See Chapter 1 for more information.)

Ampex ATR-102 (2-track)—AIR Oxford Circus became the first recording studio in the U.K. to offer 1/2" mixing when these 2-track machines were installed shortly after Dave Harries visited Village Recorders in California in the late 1970s and saw them in use there. ATR-102s were exceptionally versatile in that they were not limited to one tape width, allowing users to swap head-stacks and guides, thus permitting a single machine to handle 1/4", 1/2", and even modified 1" tape. Three ATR-102s were installed at AIR Montserrat as well.

Main Microphones

Neumann U87—Both the Oxford Circus and Montserrat facilities had a large number of these "go-to" vocal/instrument microphones on hand. Chris Michie states that a pair of these were often used to mic the studios' grand pianos, positioned "so that one was over the point where the bass strings cross over the middle strings and [the] other positioned over the high strings. Putting the mics nearer the hammers got a brighter

---

STORIES FROM THE STUDIO
To mute or not to mute?

ONE MORNING IN 1978 engineer Mike Stavrou found himself in Studio One at AIR Oxford Circus recording an orchestral overdub for a track on Art Garfunkel's *Fate for Breakfast* album. The backing tracks had been laid down in Los Angeles sometime previously, but the producer, Louie Shelton, had decided to do the sweetening at AIR because the British string players—mostly members of the London Symphony Orchestra—were deemed to be of higher caliber than those in L.A.—not to mention a little less expensive to hire.

"We had gotten a nice string sound, similar to what we usually achieved in that room," recalls Stavrou. "There was nothing special about the recording initially. But then the arranger came into the control room and admitted that he had made a big mistake. 'I wrote the part while working it out on an electronic keyboard,' he admitted sheepishly, 'and I forgot that I need-ed to allow time for the players to remove their mutes.' [*Note: A mute is a small device that clips on to a violin in order to change its tone.*]

"Now, 30 violins playing with their mutes on is a different sound altogether than 30 violins with no mutes," Stavrou continues. "And the problem wasn't just that the arranger hadn't written a rest to allow them to take the mutes off—he really didn't want a rest; at a certain point in the song, he wanted the strings to go from playing with mutes to instantly playing with no mutes.

"While everyone was scratching their heads wondering what to do, I said, 'I've got an idea. I won't explain it; just do what I tell you.'" Shelton may have been shocked at the engineer's audacity, but, as Stavrou adds with a laugh, "he really had no choice, since he was paying for this very expensive orchestra, and it was costing him a fortune every minute we sat around trying to come up with a solution."

What neither the producer nor the beleaguered arranger knew was that Stavrou had been tinkering with a new technique for several weeks prior to the Garfunkel session. "With the tape machines of the era," Stavrou explains, "any time you did a dropout [British terminology for punching out], there would be a section of tape that was blank—erased but not recorded over—for the period of time equivalent to the distance between the erase head and the record head. So you always had to pick a big gap in order not to notice the momentary silence. I'd developed a technique to get around that, and I'd been experimenting with it on pianos and on vocals, but here was the chance to try it out with a large orchestra—high risk, high reward, I thought.

"I started by having the orchestra record the entire track with no mutes. The arranger objected, saying, 'The mutes are supposed to be on in the beginning.' 'I know,' I replied, 'but trust me: Just play.' So they

sound, but [engineer] John Punter aimed for a natural sound. . . . Punter even had a three-mic setup for stereo piano, with them lined up in a row above the hammers." (See Chapter 1 for more information.)

Neumann KM84—These unobtrusive pencil condenser mics were generally used at AIR as hi-hat or drum overhead mics. (See Chapter 1 and Chapter 5 for more information.) Engineer Mike Stavrou found quite a different use for them, however, as the Story from the Studio on the following page attests!

Neumann KM86—Set on figure-of-eight polar pattern, KM86s were sometimes used as a snare drum mic at AIR. (See *CTS / The Music Centre* in Chapter 3 for more information.)

Coles 4038—Originally marketed in the U.K. as the STC 4038, this ribbon microphone was a particular favorite of Geoff Emerick, who frequently used it as a drum overhead mic. (See Chapter 1 for more information.)

AKG D12—This perennial kick drum mic was rarely used at AIR for any other purpose. (See *Lansdowne* in Chapter 3 for more information.)

AKG D212—Similar to the D202 "rocket" mic, the D212 was AKG's first dual-element microphone. This small-diaphragm cardioid offered a three-position bass rolloff switch. Because its design resulted in almost no proximity effect, it was often used at AIR on toms and for recording bass amplifiers and brass instruments. (See Chapter 6 for more information about the D202.)

AKG D224—This dynamic pencil mic was often used at AIR for miking drums; reportedly, visiting

played the song from beginning to end with no mutes. Then I instructed them to put the mutes on and told them to start again, from the beginning, and to keep playing until the tape stopped.

"Then, as I was recording over what they originally played, I took out a chinagraph pencil and, holding it loosely in one hand, dropped it down vertically behind the tape, on the oxide side, just before the erase head. Normally the tape just brushes the erase head, and then after an inch or so it would be making contact with the record head. But I knew at exactly what beat the mutes were supposed to disappear, and so, on the last beat of the bar before, I slowly and smoothly moved the tape away from the erase head by bringing the chinagraph pencil toward me, which I continued doing until the tape was no longer making contact with the record head either, at which point I hit the Stop button.

"So the tape stops, everyone wonders what's going on, I wind back, I play the tape, and sure enough there's absolutely no gap between the two takes; in fact, what was created, to everyone's amazement but mine, was a crossfade of the previous recording with the new recording—over the course of a beat, all the mutes just melted away into a non-muted string section. Essentially I had been taking over the job of the tape guide, but for a very short amount of time. And as you move the tape away from the erase head, the energy causing the tape to demagnetize dies away, so there's still some signal remaining on the tape even as the record head adds more signal to it."

The key to doing this successfully, Stavrou explains, was to keep the pencil absolutely perpendicular with the plane of the tape so that all the tracks were lifted off simultaneously—"otherwise, you'll get Track 1 fading away before Track 24." Timing was also critical: "If you move the

pencil too quickly, you'll change the tape speed and so you'll also get a little flutter during that moment; do it too slowly, and the crossfade will be too long, and too noticeable, plus there's the danger of the tape riding up the pencil." Adding to the pressure was the fact that he was doing this on the fly, with a lot of very expensive musicians looking on—a pretty ballsy move. "Fortunately," Stavrou says with a laugh, "I'd been doing this a lot during the past couple of weeks on really tricky vocal and acoustic piano dropouts. All those rehearsals made me pretty confident I could pull it off."

As a postscript, some years later Studer introduced a multitrack tape recorder that provided automatic delay compensation for seamless punch-in (drop-in) and punch-out (dropout) without a gap . . . but even that advanced machine couldn't do crossfades like the one Mike Stavrou created for Art Garfunkel on that fateful day in 1978.

producer Gus Dudgeon sometimes favored it for vocals. (See *Pye* in Chapter 2 for more information.)

Shure SM57—(See *CTS / The Music Centre* in Chapter 3 for more information.)

Sennheiser MD421—These were widely utilized at AIR for tom-toms, as well as percussion and brass instruments. (See *Pye* in Chapter 2 for more information.)

In addition, a 1979 listing indicated that AIR Oxford Circus offered Electrovoice (EV) microphones, although the exact model numbers were not specified.

Outboard Signal Processors

Neve 2254—Three of these 5-inch-square units were fitted to the meter bridge of each Neve console at AIR Oxford Circus. According to engineer Geoff Emerick, they were the only compressors at the facility that could adequately control the sound of Robin Trower's heavily effected guitar during the recording of the 1974 *Bridge of Sighs* album. (See *Pye* in Chapter 2 for more information.)

UREI 1176—AIR Oxford Circus offered two 1176s, as did AIR Montserrat. (See *Decca* in Chapter 2 for more information.)

EMT 140 plate reverbs—AIR Oxford Circus had five EMT 140 plates, with a central patch bay to for routing signal to and from any of the four control rooms. These were stashed in the crawl spaces between the studio shell and the walls of the building. AIR Montserrat had an EMT 140 as well. (See Chapter 1 for more information.)

STORIES FROM THE STUDIO
Three mics are better than one

BY THE MID-1970S, T. Rex front man Marc Bolan was a superstar in England, and someone whom Mike Stavrou very much wanted to impress, as Stavrou freely admits. In 1976, Bolan was slated to coproduce his girlfriend Gloria Jones' album *Vixen* at AIR, with Stavrou behind the board. In preparation for the upcoming sessions, the young engineer had listened to Jones' previous records, but was unimpressed with the sound of her vocals—due, he felt, to the singer's wide dynamic range, something that other engineers had not coped with effectively.

After giving the problem some consideration, Stavrou came up with an innovative solution. "If you imagine sound as being a bubble or a sphere," he explains, "it's clear that a microphone diaphragm only ever captures one tiny piece of that waveform—one small part of its radius. For a dynamic singer like Gloria, I knew that I was going to have to pull the mic further away, because that's where her sound is focusing—but of course as you move the mic further away, you capture a smaller part of that waveform. My goal was to be able to get the mic a good distance from her but still capture a large percentage of that waveform.

"So I thought, well, I can't make the mic bigger, but if I strap a few microphones together, that would in essence create a larger diaphragm to capture a bigger piece of the waveform. In this case, I used three [Neumann] KM84s, which were very well suited for that purpose because they have a very neutral sound, plus, because they are so small, you can position the diaphragms pretty much anywhere you want.

"I strapped the three mics together using rubber bands and created a sling with a large cloth—the kind of thing you'd use if you'd broken your arm—and placed it around Gloria's neck, and put her arm in it. I then gave her the cluster of mics and told her to hold them in her fist and to keep pushing against the sling as she sang. She always liked to dance around when she was singing, so if you just put her in front of a static mic stand, she'd constantly be going on and off mic, yet if you told her to stand still, it would affect her performance. Putting the mics in her fist with her arm in a sling allowed Gloria to dance around all she wanted, with the microphones chasing her instead of the other way around. Plus, by having her constantly push against the sling, it kept the mics at the distance I wanted [approximately 18 inches to two feet away]."

The three mics were brought into three different channels on the console—all at the same level and with no EQ—but were mixed to a single track so they acted as one mono signal. "By doing that," Stavrou explains, "I got a much better to signal-to-noise ratio because the noise doesn't add 6 dB per two channels, but the on-axis vocal does." In addition, Stavrou discovered that the cumulative frequency response of the cluster was also completely different from the response of each individual

EMT 240 Gold Foil—Both AIR Oxford Circus and AIR Montserrat also offered an EMT 240, which provided a slightly less dense reverb than the 140 plate and so was often used on vocals. (See *Lansdowne* in Chapter 3 for more information.)

AMS DMX 15-80—Introduced at the dawn of the digital age in 1978, this was the world's first microprocessor-controlled digital delay line, capable of monophonic 15-bit sampling as well as pitch shifting. A later version, the DMX 15-80S, supported stereo delays and sampling and eventually became a staple in recording studios the world over. AIR was said to be one of the first U.K. studios to offer digital delay to its clientele.

Other outboard equipment at AIR included an AMS Flanger and Delay; Eventide digital delays, flangers and Harmonizers; Klark-Teknik DN27 graphic equalizers; an ADR Vocal Stressor; an ADR Scamp rack outfitted with several S300 gate modules; and numerous racks of Dolby 361 noise reduction units, which were sometimes used (most often by engineer John Punter) on the sends and returns to tape echo, as well as in even more unconventional ways, as the Story from the Studio on the next page illustrates.

Film Equipment

States former AIR chief engineer Bill Price, "From the very beginning, George Martin wanted to build a film recording studio—it was just something he wanted to do. As a result, Studio One at AIR had a massive

mic, yielding an extended bottom end. "It was similar to the way Sweet Sixteens [hi-fi speakers popular in the '50s and '60s] worked," he says. "They were these big cabinets which had this incredible bottom end, but when you took the grille off, all they contained was an array of sixteen 5" speakers, all wired in phase so they moved in unison with each other to push the air as if it were a single huge cone."

Stavrou would also apply significant dynamics processing to the combined mono signal, in the form of an unconventional chain consisting of a limiter, followed by a compressor. These were patched in series (as opposed to strapping them as a bus insert), with the output of the compressor going directly to the tape machine input. "When engineers put two dynamic processors across a vocal—even today—they almost always begin with the compressor and then finish with the limiter," he explains. "But I thought I'd try it the other way around, and the result was incredible: I got twice the dynamic range with half the pumping, and with significantly reduced distortion. That's because the peak limiter would protect the low-ratio compressor, which would actually react to the voice first. Although it may seem logical to think, well, I want the compressor to react first so I'll put it upstream, and then I'll put the limiter downstream, the problem is that, by the time the limiter is getting a piece of the really loud signal, the compressor upstream is already getting totally clobbered." The limiter Stavrou used for the Gloria Jones sessions—a UREI 1176—was set to a 4:1 ratio, with a moderately fast attack and release, but with the threshold adjusted so that it would trigger only on peak signals. The compressor—an ADR Vocal Stressor—was set at a 2:1 ratio, with its slowest attack and approximately a half-second of release.

Stavrou subsequently experimented with creating clusters—something he eventually called "tri-mics"—out of combinations of different microphones, but found that the signal would inevitably add together better if three of the same model were used. He also discovered that tri-miking worked best when the mics were fairly distant from the source. "If you use it up close, you'll get phasey off-axis stuff going on," he cautions.

During Jones' vocal sessions, which were recorded in AIR's spacious Studio One, Stavrou also placed two U87s on booms and positioned them high up in the far corners of the room for ambience. These were recorded on two separate tracks in stereo, uncompressed, and then blended in with the tri-mic signal (panned directly up the center) during mixdown, with minor EQ adjustments made as necessary. The ambient tracks (but not the tri-mic track) were also routed to an EMT plate during mixing for some additional airiness.

For more details, check out Mike Stavrou's book, Mixing with Your Mind *(www.mixingwithyourmind.com).*

"Because it sounds amazing!"

MAINTENANCE ENGINEER MALCOLM ATKIN had been working at AIR Oxford Circus only a few weeks when he received a most unusual request. The band Pilot were in, doing handclap overdubs (most likely in Studio Two), with Alan Parsons as producer, and Parsons was asking if a spare Dolby rack was available—even though the tape box indicated that the recording was to be non-Dolby. At the time, AIR employed Dolby 361s, which were individual units rather than the multichannel version, and, because there was an extra charge for their use, groups of 24 modules had been installed in mobile racks and wheeled in and out of sessions as needed.

Having received an answer in the affirmative, the producer made a second, rather more enigmatic request, this time for 24 mic leads [cables]. "I wasn't quite sure why he was asking that," Atkin continues, "but I found out as soon as I wheeled in the rack and the leads."

To Atkin's considerable surprise, Parsons instructed him to plug the output of each Dolby into the input of the next one and daisy-chain the whole rig together, so that incoming signal would go into the first unit and come out of the 24th unit on the end of the chain.

"I wondered aloud why on earth he wanted me to do that, and Alan just winked at me and said, 'Because it sounds amazing!' And he was right; it did sound fantastic. Of course, it was unbelievably compressed, but what an eye-opener! That interaction stayed with me all these years, because here was this world-famous producer, and if Ray Dolby knew what he was doing with his gear, he'd have a fit! But there was simply nothing at the time that could crucify a sound the way 24 Dolbys in a chain could do."

That was the prevailing attitude in those days, according to Atkin: No matter what a piece of equipment was designed to do, as soon as it came through the door, the thinking was, *What kind of noise can this thing make?* "Engineers didn't care what the actual purpose of the piece of gear was," he says. "If they could repurpose it and come up with something unique, that's what they would do every time. Whatever the guy down the street was doing, you'd want to know, first of all, how he'd done it, and, secondly, how could you do something even more radical by plugging together the toys you had available in your toy box. The goal was to get a different noise out of your gear; it almost didn't matter sometimes what the noise was—as long as it sounded different."

screen at one end and a projection room above the control room, containing an assembly of sprocketed tape machines. Later a small dubbing theater [Studio Four] was added on the other side of the corridor.

"It was actually a bit of a bone of contention, because almost from the day we opened, we were a really busy rock 'n' roll studio, yet all this money was being diverted into this film equipment and facilities, using a technology which was in its death throes even then—all these mechanical maglinks and sprocketed machines. One of the reasons it never took off was that every one of the machines—I believe they were 4-tracks—required its own highly skilled union-pay-scale operator. At Pinewood or Denham, where they knew how to do this and did it all the time, they would have a crew scoring a picture and ten men working in the projection room, because it's really hard work spooling stuff back and cuing it up. We simply didn't have those kinds of resources."

A 1972 studio listing in *Billboard* magazine indicated that AIR offered a number of Albrecht mag film recorders and Philips 16-35mm film projectors, exact models unknown. However, by 1980 the die was cast, and virtually all of the AIR Oxford Circus film equipment was removed and sold to Abbey Road.

KEY TECHNICAL INNOVATIONS
In addition to being the first studio in the U.K. to offer half-inch mixdown and computer automation, AIR's maintenance staff were responsible for a number of "homegrown" technical innovations.

Film Synchronization
Despite the proliferation of film equipment at AIR Oxford Circus being a bit of a "white elephant," in the words of one former staffer, it did result in at least one positive, in the form of an ingenious synchronization system developed by Dave Harries—an invention that was several years ahead of its time.

Bill Price describes the history behind it thusly: "We never got any work doing film recording, despite all this money being spent [on equipment], so George [Martin] put himself forward as a film composer, and he landed quite a few contracts. The first one was a film called *The Optimists*, and I was nominated as the engineer. George asked me how I was going to record it, and I told him, 'I don't want to have anything to do with this film equipment. It's too unreliable and I don't know very much about it, so let's just record the score on 16-track [tape].' To which he quite reasonably asked, 'Well, how are we going to play it back to picture? How are we going to get it in sync?' Of course this was in the pre-synchronizer days, so there was no easy answer. But for some years I'd been using multitracks and mixing down to stereo tape machines, then flying it back in; I was actually able to do 48-track recording that way long before we had synchronizers. So I said, 'We can do something like that, George.'

"The thing about dubbing to picture," Price explains, "is that every time you do a take, the film has to be wound back, which takes a long time, because you can either rewind it by running the projector in reverse at normal speed—in which case it takes the same amount of time as playing it—or if it's a long section, you have to unlace the film from the projector, put it on a bench, wind it back, and then put it back on the projector. So it's a pretty tedious process."

Enter the redoubtable Mr. Harries. "Up until then," he says, "you could record on multitrack to picture, but if you wanted to play back to picture, you had to first create a mono mix on another bit of 35mm film. I thought, well, this is a bit silly; you ought to be able to do it by figuring out a way to start the two machines up at the same time."

What he came up with wasn't exactly a film synchronizer—it was a synchronized start link with an audio beep. But it was surprisingly effective, thanks in large part to the stability of the M56's synchronous motor and Isoloop tape path, ensuring that the tape would run almost exactly the same as the film speed. Harries' system consisted of two small boxes, one of which was attached to the projector, electrically interlocked with the start button, and the other one of which was placed in the control room, electrically interlocked with the remote of the 16-track tape recorder. The two boxes were connected via the

Notice posted at AIR Oxford Circus. It *was* the '70s, after all!
(Courtesy of Steve Nye)

audio tielines that went from the control room up to the projection room.

"When you were recording to picture, you always had a film projector running, plus a mag camera with a start tone and a 50 Hz loop," explains Malcolm Atkin. "Up in the projection room, the mag camera would start up in sync with the projector, and its 50 Hz loop would be amplified and used to drive the capstan motor of the multitrack tape machine in the control room below. A specified number of seconds later, when the projector was up to speed, the start tone would come through the gate of the mag camera and would be used to start the tape machine transport."

The AIR Montserrat control room. Note the fashionably attired maintenance engineer Frank Oglethorpe and the window to his right, which looked out over the golf course below.
(Photo by Frank Oglethorpe)

Price describes the somewhat Rube Goldberg–like procedure thusly: "When we were ready to go for a take, the tape op got a grease pencil and marked the multitrack tape, lined the mark up with the record head of the tape machine, and then sat there with his finger on the Record button (which did nothing if the transport was not moving), waiting for the projectionist to start the projector.

"As soon as the projector started, the multitrack would start up and, because the tape op's finger was on the Record button, it would begin recording. When it came time to do a playback, the tape op would rewind the multitrack machine, line it up with the grease pencil mark at the playback head, which would all be done and waiting long before the

projector was ready. Then when the projectionist would start the projector, off it would go."

"As long as you lined up the grease pencil mark properly," says Harries, "the 16-track would always start in the same place, and, as soon as it got up to speed, everything worked fine. If the projector slowed down, then the 50 Hz would also slow down, so the tape machine would slow down, too, keeping everything pretty much in sync."

As Atkin points out, "The system relied on the motor [of the M56] holding steady, which it would generally do for short periods of time. But let's face it: Most film cues are less than a minute long, and a lot of what we were doing were just 30-second adverts, so if you were a frame out by the end of a minute or so, it didn't really matter by that time." Whatever its limitations, it was a significant improvement over the primitive synchronization offered by other studios of the era, which could only provide mono, stereo, or 4-track at most when recording to picture.

Needless to say, there was hue and outcry from some corners when AIR's system became public. "I had terrible trouble with the union people, who were shouting about how there was nothing in the union rules that said we could do this," remembers Price. "They wanted to get their audio editors in to see if it was OK, and I told them, 'I can guarantee you accuracy within plus or minus 20 milliseconds at the very worst.'

"Film editing, of course, is done frame by frame," he adds, "which is 40 milliseconds, anyway. And even if there are spot edit cues, the music editor will always pull the music back and forth as needed to get the hits absolutely perfect. So I assured the union audio editors there would be absolutely no problem with this, and they finally accepted it. We did a couple of movies that way, including *Live and Let Die*."

Cue Mixers

AIR was the first studio in the U.K. to provide cue mixers. And since there weren't any in existence at the time, the staff there built their own.

Explains Dave Harries, "Geoff Emerick had just recorded the group Gallagher & Lyle at AIR [doing tracks for the 1976 album *Breakaway*], and everyone in the band always wanted something different in their cans, so he had a small mixer placed in the studio that they used to create their own headphone mixes. I thought, what a great idea—it makes things so easy for everybody! We had just installed a new Neve desk with eight aux outputs, so I said, 'Let's design and build our own little headphone mixer and feed it signal from those eight auxes; that way, artists can create their own custom headphone mixes.'"

Adds Malcolm Atkin, with a laugh, "The goal was to make a mixer that was simple enough so that even musicians would know how to use it. The design we came up with had eight little faders, eight little panpots, an overall basic EQ—bass and treble—and an overall panpot and volume control. My main problem at the time was primarily: How loud can I get it? How much voltage can I get down these headphones before

I break any laws? Which was plus or minus 50 volts at the time, so that ended up being the voltage rail.

"In fact," he says, "you could blow up a pair of Beyer headphones in a matter of 30 seconds with these mixers. I think the only person who ever complained that they weren't loud enough was Lemmy from Motörhead!"

"We put the power amplifiers in the base of the stand," recalls Harries, "which kept it all very compact and portable and also helped weigh down the unit so it wouldn't topple over. We used these little 30-watt amps, but sometimes musicians

STORIES FROM THE STUDIO
McCartney Live (and in the studio)

AIR STUDIOS' CHIEF ENGINEER BILL PRICE first used Dave Harries' synchronized start system on Paul McCartney and Wings' 1972 recording of the title track for the James Bond flick *Live and Let Die*, with producer George Martin at the helm. "It was supposed to be done in Studio One," Price recalls, "but the room was absolutely full because Paul wanted to do it live with Wings and the London Symphony Orchestra, all at the same time. So I ended up having to move the woodwind section out into Studio Two because not only was there no room for them, but I was running out of channels on the desk as well! I asked [fellow AIR engineer] Steve Nye to mix the woodwinds down to a stereo pair and send them to me so they could go straight to a couple of tracks on my multitrack machine.

"We did have to cheat a little bit—though not a hell of a lot—because, while the theory was good, in practice the separation problems of a rock band playing live along with strings made things impossible, so earlier that afternoon we recorded a backing track with Wings.

"There's one section where the orchestra stops and it goes into a reggae section," Price adds, "and that was actually done live; it wasn't edited in. We took it from a live take of Wings with the orchestra, and because the strings don't play there, it worked fine. And a lot of McCartney's vocal was live, some of it live with Wings, some of it live with the orchestra, a little bit of it overdubbed. But I do remember that I wasn't able to edit too much because there were so many tracks and so many different takes, so I mixed all the different bits and then edited the 2-track."

Sometimes you've got to take a step back to go a step forward

MIKE STAVROU JOINED AIR as a tape operator in 1974, and by the time the Montserrat studio opened in 1979, he had already worked his way up the ranks to senior engineer. "Everybody at Oxford Circus wanted to go to Montserrat," he says. "It was beautiful, it was warm, and George had built this atmospheric studio that was incredible. But the only people who got to go were engineers who actually had a gig booked, plus they would rotate the tape ops every six months."

One day Stavrou heard through the grapevine that George Martin was about to introduce Paul McCartney to Montserrat for the first time, to record tracks that would later appear on his *Tug of War* album, with Geoff Emerick engineering. "So on two separate days," he recalls with a chuckle, "I whispered into both George's and Geoff's ear, 'Look, I know how important this album is going to be, so if you'd rather kind of have a senior engineer assisting for you instead of a tape op, I just wanted you to know I'm not too proud.'

"And they took me up on it! But before I flew out, I asked George, 'What's the state of the studio? Are there a lot of faults? What are we going to find when we get there?' He said, 'Well, the tech tells me everything's perfect.'

"Now, most people, the minute they arrive in Montserrat, they hit the beach. But I locked myself into the control room and I went through every switch, every knob, every fader, every patch point, every mic, every set of cans. I swept the monitors with frequencies looking for rattles to stuff up with foam, whatever, and when George arrived three days later I showed him this fault book I'd written, with pages full of problems I'd identified."

The maintenance department was immediately instructed to work around the clock to address the issues before McCartney arrived, and Martin was so impressed with the young engineer's initiative, he appointed Stavrou studio manager right there and then. Happily, the monthlong sessions—which, in Stavrou's words, "seemed like the gig of the century, with McCartney and Stevie Wonder and Ringo Starr and Carl Perkins all there"—came off without a hitch.

"My philosophy was simple," says Stavrou. "You simply can't have anything go wrong with these guys; they're too good, they deserve the very best. If anything happens that delays what they want to do, what ingenious idea did that just abort? That was my thinking, because ev-

ery minute in sessions like that are pretty magical.

"A few days after the sessions ended, everybody except George had left, and the morning he was due to fly out, he and I were sitting in the control room and he asked me if I felt OK taking on the new job, or whether I felt it was too big a responsibility. I said, 'No, I'm fine, but, before you go, perhaps you could just tell me what my job description is?' He perched himself on the edge of the console and said, 'Ah, yes, good point, Michael,' and he thought for a second or two—George was always a man of few words. Then he just turned to me and said with a smile, 'Michael, you just have to remember one thing.' I remember sitting on the edge of my seat waiting to hear what that one thing was. And then he said: 'What you like, I like.' And that was that."

Stavrou would end up spending a year at Montserrat, serving not only as studio manager but also as tape operator on a number of sessions, including The Police's *Ghost in the Machine*, doing all he could to ensure the same level of technical perfection that had been achieved for the McCartney sessions. "Every time a new artist came in," he explains, "I wanted them to feel as though we'd built the studio especially for them."

turned them up too loud, to the point where it wasn't safe, so we put resistors in to put a limit on how loud they could go."

"After we got them installed and up and running, I was fascinated to go out into the studio and see what the musicians had actually mixed for themselves," says Atkin. "They were all the same: their own fader all the way up and everyone else down at around minus 20 or 30 [dB]. Which told you straightaway what frustra-

tion musicians had had for years, because they were constantly complaining to the engineer in the control room about the state of the foldback mix . . . and it was always the loudest ego that won! The singer, probably."

Most cue mixers today use the same basic design. And the fact that the original cue mixers built by Harries, Atkin, and company are still being used at AIR Lyndhurst today, some 40 years later, is testimony to their staying power.

SELECTED DISCOGRAPHY

- Procol Harum: *Broken Barricades* (AIR Oxford Circus)
- Jeff Beck: *Blow by Blow, Wired* (AIR Oxford Circus)
- Robin Trower, *Bridge of Sighs* (AIR Oxford Circus)
- Paul McCartney: "Live and Let Die" (single) (AIR Oxford Circus)
- Cheap Trick: *All Shook Up* (AIR Montserrat)
- Police: *Ghost in the Machine* (AIR Montserrat)
- Paul McCartney (with Stevie Wonder): "Ebony and Ivory" (single) (AIR Montserrat)

OTHER IMPORTANT STUDIOS OF THE ERA

LEVY'S / CBS / WHITFIELD STREET

From little acorns mighty oaks do grow.

It is 1921, the height of the gramophone craze in England. Brothers Morris and Jacques Levy are the owners of a popular record store in London's East End, and one day it occurs to them that profits could be further expanded if they made their own discs instead of just selling American and European imports.

And so, in 1925, the Levy brothers founded Oriole Records—the first British record label. Oriole would go on to enjoy considerable longevity and modest success (notably, it was the first U.K. label to license recordings from Tamla Motown), and its formation led to another important decision by Morris and Jacques: starting an independent recording service for aspiring artists. The enterprise, which became operational in 1931—the same year EMI's Abbey Road facility was opened—was named Levy's Sound Studios, initially located at 94-98 Regent Street, near Piccadilly Circus, until larger premises were found at 73 New Bond Street, about a half mile away.

Starting in the mid-1950s, Levy's Sound Studios was used extensively to record cover versions of the British pop hits of the day, which were released on the cut-price Embassy Records label and sold exclusively in Woolworths stores. (Levy's would eventually purchase Embassy and merge it with the Oriole label.) The Levy's recording equipment in the '50s consisted of a handful of BBC Marconi and STC condenser microphones, plus a half dozen AKG D19 dynamics; several small mixers patched together; a monophonic EMI BTR2 tape machine; and a single Tannoy 15" dual concentric speaker housed in a Lockwood cabinet, driven by the monitor amplifier in the BTR2.

Bill Johnson, who began his career at Levy's as a junior engineer in 1955, recalled in an online memoir that the control room at the time was "really quite primitive. . . . There was a central six-channel [valve] mixer . . . without any equalisation, a secondary passive mixer that took the output of the main mixer, and two Vortexion mixers purchased later. These were then fed into an equaliser with primitive top and bass controls connected to the mono tape recorder or disc cutter. . . . It was simple, but the signal was distortion-free and clean as a whistle.

"Originally, sessions were recorded direct onto disc live," he continues. "It was not until Jacques [Levy] returned from Germany at the end of hostilities clutching a Magnetophon tape machine which seemed to have fallen off a Panzer wagon, [that] they converted to prerecording on tape. . . . The [Magnetophon] ran at 30 ips and made a dickens of a noise. . . . It used open-sided European platters of quarter-inch tape, 3,250 feet long. . . . The one we had still retained the rotating scrambler head used to transmit secret messages to agents in the field, as well as normal linear heads."

Levy's good-sized studio, roughly 40' by 40', had been built into what was once an art gallery. "The acoustic engineers had built a soundproof shell within the gallery, all on a floating floor," says Johnson. "Even the control room was within the shell. Above the

A 1963 Oriole Records session at Levy's. Left to right: Engineer John Wood, producer Tony Kent, music director Conrad Wagner puffing thoughtfully on his pipe, and maintenance engineer Dag Fellner, looking concerned.
(Courtesy of Tony Kent)

control room was a void to the ceiling of the old art gallery." Yet there were nagging acoustic problems, largely due to the lack of a void above the studio. "The studio had a conical ceiling," explains former Levy's chief engineer Geoff Frost, who started work at the studio in 1959, "which meant that when you were recording a loud brass section, the sound of the instruments would go up and hit one of these huge cornices which were three or four feet in diameter, and that would send the sound down onto the string mics, which in turn would cause the preamps in the board to distort."

Eventually, studio staff got in the habit of putting the brass section in the reception area or on the stairs outside the studio when doing sessions at night— which was pretty much the only time Levy's could do any kind of loud recording, since the floor below was office space occupied by one tenant in particular who had an unsettling tendency to express his displeasure at the racket coming from over his head by rapping on the ceiling (which was, of course, the studio floor) with a broom handle. Making matters worse, vibrations would often emanate downward into the studio from the echo chamber on the roof above when it was

in use, due to the relative lack of insulation between the two. "The studio did have its problems," says engineer Mike Ross-Trevor, who joined in 1963. "But as the decade moved on, the music changed and there was more overdubbing, so the live acoustics were less of a problem since we rarely recorded everybody at the same time."

In 1962 Levy's opened a second small studio (used primarily for voice overdubs and piano demos), complete with an acoustic echo chamber. This was located in the building that housed the offices for the record label, just a few doors away at 104 New Bond Street. Also added to the 104 New Bond Street location were a cutting room, a tape copying room, and a maintenance workshop.

At around the same time, the control room at 73 Bond Street received a major refitting. A custombuilt EMI 14-channel tube (valve) mixer that enabled simultaneous mono and stereo recording (quite an accomplishment for that era!) was installed, as well as an Ampex 300 3-track machine and several rackmounted stereo and mono EMI TR90 tape machines. New outboard equipment included an EMT reverb plate, several Fairchild mic preamps, an EMI limiter, two or three Altec limiters, and both Pultec and homebuilt "Pultec-like" equalizer/compressors. Monitoring was via a pair of Tannoy/Lockwoods, powered by Quad amps. A number of tube Neumann microphones were also added to the mic cabinet, including a U47, U48, and U67, plus a KM54 and two KM56s, as well as an AKG C12.

In September 1964 the American company CBS purchased the entire Levy's empire, including Oriole/Embassy Records and its pressing plant. Levy's Sound Studios was renamed CBS Studios, and although Jacques Levy was initially retained as studio manager, he would depart after just a year. In 1967, all the operations at 104 New Bond Street were moved to the CBS headquarters in Holborn, where a small remix studio outfitted with a Neve console was constructed, along with three disc cutting rooms and two tape copying rooms.

Following the buyout, Geoff Frost departed, as did engineer John Wood (the two would go on to found Sound Techniques Studios and the manufacturer of the same name; see *Sound Techniques* below for more information), and George Balla was named technical director. Under Balla's direction, the 73 New Bond Street facility underwent a considerable makeover. First on the agenda was a change to the sound of the studio. "Prior to the mid-'60s, the trend was to have very controlled, dry studios," Ross-Trevor explains, "but as pop groups started becoming more prevalent, people wanted recording areas to sound more live, so we took all the drapes down and rolled up the carpets, and it worked very, very well."

At the same time, the control room was modernized. A 1" 4-track Studer J37 machine was brought in to replace the old Ampex 3-track, and the monitoring was changed over to Altec Lansing speakers—four of them, in fact. "It was a bizarre idea," says Ross-Trevor, "but that's what people were doing in those days: Four tracks meant four monitor speakers." A couple of years later, a second J37 was purchased, allowing 4-to-4 "reduction" recording, as popularized by the engineers at Abbey Road. (See Chapter 1 for more information.) Sometime in 1967 or 1968, Balla developed an early synchronization unit that allowed the two J37s to be linked up, essentially giving CBS Studios 8-track capability. In 1970 this makeshift system was replaced by a dedicated 8-track Studer A80; a year later, a Neve 16-track console was installed, along with a 16-track Studer A80.

John Entwistle of The Who at CBS Studios, New Bond Street, 1966.
(Photo by Chris Morphet/Redferns)

Recording engineer Mike Ross-Trevor and maintenance engineer
John Timms relaxing in the CBS Studio 1 control room, 1974.
(Courtesy of John Timms)

Yet for all of the effort and expense, it turned out these were all stopgap measures, because CBS had plans to dominate the London recording scene. Big plans.

In the early 1970s, CBS quietly began construction of a massive four-story music complex at 31-37 Whitfield Street in central London, which opened in 1972 to great fanfare. It included three full-fledged recording studios with control rooms, two remix rooms (control rooms only), three mastering studios, two dubbing rooms, and four acoustic echo chambers, plus offices and studio lounges. In contrast to the old location at New Bond Street, which was pretty much a one- or two-man operation, the new facility was staffed by three full-time engineers, three assistant engineers, three mastering engineers, two tape dubbing engineers, and a maintenance crew of four, headed up by George Balla.

The two main studios were both on the ground floor, with a third, smaller one, housed in a top-floor penthouse suite. Studio 1, with its shell-within-a-shell construction and 20' ceilings, was the largest, and was designed to offer variable acoustics, a Balla innovation. "You could either just use the four plaster walls, which made it very reverberant and great for orchestral work," explains Ross-Trevor, "or you could deploy these absorbent panels that were hung on rails. You'd wheel them out, and if you completely covered the walls with them, the sound would be completely dead; or you could vary it, with one wall dead, and another wall live; or you could have part of the wall dead and part of it live."

The panels also allowed the studio floor to be acoustically divided. "The rail ran across the middle of the room, so you could cut the studio in half completely, which is what we used to do when we recorded pop bands," Ross-Trevor says. There were also "acoustic cloud" fittings on the ceilings of both Studio 1 and Studio 2 that were adjustable by means of cables, allowing the engineer to raise or lower the height of the ceiling—another Balla idea. "You could basically create any size of room you wanted by moving the ceiling up and down or changing the wall panels, so you could pretty much design your own studio," enthuses Ross-Trevor. "If you cut Studio 1 in half and lowered the ceiling, that made it virtually the same size as Studio 2. It was incredibly versatile; in fact, it was amazing. I don't know of any other studio in England that could do that."

Yet despite innovations like this, the new complex was not without its problems. "Whitfield Street was basically a disaster," says ex-CBS mastering engineer Bill Foster, who joined in 1968. "It was designed by Americans against all of the advice of George Balla and they just didn't have a clue. They really screwed it up royally, like not being aware of London planning laws, which resulted in the ceilings in the penthouse studio at the top of the building (Studio 3) having to be lowered and the room made smaller so it could be recessed further back.

"The air-conditioning was a problem too," he continues. "The intake venting was right next to a curry house next door, and so on a Monday morning when they brewed up for the week, Studio 1 would be filled with the smell of curry. There were problems on the second floor, too, where they built three mastering rooms in a row but didn't seal them off [acoustically]. They instead used standard construction [techniques], where they put brick up to about an inch from the ceiling and then they just filled it in with plaster. You'd walk into the middle room and you could hear everything going on in the other two rooms, so we ended up with a cutting room at either end and turned the room in the middle into an office instead."

One of the mainstay precepts of the Whitfield Street design was that all three control rooms be equipped virtually identically so as to ensure continuity when projects moved from studio to studio as booking schedules dictated. Accordingly, all were outfitted with the same 24 x 16 Neve consoles and with Studer A80 16-track machines—a decision Ross-Trevor feels was shortsighted. "Twenty-four-track was just around the corner by the time the complex was built—in fact, Trident had already installed a 24-track machine, so we really should have gone 24-track, but for some reason we didn't." In fact, the three studios would continue to offer only 16-track recording until 1976—quite late in the game. Even when they finally did add MCI 24-track machines, the CBS engineers still couldn't record all 24 tracks at once because the Neve 16-bus consoles were not upgraded at the same time, though Ross-Trevor insists that didn't present a big problem. "Many of the recordings we did at that time had lots of overdubs, so you could still do a live recording on 16 tracks, leaving you with another eight for overdubs. The only time it was annoying was when you wanted to record a live orchestra on 24 tracks." In 1977, the problem was relieved when the two main control rooms received new MCI consoles—a 56 x 24 model in Studio 1 and a 42 x 24 model in Studio 2. (In an interesting example of things coming full circle, Sony would later purchase both MCI and CBS.)

In addition, all three studios had identical monitoring systems; in fact, they were initially the same Altec speakers that had been used at the old location, driven by Crown DC300A power amps. "The Altecs seemed to work well at New Bond Street," says Ross-Trevor, "but for some strange reason they didn't work at the new studios in Whitfield Street. It was something to do with the design of the control rooms—they never sounded right. So we struggled for a while. We started putting EQ on the monitors to make them sound good, and it kind of worked for a time, but they were eventually replaced by JBL 4350s with Gauss drivers and things were much better then."

The outboard racks at Whitfield Street also included virtually identical components: UREI 1176, Fairchild, and dbx limiters, Pultec equalizers, Klein & Hummel graphic equalizers, Drawmer noise gates, and, later, Eventide Harmonizers. In addition to the four acoustic echo chambers, sixteen EMT 140 reverb plates were installed in the basement of the complex, accessible via tielines, though, unusually, these were allocated to specific studios instead of being shared by all the rooms.

The demands of running three studios dictated that the microphone locker be greatly expanded, too. Large quantities of solid-state microphones were purchased, including multiple Neumann U87s and U47s, as well as dynamic mics such as the AKG D202, which replaced the D19s that had been in use since Levy's first started. Also added were models from Beyer, Sennheiser, Schoeps, Shure, and Electrovoice.

Notable artists who worked at the Levy's/CBS facility on New Bond Street included Fleetwood Mac (their "Black Magic Woman" and "Albatross"

singles were both recorded there), The Who ("Happy Jack"), Donovan ("Wear Your Love Like Heaven"), Jimi Hendrix ("Foxy Lady"), and The Byrds (the 1971 *Farther Along* album). Iggy and The Stooges' *Raw Power* album and the Clash single "White Riot" were both recorded at the Whitfield Street complex, as was "Another Day," the first single from a then up-and-coming Irish band named U2.

In 1990, CBS was bought by Sony, at which time the studio was renamed Sony Music Studios. Four years later, it would once again be rechristened, this time as Whitfield Street Studios, in order to give the facility a more independent profile apart from its record company ownership. It was purchased by producer Robin Millar in 2004 in an attempt to keep the doors open, but was sold to a developer just a year later, who converted the entire facility into offices.

STAR SOUND / AUDIO INTERNATIONAL

Star Sound Studios dated back to 1937, when an ex-BBC engineer by the name of Derek Faraday began leasing a small meeting hall / movie theater at

Exterior of Audio International, circa 1970.
(Courtesy of Tom Bullen/Air Edel)

18 Rodmarton Street, just off London's famous Baker Street, for use as a direct-to-wax disc recording facility, which he called Star Sound. The building, originally named Besant Hall, "was constructed of reinforced concrete, almost like a bunker," says Richard Millard, who was Radio Luxembourg's chief engineer from 1959 until 1969, "but it had a balcony and a stage."

There was little in the way of acoustic treatment—just several removable sheets of polystyrene suspended from the ceiling above the stage to isolate it from the balcony area—but literally thousands of programs for both Radio Luxembourg and the BBC (as well as for some American radio stations) would be recorded there. In 1949, Star Sound would become one of the first U.K. facilities to offer magnetic tape recording.

By 1969, the small control "cubicle" at the back of the Star Sound recording area was outfitted with an 18 x 4 custom console, augmented by an Ampex 6 x 2 sidecar. Tape machines consisted of a Scully 4-track and three Ampex 2-tracks, plus two mono EMI TR90s, with monitoring provided by Tannoys driven by HH amplifiers; there was even a cutting lathe off in one corner! In addition, the studio offered a "narrator's cubicle" (the precursor to a vocal booth) and projection facilities, which included a large screen, projector, and film-dubbing mixer.

But there was change in the air. Since 1952, Radio Luxembourg had been operating a small recording studio at its main U.K. office at 38 Hertford Street, in London's Mayfair district. This was used primarily to prerecord evening and late-night radio programs, including Cliff Richards' long-running and popular "Me and My Shadows" series. The control room was reasonably well equipped, with a Neve console and a Studer 4-track tape machine, but the studio had minimal acoustic isolation—just pegboard on the walls, according to Millard. This became a problem when loud rock bands like the Rolling Stones began coming in to record programs in the mid-1960s, especially since the facility was located in a residential neighborhood. As a result, in August 1970, Radio Luxembourg, along with MAM Records, decided to purchase Star Sound and lease Besant Hall in order to convert it for use as a commercial recording studio, appointing Millard general manager and tasking him with overseeing the renovation and outfitting of the new facility.

One of Millard's first decisions was to bring in Sandy Brown Associates (who had designed Lansdowne and would go on to do the same at Trident and other major studios) as the architects and McLaren Ward & Partners as the acoustic consultants. A large new studio (roughly 40' by 30') with two isolation booths was built in what had formerly been the auditorium's orchestra seating, with an 11-foot-high false ceiling installed and new walls added for acoustic isolation. Linoleum and removable carpeting were laid down over the concrete floors, but, interestingly, no bass trapping was used in the recording area; instead, fabric-covered membrane absorbers and cedar strips were mounted on the ceilings and walls to reduce boominess. The balcony was converted into a second, smaller studio used primarily for speech and language recording, with large picture windows

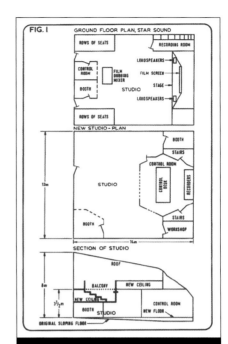

Star Sound / Audio International layout, 1971. Courtesy of *Studio Sound & Tape Recorder* magazine.

Managing director Richard Millard behind the Neve console in the Studio A control room, 1971.
(Courtesy of Richard Millard)

Engineer Peter Silver copies a vinyl record to tape in Audio International Studio B, circa 1971. Note the Neve BCM10 broadcast mixer to Silver's left.
(Courtesy of Richard Millard)

overlooking the street below; what had been the stage was transformed into a good-sized (18' by 17') control room.

By early 1971, construction was complete and Star Sound was relaunched as Audio International. The studio's mic cabinet included a complement of Neumann U87 and U47 microphones, along with AKG C12, 414, Schoeps, and various STC ribbon mics. The main control room was equipped with a Neve A210 24 x 16 console and a Studer A80 16-track tape machine (convertible to 8-track as needed), along with two Studer A80 2-tracks, plus the old Star Sound Scully 4-track; monitoring was via ceiling-suspended Tannoy Golds (later changed to HPDs) in custom-designed Lockwood cabinets, driven by HH power amplifiers (later replaced by FM Acoustics amps). Outboard gear included Neve, dbx, and UREI 1176 limiters,

STORIES FROM THE STUDIO
"Is the sound ballsy enough now?"

ACCORDING TO engineer Peter Silver, who worked at the facility from 1973 to 1988, practical jokes abounded at Audio International, perhaps no more so than in other studios, but possibly with a bit more imagination. "There were hours of hilarity to be had with the right people," he says. "For example, when the Eventide Harmonizer first appeared on the scene, it was thought to be amusing to pitch-shift the backing track in a singer's foldback and tell him or her that they were very flat or sharp, and then play the song back to prove it to them. ('It sounded in tune when I was singing!' the singer would protest.) Similarly, adding tape delay to the headphones when someone was overdubbing percussion, or adding strange sound effects to just one

of the various foldback feeds. ('Can you hear sheep, guys?' 'Nope—what have you been smoking?')"

One time an 8-track cartridge was delivered to the studio in the mail with a complaint about the quality of the recordings on it. The Audio International staff dealt with the issue in their inimitable way. "The cartridge was duly dismantled, the tape carefully pulled out and threaded on to an A80," reports Silver. "Then, across the full width of the tape and for its entire length was recorded a message along the lines of 'Our technical department has inspected this item and can find no fault with it.' It was then reassembled and mailed back to the sender."

And then there is the classic story of how one irate musician

succeeded in putting a producer in his place. "Andy Scott [guitarist with '70s glam-rock band The Sweet] always insisted on bringing enormous stage amps into sessions, some only just squeezing through the studio door," Silver recalls. "The volume created in the studio was enormous—enough to hear inside the control room without any mics. One day, just to wind him up, [producer] Mike Chapman said the sound was 'lacking balls.' Andy went over to the amp stack and appeared to make a few adjustments before turning around with a certain part of his anatomy hanging out of his trousers, and played a few riffs. 'Is the sound ballsy enough now?' he asked as we all fell about the control room laughing."

Setup work done, an unnamed staff member relaxes with a newspaper before musicians arrive for a 1971 orchestral session in Audio International Studio A. *(Courtesy of Richard Millard)*

and an ADR Scamp Rack filled with compressors and expanders, along with an AKG BX20 spring and three EMT 140 stereo reverb plates. The second studio (Studio B) was outfitted with a Neve BCM10 ten-input broadcast console (later replaced by a Soundcraft desk) and three Studer B62 tape machines.

By the end of the 1970s, Audio International had gone 24-track, and the Neve A210 board was reconfigured with the addition of Cadac input and output modules; in 1986, a Cadac 48 x 24 mixing desk—the last studio console the company ever built—was installed, along with additional outboard gear, including a Marshall Time Modulator, an Eventide Harmonizer, and a Lexicon 200 digital reverb.

Producers Mike Chapman and Nicky Chinn used

Audio International extensively throughout the 1970s and 1980s (often working with staff engineer Pete Coleman), crafting numerous hit records for Suzi Quatro, The Sweet, and Mud. Other artists to record at the facility included Harry Nilsson, Gilbert O'Sullivan, Sheena Easton, Tom Jones, Japan, and Heatwave (including their 1977 hit single "Boogie Nights"). Overdubs for Pink Floyd's 1983 *The Final Cut* (engineered by staffer James Guthrie, who would later work extensively with the group) were also done there.

In 1990, Audio International was renamed Air-Edel. The facility is still operational today, primarily used for live cast albums and film soundtrack work, and the main Air-Edel control room still uses the same Cadac console.

DE LANE LEA / KINGSWAY

The origins of De Lane Lea / Kingsway date all the way back to 1893, when one Samuel Herbert Benson set up one of England's earliest advertising agencies. The agency, called Bensons, was created at the suggestion of his former employer—Bovril, the maker of one of Britain's favorite condiments. Over the next ten years the agency acquired many other accounts, thus requiring larger premises. In 1909, Bensons moved to 129 Kingsway in Holborn, a newly redeveloped area of London that quickly became the center of the city's advertising industry due to its proximity to Fleet Street's newspaper offices. Sometime in the late 1930s, the company constructed a small 2-track studio in the basement of the building for the purpose of recording voice-overs and jingles.

In the mid-1950s, the studio was acquired by De Lane Lea, a company founded by William De Lane Lea (run by his son Jacques following William's death in 1964) that had been operating various recording facilities around London for many years. (See *CTS / The Music Centre* in Chapter 3 for more information.)

The Animals in De Lane Lea Studios, 1965. Producer Mickie Most is in the center of this posed photo, with singer Eric Burdon at far right.
(Photo by Harry Hammond/V&A Images/Getty Images)

De Lane Lea Studios, as the Kingsway facility was now renamed, was an unusually dry-sounding room, approximately 35' by 25' in size, with a relatively low 12' ceiling and little in the way of acoustic treatment other than some carpeting and a few tiles on the walls. "It was quite dark and dingy, I suppose," says former engineer Robert Zimbler, "but it had the most phenomenal sound to it. It was just a naturally good room." In 1965, the small control room was upgraded with the installation of a Sound Techniques 18 x 4 desk—the first console produced commercially by the company for an outside studio (see *Sound Techniques* below for more information)—and a modified tube Ampex 4-track tape machine to accompany the existing tube and solid-state 2-track and mono machines. (An 8-track 3M M23 would be added four years later.) Outboard gear included an EMT reverb plate and Fairchild 666 and Altec 436B compressors, and monitoring was via four Tannoy/Lockwood cabinets (driven by Quad amps)—two per side for the added volume demanded by the groups of the era and their producers. The De Lane Lea mic cabinet was particularly well stocked for a single-room facility, and included several Neumann U87, U47, and KM84 tube condensers.

Under the direction of engineer and studio manager Dave Siddle (who had also run the facility for Bensons), De Lane Lea Studios became quite popular among the rock elite of the era, and some of the most

The view from the De Lane Lea control room into the studio as the Rolling Stones record "I Wanna Be Your Man," October 7, 1963.
(Photo by Gus Coral)

important and influential records of the '60s were recorded there, including The Animals' massive hit single "House of the Rising Sun" and the Jimi Hendrix Experience classics "Hey Joe," "The Wind Cries Mary," and "Purple Haze." The Rolling Stones would record "As Time Goes By" at De Lane Lea, and The Who would lay down backing tracks for several of the songs on their 1967 *The Who Sell Out* album. The Yardbirds,

STORIES FROM THE STUDIO
Giving the neighbors an evening to remember

"IT WAS THE AGE of people experimenting and doing things in different ways," says former De Lane Lea / Kingsway engineer Robert Zimbler. In that spirit, there was one particular night when the patience of the studio's next-door neighbors was tested to the limit, as studio staff attempted to accommodate the wishes of a client.

"I was assisting on a Fleetwood Mac session back in the late '60s, when Peter Green was their lead guitarist," Zimbler recalls. "Pete used to do most of his solos as an overdub, and we'd set him up in the normal way, with

three or four U87 microphones in a long line at one end of the studio, which usually gave us this lovely rich but echoey sound. He came into the control room for a playback and his comment was, 'I like that, but I think it needs to be bigger.' Martin Birch, who was engineering, tried sending the signal to the EMT plate and it worked to a point, but it sounded too electronic. Finally, Martin turned around and said, half out of frustration, half-jokingly, 'How about if we open the fire exits and stick your amp out in the car park [parking area]?'

"To our dismay, Pete loved the idea! So we put his amp out there and ran long microphone and foldback cables out the door. I placed a mic at the other end of the car park, and he went out there and put on his headphones and started playing. When he came back in and listened to the playback, he said, straight-faced, 'Yeah, that's the sort of thing.' I don't know if we ended up using it because the sound was a bit too uncontrollable, but it certainly gave the neighbors an evening to remember!"

Ian Paice, Ritchie Blackmore, and Roger Glover of Deep Purple in De Lane Lea Studios, September 1970.
(Photo by Michael Putland/Getty Images)

Pink Floyd, Fleetwood Mac, and Deep Purple all frequented De Lane Lea, and even The Beatles themselves would record there, paying four visits to the studio in May, June, and October of 1967 to work on the George Harrison song "It's All Too Much," released on the 1969 *Yellow Submarine* album.

However, in the late 1960s, De Lane Lea was forced to relinquish the Kingsway premises and moved its operation—once again with Siddle at the helm—to Wembley in north London. (See *CTS / The Music Centre* in Chapter 3 for more information.) Interestingly, the company left the facility with much of its gear intact while continuing to pay rent to the tune of some £25,000 a year. In 1973, the studio was bought by producer Martin Birch and singer Ian Gillan, who

had recently left Deep Purple, and it was rechristened Kingsway Studios. As part of the refurbishment that followed, an acoustic echo chamber was added and the first commercially produced Raindirk console— a 30 x 24 model—was installed in the control room, along with Studer A80 16-track and 24-track machines; the monitoring was also changed over, to JBL 4350s driven by Amcron amplifiers.

Kingsway Studios closed in the 1990s and some time later the building was razed; a supermarket and drugstore now occupy the former location. De Lane Lea's multiroom movie scoring complex in Soho's Dean Street, launched in 1970, is the last remaining De Lane Lea studio still open today, owned and operated by Warner Brothers.

STORIES FROM THE STUDIO
The Tin Pan Alley studios

Denmark Street in 2013; traces of the Tin Pan Alley days still remain.
(Photo by Guy Katsav; courtesy of Denmark Street Studios, www.denmarkstreetstudios.com)

THEY CALLED IT "Tin Pan Alley," in recognition of its similarity to the passageway of the same name in New York City—a street so famous that Ray Davies immortalized it as the title of a song on The Kinks' 1970 album *Lola Versus Powerman and the Moneygoround, Part One.*

Denmark Street, just off London's Charing Cross Road, was a small thoroughfare—more like an alleyway, really—that first started being used for commercial purposes in the 19th century. Initially, metalwork was a popular trade, but it soon became the hub of Great Britain's music industry.

In 1911, Lawrence Wright, later the founder of *Melody Maker*, the oldest and most prestigious of England's weekly music newspapers, became the first music publisher to set up premises there, in the basement of Number 8, before moving to Number 19 at the end of World War I. In 1926, Campbell Connelly Music—a competitor—set up offices in Denmark Street as well. In 1952 the *New Musical Express*—a rival publication to *Melody Maker*—established offices at Number 5 Denmark Street, and by the end of the 1950s, the street housed dozens of music publishers, musical instrument retailers, and other businesses associated with the industry.

1954 saw the opening of the street's first recording studio, in a dungeon-like basement at Number 22. Tin Pan Alley Studios (TPA, for short) was founded by session musician Ralph Elman, a violinist who would later play in the string section on The Beatles' "I Am the Walrus." At a time when most studios in England were owned by major record labels such as EMI and Decca, opening an independent facility such as TPA was a big financial risk, but thanks in large part to business from the many neighboring music publishers, it ended up panning out quite nicely (pun intended); in fact, the studio remains operational to this very day.

In 1962, an eccentric businessman named James Baring began operating a small monophonic recording studio called Regent Sound at Number 4 Denmark Street, above the offices of Essex Music. Though it was little more than a demo facility, word quickly spread about the quality of the tapes coming out of Regent, thanks to the skill of house engineer Bill Farley, and despite the distinct lack of atmosphere. ("It was a shithole," producer Shel Talmy once said bluntly of the studio. "It was an awful place with egg boxes up on the ceiling for sound baffling. It really was a horrible place. I don't think it'd been cleaned since the day it was built; there were stains on the stains.") It was there that manager/producer Andrew Loog Oldham would bring his new signing in early 1964—a band by the name of the Rolling Stones—to record both their eponymous debut album and their first hit single, a cover of the Buddy Holly song "Not Fade Away."

"Both the Stones and I liked and felt comfortable in Regent Sound," wrote Oldham in his 2000 memoir *Stoned*. "It was a mono studio, and . . . everyone agreed that recording in mono would be better. Mono had the element we needed; what you hear is what you get. The studio . . . was no larger than an average good-sized hotel room [and] the control room was the size of a hotel bathroom, but for us it was magic. The sound leaked, instrument to instrument, the right way. You'd hear the bottom end of Charlie's drums bleeding through Keith's acoustic, and vice versa, Keith's guitar delay bleeding through the drum track. Put them both together and you had our wall of noise. It was our version of direct-to-disk recording, where the placement of the instrument defined the sound that you got. . . . Farley did everything he could to get the right sound, and put up with my style of direction, which requires that an engineer be more familiar with proven hits than with notes and knobs. . . . I have no doubt the feel of those early

A Rolling Stones session at Regent Sound, circa 1963.
(Pictorial Press Ltd./Alamy)

Stones records was due in no small part to avoiding the major studios."

Producer Phil Spector was present at the "Not Fade Away" session, though merely as a bystander. Contrary to popular belief, what he plays on the track is not maracas but an empty cognac bottle with an American half-dollar inside, according to singer-songwriter Gene Pitney, who was also part of the proceedings that evening. "You should have seen the [isolation] booth there," he marvels. "It was so small, it was like two people would have to have their backs against the wall to stand up in it."

In the mid-'60s, Regent Sound moved to more expansive premises at 164-166 Tottenham Court Road—about a mile north of Denmark Street—where a larger two-room facility was built. The equipment was

also substantially upgraded: The original Vortexion tube mixer used for the Stones recordings was replaced by a transistorized 12 x 4 Tiros Electronics desk custom-built by Eddie Baldwin, similar to (though somewhat smaller than) the one previously installed at Ryemuse (see *Ryemuse/ Mayfair* below), along with a Studer J37 4-track and a number of Ampex 2-track machines. Tannoy/Lockwood monitors were installed at that time, along with a complement of outboard gear that included a Pultec EQP-1A equalizer, a Teletronix LA-2A optical compressor, and a custom-designed stereo limiter; a small acoustic echo chamber was also constructed into an unused stairwell. In February 1967, the new Regent Sound was graced by the presence of the ultimate in rock royalty—The Beatles—there to record backing tracks for the song "Fixing a Hole," which would appear on their *Sgt. Pepper's Lonely Hearts Club Band* album. Staff engineer Adrian Ibbetson manned the board for that momentous session—the first time The Beatles ever recorded outside of Abbey Road. Two years later, Black Sabbath's eponymous debut album was made at Regent (the group would later return to lay down tracks for their chart-topping follow-up *Paranoid* LP); the 1969 Genesis album *From Genesis to Revelation* was recorded there as well.

Another busy Denmark Street studio was KPM (Keith Prowse Music) at Number 21, which opened the doors to its L-shaped ground-floor recording studio in 1966. The facility was designed by Ted Fletcher, then fresh off helping producer Joe Meek set up his home studio at 304 Holloway Road. (See Chapter 4 for more information.) "We did a lot of voice-over work and a lot of recording for the KPM music library whenever we weren't making interminable demos for staff songwriters Bill Martin and Phil Coulter," he recalls. "The vocals to those demos would be put down by whoever was passing—Dusty Springfield and Kiki Dee among them." The KPM control room was equipped with Tannoy Red (later Gold) monitors driven by Leak amplifiers and a homebuilt 16-input mixer with dual stereo outputs—a precursor to the Alice consoles that Fletcher would later manufacture commercially—plus a pair of TEAC TD-102 recorders (one 2-track and the other mono), which were essentially Japanese copies of the Ampex 350. "I had modified the electronics of the 2-track machine to provide 'record head replay' (sel-sync)," he says, "and we would record a sort of 'multitrack' by bouncing from one machine to the other."

Microphones included an AKG C414 and Neumann KM86, a couple of KM84s, and a handful of Shure dynamics, plus a number of homebuilt capacitor mics that Fletcher describes as being "quite nice" on vocals. Outboard equipment consisted of some homemade spring reverbs, a Langevin equalizer, Altec and Westrex compressors, and a number of additional custom-designed compressors that Fletcher says were the direct prototype of the "Joe Meek Compressor" introduced to great fanfare in the late 1990s. "We close-miked and compressed everything at KPM," he says. "We got brass sections to blow

against a wall for a bigger sound, put drawing pins in the hammers of the Chappell upright piano in the studio, and overdrove all the equipment all the time." In 1978, KPM became the in-house studio for the music publishing arm of EMI, at which time Fletcher's board was replaced by a Helios mixing desk.

An advertisement for Regent Sound, circa mid-1960s.
(Courtesy of Andy Babiuk)

There were other Denmark Street studios, too: Peer/Southern Music, at Number 8, had a recording facility on the ground floor; it was used mostly for demos, though it was also the place where Donovan recorded his second album, *Fairytale*, in 1965. Directly above the Giaconda Café at Number 9—a popular meeting place renowned for its egg and chips, bacon butties, and all the other staples of starving English musicians and recording engineers—was a small studio called Central Sound; David Bowie would record many of his early demos there. Mills Music, at Number 20, was where a young Reg Dwight worked as a teaboy (before he became much better known as

Elton John); the company had the dubious distinction of rejecting a then-unknown American singer-songwriter by the name of Paul Simon, informing him officiously that his songs "Homeward Bound" and "The Sound of Silence" were uncommercial. In the mid-1970s, manager Malcolm McLaren opened a small basement rehearsal room at Number 6; the Sex Pistols rehearsed there, recorded their first demos there, and even lived in a dingy apartment above the room for a time, until they had difficulty paying the £4-a-week rent and were unceremoniously evicted.

"There was great friendliness and camaraderie throughout Denmark Street in those days," says Ted Fletcher. "The engineers all knew each other well, and it was normal to lend and borrow expensive equipment." Many of the facilities on that famous street remained in business throughout the '80s and even into the '90s, but with the rise of home recording, they, like so many other studios around the world, began to suffer from attrition. While few of the recording studios that once predominated London's Tin Pan Alley remain operational today (sadly, even the Giaconda is gone—though on the bright side, this has undoubtedly had a positive impact on the digestive tracts of modern British hit-makers), Denmark Street still remains home to many of the country's leading musical instrument retailers.

In 2013, a commercial developer filed plans with the local authorities to raze Denmark Street and transform it into a modernized complex that would include new housing, an 800-seat underground music venue, a hotel, and new retail spaces. Sadly, the first stage of this redevelopment was begun in January 2015.

RYEMUSE/MAYFAIR

Arthur Rye was a lawyer, a real estate speculator, and an amateur composer of military band tunes. Throughout the post–World War II years he eagerly bought up property and leases in London's fashionable Mayfair district, anticipating (correctly) that the rock-bottom prices he was paying would eventually yield huge dividends.

In the late 1950s, following a chance meeting with jazz composer/saxophonist Johnny Dankworth, Rye offered the musician free premises in a building he owned at 64 South Molton Street. Excited by the prospect of having his own recording facility, Dankworth and his manager hired ex-Levy's recording engineer Bill Johnson (see *Levy's / CBS / Whitfield Street* above) and Swedish maintenance engineer Dag Fellner (who would later become chief technical director for Advision Studios; see *Advision* in Chapter 3) to do the design and installation. The studio was named Ryemuse, an amalgamation of both the benefactor's last name and the music that had inspired its construction.

The studio area was relatively small (about 30' by 25') and, other than pegboard acoustic tiles on the walls, had no special acoustic treatment. Unusually, the narrow control room (about 20' by 15') offered no direct view into the studio, being separated by a landing, and so a closed-circuit television system was used for communication. "While you would expect the lack of a window onto the studio to be a serious restriction, the artists and producers didn't seem to mind," recalls engineer John Iles with a smile. "When we were recording tracks for the first Cream album,

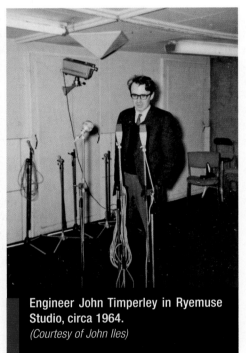

Engineer John Timperley in Ryemuse Studio, circa 1964.
(Courtesy of John Iles)

the band would often ambush producer Robert Stigwood between the studio and control room and try to put him into one of Ginger Baker's drum cases."

Though the physical facilities at Ryemuse were cramped, staff quickly learned how to make the best of the available space. "The maintenance workshop on the floor above was often used as an isolation booth," says Iles. "A toilet with access from the control room was also sometimes used as a vocal booth when everywhere else was full!" Though there were a handful of Beyer headphones on hand, they were not often used, and so the degree of foldback was usually determined by how much the toilet door was opened—a situation some of today's home recordists may be familiar with.

The Ryemuse control room housed a transistorized 8 x 2 Tiros Electronics board custom-built by Eddie Baldwin, which predated the one he constructed for Regent Sound Studios by a few years (see *The Tin Pan Alley Studios* above); this may have been the first solid-state console installed in a London studio. It was actually quite sophisticated for the time, with each channel offering high- and low-pass filtering, plus bass and treble boost or cut, as well as stereo panning, with level control on large rotary knobs. (Later, Fellner and Iles built a small transistorized six-channel mixer for mobile recording, though this was added on to the control room's main console as a sidecar when required.) Tape recorders included an Ampex 300 4-track, along with other Ampex and Philips 2-track and mono machines, including a portable

Ampex PR10. Monitoring was via four Tannoy Reds in Lockwood cabinets, driven by 50-watt Leak tube amplifiers, and reverberation was supplied by a single EMT plate buried deep in the basement. Outboard gear consisted of two Pultec equalizers, one optical tube limiter, two transistorized LDR gates, and additional transistorized equalizers based on the Pultec tube design. Microphones were almost all Neumann condensers: U67, U87, KM56, KM64, KM84, and SM2, supplemented with a few AKG C12 condensers and D202 dynamics, a Sennheiser MD 421N, and a few Beyer ribbons.

In 1968, the Ryemuse control room was upgraded with a larger 16-input Tiros console and an 8-track Leevers-Rich tape machine; in addition, the Tannoy Red monitors were replaced with Tannoy Golds, and a Leevers-Rich A501 graphic equalizer was added to the rack of outboard gear. At around that time, a production company called Spot Productions opened offices in the same building and began using the studio extensively; in the years that followed, Ryemuse would sometimes confusingly be referred to as "Spot Productions Studios" or simply "Spot Studios," although according to John Iles the staff and clientele still generally referred to it by its original name.

"The studio was popular with groups, as it had a dead acoustic and a tight sound for its day," Iles says. "Most groups worked in the evening, but during the day we were kept busy with solo artists who used session musicians." Artists who recorded at the facility included Alexis Korner, The Who, The Zombies, and Robin Gibb of The Bee Gees. Many of the *Top of the Pops* series of albums (based on the popular television

show of the same name) were done there as well, some featuring a then-unknown piano player by the name of Reg Dwight (later better known as Elton John). In addition, several tracks for the first Cream album, *Fresh Cream*, were recorded at Ryemuse in 1966. (Others were done at a small facility called RayRik Studios, the precursor to Chalk Farm Studios; see *Chalk Farm* below for more information.) The band must have had a positive experience there, because they returned a year later to record demos for their follow-up *Disraeli Gears* album. The Welsh heavy metal trio Budgie also used the facility extensively; reportedly, Marc Bolan also recorded some demos there.

In 1971, Ryemuse/Spot officially changed its name to Mayfair Studios and the following year a remix room was added, equipped with a Leevers-Rich 8-track

Four views of Ryemuse, circa 1964. Engineer John Iles, top left; John Timperley, top right, bottom left.
(Courtesy of John Iles)

Vic Keary of Chalk Farm Studios (left) and an unidentified salesperson in the Ryemuse/Spot control room circa 1969 signing a contract to purchase the Leevers-Rich 8-track machine shown in the photo. Note the 16-input Tiros console to the right.
(Courtesy of Vic Keary)

machine and the Ampex 4-track from the original control room, along with a custom 30 x 12 desk built by new chief engineer John Hudson. During the 1970s, popular bands like Orchestral Manoeuvres in the Dark and Ultravox made records at Mayfair, including the latter's hit single "Vienna," engineered by Hudson.

In 1977, John Hudson and his wife, Kate, assumed ownership of the studio and additional refurbishments were undertaken, including the installation of larger custom homebuilt mixing consoles into the main control room (a 20 x 16, followed by a 36 x 24), as well as Studer A80 24-track, 16-track, and 2-track machines, and a JBL monitoring system; new outboard gear was also added, such as Eventide Harmonizer, Delay, and Instant Phaser units. Four years later, the Hudsons moved the studio to Primrose Hill in North London. After a good three-decade run in that location, Mayfair finally closed its doors in December 2008.

MARQUEE

From the mid-1960s to the late 1980s there was no London club gig more prestigious than playing the Marquee at 90 Wardour Street, in the very heart of Soho. The list of jazz, blues, rock, punk, and post-punk artists who graced its tiny stage could fill an entire book—Johnny Dankworth, Alexis Korner, Cyril Davies, John Mayall and the Bluesbreakers, the Rolling Stones, Manfred Mann, the Yardbirds, Fleetwood Mac, The Who, Cream, Pink Floyd, David Bowie, James Taylor, Elton John, Joe Cocker, The Small Faces, Jethro Tull, Procol Harum, The Jimi Hendrix Experience, Ten Years After, Deep Purple, Supertramp, Yes, King Crimson, Roxy Music, Humble Pie, Led Zeppelin, Def Leppard, Dire Straits, U2, The Pretenders, the Sex Pistols, The Buzzcocks, Ultravox, The Human League, Squeeze, XTC, The Cure, Duran Duran, and Trans Am among them.

The Marquee was established in 1958 by Harold Pendleton, an accountant whose love of jazz had led him to become secretary of the National Jazz Federation. Originally located in the basement of the Academy Cinema in Oxford Street, the club moved to its Wardour Street location in March 1964.

Later that same year, an engineer by the name of Phillip Wood brought in some of the equipment he used in his home studio and put together a makeshift monophonic recording space in a garage behind the Marquee, at 10 Richmond Mews. It was there that he and Moody Blues manager/producer Alex Murray recorded the group's chart-topping "Go Now" single with a setup that consisted of a homemade 12-channel mixer and two secondhand Ampex tape machines (one mono and one stereo), along with a Grampian spring reverb and a borrowed Fairchild compressor, using an odd collection of old BBC ribbon microphones to capture the sound of the band, supplemented with one modern-day condenser mic (model unknown) for the vocals.

Determined to build on the success of that first recording, Pendleton and his partners (jazz trombonist and bandleader Chris Barber, along with Simon White, who was named managing director) decided to convert the space above the club into a "proper" studio, with tielines to the stage downstairs to facilitate live recording. Opened in 1966, the rather spartan 1,000-square-foot oblong-shaped studio with 13' ceilings was described by engineer Gery Collins, who started working there in 1968, thusly: "It was a long, ugly-looking room with rockwool-clad walls, some awful white Chinese lanterns hanging down here and there, and linoleum on the floors"—austere even by the standard of the day.

The small control room was initially equipped with a 24-channel mixing console that was handmade by Phillip Wood. "The desk was very impressive-looking," Collins says, "but it was absolute rubbish, with an infuriating habit of crackling at the worst possible moments; in fact, I think only about eight out of 24 channels worked at any given time." Incredibly, the desk was powered up by turning a key, similar to the way a car is started. "Phillip would say to the bands coming in, 'This is the key to your success!' on every damn session," reports Collins with a laugh. Monitoring was via Tannoy/Lockwoods powered by 12-watt Leak amplifiers. Tape recorders included 4-track, 2-track, and mono Ampexes, plus a 4-track Leevers-Rich. These were all placed in a separate machine room, with a foldback system employed to deliver instructions from the control room to the assistant engineers operating the tape recorders. Outboard gear consisted of several homemade EQ units of dubious quality, a Grampian spring reverb, and a single EMT reverb plate, originally located in the small passageway that connected the studio to the club, something that reportedly led to lots of problems in terms of spurious vibrations leaking both in and out.

Three years later, the Marquee Studio underwent a major refurbishment, courtesy of Tom Hidley and Eastlake Designs. The wall that backed onto the club was lead-lined, several isolation booths were constructed, and things were generally tidied up; the cramped control room was also enlarged, transforming it into a respectable 22' by 17' in size. Once construction was complete, the homegrown mixer in the control room was replaced by a 24 x

16 custom console, outfitted with Helios channel modules, and the studio's tape machines were finally moved into the control room, augmented with a new Ampex MM1000 8-track recorder, later upgraded to 16-track. "I think this was pretty much the first desk in the U.K. to use integrated circuits," comments former maintenance engineer Roger Pharo, "which turned out to be a bit of a mistake, as there was inadequate headroom on the channels, and the desk was prone to radio-frequency oscillation, resulting in strange chirping noises at times. Yet another problem was interference from the Coke machine which was in the lounge. Every time someone bought a Coke, a loud click came over the speakers. We got around it by dipping the playback level."

A second EMT plate was also installed during that renovation, placed in a remote location further from the club (the original EMT plate was moved there, too), and the mic cabinet was expanded with the addition of Neumann U87, U67, U47 FET, and KM84 models, along with AKG, STC, and Pearl microphones. There were a couple of changes in the monitoring, too, as Pharo explains: "We started off with ceiling-hung Altec speakers, powered by 100-watt HH amplifiers, which had a peculiar defect—after a bass drum 'thud,' they would make a loud click as they ran out of internal power. The HH amps also had a nasty habit of blowing the speakers if switched off with the volume up." Accordingly, they

Marquee control room with a view into the studio, circa 1975.
(Courtesy of Gery Collins)

The Beethoven setup

ENGINEER PHIL HARDING began his career as an assistant at Marquee Studios in 1973, where he would be based until leaving in the early '80s to work with the production team of Stock/Aitken/Waterman.

One of his strongest recollections of his time at the Marquee came the day he assisted chief engineer Geoff Calver for a string overdub on David Bowie's 1975 hit single "Young Americans," with Tony Visconti producing. "What a session!" Harding says. "I remember Tony coming into the control room saying that he'd arranged the strings on the assumption that we'd be using our standard string setup, which he really liked, even though it was anything but standard at the time . . . or so I thought.

"Usually, when recording an orchestra," explains Harding, "you arrange the musicians in what they call the 'classic semi-circle' around the conductor, with the violins on the left and the violas, celli and basses on the right, with woodwinds,

percussion, and brass behind, and the players naturally balance themselves." (See illustration below.)

"But if you think about it technically, if you use overhead mics

The "Classic Semi-Circle" orchestral setup.

instead of, or even in addition to, close mics, that really restricts you, because all your violins are on one side of the stereo image," he continues. "Besides, we didn't have enough space to do that kind of setup in our studio, since the room was long and narrow. So when we were doing string overdubs, we used to arrange the musicians in a different way: We'd have two banks of violins on either side in front of the conductor—first violins on the left and second

violins on the right. Then we'd put screens behind them and place the violas behind those screens. There would be another set of screens with the celli behind those, and then a third set with double basses and any other instruments behind them.

"On this particular evening Tony told us that there were a couple of spots in the arrangement where he had the first violins playing a part which would gradually be taken over by the second violins, so the sound would pan from left to right, across the entire stereo spectrum. I remember thinking, 'Wow, amazing—he's created this stereo soundscape out of our special setup!'

"For years, I thought that the way we recorded string overdubs was completely original, but I later learned that the Marquee configuration—arranging the musicians in long, narrow banks, one behind the other—was actually the way Beethoven liked to have his orchestras set up, centuries ago. What a revelation!"

were replaced by Amcron DC 300As, and the monitors themselves also eventually changed over to JBL drivers in Eastlake cabinets.

A second refurbishment followed when the studio upgraded to 24-track around 1973. The studio and control room floors were floated at that time, and the control room was reoutfitted with an MCI mixing board—the first in the U.K., done at the behest of producer Gus Dudgeon, who was a frequent client. This was a Model JH-416, with 32 inputs and 24 outputs (replaced soon thereafter by a JH-542 with 40 inputs and 32 outputs; just a year later, it too would

be replaced by a JH-538 38 x 32 with mix automation). At that time, Studer A80 24-track and 2-track recorders, plus a Scully 2-track, were also installed, although by 1977 these had all been replaced with a veritable arsenal of MCI tape machines: a JH-24 24-track (replaced a year later with a JH-100), a JH-140 4-track, and a JH-120 2-track. A number of Sennheiser and Electrovoice RE20 microphones were also purchased, along with some Beyer M160 ribbons and Shure SM57 dynamics. Two more EMT plates were added, and the outboard rack was enlarged to include UREI 1176 limiters, dbx 160 compressors, Teletronix LA-2A optical compressors, Pultec equalizers, ITI and APSI equalizers, a Scamp rack filled with Kepex gates and GainBrain compressors, Lexicon and Eventide digital delays, and an Eventide Omnipressor expander that former Marquee engineer Steve Holroyd recalls being used to great effect on the tom-toms on Elton John's hit single "Someone Saved My Life Tonight."

In the mid-1970s, a remix room was opened at Marquee, initially built by Eddie Veale and then redesigned by Eastlake in 1977. It was outfitted with an MCI JH-542 36 x 22 desk (upgraded by 1979 to a JH-536 36 x 32 with mix automation) and an MCI JH-114 24/16-track tape machine, plus three JH-120 2-tracks; the monitors were Eastlake TMIs, driven by Amcron DC300A amplifiers. The remix room also received a cornucopia of outboard gear virtually equivalent to that in the control room, plus a Marshall Time Modulator, Astronic equalizers, Meyer noise gates, and Orban de-essers.

Marquee Studios became extremely popular for mixing work, especially after the MCI consoles, Eastlake monitors, and bounty of outboard processors was installed. Gus Dudgeon used the control and remix rooms frequently (often to mix Elton John records), as did fellow producers Robin Cable and Mike Batt, along with Greek composer / electronic musician Vangelis. Notable artists who worked at the Marquee in the 1970s included Rory Gallagher, The Nice, Van Der Graaf Generator, The Clash, Killing Joke, and Toyah Wilcox. The 1971

Another Monty Python Record by the comedy group of the same name was also recorded there, although according to group member Terry Jones, it was a "bitter experience." "We had this horrendous time because we were recording in this rather hippy recording studio," he wrote in the book *The Pythons*. "What we hadn't realised was that the guy who was doing the recording . . . had not been making any notes. We'd end up with tapes and tapes of material with no idea of where anything was." ("A little unfair, I think," says Pharo in rebuttal. "It wasn't the normal function of the engineer in the studio to take detailed notes—that would have been the producer's job. Perhaps this was just an unfortunate misunderstanding of who was actually supposed to be doing what." (The credited producers on the record are Terry Jones and Michael Palin.)

Pendleton and Barber would eventually divest themselves of their interest in the Marquee, and in 1988 it was decided to demolish the Wardour Street site and then rebuild it as part of a plan to modernize both the club and the studio. At that time the club moved to Charing Cross and the studio operated out of Pete Townshend's nearby Eel Pie Studios, with both relocations thought to be temporary. However, changes in the property market made the redevelopment unfeasible and the project was abandoned. Marquee Studios ceased operation in 1991 when Eel Pie's lease expired; the Marquee Club would occupy six different London locations before finally closing for good in 2008.

SOUND TECHNIQUES

Sound Techniques began life as a recording studio at 46a Old Church Street in the Chelsea district of London—a building that had been a dairy since the early 19th century. Opened in the summer of 1965, it was founded by two ex-Levy's engineers: Geoff Frost and John Wood. (See *Levy's / CBS / Whitfield Street* above for more information.)

Interestingly, the lease the pair negotiated included a clause giving them permission to remove part of the second floor to give the large (50' by 20') studio

the ceiling height Frost thought necessary to get an "American sound" out of the room, based on his experience visiting Bradley's Studio in Nashville some months previously. (See the Introduction for more information.) An eighth of an inch of asphalt was also laid on the studio floor, then covered with carpet, to help dampen the sound—another trick Frost had observed during his trip to the U.S. In an idiosyncratic touch that, according to Frost, also had positive sonic implications, the original gradual slope

The tape machines in the Sound Techniques control room.
(Photo by Geoff Frost, courtesy of Matt Frost)

in the outer ends. But on their very first session, they discovered that such placement simply didn't work—the musicians in the room complained vociferously that they could not hear one another. Things were rapidly changed around, with the rhythm in the middle, the brass under the control room, and the strings under the office, and, to everyone's surprise, it worked. This then became the standard setup at Sound Techniques, and Wood eventually discovered the reason why: "The low end of the studio had a natural resonance at around 500–700 Hz, and so you would get this really big string sound from a small section. That was one of the things that I suppose we were quite lucky with—people were always going on about the great string sounds that came out of the studio."

Since the project was largely self-funded, lack of budget dictated that Frost and Wood had to build as much equipment as they could themselves. They could not afford complete Ampex tape machines, for example, so they managed to wangle a deal in which they bought just the transports, leaving Frost to build the electronics for three machines—one 4-track, one 2-track, and one mono—which they housed in secondhand consoles. Monitoring was via four 15" Tannoy Gold speakers mounted in a single homebuilt enclosure to "make things more rigid," according to Frost. These were initially driven by Quad amplifiers, later replaced by Crowns, exact models unknown.

Most importantly, Frost and Wood began building a mixing desk for the good-sized (20' by 15') control room, assembling it by hand in the middle of the studio space. This was not an altogether new endeavor for Frost—he had designed a portable 8 x 2 tube mixer for a short-lived Oriole Records mobile unit while still at Levy's—but it would lead to Sound Techniques arguably being known more as a console manufacturer than a recording studio. "We never started out to manufacture mixers for anyone other than ourselves," Frost comments. "It came as a bit of a surprise when people saw the first desk at Chelsea and said, 'Wow, this sounds great, can you make one for us?'"

in the floor from the olden days—necessary for water runoff when hosing down the cows—was retained. "Even though it was probably only a one and a half degree slope, it prevented standing waves," he says.

Other than that, there was little in the way of acoustic treatment. "We cleaned the place up, put double glazing in where it was convenient to, and where it wasn't convenient we didn't bother," said Frost in a 2008 interview with *Sound on Sound* magazine. "As far as acoustics go, John and I went around clapping our hands, and we'd say, 'Ooh, we need something up there!' but bearing in mind we were so short of money, we did as little as possible."

In his book *White Bicycles*, producer Joe Boyd described the Sound Techniques facility this way: "The control room looked down on the studio from a box above one side while the offices were built over the opposite side. It looked awkward, but the differing ceiling levels meant that you had three different acoustics in the same studio; you could move things around until you found the sweet spot for an instrument or singer." Interestingly, when the studio was first designed, Frost and Wood had expected that the middle of the room, which had twice the ceiling height, would be used for strings, with the louder brass and rhythm sections placed

The first desk built by Frost for the Sound Techniques control room had 20 input channels and four buses, plus two echo sends and two foldback sends. Each channel had an Elcom quadrant fader, a mic preamp, a wire-wound gain control, and equalization circuitry that was essentially based on Pultec functionality. "I wanted a desk where you could assign any fader to any track without it affecting the level of the other tracks," Frost adds. "The EMI desk at Levy's used what was called constant voltage mixing, so if you changed the assignment of an instrument from one track to another, the old track would go up by 2 dB and the new one would go down 2 dB, which isn't a lot but you could hear it. I'd read an article about something called constant current mixing, which is now called virtual earth mixing. I think we were the first people to do that, which meant you could freely change the assignment of each channel without affecting anything else."

The original mixing console built for the Sound Techniques studio.
(Photo by Geoff Frost, courtesy of Matt Frost)

Frost was also adamant that the new desk be solid-state and fitted with transformers. "I'd never built anything with transformers at Levy's—everything had been valves (tubes), and we did think about building a valve mixer for our studio, but we decided it would be too heavy and probably get too hot. I'd been doing some experiments and building prototype mic amps while I was at Levy's, some of which worked and some of which were rubbish, but by the time I was working at home I experimented more on that. There's nothing terribly special about the design of them, but it's the output transformer which I'm convinced is what made our boards what they are. To begin with, we couldn't buy output transformers that I liked, so John and I decided we'd wind our own, which of course saved an extraordinary amount of money too."

Sound Techniques desks would later be installed at both The Music Centre / CTS and Trident (see Chapter 3 and Chapter 6 for more information), as well as at Sunset Sound and Elektra Studios in California. Initially, they were made in the office above

the studio, though drilling and hammering would have to cease whenever the red Recording light went on. The problem was solved in 1969 when the Sound Techniques System 12 (arguably the world's first compact mixing console) began to be mass-produced at a small factory in Mildenhall, Suffolk.

Even while the first Sound Techniques mixer was being assembled, so too was other equipment being gathered for the control room. Sufficient monies were somehow found for the purchase of an EMI limiter, a couple of Altec compressors, and a slew of top-quality microphones, including Neumann U67, KM54, and KM56 condensers, as well as Sony C38 and AKG C60 condensers; AKG D19c dynamics; and RCA, Film Industries M8, and STC 4033-A ribbons. These would later be supplemented with Fairchild 660 limiters and Neumann U47 and KM88 mics. And, although Frost and Wood hoped to purchase an EMT reverb plate, their cash had run out by that point, so they opted instead to build a garage from a prefabricated kit and use that as a de facto acoustic echo chamber. However, the flimsy structure had little acoustic isolation (a particular problem on Thursday mornings when the garbage trucks would come around) and leaked whenever it rained—an all too common

Tuning the reverb . . . with a piano

"SOUND TECHNIQUES had some great EMT plates, but there were no usable acoustic echo chambers," recalls engineer Jerry Boys, who, having worked previously at Abbey Road and Olympic, had come to rely on the use of natural spaces for reverb. "To compensate, we would often do things like placing guitar amps or speakers near the piano, and then play tracks back through them. The resultant sound was somewhat similar to what you'd get from a proper echo chamber, but it wasn't exactly reverb; it was more of a harmonic room effect. If you play a chord and hold the keys down, only those hammers stay up, so only those strings resonate. Consequently, we could pretty much tune the effect so it matched the key of the song."

occurrence in London. Unsurprisingly, an EMT 140 was duly purchased as soon as funds allowed.

In the coming years, the Sound Techniques control room would replace its first mixing console with another homebuilt model, this one a 24 x 24

with dedicated 24-channel monitoring. The multitrack machines, too, would be upgraded to 8-track, then 16-track and finally 24-track (the 8-track tape recorder was a 3M model, while the 16- and 24-track machines were Studer A80s), but the basic sound and "vibe" of the facility never changed. As Boyd described in *White Bicycles*,

> When [engineer] John [Wood] heard a sound he didn't like . . . he would lumber down the stairs, muttering all the way. I began to be able to predict whether he was going to try a different microphone, reposition the existing one or shift the offending musician to another part of the studio. When I listen to records we made together in the sixties, I can still hear the air in the studio and the full dimension of the sounds the musicians created for us. I can hear the depth of Nick Drake's breath as well as his voice, the grit in the crude strings of Robin Williamson's gimbri and Dave Mattacks's drum technique spread out warmly in aural Technicolor across the stereo spectrum.

Engineers Harry Davis (foreground) and John Wood in the Sound Techniques control room, 1965.
(Photo by Geoff Frost, courtesy of Matt Frost)

The "Sound Techniques sound" was quite unique, and would come to be embodied in the folk and folk-influenced rock records that Boyd and Wood crafted for Elektra Records and, later, Boyd's Witchseason Productions company. The early projects they worked on were fast, straight-to-master-tape recordings of artists such as the Incredible String Band (who did three albums there), Martin Carthy, and Dave Swarbrick. Later, Jethro Tull would use the facility to record their breakthrough 1969 album *This Was*; the Syd Barrett–era Pink Floyd would craft their early singles "Arnold Layne" and "See Emily Play" there; and Fairport Convention would use Sound

Techniques to record eight albums between 1966 and 1971.

And it came not just from the acoustics of the room and the electronics of the equipment designed by Frost and Wood (on a shoestring budget, no less), but from subtleties such as the character of the reverb, derived from EMT plates that John Wood would endlessly tweak to perfection. "I spent a lot of time deciding how I wanted to use them at different ratios," he said. "You could put delay on them, and the sound would depend on what EQs you sent to them. You'd fiddle about with all the parameters, including the mechanical ones, until you got the sort of reverb that you wanted."

And then there were the intangibles. "[Sound Techniques] was laid-back and relaxed, with neither the clinical hospital-like feel of some studios, nor the indulgences of the rock-star lifestyle," wrote Matt Frost in a 2008 article for *Sound on Sound* magazine. "The closest thing to luxury available was a couple of pints of ale at The Black Lion pub across the road."

"There was absolutely no attempt to make it impressive or luxurious," Fairport guitarist and producer Simon Nicol said. "It was functional. The concrete staircase and the galvanised handrail could always have done with a lick of paint. It was clean, but in comparison to studios I came across later on, where some of the lobbies outdo five star-hotels—that was not the case with Sound Techniques. Function came above form, substance above style, and that was the ethos of the place. It was a very social business, too—I suppose in other places you might have ploughed a natural division between the band and the staff, but it was always just a very cool place to be."

The original Sound Techniques studio, under the purview of Frost and Wood, came to an end in 1976 after the lease to the building ran out. It was bought by Olympic, who continued to operate the studio until the early '80s, when the building was eventually sold and converted into luxury apartments. John Wood became an in-demand freelance engineer and producer, while Geoff Frost is now retired after running a successful software development company under the Sound Techniques name.

WESSEX

Any studio that can turn out hit records by the likes of King Crimson and the Sex Pistols (or Melanie and The Clash, for that matter) has to be characterized as *extremely* versatile.

Founded by brothers Robin and Mike Thompson in the mid-1960s, Wessex Studios was originally situated in Old Compton Street in London's Soho, near the future premises of Trident Studios in St. Anne's Court. The name came from the location of a recording studio the Thompson family had previously operated in Bournemouth, in the ancient English county of Wessex. In 1966, Wessex moved to new premises at a church hall situated directly behind St. Augustine's Church in the residential neighborhood of Islington, North London.

Initially, Wessex consisted of a single studio, which had the considerable advantages of being large enough (roughly 50' by 30') to house a full orchestra and having a high ceiling (approximately 15'), as well as a fairly live

A panorama of the Wessex exterior, compiled from three separate photos.
(Courtesy of Tony Harris)

acoustic, described by engineer Bill Price as "a natural club-like ambience." Unfortunately, these were outweighed by the equally considerable disadvantage of minimal acoustic isolation, which prevented the studio from operating full-time, due both to noise coming in from the outside world, and sound escaping to irritate the next-door neighbors. The Wessex control room was outfitted modestly, with just 4-track, 2-track, and mono machines (all Ampex ATR-100s), although it boasted one of the earliest Neve transistorized mixing consoles, which offered 12 input channels and seven group outputs, enabling simultaneous 4-track, stereo, and mono recording (later supplemented with an Ampex

8-track AG-440); a remix room would eventually be added, also equipped with a small Neve console. (See *Rupert Neve and the Neve console* in Chapter 2 for more information.) With the Thompson brothers doing the majority of the engineering work, Wessex quickly attracted many major British variety stars of the era, such as Tom Jones, Des O'Connor, Morecambe and Wise, Clodagh Rogers, Tommy Steele, and Frankie Vaughan.

In 1970, the control room was modernized with the installation of a new custom Neve console, this one a modular A88 with bar-graph metering, 28 input channels, and 24 group outputs to accommodate 24-track recording. This Neve board was widely

STORIES FROM THE STUDIO
Sex Pistols deconstructed

THE SOUND of '70s proto-punk group the Sex Pistols has variously been described as abrasive, caustic, and bombastic, but, love them or hate them, there's no question that they got everybody's attention. In the fall and winter of 1976, it fell to producer Chris Thomas to try to rein them in sufficiently to get their first single and one and only album recorded before the group's inevitable implosion.

"When I had recorded their single 'Anarchy in the U.K.,' they were a three-piece band, with Glen Matlock playing bass," Thomas recalls. "Glen, [guitarist] Steve [Jones], and [drummer] Paul [Cook] did the backing track, [singer] Johnny [Rotten] added his vocals, and we edited it all together and made the record in the usual way. A few months later, we went back into Wessex to start work on the album, but by this time, they'd sacked Glen, leaving Steve and Paul as the only musicians in the band. The first day of the sessions they went out into the studio, and started running through their set. I remember thinking, 'How the hell am I going

to be able to judge whether a take is any good with just the two of them playing?' There was just no interplay—nothing to work with.

"I finally decided that the only way I could really be sure if a take was a keeper was to have Steve overdub some bass on it. I told Bill Price, the engineer on the session, to keep everything Steve played as a reference, just in case he came up with something good, because he's not a bass player. Well, he went out there and simply played exactly the same thing on the bass he had just played on the guitar, and suddenly the whole thing came together!"

But that was only the first major breakthrough, as Thomas goes on to explain. "You see, I can't stand stereo; maybe it's because I'm a bit deaf in the left ear. As a result, I never liked having an instrument come out of just one speaker and not the other. Even when I was overdubbing things to death, stacking tons and tons of instruments together, I'd always mix things so that whatever came out of the left-hand side also pretty much came out of the right; pretty much the only things

that would be panned hard left and hard right would be the drum overheads and the close ambients; the distant ambient mics would usually be gated, and panned in the center.

"The problem with the Pistols is that all you ever had to work with instrumentally was bass, drums, and one guitar. So I developed this sound with them that I called 'Mono Deluxe': As soon as Steve finished recording his guitar part, I'd have him immediately double-track it. When we were mixing the song, we'd pan one guitar hard left and the other one in the center, then I would put one of the two guitars through a Harmonizer [to pitch-shift it slightly], and pan that hard right. The result was a series of very subtle imperfections, which was just as good as triple-tracking the guitar. So the basic soundscape for every Pistols song was two guitars with one of them harmonized, with a real one on one side, a real one in the middle, and the harmonized one on the other side. That way, there was always a real guitar in the middle, underlaid with a nearly duplicate bass part an octave lower beneath it."

advertised as being "London's first 24-track desk," despite the fact that studio management ordered two Ampex MM1000 16-track models instead of a 24-track machine (the MM1000 had the ability to be retroactively upgraded to 24 tracks if needed, although this never happened at Wessex), along with an Ampex AGB-440B 8-track. The monitoring facilities (most likely Tannoys) were also made "quadraphonic-ready" (four 15" Tannoy Golds in Lockwood cabinets at the front and another two at the back) at that time, and four EMT plates were added, along with air-conditioning for the studio; the remix room received the old Neve that had been in the main control room. (See *Quad: Ahead of its time, or just a bad idea?* on page 59 for more information.)

Throughout the late '60s and early '70s, Wessex began gaining popularity with many leading rock groups of the era. King Crimson recorded their first three albums there, including the groundbreaking *In the Court of the Crimson King,* and Queen was another frequent visitor to the studio, recording tracks for their 1974 album *Sheer Heart Attack,* as well as their well-known anthem "We Will Rock You," which featured the sound of a hastily gathered crowd stamping on the Wessex drum risers.

In 1975, the Chrysalis Group purchased both Wessex and AIR Studios in Oxford Circus, and AIR chief engineer Bill Price (along with recording engineer Gary Edwards and maintenance engineer Paul Nunn) was transferred to Wessex. Price was appointed a managing director and tasked with overseeing a major rebuild of the facility. Under his direction, the roof was at long last soundproofed and the control room was enlarged. The control room and remix room were re-equipped with Cadac mixing desks (a 32 x 24 model in the control room, and a 32 x 8 in the remix room) as well as 3M M79 24-track and Studer A80 4-track and 2-track machines, and were outfitted with new Tannoy monitors driven by HH, Studer, and Turner amplifiers. An array of outboard gear was also added, including Neve, UREI and dbx limiters; UREI and Orban equalizers; Marshall Time Modulators; and Eventide Flangers and Harmonizers. The microphone locker was also expanded at that time to

STORIES FROM THE STUDIO
Brass in pocket . . . and PA in studio

JUST ABOUT EVERY ENGINEER who's worked with a young, inexperienced band has a story about a group carting their live sound system into the studio with them, only to learn to their embarrassment that it wasn't the least bit necessary. But veteran producer Chris Thomas, who first cut his teeth working with The Beatles as George Martin's assistant, found a creative use for a PA system when working with the Pretenders at Wessex in 1979.

"The idea was basically borne out of the fact that I was frustrated about the studio being so dead because there were carpets everywhere," he explains. "I felt that if we brought in a PA system and fed the drum mics through it, we'd be able to replicate what you might hear if you were standing onstage, listening to the drummer coming through the monitors. It was really just an effort to bring some life to the sound.

"The problem is, it worked so well, I almost used that idea forever! In fact, when we were doing the song 'Private Life,' I put Chrissie Hynde's vocal through the PA as well. Later, when I recorded the INXS single 'What You Need' in Australia, I not only put the drums through the sound system, I'd feed in drum-machine effects like handclaps, too. If you listen to the record closely, you'll hear what's coming through the PA almost as much as the close-miked parts."

include a large selection of models from Neumann, AKG, Sennheiser, STC, and Sony.

In October 1976 the Sex Pistols formally ushered in the punk era when they rolled into Wessex to record demos with engineer Tim Friese-Greene. They would return a short time later to record the single "Anarchy in the U.K.," followed by their one and only album, *Never Mind the Bollocks, Here's the Sex Pistols,* credited, interestingly enough, as being "Produced by Chris Thomas or Bill Price." (See *Sex Pistols deconstructed* on the previous page for more information.) The Pistols having paved the way, fellow punk rockers like The Clash (*London Calling*), Generation X, The Damned, and Siouxsie and the

Banshees followed, along with post-punk groups like the Pretenders, The Boomtown Rats, Public Image, and the Specials.

In 1993, Wessex was put up for sale by Chrysalis. It was eventually bought by Matrix Studio owner Nigel Frieda, who rebranded it as Matrix-Wessex. (See *Matrix* later in this chapter.) In 2003, the studio was closed for good and the building was sold to a developer, who converted it into a block of nine luxury apartments.

MORGAN

Morgan Sound Studios was founded in 1967 by four musicians who owned a jazz record label operating out of Lansdowne studios: Barry Morgan, Monty Babson, Jerry Allen, and Leon Calvert. A desire for office space of their own led to their finding premises at 1 Maybury Gardens in Willesden, Northwest London, where they decided to build a small recording studio as well, with Calvert tasked with the design and Babson appointed managing director in charge of day-to-day operations.

Morgan Studios exterior.
(Courtesy of Tony Harris)

Morgan Studios' first hire was Terry Brown, an ex-Olympic engineer whom the owners had met when he was working at Lansdowne. Brown was appointed studio manager and invited to take an active role in the planning of the new studio; he also appointed the studio's first chief engineer—Andy Johns, formerly of Olympic and brother of famed engineer Glyn Johns. Another burgeoning star at Morgan was assistant engineer Roy Thomas Baker, who would later find fame as a producer/engineer at Trident.

Both the modest recording area (approximately 20' by 20' in size) and small control room (roughly 17' by 10') were on the ground floor, at the rear of the building. The control room was equipped initially with a Scully 1" 8-track and Ampex 4- and 2-track machines, later upgraded to 3M and Studer models. Notably, the mixing console was by a new English company called Cadac—the very first one ever manufactured, in fact. "Terry [Brown] knew that I was designing a new desk for Lansdowne," explains Cadac founder Clive Green, "and he asked if he could buy the designs. I told him it would be better if we built the desk for him. That was actually how the company came to be formed." In late 1967, the custom-built hand-wired desk, an 8-track split-console design with transformerless balanced inputs and outputs, was delivered to Morgan. This would later be replaced by a 24 x 24 model. (See *Lansdowne* in Chapter 3 for more information.)

Artists began flocking to the studio, attracted at least in part by the extremely clean sound of the Cadac desk. By 1969, Morgan had become busy enough to justify adding another room. For some reason, the existing studio was renamed Studio 2 and a new, larger Studio 1 was built upstairs, occupying two floors, with a control room overhead. It quickly became apparent, however, that there was insufficient acoustic separation between the two rooms, so the original studio on the ground floor was moved to the front of the building, with the rear space converted to a restaurant/bar. The new Studio 1 control room was equipped with another Cadac desk (this one a 24 x 16 model and modular in design), paired with a 3M 16-track tape recorder, along with a 2-track Studer A80 and a 2-track C37. In 1978, a 36 x 24 Harrison console with parametric equalization and Allison automation was installed, replacing the Cadac.

1972 saw the opening of a much larger Studio 3, again designed by Leon Calvert, situated on the ground floor of a building across the street. Its control room, like that of Studios 1 and 2, was located in a corner and could be reached only by walking through the recording area—an odd Calvert touch that sometimes caused problems in the middle of sessions. It was equipped initially with a 24 x 24 Cadac console (later replaced by an automated 40 x 32 model with quad joystick panners; see *The Vortex* below) and a 3M M79 24-track recorder. (See *Quad: Ahead of its time, or just a bad idea?* on page 59 for more information.)

In 1974, another property was purchased around the corner, which was converted to become Studio 4. Initially designed by a "specialist" company, it was quickly changed over to a Leon Calvert specification to match that of the existing studios, although one end had wooden floors, and so it yielded a significantly more live sound than the other three rooms, which were carpeted and therefore quite dead acoustically. Studio 4 (often referred to as "The Laundry" by Morgan staff since the building's previous tenants had used the space for that purpose) was a sizable square room with no isolation booths—the largest recording area in the Morgan complex. Its control room housed a 28 x 24 quad-ready Cadac desk and had the distinction of receiving the first Ampex 24-track tape machine in England, later replaced by a Studer A80. In fact, by 1979 *all* the tape machines at Morgan—multitrack and 2-track—were Studer A80s, including five 24-track models. (There were two of them in Studio 2, time-code synchronized for 46-track recording.)

Monitoring in all four Morgan control rooms was initially via 15" Tannoy Gold dual concentric speakers mounted in "Lockwood-like" cabinets and driven by 40-watt Radford tube amplifiers. As rock music began to get louder, these were later replaced by Tannoy HPD speakers (in the same

STORIES FROM THE STUDIO
His aim was true

JUST A FEW MONTHS AFTER joining Morgan at the tender age of 19, engineer Robin Black had the good fortune of spending a day in the studio with Paul McCartney as the legendary ex-Beatle performed overdubs on the song "Kreen-Akrore," which would appear on his first solo album, *McCartney*, released in 1970.

"Paul came in excitedly talking about this program he'd seen on television about a tribe in Brazil," Black remembers. "While I was busy doing some tape transfers for him [to Morgan's 8-track machine; most of the songs had been recorded in McCartney's home studio on a Studer J37 4-track], he said, 'I'm just

off to Harrods.' He came back with a bow and arrow and a target and explained that he wanted the sound of the arrow flying through the air overdubbed onto this sort of jungle music he'd recorded.

"I set up a number of valve [tube] mics—mostly U47s and U67s—across the room to try and capture the release of the arrow, the 'swoosh' sound as it went through the air, and the thud as it hit the target. Paul stood at the entrance of the studio area with the door shut and we put the target as far away as possible. I was just hoping he wasn't going to hit any of the microphones with the arrow because they're quite expensive,

but, no, he was actually quite a good shot!

"In the control room, I had to turn the preamps up really loud, and I equalized each microphone a little differently, applying more top end to some to catch the swoosh and more bottom end to others to capture the thud as it hit the target. I was just trying whatever my ears told me—whatever felt and sounded good, and whatever Paul was happy with. In the end, we did manage to capture what he was after, and on just the first or second take, as I recall. You can't quite hear it on the final record, but at the time I was really pleased with what we'd gotten down on tape."

cabinets), ultimately upgraded to stock JBL monitors. Each control room had its own three dedicated EMT reverb plates (including later-model units with quad outputs), as well as two Pye and UREI 1176 limiters, supplemented later by Kepexes, Gain Brains, and Eventide Harmonizers, Flangers, and Instant Phasers. Notably, there were no outboard equalizers; apparently, the internal EQ circuitry in the Cadac desks was deemed to be more than sufficient. Microphones included Neumann U47s, U67s, and KM84s, as well as models from Schoeps, Sennheiser, Beyer, Calrec, and AKG (including a number of tube C12A mics and the ubiquitous D12 for bass drum). Unusually, there was no mic locker (or cupboard, in the English vernacular) at Morgan; all the studio's microphones were left mounted on dedicated stands with their coiled cables attached, and engineers would simply wheel them from room to room as needed.

Many important recordings of the late 1960s and 1970s were made at Morgan, including five albums from Jethro Tull (*Stand Up*, *Benefit*, *Thick as a Brick*, *War Child*, and *Songs from the Wood*, all recorded in Studio 2 and engineered by Robin Black), The Kinks' *Muswell Hillbillies* (for which Ray Davies insisted on using vintage microphones only, in order to give the album an antiquated feel), Mott the Hoople's eponymous *Mott the Hoople*, Yes's *Tales from Topographic Oceans*, Black Sabbath's *Sabotage*, and The Cure's *Three Imaginary Boys*. Other major artists who recorded at the studio included Paul McCartney, Donovan, Pink Floyd, Ten Years After, Joan Armatrading, Cat Stevens, Rod Stewart, and UFO.

Morgan Studios was eventually sold in pieces. In 1980, Studios 3 and 4 were purchased by Zomba Records, which rechristened them Battery Studios; they are still operational today as Miloco / Assault & Battery Studios, co-owned by the Miloco corporation and producers Alan Moulder and Flood. Studios 1 and 2 were sold to producer Robin Millar in 1984 and renamed Power Plant Studios; that facility closed six years later.

STORIES FROM THE STUDIO
The strings are revolting

GREGG JACKMAN stakes an unusual claim: He states that he was the first British engineer to get an entire string section to wear headphones. "My eldest brother, Andrew, was a busy orchestrator when I was cutting my teeth at Morgan Studios back in 1971," he explains. "Standard practice for a string section overdubbing on a pop record at the time was to give them the backing track on foldback speakers—studios usually didn't have enough headphones for a big section anyway, and then there was the theoretical zero ohms reached by chaining enough of them together on the same amp.

"But I got fed up with having my strings covered in backing track," he continues. "The string players always asked for it to be turned up, and they were never happy with how quiet I wanted it to be. The spill was simply an annoyance."

One day an orchestral session was booked into Morgan Studio 2 with a small enough string section—"probably 14 violins, four violas, and two cellos," he recalls—to allow him to give headphones a try . . . although Jackman also remembers setting up the usual foldback speakers as a backup, just in case the section revolted.

"Since the conductor was my brother, we had a fighting chance of getting away with this outrageous suggestion. We found the musicians were on the whole OK with it as long as they could leave one ear off to hear their own instrument acoustically. When something like this occurs, it's not long before word spreads, and within weeks I heard that others were doing the same. Eventually Beyer started making one-eared headphones specifically for this purpose.

"My brother was soon conducting the entire London Symphony Orchestra on pop sessions at Abbey Road," Jackman adds as a footnote. "He got brave enough to start issuing headphones to the entire LSO string section so they could overdub and not have their parts smothered in brass and drum kits. Between Abbey Road's own headphones and those they borrowed from AIR and RAK, they were able to manage it. Later the studio bought enough to outfit an entire symphony orchestra!" (See Chapter 7 and *RAK* below for more information.)

"I DISCOVERED a pretty unique technique for recording guitars back in those days," says producer Chris Tsangarides, who started as an assistant engineer at Morgan in 1975, initially working 18-hour shifts that typically ended at four in the morning. "It started when I was assisting on a Brand X album, which was Phil Collins' fusion jazz side project whenever he wasn't playing with Genesis or making solo records.

"This one track was a bit self-indulgent," he continues. "Every one of the musicians had a solo: drum solo, bass solo, keyboard solo—time for the guitar! But the producer and the engineer weren't interested in guitars at all; they were saying, 'That's not for jazz,' that kind of thing. So they took a break and left it to me and John Goodsall, the guitar player, to record this solo. Their one direction to me was 'Make it really loud.' I wasn't sure how to go about doing that at first, but then it came to me in a blinding flash of inspiration: 'Let's build a great big bass bin out of the speaker cabinet

you've got,' I said to John. He had a Marshall stack with JBL speakers in it, and so I built these flares out of partition screens which extended out to about 15 feet on either side, making it act like a massive bass bin. It certainly did make it sound a lot louder, because everything was directed at the microphone I was using to record it a few feet away— probably a [Neumann] U87.

"But in addition to the U87, I also set up a bunch of U67s around the room; I miked the walls, the floor, the ceiling, everything I could think of, with each going to a separate track. Then I started messing around with the Cadac desk we had at the time. It was quad-ready, so it had a matrix of joysticks that you could use to pan tracks around the four speakers. As John was playing away I began wiggling these joysticks, just having a great time in the control room because I really didn't know what I was doing—I'd only been at the place for a few months, to be fair.

"When John came in for a playback, I started panning these vari-

ous tracks the way I had done while he was out there playing, just for fun. Even listening to it in stereo was amazing! There were just these random notes coming out louder first on the right side, then the left, and the whole thing was constantly moving all over the place. I said, 'Listen to that!' And John said, 'Yeah, man, it's brilliant. It's the vortex!'

"So that's what I called this technique—'The Vortex'—and I've used it often, though I've modified it a bit over the years. These days I tend to use just two microphones—a close mic and a room mic in the sweet spot—with each panned to a different side. What I've found is that, as the guitarist is playing his run, there are certain frequencies that will go out of phase with each other depending on the distance of one microphone from the other, creating a standing wave. It basically cancels out on one side or the other, giving the impression of pan and movement. People sometimes ask me, 'Where can I buy a Vortex?' and the answer is: You can't!"

CHAPPELL

Chappell Studios had deeper roots than any other recording facility in England—possibly even the world. The music publishing company of the same name was founded in 1811—a time when Napoleon was still emperor of France. In 1819, a promising German composer by the name of Ludwig van Beethoven sent them three sonatas for publication.

Originally based at 124 New Bond Street in central London, Chappell Music would move a few doors down, to 50 New Bond Street, in the 1850s. A century

later (!), a small demo studio was constructed in the basement, beneath the company offices. Unfortunately, a devastating fire burned the building to the ground in 1965. Chappell managing director Teddy Holmes decided to use the opportunity to not only rebuild, but also to construct a new, state-of-the-art professional recording facility in the floor above the company's retail music shop around the corner, at 52 Maddox Street. Accordingly, he hired recording engineers John Timperley and John Iles (both formerly with Ryemuse;

THE STAFF

The Chappell Recording Studio, in its short history, has proved to be successful artistically and technically.

Its experienced Recording Engineers are capable of meeting to-day's high demand, in every way, for the imagination required, for sound recording at the present time.

CHIEF ENGINEER
JOHN TIMPERLEY

Technical & Balance Engineer
JOHN ILES

Balance Engineer
ROBERT BECKER

Balance Engineer
GAVIN RUSSELL

Studio Bookings
RUTH ROSENTHAL

Staff and a good view of the Chappell control room, circa 1967.
(From studio brochure)

see *Ryemuse/Mayfair* above for more information) to oversee the design and installation; Timperley was named studio manager and Iles technical director.

Blessed with a healthy budget, the two spared no expense. Sandy Brown, who had overseen the treatments at Lansdowne and at Audio International and would go on to do the same at Trident (see *Star Sound / Audio International* above and Chapter 3 and Chapter 6), was brought in to do the acoustic design for the facility, which included a main studio and a remix room (45' by 25' and 30' by 15' in size, respectively). At his direction, triple wall construction was employed and floating floors put in. Because the two rooms had relatively low ten-foot ceiling heights due to space constraints, Brown utilized a unique design that incorporated rockwool acoustic traps above a suspended false ceiling. "Some thought that we wouldn't be able to get a good string sound," says John Iles. "In fact the opposite was true, and the reasonable separation and the slightly more live acoustic at one end of the main studio worked well."

On the recommendation of CTS technical director Peter Harris (who acted as a consultant on the project), a Neve 20 x 4 console—the first ever constructed by the company with space-saving narrow modules—was installed into the good-sized (17' by 15') control room. Unusually, four graphic equalizers (manufacturer unknown) and four Pye TVT limiter/compressors were built into the console; the latter used pulse width modulation to "chop up" the signal at high frequency to reduce output level in response to fluctuations in input level—an innovative approach to dynamics processing for the era.

The tape recorders at Chappell initially consisted of Ampex AG300 4-track machines, along with 2-track and mono Ampexes, all operating at 110 volts with the use of a central transformer. Monitoring was via 15" Tannoy Reds in Lockwood cabinets, driven by tube Quad amplifiers (later replaced by solid-state HH models), and there were three EMT plates for reverb; in addition, the facility's elaborate marble staircase was sometimes employed at night as a de facto acoustic echo chamber—some singers, like Dusty Springfield, actually preferred performing live there. Microphones included models from Neumann (U87, U67, U64, KM84, and SM69 among them), an AKG C12A and D202, an Electrovoice RE20, two STC 4038s, and other Westrex and RCA ribbon microphones, plus two BBC PGS ribbons (predecessors to the 4038).

The revamped Chappell Studios opened its doors for business in early 1967 and almost immediately attracted major artists like The Animals, The Bee Gees, and The Hollies. EMI producer Norman Newell, head of the Columbia Records division, often used the facility, and George Martin worked there several times before accompanying The Beatles on the 22nd and 23rd of August 1967, when they recorded the song "Your Mother Should Know" (used in the *Magical Mystery Tour* soundtrack) at Chappell. The latter session occurred just four days before manager Brian Epstein's death, and was the last Beatles session Epstein would ever attend. In a strange example of life imitating art, the comedy album *The Rutles*, recorded by the Beatles parody band of the same name (featuring Monty Python's Eric Idle), was recorded at Chappell a decade later.

Chappell Recording Studio, circa 1967.
(From studio brochure)

Engineer John Iles in the Chappell control room, 1974.
(Courtesy of John Iles)

Unfortunately, just a year after its opening, Chappell was forced to sell its music publishing division and studio to Philips in order to meet the onerous tax liabilities that had resulted from the death of the company's owner, Louis Dreyfus. Philips decided to continue to operate the facility under the name Chappell Studios, and although there was reportedly some corporate resentment at the level of expenditure required to keep the studio modernized, there were nonetheless significant upgrades in the years that followed. By the early 1970s, the equipment in Chappell's main control room included a new Neve 24 x 24 console, along with Ampex MM1000 8-track machines (later modified to 16-track), plus home-built multiband compressor/limiters and frequency shifters for flanging and phasing effects.

By 1978, the console had been replaced by a larger Neve 30 x 24, and Studer A80 24-track, 16-track, and 2-track machines were installed, in addition to Ampex ATR-100 and AG-440 2-track and 4-track recorders, plus several Philips PRO 51 machines. There was also an odd piece of Philips equipment made in Holland that was "rather forced upon us by management," according to Iles. This was the Phonogram "Magnetic Audio Delay Wheel" (described in the *Philips* section in Chapter 2), somewhat similar to the "delay drum" developed by EMI and used at Abbey Road in conjunction with their experimental Ambiophony system (see *Ambiophony* in Chapter 1 for more information). Iles describes it as being "a very large motorized drum that had magnetic tape wound around its circumference and several heads arranged close to the tape. We used it in series with the send to the EMT plates to act as a short delay."

Chappell Studios closed in 1979, shortly before the formation of PolyGram Records that resulted from the merger between Polydor and Phonogram (the renamed Philips label). (See *Philips* in Chapter 2 for more information.)

CHALK FARM

The primary moving force behind Chalk Farm Studios was Vic Keary, a man of many hats. After a few years working in television, Keary took a job as a maintenance engineer at Lansdowne Studios in late 1959, literally a day after Joe Meek's departure. He would follow in Meek's footsteps in many different ways, progressing rapidly through the ranks to become a recording engineer under Adrian Kerridge's tutelage before leaving to strike out on his own in 1961. (See *Lansdowne* in Chapter 3 for more information.)

Shortly thereafter, Keary opened a studio called Maximum Sound, equipping its control room with a 10 x 8 mixing desk he built himself, based on the design of the EMI console at Lansdowne that had been constructed to Meek's specifications, although sans equalization. Although it was forced to move premises at one point, Keary's new studio would eventually acquire a significant reputation for recording reggae music, which was fast becoming popular in England at that time; one of its primary attractions was a cutting lathe with electronics intended for cutting 78-rpm records instead of 45s. As a result, in Keary's words, "it really pumped out the bass end, so the reggae guys loved the records we cut there."

Four years later, Keary sold Maximum Sound to keyboardist Manfred Mann and drummer Mike Hugg and purchased a small rehearsal/recording facility called RayRik Studios, located at 1a Belmont Street in the Chalk Farm area of Camden, North London. (RayRik's main claim to fame was that several tracks for the 1966 debut Cream album *Fresh Cream* were recorded there; see *Ryemuse/Mayfair* above for more information.) Renaming it Chalk Farm Studios, Keary once again installed his hand-built mixing desk into the tiny control room, along with a newly purchased Leevers-Rich 8-track recorder, Ampex and Studer 2-tracks, a couple of Altec 436 compressors, eight graphic equalizers, and a spring reverb. Monitoring was initially via the same Tannoys used at Maximum Sound, but these were quickly replaced with Altec speakers in custom-built bass reflex cabinets (positioned, unusually, at the back of the control room due to space constraints). The Chalk Farm mic locker included two AKG C12A condensers and D20, D202, and D224E dynamics, plus Shure SM57 and Calrec 1050c dynamics and a pair of RCA KU54A ribbon mics. In addition, the studio owned a pair of Fi-Cord tube condenser mics, which, according to Keary, were "vastly underrated and probably my best vocal mic."

The acoustic treatment in the good-sized studio—about 45' by 15', with unusually high ceilings—was minimal, according to Keary: "All we had to do was put a new carpet down and put some foam and wood over the windows." A small drum booth, custom-designed by Keary, was also constructed in the studio, yielding what he describes as an "unusually tight" drum sound and making it possible for full bands to play together with minimal leakage. There was also a mastering room on the floor above, outfitted with a Lyrec/Ortofon lathe, a pair of Ampex 2-track tape machines, a Fairchild 670 stereo limiter (which floated between the cutting room and the control room), a Sean Davies–built limiter, and various equalizers.

The Chalk Farm control room, upgraded to 16-track and outfitted with Vic Keary's second-generation mixing console. *(Photo by Vic Keary)*

Chalk Farm quickly achieved a good degree of success, initially in the same genre Keary had excelled in at Maximum Sound—reggae music—although later the studio would enlarge its focus to encompass other kinds of popular music, including blues, soul, and ska music, the latter becoming a craze in England throughout the early and mid-1970s. Trojan Records' star producer Dandy Livingston made Chalk Farm his London studio of choice, often using it to overdub strings on backing tracks recorded in Jamaica (usually with Fi-Cord pencil condenser mics similar to the AKG C28, suspended high above the musicians), and producer Harry J recorded Jamaican vocal duo Bob and Marcia's 1970 single "Young, Gifted and Black" there—the studio's first hit—with a unique delay on the strings that, according to Keary, was achieved by mixing the output from both the sync and replay heads on the 8-track machine. At its height, Chalk Farm was rivaled only by Gooseberry Sound in Soho for reggae work; they were widely

viewed by producers as being the only two studios in England capable of accurately replicating the sound of the records coming out of Jamaica.

As Chalk Farm evolved to offer 16-track and then 24-track recording, it outgrew the original console, so Keary built a larger 20 x 16 version of the board that offered a separate monitoring section. In addition, a great deal of new equipment was acquired following the success of "Young, Gifted and Black," including a Studer 2-track machine and several items purchased from Lansdowne, including EMI mic preamps, a Joe Meek–designed tube "black box" equalizer, and a reverb plate. Also installed at that time were an EMT 140 and a 240 Gold Foil, and a number of Neumann condensers (U87, U47 FET, KM84) were added to the arsenal of microphones.

Notable artists to record at Chalk Farm included Dave Davies (of The Kinks), The Nice, Dire Straits, Mungo Jerry, and Georgie Fame. Unfortunately, with the changing economic times, Keary was forced to close Chalk Farm Studios in 1982. He remains active in the professional audio business today and heads up Thermionic Culture, a manufacturer of analog tube studio recording equipment.

APPLE

The mixing console was a piece of plywood with four faders at either end and a small green oscilloscope set in the middle. There were eight tiny speakers on the control room wall—one for each channel (!)—and there was an audible "twitter" when you stood in the corner. There were no holes in the connecting wall to the studio, so cables had to be run through an open door and down the corridor. And there was virtually no acoustic isolation between the studio and the Tube train that ran below or the adjacent boiler room, which meant that every now and then sessions were interrupted by deep rumblings beneath the concrete floor or what sounded like a small airplane taking off directly next door.

Other than that, it wasn't a bad start.

Such were the dire circumstances that faced George Martin and engineer Glyn Johns when they arrived at the newly built Apple Studios in January of 1969 to begin recording what was to become The Beatles' *Let It Be* album. By the mid-'60s, the group had become so wealthy that their business advisors warned that they needed to start spending large amounts of money on business-related projects to avoid massive tax bills. What better way than to build their own recording studio—a private playground where they could both capture their muse and party with friends, away from the sterility of Abbey Road and its besuited recording engineers and white-coat-clad maintenance engineers?

In June 1968 Apple acquired premises at 3 Savile Row in London's Mayfair district, a five-story Geor-

Cover of the Apple Studios brochure, circa 1971.
(From studio brochure)

gian town house that had once been a gentleman's club, but had been used as office space for decades before The Beatles purchased it. Their plan was to convert the building's basement—essentially just a corridor with several small rooms off of it that had been used for storage—into a recording studio.

And they decided to put the job in the hands of an individual with dubious credentials whom John Lennon had met at a party—"Magic" Alex Mardas. Alex had them convinced that he could build a studio that would far outstrip EMI's Abbey Road facilities—their long-serving base of operations—in terms of both comfort and technical innovation. He had promised them miraculous things—72-track tape machines, wall paint that could change colors, even an invisible spaceship that they could presumably use to fly to and from sessions—but none of them had come to pass.

And now it had come to this.

With the aid of borrowed gear from EMI, Martin and Johns made the best of a bad situation, with "Magic" Alex banned to an electronics workshop several miles away. (Perhaps the only truly magical thing about him was that he somehow avoided being fired!) But it was clear that Apple Studios needed help—professional help—and that aid came in the form of EMI engineer Geoff Emerick, who was hired away by the group in the spring of 1969 and given the monumental task of rebuilding Alex's folly into a workable studio.

"It was bloody hard work getting that studio designed and built," wrote Emerick in his 2006

STORIES FROM THE STUDIO

"Um, I think we should get out of here . . ."

IN THE BRIEF YEARS of its existence, Apple was renowned for the opulence of its annual Christmas parties, funded, of course, from the deep pockets of its owners, the four Beatles. But, according to Geoff Emerick, the 1969 Christmas bash was especially notable in that it very nearly marked the end of the company . . . literally. "The demolition phase of the studio project had been completed by then, although the construction had not yet begun," he explained in *Here, There and Everywhere*. "As you gazed out the second floor window, where the party was being held, you looked straight down into this pit, this great, gaping hole where the basement had once been. The contractors had put in just enough support beams for a hundred people jumping up and down and dancing—that's how many had been invited—but two hundred had turned up. As the festivities went on into the wee hours and the room got more crowded, I began to get increasingly concerned.

"As carefully as I could, I began walking around having a quiet word in everyone's ear, saying, 'Um, I think we should get out of here—the floor's about to cave in.' Amidst the din and the free-flowing booze, nobody paid me much mind—they just assumed I was kidding around, but I wasn't. Actually, I was scared to death that the whole building was going to collapse, taking all of us and assorted Beatles and Beatle wives with it. Somehow it didn't happen, but I can't help but think that if one more uninvited guest had shown up, my place in Beatles history would have been quite different."

memoir *Here, There and Everywhere*. "There was absolutely nothing straightforward about the project; at one time or another we encountered every problem you could possibly encounter. For one thing, physical access at Savile Row was extremely limited. Not only was it a very small premises to begin with, we were building a room within a room, and so we had to hire extra-thin workmen to fit in the void between the walls. The noise coming from the underground train that ran nearby was another huge problem, forcing us to float everything on special shock-absorbing pads. Designing the air conditioning system was a nightmare; building an echo chamber was problematic because of leakage; there were delays [and] constant aggravation."

The band had specifically requested that the recording area sound acoustically like Abbey Road's Studio Two, where they had spent so much time over the years, and where most of their greatest hits and most ambitious recordings had been crafted. But Apple was considerably smaller (the studio area was a modest 30' by 45', with just 11' ceilings, while the control room was only 12' by 22'), so the best that could

A collage put together for a 1970 Apple Christmas card. Left to right: Mastering engineer Malcolm Davies, maintenance engineer Claude Harper, recording engineer John Smith, and studio manager Geoff Emerick.
(Courtesy of John Smith)

Page from Apple Studios brochure, circa 1971.
(From studio brochure)

Eddie Klein, Ron Pender, and Claude Harper—turned their attention to equipping the studio, with the mixing board the first and largest item to consider. Emerick's initial preference was to have Neumann build Apple a custom console built around the EMI TG design, with compressor/limiters on every channel—a mixer that would be way ahead of its time, with every bell and whistle an engineer would ever need. But the band's newly appointed manager, Allen Klein, balked at the cost, causing a considerable delay. With the studio standing idle for so long

be achieved by Emerick and acoustic designer Ken Shearer (who had designed the Royal Albert Hall) was to re-create the same room decay time. Nonetheless, writes Emerick, "I was quite pleased with the results: in the end, the room sounded much larger than it actually was."

As the construction phase came to an end, Emerick and his newly hired maintenance staff—

while the idea was being debated, a decision was finally made to instead purchase a 36 x 16 Helios that was immediately available. This had the bonus of being significantly smaller than the planned Neumann desk, thus freeing up valuable space in the cramped control room. Also installed were Studer and 3M 16-track tape machines, Cadac monitors and amps, and four EMT 140 plate reverbs, which supple-

Reverse tape copying—gniypoc epat esreveR

THE APPLE STUDIOS were built with a mandate to create the most advanced recording environment in the world. To that end, studio manager Geoff Emerick and his engineers were constantly experimenting to come up with innovative techniques that would keep them one step ahead of the competition.

"I'd long been wrestling with the problem of transient overload," Emerick remembers. "The tape machines and amplifiers of the time weren't that good at dealing with

spikes in level—in fact, transients wouldn't even register on VU meters, so you never knew when one had passed. All too often, the equipment would distort when one of those little gremlins hit the circuitry, and it frustrated me no end."

The problem became exacerbated further still when making tape copies, because for some reason second-generation transients tended to overload even worse than the original ones. Ultimately, it was Apple engineer John Smith

who came up with a simple solution: copy the tapes backwards. "That would give the circuitry a chance to react a lot better to those spikes," Emerick says, "because the signal would build up to it instead of it just hitting all of a sudden. As a result, the copies sounded a whole lot better when threaded in reverse and played back normally." Thus, an easy fix to a perplexing problem, and one which gave clients yet another reason to book the facilities at 3 Savile Row.

Power to the people—but less to the cutting lathe

WHEN JOHN LENNON came into the Apple cutting room to master his new single "Power to the People," he made it abundantly clear how he wanted the 45 to sound: loud. To fulfill the request, the mastering engineers at the studio devised a method of cutting the disc at half speed—the first time that had ever been done, according to former Apple engineer John Smith. Playing back the master tape at half speed was simple; the problem was that the slowest the room's Neumann lathe could go, with a slight mechanical adjustment, was just under 33 1/3 rpm, not to the 22.5 rpm that was required. "But our guys discovered that if you stepped down the voltage of the power going to the platter," Smith relates, "you could bring it all the way down to half speed, or even lower. By cutting with both the lathe and the tape machine going at half speed, you could not only put more level on the acetate, but also with a much better low end. We always used to say that if Neumann had gotten wind of this, they would have thrown our warranty right out the window!"

That wasn't the only unusual thing about "Power to the People," as it turned out. "For some reason," Smith says, "it was cut at least six months before it went off to the pressing plant. I'm not really sure why—maybe there was some sort of legal reason—but for a long time it just sat in a can on a shelf waiting to go to the factory and we swore that when we finally got the white-label pressing back to us, it had this real hard edge to it. Our understanding was that, over those six months, the actual acetate had become physically harder—it wasn't as soft as when you would typically send it to the factory—and that seemed to have affected the sound by making it harder, too."

mented the studio's good-sized acoustic echo chamber. In addition, the stack of Dolby noise reduction units were double-bussed, allowing clients to monitor off tape without repatching.

Emerick was determined to make Apple Studios a pleasant place to work, a space that would encourage the creative flow. Accordingly, a great deal of thought and effort had gone into the interior design, with muted lighting and polished parquet floors everywhere. The reception area was decorated with elegant Regency furniture and brass fittings. The control room walls were covered with a soft blue fabric, while the mastering room walls were decorated with a purple and mauve zigzag fabric evocative of sound waves; even the tape copying room got the decorator's touch, with walls covered by a blue fabric that had a circular pattern that looked like flying discs. The studio ceilings were covered with angular panels that were specially designed to give the

Clowning around in the Apple control room, 1972. Left to right: Mastering engineer George (Porky) Peckham, engineer Claude Harper, and assistant engineer Mike O'Donnell.
(Courtesy of Claude Harper)

Covering up

WHEN HE WAS ASSIGNED to engineer Jack Jones' album *Write Me a Love Song, Charlie* at Apple Studios in 1974, John Smith faced an unusual dilemma: The microphone he wanted to use on the singer's voice looked too old. "I really wanted to use a [STC] 4038 for the vocals, even though it's unusual to use it for that purpose because, being a ribbon microphone, it pops so readily. But I thought, 'Well, I'm not working with a rocker here; I'm working with a jazz singer, somebody who knows how to work a mic, so I'll give it a try.' It was a new mic, but having been designed by the BBC in the 1950s, it looked old, and since Jack and his producer had chosen to come into a studio that was renowned for being current in terms of the technology at the time, I decided that I wasn't going to scare them off by showing them this old-fashioned mic. Instead, I covered the microphone with a wind sock, so all they saw was this big wind sock on a mic stand.

"And you know what? It worked great. That thing probably popped maybe twice in all the time that we were doing vocals. All you had to do was take a whole load of low end off of it, and the vocal just came right at you. As a result, when it came time to mix the tracks, you could bring the orchestration up quite high compared to the vocal—that's how well the vocal cut through. That was the only time I ever used a 4038 to record lead vocal, because it popped so much. But Jack was the kind of artist that I could take that kind of risk with. And to the best of my knowledge he never did find out that that was what I was using."

appearance of height; the walls were also covered in panels, with lamp recesses along the floor that allowed the walls to be underlit in any color by sliding in different colored gels.

The redesign and refurbishment took more than two years. Apple Studios reopened in September 1971, with George Harrison as the only Beatle to attend the launch party. The Apple mastering room in particular quickly gained a solid reputation as one of the best in the world, thanks to ex-EMI mastering engineer Malcolm Davies' skill, both at the cutting lathe and as the room's designer. Not only had he hand-selected the equipment, he had also specified that rubber shock mounts be placed underneath the lathe in order to insulate the platter from spurious vibrations—both from the street and the nearby underground railway—which could degrade the sound. In 1972, Davies was joined by a second highly regarded mastering engineer, George "Porky" Peckham, whose discs were embellished with his signature "A Porky Prime Cut" engraved on their run-out grooves.

Mechanical de-essing

SIBILANCE WAS ALWAYS the mastering engineer's worst enemy back in the days of cutting to vinyl. Says former Apple engineer John Smith, "You'd occasionally get in a tape that seemed perfectly fine when you listened to it, but when you'd go to cut it, sometimes the mechanics of getting an 's' onto a platter just broke down where it would just go 'splat' instead. Lynsey de Paul, for example, was one artist whose 'esses' went right the way through the stratosphere. We had limiters in our cutting chain that did de-essing reasonably well,

but on occasion it wasn't enough. Alternatively, you could bring down the overall level, but sometimes you'd have to bring it down so much that the record company would reject it."

To meet the challenge, Apple mastering engineer Malcolm Davies came up with a couple of ingenious solutions. "Sometimes we would cut out the offending 's' from the tape altogether—using a razor blade to remove just a tiny sliver," he explains. "Other times we'd put a little bit of splicing tape on the oxide side of the tape, just for that very short length

of time, which would cause the tape to lift off the head at that point, and it would tone the sibilance down just enough. It was like a mechanical de-esser, you might say."

Asked if the same thing could have been accomplished with EQ or a notch filter, Smith's reply is, "Possibly, but then you'd have to switch it in and out incredibly fast or it would be an obvious tonal change, an obvious loss of presence. Using that little tiny bit of splicing tape ensured that it would only happen for that one split second, and that most people wouldn't notice it."

In the months following its reopening, the studio would be used by Apple Records artists like Badfinger and Lon and Derrek Van Eaton, as well as outside artists like Stealers Wheel (their debut album and hit single "Stuck in the Middle with You" were recorded there, with Jerry Leiber and Mike Stoller producing, and Geoff Emerick engineering), Tim Hardin, Nazareth, Fanny, and Mark Wirtz. Ironically, George Harrison would be the only Beatle to record at Apple, laying down a few tracks for his 1973 *Living in the Material World* album. (Most of the album was recorded at Harrison's home studio, constructed during the long wait for Apple to be completed.)

Sadly, less than a year after the studio reopened, the upper floors of the building were demolished because Ringo Starr wanted to convert the Apple offices into a film scoring complex. It was a project that never got completed. Worse yet, it had the unin-tended consequence of throwing the basement studio operations into chaos, which, along with the collapse of Apple Corps as a viable company, led to the entire facility being closed in 1975.

In the eyes of many, Apple is seen as a failed experiment, a relic of the '60s. Yet the fact remains that the studio and cutting room housed in the basement of 3 Savile Row were consistently prof-itable—one of the few Apple ventures that actu-ally made money. More importantly, they served as the prototype for a slew of British artist-owned commercial recording facilities in the years and decades that followed, including Ringo Starr's Startling Studios, The Who's Ramport, Pete Towns-hend's Eel Pie, Pink Floyd's Britannia Row, Jethro Tull's Maison Rouge, The Kinks' Konk Studios, 10cc's Strawberry Studios, Paul Weller's Solid Bond Studios, and Dire Straits guitarist Mark Knopfler's British Grove Studios.

ISLAND / BASING STREET

Island Studios was established by Island Records founder Chris Blackwell in early 1970. It was located in the same building that housed the offices for Island Records: an old church at 8-10 Basing Street, near Portobello Road in West London.

Studio One, designed to accommo-date some 80 musicians, was at ground-floor level. It was some 60' by 40' in size, with 25' ceilings, included a large screen for recording to film, and had a separate projection room above the control room. Studio Two, in the basement, was approxi-mately 30' by 20' in size, with 10' ceilings. (A small upstairs copying room was added during a 1973 refurbishment.) According to engineer Phill Brown, the two studios were the first to be built using a "concrete inner room" design, suspended in air voids on rubber pillars. Both control rooms had heavy brown carpet on their walls, ceiling, and floor, with a resultant sound that Brown describes as "very dead."

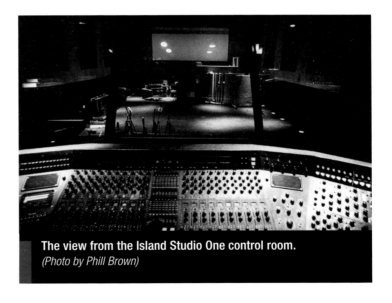

The view from the Island Studio One control room.
(Photo by Phill Brown)

In 1975, Island Studios was renamed Basing Street Studios and was put under the direction of A&R man / producer Muff Winwood (brother of Steve Winwood). Island / Basing Street Studios played host to dozens of

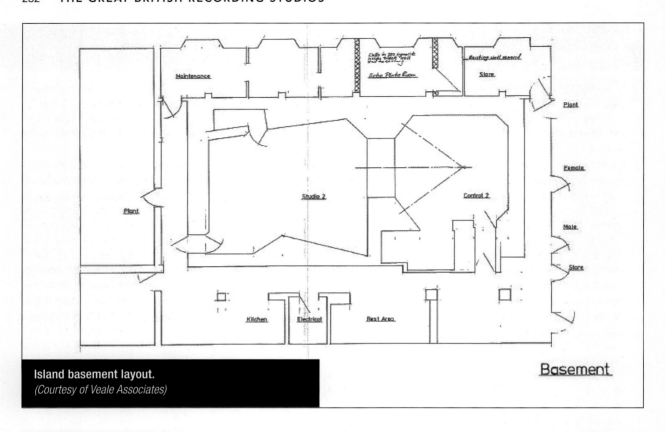

Island basement layout.
(Courtesy of Veale Associates)

major artists in the 1970s, including Bob Marley and the Wailers, the Rolling Stones, Traffic, Led Zeppelin, Jethro Tull (their definitive *Aqualung* album was recorded there), Roger Waters, Spooky Tooth, the Eagles (*Desperado*), Stephen Stills, Genesis, Black Sabbath, Mott the Hoople, Brian Eno, and Dire Straits.

STORIES FROM THE STUDIO
The birth of Helios

ISLAND RECORDS head honcho Chris Blackwell liked the console that Olympic maintenance engineer Dick Swettenham had built for the facility's large Studio One. In fact, he liked it a lot. Blackwell was planning on opening his own two-room recording facility soon, and felt that having Swettenham's consoles there would be a major attraction and thus help the studio turn a profit.

There was only one problem: How to get an Olympic employee to build a mixing desk for a competitor? Blackwell discussed his dilemma with producer/engineer Glyn Johns, who suggested that the Island executive form a company with Swettenham and go into the business of designing and manufacturing the consoles. And so Helios was born.

Ultimately, seven Helios desks would be built for Island, including one for its mobile studio. (See Chapter 9 for more information.) Geoff Emerick ordered one for Apple Studios. So too did Pete Townshend, for Ramport Studios, and Ian Stewart, for the Rolling Stones Mobile. Even one of Blackwell's fiercest competitors—Virgin Records, run by Richard Branson—would order three Helios consoles: one for The Manor, one for the Manor Mobile, and one for Townhouse Studios. In the end, some 125 Helios consoles would be installed in studios throughout England and Europe— every one of them custom-built to order—and they would continue to be produced right up until the end of the 1970s, putting their distinctively clean sonic stamp onto hundreds of iconic recordings. Clearly a sound investment (pardon the pun) for Mr. Blackwell!

"You'll see: This one builds really well"

"I REMEMBER THAT ONE really well," said famed engineer/producer Andy Johns in a 1999 interview with the author, "and not because of what people thought about it after it came out, but because doing it was very special."

The track he's talking about is one of the most famous Led Zeppelin songs—heck, one of the most famous songs, period: "Stairway to Heaven," recorded at Island Studios in late 1970. "At the time," he continued, "I was having a competition in my own mind with my brother [Glyn Johns] about this song he'd done with the Steve Miller Band that was a complete rip-off of 'Jumpin' Jack Flash.' The way my brother had mixed it, it started off fine and just kept getting louder and louder, more and more. Your mind would just be going, man, it can't get any bigger. But it would! So I'd said to Jimmy [Page], 'What we need is a building song on this album [*Led Zeppelin IV*]; what do you think?' And he replied, 'I've got something, we'll do it tomorrow—you'll see: This one builds really well.'

"We tracked it the next day with acoustic guitar, drums, and John Paul [Jones] was playing a Hohner electric piano, which looked like a miniature upright; quite a charming little thing. Because there was no bass, I spent quite a lot of time figuring out how to make the left hand have bottom end so they'd have something to play to. And that can't have been more than an evening doing that, it probably only took a couple of hours to get it on tape, maybe three hours. It's an amazing [basic] track.

"There really aren't that many overdubs on there. Obviously, John would have played bass, which he'd have done very quickly. Then Jimmy announced that he wanted to put Rickenbacker 12-strings on, and I remember saying, 'Well, let's do them direct,' through some compression so it's nice and glassy and sparkly. One of them, in actual fact, is a little bit distorted on one side.

"Then Page did the lead line, and the thing just kept getting better and better; it was becoming monstrous. Then John Paul came in and he had the idea for the recorders, which is a four-part thing. And Robert sang very quickly. The vocal for 'Stairway to Heaven,' I'm sure, couldn't have been more than two, two and a half takes. And he hadn't finished the lyrics, either! I remember him saying, 'Oh, is it my turn to sing now? Hang on, play that again because I haven't finished the lyrics . . .'

"But the solo took time; that was a long afternoon downstairs at Island. [*Note: Jimmy Page's guitar was recorded several months after the backing tracks.*] It was one of those paranoia things: 'How was that one, Andy?' 'It's really good.' 'No, it's horrible; let me do another one.' And I'm getting very paranoid, because I can see he's freaking out. After about two hours, Jimmy says, 'You're making me paranoid,' and I said, 'No, you're making *me* paranoid!' We both decided, let's both stop being paranoid and—voilà! In another 20 minutes, he'd done it. And it's a great solo.

"There's something else that's interesting. If you listen very hard, at the very end, when [Robert is] singing the last line—'And she's buying / The stairway to heaven'—[you'll hear] a little crackling sound. In those days, you used to get what was called 'bias bubble,' so when [the tape was] getting signal, it would go [*makes crackling noise*] right on the very, very end."

The Studio One control room was equipped with a Helios 28 x 16 console, replaced in 1973 by a Helios 32 x 24; the Studio Two control room had a 20 x 16 model, upgraded in 1974 to 32 inputs. In the late '70s, both control rooms were refitted with MCI 500-series desks. All the multitrack tape recorders at Island were 3M models: 24-track, 16-track, and 8-track; the 2-tracks were 1/4" Philips machines. Monitoring was via 15" Tannoy Reds inside Lockwood cabinets, driven by Crown amplifiers. Unusually, the speakers were suspended from the ceiling on a custom-built curved track. In 1973, the monitors in Studio Two were changed to JBL 4350s and EPI 50s, amplifiers unknown. Outboard equipment included four EMT 140 reverb plates and four blackface UREI 1176 limiters, as well as Pultec equalizers, and a rack of Kepex expanders and GainBrain compressors. Later, an Eventide Digital Delay, Harmonizer, and Phaser were added.

Go

IN FEBRUARY OF 1976 engineer Phill Brown began work on Japanese composer Stomu Yamashta's ambitious recording *Go* at Island Studios' main tracking room (Studio One). Labeled a "rock/classical concept album"—a popular genre at the time—the banal phraseology belied the incredible complexity of the project.

For the album, Yamashta had assembled an all-star group of musicians that included Steve Winwood, Al Di Meola, Klaus Schulze, and Michael Shrieve, and he insisted that all recording be done live, essentially treating the band as if they were a symphony orchestra. In addition, he ordered full-sized projections of the 1969 NASA moon landing to be shown on the walls and ceiling of the studio in order to inspire the best performances from the somewhat puzzled musicians.

But that wasn't the only trick up Yamashta's sleeve. "Down the center of the studio was a collection of sculptures from Instruments Sonores des Freres Baschet in France, a phenomenon Stomu had [discovered] during his months of touring," Brown relates in his book *Are We Still Rolling?* "The instruments consisted of 16' springs that could be made to vibrate when struck and glass tubes of varying length that, when stroked, gave off sounds similar to using a moistened finger on the rim of a wine glass."

Complicating things further still, there were no fewer than three producers on the project—Dennis McKay, famed arranger Paul Buckmaster, and Yamashta himself—with additional production input from Winwood and Shrieve. "This presented some problems with individual sounds," says Brown in a master of understatement, "as there were six different opinions—including mine—on offer.

"We recorded with very few acoustic screens up," he continues, "and in employing a classical approach, there was a large amount of leakage." In all, Brown reports using no less than 22 microphones and eight DI boxes on the collection of instruments set up on the studio floor—something that stretched the capacity of the control room's 32-input Helios desk. "With the large number of microphones, leads and headphones used, and the outboard equipment of compressors and limiters, we were technically pushed to the limit," Brown says. "The sessions were intense and became more difficult as the days progressed. This was mainly due to the combination of technical requirements, the number of producers and musicians . . . and the clash of various musical egos. From the moment the session started I would be required to work at maximum pace, both physically and mentally, while I looked after 32 microphone and line inputs, attended to the requirements of six musicians and five producers and operated the desk and tape machines."

It turned out that Brown and his assistant Robert Ash were not only pushing the equipment and their concentration to the limit, but their ingenuity as well—and it was only fast thinking and complete familiarity with the music being recorded that saved the day. Brown explains: "One night we were working on the first six-minute section of the album. We had recorded a couple of run-throughs and were now on take three, which unfortunately broke down before the last chorus. There was easily enough tape left for one more version of the piece, so I left the machine in record and said, 'OK, we're still rolling. Take four,' and we were off again. I looked down into the studio and nine guys were playing, heads bowed.

"As it reached what should have been the end, Klaus unexpectedly went into the next track. Now we had a problem, as we found ourselves at the beginning of a five-minute song with only about two minutes of tape. I felt reluctant to stop the musicians for two reasons: Firstly, I didn't want a technical glitch to interrupt this excellent atmosphere, and secondly, this was a heavy bunch of musicians and the thought of having to say, 'Sorry, guys, we ran out of tape' down the talkback system was horrendous."

Fortunately, both Brown and Ash had previously worked in the Island Mobile—an experience that immediately paid dividends. "I realized we could use the other multitrack machine," Brown says, "even though it was only a 16-track. Luckily, on this song we were only recording to 18 tracks of the studio's 24-track machine, and two of the 18 were recording signal from our ambient mics, which I thought we could probably manage without.

"We loaded up the 16-track machine with new tape and got ready. Due to the way the Dolby noise reduction was wired up, the signal could be sent to either machine, but not to both at once, so it was going to be necessary to switch between them on the fly. I had never found a need to do this before and did not know if it would work at all, or if it did work, whether or not there would be any clicks.

"The familiar Moog wind and intergalactic atmospherics were floating through the speakers and the lunar module was getting ever closer to the moon's surface. I checked all the levels reading at the desk on the first 16 tracks.

"'God, Robert,' I said, moving over to him at the tape machines. 'Do you realize that wherever we switch will have to be my edit point? How quick do you think this switching works?' The Moog continued to build in dynamics and power.

"'I don't know,' said Robert, 'but I think you should pick your spot and count me in, and pretty quick.' Just at that moment Michael Shrieve played the drum entry and everyone picked up the new song. Our remaining length of tape on the 24-track machine was growing alarmingly short.

"Robert put the 16-track machine into record. 'I've got the rhythm of the song,' he said. 'Let's go, in two bars.'

"'OK, but switch just before the snare beat.' I took a deep breath and counted. 'One bar . . . one . . . two . . . three . . . and . . .'

"Robert switched, and the meters immediately began to move. We did not know, however, whether it had worked or not—we would only find that out on playback. Below me in the studio, unaware of our activities, the band was already building the track with percussion, timpani and piano to Winwood's fragile vocal entry. 'When you're caught / the other side . . .' he sang as he played along on piano, '. . . possibilities aren't always what they seem / reject them and all your choices will be free / crossing the line.'

"'These lyrics seem strangely relevant,' I thought."

As luck would have it, both the songs recorded that night turned out to be the masters. Since there was almost no way to play them back-to-back due to the way they had been recorded, Brown and Ash quickly copied the 16-track over to fresh tape on the 24-track machine and then edited the two parts together. "With fingers crossed, I hit the play button," Brown recalls. "Surprisingly it had worked, with only a slight variation in hiss level. I felt it had been a complete accident, as it could so easily have gone either way."

The Island / Basing Street mic cabinet included Neumann U87s and numerous AKGs (including D12, D20, D25, C28, D224E, C414, C451), as well as Shure SM57s, a Beyer M160, and various Coles ribbon microphones. In a 2011 online interview for The Jethro Tull Forum, engineer John Burns described the typical mic setup he used while recording the backing tracks for *Aqualung*: "I would have had an AKG D20 on the bass drum; a D25 or a D20 on the floor tom, mid tom, and top tom, or possibly Neumann U87s; an AKG 224E on the snare; an AKG 451 on the hi-hat; and two Neumann U87s on the overheads. On the amps I would have had an AKG D25 on the bass, a D20 close up on the guitar, and probably a U87 forty centimeters away so I had two mics to mix together. Piano would have been two Neumann U87s; vocals would have been a U87 or possibly a U67."

In 1982, Basing Street Studios was purchased by ZTT Records (part of the Sarm group) and renamed Sarm West. (See *Sarm* below.) In November 1984, Studio One served as the venue for the recording of the best-selling single "Do They Know It's Christmas" by the members of Band Aid in support of relief efforts for the famine in Ethiopia. A year later, architect Eddie Veale was brought in to oversee an extensive redesign, during which two small additional studios were constructed and three large isolation booths added to Studio One; the Studio One control room was also moved from one end to the other at that time. Sadly, Sarm West closed its doors in late 2014.

Island Studio One session setup, 1972.
(Photo by Brian Cooke/Redferns)

Doing the nasty

FOR MORE THAN three decades, Robert John "Mutt" Lange was one of the most innovative and influential record producers in the world. Starting in 1976, he crafted hit after hit for artists as diverse as The Boomtown Rats, AC/DC, Foreigner, Def Leppard, and Bryan Adams, as well as enjoying a string of successes with country singer (and ex-wife) Shania Twain.

"Working with Mutt, you were always experimenting one way or another," says Tony Platt, who worked side by side with the producer, engineering The Boomtown Rats' 1979 album *Fine Art of Surfacing* in Basing Street Studio One.

"This was in the days before samplers and all those sort of things, and Mutt wanted to get a white-noise kind of sound on the snare drum. We tried generating some white noise from a piece of test equipment, but it was a little bit too much of what he was after.

"I thought about it for a while and suddenly remembered that the mic cupboard at the end of Studio One was a particularly nasty-sounding room with plaster walls. So we put a big old Altec horn-loaded speaker in there and an AKG 451 mic, and we sent the sound of the snare, gated, through the speaker. Then we squashed the

hell out of the signal coming back from the microphone, probably by overloading the mic amp on the Helios console. It ended up being the perfect kind of white noise to put underneath the snare to add a particularly punky sound to the whole thing.

"I think I knew that the cupboard sounded that way because I'd probably tried to use it as an isolation booth. Sometimes you'd have an amp that you wanted to stick away in order to isolate the sound from the main room. I'd probably used it at some point for that reason and decided that the sound in there was particularly nasty."

PATHWAY

It was tiny. It was minimally equipped and had no real acoustic treatment. It smelled, too—an unpleasant mixture of mildew, cigarettes, and stale beer.

And yet, somehow, it worked.

Launched in 1970, Pathway Studios was located at 2A Grosvenor Avenue in the then highly unfashionable (since highly gentrified) North London neighborhood of Islington. The building had previously been a workshop accessible via a tiny alleyway that had room for one or two cars, or, if you didn't mind just three inches of space on either side, a small transit van of the variety typically used by musicians to transport their equipment. In other words, it had free parking . . . if you mentioned to get to the driveway before anyone else.

Pathway's owners were producer/songwriters Mike Finesilver and Pete Ker, and its construction was largely funded with the royalties Finesilver had received as cowriter of the classic '60s single "Fire" by The Crazy World of Arthur Brown. (See *Advision* in

Chapter 3 for more information.) Originally intended for use as a private facility, it quickly became a popular demo studio for many up-and-coming bands, not just for its low hourly rates and decidedly relaxed atmosphere, but because the tapes that came out of Pathway sounded surprisingly good.

The reason is hard to fathom. The recording area was small (some 25' by 25' in size), square, and carpeted, with low ceilings and nothing in the way of acoustic treatment save a few pegboard panels nailed to the walls. But it was a palace compared to the minuscule control room, which was approximately the size of a walk-in closet and could barely fit three people if one of them were dieting; its cramped dimensions also meant that the ceiling-hung 12" dual concentric Tannoy monitors were essentially large headphones for the engineer seated directly beneath them.

The Pathway console was a homemade 16 x 8 mixer built by maintenance engineer Barry "Bazza" Farmer based on a design he saw in a magazine; it was trans-

The very cramped control room at Pathway, with Glen Tilbrook of Squeeze and an unknown engineer: "Approximately the size of a walk-in closet, and could barely fit three people if one of them were dieting."
(Photo by Lawrence Impey)

former coupled, with all discrete electronics and inductor-based EQ, and it was clean and relatively quiet, but it was no Neve, either. The tape recorders were similarly adequate but nothing exceptional: a Brennell 1" 8-track, later replaced by an Otari, coupled with three Revox 1/4" 2-track machines—two A77s and a B77. In a space-saving measure that proved to be ingenious, the two A77s were placed side by side on a shelf; they both ran at 7.5/3.75 ips and were equipped with Varispeed controls, but when this wasn't slow enough, the tape reel could be placed on the machine to the left and the take-up reel on the machine to the right, allowing the delay time to be adjusted simply by moving the two machines closer or further apart.

The outboard gear consisted of little more than a couple of Bazza-built compressors, an ADR Vocal Stressor, two A&D limiter/compressors, an EMT reverb plate, and an old spring reverb (model unknown, but probably taken from the back of a guitar amplifier), the former housed in the upstairs office, and the latter tucked away in an alcove at the top of the steep staircase outside the studio door leading to the office, toilet, and tape library. The microphone collection at Pathway was also largely undistinguished, consisting of a dozen or so Shure and Electrovoice dynamics, plus an AKG D12 always used on bass drum, and a Beyer M160 favored for guitar recording. It was, however, enhanced with three vintage Neumann mics—a U47 and two U87s,

Squeeze drummer Paul Gunn standing by the control room door during a 1976 demo session.
(Photo by Lawrence Impey)

all powered by stand-alone "lunch boxes" since the primitive console did not provide phantom powering facilities.

Yet there was a certain indefinable "something" about the facility, and by the mid-1970s Pathway was not only considered one of the top demo studios in London, it even began turning out releasable master recordings. The studio became a favorite of Jake Rivera and Dave Robinson, founders of Stiff Records, and numerous Stiff punk and post-punk artists began working (and drinking) there extensively, including The Damned, Wreckless Eric, Tenpole Tudor, Lene Lovich, Dave Edmunds, Nick Lowe, and Ian Dury, plus a then-unknown singer-songwriter by the name of Elvis Costello, who recorded his entire debut album, *My Aim Is True*, at Pathway, reportedly in a total of just 24 hours of studio time. Three years later, he would return to the studio to record demos for his *Imperial Bedroom* album with one of the studio's staff engineers behind the board, an American by the name of Howard Massey (who would later write a book about the Great British Recording Studios . . . this one, in fact).

Other notable artists to record at Pathway included Alvin Stardust, Squeeze, the 101ers, Link Wray, Thomas Dolby, Spandau Ballet, John Foxx, and Madness (whose first single, "The Prince" was mixed by Massey—the first session he ever engineered). In addition, a number of well-known producers worked at Pathway, including Shel Talmy, Clive Langer, Alan Winstanley, Peter Collins, and Pete Waterman (later of Stock/Aitken/Waterman fame). 1977 in particular was a bumper year for the studio: Dire Straits came in to record a demo of "Sultans of Swing," and a newly formed band named The Police booked a session to record their first demos, returning later that same year to record several more tracks with John Cale producing. John Cleese also used Pathway to record voice-overs for his post–Monty Python industrial training films.

Despite some minor equipment overhauls in the 1990s to incorporate digital recording gear, Pathway closed sometime in the early 2000s and the building was converted into two small apartments.

THE MANOR

Based in the quaint village of Shipton-on-Cherwell in Oxfordshire, England, and opened in 1971, The Manor was the second residential recording studio in the U.K. (the first was Rockfield Studios in South Wales, opened in 1964). The 35-acre estate and 16th-century manor house was owned by Virgin Records CEO and '70s wunderkind Richard Branson. Opulent amenities were made available to artists using the facility, including eight double bedrooms, tennis courts, a swimming pool, a billiards room, and the services of a private chef advertised as being capable of preparing "anything from macrobiotic cooking to French haute cuisine."

Interestingly, Virgin was initially unable to get planning permission to run the facility at night because of objections from the neighbors, and so the local constabulary were often summoned when sessions ran late. Eventually, this problem was ameliorated when studio management posted a guard at the gate, with instructions to press an alarm button to alert the studio staff when the Old Bill paid a midnight call; this would give everyone a chance to stop what they were doing and gather innocently around the communal kitchen drinking cups of tea instead of doing noisy recording (and/or partaking of whatever illegal substances might have been on offer—this was, after all, the '70s).

The studio was in a separate building on the side of the residence, a good-sized area (approximately 50' by 20') that originally been a coach house but in more recent years had been used as a squash court; a balcony overhead was converted into a smallish control room. The multitrack machine was a 16-track Ampex MM 1000 and the main 2-track was an old tube Ampex Model 300; varispeed was provided by a monstrous contraption called The Savage, recently purchased from Pye Studios. (See *Pye* in Chapter 2 for more information.)

Paired with these was a 20 x 16 mixing console made by an obscure company called Walsall Timing Developments (later Rebis / Audio Developments). Virgin technical director Philip Newell (who started

The Manor control room.
(Courtesy of Mick Glossop)

The Manor control room, 1976, during sessions for the Mott album *Shouting and Pointing*. Left to right: Producer/engineer Eddie Kramer, band member Ray Majors, and then–assistant engineer Mick Glossop. *(Photo by Morgan Fisher)*

at The Manor several months after it opened) quickly found out that the mixing console was totally unsuitable for the task at hand. "The desk had a very inflexible way of working," he says. "It was basically a PA desk, and it wasn't easy to do overdubs or many of the other things that were absolutely necessary [to make records in that era]." Monitoring was initially via Tannoy 15" Golds, soon changed to JBL 4320s.

Not only was some of the equipment idiosyncratic, so too was the original acoustic design. "The acoustics in the control room were terrible," says former Manor (and later Townhouse) chief engineer Mick Glossop, "and there was virtually no acoustic treatment in the studio, either. When I started working there [in 1973] it was very rough and ready and technically a very funky sort of place. A lot of people went up there thinking it would be a nice place to record, but they quickly got very frustrated with the studio and never went back.

Lots of stuff was recorded there in the first couple of years because it was a very novel idea, but it didn't have the facilities and it really didn't have a lot of gear, either; the reputation of the studio was going downhill."

That was to change fairly quickly. A year after opening The Manor, Richard Branson had signed a 19-year-old composer/multi-instrumentalist by the name of Mike Oldfield to the newly formed Virgin Records label. With Branson's blessing, Oldfield took up residence at the studio, where he would work with coproducers Tom Newman and Simon Heyworth for more than six months recording his debut album, *Tubular Bells*. This would be the first release for the fledgling label and its greatest commercial success, selling some 15 million copies worldwide; a year later its theme song was adopted as an integral part of the soundtrack to the hit movie *The Exorcist*, giving sales a further boost. *Tubular Bells* would, in essence, provide the financing for the expansion of the Virgin empire into areas such as aviation; it would also more than cover the costs of a badly needed refurbishment for The Manor, which began in 1975.

Tom Hidley of Eastlake was brought in to do the acoustic treatment, under the direction of Newell and Glossop. The Manor would be only the second studio in Europe to undergo such transformation, Threshold Studios at Decca being the first. During the yearlong renovation, the original control room was demolished and a new one built at the opposite end of the studio—a typical Westlake design, with heavy trapping in the form of a series of "acoustic blankets"—long narrow strips of fiberboard, covered with fiberglass and hung at predetermined intervals on the ceiling and walls. These were said to be tuned for resonance and absorption at certain frequencies, "the idea being that certain frequencies were supposed to zoom in there and not come out again," says Glossop. "It was an exotic mix of different sorts of reflective and absorbing materials, all blended in this kind of acoustic-chef-like design to produce, theoretically, an incredibly flat response." The monitoring was also changed drastically, with JBL tweeters and midrange horn drivers, coupled with Gauss bass units, housed in massive Westlake cabinets at each corner of the control room, making it fully quad-ready. "They were

a little hard-sounding," says Glossop, "but it was pretty cutting-edge stuff at the time." (See *Quad: Ahead of its time, or just a bad idea?* on page 59 for more information.) Accompanying the huge new bi-amped monitors was a rack full of power amps, crossovers, and third-octave graphic equalizers to compensate for small acoustic variations in the room, as well as a pair of tiny Auratone 5C monitors—a staple of the '70s.

At the urging of Newell, who had positive experiences with the Helios installed in the Pye Mobile (later the first Manor Mobile; see Chapter 9 for more information), a quad-ready Helios 32-into-24 mixing desk in a wraparound console (necessary to meet the space limitations of the asymmetrical Westlake design) was installed in the new control room, complete with an early Allison automation system. "The Helios looked fantastic and it worked extremely well," enthuses Newell. "It was very advanced, too, with four-band parametric equalizers on each channel, which was unheard of on mixing consoles at the time. Most importantly, it gave us a great deal of flexibility, plus a lot of high headroom for a cleaner sound. You could turn things up or down freely without having to worry a lot about the gain structure."

The new control room was equipped with a full complement of signal processors, including Kepex noise gates, dbx companders, ADR F760 compressor/expanders, Neve compressor/limiters, UA 1176 limiters, Teletronix LA-3a compressors, UREI graphic equalizers, an Orban de-esser, a UREI Little Dipper notch filter, and an Eventide Phaser, plus two EMT 140 plates and two Master Room reverbs, supplemented by a Pandora Time Line ("So noisy that it was almost unusable," in Newell's words) and one of the first AMS delay lines in the U.K. The complement of tape machines was upgraded, too, with an Ampex MM1100 24-track recorder and both 4-track and 2-track Ampex AG-440C machines. The mic locker at The Manor was equally bountiful and included a large number of Neumann mics (U87, U77, U67, U47, KM84, KM64, M49) as well as AKG

STORIES FROM THE STUDIO
One for the birds

THE MANOR PROVIDED a singularly bucolic setting for the creation of music, and producer Tom Allom has a fond memory of the positive effect the facility's lush ambience had on the resultant sound. "I remember working on Dave Cousins' solo album *Two Weeks Last Summer* there," he says, "and it was indeed high summer, and there was a gentle, soulful song to be recorded—just vocal, acoustic guitar, and dobro—and so we decided we would record it out in the garden. I put a pair of [Neumann] U67s about 20 feet from the two musicians, and then I sat beside this beautiful old stone wall to watch and listen. It was fairly late in the evening, and, amazingly, as soon as the musicians started playing, the birds starting singing in response. You can hear this quite clearly in the record because the mics were so far back; in some sections the birds are quite audible. Unfortunately, so was the traffic from the main road, which was a quarter of a mile away! But the combination of the birds and the reflection off the stone wall made for a lovely sound."

Dip a gong; get it on

ONE OF THE BIG ADVANTAGES of recording in a residential studio like The Manor was that there were lots of odd places to put instruments and get unusual sounds—way more than were normally available in the relatively cramped recording facilities in London.

"[Visiting producer] Eddie Kramer started the fashion for recording drums in the billiard room at the far end of the house," recalls former Manor maintenance engineer Rod Duggan, "and so it was with subsequent bands. Roger Taylor had his kit in there when Queen were in [recording tracks for their 1976 *A Day at the Races* album]. The mic leads would go out of the window [of the billiards room], across the lawn, and then through the door of the control room. Every morning there was at least one broken lightbulb on the billiard table that had rattled out of its holder—Roger had an enormous kit in there, and all the lightbulbs were shaking out of the billiard lamps onto the green felt."

Producer Mike Howlett has a similar recollection. "That room got used a lot," he says. "People really liked the sound of it. It had big flagstone floors and plaster walls and a hard, low ceiling—a very bright, live hard room. At one point when I was playing bass with [the group] Gong, we thought, 'What would happen if we recorded all the billiard balls smashing into each other?' We put some mics all around the room and made this noise, which we ended up using on a track called 'A Sprinkling of Clouds' [on the 1974 album *You*]."

But that wasn't the only oddball place where musicians found themselves while working at The Manor. "Saxophones were often recorded in the tiny downstairs toilet just beside the kitchen," Duggan reports. "You'd go in for a pee and there would be a U87 on a stand in there and a lead going out the window." Studio lore had it that a gong had once been recorded in the swimming pool, too. "That was before I joined," says Duggan, "but I was told they put a mic by the pool and then they hit this gong and immediately dipped it into the water so it would make this weird phasing sort of sound. Everything we did was a bit experimental in those days."

(D12, D202, D224) and Beyer (M69, M88, M160, M360, Soundstar) models, plus a Schoeps CMC 56, an STC 4038 ribbon, and several Shure 456 mics.

During the refitting, the studio too was modified into a typical Westlake design popular in the era, with heavy trapping installed, minimizing the need for separation screens and making it easier for large numbers of musicians to play together in the same room. "Tom Hidley's theory was that instead of screening off instruments, you just positioned them next to a trap so that musicians didn't feel like they were confined by being in a booth or something," explains Glossop. "It worked quite well, depending on the relative volume of the other instruments."

At one point during the demolition/construction process, one of the walls in the studio actually collapsed, leading to an unexpected opportunity. "One of the byproducts was that a big window previously covered by plasterboard opened up and we all thought, 'Wouldn't it be fantastic to have daylight in the studio?'" Newell recalls. "And so we spoke to Tom [Hidley] and he didn't think they would present any problems with sound isolation, so we got to have our big windows. That's when I said, 'Can we keep those stone walls underneath, too?' because all the plaster had to come off. Tom was saying, 'No, you can't do that!' but Mick and I eventually decided otherwise.

"That was pretty significant, because, at that point in time, the general consensus was to have a very, very neutral acoustic in studios, hence Tom's system of trapping everything. But what we had learned with from our experience with the Manor Mobiles was that that wasn't necessarily the way you got the most interesting sounds. We would have never had the confidence to leave the wall like that if we hadn't used the Mobiles to make successful recordings in venues with stone walls, such as old castles." (See Chapter 9 for more information.) This would also lead to the deliberate construction of the fabled "Stone Room" when Virgin's Townhouse Studio was designed several years later. (See *Townhouse* below for more information.)

Throughout the 1970s, a who's who of Virgin artists would record at The Manor, as well as a number of artists signed to outside labels. These included the Bonzo Dog Band (who did the inaugural session in November 1971), Van Morrison, John Cale, Queen, Elton John, Gong, Tangerine Dream, the Strawbs, Sandy Denny, Dave Cousins, Claire Hamill, Split Enz, Public Image Ltd., XTC, and, of course, Mike Oldfield.

During a 1980 refurbishment, an isolated "Stone Room" extension similar to the one at Virgin's Townhouse Studios was built. "It was twice the size [of the one at Townhouse] and although it had the same characteristics and was intended to sound the same, it never did because the reverb time was much longer and it didn't compress in the same way because it wasn't small enough," comments Glossop. (See *Townhouse* below for more information.) At the same time, the Helios board in the control room was replaced with an SSL 4000 E-series 40 x 24 console and extra amenities were added, including a gym, a sauna, and an artificial lake complete with the obligatory two swans.

In April 1995, three years after EMI purchased Virgin Records, the recording studio was closed and the building sold to the Marquess of Headfort for £750,000. In 2010, The Manor was once again put up for sale, this time with an asking purchase price in excess of £5.75 million.

SCORPIO SOUND

Located on the ground floor of Euston Tower in central London (not coincidentally, the same building that housed both Capital Radio and the London headquarters of Thames Television), Scorpio Sound opened in 1972. Although originally intended to specialize in providing recording services for radio, it eventually became a popular studio for music recording and mixing, as well.

Despite being built into a high-rise office tower, Scorpio had a good-sized recording area—32' by 24', with 10' ceilings. The room was designed by BBC engineers, and so the initial acoustic treatment it received consisted mainly of the installation of special absorber boxes,

scorpio sound

Brochure page showing the Scorpio Sound exterior and reception area.
(From studio brochure)

giving it the same neutral sonic characteristic of most BBC studios. As studios trended toward livelier acoustics in the late 1970s, many of the original BBC absorbers were covered with hardwood. The 22' by 20' Scorpio control room was located side-on to the recording area—a very unusual layout, although there was a large window that ran virtually the entire length of the studio and isolation booth, yielding a good line of sight. The control room's original acoustic treatment was identical to the studio; however, by 1975 the BBC-style absorber boxes were removed and replaced with treatments designed by technical director Sean Davies, formerly of IBC.

The Scorpio control room was initially outfitted with a 24 x 16 Cadac console and an Ampex MM1100 16-track recorder, along with three Studer 1/4" 2-track machines: two A80s and a B62. Main monitoring was via Altec speakers, replaced a year later by cabinets that housed three 15" Tannoy HPDs per side, amplification unknown. Outboard gear included a rack of custom noise gates built by Davies, a pair of blackface UREI 1176 limiters, Allison Gain Brain compressors, and both mono and stereo Fairchild compressors, along with a Cooper Time Cube and EMT 140 and 240 reverb plates. The studio's mic cupboard was well stocked with Neumanns (U87, U67, U48, U47 [both tube and FET], KM84, and M49), a Telefunken ELA M251, an RCA 44, and a number of Shure and Electrovoice dynamics, plus Beyer and STC/Coles ribbons.

In 1978, Scorpio upgraded to 24-track and the control room was completely rebuilt and outfitted with a larger 28 x 24 Cadac console. (This would later be upgraded to a 32 x 24 and, finally, a 36 x 24 Cadac model.) A Telefunken 24-track tape machine was installed at that time, although problems quickly surfaced and this was soon replaced by a 3M M79, which itself was ultimately supplanted by a Studer A80 MkII recorder. As part of the refitting, a pair of gigantic (seven-foot-tall) Cadac "Power House" speakers with twin 18" bass units were also installed, supplemented some time later by UREI 813s—a first for U.K. studios. (See *The best of both worlds* on the following page.) The complement of outboard gear at Scorpio was also expanded at that time to include vintage Pultec equalizers, plus modern gear from ADR, Orban, MXR, and dbx.

Despite the investment in first-class equipment, Scorpio management's initial efforts to fill the bookings calendar fell disappointingly short, largely because the studio's decor was pure BBC—an environment that was simply not appealing to the artists of the era, who were starting to move away from institutional-style recording facilities like Abbey Road, Decca, and Pye and into rooms that offered more in the way of amenities and were better suited to their casual lifestyle. Fortunately, Scorpio received a lifeline when its upstairs neighbor, Capital Radio, realized that it could get around

Brochure page showing the Scorpio Sound studio and control room.
(From studio brochure)

T. Rex (Marc Bolan and Steve Currie) with singer Gloria Jones at Scorpio Studios, 1974.
(Photo by Estate of Keith Morris/Redferns/Getty Images)

needle-time restrictions by recording bands specifically for broadcast. Since Capital's own 8-track studio was far too small for most bands, the logical choice was to book Scorpio's big 16-track room just downstairs. Hence, throughout 1974 and into 1975, just about every chart act came through Scorpio's doors, receiving exposure to the technically excellent, if somewhat questionably decorated, studio. It was also at around this time that American engineer Dennis Weinreich joined the staff, providing crucial connections to L.A.-based producers like Val Garay and early exposure to equipment being used in the U.S. studios of the era. (See *The best of both worlds* below.)

Major 1970s artists to record and mix at Scorpio included Neil Diamond, Supertramp, Stanley Clarke, Billy Cobham, Jack Bruce, Cockney Rebel, Mick Ronson, and UFO; producer Roy Thomas Baker would also use the facility to overdub tracks on Queen's 1975 album *A Night at the Opera*.

In the early 1980s, Scorpio changed ownership and the Cadac console was replaced with an SSL 4000E; the Studer 24-track was also replaced with an Otari MTR-90. The studio continued in operation until 1997, when Capital Radio left Euston Tower, at which time Scorpio also closed its doors. The space that once housed Scorpio Sound is now a supermarket.

STORIES FROM THE STUDIO
The best of both worlds

"LIKE ALL 70'S STUDIOS, Scorpio [did indeed have] eccentricities," writes Los Angeles native and former Scorpio engineer Dennis Weinrich in an essay posted on philsbook.com. "The Cadac Power House monitors . . . sounded amazing and were loud (during the mixing of the Supertramp album *Crime of the Century* we received numerous calls from the Capital engineers saying we were breaking through the structure and could be heard on air!) . . . but they did not work particularly well at low levels. . . . Their HF characteristics were quite unique and it took some . . . time to adjust to them. They were also prone to blowing drivers."

Fortunately, Weinrich's U.S. connections paid off when it came time to resolve the problem. Some months after the installation of the Cadacs, L.A.-based engineer/producer Val Garay came to Scorpio to make an album with the group Mr. Big. On the recommendation of fellow U.S. engineer Bill Schnee (who had previously worked at Scorpio, recording an album with Neil Diamond), Garay brought with him a pair of Altec 604s with

Mastering Lab crossovers to use as reference monitors, along with a new speaker that Yamaha was thinking of marketing called the NS10, plus, in Weinrich's words, "some gizmo the Sunset Sound engineers were experimenting with called an Aphex Aural Exciter." So impressed were Scorpio's engineers with the NS10s—which would eventually become the standard "consumer speaker" reference monitor in studios the world over—that they attempted to buy a pair from Yamaha UK but were met with complete denial that the speakers even existed!

Soon after the Mr. Big project was completed, Weinrich traveled to L.A. to engineer a project at United Western. While there, he moved between two studios, one outfitted with a pair of Altec 604s identical to those Garay had brought with him, and another with a pair of prototype Altec UREI 813s—604-based monitors with time-aligned crossovers. Weinrich became convinced that the 813s addressed all of the shortcomings of the Cadac monitors back at Scorpio, and so upon his return from L.A. he promptly at-

tempted to place an order for them with his local U.K. audio dealer . . . only to have them inform him that they had no intention of importing 813s to the U.K. because doing so would conflict with products they were already carrying from competitors. A frustrating call to UREI followed, during which the company explained that it would not sell the speakers directly to Scorpio, either. In the end, a pair was purchased from a retailer in Los Angeles and shipped to Scorpio.

The UREIs were initially mounted on custom-made hydraulic steel stands that allowed them to be wheeled into the Scorpio control room, raised to the proper height in front of the desk, and then lowered and wheeled out for clients who preferred to instead use the Power Houses. With both sets of monitors being used equally (albeit by different clients), this quickly became an untenable situation, and so management eventually decided to have the control room rebuilt (at no small expense!) to provide permanent mounting for both pairs, thus giving Scorpio's clients the best of both worlds.

CHIPPING NORTON

Chipping Norton exterior.
(Photos by Tony Harris)

Brothers Mike and Richard Vernon were blues fans who owned a specialist record shop in Camden, North London. They even had their own fledgling record label—Blue Horizon—through which they'd been releasing various obscure blues recordings since 1965. Older brother Mike had a day job, too: producing records for Decca, where he had worked since 1962. Four years later, brother Richard would join the staff of CBS Records.

In 1966, Mike Vernon produced John Mayall's classic *Bluesbreakers with Eric Clapton* LP (better known in Britain as the "Beano" album, after the title of the comic book Clapton is seen reading on the cover). It was through that association that he came to meet Clapton's successor in the band, fellow blues enthusiast Peter Green. When Green left to form his own band with drummer Mick Fleetwood and bass player John McVie (appropriately enough named Fleetwood Mac), he was insistent that Vernon not only produce the band's debut album but also release it on Blue Horizon (distributed worldwide by CBS Records), giving the label its first high-profile artist.

Shortly thereafter, Mike Vernon left Decca to become an independent producer, and Richard soon followed to concentrate full-time on the Blue Horizon label. Other artists were duly signed, and the label began to enjoy tremendous success, culminating in Fleetwood Mac's single "Albatross" topping the U.K. charts.

In 1970, the Vernon brothers began contemplating building their own recording facility. Their original idea was to open a studio in the back room of the record shop, but it soon became apparent that the available space was too limited, and so the Vernons began looking further afield. One day, on their way home after viewing a potential site, they found themselves driving through the small but picturesque market town of Chipping Norton in Oxfordshire, about 75 miles northwest of London. There they spotted an old (circa 1853) schoolhouse, a building that had closed in 1966 but was now vacant and for sale. It offered thick stone walls, spacious rooms, and high ceilings, plus an adjacent headmaster's house, making it ideal for a recording studio complex. Recording engineer

Dave Grinsted was recruited from Decca Studios, and the trio began construction and planning for the new facility, which would take its name from the town in which it was located.

By 1972, renovations were nearly complete, and in October of that year, Chipping Norton Studios opened its doors for business. The recording area was built in what had been the old school auditorium (assembly hall) on the ground floor, and an adjacent classroom was converted into a control room. Other floors provided office space and residential facilities, including a lounge, a spacious kitchen, and six bedrooms. Although their intention had been to make the complex available to Blue Horizon artists only, by the time construction was completed, the Vernons decided to operate the studio as an independent commercial entity

The recording area (32' by 16') had an unusually high 12' ceiling, and other rooms in the building were fitted with audio tielines, thus giving access to a wide selection of ambient acoustics. The square-shaped control room (16' by 16' before acoustic treatment, with 8' ceilings) was located above and alongside the studio, giving the engineer a good view of the recording area.

In 1977, American acoustician John Storyk was brought in to carry out an acoustic redesign. His approach was rather unorthodox for the time in that it did not rely on large Eastlake-style traps, but rather on smaller treatment areas to suit a particular environment. At his direction, the control room monitors were soffit-mounted into the walls and a fulcrum rostrum (used for piano) was added to the studio, along with custom-designed recesses in the walls to house amplifiers. As part of the redesign, the walls in both rooms were covered with a combination of wood paneling and stone facings.

The control room initially housed an 18 x 8 Trident console—the second B-Range ever built. It had been Dave Grinsted's friendship with producer/engineer Roy Thomas Baker that led to the order, which in turn convinced Trident owners Norman and Barry Sheffield to set up Trident Audio Developments (TRIAD) as a separate console manufacturing business. (See Chapter 6 for more information.)

Chipping Norton began life as a 16-track facility equipped with an MCI JH-16 tape machine. In 1975, the studio upgraded to 24-track and installed an MCI JH-100 24-track recorder, along with a 30 x 24 Trident A-Range mixer. A third Trident desk was installed in 1980—a 32 x 24 TSM, along with an MCI JH-24 machine, two Studer A80 2-tracks, and two Revox A77 stereo machines used for delay. The control room monitoring was supplied by JBL 4326 speakers driven by a Crown DC300A amplifier, along with small Auratones driven by Quad amps; outboard equipment included UREI 1176LN limiters, dbx 160 and dbx 165 limiter/compressors, Allison Research noise gates, Orban Parasound stereo parametric equalizers and de-essers, a Marshall Time Modulator, a Bel stereo flanger, an Eventide 1745M digital delay line and H910 Harmonizer, and an AMS DMX15 digital delay line and RMX 16 digital reverberation system. Although the exact models are unknown, the studio's microphone collection included 16 Neumann mics, six AKGs, two Beyers, one Electrovoice, and four Sennheisers, Shures, and Amcron PZMs.

In early 1986, the control room was enlarged and the monitoring upgraded to Questeds during a major acoustic revamp by Neil Grant's company Discrete Research, which included the installation of RPG diffusors. By that time, the accommodations at Chipping Norton had also grown extensively and included 15 double bedrooms in five different locations within the L-shaped complex.

Chipping Norton held a particular attraction for singer-songwriters, who used the studio a great deal in the 1970s. These included Richard and Linda Thompson, Chris Rea, Richard Digance, Ralph McTell, and Gerry Rafferty, who recorded his hit single "Baker Street" there. Other major artists of the '70s and beyond who recorded at Chipping Norton include Status Quo, the Bay City Rollers, Dexys Midnight Runners, Duran Duran, Marianne Faithfull, Jeff Beck, XTC, Alison Moyet, Robbie Williams, Noel Gallagher, and Radiohead.

On October 31, 1999, ex–Black Sabbath guitarist Tony Iommi completed what would be the last session at Chipping Norton and the studio closed shortly afterward. The property was converted into private residences, one of which now houses a dental practice.

RAMPORT

The Who were a band that loved recording. While most groups of the era tended to stick with one studio most of the time (e.g., The Beatles / Abbey Road, the Rolling Stones / Olympic, The Kinks / Pye), The Who recorded all over London—IBC, Advision, CTS, Olympic—and their leader, Pete Townshend, was a songwriter who loved making demos, usually playing all the instruments himself at his well-equipped home studio.

It was almost a given, then, that The Who would eventually open a studio of their own. And so they did, in 1973, in a dilapidated building at 115 Thessaly Road in London's Battersea district. The facility was initially called "The Kitchen," but was later renamed Ramport Studios. It was originally intended to be a private studio for the band's own use, but so run-down was the building that it had to be completely renovated at huge expense, necessitating it becoming a commercial facility in an attempt to recoup some of the cost.

Initially, Ramport was outfitted with a wraparound Helios 32 x 24 quad-ready desk and 3M M79 24- and 16-track tape machines. (See *Quad: Ahead of its time, or just a bad idea?* on page 59 for more information.) Outboard gear included two EMT 140 reverb plates; an AKG BX20 spring reverb; Teletronix and Universal Audio limiters; ADR F700 compressors; Roger Mayer and Alice gates; ITI and

Who bassist John Entwistle at the Helios mixing desk in Ramport Studios, 1974.
(Photo by Michael Putland/Getty Images)

Acousta-voicette equalizers and Aengus EQ modules; and Eventide delay lines and phasers.

In 1976, the Helios was sold and replaced by a Neve desk. A year later, a second Neve—this one a Series 8088 40-input console—was installed, along with a second 3M M79 24-track tape machine and a 16-track Studer A80.

In 1983 the studio was bought by Virgin Records and renamed Townhouse 3. (See *Townhouse* below.) Two years later, it received the Helios 40 x 32 desk from Townhouse Studio 1. The console would be sold in 1988 and replaced by a Neve 8078.

Artists who recorded at Ramport included Bryan Ferry, Jeff Beck, Supertramp, Gentle Giant, Procol Harum, Thin Lizzy, Motörhead, Carlene Carter, Joan Jett, and, of course, The Who (tracks for their *Quadrophenia* and *Who Are You* albums, although the former also required the services of the Ronnie Lane Mobile; see Chapter 9 for more information).

In 1995, Ramport / Townhouse 3 was closed by Virgin's new owners, EMI, and the studio was sold a year later. The building that once housed Ramport is now used as a doctor's clinic.

SARM

London's East End is known for many things: Cockneys, docklands, street markets, beigels, salt beef (the latter two being the English equivalent to American bagels and corned beef). What it is *not* particularly well known for is recording studios, with one notable exception: Sarm.

Actually, there had been one studio operating in that part of the city, since 1960. It was called The City of London Recording Studios—a small basement operation at 9-13 Osborn Street in Aldgate that was mono-only and used mostly to record radio programs and narration for newsreels. The facility went out of business in 1972, and shortly afterward the premises was purchased by a consortium consisting of two experienced recording engineers formerly of Command Studios—Gary Lyons and Barry Ainsworth (who had previously also worked at Pye)—along with businessman David Sinclair, who provided the financing. (Ainsworth would leave the operation in 1975, at which time ex-Trident engineer Mike Stone would take his place as codirector.) For some months previously, Lyons and Ainsworth had been operating a tape copying service called Sound and Recording Mobiles, and they used an acronym of its name—Sarm—to christen the studio they opened at the Aldgate location in July 1973.

The recording area they designed (along with Sinclair's son John, who later became a codirector, along with his sister Jill) may have been somewhat

9-13 Osborn Street, Aldgate: the home of City of London Studios, and later, Sarm Studios.
(Photo by Tony Harris)

modest in size (approximately 30' by 20', with 12' ceilings) but Sarm was possibly the first operational 24-track studio in the U.K. Its small control room (some 20' by 10', with 10' ceilings) was initially outfitted with a 28 x 24 Trident B-Range desk—the third one to be built. (This would later be replaced by a larger 40 x 24 B-Range.) Tape recorders included a 3M 24-track and an MCI 2" machine (the latter with both 16-track and 24-track head blocks), as well as Studer A80 2-tracks—one 1/2" and the other 1/4"—and Revox stereo machines for delay. Monitoring was via Tannoy/Lockwoods, and there was quite an extensive collection of outboard gear, including UREI 1176 limiters, Teletronix LA-2A optical compressors, dbx 160 and 165 compressors, Westrex valve (tube) compressors, Marconi valve (tube) limiters, Kepex noise gates, UREI and Aengus graphic equalizers, Orban and TRIAD parametric equalizers, a UREI Little Dipper filter set, and an Eventide Omnipressor, Digital Delay, Phaser, and Flanger; there was also an EMT reverb plate, and, unusually, both Dolby and dbx noise reduction were available. It was with this setup that producer Roy Thomas Baker mixed Queen's classic single "Bohemian Rhapsody," as well as many of the tracks for their 1975 and 1976 albums *A Night at the Opera* and *A Day at the Races*. The mic cabinet at Sarm offered various models from Neumann, AKG, STC, RCA, Shure, and Sennheiser, including a Sennheiser dummy head that studio staff nicknamed Horace.

Unfortunately, Sarm suffered extensive water damage as a result of a March 1978 fire, forcing a major renovation, including a control room redesign by Eddie Veale. The studio was also remodeled at the time and a specific drum area added at one end. Interestingly, the acoustics of that area could be varied by hanging sheets of plywood or corrugated tin on wall hooks, similar to the treatments used in the isolation booth at Tony Visconti's Good Earth Studios (see *Good Earth* below for more information). Another unique feature at Sarm was a large erotic sculpture—approximately ten feet long and three feet high—directly behind the studio's 9'6"

Bösendorfer grand piano. Ex-Sarm engineer Gary Langan states unequivocally that its placement was more for acoustic than aesthetic reasons. "That sculpture acted as a very effective diffusor," he says. "Its uneven surfaces acted to dissipate the sound waves coming off the front lid of the Bösendorfer and made the piano sound absolutely enormous."

The control room also received a new 40 x 40 Trident TSM console—the largest one ever built—customized with PPM meters and a phase correlation meter, and fitted with an early Allison computer automation system that recorded fader moves using two tracks on the multitrack machine, updated by bouncing between them. The 3M and MCI multitrack machines were also replaced by a pair of Studer A80s linked by a Studer TLS synchronizer to allow for 48-track recording, and the monitoring changed over to Cadacs driven by Audix amplifiers, plus small Auratone cube speakers. Several Calrec microphones were purchased and new outboard equipment included an Eventide H910 Harmonizer, a Survival Projects panner, a Lexicon 224 digital reverb, and an AMS digital delay.

Producer and ex-Buggle/ex-Yes bass player Trevor Horn was one frequent client, and, following his marriage to studio manager Jill Sinclair in 1980, Sarm would become his regular base of operations. Over the next two decades Horn would craft hit records there for many top artists, including the Buggles, Yes (*Drama* and *90125*), ABC (*Lexicon of Love*), Frankie Goes to Hollywood (*Welcome to the Pleasuredome*), and The Art of Noise.

In 1982 the studio took delivery of a 32-input SSL 4000 desk—one of the first SSLs in London—later upgraded to a 40-input model with a remote patch bay to maximize space in the control room. A year later, Horn and Sinclair set up ZTT Records and purchased Island Studios in Basing Street, rebranding it as Sarm West. (See *Island / Basing Street* above.) The Osborn Street location, renamed Sarm East, would continue in operation until 2001, when it was sold. An audio school and facility called The London Recording Studios now occupies the former premises of Sarm East.

Sawmills exterior.
(Courtesy of Sawmills Studios)

SAWMILLS

First opened in 1974, Sawmills is, as of this writing, one of the longest-running residential recording facilities in the U.K. Located near the village of Golant in Cornwall, some 200 miles west of London, the main building that houses the studio is a former 17th-century water mill, and the site has documented history dating all the way back to the 11th century. Sawmills is not only historic, it's also unique in that it can be accessed only by boat . . . or, if the tide is out, by a two-mile walk down the railway line that runs behind the studio.

The studio was founded by folk-rock record producer Tony Cox, who also worked with Yes on their 1970 album *Time and a Word*. Cox was a frequent client at Sound Techniques Studio in London (see *Sound Techniques* above), and at one point someone jokingly commented that he'd been spending so much time there, he might as well buy his own studio. Apparently this struck a nerve with Cox, and he duly began scouting for possible locations. The Cornwall property that he even-

tually settled on had been previously owned by Welsh author Denys Val Baker. It was described by drummer Alan Eden, who was in a band that was in preproduction rehearsals with Cox at the time, as being "an old building situated in splendid isolation on the bank of the River Fowey."

However, Eden reports, the structure was also in a somewhat dilapidated state, "with only half a roof and no windows. . . . Tony, however, decided it was totally unique, had grace and charm, and promptly set the wheels in motion to purchase it." Although some questioned the producer's decision to open a studio in such an inaccessible location, at the time it was becoming increasingly fashionable for artists to escape to the countryside to record their next masterpiece. Not only were bands making records in makeshift barns and cottages all over the U.K., but Richard Branson's Manor in Oxfordshire and Rockfield Studios in South Wales were actually offering fully professional recording facilities in rural surroundings with considerable success.

Cox's vision was to set up an in-house production team, complete with house band, as Motown, Stax, and Muscle Shoals studios had done in America. The incoming production work, he hoped, would generate the income required to build the facilities and at the same time create a relaxed environment conducive to making music.

His first task was to hire someone to oversee the construction of the studio and installation of its equipment. Fortunately, Sound Techniques' chief engineer Jerry Boys—someone with whom Cox was already well acquainted—was available, having recently decided to relocate to Cornwall. It was a perfect match: Not only did Boys have all the required technical skills, he also had his own client base, and so he was promptly brought on board as chief engineer.

"It was hard work keeping such a remote studio running smoothly," commented Eden, who became involved in the facility's day-to-day logistics. "When a band arrived, they and their gear had to be brought in by boat down the creek, and if a piece of equipment was needed or broken, you couldn't just nip out and get a replacement. More often than not we worked a 24-hour day . . . the tide table became our most-used item of reference."

The walls in the Sawmills recording area were lined with rough stones, but a unique ceiling design kept the sound from being overly live. "Although it's low for the application—from 8 to 15 feet in the middle—it is absolutely dead, eliminating the vertical dimension in the acoustic sense," wrote journalist Frank Ogden in a 1976 article for *Studio Sound* magazine. "The ceiling has been constructed in three layers. The lowest consists of absorbing tiles enclosing a 'trap' some 20 centimetres deep filled with rockwool enclosed between the false and real ceiling. This method of construction has been used over the entire area and apparently works efficiently, even at the low bass end. The overall resulting sound feels bright but not echoey." "Because the walls are old stone and very rough, the tops bounce off and rapidly diffuse as opposed to going backwards and forwards as with smooth walls," added Boys in that same article. "The sound comes back as a general 'live' feeling to the studio."

The Sawmills control room was initially outfitted with a 20 x 4 Sound Techniques mixing console, a 3M M79 16-track recorder and assorted Studer 2-track tape machines, and custom Tannoy monitors. Outboard gear consisted of a Fairchild 660 compressor, four ADR parametric equalizers, two A & D stereo limiters with built-in noise gates, and an AKG BX20 spring reverb. Microphones included models from Neumann (U47, U67, U87, and U88), AKG (C12A tube condensers, as well as D12, D190, D224, and D202 dynamics). In 1986, a 56 x 24 Trident Series 80B with mix automation replaced the Sound Techniques board; at the time of this writing it was still in use at the studio.

In his book *Are We Still Rolling?* engineer Phill Brown writes eloquently of a 1978 visit to Sawmills

STORIES FROM THE STUDIO
Just how wet do you want it?

"ONCE, when I was doing a Michael Chapman album at Sawmills Studios," producer Tom Allom recalls, "I ended up using a creek as an echo chamber. The sawmill itself was over an inlet from a tidal river, so the level of the water in the creek varied quite a lot. I positioned this terrible old Altec speaker over the creek—it was basically good for nothing anyway—and I placed a couple of [Neumann] U67s in the driveway behind the house, where they couldn't pick up the Altec directly, but they could pick up the reflection of it off the woods on the other side of the creek. The resultant sound wasn't so much a reverb as it was a series of slap echoes coming off the contours of the hillside, but it was quite effective, and it was stereo, of course. Plus, since the creek was tidal, the sound would change quite drastically depending on the time of day. I found it optimum when the tide was in, because there were better reflections off the water—the sound would travel forever."

Former Sawmills chief engineer Jerry Boys confirms that the creek was frequently used as a makeshift echo chamber, but, interestingly, his recollection is that "we always got a better sound when the tide was out—less absorption, literally! That's because there was more mud, with the water being more reflective than the mud, so you got a purer bounce off the trees on the other side when the water wasn't there." Proof positive that if you put two audio engineers in a room, you'll get three different opinions on the sound!

to record an album with ex–Roxy Music members Andy Mackay, Phil Manzanera, and Paul Thompson:

> We loaded our equipment into a small outboard-powered boat, and towing a barge laden with the larger items, headed downstream from the small harbour at Golant. We passed many small dinghies, loaded with china clay, regularly headed down to Plymouth Sound and the English Channel. At 3 mph we chugged into the creek, which was also only accessible at high tide. We moored the boat and barge at the quayside. It was incredibly quiet, with just the sound of a few birds and rustling trees. We unloaded our bags and equipment and walked the 50 yards to the large, three-storey building. It all looked very rough-and-ready and supplied only basic living conditions. Many of the upstairs rooms were furnished only with assorted single beds and cushions on the floor. The kitchen had a scruffy, lived-in look, with piles of wood drying by a large stove. . . . After a cup of tea, we were shown around.

There was a separate building that housed a small live studio with an even smaller control room. There were additional living quarters in a wooden chalet hidden up the creek amongst trees. This could sleep four people, but the main accommodation was up in the large mill house. On one side it was enclosed by trees, and on the other the creek and the River Fowey. It was a beautiful location and an excellent place to live, regardless of the studio. (*Reprinted by kind permission of the author.*)

In the mid-'70s, Sawmills briefly had its own record label, distributed by the Swedish company Sonet Records, which was interested in releasing the work of artists coming through the facility. Major artists who worked at Sawmills in the 1970s included Fairport Convention, Back Street Crawler (featuring ex-Free bassist Paul Kossoff), ex–Roxy Music saxophonist Andy Mackay, Michael Chapman, and the prog-rock band Gryphon. In more recent years, the studio has been host to Robert Plant, Oasis, The Verve, and Muse, as well as Supergrass, who recorded their first three albums there.

ROUNDHOUSE

The Roundhouse was one of the most popular concert venues in London in the '60s and '70s. It was literally that—a large round building that had once been a railway engine shed. Located in Chalk Farm, North London, it was converted into a performing arts center in the mid-1960s.

In late 1975, producer Gerry Bron opened a recording studio in the basement of an office block next door and gave it the same name as their famous next-door neighbor. Bron, a regular client at Lansdowne Studios, poached two of their staffers—Peter Gallen and Ashley Howe—to serve as his recording engineers, with Gallen named studio manager. The Roundhouse Studio was designed by famed architect Eddie Veale, who gave it a fairly dead acoustic, though the center of the good-sized room (43' by 22', with fairly high ceilings) was somewhat more live than the outer edges.

The large Roundhouse control room—about six times the size of the one at Lansdowne, according to Gallen—was built to handle both stereo and quadraphonic mixing (see *Quad: Ahead of its time, or just a bad idea?* on page 59), with large Cadac monitors positioned in the four corners of the room (soon replaced by JBL 4350 speakers powered by Yamaha B1 amplifiers). The mixing console was a 36 x 24 L-shaped Cadac, and there were Studer A80 24-track and 4-track tape machines, plus three A80 2-tracks. Main microphones were Neumann U67, KM54, and M49s, supplemented with various AKG, Sennheiser, and Shure mics; outboard gear included Fairchild, UREI, and Teletronix limiters, dbx 160 compressors, a Delta T digital delay line, and an Eventide Flanger and Harmonizer. For echo, the facility had three EMT 140 reverb plates. There were also audio tielines and a closed-

Roundhouse Recording Studio the only 32 track digital recording facility in the UK.

Phone 01-485 0131. 100 Chalk Farm Road, London NW1 8EH.

3M
Digital Mastering System

A Roundhouse trade advertisement circa 1980, shortly after the studio's installation of 3M 32-track and 4-track digital machines.

circuit television link to the stage of the Roundhouse Theatre next door, but ultimately, little live recording was done there because the acoustics of the venue were too reverberant to yield satisfactory results.

"The facility was clearly built to satisfy artists signed to Gerry's label, Bronze Records, so they didn't have to spend money hiring other studios and could do their recording under his watchful eye," says Gallen, who points out that, despite that intention, the majority of the studio's clients ended up being artists signed to other labels. "But it was always designed to be a very comfortable place to work in, unlike other studios from the era, which tended to be fairly grim places: dark, poky, and with dodgy [beat-up] furniture. They were not particularly comfortable places to be in, whereas the Roundhouse actually employed an interior designer, who, among other things, put reflective

wallpaper in the reception area and down the main corridors to the studio—something we became quite well known for. It was almost like having aluminium [aluminum] foil on the walls, though it scuffed quite readily." There was also a kitchen with a well-stocked refrigerator, a microwave, and "enough tea, coffee and Coca-Cola to sink a battleship," in the words of one exuberant journalist of the era—an amenity which proved to be very popular with clients and may have served as a partial inspiration to Richard Branson when he conceived of his Townhouse Studios some time later. (See *Townhouse* below.)

A few years after its opening, Roundhouse was given a complete overhaul, overseen by acoustic designer Ken Worrell. The control room was stripped to its bare walls, and bays built out of concrete blocks were constructed, each lined with rockwool to

STORIES FROM THE STUDIO
"We had to wait for the ceiling to warm up"

"THE STUDIO ITSELF was actually pretty universal; not only could you record acoustic instruments there, it was also very good for band recordings," says former Roundhouse studio manager Peter Gallen. "The one problem we had with it was the ceiling, which was composed of aluminium [aluminum] slats with some insulation behind it. But what hadn't been accounted for was that the ceiling also held a number of lighting fixtures that generated quite a bit of heat.

"Normally we'd be running the studio all day with all the lights and air-conditioning on," he explains. "But there was this one evening when I made the mistake of going out to eat dinner with the client and switching the lights off in the studio as we left, because we were forever overstretching the air-conditioning so I thought we'd give it a rest. When we came back and turned the lights on, the slats in the ceiling all started to creak because they were expanding back into place.

"Here I was trying to record the *Carnival of the Animals* [*a musical suite by the French Romantic composer Saint-Saëns*] with a small classical orchestra, and when it came to the solo flute part, there were so many cracking noises going on in the background, we ended up having to wait for an hour for the ceiling to warm up!"

complement the acoustic treatment of the room as a whole. In keeping with the initial design, the rebuilt control room was completely decked out in Rosewood veneer—"a very classy finish," says Gallen.

Once construction was complete, a 48-channel Harrison desk was installed in the control room, positioned sideways to the studio area to allow for a wider spread of the main monitors, which were now customized Eastlake TM-3s driven by HH power amps and voiced with White room equalizers.

It had not escaped studio management's attention that much of the work coming into Roundhouse was mixing, not recording, and so a small dedicated remix room was also constructed, shoehorned into a space previously occupied by the maintenance workshop and tape library. It was outfitted with a 32 x 32 Harrison desk with "Autoset" mix automation, along with three Studer A80 stereo machines; monitoring was via JBL

4343 speakers. Outboard gear in the remix room included UREI, Teletronix, and dbx compressors and limiters, as well as Kepex noise gates, an Aphex Aural Exciter, a Delta T digital delay line, a Marshall Time Modulator, and an Eventide Harmonizer.

Among other achievements, Roundhouse may have been the first recording studio in Great Britain to offer digital recording when, in 1980, it installed 3M 32-track and 4-track digital machines. At around that time, the studio also installed a home-brewed wireless foldback system called Cuemix. This allowed musicians to create individual headphone mixes by means of compact portable mixers that received multichannel signal from the control room via RF. There was a subsequent attempt to market the product commercially, with limited success. "One of the problems was that the transmission of the signal across the studio tended to be a bit patchy, so in the end it didn't really take off," says Gallen. "But it was typical of the kind of thing Gerry [Bron] was into, always experimenting with technology."

Major groups who worked at Roundhouse include Queen (tracks for their 1975 *A Night at the Opera* album), The Small Faces, Yes, AC/DC, and Bronze Records artists Motörhead (*Bomber, Overkill*), Hawkwind (*Levitation*), Osibisa (*Black Magic Night*), Colosseum (*Colosseum II*), and Uriah Heep, who recorded three albums there: *Firefly, Conquest*, and *Abominog*.

In common with other London recording facilities, Roundhouse Studios ran into financial difficulties in the mid-1980s as studio rates fell and rents soared, eventually forcing the closure of the Camden site and a move to the more affordable City of London.

Roundhouse Studio is still operational at that location today, as is the original Roundhouse Theatre, which remains in Chalk Farm and continues to present concerts and other arts-related events.

RAK

48 Charlbert Street in St Johns Wood, home of RAK Studios.
(Courtesy of RAK Studios)

Record producer Mickie Most (born Michael Peter Hayes) was a major U.K. hit-maker in the 1960s and 1970s, with a personality that was larger than life, a predilection for motorcycles and fast cars, and a discography that was the envy of the industry. He discovered The Animals and produced their monster hit "House of the Rising Sun" (reportedly recorded in a single take), as well as crafting Herman's Hermits classic "I'm Into Something Good," the Nashville Teens' "Tobacco Road," and Lulu's "To Sir with Love." Most also churned out a string of hit singles for Donovan, including "Sunshine Superman," "Season of the Witch," "Mellow Yellow," "Jennifer Juniper," and "Hurdy Gurdy Man," many of them featuring

session musicians (and future superstars) Jimmy Page on guitar and John Paul Jones on bass.

Building on his success, Most started three companies at the end of the '60s: RAK Records, RAK Publishing, and RAK Music Management. (The origin of the RAK name is somewhat shrouded in mystery, but reportedly it was a shortened version, and a deliberate misspelling, of the word "rackjobbing," an industry reference to the practice of selling records in unusual places such as gas stations and supermarkets.) By this time, Most had established an uncanny knack for picking hit songs, and his record label was formed with the stated goal of pairing those songs with the perfect artists to present them. The

Mickie Most.
(Courtesy of RAK Studios)

Since 1974, Most had owned a mobile studio also called RAK (see Chapter 9 for more information), but he was still doing most of his recording work in London studios. At a certain point, he reached an epiphany. "Mickie was saying, 'Why am I spending all this money on studios? I'm going to find somewhere and build my own,'" recalls RAK studio manager Trisha Wegg, who also managed the RAK Mobile. The place he found was 48 Charlbert Street in St Johns Wood, not far from the EMI facilities at Abbey Road, an expansive Victorian building that had once been a school but had more recently been owned by ATV and used for television program rehearsals.

singles released on the RAK label were, to be sure, on the lightweight side and very much *au courant*—of their time—but they nonetheless provide a good representation of where popular disco-influenced music was heading in England in the mid-1970s, with titles like "Tiger Feet" by Mud, "Can the Can" by Suzi Quatro, and "You Sexy Thing" by Hot Chocolate.

The doors to RAK Studios opened in 1976. Originally, the facility consisted of two good-sized recording studios: the larger Studio 1 is 49' by 27', with a sloping ceiling and a wooden floor. Studio 2, at the back of the building, was originally planned to be a remix room and so is considerably smaller—

STORIES FROM THE STUDIO

Two studios, one plate

ENGINEER TIM SUMMERHAYES recalls that the only reverb device at RAK in the 1970s was a single EMT echo plate. An ingenious system therefore had to be devised to make it available to either of the two studios, without the other being able to steal it back. He explains how it worked: "Each control room had a panel fitted that contained a 'Select' button with an associated green light, and a red light to indicate that the other control room

was using the plate; I think there was also a 'Call' light and switch on the panel. There were many complaints about the number of clunky old relays that were used to make this all happen—there was no electronic switching, because of course the purity of the signal path overrode everything—but the plate had to be released by one studio before the other one could use it. It really was very clever."

There were also problems associ-

ated with the location of the plate, which lived downstairs in the RAK tape library. "Although we took care to be quiet when down there," he says, "the door was spring-loaded, and I lost count of the number of times the banging door caused a massive 'boom!' on the control room speakers, sometimes followed by an embarrassed assistant putting his head around the door to say, 'Sorry!' Other times, everyone just denied everything!"

Punk drums

TIM SUMMERHAYES was promoted from assistant to full engineer at RAK during the height of the punk era in the late 1970s. "Drum sounds were always the engineer's favorite competition," he says. "And make no mistake: it *was* a competition. RAK had—and still has—a reputation for having one of the best-sounding drum rooms in the U.K., it being a big wooden studio with huge windows. But punk had to be different: nothing posh, nothing ordinary. In particular, we needed to find a dense, roomy re-verb for the snare drum, and the EMT plate just couldn't deliver that—it was a good, industry-standard reverb device, but primarily for generating smooth, lush effects for vocals and instruments.

"So we experimented with putting the snare drum in the stairwell. Acoustically, it sounded huge! We placed mics at varying distances from the drum and found we had the basis of a new and dense reverb." But it took one last piece of gear to seal the deal—something called the Scamp Rack, which Summerhayes describes as being "a set of incredibly violent dynamic processors, nothing smooth like the UREI or Neve ones. The Kepex noise gates in the rack could be triggered via their sidechain inputs," he explains, "so we could effectively time the opening and closing of the new snare drum sound with its attached stairwell reverb from a click track or even the original drum hit. The gated sound could then be compressed to a degree that was unheard of in conventional recording."

just 17' by 17'—but at the last minute it was decided to add a small L-shaped overhead control room, accessible from the studio floor by a flight of stairs (somewhat similar to the arrangement at Abbey Road Studio Two; see Chapter 1 for more information). The Studio One control room is quite spacious (25' by 16'), although it has relatively low false ceilings. It is located at the front of the building and is dominated by three tall windows overlooking Charlbert Street. Because of the obvious need to avoid sound leakage (both in and out), these are fitted with 1-inch-thick plate glass, with curtains that can be electronically closed for those engineers who preferred to work in the artificial light conditions prevalent in most studios.

RAK's two control rooms initially housed identical 32 x 24 API consoles (state of the art at the time), coupled with Lyrec TR532 24-track tape machines (the first in the U.K.) and Studer B67 2-track machines. Monitoring was also identical in the two control rooms and was via Tannoy HPDs in Lockwood cabinets, hung from the ceiling and driven by Amcron DC300 amps (there were also ubiquitous Auratone cubes, driven by smaller Amcron DC60s). A 1978 refitting saw the installation of a larger 48 x 48

A Donovan session in the RAK Studio 2 control room with producer Mickie Most and members of the group Smokie. *(Courtesy of RAK Studios)*

extensively throughout the '80s, the former making records with the Pet Shop Boys, Orchestral Manoeuvres in the Dark, and New Order, and the latter recording Paul Young, the Q-Tips, and ABC, as well as overdubs for the Buggles' hit single "Video Killed the Radio Star."

Now fully modernized with the addition of a third studio and outfitted with a combination of contemporary digital and vintage analog gear, RAK Studios continues in operation today at the original location, used by artists like Adele, Arctic Monkeys, and Shakira. And although Mickie Most passed away in 2003, his office remains exactly as it was when he last sat behind his massive desk, carefully preserved as both a legacy and an inspiration to future generations of hit-makers.

UTOPIA

Producer Phil Wainman opened Utopia Studios in October of 1976. Wainman had been a busy session drummer before forming a partnership with songwriting team Nicky Chinn and Mike Chapman. Together they crafted a series of hit records for The Sweet, before Wainman left and branched out on his own to produce '70s pop phenoms the Bay City Rollers. Wainman would go on to work with other popular '70s bands such as Mud and Butterscotch, as well as Generation X, and would also produce the 1979 Boomtown Rats hit single "I Don't Like Mondays."

Located at 7 Chalcot Road in Primrose Hill, just north of London's Regents Park, Utopia initially consisted of a single recording studio, designed by Eastlake. It was square in shape (32' by 32', with 11' ceilings) and contained a single large isolation booth, used mostly for drums. The studio was also decorated rather opulently, with marble flooring, plush carpeting and a flexible lighting system, with mirrors and several distinctive murals on the wood-paneled walls. A disc cutting room was opened in early 1977; a few years later, a more modest second studio (20' by 13', with 8' ceilings) and a remix room with vocal overdub booth would be added as well.

Utopia's first studio manager was John Mackswith, formerly an engineer at Lansdowne and Advision, and among his staff was James Guthrie, who would go on to a long career engineering and producing for Pink Floyd. The expansive Studio 1 control room featured a large Neve 40 x 32 mixing console and Studer A80 24-track and 4-track machines, plus two A80 2-tracks, with Eastlake monitors fitted with Gauss speakers and Emilar high-frequency drivers, powered by Crown DC300 amps. Outboard equipment included UREI 1176 limiters, along with Neve and dbx compressors, Klein and Hummel parametric equalizers, an ADR Vocal Stressor, a Scamp rack with Kepexes and Gain Brains, an Eventide Harmonizer and Flanger, and a Marshall Time Modulator, plus two EMT reverb plates (two more were added at a later date). The remix room

Utopia's main studio.
(From studio brochure)

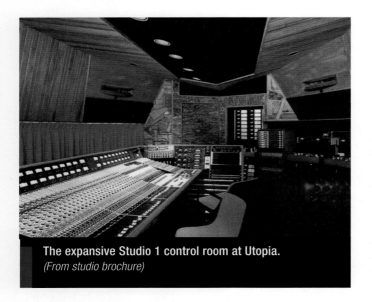

The expansive Studio 1 control room at Utopia.
(From studio brochure)

was outfitted identically to the Studio 1 control room, but with an enormous 52 x 8 Neve desk with NECAM mix automation. The somewhat smaller Studio 2 control room had an Amex 20 x 16 console (later replaced by a Soundcraft 2400) and Studer A80 24-track and 16-track tape machines, plus Studer B62 2-track recorders; monitoring was via Tannoy HPDs driven by Quad amplifiers, later changed over to East-

lakes driven by Crown DC300 amps. The Utopia mic cabinet included models from Neumann, AKG, STC, Electrovoice, Sennheiser, and Shure, including several tube microphones.

In early 1978, Wainman launched his own label—Utopia Records, distributed in the U.K. by Phonogram. It would score a novelty Top 20 hit later that same year with the Richard Myhill single "It Takes Two to Tango." Utopia Studios enjoyed considerable success over the 15 years of its operation; its cutting room was especially popular, and the remix room would eventually be converted to a video postproduction facility. Artists who worked at Utopia included Donovan, Duran Duran, Bryan Ferry, the Strawbs, Ian Hunter, John Miles, Judas Priest, Nils Lofgren, Landscape, Slade, and Spandau Ballet.

Utopia Studios was sold in 1991 to John and Kate Hudson, owners of Mayfair Studios (see *Ryemuse/ Mayfair* above) and was rebranded for a short time as Mayfair Village, but unfortunately the new enterprise shut its doors in August 1994. The complex that once housed the studios has been renamed Utopia Village and is now used as office space.

GOOD EARTH

Owned by producer Tony Visconti, Good Earth opened in 1976 in the basement of 59 Dean Street in London's Soho. It had been the former site of Zodiac Studios, a film preproduction facility since the 1950s.

The studio was a mid-sized L-shaped room (approximately 600 square feet), with a 22' by 20' "live end," and a 14' by 10' "dead end"; in addition, there were two isolation booths. Of particular note was the large split-level control room; the higher level was behind the engineer position at the mixing desk, giving visitors and guests a clear view of proceedings in the studio.

Acoustic treatment was by Westlake, who eliminated the one funky standing wave that initially plagued the control room. "We got rid of it eventually by building a bass trap, which is still there today," says

Visconti. "It was just a little box attached to the wall, and the front facing is slanted downwards so that it's larger at the top than at the bottom. Inside there is a very carefully piece of measured plywood hanging on hooks, and that absorbs the sound wave. It worked great, and it got rid of our standing wave completely."

Zodiac's original tiny control room was converted into a drum iso booth with exceptionally good soundproofing. "We were able to have the loudest drummers in the world in there," recalls Visconti, "and the sound wouldn't leak into the adjacent studio, even if it was just a singer on a nearby mic.

"The iso booth was, however, a little deadsounding," he continues, "so I bought some sheets of rippled galvanized steel, and if you put one or two of them up against the wall, near the drummer, it would add a little half-second decay to the signal by picking up reflections off the drum kit. Eventually, we bought enough to line all of the walls. We put up hooks so you could hang the sheets up as needed so they were actually free-moving; they could move a bit more than just being leaned up against the wall, and it made all the difference in the drum sound. I ended up putting PZM mics behind them, too, so the whole booth would act like a very cool plate reverb."

Good Earth's control room was initially outfitted with a Trident B-Range 24 x 16 desk and an MCI 16-track machine (both of which had come from Visconti's home studio in Shepherd's Bush, where he had mixed David Bowie's *Diamond Dogs* and recorded the band Sparks), augmented by a Trident Fleximix sidecar with ten inputs and, in Visconti's words, "the beginning of the TSM equalizers with that real severe EQ. I loved recording drums through that sidecar! I'd basically just use the B-Range for monitoring."

Once the Trident TSM became available, the control room was upgraded with a 32 x 24 TSM console and a Lyrec TR532 24-track, which had the unique facility of 100 percent varispeed, both up and down. This allowed for some unusual effects, although by some accounts it could be nerve-racking to watch a master flying through the heads at 60 ips! Mastering and tape echo was provided by Studer B62s and B67s (later replaced by 1/4" and 1/2" Studer A80s) and two Revox A77s with varispeed. Monitoring was originally via JBL 4333s powered by Studer amps or Klein and Hummel Telewatts, later replaced by Eastlakes with TAD and JBL components, as well as Westlake BBSM4s. The studio's mic cabinet included two vintage tube U47s acquired from Twickenham Film Studios.

Thanks to Visconti's long string of chart successes with artists like Bowie, Marc Bolan, and Thin Lizzy, Good Earth's battery of outboard gear rivaled that

▶ *GOOD EARTH STUDIOS*

ADDRESS: 59 DEAN STREET, LONDON W1V 5HH
TELEPHONE: (01) 439 1272 TELEX: 297616 ORDER G FAX: (01) 437 5504
STUDIO MANAGER: PAUL CARTLEDGE
BOOKINGS CONTACT: SAMI WALTER

Good Earth is a world class studio located in the heart of London's West End. Dozens of gold and platinum artists have recorded there including David Bowie, Wham!, Duran Duran, The Smiths, Tina Turner, The Moody Blues, U2, The Cult, The Alarm, Living In A Box, Lloyd Cole & The Commotions, Nana Mouskouri, Elaine Paige, Terence Trent D'Arby and others.

It features: a) A large control-room 20 ft x 20 ft; b) A "live end/dead end" main studio of 600 sq ft; c) An isolation booth 14ft x 10 ft; d) A live room 22 ft x 20 ft; e) A programming suite with 24-track recording and many keyboards; f) A large amount of outboard including Publison IM90, Lexicon 224XL, PCM 42, PCM 70, AMS 15-80S, Quantec, EMT Plate and Foil, REV 5, SPX90 and much more.

▶ *EQUIPMENT*
CONSOLE: SSL 4048E, TOTAL RECALL
TAPE MACHINES: 2xOTARI MTR90, OTARI MTR 12½", STUDER A80 ½"/¼", SONY PCM F1, SONY DAT, STUDER A710
MONITORS: EASTLAKE (TAD/JBL COMPONENTS), WESTLAKE BBSM4's, YAMAHA NS10M, E.A.R.
OTHER EQUIPMENT: PUBLISON INFERNAL MACHINE, ECHO PLATES, GATES, COMPRESSORS ETC AND WIDE RANGE OF MICS

▶ *FACILITY CHARGES*
24-TRACK: DAILY, £850
48-TRACK: DAILY, £950
COPYING CHARGES: ON REQUEST
OVERTIME RATE: NO OVERTIME CHARGES

Studio listing circa mid-1980s showing the Good Earth recording area.

of much larger studios. "It was my studio so I could do whatever I wanted," he says. "So as soon as a new piece of equipment came out that I liked, I would get it. I was already a hit producer and I was making a lot of money, which meant I was also liable for a lot of tax, so it made sense to pour the money into new equipment; as a result I had no budget constraints."

That purchasing freedom translated into no fewer than fourteen limiters and compressors, including vintage UREI 1176s and modern units from Allison Audio and ADR. In addition, there were Eventide

Scary Kepexes

"GIVING A PRODUCER HIS OWN STUDIO means that he can do whatever he wants, and that's exactly what I did," says Tony Visconti with a laugh.

At Good Earth, that translated into a virtual treasure trove of outboard gear. Visconti was particularly partial to Valley People (formerly Allison Research) gear like Kepexes and Gain Brains; as a result, he had literally dozens of them. And he used them in especially creative ways, too: "I really got into triggering things—tricks like, if a snare drum sounded a little thin, I would dial up a 100 Hz sine wave tone on a Moog synthesizer and have the snare drum trigger the sine wave, which added body to it. You couldn't do that with any gates before the Kepex was invented; the Kepex was a fast motherfucker! It was built for this kind of stuff.

"On the *Scary Monsters* title track I used the Kepex on the vocal, keying it from a 20 Hz tone coming from the desk oscillator—that was the hidden source. I played with the threshold until it sounded like a tremolo effect on the voice. I also loved the Valley People Gain Brain—it was a remarkable piece of gear. I used to put bass through one of those and it would give me a sweet, punchy sound."

and Delta Lab delay lines, a Quad Eight spring reverb, and an EMT 140 plate and 240 Gold Foil.

As a result, Good Earth became highly acclaimed as a mixing facility; Bowie's *Stage* and *Scary Monsters* were mixed there, as was Thin Lizzy's *Live and Dangerous.* Notable '70s albums credited as having been done at the studio include Hazel O'Connor's *Breaking Glass,* Magazine's *Secondhand Daylight,* Philip Lynott's *Solo in Soho,* Radiators' *Ghostown,* and Sparks' *Indiscreet.* According to Visconti, there were a number of uncredited projects as well. "Some of our clients liked to, shall I say, pretend that their entire album was created overseas, for tax purposes," he explains. "It started with Marc Bolan, who actually was true to his word—he would do all his recording outside the country, but we would mix at Good Earth. He would attend his mixes, but he wouldn't record anything in England. He could sit in the control room with me and say, 'I want more vocal' or 'I want more guitar,' but he couldn't sing or play. That's why you won't see Good Earth credited a lot of times—we had to keep the name off the credits, or the tax man would get suspicious. It was a shame, but that was the reason."

Good Earth was sold to a music production company in 1989; since 2007 it has been operating under the name Dean Street Studios.

MATRIX

Matrix Studios opened in 1977, owned by producer Nigel Frieda, who had outgrown the home studio in his Notting Hill flat. The facility was constructed in the basement of 35 Little Russell Street in London's West End—a building that had once been a dairy; reportedly, the recording area occupied what had once been a stable for the horses who pulled the milk wagons.

Frieda's first hire was ex-Trident engineer Nick Bradford, who helped in the design of the new facility, with advice from acoustician/architect Eddie Veale. Initially, Matrix consisted of a single mid-sized studio (Studio 1) that measured 38' by 25' and incorporated a raised drum area. Its control room was outfitted with a homebuilt 30 x 30 desk designed by Dick Swettenham colleague Tim Isaacs (see *The birth of Helios* on page 262) and an MCI 24-track tape recorder, along with MCI and Scully 2-track machines. Outboard gear included UREI, Rebis, and Valley People limiters, an AMS Digital Delay Line and Harmonizer, and a Marshall Time Modulator. Following the construction of Matrix Studio 2 (see below), the original 28 x 24 A-Range mixer used at Trident Studios was purchased by Matrix and installed in the Studio 1 control room. (See Chapter 6 for more information.)

STUDIO 1

The studio: The larger of the two studios, some 38 by 25 feet suitable for large backing tracks. It has a fine Bechstein grand piano, raised drum area and also a live echo room.

The control room: A fully comprehensive recording and mixing room with both 16 and 24 track capability. The 28 into 24 Triad A Range mixer is served by MCI Multitrack and Scully and MCI stereos.
Comprehensive delay and reverberation systems are backed up with the usual compliment of outboard gear and noise reduction.
The room is spacious and fully air conditioned.

STUDIO 2

The studio: Measuring some 22 by 15 feet, it has full backing track capability while offering an intimate over-dubbing situation. It is fully air conditioned and has a Schmidt-Flohr upright piano.

The control room: A comprehensive control room featuring a Telefunken 24 track recorder with programmable autolocate, a Studer two track, and a custom built 30 into 30 desk.
Dolbied throughout and with the usual variety of outboard gear: reverberation, plate echo, flangers, phasers, digital delay, etc. As in studio 1 monitoring is through Tannoys.

Page from a Matrix brochure circa 1978 showing the Studio 1 and 2 recording areas and control rooms.
(From studio brochure)

A small Studio 2 (roughly 22' by 15') was added shortly after Matrix opened, at which time the custom Isaacs console was moved from the old control room into the new one, along with a Telefunken 24-track machine. The complement of outboard equipment in the new Studio 2 control room included UREI 1176 limiters, dbx 160 compressors, and AMS Digital Delay Line, Flanger, and Harmonizer, and a Master Room reverb.

Monitoring in both control rooms was provided by Tannoy speakers (exact models unknown). The Matrix facility also had several EMT reverb plates and Gold Foils available to both control rooms via tielines, as well as a live echo chamber off Studio 1 that the staff nicknamed "The Dungeon."

By 1980, Matrix had added a dedicated remix room, which housed a Trident TSM 32 x 24 console and a good complement of outboard gear, with monitoring via Tannoy Super Reds. The multitrack in the remix room was an unusual hybrid machine that consisted of a Lyrec transport and electronics that had been modified to incorporate a noise gate for every channel, triggerable from the sync head in order to reduce tape hiss during mixdown. A small recording area was later constructed directly adjacent, at which time the remix room was renamed Studio 3.

Unfortunately, a flood from an upstairs restaurant in 1985 caused significant damage and necessitated a major rebuild. Studio 2 was reborn as a remix room at that time, with its control room converted to a vocal booth, and the tape machines in all three control rooms were replaced by Otari MTR-90s.

The hourly rate at Matrix was considerably lower than at other London 24-track rooms, and the facility also provided a communal feel that was missing in many other competing studios, with a central recreation area onto which all the control rooms opened. As a result, the studio quickly became popular with independent artists and record labels in the punk and post-punk eras. The Matrix client list included The Police, The Smiths, Stiff Little Fingers, Adam and the Ants, and XTC. Marianne Faithfull also recorded her 1979 breakthrough album *Broken English* at Matrix, along with tracks for her follow-up LP, *Dangerous Acquaintances*.

Matrix continued in operation throughout the 1990s, but after the Little Russell Street building was sold, Frieda bought an old church hall in Parsons Green, London, with the idea of moving premises. However, a sudden surge of work allowed him to not only keep both locations open but also to purchase Jethro Tull's Maison Rouge Studios, as well as Wessex Studios, all rebranded with the Matrix name. At one point there were ten different Matrix rooms spread across London, all operating simultaneously!

However, the rise of home recording at the end of the decade caused a commensurate decrease in studio business, and by 2000 Frieda had not only sold the original Matrix Studios but all the other facilities as well. Matrix still occupies the Parsons Green location and operates as a complex that houses various music and media-related businesses, including remix rooms, programming rooms, and office space.

TOWNHOUSE

After a somewhat rocky start, Richard Branson's residential studio in Oxfordshire, The Manor, had turned into a commercial success. Branson understood that artists had flocked there to enjoy the bucolic countryside and peaceful isolation that came with it (not to mention the freedom to record 24 hours a day) as much as its technical facilities. But the British music industry, along with most of its recording artists, was based in the capital city. Why, then, not try to offer something similar—sans the bucolic countryside—in West London?

In 1978 he did just that, opening Townhouse Studios (officially named The Town House) at 150 Goldhawk Road, a building that had previously housed Goldhawk Film Studios. It originally consisted of two studios (called Townhouse 1 and Townhouse 2), along with mastering rooms, recreation rooms, a restaurant, *and* accommodations, all under one roof—essentially giving artists the best of both worlds.

Designed by Eastlake's Tom Hidley, in collaboration with Virgin technical director Philip Newell and chief engineer Mick Glossop, Townhouse 1 was the largest studio in the complex. It was actually on two levels: the main studio floor at ground level and above it a live room with smoke glass mirrors and wood-paneling on the wall. "The acoustics were built from experience, certainly not from any measurements," says Newell. "We did use quite a lot of Tom Hidley's bass traps, although they're not actually bass traps—they're wide-band absorbers and they absorb high frequencies even better than low ones—strategically placed to control any nasty resonances in the room. They were huge and they took up a lot of floor space—they were 10 feet high and 15 feet across, and there were several of them—but the laws of physics demand that, until you get to about 20 percent of a room's surface, you're not going to significantly start to hear any difference in the sound. People were saying, 'But we've lost all this floor space,' and I was saying to them, 'You haven't lost anything! What's the point of having 20 square meters more floor space and a lousy sound?'

"We also used quite a lot of glass," he continues, "because we always felt that line of sight was important even if it sometimes compromised the acoustics. When the musicians can see each other playing, they play differently. They often play a lot tighter. They like the eye contact."

The Townhouse 1 control room was originally equipped with a 40 x 32 Helios desk with Allison automation, replaced by an SSL 4000E

The Townhouse exterior.
(Courtesy of Tony Harris)

The Townhouse control room, showing the original Helios console.
(Photo courtesy of Shorefire Studios)

STORIES FROM THE STUDIO
The drum shot heard around the world

SOMETIMES THE BEST RESULTS come by accident, not by design. One perfect case in point is the "drum shot heard around the world"—the classic gated snare sound made famous in the Phil Collins smash hit single "In the Air Tonight," a sound that dominated so many of the records of the 1980s.

It's a tale that begins in Townhouse Studios' famous "Stone Room" in late 1979. "The room was live, with a stone-slabbed floor, which was done at least 50 percent for aesthetic reasons," engineer Mick Glossop recounted in *Behind the Glass*. "Actually, given the context of the day, it was *very* live. If you hit a snare drum in the room, it was so loud, it was incredible. We were contemplating changing the acoustics in there because we felt it was a bit uncontrollable, but it went on to become the vehicle for a classic drum sound!

"Peter Gabriel had decided before he even went in the studio [to record his third solo album, sometimes referred to as *Melt*, due to its distinctive cover] that he wanted to restrict the choice of percussion sounds inasmuch as he didn't want any cymbals on the album—no crashes, rides, or hi-hats. So the rhythmic components that were traditionally played on hi-hats and rides had to be played on floor toms and that kind of thing.

"On the Townhouse SSL, there was a talkback system that used a mic rigged up in the ceiling, connected to a really vicious compressor—so vicious that if somebody hit a drum, the volume of that drum was the same as the level of their voice, which is exactly what you want [in a talkback system]. Phil Collins was playing the drums at the time; the musicians were talking about something, and he started playing, and in the control room they suddenly heard this amazingly compressed drum sound. Peter Gabriel heard it and said, 'Wow, that's fantastic! Put it on the record!' So [engineer] Hugh [Padgham] then set about using the SSL channel compressors to reproduce the sound of the talkback compressor. In the course of doing that, he was playing around with the gate, and again Peter responded, because Phil hit the snare and the gate chopped off the reverb—which is the classic sound that has become legendary. It was really Peter who insisted that the sound be used, though it came about by accident.

"The point is, if they had been using cymbals with that kit, they wouldn't have been able to use that sound, because the gating would have chopped off all the cymbal decays in a very haphazard way, which would have messed up the sound. The sound is basically the sound of a drum being hit and the ambience compressed and then, as the ambience tails off, it chops off sharply because the gate's got a short release. It just doesn't work if you play cymbals as part of the rhythm. So it was only possible to get that drum sound without using cymbals. That's an example of a massive sonic creative effect being made possible only by a restriction of choice and a series of accidents."

following the purchase of Ramport Studios in 1984 (see the next page for more information). Unusually, the multi-track was a Telefunken M15 32-track tape recorder (replaced in 1984 by two Studer A800 24-track machines), augmented by 1/2" and 1/4" Ampex ATR-102 and ATR-104 2-track machines. Monitoring was by Eastlake Audio. A wide selection of outboard gear was available, including Rebis parametric equalizers, a Scamp rack with Allison Gain Brains and Kepex gates, UREI 1176 limiters, Teletronix LA-3A limiters, an EMT 251 digital reverb, digital delay lines from Eventide, MXR, and Lexicon, and assorted other processors from dbx and Rebis. There were also three EMT 140 reverb plates, accessible to all the Goldhawk Road studios via tielines.

According to Newell, Townhouse 2 was originally intended to be a rehearsal room, but the plan changed a few months before the studio opened. Like Townhouse 1, it was designed by Tom Hidley, with a typical Eastlake approach to room acoustics. Especially popular, especially after the release of Phil Collins' hit single "In the Air Tonight," was its high-ceilinged, exceedingly live "Stone Room" off to one side of the main recording studio and about half its size. (See *The drum shot heard around the world* on this page for more information.)

"I did lots of recording in the Stone Room with guitars, horns, all kinds of things," says Glossop, "and I got good results but it was not easily controlled. You'd probably never design a room like that for normal recording because you'd want to have a flatter frequency response and more even decay time at different frequencies, things like that. But then again, that's why rooms have character—because they're not flat, they're not even. That's what makes them interesting." Beneath the floor of the Stone Room lay a trapdoor that led to an acoustic echo chamber below, built into what had once been an indoor swimming pool used by the previous tenants—Goldhawk Film Studios—to do underwater shots.

The Townhouse 2 control room was home to the first large SSL console in the U.K., a 32-channel 4000B, later upgraded to a more advanced SSL 4048E in 1984. Glossop recalls the thinking that went into the decision to place an order with the then fledgling company: "When we started the planning for the second control room at Townhouse, Phil Newell and I had decided we didn't want to put in another Helios— we wanted something different. The contenders were Neve, Cadac, Harrison, and MCI, but in the end we decided there were things about all of them that we didn't like. Of course, we'd been spoilt by having custom consoles!

"At the time there was a guy doing weekend maintenance at The Manor who was working for a company called Solid State Logic during the week," continues Glossop. "SSL had been founded by a fellow named Colin Sanders; they manufactured logic-controlled systems for church and cathedral organs. Colin was also very musical and had built himself a small 16-track home studio, and it was that experience of recording in a studio, combined with his own sense of imagination and his design capability, that led to the SSL console. We met Colin and he basically described what the console was all about, and we thought the layout and channel strip was perfect: everything seemed to fit in the right way. Then he talked about the dynamics module and the compressor and the noise gate on every channel. By the time he finished describing the automation system, which was much better than anything we'd seen, Phil and I went, 'Wow, this is amazing!'"

The outboard equipment lineup in the Townhouse 2 control room was similar to that of Townhouse 1, albeit with fewer dynamics processors due to the SSL board providing noise gates and compressor/limiters on every channel.

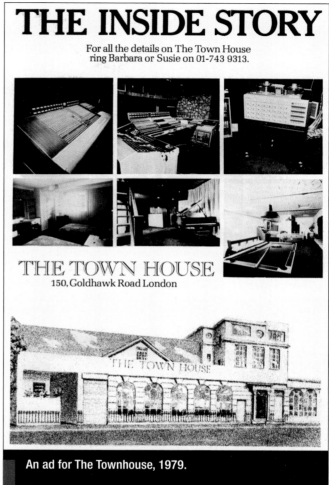

An ad for The Townhouse, 1979.

In 1984, the Virgin Group purchased Ramport Studios from The Who and, despite it being located miles away from the main facility, designated it Townhouse 3. (See *Ramport* above for more information.) Shortly after reopening under the new name, the Townhouse 3 control room was reequipped with the Helios desk from Townhouse 1.

A few years later, a third studio, designated Townhouse 4, was added to the Goldhawk Road premises and outfitted with a 56-channel SSL 4000 and Studer A800 multitracks. The first room in England to be designed by Sam Toyashima, the recording area offered variable acoustics with the use of motorized rotating absorbent panels in the walls and ceiling.

The Townhouse's four studios hosted a slew of artists throughout the '70s, including Peter Gabriel, Phil Collins, Sting, Eric Clapton, Jeff Beck, Yes, Van Morrison, Frank Zappa, Mike Oldfield, Kate Bush, Joan Armatrading, The Jam, Human League, Simple Minds, XTC, The Cure, Duran Duran, and the short-lived but groundbreaking Buggles. (The backing tracks for their 1980 *Age of Plastic* album were recorded at Townhouse, including those for the hit single "Video Killed the Radio Star"—the first video ever played on MTV.)

The Virgin Studios Group, which included both Townhouse and The Manor, was acquired by EMI as part of the 1992 sale of Virgin Records. The Sanctuary Group bought Townhouse from EMI in 2002; six years later, Universal closed it after purchasing Sanctuary. Planning permission was requested in 2012 to convert the Goldhawk Road building into residences, with an intriguing provision that the new planned complex "re-provide an element of recording studio space."

RIDGE FARM

Ridge Farm Studio was a residential recording facility located about 40 miles south of London, near Dorking in West Sussex. It was built into the barn of a mid-17th-century farmhouse and surrounded by 12 acres of land that included gardens, orchards, meadows, and woodland—later supplemented with an outdoor swimming pool.

The studio's owners were a lighting technician named Frank Andrews and his brother, Billy Andrews. Frank, who had toured extensively with

top bands like Queen, Bad Company, the Rolling Stones, the Doobie Brothers, and ABBA, had good industry contacts and felt that many artists would be attracted to the lush surroundings and relaxed environment the property afforded. When Ridge Farm first opened in 1975, it was just a rehearsal space, but it wasn't long before clients like Back Street Crawler (featuring ex-Free guitarist Paul Kosoff) and Queen (who reportedly wrote "Bohemian Rhapsody" there) began taking advantage of the barn's outstanding acoustics to make recordings on site, using mobile facilities. "We used the Manor Mobile to record the band Magazine at Ridge Farm in early 1978," says producer John Leckie. (See Chapter 9 for more information.) "Most of the tracks were recorded live in the barn. Although the space was good, I remember the accommodation was a little cramped. We had to share rooms with the family and keep the noise down, and breakfast and dinner was served in the house after Frank's family had eaten. We also had to beg Frank to let us watch *Top of the Pops* on TV in the family lounge! At

Ridge Farm exterior.
(Courtesy of Tony Harris)

first he said no because his mother was watching *Coronation Street*."

The logical next step was to turn Ridge Farm into a proper recording studio. In the winter of 1978, the Andrews brothers converted the barn into a soundproofed 1,200-square-foot studio, with acoustic design by ex-EMI and ex-AIR technical engineer Keith Slaughter. The main recording area was given a wood floor and, other than a single isolation booth (which served for a time as a temporary control room), was essentially one big open space, with separation provided by acoustic screens

A view of the Ridge Farm studio.
(Courtesy of Tony Harris)

when necessary. A separate control room was fully floated on rubber pads to isolate it from the main structure and was also slightly elevated to provide good line of sight to the recording area below.

The Ridge Farm control room was initially outfitted with equipment rented from Yes singer Jon Anderson. This included a 28-channel MCI JH-400 mixing console and an MCI JH-24 2" 24-track tape recorder, along with an MCI 1/4" 2-track machine, with monitoring by JBL 4341s and Tannoy Reds in Lockwood cabinets, driven by Amcron and Quad amps. Outboard equipment included UREI limiters, an Eventide DDL, Harmonizer and Flanger, and an EMT Gold Foil, with microphones from Neumann, AKG, Beyer, Electrovoice, and Schoeps.

That was the gear used to record the 1979 Roxy Music album *Manifesto*, among other projects, but by 1982 Ridge Farm had purchased its own equipment, which included a 32-channel SSL 4000E mixing console and a Telefunken 15A 24-track, as well as a pair of Ampex ATR-100 2-track tape machines. The outboard gear, which was housed in a sweeping curve-shaped rack mounted on wheels, included an AMS ADR FX760 Compex limiter, DMX15-80 digital

delay line, and DM2-20 phaser/flanger; an Eventide Harmonizer; a Lexicon 224 digital reverb and Primetime; an MXR Flanger; a PanScan autopanner; and a pair of Lindsay 7607 graphic equalizers. Several additional mics (including models from Sennheiser) were also purchased and an EMT 140 stereo reverb plate installed.

There was a further equipment upgrade in 1985, at which time the control room was also enlarged, and three years later the studio was divided into two separate areas with the construction of a permanent partition.

Ridge Farm Studio closed in early 2003, with Joe Jackson the last artist to record there, and the property is now used as a facility for weddings, banquets, and meetings. But in the nearly quarter of a century during which it was operational, the studio attracted an enviable client list that included Bad Company, Thin Lizzy, Frankie Goes to Hollywood, A Flock of Seagulls, The Smiths (*Meat Is Murder*), Magazine (*Real Life*), Ozzy Osbourne (three solo albums, including *Diary of a Madman*), Oasis, Muse, and Supergrass. Pearl Jam's 1991 debut album, *Ten*, was also mixed at Ridge Farm.

ODYSSEY

Odyssey was the last major U.K. studio to open in the 1970s. Located at 23-25 Castlereagh Street, a cul-de-sac near Marble Arch, it was launched in July 1979, set up by owner/producer Wayne Bickerton as an extension of State Records, the independent label he had formed with partners Tony Waddington and John Fruin in 1975.

Funded with the proceeds Bickerton had received from the hit records he'd made with the faux pop group the Rubettes (kind of a '70s English version of The Monkees), Odyssey was a purpose-built recording facility with expansive premises and state-of-the-art equipment. Ex-EMI technical engineer Keith Slaughter, who had also played an integral role in the design of AIR Studios, was recruited to do the acoustic treatment. Initially the Odyssey complex consisted of one very large main studio and a remix room with a small studio area; a third voice-over and radio production studio was added later. (A mastering suite was also planned but never came to fruition.)

Under Slaughter's direction, the entire complex was isolated on neoprene pads for sound isolation. The large Studio 1 incorporated a drum booth and a piano trap, and had an unusually high 18' undulating ceiling treated with a patented strip system that provided a random reflective plane. The studio had a partially carpeted, partially wooden floor and wall treatments to match. In addition, there was a large sectionalized runner curtain that extended from floor to ceiling, allowing effective acoustic division of the studio floor. One very unusual feature at Odyssey was the U-shaped balcony that swept above the control room and offered a different acoustic; brass and woodwind instruments were frequently placed up there.

The control room and the remix room at Odyssey were about the same size (approximately 320 square feet) and were equipped more or less identically. The mixing consoles were custom MCI JH-500 56-channel desks with full automation, and the tape recorders were also all MCI, including 24-track, 16-track, and 2-track machines. Odyssey was originally going to be the U.K.'s first 56-track facility, incorporating both 24-track and 32-track recorders, but MCI's plans for a 32-track machine (which used 3" tape running at 20 ips) never got beyond the prototype stage, so both the control room and the remix

Odyssey Studios exterior.
(Courtesy of Tony Harris)

room ended up operating as 48-track, using two synchronized MCI JH-24 24-track machines.

The monitoring in both rooms was via Audicon units containing JBL drivers (later changed to UREI 813s), bi-amped from BGW 750-watt power amplifiers, plus a pair of Auratones. Outboard gear included a wide variety of UREI and ADR compressors and limiters, Klark-Teknik graphic equalizers, and AMS, Eventide, and Bel digital delay lines and time processors; there were also a number of EMT reverb plates. The studio's mic cabinet included Neumann and AKG condensers, as well as AKG dynamics.

Odyssey closed in 1989 and was sold to a major FM radio station. Major artists who worked at the

A panoramic view of Odyssey's main studio presented in a studio brochure circa 1980.
(From studio brochure)

facility include Black Sabbath, Gerry Rafferty, Kate Bush, Men Without Hats, the Pat Metheny Group, Roger Daltrey, Thin Lizzy, and XTC. The Who also recorded their 1981 album *Face Dances* at Odyssey.

MOBILES

"A recording studio is an immediate imposition
as compared to sitting around a fire strumming."
—Robert Plant

"We needed the sort of facilities where we could have a cup of tea
and wander round the garden and then go in and do what we had to do."
—Jimmy Page

Remote recording was being done in England as far back as the early 1920s, when The Gramophone Company (later to evolve into EMI) dispatched its two-ton Lancia truck to record classical concerts at Queen's Hall near Oxford Circus and Kingsway Hall in the City of London as well as at events like the annual Aldershot Military Tattoo. The truck was filled with a broad selection of recording equipment of the day—primitive microphones and rudimentary homebuilt amplifiers and two- or three-channel mixers, supplemented with two "portable" wax-cutting lathes, each weighing hundreds of pounds—all carefully packed into wooden crates. So heavy and cumbersome was the rig that a jacking system was required to support each corner of the truck during recording in order to level the lathes, which used 55-pound lead weights as gravity motors. The power for the amplifiers and for the suction and heating of waxes was derived from batteries that were recharged during rest periods.

In the 1930s, Decca—EMI's closest competitor—would do the same, even going to the extent of setting up a small, semipermanent control room area at Kingsway Hall (as did EMI, even though its microphone connectors were purposely wired the opposite way! [see Chapter 2 for more information]). Following World War II, IBC joined the fray, launching its own remote recording unit, frequently deployed to nearby Conway Hall (where IBC maintained a very small monophonic control room; signal would be piped in via standard telephone lines so that ambience from the studio's echo chamber could be added during recording and broadcast [see Chapter 3 for more information]) and other venues, including the Royal Albert Hall and places as far-flung as Dublin. Like other IBC recording facilities, it was equipped with custom mixing desks built by the maintenance department—initially with a "tall valve [tube] console

The IBC Mobile recording equipment set up in a remote location, 1965.
(Photo by Peter Smith)

Olympic's mobile recording unit, circa 1964:
an ex-Daimler ambulance.
(Photos by Frank Owen)

concert halls. Two modest transit vans (one Renault and one Ford) were duly purchased and pressed into service to transport the various pieces of recording equipment assembled by Auger, all carefully packed in cases, then carried into each venue by a hired moving company. These included an Ampex 3-track tape recorder and a pair of Tannoy Lockwood speakers with built-in Leak 25 amplifiers, as well as two mixers: one homebuilt by Pye's chief maintenance engineer Ken Atwood, and the other a good-sized Neumann mixer designed to be placed on a wooden plinth that bolted to the base of its case. The mixers were simple 12-input / 4-output models, with old-fashioned rotary Bakelite knobs and rudimentary EQ, basically just a treble and bass control. Eddie Kramer, who would later gain fame for his work with Jimi Hendrix and Led Zeppelin, often assisted Auger on those early outings; reportedly, a favorite mic technique was placing three Neumann U47s strategically to the left, right, and directly in front of the orchestra—each assigned to one of the three tracks, enabling a correct balance to be crafted when mono mixes were done back at Pye Studios.

A year or two later, Olympic purchased an ex-Daimler ambulance, recently retired from service transporting the injured and ill around London, and outfitted it with recording equipment. Clive Green's recollections of it are vivid: "Joseph Yu and Frank Owen and I would traipse to different places around the country and record concerts; we did a fair amount of work for a Radio Luxemburg show called *Double Your Money*. Of course, we couldn't see what was going on because there was no closed-circuit television at the time. The tape recorders were stereo valve [tube] Telefunkens—monster contraptions—and we had two of these so we could record the program continuously on reel-to-reel." Ex-Olympic engineer George Chkiantz recalls seeing the 8-in mono-out tube mixer used in the ambulance. "It had a single slant panel with rotary faders and used EF86 valves with wire-wound resistors to keep the noise down," he reports. "And it had a really cheapskate tone

on wheels," in the words of former engineer Sean Davies, replaced in 1964 with a compact transistorized 9 x 3 mixer, along with domestic Grundig and/or EMI TR51 monophonic tape recorders, supplanted eventually by Ampex 3-track machines.

In the early 1960s, Pye's chief engineer Bob Auger talked his employer into setting up a similar kind of rig for recording symphony orchestras at outside

Maintenance engineer Philip Newell with the three sections of one of the Pye van's "portable" 8-track tape recorders, recording the Who *Live at Leeds* concert, 1970.
(Photo by Simon Heyworth)

control circuit which gave bass and treble cut and lift with a bare minimum of components."

Following the studio's move to Barnes in 1966, Olympic's Daimler was apparently retired,* but the Pye Mobile continued going strong. By the late 1960s, it was upgraded with two large and bulky 3M M23 8-track recorders. (Dual tape machines were a necessity on remote recording rigs, since they allowed for overlapping recording in case performances exceeded the length of a single reel of tape.) This was the configuration of the Pye Mobile that was used to record The Who's epic *Live at Leeds* album in February 1970. (See *Crackles are OK* on the following page.) A few months later, the two portable mixers in the van—one Pye-built, the other a contraption lovingly

called the "Smellotron" (three Vortexion mixers linked together)—were replaced by a pair of early solid-state Neve Series 80 desks custom-designed so that each could be split in half for transport and later reassembled at the venue.

Alan Perkins, who came on board in 1969, elaborates on the design of the Neve desk used in the Pye Mobile: "There were two input sections that provided 12 microphone input channels each, with the usual array of Neve mic amps, EQ, foldback, and faders. Each section had four handles on the side and would be mounted on a metal stand. They were bloody heavy, too! Then there were two output units, which had eight bus sends each, plus aux and echo master sends, and 8-track monitoring.

"All four sections were the same size, and they would clip together and interconnect with multicore cable so you could hook them up in any kind of configuration," Perkins continues. "For example, you could have two completely separate 12-in / 8-out

---

* Liner notes to the contrary, the Olympic Mobile was *not* used to record the music performed during the *Rolling Stones Rock and Roll Circus* television show filmed on December 11, 1968. Instead, according to former Olympic and Rolling Stones Mobile engineer Mick Mckenna, it was recorded by Glyn Johns using equipment provided by IBC.

Crackles are OK

ALAN PERKINS joined Pye Studios as a trainee assistant engineer in 1969. As fate would have it, Vic Maile, who was doing much of Pye's remote recording at the time, had just lost his driver's license. And so the young Perkins was dispatched to take over driving duties, as well as to assist Maile.

In February of 1970 their travels took them to the University of Leeds, where The Who were scheduled to perform. The concert—with the aid of Maile and Perkins—was soon to be immortalized in the album *Live at Leeds*. "We basically wrapped our two small mixers up in sleeping bags and everything would get piled into these two transit vans," recalls Perkins. "Then we'd drive off to the gig, unload the gear, set it all up, set the mics up, and do the recording. It was great fun, but everything was so incredibly heavy!"

During the performance, Maile and Perkins, accompanied by two other Pye engineers, were ensconced in a makeshift control room set up in a cloakroom underneath the auditorium. "At the end, when the band finished their set, the audience were all stamping on the floor right above our heads," Perkins remembers. "The noise was like thunder! But it was a very good recording—apart from one thing: There was a power cable that we had running across the staircase that must have had some sort of a problem, because whenever anyone walked on the staircase, you'd get a crackle on the recording. We didn't have time to unplug everything and try and work out where this was coming from—I don't know if we even got a sound check to go through everything before the show actually started; in fact, I have a feeling we went straight into it cold. So we had this intermittent crackling problem and there was nothing we could do about it.

"Sure enough, when the album came out few months later, on the label it said, 'Crackles are OK,' because obviously all the way through the mixing and mastering and pressing process, they couldn't get rid of them!"

boards for two different gigs in different parts of the country, or you could have one 12-input section hooked to a single 8-output section, or two 12-ins to one 8-out so you could have 24 microphones going to an 8-track machine, plus have separate 8-track monitoring." One problem that came up if you were working in 16-track was that, because each output section was separate, there were two monitor gain pots—one for each set of eight outputs—so it wasn't possible to turn all the monitors down with a single knob." As a result, a separate small monitor mixer was later added to combine the output from the two sections together.

By the mid-1960s, there was yet another remote recording facility in the mix: Granada Recordings (later Bob Auger Associates), formed by former Pye chief engineer Bob Auger, with funding from Granada Television. This included both mobile facilities and a land-based remix room, located initially near the Oval in South London, later moved to Auger's home near Henley-on-Thames. Granada Recordings initially offered a selection of Neve modules that could be custom-assembled into a large or small desk (up to a 24 x 8 configuration) as needed, along with Ampex 4- and 8-track recorders, Tannoy Red monitors in Lockwood cabinets, and a selection of Neumann, AKG, and Calrec microphones, including Auger's favorite Neumann M49, M50, and U87 tube mics. This was supplemented in later years by an Ampex MM1100 16-track machine and various submixers, as well as Westrex tube limiters and some ADR outboard equipment—all of which would be packed in cases and hauled to venues such as Ronnie Scott's jazz club in Soho, in an overstuffed transit van. At its peak, the company employed four full-time engineers (including Auger) and was recording some 300 LPs a year.

Things were getting quite sophisticated, yet despite the evolution of equipment and facilities, the state of the art in remote recording in England at the end of the 1960s was far from ideal, for a number of reasons. One was the time and the amount of manpower required to unload, set up, and pack down the rig. Ex-Pye maintenance engineer Philip Newell (who would go on to oversee the assembly of the later

Manor Mobile) writes in his 2003 book *Recording Studio Design*: "It took four people to lift each section [of the Neve console], and two people to lift each of the three sections of the 'portable' 3M M23 8-track tape recorders." "We were up and down stairs and all over the place with these things," he remembers. "It was backbreaking work, especially with those gigantic Lockwood loudspeakers."

But a much bigger problem was the lack of standardized monitoring. Even though the Pye Mobile (and some of its earlier predecessors) carried professional studio speakers and amplification, the gear was always simply carted into the venue and then,

as Newell writes, "set up in the best available space for each recording: dressing rooms, hallways, and the like. Obviously, this meant that the monitoring conditions varied wildly, so apart from listening for noises or distortions, and perhaps assessing the relative musical balance of a section of instruments, not much could be done in the way of judging the timbre of an instrument, especially at the lower frequencies."

Ironically, it would be the Rolling Stones—the quintessential antiestablishment (and, arguably, antitechnology) band of their day—who would be first to provide the solution.

THE ROLLING STONES MOBILE

By the late 1960s, The Beatles, in the guise of their doppelgänger Sgt. Pepper's Lonely Hearts Club Band, had changed the way major artists made records. The studio had evolved from a place to capture the sound of live performance to a kind of sonic playground, a place for experimentation. It wasn't long before albums began taking many weeks, if not months, to complete.

Somewhat predictably, the always competitive Rolling Stones had taken things a step further. Guitarist Keith Richards had adopted the technique of putting the band through endless hours of studio jamming in search of some kind of elusive (im)perfection that only he could perceive. To Richards, the studio was not so much a place to experiment with new sounds or genres but a glorified rehearsal room, a place where a riff could be fed to musicians he trusted in order to see just how far they could take it, by means of studied—often stupefying—repetition.

Keith may have been the musical leader of the group, but the pennies were being counted by fellow Glimmer Twin Mick Jagger, an astute businessman who made a point of keeping a close eye on the alarmingly mounting studio bills. Nor did it escape Mick's attention that his friendly archrivals from Liverpool were making noises about building their own recording studio in order to escape the insti-

tutional clutches of the not-so-friendly confines of EMI's Abbey Road studios. (See *Apple* in Chapter 8.)

Early in 1970, Jagger purchased a mansion in southern England named Stargroves, and it occurred to him that it could serve as a suitable place to record Keith's interminable jams, but without the commensurate bills; all that was required was transporting the necessary recording equipment to the house. In the process of planning the logistics of such a move, the group's road manager (and occasional pianist), Ian Stewart, came up with the idea of building the control room inside the truck itself. This would not only negate the necessity of doing any construction work on Jagger's home, it would also allow the equipment to easily be moved to other recording locations.

Thus was born the modern mobile studio—a control room on wheels that provided standardized monitoring and avoided most of the backbreaking labor required by its predecessors, since almost everything (apart from the microphones, mic cables, and foldback equipment) would remain on the truck, fixed in place, instead of having to load gear in and out of each venue. Glyn Johns was brought in as a consultant and Sandy Brown hired to do the acoustic design, with the electronics and desk provided by Dick Swettenham and his new Helios company. (See *Mixing Consoles* below and Chapter 5 for more information.)

The Rolling Stones Mobile.
(Photo by Mick Mckenna)

Interior of the RSM.
(Photo by Chris Pearsall, www.cpphoto.com)

In the summer of 1970, the Rolling Stones Mobile (or "RSM," as it came to be known, though internally it was generally referred to as the "Mighty Mobile" or the "Stones Truck") was driven down to Stargroves for the recording of numerous tracks that would make their way onto the band's *Sticky Fingers* album. A year later, the Stones decamped for Europe to avoid the astronomical tax rate imposed by the British government. That summer, the RSM was moved to Nellcôte, a mansion in southern France rented by Keith Richards. With ex-Olympic engineer Andy Johns manning the board out in the truck, the band spent many long hours recording the album *Exile on Main St.* in the villa's massive basement.

During the Rolling Stones' 1973 European tour, ex-Olympic engineer Mick Mckenna was brought in to oversee the future development of the unit, in consultation with Ian Stewart. Over the next two years, the RSM went from 16-track to 24-track capability and the onboard Helios console was expanded from 20 inputs to 32. In addition, significant work was done to improve the acoustics of the truck's interior. Renting the RSM to other artists was never part of the original plan, according to Mckenna, but inquiries soon started flooding into the Stones' office— a golden business opportunity that must have appealed tremendously to the group's notoriously parsimonious lead singer.

The "Mighty Mobile" would be used by Led Zeppelin at Headley Grange to record tracks for *Led Zeppelin III*, *IV*, and

"I remember being very bored but having the time of my life"

WHEN ASKED in a 1999 interview to comment on the making of *Exile on Main St.*, engineer Andy Johns (who passed away in 2013) summed it up in three words: "It was tough."

"It was a lovely, gorgeous, stunning place," Johns said of Nellecôte, Keith Richards' temporary home in exile, "and there was a proper basement, not a wine cellar. There was one big room down the end which [had been converted] into a kitchen, and there were several [other] rooms. I put [session keyboardist] Nicky Hopkins in one room; [bassist] Bill Wyman's amp was under the stairs, outside the door; Charlie [Watts] and Keith were next to each other, and Mick Taylor was in that room, too. But it was stone and plaster, so it was difficult working in there. And the electricity was always going on and off because it was the south of France, and it was incredibly humid and very hot; there was just one little fan in a window at ground level, so the guitars

would constantly go out of tune halfway through a song. The drum sounds were never quite right—there was always this bloody compromise—and Mick would often have a vocal mic in the studio so he could cavort with the boys. You'd pull that up and think, boy, those drums sound good, but we can't use it because it's got all the other stuff leaking into it.

"Plus," he continued, "the Stones being the Stones, you'd show up at six, Bill might get there at nine, Keith would come downstairs at ten, Mick just went off somewhere, so you really didn't get things going productively until about 11 or 12. And you might get two or three good hours and then things would fall to bits again. We were there for six months."

Making matters worse, singer Mick Jagger had just gotten married to his first wife, Bianca, which caused him to be somewhat, in Johns' words, "distracted."

"So Mick wasn't paying as much attention as Keith might have liked," Johns explained, "but [there was] the boredom factor [too]. Showing up in someone's house, it's not like going to the studio, . . . it's where someone lives, so there's the kids and servants and all that, and I don't know whether Mick liked that.

"Most of the time," he added with remarkable candor, "they were the worst band on the planet. Out of time, out of tune, and no one's going, 'Hey, man, this sounds awful, we've got a problem'; no one's going, 'How about you just tune up?' It's just this rubbish noise. And then, it might take a few hours or a few days, and it would just come together. Bill might get up out of his chair and start playing; Keith would go stand next to Charlie, and this magic thing would happen, and boing, you'd have this off-planet experience. I just remember being very bored but having the time of my life."

Houses of the Holy, and it would also be pressed into service by numerous other major artists of the era, including Bad Company, Ten Years After, and Fleetwood Mac. The RSM—newly painted in camouflage because the original silver color was too reflective for the cameras (it would eventually be repainted dark blue)—would also be featured in the 1971 Frank Zappa film *200 Motels* and used to record the soundtrack album.

Following the untimely death of Ian Stewart in 1985, the Stones sold the truck to their bassist, Bill Wyman. "When the band decided to give up collective ownership of our mobile studio, I took it over," Wyman recalled in his 1990 autobiography *Stone Alone*. "I then launched AIMS—Ambition, Ideas, Motivation, Success—and together with sponsor-

ship . . . we were able to give free recording facilities to 50 bands, out of 1,200 applicants in England. My purpose was to encourage young live bands in an age when producers were taking over." The AIMS project ended with a final concert at the Royal Albert Hall in 1988, and the "Mighty Mobile" was retired in 1993 after a final recording by Mick Jagger's brother Chris and his band. Three years later, the truck was sold at auction and shipped to New York, where it underwent some technical refurbishing before being put back into service, doing a short residency at the famous punk club CBGB's, where live shows by the Ramones, Patti Smith, and others were recorded.

The Rolling Stones Mobile is currently owned by the National Music Centre in Calgary, Alberta, Canada, where it is undergoing a major restoration.

A Rolling Stones Mobile ad, circa early 1970s. Mick Jagger's mansion Nellcôte is shown in the top photo, with the RSM truck parked outside. The bottom left photo shows the Nellcôte basement, as set up for the recording of the Stones' *Exile on Main St.* album. Bottom right, Stones road manager (and occasional pianist) Ian Stewart behind the board in the RSM.
(From studio brochure)

KEY PERSONNEL

Ian Stewart, Mick Mckenna, Jeremy Gee, Tapani Tapanianen, Peter "The Fish" Stevens, Charlie McPherson, Arnold Dunn, Les Kingham, Mick Williams, Malcolm Rogers

PHYSICAL FACILITIES

The box and trailer construction of the Rolling Stones Mobile was by Bonnallack Freight Containers of London, built onto a 1971 J-registration BMC Laird truck. Nearly half of the 90 square feet of interior space was taken up by a large isolation booth, although this ended up being used most often as a storage area. "It was designed to emulate a studio control room," says Mckenna. "Not only did it have a fixed console and monitors, it had air-conditioning too. But everything on the truck had to have a place so you could find things easily.

"What would usually happen, if we were doing a live show, was we'd get the cables out, tie up with the PA guys, and then I would specify where I wanted things on the board, especially in the early days when the RSM mixer only had 20 inputs [an extra 12 channels were added in late 1974], so it was quite limited. For the early live work we did, it wasn't a problem, but as the shows got bigger and bigger, the lack of input channels presented quite a challenge, and recording albums on location was an even more tenuous operation. I think the largest tally of channels I ever had to deal with during a show was 144, and at that point the desk still had only 32 inputs, so you can imagine how much ancillary equipment was brought into play."

At the same time the additional channels were installed, the mixing console was also upgraded to 24 outputs in order to accommodate the RSM's brand-new 24-track tape recorder. Incredibly, this also marked the first time that the mobile was outfitted with connector panels for the tape machines—up until then, all connections were directly hardwired with loose cabling. In addition, the electrical feeds were split, with the equipment on one circuit and the lights and air-conditioning on the other, allowing much more flexibility in situations where power was unreliable.

According to Mckenna, an ongoing problem was trying to figure out where to park the large truck between gigs, especially since a nearby workshop was always needed to facilitate maintenance. In the early days, it was kept at Stargroves, but after Mckenna came on board he began looking for a place nearer to London for the sake of convenience. Eventually he found a rehearsal place in Little Chalfont, run by drummer Trevor Morais (converted in the late '70s to Farmyard Studios), where the truck could work and be serviced (albums by Alan Price and Simple Minds were recorded there), but then The Who offered to look after it at the space they were temporarily renting at Shepperton Film Studios in Surrey. When Shepperton converted to all film work, The Who, Mckenna, and the RSM all found a temporary new home at an industrial estate near Heathrow airport, though the truck was ultimately moved to Pinewood Studios in Buckinghamshire. There, in addition to music recording and TV work, the RSM tied into Pinewood's sound department to provide multitrack facilities for various film projects.

Acoustic Treatments

The exterior skin of the Rolling Stones Mobile was aluminum. Initially, the interior walls were coated with foam rubber covered by burlap (or "hessian" in the English vernacular), along with some hardboard and rockwool.

In late 1974, on the advice of acoustic consultant Eddie Veale, more rockwool was added to the interior walls, placed underneath aluminum pegboards for additional absorption and diffusion.

At a later date, the roof of the RSM was peeled back and filled with rockwool, too, something that really helped the bottom end, according to Mckenna.

KEY EQUIPMENT
Mixing Consoles

Initially, the mixing board in the RSM was a custom-built Helios 20-input / 16-output model, similar to the one installed in Olympic Studio Two in 1969. (See Chapter 5 for more information.) "One of the nice things about the desk was that it had troughs and recessed switches, so it was quite good for soloing and muting," says Mckenna.

In late 1974, the Helios was refitted with an additional five full channels and eight more bus outputs. The first eight main gains were now on faders (the rest were still on knobs), and the

---

STORIES FROM THE STUDIO
Smoke on the water

TOWARD THE END of 1971, the Rolling Stones Mobile was driven to Montreux, Switzerland, where Deep Purple had decided to record their next album onstage, using the natural acoustics of a local theater called the Pavilion; their concept was to make a live album sans audience.

The day before they were due to start recording, the RSM was parked next to the Casino, an arena that was part of a complex of gambling halls, restaurants, and theaters. While Frank Zappa and the Mothers of Invention were playing onstage, a fire was ignited when an audience member shot a flare into the ceiling. The Casino burned to the ground, but the Mighty Mobile was moved to the nearby Grand Hotel in time to escape damage, and it was decided that the Deep Purple album would be recorded there instead. But it was the sight of the smoke spreading over Lake Geneva that served as the inspiration for the band's best-known song, "Smoke on the Water," which immortalized the (slightly skewed) "Rolling truck Stones thing" in its lyrics.

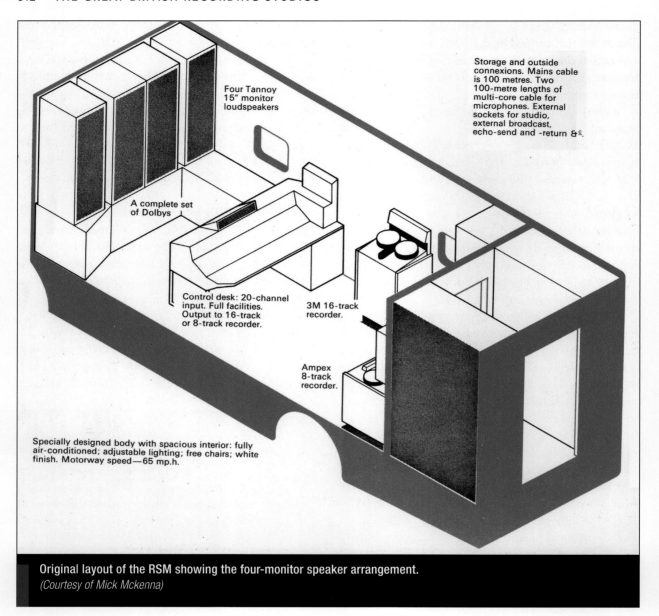

Four Tannoy
15" monitor
loudspeakers

Storage and outside
connexions. Mains cable
is 100 metres. Two
100-metre lengths of
multi-core cable for
microphones. External
sockets for studio,
external broadcast,
echo-send and -return &ᶜ.

A complete set
of Dolbys

Control desk: 20-channel
input. Full facilities.
Output to 16-track
or 8-track recorder.

3M 16-track
recorder.

Ampex
8-track
recorder.

Specially designed body with spacious interior: fully
air-conditioned; adjustable lighting; free chairs; white
finish. Motorway speed—65 mp.h.

Original layout of the RSM showing the four-monitor speaker arrangement.
(Courtesy of Mick Mckenna)

jackfield was pushed out and extended. Additionally, "mini channels" (a Mckenna innovation) were added: seven channels in a minimal rack space, each containing a Helios mic amp, with access to the mix buses and sends to the echo, foldback and monitor systems, but no EQ other than a three-position high-pass filter. (If necessary, external equalizers could be inserted into the "mini channels" via the patch bay.) This upgrade brought the console to 32 in, 24 out.

Monitors

Initially, the RSM had a four-speaker setup, as was used at Olympic, Pye, and other English studios of the era. These were 15" Tannoy Reds in Lockwood cabinets. (See Chapter 1 for more information.) After the 1974 refurbishment, this was changed to a standard two-speaker stereo setup.

In the late 1970s, these were temporarily replaced by Altec 604-8G monitors, although after a short period the decision was made to go back to Tannoys.

Tape Machines

The multitrack carried by the RSM was a 3M M56 2" 16-track recorder, with an Ampex AG-440 8-track as backup. (See *Decca* in Chapter 2 and Chapter 6 for more information.)

Following the 1974 refurbishment, both machines were replaced by two 3M M79 2" 24-tracks with a modification allowing for the use of 14" reels—particularly important when recording live performances. (See Chapter 5 for more information.)

Main Microphones

The most favored microphones on the RSM were Shure SM58s, SM81s, and SM7s, along with AKG D25s and C34s, but there were also models from Neumann (including U47s, U67s, U87s, and a stereo SM69), Beyer, Countryman, Sennheiser, and Sony.

"I didn't always need to use a lot of mics," says Mckenna. "Some nights it might just be couple of drum overheads and audience miking. I did like using an AKG C34, positioned in the middle of the lighting truss looking down at the audience. That was a good way to maintain timing rather than picking up a lot of slap echo. I might supplement that with a couple of shotgun mics, depending on the venue."

Outboard Signal Processors

Because the Helios board on the RSM had no signal-splitting facilities and only minimal foldback capability, one of Mick Mckenna's first projects upon joining the RSM in 1974 was designing and building

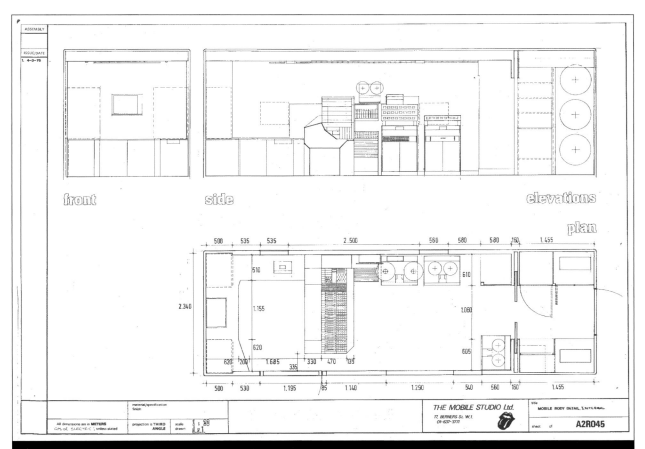

RSM layout following a 1975 refit.
(Courtesy of Mick Mckenna)

splitter boxes with built-in foldback for live work. "I built five or six them in blocks of ten so they were reasonably portable and could pack well," he explains, important since everything had to be well secured for travelling. Many of the PA companies of the era had passive splitters, which Mckenna felt were less than ideal due to signal reflections and level changes. Accordingly, the boxes he built had active electronics and used Nagra recessed ground lift switches—key because they couldn't be accidentally activated. "They were very expensive, but worth it," Mckenna says. Also added at around the same time was an early Wollensak cassette deck and some quite complex Dolby switching, accomplished by installing tiny relays on boards in the back of the 3M tape machines so that both the Dolbys and the foldback boxes could be switched simultaneously, allowing independent mixes to be created.

Other outboard gear on the RSM included numerous compressors, Pultec, UREI, ESS and Orban equalizers, Kepex gates, a Bel flanger, an Eventide H910 Harmonizer, a Lexicon 224 digital reverb, and even, for a while, an EMT 240 gold foil.

SELECTED DISCOGRAPHY

- Rolling Stones: tracks for *Sticky Fingers*, *Exile on Main St.*, *Black and Blue*, and *Tattoo You*
- Led Zeppelin: tracks for *Led Zeppelin III*, *Led Zeppelin IV*, and *Houses of the Holy*
- Deep Purple: *Machine Head*, *Who Do We Think We Are*, *Burn*, "Smoke on the Water" (single)
- Bad Company: *Run with the Pack*
- Bob Marley: "No Woman No Cry" (single)
- Neil Young: "A Man Needs a Maid" and "There's a World" (tracks for *Harvest*)
- Frank Zappa: *200 Motels*

THE PYE MOBILE

The success of the Rolling Stones Mobile did not escape the attention of the boffins at Pye, particularly those who had been involved in the company's early remote recording efforts; in fact, it spurred them on to build a competitive mobile facility of their own. As Philip Newell wrote in *Recording Studio Design*, "Together with the monitoring variability, the great loss of time for rigging and derigging led Pye to build their first dedicated mobile vehicle in 1971, which went on the road just after the Rolling Stones mobile. It was immediately appreciated that this gave a new consistency in monitoring conditions, which, even if they were wrong, at least they were always the same. The crews could learn how to come to terms with their 'wrongness,' which was something which was very difficult when portable equipment was set up in a different room for each recording venue."

Pye Studios technical manager Ray Prickett was tasked with the job of overseeing the design and outfitting of the new Pye Mobile, which, like the RSM, was to be a "control room on wheels" with acoustic treatment and fixed monitoring and recording equipment. However, since the truck selected for these

duties was less powerful than the RSM ("desperately underpowered," in the words of some of the onboard crew), a second transit van would follow wherever the Pye Mobile was dispatched, carrying all the equipment that would have to be brought into the venue itself—things like microphones, mic stands, cabling, splitter boxes, and DI boxes.

There was another reason behind the decision to deploy two vehicles instead of one: The heavier the truck, the higher the class HGV (Heavy Goods Vehicle) license the driver had to hold. The Pye Mobile was therefore built into a semitrailer with a transit front end, which only required the driver to carry a Class 4 license, as opposed to the more expensive (and harder to obtain) Class 1 license. Needless to say, this put a significant limitation on what could be installed inside, but it must have seemed like a worthwhile trade-off to Pye management.

Maintenance engineer Peter Duncan was given the assignment of fitting out the new purpose-built Pye Mobile and making a more permanent union of the portable Neve desks prior to installation. Because there was insufficient room in the maintenance workshop, the console was assembled at his home in East Anglia with assistance from fellow technical engineer Philip Newell and recording engineer Vic Maile, and then moved into the truck parked outside. Unexpectedly, the Pye Mobile ended up being used mostly by artists not signed to the label, according to Alan Perkins, who became the mobile's chief engineer following Maile's departure in 1971.

In 1973, the truck was redesigned by Ray Prickett and equipped for 16-track recording, complete with two 16-track Studer A80 tape recorders with Dolby, new Tannoy speakers, and CCTV. The Pye Mobile was sold to The Manor a year later and rechristened Manor Mobile Two. (See *The Manor Mobiles* below for more information.)

KEY PERSONNEL

Ray Prickett, Peter Duncan, Vic Maile, Alan Perkins, Philip Newell, Neville Crozier, Alan Florence, Steve Muirfield, Bob Harper

KEY EQUIPMENT
Mixing Consoles

The same four-section custom Neve console used by the original Pye Mobile was built into the truck used for the mobile's second incarnation as a "control room on wheels." However, this was not without its difficulties.

"The problem was that the permanent mobile truck had a 16-track machine," says Perkins. "That meant we needed to monitor 16 tracks, but the Neve wasn't set up for that." This was solved with the addition of a sidecar monitor mixer. But there was another problem, one that was not so easily resolved. "It turned out that the truck wasn't wide enough to have all four [Neve mixer] sections side by side," he explains. "So

The Pye Mobile at the Isle of Wight Festival, 1970. Left to right: Recording engineers Alan Perkins and Neville Crozier, and maintenance engineer Tony Carey.
(Courtesy of Neville Crozier)

what we ended up doing was placing three of the units in a row—the two input sections and one of the output sections—and we had the other output section to the right of the first one, making the whole console L-shaped. It was far from ideal, but it was workable."

Monitors

Monitoring in the Pye Mobile was via 15" Tannoy HPD speakers in Lockwood cabinets.

Tape Machines

Initially, the Pye Mobile was outfitted with an Ampex MM1100 16-track tape recorder, but following the 1973 redesign, two Studer A80 16-track machines were installed instead. The two 3M M23 8-track machines from the original Pye Mobile were also retained and used as backup.

8

Main Microphones

The microphones carried by the van that accompanied the Pye Mobile included Neumann U87s and U67s (the latter, according to Perkins, were frequently used as drum overheads), along with a number of KM84s, used mostly for orchestral work. In addition, there were several AKG 224Es, used primarily for vocals and snare drum, along with Sennheiser MD421s, used for bass drum and bass. Because there were no splitter boxes, Perkins recalls having to gaffer-tape the recording mics to the PA mics at every venue.

Outboard Signal Processors

By all accounts, there was little outboard gear carried by the Pye Mobile, other than a handful of DI boxes (used mostly for bass), and a talkback system so the engineer in the truck could talk to his assistants onstage. "We didn't need much since we were just trying to get the sound down," says former Pye Mobile engineer Neville Crozier. "Everything would be done later, at the mixing stage."

"There were four Neve compressors and that's all," recalls Perkins. There was no reverb either, at least to begin with. Following the 1973 refitting, a Master Room spring reverb was added. "It was fixed length, so you couldn't adjust the decay, but it didn't sound too bad," Perkins says. "Plus, it was sturdy enough to withstand being bumped around in the back of the truck as we traveled from place to place."

RONNIE LANE MOBILE

Ronnie Lane had a long-standing desire to build a mobile studio in an Airstream trailer. "So when he got off an American tour [in 1972], he brought one back with him," said producer Ron Nevison in a 1998 interview with *Studio Sound* magazine. "And I got the commission to do the job."

Lane had been the bass player for the popular mid-'60s English band known as The Small Faces, later renamed just "The Faces" after singer Rod Stewart and guitarist Ronnie Wood joined forces with the remnants of the group (following Steve Marriott's departure) in 1969. The American-born Nevison had begun his career as a live sound engineer, doing FOH [Front of House] mixing for the band Traffic when Chris Blackwell offered him a job at Island Studios in London. The common denominator between the two was Who guitarist Pete Townshend, who had done some work with Nevison and was close friends (and an occasional musical collaborator) with Lane. And the job Nevison refers to was that of converting the 26-foot Airstream trailer into what would become the Ronnie Lane Mobile, better known as the LMS (short for Lane Mobile Studio).

Painted pastel blue, with shag pile carpeting lining the aluminum shell, the LMS became operational by 1972. The sound of the "room" inside was considered to be exceptionally accurate, largely due to the concave shoulders that ran across the entire length and width of the vehicle. This had the effect of both reinforcing the low end and reducing standing waves.

The LMS was initially outfitted with a custom wraparound Helios console, an 8-track Studer A80, Tannoy monitors, an AKG BX20 spring reverb, and a large selection of tube mics. However, it wasn't long before a major upgrade was required, at the request of Who guitarist Pete Townshend.

In 1973, Townshend was getting ready to record the *Quadrophenia* album. At the time, The Who were in the process of building their own studio, Ramport, in the Battersea district in southwest London. (See *Ramport* in Chapter 8.) The construction and acoustic design of the studio was done, but the equipment installation was not quite complete. As a result, the Ronnie Lane Mobile was parked outside so that the band could lay down basic tracks in their studio and record it with the LMS equipment. The project took nearly a year, with Ron Nevison spending weekends on the Cornwall beach with a Nagra recorder and four Neumann U87s recording sound effects like the sea rolling in and train whistles in the distance. It soon became apparent, however, that eight tracks were not enough.

The LMS upgrade to 16-track—which, amazingly, Nevison pulled off in a single weekend—was not without its difficulties. "If you're not familiar with an Airstream, [it's] like a tube," he said. "And in those days, the tape machines were enormous. There wasn't enough space to go up to 16 tracks without putting the tape machines right in the middle of the room. So we had to put eight tracks down at the bottom, and eight tracks up top, and then I got into all sorts of problems with hum, because it was right next to the motor. We finally got it all sorted out. In fact, it was the very first eight-up, eight-down Studer A80 [*Note: a 2" 16-track tape deck configured so that the electronics for eight tracks were above the deck and eight below it*] in history."

Exterior of the Ronnie Lane Mobile.
(From studio brochure)

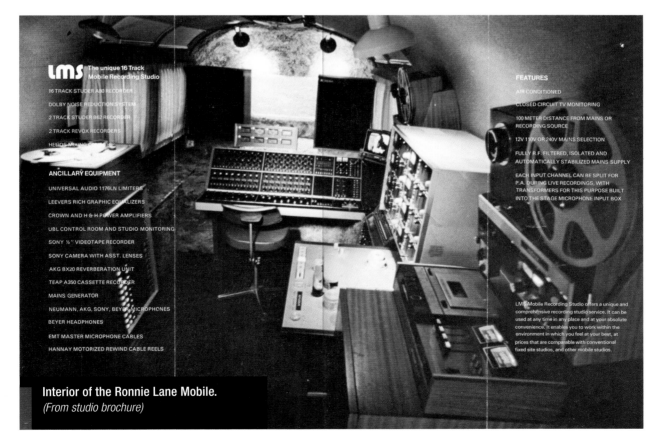

LMS The unique 16 Track Mobile Recording Studio

16 TRACK STUDER A80 RECORDER
DOLBY NOISE REDUCTION SYSTEM
2 TRACK STUDER B62 RECORDER
2 TRACK REVOX RECORDERS
HELIOS MIXING CONSOLE

ANCILLARY EQUIPMENT

UNIVERSAL AUDIO 1176LN LIMITERS
LEEVERS RICH GRAPHIC EQUALIZERS
CROWN AND H & H POWER AMPLIFIERS
UBL CONTROL ROOM AND STUDIO MONITORING
SONY ½" VIDEOTAPE RECORDER
SONY CAMERA WITH ASST. LENSES
AKG BX20 REVERBERATION UNIT
TEAP A350 CASSETTE RECORDER
MAINS GENERATOR
NEUMANN, AKG, SONY, BEYER MICROPHONES
BEYER HEADPHONES
EMT MASTER MICROPHONE CABLES
HANNAY MOTORIZED REWIND CABLE REELS

FEATURES

AIR CONDITIONED
CLOSED CIRCUIT TV MONITORING
100 METER DISTANCE FROM MAINS OR RECORDING SOURCE
12V 110V OR 240V MAINS SELECTION
FULLY R.F. FILTERED, ISOLATED AND AUTOMATICALLY STABILIZED MAINS SUPPLY
EACH INPUT CHANNEL CAN BE SPLIT FOR P.A. DURING LIVE RECORDINGS, WITH TRANSFORMERS FOR THIS PURPOSE BUILT INTO THE STAGE MICROPHONE INPUT BOX

LMS Mobile Recording Studio offers a unique and comprehensive recording studio service. It can be used at any time in any place and at your absolute convenience. It enables you to work within the environment in which you feel at your best, at prices that are comparable with conventional fixed site studios, and other mobile studios.

Interior of the Ronnie Lane Mobile.
(From studio brochure)

"He was adamant about not having microphones near his drums"

IN 1974, Ron Nevison and the Ronnie Lane Mobile were commissioned to record Led Zeppelin's *Physical Graffiti* album at Headley Grange, the same mansion in the English countryside where several of the tracks for their previous release, *Houses of the Holy*, had been recorded with the Rolling Stones Mobile.

At the band's insistence, he employed pretty much the same recording setups that had given them such a distinctive sound on their previous records. "I only used two microphones on John [Bonham]'s kit—a pair of [Neumann] U87s, set up on the second floor looking down on the kit, about ten feet above them," Nevison explained in an interview with *Studio Sound*. "John was adamant about not having microphones near his drums. I wanted to put some backup microphones behind the kit, but he wouldn't let me. Still, the kick and the snare come through large. It's all in how he played, the acoustics of the room—which had a beautiful stone floor and mahogany walls, but not so big that you couldn't contain the sound—and the drums themselves. It would be impossible to re-create that sound again without all of those components."

Nevison did manage to bring his own distinctive touch to the Zeppelin drum sound, though. "On [the track] 'Kashmir,' I ran one of the two 87s through an Eventide phaser and recorded that to a third track. If you listen to the song, you can tell we ended up using that."

The remainder of the *Quadrophenia* backing tracks were recorded in 16-track, with the earlier backing tracks copied from 8-track to 16, so the entire album ended up being 16-track. Nevison would go on to record two albums with Bad Company using the LMS: their first, eponymously titled album (done at Headley Grange), and their follow-up, *Straight Shooter*, recorded at Clearwell Castle in west Gloucestershire.

After he left The Faces in 1973, Lane parked the LMS on his farm in Wales. There he recorded his first solo album, *Anymore for Anymore*, followed two years later with *One for the Road*, which featured a picture of the mobile on the album cover. Lane passed away in 1997.

The LMS was sold in 1982, and has since been used by a series of private clients. It underwent a major overhaul in 2009, when the original Helios board was replaced with a Cadac, and the Tannoy monitors upgraded to JBLs, and is still operational today.

SELECTED DISCOGRAPHY

- Ronnie Lane: *Anymore for Anymore*, *One for the Road*
- Eric Clapton: *Rainbow Concert*
- The Who: *Quadrophenia*, *The Who by Numbers*
- Rick Wakeman: *Journey to the Centre of the Earth*
- Bad Company: *Bad Company*, *Straight Shooter*
- Led Zeppelin: *Physical Graffiti*

THE MANOR MOBILES

On July 30, 1973, a truck filled with state-of-the-art recording equipment drove through the gates of millionaire Richard Branson's residential Oxfordshire recording studio, The Manor (see Chapter 8 for more information), and hit the open road for the first time. Its birth had come about as a result of an unusual deal struck between Branson and the studio's new chief technical director, Philip Newell, recently departed from Pye.

"I had brought a lot of redundant [unwanted] equipment with me from Pye," Newell explains, "My plan was to install the gear into a van I owned and turn it into an 8-track mobile recording studio because I still enjoyed doing mobile recordings. The van was parked at The Manor, on Richard's land, and I guess he got wind of what I was doing and wasn't too happy about it. So on New Year's Day 1973, I was told he wanted to see me. We sat in the studio lounge and he gave me an ultimatum: either I took my things and left, or I gave him all my equipment—everything—and in exchange he would give me 20 percent of a new company and the resources to build the world's most advanced mobile recording truck. Obviously, I opted for the latter."

The Manor Mobile, built into a standard 20' freight container, would indeed be the world's first purpose-designed 24-track mobile recording studio, carrying a crew of three to venues all over the U.K. and Europe. Interestingly, at first, the recordings it was making couldn't be mixed at The Manor itself, which was still only 16-track. As a result, two years later, the control room in the studio was rebuilt and upgraded to 24-track—a perfect example, perhaps, of the tail wagging the dog.

The Mobile met with immediate success, with bookings coming in not only from artists signed to Branson's rapidly expanding Virgin label (who received a significant discount), but also from other record companies and the BBC. It soon became apparent that there was sufficient demand to warrant launching a second vehicle, and so, when the Pye Mobile came on the market at the end of the year, it was purchased and repurposed as Manor Mobile Two.

However, the Pye truck was eventually deemed as being too different from the existing Manor Mobile, not only in physical construction, shape, and size, but also in acoustic treatments and monitoring speakers, all making for a completely different sound. Accordingly, as Newell writes in *Recording Studio Design*, "not only was [the Pye Mobile] updated and expanded, but it was refitted into a new vehicle, very similar to the first Manor Mobile. This was specifically done to try to ensure the closest match of monitoring conditions between the two. The crews therefore did not have to remember which truck they were in, or which mental compensation to make."

The Manor Mobile, parked outside its namesake.
(From studio brochure)

The Manor Mobile 24/16/8 track recording truck was primarily designed for the recording of live concerts and for use as a mobile control room when bands wanted to record at places other than conventional studios (country houses etc.). However, it also carries all the necessary equipment for mix-downs and overdubs, and an increasing amount of its available time is now being used for these purposes. Almost every available facility of a normal studio is contained within this unit.

This is one of the most sophisticated mobile recording units in existence today; apart from the many albums which have been recorded with the truck, it is also responsible for a great number of television music programmes and film sound tracks where its flexibility and the experience of its crew are invaluable. The truck has been successfully used for the recording of everything from rock bands to symphony orchestras, solo artists, folk groups, big bands, vocal groups and choirs, indoors and outdoors. Should a band wish to use their own engineer, he will have the full co-operation of the permanent crew.

A Manor Mobile brochure from the mid-1970s showing two views of the truck interior.
(From studio brochure)

A close-up of the Helios submixer used in the Manor Mobile.
(Photo by Philip Newell)

Following the refitting (which occurred in the mid-1980s), the main difference between the two Manor Mobiles was in their consoles—a Helios in the original truck, and a Neve (inherited from Pye) in Mobile Two, as it came to be known. Unfortunately, almost as soon as the new truck was finished, its equipment was stripped out and moved to Virgin artist Mike Oldfield's house to record his *Ommadawn* album, delaying the launch of Mobile Two for almost a year.

"The trucks were like universities because you had to adapt to so many different recording environments," says Newell. "Our experiences using the Manor Mobiles to record in places like castles and stately homes actually influenced the redesign of The Manor studio in 1975 (and later, at Townhouse Studios), because we realized everything didn't have to be of traditional studio design—you could get amazing recordings from 'unconventional' rooms with stone walls, too!" (See Chapter 8 for more information.)

The original Manor Mobile was sold in the early 1980s, shortly after a new vehicle had been built. It was refitted with digital Tascam recorders and a Raindirk console and remained operational into the mid-1990s. Mobile Two was sold in December 1980 and was eventually dismantled.

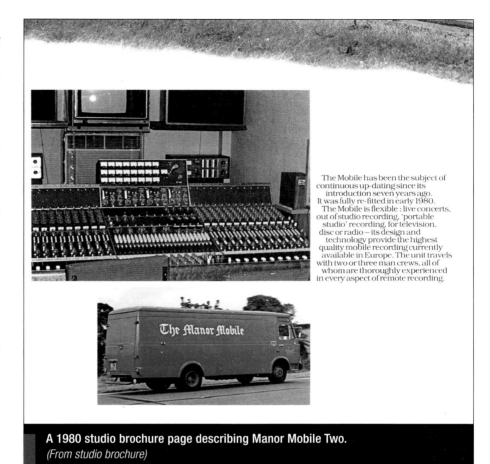

The Mobile has been the subject of continuous up-dating since its introduction seven years ago. It was fully re-fitted in early 1980. The Mobile is flexible : live concerts, out of studio recording, 'portable studio' recording, for television, disc or radio – its design and technology provide the highest quality mobile recording currently available in Europe. The unit travels with two or three man crews, all of whom are thoroughly experienced in every aspect of remote recording.

A 1980 studio brochure page describing Manor Mobile Two.
(From studio brochure)

KEY PERSONNEL
Philip Newell, Ken Capper, Chris Blake, Alan Perkins, Simon Heyworth, Steve Cox, Chris Hollebone, Peter Greenslade, Phil Becque

KEY EQUIPMENT
Monitors
Monitoring in the original Manor Mobile was initially via 12″ Tannoy HPD speakers, later replaced by Altec 604Es.

For more information about the monitoring in Manor Mobile Two, see *The Pye Mobile* above.

Mixing Consoles
The Helios console installed in the original Manor Mobile was a 24 x 24 configuration with basic equalization facilities. A number of ten-channel and six-channel Helios submixers were later installed, giving engineers a total of 40 inputs. "The main

reason for our choice of Helios was because they'd done the desk for the Rolling Stones Mobile and that was getting a very good reputation," says Philip Newell. "It was flexible and it had a very musical sound, plus it was quiet and clean—all things which are especially important in a mobile because you've got to do such a wide range of work, so you can't really have a mixing console that only gets a great sound for a certain type of music."

An additional factor was the electrical efficiency of the Helios desk. "I wanted to run this mobile off a single 13-amp plug because I knew we could get that feed from anywhere and I didn't want to carry a generator around," explains Newell. Another key concern was headroom. "The Helios allowed us to plug things in in ways that you couldn't imagine," he states. "Everything was balanced—even the inserts—and operating at high levels so we could work with television people and take feeds from PAs. After a while, we really started to appreciate how good that console was."

For more information about the Neve console in Manor Mobile Two, see *The Pye Mobile* above.

Tape Machines

The first Manor Mobile was initially equipped with a prototype Ampex MM1100—one of the first ten made and the only 24-track unit in that factory run (all the others were 16-track configurations). "It was a fabulous-sounding machine but terribly unreliable," says Newell. A few years later, this was replaced with two MM1200 24-track machines, a model that was deemed much more trustworthy; in 1980, these were upgraded to either Ampex ATR-124s or Studer A80s.

For more information about the tape machines in Manor Mobile Two, see *The Pye Mobile* above.

Main Microphones

Each Manor Mobile carried a dozen or more Neumann microphones (largely U87s and KM84s), as well as numerous Calrecs and mics from Beyer, AKG and Shure. SM57s and SM58s were most often used for vocals, while a stereo pair of Calrec 1050s were typically hung high above the stage, about 20 yards apart, to capture audience sound.

Outboard Signal Processors

A battery of UREI 1176 limiters served as the mainstay of the Manor Mobile outboard gear rack. "The large amount of headroom supplied by the Helios and Neve desks, as well as the Ampex multitracks, was very, very useful," says Newell, "and that's why we relied so heavily on the 1176s—the needle could go right down to the end and it still didn't sound like it was overcompressed. That would stop you from overloading the tape, but at the same time it wouldn't give you a squashed sound that you couldn't recover from. A lot of the equipment on the Manor Mobile was chosen because it was highly tolerant. Whenever you did a sound check, people would always say, 'Oh, we're definitely not going to play louder than this, definitely not,' but you could almost guarantee that you'd have to leave a 10 dB margin before the concert because during the performance it would be 10 dB louder as they get more of a PA sound, more excitement from the audience, more adrenaline, more everything." (See Chapter 5 for more information.)

The original Manor Mobile also carried an AKG BX20 spring reverb unit, as well as an EMT 240 gold foil.

SELECTED DISCOGRAPHY

- Queen: *Live Killer*
- Mike Oldfield: *The Orchestral Tubular Bells, Exposed*
- Magazine: *Real Life, Secondhand Daylight*
- Frank Zappa: *Sheik Yerbouti*
- Also live recordings by Jethro Tull, Genesis, Yes, The Buzzcocks, XTC, The Band, Joni Mitchell, Little Feat, The Grateful Dead, and Crosby, Stills, Nash & Young

THE ISLAND MOBILE

The Island Mobile was owned by Chris Blackwell's Island Studios (see Chapter 8 for more information). It became operational in 1973 and typically carried a crew of four, along with a backup 12-kilowatt power generator—a new concept for the time. Built with a similar construction to that of the Rolling Stones Mobile, it was outfitted with a 24 x 24 Helios desk, later upgraded to 40 inputs. Also installed were dual 24-track 3M M79 tape recorders and dual Studer A80 1/4" 2-track recorders, with monitoring via JBL 4311s, power amps unknown. Outboard gear included an EMT 240 gold foil and four UREI 1176 limiters. The Island Mobile was used by Marvin Gaye, The Who, John Denver, the Carpenters, Genesis, Roxy Music, and the Wailers.

KEY PERSONNEL

Frank Owen, Robert Ash, Phill Brown, Ray Doyle, Barry Sage

THE ISLAND MOBILE

The clientele say it all - Marvin Gaye, The Who, John Denver, The Carpenters, Genesis, Roxy Music and The Wailers have all recorded highly successful 'live' albums on the truck. During the last two years we have also been first choice for countless major American and U.K. Artists for their T.V. and film soundtracks. We are especially proud of our talented four man crew (Resident Engineer, Assistant Engineer, Technical Engineer and Driver) whose wealth of experience ensure superb results and no problems.
If clients wish to supply their own engineer we are happy to accomodate them, and give every assistance. The Mobile has a custom designed Helios console with 40 inputs and 24 outputs. And the great sound you hear comes from the twin JBL 4311's.
All ancillary equipment is identical to Basing Street Studios. However, the truck boasts 2 x 24 track machines which ensures no stopping for reel changes during 'live' recording. This facility also enables us to drive to your door and do any 24 - 24 transfers or 16 - 24 copies. All this, plus T.V. and sound communications from truck to stage and its own 12 kilowatt generator, means you will get the best results whether you are touring Europe, making an album at a country hideaway, doing a gig in a pub in Leeds, playing a week at Earls Court or making a Movie. (We do them all the time.)

A brochure page showing the Island Mobile, interior and exterior.
(From studio brochure)

The making of *One World*

IN THE SUMMER of 1977, Island CEO Chris Blackwell asked Phill Brown to bring the Island Mobile to his Woolwich Green farm in order to cut tracks for John Martyn's upcoming LP *One World*. "This is where I had recorded overdubs for Robert Palmer's *Pressure Drop* album, two years earlier," wrote Brown in a 1999 Internet posting, "and Chris [liked] the idea of recording outside. He had been impressed by the apparent ease of working this way, the great sound and ambience of vocals and instruments and the extra freedom when working from home. The house was almost totally surrounded by a flooded disused gravel pit, [so it was like] a large lake with a house in the middle."

The Mobile was parked in the courtyard, which provided easy access to a barn and a converted four-bedroom stable block, where Brown, driver Ray Doyle, assistant engineer Barry Sage, and Martyn himself would be living during the course of making the album, using a large self-contained apartment (flat) at the far end as the studio. There was a practical reason for living and recording in the same place. "Doing it out at Chris' house . . . he [always] knew where John would be," Brown wrote in the album's liner notes. "John has his wayward ways and likes disappearing off at certain opportunities . . . [but at Blackwell's house] he couldn't escape!"

Martyn and his guitars, amplifiers, and effects pedals were carefully positioned in the apartment's main 15' by 12' room. "I took direct injection feeds from the guitar and every effects pedal," wrote Brown, "as well as miking up the amplifier. We spent a great deal of time making sure the feeds were as clean as possible."

A PA system was also set up on the far side of the stables, facing out across the lake. "I used two Neumann U87s on the opposite side of the house to mic up the outdoor PA sound coming back off the lake," Brown explains. "A further two Neumann U87s were placed close to the water's edge, as far away as our leads would allow. These picked up . . . a distant strangled sound on the guitar which was perfect for lead solos . . . [They] also recorded scurrying animals, birds, and the sounds of water lapping at the water's edge." Despite the remoteness of the farm, there were occasional interruptions with planes and traffic, so most of the recording done with outside mics was accomplished at night.

"We tried to protect the microphones from the damp night air using polythene [plastic], with limited success," reports Brown. "When they went down, on particularly wet nights or because of a heavy dew, we replaced them and then dried out the originals. Between 3 am and 6 am was the toughest time on the mics, but those quiet hours before dawn created the most magical atmosphere for recording." "I remember thinking this is fucking wonderful," wrote Martyn in the liner notes, "recording from a speaker a half a mile away across a load of water. It was just a cool thing to do. That was *real* ambience."

Continues Brown, "we fell into a routine, starting at about two in the afternoon and working through until five in the morning. . . . It was an idyllic way to record an album. I used six tracks for the guitar, two for the outdoor returns and two more for vocal and basic drum machine. I had control over the blend of the six main guitar sounds because of our separate DI feeds. These included one feed straight out of John's guitar, another after his compressor, one each pre and post F/X and echoes, and finally, one with everything but preamplifier.

"Some of the songs were arranged and recorded quickly and easily. Others were played repeatedly for many hours. Chris and I would then edit the multitrack into an arrangement of verse, chorus and instrumentals, from time to time taking bets on which bar we were on.

"We changed the reels of tape every half hour (we were recording at 15 ips) and took breaks every three or four hours for tea."

Guest musicians like Andy Newmark, Steve Winwood, and Danny Thompson also came by at various times, set up in the self-contained flat with electric piano, Moog, and bass. Most of the songs that ended up on the album included live vocals from Martyn, who, in Brown's words, "at one moment might be sounding warm, mellow and easily in control and at the next would travel to a place of uncomfortable darkness, becoming someone obviously on the edge of his emotions."

(Reprinted with the kind permission of Phill Brown.)

THE RAK MOBILE

As early as 1969, former BBC engineer Doug Hopkins had begun drawing up plans to build a mobile recording truck to use at remote television broadcast locations. Four years later, he was able to realize that dream with the construction of the Trans European Audio Mobile (TEAM). The TEAM was equipped with a customized API 2488 desk that had 24 full channels with EQ, plus an additional 30 auxiliary input channels, for a total of 54 inputs; the board also offered 24 outputs. Other equipment included two 16-track 3M M79 recorders, linked by a Maglink synchronizer, Aengus graphic EQs, an EMT 140 echo plate, and closed-circuit TV.

"The TEAM mobile was designed around what was really the smallest comfortable size that we could actually get all the equipment and two or three people working within it," said Hopkins in a 1984 interview for *Studio Sound* magazine. "That was especially important since the truck itself was below the limit that would require its operator to carry a special HGV license, allowing the engineer himself to drive it."

After about a year of operation, Hopkins received a phone call from producer Mickie Most, who wanted to hire the TEAM mobile to do some long-term recording projects in France. Quickly calculating the rental costs, Hopkins made a joke about how Most should buy the truck instead of renting it . . . and a week later the producer did just that, renaming it the RAK Mobile, predating the land-based RAK Studios by more than two years. (See Chapter 8 for more information.) Following his acquisition, the M79 16-track recorders were replaced by a pair of M79 24-track machines, also linked by a Maglink synchronizer,

The RAK Mobile.
(Courtesy of RAK Studios)

Mickie Most with his pride and joy.
(Courtesy of RAK Studios)

presser, and digital delay line. Usually manned by engineer Tim Summerhayes, the RAK truck carried Neumann, AKG, Beyer, Schoeps, and Shure microphones, several of them condenser models.

The RAK Mobile would be used to record Wings' massive hit single "Mull of Kintyre"—the first record in the U.K. to sell more than two million copies—at Paul and Linda McCartney's farm in Scotland, as well as tracks for McCartney's 1979 *Back to the Egg* album, done at Lympne Castle in Kent. Duran Duran would later record demos for their 1983 album *Seven and the Ragged Tiger* with the RAK Mobile at a chalet

and a pair of 2-track Studer B62s (one a portable model) were added. The monitoring was upgraded to JBL 4310s driven by an Amcron power amplifier, and additional outboard equipment included a UREI limiter and Eventide Phaser, Harmonizer, Omni-

near Cannes in the south of France.

KEY PERSONNEL

Doug Hopkins, Neville Crozier, Tim Summerhayes, Bob Harper

Sitting on the can with cans on

"WE USED TO GO off to France and use a small hotel just outside Paris," RAK Mobile designer and engineer Doug Hopkins recalled, speaking of the early days spent on the road with producer and Mobile owner Mickie Most. "They said if we booked ten people into it, we could have the whole place. It was a little country hotel in the middle of a forest, and it was lovely. There was a period of time when

we were spending something like three months of the year there.

"We generally used their basement for recordings, but I can remember one particular time when we wanted a very live drum sound for a Chris Spedding album we were doing. Mickie always used two drummers to get his particular type of sound and on this occasion we had Tony Carr and Brian Bennett. We

wanted to get an especially 'live' snare sound, and the only place that we could really make it work properly was in a gent's toilet that was all marble. There were two cubicles side by side, so we took the doors off, and then on the closed-circuit television link we could see Brian and Tony actually sitting there playing the snares—both of them sitting on the can with cans on."

MAISON ROUGE MOBILE

The Maison Rouge Mobile, which, like the RAK Mobile, predated the land-based studio of the same name, was owned by the band Jethro Tull. By the mid-'70s, the group had become so successful they had to leave the U.K. for tax reasons, relocating, like the Stones before them, to France. A mobile studio was duly constructed to allow them to record overseas. It became operational in 1975.

Interior of the Maison Rouge Mobile.
(From studio brochure)

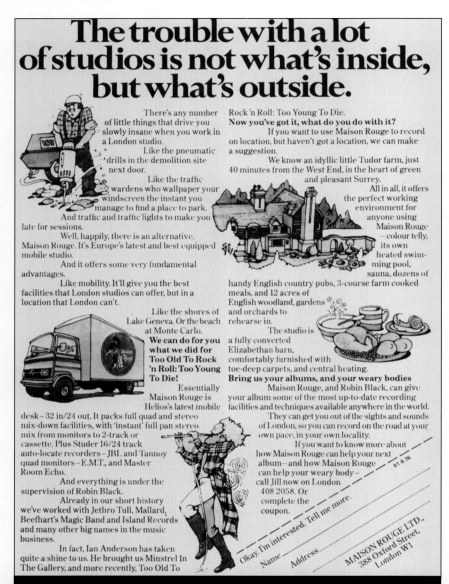

The trouble with a lot of studios is not what's inside, but what's outside.

There's any number of little things that drive you slowly insane when you work in a London studio.

Like the pneumatic drills in the demolition site next door.

Like the traffic wardens who wallpaper your windscreen the instant you manage to find a place to park.

And traffic and traffic lights to make you late for sessions.

Well, happily, there is an alternative. Maison Rouge. It's Europe's latest and best equipped mobile studio.

And it offers some very fundamental advantages.

Like mobility. It'll give you the best facilities that London studios can offer, but in a location that London can't.

Like the shores of Lake Geneva. Or the beach at Monte Carlo. **We can do for you what we did for Too Old To Rock 'n Roll: Too Young To Die!**

Essentially Maison Rouge is Helios's latest mobile desk – 32 in/24 out. It packs full quad and stereo mix-down facilities, with 'instant' full pan stereo mix from monitors to 2-track or cassette. Plus Studer 16/24 track auto-locate recorders – JBL and Tannoy quad monitors – E.M.T., and Master Room Echo.

And everything is under the supervision of Robin Black.

Already in our short history we've worked with Jethro Tull, Mallard, Beefhart's Magic Band and Island Records and many other big names in the music business.

In fact, Ian Anderson has taken quite a shine to us. He brought us Minstrel In The Gallery, and more recently, Too Old To

Rock 'n Roll: Too Young To Die.
Now you've got it, what do you do with it?

If you want to use Maison Rouge to record on location, but haven't got a location, we can make a suggestion.

We know an idyllic little Tudor farm, just 40 minutes from the West End, in the heart of green and pleasant Surrey.

All in all, it offers the perfect working environment for anyone using Maison Rouge – colour telly, its own heated swimming pool, sauna, dozens of handy English country pubs, 3-course farm cooked meals, and 12 acres of English woodland, gardens and orchards to rehearse in.

The studio is a fully converted Elizabethan barn, comfortably furnished with toe-deep carpets, and central heating.

Bring us your albums, and your weary bodies

Maison Rouge, and Robin Black, can give your album some of the most up-to-date recording facilities and techniques available anywhere in the world.

They can get you out of the sights and sounds of London, so you can record on the road at your own pace, in your own locality.

If you want to know more about how Maison Rouge can help your next album – and how Maison Rouge can help your weary body – call Jill now on London 408 2058. Or complete the coupon.

Okay, I'm interested. Tell me more.

Name _____ Address _____

MAISON ROUGE LTD.,
388 Oxford Street,
London W1

An ad for the Maison Rouge Mobile, 1976.

Designed by Peter Smith (formerly of IBC) and operated by ex-Morgan engineer Robin Black, the Maison Rouge Mobile was housed in a Mercedes truck and equipped with a 32 x 24 Helios desk, Studer A80 16- and 24-track recorders, Tannoy and JBL monitors, and both Master Room and EMT 240 reverbs. It became operational in 1975 and was used for the Tull albums *Minstrel in the Gallery* and *Too Old to Rock 'n' Roll: Too Young to Die*, both recorded in Monte Carlo; it was also used by Queen and other popular English bands of the era.

When it was not on the road, the truck was parked a special soundproofed garage next to Maison Rouge Studios in Fulham, London, with tielines to the main studio to allow for multitrack copying; this also enabled the mobile to be used as a remix room during idle periods.

The Maison Rouge Mobile was sold by the band when they returned to the U.K. in 1979 and remained unused for four years. Incredibly, it was stolen in 1983 and vanished without a trace!

GLOSSARY

A&R—An acronym for "Artists and Repertoire," a title for a person at a record company tasked with finding artists to sign and obtaining material for them to record.

absorber—A box, panel, or frame (usually wooden) designed to absorb sound at certain specific frequencies. Absorbers are normally filled with dense materials like fiberglass and covered with fabric such as burlap in order to minimize reflections. (See **reflections**.)

acoustic treatment—Refers to the techniques and materials used to alter a space in order to improve its sonic characteristics.

ADT—An acronym for "Artificial Double Tracking" (sometimes called *Automatic Double Tracking*), a tape-based doubling technique invented by Ken Townsend at Abbey Road.

AES—An acronym for the Audio Engineering Society, an international professional organization.

ambient sound—Diffuse, reflected sound coming from the walls, ceiling and floor of a space, as opposed to direct sound. (See **diffusion**, **direct sound**, and **reflected sound**.)

analog—In recording, refers to the process of converting a sound to an electrical signal (the function of a microphone), amplifying that signal to a sufficiently high level (the function of a mic preamp), then converting it to magnetic signal (the function of a record head) and storing it on tape (or converted to physical movement and storing it on vinyl [the function of a cutting lathe]), and, finally, playing it back through monitors, where the signal is converted back to a sound. (See **condenser microphone**, **cutting lathe**, **mic preamp**, **monitor**, and **record head**.)

assistant engineer—An entry-level position at a recording studio, sometimes known in the U.K. studios of the '60s and '70s as a *teaboy*. Assistant engineers can be responsible for anything from making the coffee (or tea) to setting up and tearing down the equipment and microphones needed for a session. In the days of analog recording, they were also generally responsible for operating the tape machine(s), hence the alternate names *tape operator*, or, simply *tape op*.

attack time—In a dynamics processor such as a compressor, limiter, expander, or noise gate, the amount of time it takes for the gain of a signal to initially be altered. Fast attack times catch transients, altering their level and thus, in the case of compressors and limiters, "softening" the sound. Slower attack times allow transient signals to pass through unscathed. (See **compressor**, **dynamics processor**, **expander**, **gain**, **limiter**, **noise gate**, **overshoot**, and **transient**.)

attenuation—The reduction of signal level.

attenuator—A device which reduces signal level. (See **attenuation** and **pad**.)

aux—Short for "auxiliary." (See **auxiliary**.)

auxiliary—On a mixing board, a secondary input, output, send, or return. (See **input**, **mixing board**, **output**, **return**, and **send**.)

backing track—The basic instrumental foundation of a song (usually consisting of bass, drums, and rhythm guitar and/or keyboard, plus a rough, or "guide" vocal), or the overall instrumental accompaniment to a song with vocals. (See **tracking**.)

baffle—A movable acoustic barrier, sometimes called a *gobo*. Also refers to the boxlike enclosure for a loudspeaker or monitor. (See **monitor**.)

balanced—An audio connection in which the signal is carried by two conductors, one out of phase with the other (and neither connected to the braided metal shield, which serves as ground) in order to reduce hum and electrostatic or electromagnetic noise, as well as to minimize signal loss, thus allowing the use of long cable runs. (See **unbalanced**.)

band—In equalizers, refers to the range of frequencies that can be boosted or cut. (See **boost**, **cut**, **equalizer**, **frequency**, and **graphic equalizer**.)

bandwidth—In a parametric equalizer, refers to the range of the frequency band being affected. Sometimes used interchangeably with the term *frequency response*. (See **frequency response** and **parametric equalizer**.)

bass trap—A special type of absorber designed to reduce low frequencies and/or eliminate standing waves. (See **absorber**, **low-frequency**, **standing wave**, and **trapping**.)

bidirectional—A type of microphone that mostly picks up sounds coming from the front and the rear, as opposed to sounds coming from the sides. Sometimes referred to as a *figure-of-eight* polar pattern. (See **figure-of-eight** and **polar pattern**.)

board—See **mixing board**.

boost—In audio, to raise the level of a signal.

bottom end—See **low-frequency**.

bus—In audio, a signal path capable of routing multiple ("grouped") input signals to a particular destination. (See **group**.)

bussing—The act of routing one or more input signals to a particular destination or destinations. (See **bus** and **group**.)

capstan—In a tape recorder, the rotating vertical shaft (driven by a specialized motor) that moves the tape past the tape heads. (See **tape head**.)

cardioid—A directional microphone with a polar pattern that mostly picks up sounds coming from directly in front while less sensitive to sounds coming from the sides and the rear. (See **directional**, **hypercardioid**, and **polar pattern**.)

CCIR—An acronym for the European standards organization Comité Consultatif International pour la Radio.

channel—On a mixing board, refers to an input signal (which may come from a microphone or a line-level input such as a recorded track or an external signal processor). The corresponding *channel strip* allows gain control, panning, equalization, and bussing of the signal, as well as enabling it to be routed to various outboard signal processors via auxiliary sends and returns. (See **auxiliary**, **bussing**, **equalization**, **line-level**, **outboard**, **panning**, **return**, **send**, and **signal processor**.)

coaxial—A loudspeaker design in which the individual driver units radiate sound from the same point or axis. (See **driver**.)

compander—A device which **com**presses an incoming signal and then correspondingly ex**pand**s it upon output, thereby restoring it while significantly reducing the level of noise coming from tape. Noise reduction devices made by companies such as Dolby and dbx were specialized companders. (See **compressor**, **expander**, and **noise reduction**.)

compression driver—A type of speaker design (originally developed by Bell Labs in the 1930s) in which a tiny driver is placed on the small end of a horn, with the driver providing a relatively high sound pressure at the throat of the horn, and the mouth of the horn providing a large area of low pressure to radiate the sound efficiently into the air. (See **driver**.)

compression ratio—In a compressor, the amount of increase in input signal required to cause a 1 decibel increase in output. A ratio of 1:1 means that for every 1 dB (decibel) of increase in input level, there is a 1 dB increase in output level; in other words, there is no compression being applied. A ratio of 8:1 means that an 8 dB increase in input is required to produce only a 1 dB increase in output. (See **compressor** and **decibel**.)

compressor—In audio, a device in which the level of a sound is automatically reduced during louder passages, thus constraining the overall dynamic range and making it easier to hear quiet passages. Compressors also typically add "punch" to a signal. Devices called *limiters* do much the same thing, but in a more severe fashion. (See **dynamic range** and **limiter**.)

condenser microphone—A type of microphone comprised of a thin stretched diaphragm near a metal disk (called a *backplate*) which receives power from an external voltage source. Incoming sound causes the diaphragm to move slightly, thus causing equivalent ("analog") variations in the voltage output. Condenser microphones tend to have better frequency and transient response than dynamic microphones and by their nature are omnidirectional; however, design changes can cause them to exhibit different polar patterns, such as cardioid, hypercardioid, or figure-

of-eight. (See **analog**, **cardioid**, **dynamic microphone**, **figure-of-eight**, **hypercardioid**, and **omnidirectional**.)

console—See **mixing board**.

control room—A specialized room housing a mixing board, monitors, recording equipment, and signal processors. Control rooms generally receive acoustic treatment in order to provide an accurate listening and mixing environment. (See **acoustic treatment**, **mix**, **mixing board**, **monitors**, and **signal processor**.)

copying room—A room (generally with some acoustic treatment) housing two or more playback/recording devices and one or more pairs of monitors, designed to allow accurate copies of recordings to be made. (See **acoustic treatment** and **monitors**.)

crossover—A filter inside a loudspeaker that splits up the incoming signal into different frequency areas (at the *crossover frequencies*), which are then routed to the appropriate speaker drivers. For example, in a 2-way speaker, the high (treble) frequencies are routed to a tweeter, while the low (bass) frequencies are routed to a woofer. (See **filter** and **frequency**.)

crosstalk—Signal leaking from one channel or track onto another. (See **channel** and **track**.)

cue mixer—A compact headphone mixer which receives multiple channels of foldback signal from the mixing board, thus allowing musicians in a studio to adjust individual levels during performance. (See **channel**, **foldback**, and **mixing board**.)

cut—In audio, refers to the reduction of signal. (See **attenuation**.)

cutoff frequency—The frequency at which a filter begins to significantly affect a sound. (See **filter**, **frequency**, **high-pass filter**, **low-pass filter**, **notch filter**, and **shelving filter**.)

cutting lathe—A large, heavy machine on which grooves are cut into a wax, vinyl or acetate disc. (See **disc cutting**.)

cutting room—See **mastering room**.

dB—Shorthand for decibel. (See **decibel**.)

dead—In acoustics, refers to a room with little reflected sound. Interior treatments that contain a lot of hard surfaces such glass, stone, or metal result in a "live" sound, while room treatments comprised of soft or porous materials such as carpeting, draperies and upholstered furniture, cause the sound to become more "dead." (See **live** and **reflected sound**.)

decay time—The amount of time it takes for a signal to die away to silence.

decibel—A logarithmic unit of measurement that indicates relative sound intensity. (See **dB**.)

de-esser—A specialized kind of dynamics processor designed to reduce vocal sibilance. De-essing is essentially frequency-sensitive compression in which the frequencies in the 3–7 kHz range are boosted on a sidechain input signal, while all other frequencies are cut. The compressor's detector therefore reacts to and reduces the gain of that portion of the signal alone (See **boost**, **cut**, **dynamics processor**, **high-frequency**, **low-frequency**, **midrange**, **sibilance**, and **sidechain**.)

delay—In audio, refers to a discrete echo. In the jargon of the '60s and '70s, signal processors (both analog and digital) that delayed signal were sometimes called *delay lines*. (See **echo**, **signal processor**, and **tape delay**.)

desk—See **mixing board**.

DI—Short for "Direct Injection." A DI box converts the low-level unbalanced signal coming from an electric bass (or guitar) into a higher-level balanced signal that can be connected directly to a line-level input of a mixing board. (See **balanced**, **line-level**, **mixing board**, and **unbalanced**.)

diaphragm—In microphones, refers to an element which moves in response to changes in air pressure, not unlike the eardrum. Generally speaking, small-diaphragm microphones (i.e., those with diaphragms that have diameters of less than an inch) offer better transient and high-frequency response than large-diaphragm mics; however, large-diaphragm mics have improved low-frequency response and less self-noise, and can often withstand higher sound pressure levels (SPLs) without distorting. (See **high-frequency**, **low-frequency**, **SPL**, and **transient**.)

diffusion—In audio design, refers to the degree to which sound waves are scattered. Diffusion reduces or eliminates discrete echoes (which can blur or destructively combine with the direct sound), instead spreading the sound evenly throughout a room in a broad array of reflected sound. (See **direct sound**, **echo**, and **reflected sound**.)

digital—In recording, refers to the process of converting sound into a stream of binary numbers (that is, the numbers 0 and 1) at a high rate of speed (called the *sampling rate*) and with a particular degree of definition (called *bit resolution*). While proven in theory as early as 1929, digital technology as applied to audio did not become practical until the early 1970s.

direct sound—The sound emanating from the source, as opposed to *reflected sound*, which is produced by the direct sound bouncing off hard surfaces such as walls, floors, and ceilings. (See **reflected sound**.)

directional—In acoustics, refers to the degree to which the location of a sound source can be identified ("localized"). Also refers to microphones with cardioid or hypercardioid polar patterns, which are mostly sensitive to sounds coming from directly in front, as opposed to sounds coming from the sides and the rear. (See **bidirectional**, **cardioid**, **hypercardioid**, **omnidirectional**, and **polar pattern**.)

disc cutting—Refers to the process of cutting grooves into a wax, vinyl or acetate disc. (See **cutting lathe** and **mastering room**.)

disc cutting room—See **mastering room**.

double-track—Recording two versions of the same material in order to thicken the sound. In rock music, vocals and guitars are often double-tracked.

driver—In audio, refers to the individual components in a loudspeaker system that produce sound. A high-frequency driver is sometimes called a *tweeter*, while a low-frequency driver is sometimes called a *woofer*. (See **high-frequency** and **low-frequency**.)

dropout—See **tape dropout**.

dropping in—Engaging recording while a track is playing back so as to replace previously recorded material. Sometimes called *punching in*.

dropping out—Stopping recording while a track is playing back in order to stop the replacement of previously recorded in material. Sometimes called *punching out*.

drum booth—An isolation booth specially designed to house a drum kit and drummer. (See **isolation booth**.)

dual concentric—A type of coaxial speaker design (trademarked by Tannoy) which places the tweeter behind the center of the woofer. (See **coaxial**.)

dubbing—The act of adding sound to film.

dubbing theater—A specialized room designed for dubbing to film. Dubbing theaters are equipped with both audio and film equipment as well as a projection screen and normally offer at least one isolation booth, along with cinema-like seating and sound system. (See **dubbing**.)

dynamic microphone—A type of microphone comprised of a plastic diaphragm attached to a coil of wire that sits inside a magnet. Incoming sound causes the diaphragm and attached coil to move slightly, thus causing equivalent ("analog") variations in the magnetic field and voltage output. Unlike condenser microphones, dynamic microphones do not require external power and are generally more rugged and able to withstand higher sound pressure levels (SPLs). (See **analog**, **condenser microphone**, and **SPL**.)

dynamic range—A measure of the ratio between the loudest and softest parts of a sound, measured in decibels (dB). (See **decibel** and **dynamics processor**.)

dynamics processor—A device (such as a compressor, limiter, or expander) that alters the dynamic range of a sound. Compressors and limiters decrease the dynamic range by reducing the level of the loudest parts of a signal, while expanders increase the dynamic range by reducing the level of the softest parts of a signal. (See **compressor**, **dynamic range**, **expander**, and **limiter**.)

echo—In audio, a repetition of a sound. (See **delay**.)

echo chamber—A small room, usually with live acoustics, that houses a loudspeaker into which selected signal is routed, along with one or more microphones to pick up the resultant reverberant ("wet") sound, which is then returned to the mixing board in order to be added to the original "dry" signal. (See **live**.)

echo return—On a mixing board, an auxiliary input normally used to receive signal from a device producing echo, delay, or reverb. (See **auxiliary**, **delay**, **echo**, **mixing board**, **return**, and **reverb**.)

echo send—On a mixing board, an auxiliary output normally used to send signal to a device producing echo, delay, or reverb. (See **auxiliary**, **delay**, **echo**, **mixing board**, **reverb**, and **send**.)

edit—In analog recording, this is accomplished by physically cutting and splicing together different pieces of tape.

EQ—An acronym for "equalization" or "equalizer." (See **equalization** and **equalizer**.)

equalization—The process of altering specific frequency areas within a signal. Most mixing boards provide equalization controls on a per-channel basis, though this can often be accomplished with greater precision by using standalone outboard equalizers. (See **channel**, **equalizer**, **mixing board**, and **outboard**.)

equalizer—A device (most usually outboard) which provides controls for altering specific frequency areas in a signal. Among the most common kinds of equalizers are *graphic equalizers* and *parametric equalizers*. (See **equalization**, **frequency**, **graphic equalizer**, **outboard**, and **parametric equalizer**.)

erase head—The tape head which demagnetizes the tape (thus erasing any signal which might have been previously recorded) before it reaches the record head. (See **record head** and **tape head**.)

expander—A device that increases the dynamic range of a sound by reducing the level of the softest parts of the signal. (See **dynamic range** and **noise gate**.)

fader—A linear potentiometer most often used to control the level of a signal. Each channel on a mixing board typically includes a fader so that the engineer can alter levels in real time while blending ("mixing") multiple signals together. (See **channel**, **mixing**, **mixing board**, and **potentiometer**.)

feedback—In audio, the howl that results when a transducer such as a microphone or guitar pickup is placed too close to the speaker reproducing the sound. (See **transducer**.)

FET—An acronym for "Field-Effect Transistor," a specialized solid-state component sometimes found in microphones or amplifiers, typically used for amplifying or switching electronic signals. (See **MOS-FET**.)

figure-of-eight—A bidirectional polar pattern. (See **bidirectional** and **polar pattern**.)

filter—In audio, a type of equalizer which reduces or removes ("filters out") specific frequency areas of a signal. (See **equalizer**, **frequency**, **high-pass filter**, **low-pass filter**, **notch filter**, and **shelving filter**.)

flanging—An effect made popular in the '60s whereby a signal is combined with a slightly delayed version of itself, with the amount of delay changing over time. In the days of tape recording, this variation would be accomplished with the use of a manual varispeed control or a tape operator's finger against the flange of the delay machine's tape reel (hence the name); alternatively, the modulation can be accomplished through the application of a control voltage from a low frequency oscillator (LFO) or via digital signal processing. However flanging is derived, the result is a characteristic sound similar to that of a jet airplane passing overhead. (See **phasing** and **varispeed**.)

flat—In recording, refers to a response without any appreciable cut or boost in any frequency area. (See **boost** and **cut**.)

Fletcher-Munson curve—A graph that illustrates how the human brain perceives different frequencies at different levels. Sometimes referred to as an "equal-loudness contour." (See **frequency** and **level**.)

flutter—Slight unwanted rapid variations in speed. (See **wow**.)

foldback—The section of an audio system that provides amplified sound to the musicians in the studio so that they can hear themselves while recording and overdubbing. (See **overdubbing**.)

frequency—In audio, a measure of how many times per second a sound wave repeats itself, measured in hertz (Hz) and kilohertz (kHz). The human ear can generally detect sounds with frequencies between approximately 20 Hz and 20 kHz; this is known as the *audible range*. Low frequencies (waves with lower repeat rates, such as those emanating from bass drums and the lowest notes on a piano) are felt as rumbles and are mostly non-directional (that is, they appear to be coming from everywhere), while higher frequencies (those with faster repeat rates, such as those emanating from cymbals and high guitar notes) can be piercing and are highly directional (that is, they appear to be coming from a particular location). Sounds above the audible range are termed *ultrasonic*, while those below are termed *subsonic* or *infrasonic*. (See **high-frequency**, **Hz**, **kHz**, and **low-frequency**.)

frequency response—A measure of how well a device reproduces signal across different frequency areas, sometimes referred to as *bandwidth*. (See **frequency**.)

gain—In audio, the amount of increase in the power of an output signal relative to the input signal; for example, the increase in the raw signal from a microphone before it is routed into other electronic components. Each channel of a mixing board typically has a gain control, used to raise the input signal to a sufficient level for the rest of the controls on the board to work properly. Sometimes used interchangeably used with *level* and *volume*, though technically different. (See **channel**, **input**, **level**, **mixing board**, **output**, and **volume**.)

gate—See **noise gate**.

gobo—See **baffle**.

graphic equalizer—A specialized type of equalizer that offers numerous frequency areas, or *bands*, each controlled by a slider that applies cut or boost, thus providing a graphic view of the equalization curve. (See **boost**, **cut**, **equalizer**, and **parametric equalizer**.)

group—In audio, another name for a bus (a signal path capable of combining multiple input signals so they can be routed to a particular destination). Sometimes referred to as a *subgroup*.

Harmonizer—A specialized signal processor capable of altering the pitch of an incoming signal. The output of a

Harmonizer is normally combined with the original in order to produce thickening effects or two- (or more) note harmony. (See **signal processor**.)

headblock—An assembly of three tape heads mounted on a rigid base plate, in the following order from left to right: erase head, record (sync) head, then playback (repro) head. Sometimes called a *head stack*. (See **erase head**, **playback head**, **record head**, **sync head**, and **tape head**.)

headroom—A measure of the difference between the highest level of an input signal and the maximum level a recording device or power amplifier can output without noticeable distortion. The more headroom, the less distortion, even at high volumes.

hertz—See **Hz**.

hessian cloth—British vernacular for burlap, a coarse fabric often used to cover studio and control room walls, as well as baffles and acoustic absorbers. (See **absorber** and **baffle**.)

high-frequency—Generally refers to frequencies in the range of 5 kHz (5,000 wave cycles per second) to 20 kHz (20,000 cycles per second). Sometimes called *treble* or *top end*. (See **frequency**, **Hz**, and **kHz**.)

high-pass filter—A specialized filter which reduces or removes frequencies below a user-specified *cutoff frequency*, thus allowing frequencies above that point to pass through unaltered. (See **cutoff frequency**, **filter**, **frequency**, **low-pass filter**, and **notch filter**.)

hypercardioid—A highly directional microphone with a polar pattern that mostly picks up sounds coming from directly in front while less sensitive to sounds coming from the sides, and almost completely rejecting sounds coming from the rear. (See **cardioid**, **directional**, and **polar pattern**.)

Hz—Shorthand for hertz, a unit of measurement that indicates one wave cycle per second.

IEC—An acronym for the European standards organization International Electrotechnical Commission. (See **CCIR**.)

input—On a mixing board, the point at which a signal enters.

insert—On a mixing board, a point in a channel at which signal flow can be broken. Insert jacks are usually three-conductor, with connections for both an input (the *insert return*) and an output (the *insert send*). Inserts are generally used to route signal to and from outboard signal processors at line level. (See **channel**, **input**, **mixing board**, **outboard**, **output**, **return**, **send**, and **signal processor**.)

ips—An acronym for inches per second, used to indicate tape speed; generally, the higher the tape speed, the better the sound quality.

isolation booth—A small, generally windowed room within a recording studio in which a vocalist or musician can be placed (along with a microphone and headphones) in order to be acoustically isolated from the other performers.

kHz—Kilohertz, or 1,000 hertz (1,000 wave cycles per second). Sometimes referred to simply as "k" (as in "10k"). (See **Hz**.)

kilohertz—See **kHz**.

lathe—See **cutting lathe**.

leakage—In recording, refers to the amount of unwanted sound ("bleed") from an instrument to the microphone(s) capturing the sound of other instruments or vocalists in the same room.

Leslie—A wooden cabinet containing a biamplified speaker system where the top speaker rotates in order to introduce a distinctive vibrato (periodic wobbling of the pitch). Originally designed for use with the Hammond organ, The Beatles popularized its use as a guitar amplifier and outboard signal processor. (See **outboard** and **signal processor**.)

level—In audio, a term used to describe the magnitude of a sound in SPL (sound pressure level). Sometimes used interchangeably with *gain* and *volume*, though technically different. (See **gain**, **SPL**, and **volume**.)

leveling amplifier—A term commonly used in the '50s and '60s to describe compressors such as the Teletronix LA-2A (which "leveled" a sound by reducing its dynamic range). (See **compressor** and **dynamic range**.)

lift—British terminology for "boost." (See **boost**.)

light orchestra—A mainly British style of music which features short orchestral pieces and suites designed to appeal to a wider audience, as opposed to more "serious" classical compositions.

limiter—A dynamics processor in which the level of a sound is automatically reduced severely during the loudest passages, thus preventing overload and distortion. Compressors are more gentle forms of limiters. (See **compressor** and **dynamics processor**.)

line-level—Refers to the relatively high signal level (typically 1.228 volts in the case of professional-grade equipment) provided by the output of preamplifiers, recording devices, DI boxes, and signal processors. Line-level inputs (which are significantly "hotter" than mic-level inputs) are sometimes referred to simply as "line" inputs. (See **DI**, **mic-level**, **mic preamp**, and **signal processor**.)

lineup tape—A special tape prerecorded with test tones at various levels, used to assist in making adjustments on tape machines such as azimuth (head gap alignment).

live—In acoustics, refers to a room with a good deal of reflected sound. Interior treatments that contain a lot of hard surfaces such glass, stone, or metal result in a "live" sound, while room treatments comprised of soft or porous materials such as carpeting, draperies and upholstered furniture, cause the sound to become more "dead." (See **dead** and **reflected sound**.)

Live End / Dead End—Sometimes referred to by the trademarked acronym LEDE, this was a form of control room acoustic treatment popularized in the 1970s in which the area around the monitors was significantly deadened, while the remainder of the room (behind the listener) was made "live" (reflective). Its main purpose was to stagger the arrivals of direct and reflected sound so as to minimize interference between the two during monitoring. (See **control room**, **dead**, **direct sound**, **live**, **monitor**, **monitoring**, and **reflected sound**.)

low end—See **low-frequency**.

low-frequency—Generally refers to frequencies in the range of 20 Hz (20 wave cycles per second) to around 400 Hz (400 cycles per second). Sometimes called *bass* or *low end*. (See **frequency** and **Hz**.)

low-pass filter—A specialized filter which reduces or removes frequencies above a user-specified *cutoff frequency*, thus allowing frequencies below that point to pass through unaltered. (See **cutoff frequency**, **filter**, **frequency**, **high-pass filter**, and **notch filter**.)

machine room—An acoustically isolated room in a recording studio in which recording devices and power amplifiers are housed, along with patch bays that allow tieline access to the equipment from other areas such as the control room(s). (See **patch bay** and **tieline**.)

mains—English terminology for the electric power supply.

maintenance engineer—In a recording studio, a person tasked with repairing, maintaining (and sometimes setting up, installing, customizing, and/or designing) equipment. In the U.K., maintenance engineers are often referred to as *technical engineers*.

mastering—The process of taking a mix and making global (and usually very fine) sonic adjustments such as the application of equalization and dynamics processing in order to optimize fidelity prior to cutting the signal to disc or creating a master tape or hard drive. Mastering also often involves level matching and song sequencing and is the final step prior to manufacture and/or distribution. (See **disc cutting**, **mastering engineer**, and **mastering room**.)

mastering engineer—An engineer skilled in the art of mastering. (See **mastering**.)

mastering room—A specialized room in a recording studio outfitted with playback and recording devices as well as signal processors designed specifically for mastering purposes. (See **mastering**.)

matrix—In audio, refers to the routing of multiple signals to multiple destinations.

mic—Short for "microphone."

mic-level—Refers to the extremely low-voltage signals typically generated by microphones (usually on the order of 1 millivolt, or one thousandth of a volt). Mic-level input signals (which are significantly lower in voltage than line-level input signals) are sometimes referred to simply as "mic" inputs. (See **DI**, **line-level**, **mic preamp**, **preamp**, and **signal processor**.)

mic preamp—An amplifier specifically designed to increase a mic-level signal to line-level in a transparent or sonically pleasing fashion, and with minimal distortion. Each channel of a mixing board will contain a mic preamp (sometimes called *mic pres* or *mic amps*) but they are also available as standalone outboard devices. (See **channel**, **line-level**, **mic-level**, **mixing board**, and **outboard**.)

mid—Short for "midrange." (See **midrange**.)

midrange—Generally refers to frequencies in the range of 400 Hz (400 wave cycles per second) to 5 kHz (20,000 cycles per second). These are sometimes further divided into low-midrange (400 Hz to 2.5 kHz) and high-midrange (2.5 kHz to 5 kHz); the latter is sometimes called *presence*. (See **frequency**, **Hz**, and **kHz**.)

millisecond—A thousandth of a second.

mix—The process of combining the recorded tracks for a song into a mono or stereo signal. This involves carefully creating a balance by adjusting each track's level, panning, equalization and dynamics, and adding effects such as reverb, delay, and time-based modulation such as flanging or phasing (to individual tracks, groups of tracks, or the entire blend) as desired. Sometimes also refers to the final result of the mixing process. (See **delay**, **dynamics processor**, **equalization**, **flanging**, **group**, **level**, **mono**, **panning**, **phasing**, **reverb**, and **track**.)

mix automation—Computer-assisted mixing. (See **mixing**.)

mixing—The process of creating a mix. Sometimes referred to as *remixing*, even when it is the first time a song is being mixed. (See **mix**.)

mixing board—A device which allows multiple signals to be combined in various ways. Mixing boards typically provide numerous channels, each of which are outfitted with mic preamps, faders, mute and solo switches, equalization (and sometimes dynamics processing) controls, echo sends and returns, and auxiliary inputs and outputs, as well as a dedicated monitoring section and a foldback system. Sometimes referred to as a *mixing console*, *mixing desk*, or simply *board*, *desk*, or *console*, this is typically the largest, and most expensive, piece of equipment in a recording studio. (See **auxiliary**, **channel**, **dynamics processor**, **echo return**, **echo send**, **equalization**, **fader**, **foldback**, **mic preamp**, **monitoring**, **mute**, and **solo**.)

module—In recording, a group of electronic components designed to act together on an audio signal. A mixing board or tape recorder with a modular design incorporates a series of identical modules (one or more per channel or track), making it easy to service. (See **channel** and **track**.)

monitor—A studio-quality loudspeaker.

monitoring—Listening to material (live or recorded) over studio-quality loudspeakers.

mono—Refers to single-channel audio (as opposed to dual-channel *stereo*), where each loudspeaker reproduces the same signal, even if multiple loudspeakers are used.

MOS-FET—An acronym for Metal-Oxide-Semiconductor Field-Effect Transistor. (See **FET**.)

ms—Short for "millisecond." (See **millisecond**.)

multitrack—A tape machine (or any recording device) that provides more than two tracks for recording. (See **track**.)

mute—On a mixing board, a switch that temporarily turns off a channel.

NAB—An acronym for the American standards organization National Association of Broadcasters.

noise gate—Essentially an extreme form of an expander, a noise gate is a device that turns off or severely reduces the level of a signal when that signal drops below a user-specified threshold. (See **expander**.)

noise reduction—A process for reducing the noise coming off tape. The two most popular types of tape noise reduction devices in the 1970s and beyond were essentially specialized companders made by the American companies Dolby and dbx. (See **compander**.)

notch filter—A specialized filter which provides two or more user-specified *cutoff frequencies*, so that multiple frequency areas can be affected simultaneously. (See **cutoff frequency**, **filter**, and **frequency**.)

omni—Short for "omnidirectional." (See **omnidirectional**.)

omnidirectional—A type of microphone that is equally sensitive to sounds coming from all directions. Sometimes referred to as *omni* for short.

oscillator—An electronic device which generates a periodic signal at a particular frequency, typically used for testing audio equipment. (See **frequency**.)

outboard—Refers to equipment that is external to a mixing board, such as signal processors, reverb devices, etc. The inputs and outputs to and from outboard gear are typically accessed via a patch bay. (See **mixing board**, **patch bay**, and **signal processor**.)

output—On a mixing board, the point at which a signal exits.

overdub—New material added to previously recorded material.

overdubbing—The act of adding instruments or vocals to previously recorded material.

overshoot—The initial excessive amount of signal level that passes through a compressor or limiter with an insufficiently fast attack time. (See **attack time**, **compressor**, and **limiter**.)

pad—An attenuator, usually with a fixed amount of signal reduction. (See **attenuation** and **attenuator**.)

panning—The act of positioning or moving a sound across the left-right stereo soundfield, usually accomplished with a panpot. (See **panpot**.)

panpot—A potentiometer (usually rotary) specially designed to route signal to any continuous point in a left-right stereo soundfield. (See **panning** and **potentiometer**.)

parametric equalizer—A specialized type of precision equalizer which offers variable "Q" (bandwidth) in addition to selectable frequencies and cut/boost controls. (See **bandwidth**, **boost**, **cut**, **equalizer**, and **frequency**.)

passive—In recording, refers to any device which contains no amplification circuitry and thus needs no external power to operate.

patch bay—A panel containing a collection of jacks which enable equipment to be interconnected with the use of short, specialized cables known as *patch cords*.

patching—The act of plugging and unplugging patch cords into a patch bay in order to interconnect equipment. (See **patch bay**.)

phantom power—The power required by condenser microphones, generally +48 volts. (See **condenser microphones**.)

phase—A measure, in degrees, of the position of a sound wave (or an analog or digital representation of a sound wave) at a certain point in time. When two or more input signals of different phase (i.e., "out-of-phase" signals) are combined—for example, from two microphones at differing distances from a single sound source—cancellations result, often degrading the audio. For this reason, many mixing boards provide phase reversal controls on each channel.

phasing—A "swooshing" effect caused by the phase cancellations that occur when an audio signal is combined with a slightly delayed (and sometimes slightly filtered) copy of itself. Sometimes called *phase shifting*. (See **flanging** and **phase**.)

pink noise—A type of noise which contains equal amounts of energy in each octave band. Pink noise is derived by filtering random *white noise*. (See **white noise**.)

plate—See **reverb plate**.

playback head—The tape head which senses the magnetic flux recorded on tape and converts it to electrical signal which can then be amplified to drive a speaker system in order to be heard as sound. Sometimes referred to as the *reproduce head* or *repro head*. (See **tape head**.)

polar pattern—A plot of the sensitivity of an audio device as a function of various angles around the device. In microphones, the polar pattern describes directional sensitivity—important since it tells the user how to position a particular make and model of microphone in order to obtain the optimal sound. Common mic polar patterns include *cardioid*, *hypercardioid*, *omnidirectional*, and *figure-of-eight*. (See **cardioid**, **figure-of-eight**, **hypercardioid**, and **omnidirectional**.)

pop shield—An acoustically transparent piece of material such as foam or nylon, placed over or in front of a microphone in order to reduce wind noise or plosives such as popping "p's." Sometimes referred to as a *pop filter*, *windscreen*, or *windsock*.

pot—Short for "potentiometer." (See **potentiometer**.)

potentiometer—A variable resistor controlled by a rotary knob or linear fader, typically used in audio devices to control volume or tone. (See **fader**.)

PPM—Short for "Peak Program Meter," a type of meter that responds to the peak (maximum) level of a signal (as opposed to a *VU meter*, which responds to average level). (See **VU**.)

preamp—See **mic preamp**.

pre-delay—An effect that simulates the acoustic response of large concert halls, where there is an audible delay between the initial impulse (the direct sound) and the onset of reverb occurring from reflected sound. In the studios of the '60s and '70s, this was often accomplished by routing signal to a tape machine before sending it to a reverb plate; the gap between the record and playback heads (the timing of which could be lengthened or shortened by adjusting the tape speed) was responsible for creating the pre-delay. (See **direct sound**, **playback head**, **record head**, **reflected sound**, **reverb**, and **reverb plate**.)

presence—High-midrange frequencies (2.5 kHz–5 kHz). (See **midrange**.)

producer—Roughly equivalent to a film director, a producer is the person in charge of overseeing a recording. The producer's tasks may include selecting and booking the studio and/or musicians, choosing the material to be recorded, helping to create the musical arrangements, issuing instructions to the engineer (or directly engineering the session), supervising the mix and mastering, and acting as the artist's advisor and/or private therapist. (See **engineer**, **mastering**, and **mix**.)

pulse—In audio, refers to an impulse wave (an extremely short transient) used in testing equipment. (See **transient**.)

pumping—Audible changes in level mid-signal, usually caused by improper (or sometimes deliberate) compressor/limiter settings. (See **compressor** and **limiter**.)

PZM—Short for "pressure zone microphone," a small condenser mic mounted on a flat aluminum plate and designed to be placed on a wall, floor, piano lid, or other large reflective surface in order to pick up ambient sound. (See **ambient sound**.)

Q—See **parametric equalizer**.

quad—Short for "quadraphonic." (See **quadraphonic**.)

quadrant fader—An early type of fader widely used in British recording studios (and the BBC) in the 1950s and early 1960s. They were constructed by mounting a rotary control side-on and buried inside a panel, with a lever arm attached and extended to the panel surface, causing the arm to travel over an arc, but in a linear direction. An English company named Painton made quadrant faders in various forms, some with continuous carbon tracks, some with stud tracks (switching level in steps of 1 or 1.5 decibels). Interestingly, quadrant faders were sometimes deliberately mounted in mixing boards in reverse, so that moving them away from the engineer resulted in the signal being attenuated rather than boosted. (See **attenuation**, **boost**, **decibel**, and **fader**.)

quadraphonic—A technology developed in the 1960s whereby audio was mixed onto four discrete tracks instead of two, so that independent signals could be routed to four speakers—the traditional two stereo speakers in front of the listener, and an additional two behind (rear left and rear right), arranged in a square pattern. (See **mix** and **track**.)

record head—The tape head which magnetizes tape in response to incoming electrical signal, thus creating an equivalent analog magnetic flux field on the tape. Record heads that are capable of playing back the signal off tape as well (in order to enable overdubbing) are called *sync heads*. (See **analog**, **sync head**, and **tape head**.)

recording engineer—The person who operates the audio equipment and crafts the sound of a recording, sometimes under the supervision of the producer (just as a film cinematographer crafts the look of a scene under the supervision of the director). The ultimate purpose of the recording engineer is to ensure that all the sonic components get successfully recorded and/or mixed. (See **mixing**.)

recovery time—See **release time**.

reflected sound—Sound that has bounced off hard surfaces such as walls, floors, and ceilings, as opposed to *direct sound*, which emanates from the source. (See **direct sound**.)

reflections—Reflected sound waves. (See **reflected sound**.)

release time—In a compressor or limiter, refers to the time it takes for a signal to return to its initial (pre–gain reduction) level after it drops below the user-specified threshold point. If the release time is set too short for the material, "pumping" artifacts can occur, due to the rapid rise of background noise as the gain is increased. If the release time is set too long, however, a loud section may cause gain reduction that persists through a soft section, rendering that section inaudible. Sometimes referred to as *recovery time*. (See **compressor**, **limiter**, **pumping**, and **threshold**.)

remix—See **mix**.

remix room—A specialized control room in a recording studio outfitted with equipment (including, typically, a plethora of signal processors) designed specifically for mixing purposes. (See **mixing** and **signal processor**.)

repro head—Short for "reproduction head." (See **playback head**.)

return—On a mixing board, the point at which a signal is input at line-level. (See **input**, **line-level**, **mixing board**, and **send**.)

reverb—Short for "reverberation," the persistence of a sound after it has been produced. A reverb is created acoustically when reflections build up and then die away over time. It can also be generated by electro-mechanical devices such as *reverb plates* or *spring reverbs*, or via digital signal processing. (See **echo chamber**, **reflections**, **reverb plate**, and **spring reverb**.)

reverb plate—A large metal plate suspended vertically from springs so that it can freely resonate in response to an incoming signal applied by a speaker-like driver. Reverb plates normally include dampers so that reverb times can be shortened if required. Sometimes referred to simply as a *plate*. (See **driver** and **reverb**.)

reverb time—Technically, the time it takes for the sound pressure level (SPL) to decay to one-millionth of its former value (a 60 dB reduction). (See **dB** and **SPL**.)

ribbon microphone—A type of microphone comprised of a small corrugated strip of very thin aluminum hanging loosely within a strong magnetic field. Incoming sound causes the ribbon to move slightly, thus causing equivalent ("analog") variations in the voltage output. Ribbon microphones require no external power to operate and by their nature have a figure-of-eight (bidirectional) polar pattern. (See **bidirectional**, **figure-of-eight**, and **polar pattern**.)

rockwool—A matted mineral fiber used for soundproofing and/or insulation.

rolloff—Another term for attenuation. (See **attenuation**.)

RPM—An acronym for "Revolutions Per Minute," used to describe the rotational speed of a vinyl disc.

send—On a mixing board, the point at which a signal is output at line-level. (See **input**, **line-level**, **mixing board**, and **return**.)

separation booth—See **isolation booth**.

shelving filter—A type of filter that gradually rolls off frequencies above or below a particular frequency. Sometimes called a *shelf filter*, *shelving equalizer*, or *shelving control*. (See **filter** and **frequency**.)

shotgun mic—A highly directional microphone that prioritizes sound coming from directly in front and almost completely rejects sound coming from the sides and rear. Shotgun mics typically have long barrels, hence their name.

sibilance—The vocal "s" sound, most predominant in the 3 to 7 kHz range. Sibilance can usually be effectively removed with a device called a *de-esser*. (See **de-esser** and **kHz**.)

sidecar—An auxiliary mixing board, typically used to add extra inputs and/or for monitoring.

sidechain—A secondary input to a dynamics processor that allows it to "listen to" and respond to a signal other than the one that is actually being affected. (See **dynamics processor**.)

signal path—A description of the routing of a signal, from input to output (and every point in between). For example, the typical signal path for recording a vocal would be microphone ➜ mic preamp ➜ dynamics processor ➜ equalizer ➜ recording device. (See **dynamics processor**, **equalizer**, and **mic preamp**.)

signal processor—An outboard device which alters an audio signal, such as compressors, limiters, equalizers, delay/reverb units, phasers, flangers, Harmonizers, etc. (See **compressor**, **delay**, **equalizer**, **flanger**, **Harmonizer**, **limiter**, **outboard**, **phaser**, and **reverb**.)

soffit—The underside of any construction element. Large monitors in control rooms are often *soffit-mounted* (i.e., hung from the ceiling and sealed inside an enclosure that is acoustically isolated from the wall). (See **monitor**.)

solo—On a mixing board, a switch that temporarily turns off all other channels, allowing only the soloed channel to be heard. (See **channel** and **mixing board**.)

SPL—An acronym for "Sound Pressure Level," a measure of how loud a sound is.

splicing tape—A relic of the tape recording era, this was a special kind of sticky tape designed to hold together splices (sections) of audio tape.

spooling—Fast-forwarding or rewinding tape at a high speed.

spot mic—Refers to any microphone being used to capture a specific instrument or group of instruments in a large ensemble such as an orchestra.

spring reverb—A device containing a transducer at one end of a metal spring and a pickup at the other, similar to those used in plate reverbs, to create and capture vibrations within the spring. Spring reverbs are often built into guitar amplifiers, and are sometimes also used as outboard signal processors. (See **outboard**, **reverb**, **reverb plate**, **signal processor**, and **transducer**.)

standing wave—An acoustic phenomenon that occurs when a sound wave in a room is reflected back onto itself between two opposite surfaces, resulting in reinforcement and a resultant exaggerated response in that frequency area. This typically occurs with low-frequency waves, making a room sound "boomy." Standing waves can be reduced or eliminated with the addition of bass traps and/or other kinds of acoustic absorbers. (See **absorber**, **bass trap**, **low-frequency**, and **reflected sound**.)

subgroup—See **group**.

sweep EQ—Refers to any equalization or test circuit that allows the continuous selection (a "sweeping") of frequencies.

sync—Short for "synchronize" or "synchronization."

sync head—A record head which is also capable of playing back signal off tape. This enabled overdubbing; however, in most tape machines of the '60s and '70s, the frequency response of the sync head was inferior to that of the playback head. (See **frequency response**, **overdubbing**, **playback head**, and **record head**.)

synchronizer—A device that causes two or more tape machines to run at the same speed. Some advanced synchronizers of the '70s also enabled multiple machines to start or stop at the same time.

take—A recorded performance. A *first take* is the first time a performance is recorded. Various takes of anything from entire performances to specific vocals or instruments are often edited together. (Vocals in particular usually receive this treatment, where the best parts of various takes are used to create a composite, or "comp" track.)

talkback—The microphone/speaker system that allows communication between the control room and the studio.

tape copying room—See **copying room**.

tape counter—A device that displays tape position, either as an abstract number or as minutes / seconds / fractions of a second.

tape delay—An echo caused by the distance between a tape recorder's record head and its playback head. The timing of the delay can be varied by altering the tape speed. Sometimes referred to as *tape echo*. (See **delay**, **playback head**, and **record head**.)

tape dropout—The brief loss or sudden decrease in signal level (volume) caused by a defect in the oxide coating on a tape. Dropouts can also be caused by damage to the tape itself, a temporary clogging of the record head during recording, or a clogging of the playback head during playback. (See **playback head** and **record head**.)

tape echo—See **tape delay**.

tape head—A small transducer in a tape recorder which consists of a two-part core of soft iron or other ferro-magnetic material with a coil of wire wrapped around it; between the two parts of the core is a tiny gap over which tape is moved. There are three basic types of tape heads, each with its own particular function: an *erase head*, a *record/sync head*, and a *playback head*. (See **erase head**, **playback head**, **record head**, **sync head**, and **transducer**.)

technical engineer—English terminology for "maintenance engineer." (See **maintenance engineer**.)

telecine—The process of transferring motion picture film to video.

threshold—In a dynamics processor, the user-specified level at which the signal starts to be affected. In the case of a compressor or limiter, signal above the threshold is reduced; in the case of an expander or noise gate, signal below the threshold is reduced. (See **compressor**, **dynamics processor**, **expander**, **limiter**, and **noise gate**.)

tieline—An audio line that enables signal to be routed from one room to another. Tielines are usually hidden inside walls or floors, and are accessed from connector panels or patch bays. (See **patch bay**.)

time code—A special signal that designates elapsed time, enabling precise synchronization between two or more audio and/or video devices.

top end—See **high-frequency**.

track—In audio, refers to an area in a recording device in which specific audio information is stored. Stereo recorders offer two tracks, while multitrack recorders offer more than two. (See **multitrack**.)

tracking—Refers to the process of recording a backing track. Once tracking is done to everyone's satisfaction, overdubs and final vocals will typically be added until the song is complete, at which point it will be mixed. (See **backing track**, **mixing**, and **overdub**.)

transducer—A device which converts one form of energy into another. Examples of transducers include microphones (which convert mechanical energy from moving air to equivalent [analog] electrical signal), speaker drivers (which do the reverse) and tape heads (which convert electrical signal to magnetic flux, and vice versa). (See **analog**, **driver**, and **tape head**.)

transformer—A device consisting of two or more coils of wire wound around a core of soft iron or other ferro-magnetic material. Audio transformers are used to step voltages up and down so that signal can be routed between microphones, mixing boards, outboard signal processors, and recording devices. (See **mixing board**, **outboard**, and **signal processor**.)

transformerless—Refers to any piece of audio equipment that has no transformers.

transient—An audio signal of extremely brief duration, such as the "crack" of a snare drum or the initial attack of a guitar or bass string prior to the sustained tone.

trapping—The use of absorbers or bass traps to tune a room acoustically and reduce or eliminate standing waves. (See **absorber**, **bass trap**, and **standing wave**.)

tube—In audio, short for "vacuum tube," forerunner to the modern transistor.

tweeter—A high-frequency speaker driver. (See **driver** and **high-frequency**.)

unbalanced—A single-conductor audio connection, where the shield acts both as the return path for the signal and as ground. Sometimes also refers to the state of mind needed to achieve success in the music industry. (See **balanced**.)

valve—English terminology for a vacuum tube. (See **tube**.)

varispeed—A circuit or device used to change the speed of a tape recorder.

vocal booth—An isolation booth specially designed to house one or more vocalists. (See **isolation booth**.)

void—In acoustic design, an empty space.

volume—In audio, a term used to describe the power level of a signal. Sometimes used interchangeably with *gain* and *level*, though technically different. (See **gain** and **level**.)

VU—Short for "Volume Unit," a measure of average signal level. A *VU meter* shows the continuous change in Volume Units when audio signal is present. (See **PPM**.)

white noise—An audio signal consisting of random frequencies at equal intensities. (See **pink noise**.)

windscreen—See **pop filter**.

windsock—See **pop filter**.

woofer—A low-frequency speaker driver. (See **low-frequency** and **driver**.)

wow—Slight unwanted slow variations in speed. (See **flutter**.)

BIBLIOGRAPHY

Audio Technology magazine, various issues.

The Beatles. 2000. *The Beatles Anthology*. San Francisco: Chronicle.

The Beatles Monthly Book, Number 33, April 1966. London: Beat Publications.

Beyond the Pale (Procol Harum fan site). http://www.procolharum.com.

Billboard magazine, various issues.

Brown, Phill. 2010. *Are We Still Rolling?* Sacramento: Tape Op Books.

Cleveland, Barry. 2013. *Joe Meek's Bold Techniques (Second Edition)*. Cambridge, UK: ElevenEleven.

Coral, Gus. 1995. *The Rolling Stones: Black and White Blues, 1963*. Atlanta: Turner.

Emerick, Geoff, and Howard Massey. 2006. *Here, There, and Everywhere: My Life Recording the Music of the Beatles*. New York: Gotham.

Garrison, Mark. 2011. *The Encyclopedia of Home Recording*. CreateSpace Independent Publishing Platform.

Hayward, Keith. 2013. *Tin Pan Alley: The Rise of Elton John*. London: Soundcheck Books.

Irwin, Mark. 2007. "Take the Last Train from Meeksville: Joe Meeks's Holloway Road Recording Studio, 1963–7." *Journal on the Art of Record Production*: ISSN: 1754-9892.

Jansen, Arian. 2008. "A Universal NAB to IEC Playback Equalization Converter for Reel to Reel Recorders." http://laocaudiosociety.net/tech/NABtoIEC.pdf.

The Jethro Tull Forum website. Q&A with John Burns (*Aqualung* engineer). http://jethrotull.proboards.com/thread/1751/aqualung-john-burns-engineer.

Joe Meek Society website. http://www.joemeeksociety.org/.

Johns, Glyn. 2014. *Sound Man*. New York: Blue Rider Press.

Lewisohn, Mark. 1989. *The Beatles Recording Sessions: The Official Abbey Road Studio Session Notes, 1962–1970*. New York: Harmony.

Lewisohn, Mark. 2013. *Tune In*. New York: Crown.

Mankowitz, Gered. 2014. *Gered Mankowitz: 50 Years of Rock and Roll Photography*. London: Goodman.

Martin, George. 1979. *All You Need Is Ears*. New York: St. Martin's Press.

Massey, Howard. 2000. *Behind the Glass*. San Francisco: Backbeat Books.

Massey, Howard. 2009. *Behind the Glass Volume II*. New York: Backbeat Books.

MIX magazine, various issues.

Museum of Magnetic Sound Recording website. http://www.museumofmagneticsoundrecording.org.

Myers, Mark. 2014. "The Making of Led Zeppelin's 'Whole Lotta Love.'" *Wall Street Journal* online. http://www.wsj.com/articles/the-making-of-led-zeppelins-whole-lotta-love-1401390281.

Newell, Philip. 2011. *Recording Studio Design*. New York: Focal Press.

Notes from the Edge website. Interview with Eddy Offord. http://www.nfte.org/interviews/eo234.html.

Oldham, Andrew Loog. 2000. *Stoned*. London: Secker & Warburg.

Peter Miller's website. http://www.bigboypete.com.

Philsbook.com website. http://philsbook.com.

The Polymath Perspective. www.polymathperspective.com.

Record Collector magazine, various issues.

Repsch, John. 2001. *The Legendary Joe Meek: The Telstar Man*. London: Cherry Red Books.

Robb Huxley's website. http://www.silvertabbies.co.uk/huxley.

The Rolling Stones Chronicle 1964. http://www.timeisonourside.com/chron1964.html.

Ryan, Kevin, and Brian Kehew. 2006. *Recording The Beatles*. Houston: Curvebender.

Sheffield, Norman. 2013. *Life on Two Legs*. London: Trident Publishing.

Sound on Sound magazine, various issues.

Sound Techniques website. http://www.soundtechniques.co.uk/.

Southall, Brian, Peter Vince, and Allan Rouse. 2002. *Abbey Road*. Cambridge, UK: Patrick Stevens.

Studio Sound magazine, various issues.

Thompson, Daniel M. 2005. *Understanding Audio*. Boston: Berklee Press.

Thompson, Gordon. 2008. *Please Please Me*. New York: Oxford University Press.

Time Is on Our Side website. http://www.timeisonourside.com/lp12X5.html.

Tobler, John, and Stuart Grundy. 1982. *The Record Producers*. New York: St. Martin's Press.

Valentine, Penny, and Vicki Wickham. 2001. *Dancing with Demons: The Authorized Biography of Dusty Spring-field*. New York: St. Martin's Press.

Weindling, Dick, and Marianne Colloms. 2013. *Decca Studios and Klooks Kleek*. Stroud, Gloucestershire, UK: The History Press.

White, Glenn D. 1991. *The Audio Dictionary, Second Edition*. Seattle: University of Washington Press.

Woram, John M. 1989. *Sound Recording Handbook*. Indianapolis: Howard W. Sams & Company.

Wyman, Bill. 1990. *Stone Alone*. New York: Viking.

INDEX

10cc, 192
200 Motels (album), 309
200 Motels (film), 309
304 Holloway Road, 133–147, 235
3M tape machines. *See* tape machines
90125 (album), 279

A&R (studio), 2
Abbey Road (album), 10, 179
Abbey Road Studios. *See* EMI Studios
ABC, 279, 289
Acousta-voicette equalizers, 278
Adams, Cliff, 150, 153
Adams, Dave, 133–135, 141, 147
Addey, Malcolm, 16, 31
ADR (Audio & Design Recording), 95, 106, 115, 213,
    291, 306
    F600 stereo limiter, 167
    F700 compressor, 277
    F760 compressor/expander, 270
    S300 noise gate modules, 213
    Scamp rack, 95, 213, 229, 241, 287, 288, 289, 296
    Vocal Stressor, 213, 267, 289
ADT (Artificial Double Tracking), 13, 26, 27, 28, 33–34, 35,
    36, 171, 172
Advance oscillator, 144
Advision Studios, 5, 6, 10, 13, 87, 107–118, 186, 236, 277, 289
Aengus equalizers, 278, 279, 325
Age of Plastic (album), 298
AIMS project, 309
Ainsworth, Barry, 75, 278
AIR Lyndhurst, 198, 205, 218
AIR Montserrat, 197–219
AIR Studios (Oxford Circus), 8, 13, 48, 72, 195–219, 247, 300
Air-Edel, 229
AKG, 59
    BX20 spring reverb, 62, 167, 229, 277, 281, 316, 322
    microphones. *See* microphones
"Albatross," 226, 275
Albert Hall. *See* Royal Albert Hall
Albrecht film recorders, 117, 214
Alchemy Live (album), 204
Alice
    gates, 277
    mixing board. *See* mixing boards
All You Need Is Ears (book), 130, 195, 198, 201, 203
"All You Need Is Love," 19, 171
Allen, Jerry, 248

Allison automation, 249, 270, 279, 295
Allison Research, 168, 272, 276, 291, 296
Allom, Tom, 51, 61, 270, 281
Altec
    436 compressor, 254
    436B compressor, 30, 143, 231
    436C leveling amplifier, 168
    438A leveling amplifier, 143
    compressors, 30, 106, 235, 243
    leveling amplifiers, 143, 222
    monitors. *See* monitors
    microphones. *See* microphones
Ambiophony, 38–39, 74, 254
Amcron amplifiers. *See* amplifiers/Crown
America (group), 206
Amex mixing board. *See* mixing boards
amplifiers
    Audix, 279
    Avantics, 161
    BGW, 301
    Crown, 6, 112, 185, 263
    Crown D150, 126
    Crown DC300, 104, 289, 290
    Crown DC300A, 225, 276
    FM Acoustics, 228
    HH, 126, 185, 226, 228, 239, 247, 253, 284
    HH V800 MOSFET, 207
    Klein & Hummel Telewatt, 291
    Leak 25, 304
    Leak TL12, 81
    Leak TL50, 138
    Leak TL50+, 162
    Quad 303, 162
    Quad AC88, 137
    Quad II, 162
    Radford, 6, 73, 112, 162, 185, 249
    Radford MA25, 81
    Radford STA25, 93
    Radford STA100, 94
    RCA Model LM1/322, 138
    Sagatone, 138
    Studer, 247
    Turner, 247
    Westrex, 161
    Yamaha B1, 282
AMS
    ADR FX760 Compex limiter, 299
    digital delay, 190, 213, 270, 279, 292, 301

AMS *(continued)*
    DM2-20 phaser/flanger, 299
    DMX15 digital delay, 276
    DMX 15-80 digital delay, 213, 299
    DMX 15-80S digital delay, 213
    Flanger, 213
    harmonizer, 292, 293
    RMX 16 digital reverb, 276
"Anarchy in the U.K.," 246, 247
Anderson, Jon, 299
Andrews, Billy, 298–299
Andrews, Frank, 298–299
Animals, The, 12, 89, 119, 177, 230, 231, 253, 285
"Another Day," 226
Another Monty Python Record (album), 241
Anymore for Anymore (album), 318
Aphex Aural Exciter, 274, 284
API
    MagLink synchronizer, 115, 117
    mixing board. *See* mixing boards
Apple Corps, 261
Apple Studios, 196, 256–261, 262
APSI equalizers, 241
Aqualung (album), 262, 265
Are We Still Rolling? (book), 151, 158, 264, 281
"Arnold Layne," 244
Art of Noise, The, 279
"As Time Goes By," 231
Ash, Robert, 264, 322
Associated Independent Recording (AIR), 195
Astronics graphic equalizers, 189
Atkin, Malcolm, 13, 198, 199, 200, 201, 202, 204, 205, 206,
    208, 215, 217
Atlantic Records, 10, 117
Atlantic Studios, 4, 185
ATOC (Automatic Transient Overload Control), 14, 38
Atwood, Ken, 75, 80, 81, 304
Audio & Design Recording. *See* ADR
Audio International, 226–229
Audix amplifiers. *See* amplifiers
Auger, Bob, 75, 77, 82, 157, 304, 306
Austin, Louis, 121, 123
Avantics amplifiers. *See* amplifiers

Babson, Monty, 248
"Baby You're a Rich Man," 160, 175
Back Street Crawler, 282, 298
Bad Company, 298, 299, 309, 318
Baker, Denys Val, 279
Baker, Ginger, 78, 157
Baker, Roy Thomas, 43, 179, 184, 192, 248, 274, 276, 279
"Baker Street," 276
Baldwin, Eddie, 234, 236
"ball and biscuit" microphone. *See* microphones/STC 4021
Balla, George, 223, 224, 225
Band Aid, 265

Banks, Major Wilfred Alonzo, 133
Bannister, Arthur, 43, 50, 61
Barber, Chris, 239, 241
Barclay, Michael, 97
Baring, James, 233
Barker, George, 106
Barnett, George, 16, 195, 198
Barrow, Howard, 75, 78, 82, 84
Basing Street Studios. *See* Island Studios
Batt, Mike, 241
Battery Studios, 250
Bay City Rollers, 276, 289
BBC, 15, 26, 29, 75, 77, 88, 89, 93, 95, 102, 107, 161, 169,
    181, 183, 192, 226, 260, 272, 273, 319, 325
    limiter, 142
    microphones. *See* microphones
BBC Broadcast House, 107
Beach Boys, the, 2, 7
Beatles, The, 1, 2, 3, 4, 5, 6, 7, 8, 9, 10, 12, 14, 16, 17, 18, 19,
    20, 21, 23, 24, 25, 27, 29, 31, 33, 34, 36, 38, 39,
    54–55, 66, 72, 89, 97, 106, 119, 130, 133, 143, 150,
    160, 171, 173, 175, 178, 186, 188, 195, 196, 206,
    232, 233, 234, 247, 253, 256, 257, 277, 307
Beatles Anthology (album), 55
Beatles Anthology, The (book), 3, 8
Bee Gees, The, 158, 237, 253
Beggars Banquet (album), 154, 155
Behind the Glass (book), 5, 6, 7, 8, 11, 296
Bel
    digital delay, 301
    flanger, 276, 314
Bell Sound, 113
Bender, Ariel, 115
Benefit (album), 250
Bennett, Brian, 326
Benson, Samuel Herbert, 230
Bensons advertising agency, 230
Besant Hall, 226, 227
Best, Pete, 54
Beyer
    headphones, 217, 236, 250
    microphones. *See* microphones
BGW. *See* amplifiers
Bickerton, Wayne, 300
Billet, Charles, 103
Binson Echorec, 38, 139
Birch, Martin, 121, 231, 232
Black, Cilla, 16, 203
Black, Robin, 249, 250, 328
"black box"
    compressor/limiter, 106, 141
    equalizer, 255
    spring reverb, 96, 141
"Black Magic Woman," 226
Black Sabbath, 4, 262, 276, 301
Blackham, Denis, 94

Blackwell, Chris, 261, 262, 316, 324
Blind Faith, 157
Blue Horizon Records, 275, 276
Bluesbreakers with Eric Clapton (album), 68, 275
Blumlein, Alan, 32
Blumlein Pair, 13, 32, 33
Bob and Marcia, 255
"Bohemian Rhapsody," 192, 279, 298
Bolan, Marc, 179, 212, 237, 273, 291, 292
Boland, Jock, 35
"Bold As Love," 172
Bonham, John, 159, 318
"Boogie Nights," 229
Boomtown Rats, The, 248, 266, 289
Bott, David, 103
Bowie, David, 1, 5, 8, 11, 179, 186–187, 191, 235, 238,
    288, 291
Bown, Peter, 6, 16
Boyce, Tommy, 160
Boyd, Joe, 1, 242, 244
Boys, Jerry, 244, 281
Bradford, Nick, 179, 292
Bradley's Studio, 7, 241
Brand X, 251
Branson, Richard, 151, 262, 268, 269, 283, 294, 318
Breakaway (album), 217
Bride, The (film), 131
Bridge, Tony, 12, 123
Bridges, Denny, 198, 202
Britannia Row Studios, 261
British Grove Studios, 261
Bron, Gerry, 282, 284
Bronze Records, 283, 284
Brooker, Gary, 209
Brosius, Ham, 113
Brown, Phill, 151, 154, 158, 163, 261, 264, 281, 322, 324
Brown, Sandy, 13, 71, 102, 181, 227, 252, 307
Brown, Terry, 101, 102, 150, 151, 155, 172, 248
Bruford, Bill, 117
Buckmaster, Paul, 264
Budgie, 237
Buggles, the, 279, 289, 298
Burgess, John, 195
Burns, John, 43, 265
Burton, Richard, 118
Butterscotch, 289
Butterworth, Bob, 2, 101, 106
Byrds, The, 226

Cable, Robin, 179, 241
Cadac, 5, 13, 92, 103, 151, 183, 207, 248
    automation. *See* CARE
    mixing boards. *See* mixing boards
    monitors. *See* monitors
Calver, Geoff, 75, 240
Calvert, Leon, 248, 249

Cameron, Roger, 5, 108, 109, 110, 111, 112, 113, 114, 115,
    116, 117, 118
Campbell Connelly Music, 233
"Can Can 62," 146
"Can the Can," 286
Capital Radio, 272, 273, 274
Capitol Records, 12, 13
Capitol Studios/Capitol Tower, 2, 6, 186
CARE automation, 80
Carr, Tony, 326
Cattini, Clem, 78, 189
CBS, 222, 224, 226
CBS Records, 275
CBS Studios, 222–226
CCIR (Comité Consultatif International pour la Radio), 11,
    12, 27, 184, 187
Chalk Farm Studio, 237, 238, 254–255
Chandler, Chas, 89, 92
Chapman, Michael, 281, 282
Chapman, Mike, 228, 229, 289
Chapman, Phil, 151, 152, 156, 161, 164, 166, 167, 168, 169,
    175
Chappell Music, 251, 254
Chappell Studios, 70, 73, 251–254
Chevin, Gerald, 108, 110, 114, 116
Chinn, Nicky, 229, 289
Chipping Norton Studios, 192, 275–276
Chkiantz, George, 81, 151, 154, 155, 156, 157, 158, 159, 160,
    161, 162, 163, 164, 165, 166, 167, 168, 169, 170,
    171, 172, 175, 304
Chrysalis Group, the, 197, 247, 248
City of London Recording Studios, The, 278
Clapton, Eric, 5, 198, 275, 298
Clarke, Tony, 43, 61, 63, 64
Clash, The, 1, 226, 241, 245, 247
Cleese, John, 268
Clegg, Jack, 43, 51, 89, 92, 95, 121, 130, 196, 198, 203
Cleveland, Barry, 101, 144
Climax Blues Band, 197
Clouston, George, 89
Coleman, Pete, 229
Coles microphones. *See* microphones/STC
Collins, Gery, 239
Collins, Peter, 268
Collins, Phil, 7, 205, 251, 296, 298
Colosseum, 284
Columbia Records, 15, 36, 68, 69, 253
Command Studios, 278
Congas, John, 192
Conway Hall, 89, 92, 303
Cook, Paul, 246
Cooper, Duane H., 73
Cooper Time Cube, 63, 64, 273
Copeland, Stewart, 205
Costello, Elvis, 267
Coulter, Phil, 235

Countryman microphones. *See* microphones
Cousins, Dave, 270, 272
Cox, Tony, 280, 281
Crazy World of Arthur Brown, The, 116, 118, 266
Cream, 1, 4, 98, 236, 237, 238, 254
Crime of the Century (album), 274
Cronin, Dan, 113
Crown. *See* amplifiers
Crozier, Neville, 315, 316, 326
Crystalate Manufacturing Company, 41, 42
CTS, 87, 118–131, 196, 203, 243, 252, 277
Cuemix, 284
Cure, The, 238, 298
Curvebender. *See* EMI RS56

Dahlstedt, Stellan, 108
Daltrey, Roger, 110, 301
Dankworth, Johnny, 236, 238
Dark Side of the Moon (album), 27, 28, 39
Dart, F. H., 15
Darts, 160
Dave Clark Five, 104, 105, 106
Davies, Dave, 77, 91, 255
Davies, Malcolm, 32, 257, 260
Davies, Ray, 77, 91, 233, 250
Davies, Sean, 89, 90, 92, 94, 95, 98, 255, 272, 304
Day at the Races, A (album), 271, 279
dbx
        160 compressor, 240, 276, 279, 282, 293
        165 compressor, 276, 279
        companders, 270
        compressor/limiters, 64, 106, 225, 228, 247, 273, 284,
            289, 296
        noise reduction, 11, 64, 86, 279
De Lane Lea, Jacques, 230
De Lane Lea, William, 119, 230
De Lane Lea Music, 119
De Lane Lea Studios, 12, 119, 192, 230–232
de Paul, Lynsey, 260
"Dear Prudence," 179
Decca, 7, 9, 14, 33, 41, 87, 88, 89, 146, 195, 196, 275, 303
        compressor/limiter, 14, 61, 62, 64
Decca Records, 41, 57, 66, 88, 146, 275, 303
Decca Studios, 7, 9, 26, 29, 33, 41–68, 97, 146, 149, 191, 270,
        273, 276
Decca Studios and Klooks Kleek (book), 51
Decca Tree, 13, 32, 33, 58, 65, 66, 68
Dee, Kiki, 235, 288
Deep Purple, 91, 119, 156, 232, 238, 311, 319
delay drum, 38, 74, 254
Delta T digital delay line, 282, 284
Denton, Kenny, 75, 78, 120, 121, 122, 124, 127, 129,
        130, 131
Desperado (album), 262
DI (Direct Inject), 13, 35, 264, 314, 316, 324
Di Meola, Al, 264

Diamond, Neil, 274
Diamond Dogs (album), 291
Diary of a Madman (album), 299
Dire Straits, 70, 204, 238, 255, 261, 262, 268
Disraeli Gears (album), 4, 237
"Do They Know It's Christmas," 265
Dolby, Ray, 37, 191, 214
Dolby Labs, 37
Dolby noise reduction, 11, 27, 37, 64, 86, 114, 190, 191, 213,
        214, 259, 264, 279, 314, 315
Donegan, Lonnie, 106, 146
Donovan, 86, 106, 226, 235, 250, 285, 287, 290
Dorset, Ray, 82
Dowd, Tom, 4, 10, 185
Dowler, Jim, 151, 159, 160, 167, 168, 169, 175
Doyle, Ray, 322, 324
"Dr. Dutton" speaker. *See* monitors/EMI RS143
Drake, Nick, 244
Drama (album), 279
Drawmer
        DS201 dual noise gate, 168
        noise gate, 225
Drawmer, Ivor, 168
Dreyfus, Louis, 254
Dudgeon, Gus, 43, 61, 149, 212, 240, 241
Duggan, Rod, 271
Duncan, Peter, 75, 82, 121, 122, 123, 314, 315
Duran Duran, 238, 276, 290, 298, 326
Dutton, Dr. Gilbert, 25, 38
Dwight, Reg. *See* John, Elton
Dyna PAS/2 stereo preamplifier, 136
Dynaudio, 206, 207

Eagles, the, 5, 150, 262
Eastlake, 71, 78, 201, 239, 240, 241, 276, 289, 296
Eastlake amplifiers. *See* amplifiers
Eastlake monitors. *See* monitors
echo chambers, 4, 20, 21, 22, 29, 32, 49, 74, 77, 78, 79, 81, 85,
        91, 109, 115, 124, 158, 204, 224, 226, 244
Eden, Alan, 280, 281
Edwards, Gary, 247
Eel Pie, 241, 261
Egan, Rusty, 179
Elcom faders, 243
Electrovoice microphones. *See* microphones
Elektra Records, 244
Elektra Studios, 243
Elgar, Sir Edward, 15, 16
Elman, Louis, 119, 121
Elman, Ralph, 233
Eltham, Stuart, 16, 21, 30
Embassy Records, 221, 222
Emerick, Geoff, 3, 7, 8, 10, 12, 13, 16, 20, 24, 29, 30, 31, 38,
        160, 196, 198, 200, 206, 211, 212, 217, 218, 256,
        257, 258, 259, 261, 262
Emerson, Lake & Palmer, 107, 111, 118, 175

EMI, 6, 7, 9, 10, 12, 14, 15, 16, 20, 22, 24, 25, 26, 27, 28, 30, 31, 32, 33, 34, 35, 36, 37, 39, 41, 49, 55, 66, 67, 68, 69, 74, 84, 87, 88, 160, 186, 192, 195, 233, 235, 253, 254, 256, 260, 272, 278, 298, 299, 300, 303
    843 passive equalizer, 143
    844 passive equalizer, 143
    limiters, 222, 243
    mic preamps, 255
    mixing boards. *See* mixing boards
    monitors. *See* monitors
    RS56 Universal Tone Control ("Curvebender"), 14, 31, 32, 37
    RS114 limiter, 31
    RS124 compressor, 30
    tape machines. *See* tape machines
EMI Studios, 4, 10, 15–39, 90, 97, 99, 102, 171, 172, 183, 195, 206, 286
Emilar speaker drivers, 289
EMT
    140 reverb plate, 32, 49, 61, 62, 74, 79, 60, 86, 90, 95, 106, 115, 122, 123, 129, 167, 179, 182, 190, 209, 212, 213, 222, 226, 229, 231, 237, 239, 240, 243, 244, 245, 247, 250, 253, 254, 255, 258, 263, 267, 270, 273, 277, 279, 282, 286, 287, 288, 289, 292, 293, 296, 301, 325
    240 Gold Foil, 62, 106, 167, 213, 255, 273, 292, 293, 299, 314, 322, 328
    251 digital reverb, 296
"End, The," 10
Eno, Brian, 202
Entwistle, John, 223, 277
EPI monitors. *See* monitors
Epstein, Brian, 4, 54, 55, 253
ESS equalizers, 314
Essex, David, 118
Essex Music, 233
Euston Tower, 272, 274
Evans, Dame Edith, 103
Evans, Mal, 20
"Evening in Paris," 134, 136, 147
Eventide
    1745M digital delay, 74, 106, 115, 190, 213, 238, 241, 263, 276, 278, 279, 288, 291, 292, 296, 299, 301, 326
    FL201 Instant Flanger, 190, 213, 247, 250, 282, 289, 299
    H910 Harmonizer, 74, 115, 129, 130, 213, 226, 228, 229, 238, 247, 250, 263, 276, 279, 282, 284, 288, 289, 299, 314, 326
    Instant Phaser, 63, 238, 250, 263, 270, 278, 279, 318, 326
    Phaser/Flanger, 106, 115
    Omnipressor expander, 241, 279, 288, 326
Exile on Main St. (album), 308, 309, 310, 314
Exorcist, The (film), 269

Face Dances (album), 301
Faces, The, 316, 318
Fairchild, 6, 7, 30, 95, 142, 143, 174, 189, 225, 238, 272,

273, 282
    658 Reverbertron, 141
    660 compressor/limiter, 31, 62, 106, 143, 169, 243, 281
    661 AUTO TEN noise gate, 143
    663 compressor/limiter, 143
    666 compressor, 31, 231
    670 stereo compressor/limiter, 106, 143, 145, 255
    673 Dynaliser, 143
    mic preamps, 222
Fairport Convention, 244, 245, 282
Faithfull, Marianne, 20, 106, 154, 276, 294
Fantasia (film), 170
Faraday, Derek, 226
Farley, Bill, 233, 244
Farmer, Barry "Bazza," 266, 267
Farther Along (album), 226
Fate for Breakfast (album), 210
Fautley, Peter, 89, 94
Fellner, Dag, 108, 111, 113, 222, 236
Ferranti disc cutter, 143
Ferrograph tape machines. *See* tape machines
Ferry, Bryan, 202
FFRR (Full Frequency Range Recording), 60, 67, 68
FFSS (Full Frequency Stereophonic Sound), 68
Fi-Cord microphones. *See* microphones
Film Industries microphones. *See* microphones
Final Cut, The (album), 229
Fine Art of Surfacing (album), 266
Finesilver, Mike, 266
"Fire," 116, 118, 266
"Fixing a Hole," 234
flanging, 36, 254
Fleetwood, Mick, 275
Fleetwood Mac, 119, 131, 226, 231, 232, 238, 275, 309
Fletcher, Guy, 135
Fletcher, Ted, 138, 139, 140, 142, 144, 145, 146, 147, 235
Flodthart, William, 99
Flood, 250
Florence, Alan, 75, 77, 78, 79, 81, 83, 89, 119, 121, 122, 128, 315
Flowers, Herbie, 189
FM Acoustics amplifiers. *See* amplifiers
Foster, Bill, 77, 82, 225
Four Weddings and a Funeral (film), 120
"Foxy Lady," 226
Fragile (album), 116
Frankie Goes to Hollywood, 279, 299
Franz, John, 69
Fresh Cream (album), 237, 254
Frewin, Arthur, 96, 146
Frieda, Nigel, 248, 292, 294
From Genesis to Revelation (album), 234
Frost, Geoff, 6, 13, 124, 127, 222, 241, 242, 243, 245
Fruin, John, 300

Gabriel, Peter, 296, 298
Gain Brain compressor. *See* Allison Research
Gallagher & Lyle, 217, 288
Gallen, Peter, 101, 282, 283, 284
Garay, Val, 274
Garfunkel, Art, 210, 211
Gaumont Kalee projectors, 169
Gauss speaker drivers, 225, 270, 289
Generation X, 247, 289
Genesis, 1, 179, 191, 192, 234, 251, 262, 322
Gentle Giant, 107, 278
Ghost in the Machine (album), 205, 218, 219
Giaconda Café, 235
Gibb, Robin, 237
Gibson, Brian, 16
Gillan, Ian, 232
"Gloria," 57
Glossop, Mick, 13, 269, 270, 271, 272, 294, 296, 297
Go (album), 264
Goddard, Geoff, 133, 136, 145
Godwyn, Ron, 44, 70, 71, 72, 73
Gold Star Recording, 71
Goldblatt, Richard, 79, 81, 120, 121, 122, 123, 125
Goldhawk Film Studios, 294, 297
Gong, 271, 272
Good Earth Studio, 279, 290–292
Goodman, Bob, 44, 51
Goodsall, John, 251
Gooseberry Sound, 255
Graham, Bobby, 57, 91
Gramophone Company, The, 15, 303
Grampian spring reverb, 141, 238, 239
Granada Recordings, 306
Granada Television, 306
Grand Hotel (album), 209
Grant, Keith, 13, 78, 89, 90, 93, 98, 112, 149, 150, 151, 152, 153, 155, 156, 158, 159, 160, 161, 162, 164, 165, 166, 169, 172, 173, 174, 175
Grant, Neil, 276
Grant, Robertson, 13, 78, 155, 156
Grech, Ric, 157
Green, Clive, 13, 102, 103, 104, 105, 151, 158, 169, 172, 174, 175, 248
Green, Peter, 231, 275
Greenslade, Arthur, 57
Grinsted, Dave, 43, 276
Grundig tape machines. *See* tape machines
Guthrie, James, 229, 289
Guy de Bere Studios, 107

"Had to Cry Today," 157
Haddy, Arthur, 41, 42, 43, 57, 65, 67
Hague, Stephen, 288
Halling, Patrick, 173
Hamilton-Smith, David, 151, 173
Hammond organ, 102, 151

"Happy Jack," 226
Harding, Phil, 240
Harmonizer. *See* Eventide
Harper, Claude, 257, 259
Harries, Dave, 10, 13, 16, 25, 30, 35, 195, 198, 199, 200, 201, 203, 204, 205, 206, 207, 210, 214, 215, 216, 217, 218
Harris, Peter, 89, 118, 121, 125, 252
Harrison, George, 4, 54, 182, 193, 232, 260, 261
Harrison, mixing boards. *See* mixing boards
Harry J, 255
Hartley, Richard, 160
Hawkwind, 284
Heatwave, 229
Helios, 5, 13, 92, 160, 183, 262, 307
    channel modules, 239
    compressor/limiters, 168
    mic amp, 312
    mixing boards. *See* mixing boards
    RE24 equalizer, 190
Hendrix, Jimi, 89, 119, 150, 168, 172, 175, 226, 231, 238, 304
Hentschel, David, 179, 190
Here, There, and Everywhere (book), 3, 7, 257
Herman's Hermits, 285
"Hey Joe," 231
"Hey Jude," 10, 39, 178, 179, 188, 191, 193
Heyworth, Simon, 269, 321
HH amplifiers. *See* amplifiers
Hibberd, Kevin, 107, 111
Hidley, Tom, 43, 71, 78, 239, 270, 271, 294, 296
Hind, Chris, 155, 156
Hitchcock, Peter, 99, 101
HMV microphones. *See* microphones
Holbrook, John, 95
Holder, Noddy, 169
Holder, Pete, 144
Hollies, The, 16, 253
Holmes, Teddy, 251
Holroyd, Steve, 241
"Homeward Bound," 235
"Honey Pie," 12, 179
Hoople, The (album), 115
Hopkins, Doug, 325, 326
Hopkins, Nicky, 309
Horn, Trevor, 279, 288
Hot Chocolate, 286
"House of the Rising Sun," 12, 119, 231, 285
Houses of the Holy (album), 175, 309, 314, 318
"How to Give Yourself a Stereo Checkup," 61
Howe, Ashley, 282
Howe, Steve, 117
Howlett, Mike, 271
Hudson, John, 238, 290
Hugg, Mike, 254
Humphries, Brian, 75
"Hurdy Gurdy Man," 285

Huxley, Robb, 144
Hynde, Chrissie, 247

"I Am the Walrus," 233
"I Don't Like Mondays," 289
"I Want You (She's So Heavy)," 179
Ibbetson, Adrian, 234
IBC, 3, 64, 87, 88, 89, 90, 91, 92, 93, 94, 95, 96, 97, 98, 99,
    107, 133, 303, 305
    CU-3H equalizer, 143
    limiter, 64
    Mobile, 303
IBC Studios, 3, 75, 87, 88–98, 107, 133, 139, 143, 144, 145,
    146, 149, 185, 191, 272, 277, 328
Idle, Eric, 253
IEC (International Electrotechnical Commission), 11, 12,
    209
Iggy and The Stooges, 226
Iles, John, 236, 237, 251, 252, 253, 254
"I'm Into Something Good," 285
"I'm Not in Love," 84
Imperial Bedroom (album), 267
"In the Air Tonight," 7, 296
In the Court of the Crimson King (album), 247
"In the Summertime," 82, 86
Indiscreet (album), 292
INXS, 247
Iommi, Tony, 276
Isaacs, Tim, 292
Island Mobile, 264, 322–324
Island Records, 261, 324
Island Studios, 261–266, 279, 316, 322
Isoloop, 28, 56, 163, 215
"It Takes Two to Tango," 290
"Itchycoo Park," 172, 175
ITI
    equalizers, 241, 277
    ME-230 parametric equalizer, 85
"It's All Too Much," 232

Jackman, Andrew, 250
Jackman, Gregg, 250
Jackson, Joe, 299
Jackson, Michael, 198, 288
Jagger, Mick, 2, 20, 67, 154, 156, 307, 309
"Jaywalker," 146
Jaywalkers, Peter Jay and the, 133, 146
JBL
    components/speaker drivers, 53, 112, 240, 270, 291,
        301, 328
    monitors. See monitors
Jeff Wayne's Musical Version of The War of the Worlds
    (album), 118
"Jennifer Juniper," 285
Jethro Tull, 238, 244, 250, 262, 265, 322, 327, 328
Joe Meek's Bold Techniques (book), 101, 144

John, Elton, 78, 149, 179, 191, 193, 198, 235, 237, 238,
    241, 272
"Johnny, Remember Me," 146, 147
Johns, Andy, 151, 157, 163, 248, 263, 308, 309
Johns, Glyn, 3, 13, 89, 91, 149, 151, 154, 156, 158, 166, 169,
    170, 171, 172, 174, 248, 256, 262, 263, 305, 307
Johnson, Bill, 221, 236
Johnson, Terry, 43, 54, 57, 64, 89, 121
Jones, Brian, 20, 154
Jones, Gloria, 212, 213, 273
Jones, Jack, 260
Jones, John Paul, 263, 285
Jones, Steve, 246
Jones, Terry, 241
"Jumpin' Jack Flash," 263

"Kashmir," 318
Kavan, Clive, 121, 151, 161
Keary, Vic, 101, 238, 254, 255
Keating, Martin, 50, 58, 61
KEF monitors. See monitors
Keith Prowse Music, 234
Kent, Tony, 222
Kepex noise gate. See Allison Research
Ker, Pete, 266
Kernon, Neil, 179, 189
Kerridge, Adrian, 13, 89, 93, 94, 96, 97, 99, 101, 102, 103,
    104, 105, 106, 120, 141, 145, 146
Kimsey, Chris, 151, 170, 174
King, Dennis, 89, 93, 95, 98
King Crimson, 238, 245, 247
Kingsway Hall, 15, 41, 42, 50, 66, 303
Kingsway Studios, 119, 124, 230–232
Kinks, The, 75, 77, 80, 86, 91, 98, 233, 250, 255,
    261, 277
Kinks Are the Village Green Preservation Society, The (album),
    77, 86
Klark Teknik
    DN27 graphic equalizer, 213
    DN34 delay line, 95
    graphic equalizer, 106, 130, 301
Klein, Allen, 258
Klein, Eddie, 258
Klein & Hummel
    amplifiers. See amplifiers
    graphic equalizer, 225
    UE400 equalizer, 86
Konk Studios, 261
Korner, Alexis, 160, 237, 238
Kossoff, Paul, 282, 298
KPM. See Keith Prowse Music
Kramer, Billy J., 35
Kramer, Eddie, 75, 79, 82, 108, 112, 151, 152, 154, 159, 166,
    168, 171, 269, 271, 304
"Kreen-Akrore," 249
Kurlander, John, 16, 30, 32, 33

Lambert, Kit, 116
Lane, Ronnie, 316, 318
Langan, Gary, 279
Lange, Robert John "Mutt," 266
Langer, Clive, 268
Langevin
    compressor/limiter, 142
    EQ251-A equalizer, 81
    EQ252 equalizer, 81
    equalizer, 7, 235
Lansdowne Studios, 2, 13, 87, 89, 96, 99–106, 115, 120, 133,
    141, 142, 145, 227, 248, 252, 254, 255, 282, 289
Leak amplifiers. *See* amplifiers
Leckie, John, 16, 298
Led Zeppelin, 1, 63, 150, 166, 175, 238, 262, 263, 304, 308,
    314, 318
Led Zeppelin IV (album), 263, 308, 314
Leevers-Rich
    A501 graphic equalizer, 237
    tape machines. *See* tape machines
Legendary Joe Meek, The (book), 138
Lennon, John, 2, 3, 20, 30, 33, 34, 35, 54, 180, 256
Lenny, Malcolm, 134, 136, 137
Leon, Craig, 8
Let It Be (album), 39, 256
Levy, Jacques, 221, 222
Levy, Morris, 221
Levy's Sound Studios, 6, 221–226, 236, 241, 243
Lewis, Sir Edward, 41, 43
Lexicon
    200 digital reverb, 229
    224 digital reverb, 279, 299, 314
    digital delay, 241, 296
    Primetime digital reverb, 299
Lexicon of Love (album), 279
Leyton, John, 146, 147
Lilley, Arthur, 42, 43, 50, 54, 58
Lindsay 7607 graphic equalizer, 299
Lion Television, 192
"Live and Let Die," 217, 219
Live and Let Die (film), 217
Live at Leeds (album), 305, 306
Living in the Material World (album), 261
Livingston, Dandy, 255
Lock, James, 43, 51, 66, 88, 89, 90, 92, 96
Lockwood cabinets, 6, 25, 53, 54, 81, 93, 108, 112, 126, 137,
    154, 161, 183, 185, 204, 221, 228, 231, 234, 237,
    247, 249, 253, 263, 287, 299, 304, 306, 307, 312, 315
Lockwood Major, 161
Lola Versus Powerman and the Moneygoround, Part One
    (album), 233
London Calling (album), 247
London Symphony Orchestra, 15, 50, 68, 210, 217, 250
Lord, Jon, 91
Lulu, 285
Lush, Richard, 16, 36

Lynott, Philip, 292
Lyons, Gary, 278
Lyrec, 294
    cutting lathe, 95, 116, 255
    tape machines. *See* tape machines

Mackay, Andy, 202, 282
Mackenna's Gold (film), 191
Mackswith, John, 101, 103, 106, 108, 289
Madness, 268
Madras, "Magic" Alex, 196, 256
Magazine (band), 298, 299, 322
"Magical Mystery Tour," 36
Magical Mystery Tour (album), 39, 253
Magna-Tech, 117
Magnetophon tape machine. *See* tape machines
Maile, Vic, 75, 306, 315
Mailes, Mike, 43, 50
Maison Rouge Mobile, 327–328
MAM Records, 227
Manfred Mann, 70, 238, 254
Manor, The, 151, 262, 268–272, 280, 294, 297, 298, 315, 318
Manor Mobiles, 262, 270, 271, 298, 307, 315, 318–322
Manzanera, Phil, 282
Marconi, 84
    limiter/compressors, 86, 106, 279
    microphones. *See* microphones/BBC
Marcus Studios, 120
Marquee Club, 177, 192, 238, 241
Marquee Studio, 238–241
Marriott, Steve, 78
Marshall Time Modulator, 229, 241, 247, 276, 284, 289, 292
"Martha My Dear," 12, 179
Martin, Bill, 235
Martin, George, 1, 2, 4, 6, 8, 14, 15, 16, 27, 35, 130, 171, 172,
    195, 196, 198, 201, 203, 206, 213, 214, 217, 218,
    253, 256
Martyn, John, 324
"Mary Had a Little Lamb," 169
Massenburg, George, 6, 85
Master Room spring reverb, 64, 270, 293, 316, 328
Matlock, Glen, 246
Matrix Studios, 248, 292–294
Mattacks, Dave, 244
Matthews, Anton, 151, 164
Maximum Sound, 254, 255
Mayall, John, 68, 238
Mayfair Studios, 237, 238, 290
McBride, Jim, 151, 160, 167, 169
McCartney (album), 249
McCartney, Paul, 2, 7, 8, 12, 17, 24, 54, 169, 192, 198, 217,
    218, 219, 249, 250
McDonald, Phil, 16, 20
MCI, 114, 207, 225
    mixing boards. *See* mixing boards
    synchronizer, 209

tape machines. *See* tape machines
McKay, Dennis, 264
Mckenna, Mick, 151, 305, 308, 310, 311, 312, 313, 314
McKenna, Rafe, 121, 123, 126, 128, 130
McKenzie, Angus, 149, 150
McLaren, Malcolm, 235
McLaren Ward & Partners, 227
McVie, John, 275
Meek, Joe, 13, 14, 87, 89, 94, 96, 97, 99, 100, 101, 102, 106, 133–147, 235, 255
Melanie, 245
Mellotron, 64, 84, 98
"Mellow Yellow," 106, 285
Melody Maker (periodical), 233
Meyer noise gates, 241
Michie, Chris, 199, 209, 210
Micro Kit microphones. *See* microphones
microphones
    AKG, 60, 74, 127, 140, 141, 166, 239, 247, 250, 279, 282, 288, 290, 299, 301, 306, 322, 326
    AKG C12, 128, 164
    AKG C12A, 128, 164, 187, 250, 253, 255, 281
    AKG C24, 95, 165
    AKG C28, 57, 59, 64, 95, 115, 187, 255, 265
    AKG C34, 313
    AKG C414, 74, 95, 129, 235, 265
    AKG C414 B-ULS, 129
    AKG C451, 74, 165, 166, 187, 265
    AKG C535, 74
    AKG D12, 74, 105, 129, 166, 187, 189, 211, 250, 265, 267, 271, 281
    AKG D19, 49, 60, 140, 221, 226
    AKG D19c, 29, 30, 243
    AKG D20, 30, 74, 166, 255, 265
    AKG D24, 74
    AKG D25, 74, 166, 265
    AKG D30, 159, 166, 170
    AKG D60, 141
    AKG D190, 74
    AKG D190E, 74
    AKG D202, 188, 211, 226, 237, 253, 255, 271, 281
    AKG D224, 82, 83, 166, 188, 211, 271, 281
    AKG D224E, 74, 255, 265
    Altec 639A, 29, 141
    Altec 639B, 141
    BBC/Marconi, 221, 238
    BBC/Marconi AXBT, 84, 95, 105
    BBC PGD, 166
    BBC PGS, 166, 253
    Beyer, 95, 188, 237, 250, 273, 299, 313, 322, 326
    Beyer M23, 141
    Beyer M61, 141
    Beyer M66, 74
    Beyer M67, 74
    Beyer M69, 271
    Beyer M88, 84, 271
    Beyer M160, 84, 166, 240, 265, 267, 271
    Beyer M201, 74
    Beyer M260, 74
    Beyer M360, 271
    Beyer Soundstar, 271
    Calrec 1050, 322
    Calrec 1050c, 255
    Countryman, 313
    Electrovoice RE20, 84, 129, 188, 240, 253
    Fi-Cord, 255
    Film Industries M8, 243
    HMV 235CH, 141
    Micro Kit Omni Capacitor, 141
    Neumann CMV 3, 60
    Neumann KM53, 21, 29, 58, 65, 128
    Neumann KM54, 29, 59, 103, 105, 128, 164, 187, 189, 222, 243, 282
    Neumann KM56, 29, 58, 65, 83, 128, 141, 187, 237, 243
    Neumann KM64, 59, 74, 128, 237, 270
    Neumann KM66, 128
    Neumann KM84, 30, 59, 74, 94, 128, 164, 187, 211, 231, 237, 239, 253, 255, 270, 273
    Neumann KM86, 74, 128, 164, 211, 235
    Neumann KM88, 128, 243
    Neumann M49, 29, 58, 60, 83, 94, 105, 128, 164, 270, 273, 306
    Neumann M50, 29, 30, 58, 60, 65, 306
    Neumann SM2, 141, 237
    Neumann SM69, 74, 164, 253, 313
    Neumann U47, 29, 30, 58, 60, 78, 83, 94, 105, 128, 138, 140, 141, 164, 170, 222, 228, 231, 239, 243, 255, 267, 270, 273, 281
    Neumann U48, 29, 83, 222, 273
    Neumann U64, 115, 253
    Neumann U64D, 74
    Neumann U67, 29, 58, 74, 83, 94, 105, 115, 128, 154, 164, 187, 189, 222, 237, 239, 243, 253, 265, 270, 273, 281, 282, 288
    Neumann U77, 83, 270
    Neumann U87, 29, 30, 58, 74, 83, 94, 105, 115, 128, 164, 166, 210, 228, 231, 237, 239, 251, 253, 255, 265, 270, 271, 273, 281, 306
    Pearl, 239
    RCA, 6, 141, 243, 253, 279
    RCA 44-BX, 30, 84, 115
    RCA BK 6B, 60
    RCA KU54A, 255
    RCA ribbon, 253
    RCA Type 77DX, 59, 84
    Reslosound Ribbon, 140
    Schoeps, 6
    Schoeps CMC56, 271
    Sennheiser, 58, 95, 226, 240, 247, 250, 276, 279, 282, 288, 290, 299, 313
    Sennheiser MD421, 84, 129, 205, 212, 316
    Sennheiser MD421N, 273

microphones (*continued*)
  Sennheiser MD441, 188
  Shure, 456, 271
  Shure SM57, 6, 85, 129, 205, 212, 240, 255, 265, 322
  Shure SM58, 85, 129, 157, 313, 322
  Sony C38, 243
  Sony C38B, 188
  STC Coles 4021, 79, 85, 95, 102, 105, 109, 115
  STC 4033-A, 29, 95, 243
  STC (Coles) 4038, 29, 60, 85, 105, 166, 188, 205, 211, 253, 260, 271
  Telefunken, 6
  Telefunken ELA M250, 141, 164
  Telefunken ELA M251, 60, 95, 141, 164, 170, 273
  Telefunken NSH, 141
  Westrex ribbon, 253
Millar, Robin, 226, 250
Millard, Richard, 226, 227
Miller, Jimmy, 154, 157, 174
Miller, Peter, 133, 135, 136, 137, 139, 141, 144, 145, 146
Mills Music, 235
mixing boards
  Alice, 235
  Amex, 290
  API, 52, 206, 287, 288
  API 2488, 325
  Cadac, 103, 104, 229, 247, 248, 249, 250, 251, 272, 273, 274, 282, 297, 318
  EMI, 102, 105, 222, 243, 254
  EMI REDD, 13, 22, 23, 24, 37
  EMI REDD.17, 22
  EMI REDD.37, 22
  EMI REDD.51, 22, 23, 24
  EMI TG, 24, 25, 37, 258
  EMI TG12345, 23, 24
  EMI TG Mk IV, 37
  Harrison, 249, 284, 297
  Helios, 160, 183, 235, 258, 262, 263, 264, 266, 270, 272, 277, 278, 295, 297, 308, 311, 313, 316, 318, 320, 321, 322, 328
  MCI 500-series, 263
  MCI JH-400, 299
  MCI JH-416, 240
  MCI JH-500, 300
  MCI JH-536, 241
  MCI JH-538, 240
  MCI JH-542, 240, 241
  Neumann, 72, 79, 81, 258, 304
  Neve, 5, 25, 53, 70, 72, 73, 80, 81, 85, 111, 124, 125, 126, 130, 197, 205, 206, 212, 217, 222, 223, 225, 227, 246, 247, 252, 254, 278, 289, 290, 305, 307, 314, 315, 320, 322
  Neve 8078, 278
  Neve 8088, 278
  Neve A27, 205
  Neve A29, 205
  Neve A45, 205
  Neve A88, 246
  Neve A210, 228, 229
  Neve A4792 "AIR Montserrat," 13, 205, 207
  Neve BCM10, 228, 229
  Neve Series 80, 80, 305
  Phonogram, 72, 73, 74
  Quad Eight, 111, 112, 117, 118
  Raindirk, 161, 232, 321
  Rebis, 268
  Sound Techniques, 13, 124, 125, 126, 180, 182, 183, 184, 190, 231, 243, 244, 281
  Sound Techniques System 12, 243
  Soundcraft 2400, 290
  SSL 4000, 279, 297
  SSL 4000B, 297
  SSL 4000E, 272, 274, 295, 296, 299
  SSL 4048E, 297
  Telefunken, 124
  Tiros Electronics, 234, 236, 237, 238
  Trident A-Range, 13, 180, 183, 184, 185, 192, 276, 292
  Trident B-Range, 184, 192, 276, 279, 291
  Trident Fleximix, 192, 291
  Trident Series 80, 184, 185, 192
  Trident Series 80B, 281
  Trident TSM, 13, 180, 185, 192, 276, 279, 291, 293
  Vortexion, 221, 234, 305
  Vortexion 4/15/M, 136
  Walsall Timing Developments, 268
Mixing with Your Mind (book), 213
monitors
  Altec, 104, 272, 281
  Altec 604, 6, 274, 312
  Altec 604E, 321
  Altec 605A, 25
  Auratone, 127, 279, 287, 288
  Auratone 5C, 270
  Cadac, 258, 282
  Cadac "Power House," 273
  Eastlake, 240, 241, 289, 296
  Eastlake TM-3, 81, 284
  Eastlake TMI, 241
  EMI RLS 10 ("White Elephant"), 25
  EMI RS143 ("Dr. Dutton" speaker), 25
  EPI Model 50, 263
  JBL, 6, 26, 54, 113, 185, 238, 250
  JBL 4310, 326
  JBL 4311, 208, 322
  JBL 4320, 269
  JBL 4326, 276
  JBL 4333, 291
  JBL 4341, 299
  JBL 4343, 284
  JBL 4350, 112, 185, 206, 207, 208, 225, 232, 263, 282
  KEF Slimline, 79, 81
  Tannoy, 6, 25, 49, 53, 54, 73, 81, 108, 109, 126, 137, 138,

204, 205, 206, 207, 221, 222, 226, 231, 234, 239, 247, 254, 266, 279, 281, 293, 304, 315, 316, 318, 328
Tannoy Gold, 21, 25, 126, 127, 162, 207, 242, 249
Tannoy HPD, 207, 208, 249, 315, 321
Tannoy Lancaster, 81
Tannoy Red, 137, 162, 185, 235, 237, 306
Tannoy Silver, 161
Tannoy Super Red, 161, 294
UREI 813, 273, 274, 301
Westlake, 47, 53
Westlake BBSM4, 291
Yamaha NS10, 274
Montserrat. *See* AIR Montserrat
Monty Python, 63, 241, 268
Moody Blues, The, 42, 43, 61, 63, 64, 66, 68, 98, 238
Moog synthesizer, 264, 265, 292, 324
Morais, Trevor, 311
Morgan, Barry, 103, 248
Morgan Studios, 103, 157, 248–251, 328
Moriarty, Mick, 70, 72
Morrison, Van, 57, 272, 298
Most, Mickie, 2, 38, 230, 285, 286, 287, 289, 325, 326
Motörhead, 217, 278, 284
Motown, 2, 3, 7, 10, 221, 281
Mott the Hoople, 115, 118, 250, 262
Mott the Hoople (album), 250
Moulder, Alan, 250
Move, The, 70, 74, 107
Mr. Big, 274
MSS disc cutter, 143
Mud, 289
"Mull of Kintyre," 326
Mullin, Jack, 9
Mungo Jerry, 82, 86, 255
Murray, Alex, 238
Murray, Barry, 82
Muscle Shoals Studios, 281
Music Centre, The, 118–131
Muswell Hillbillies (album), 250
MXR, 273
    digital delay, 95, 296
    Flanger, 299
    phaser/flanger, 106
My Aim Is True (album), 267
Myhill, Richard, 290

NAB (National Association of Broadcasters), 11, 12, 27, 184, 187, 209
Nagra tape machine. *See* tape machines
Nashville Teens, 285
NECAM. *See* Neve
Neumann
    lathe, 259
    microphones. *See* microphones
    mixing boards. *See* mixing boards
Neve, 72, 85, 92, 111, 183, 205, 297

2254 limiter/compressor, 130, 212
AIR Montserrat mixing board. *See* mixing boards/ Neve A4792
compressors/limiters, 228, 248, 270, 287, 288, 289, 316
mixing boards. *See* mixing boards
modules, 306
NECAM automation, 72, 205, 290
Neve, Rupert, 72, 73, 198, 206, 207
Never Mind the Bollocks, Here's the Sex Pistols (album), 247
Nevison, Ron, 203, 316, 317, 318
New Musical Express (periodical), 233
Newell, Norman, 69, 253
Newell, Philip, 13, 75, 81, 83, 85, 268, 270, 271, 294, 296, 297, 305, 306, 314, 315, 318, 319, 320, 321, 322
Newman, Tom, 269
Newmark, Andy, 2, 324
Nicol, Simon, 245
Night at the Opera, A (album), 274, 279, 284
"Not Fade Away," 234
Nunn, Paul, 198, 247
Nye, Steve, 198, 217

O'Connor, Hazel, 292
O'Duffy, Alan, 77, 157
Odyssey Studios, 300–301
Offord, Eddy, 117
Oldfield, Mike, 269, 272, 298, 320, 322
Oldham, Andrew Loog, 2, 89, 172, 234
Oliff, Peter, 70, 71
Olympic Studios, 4, 5, 6, 13, 39, 78, 81, 89, 90, 93, 102, 112, 149–175, 178, 244, 245, 248, 262, 277, 304, 305, 308, 311, 312
Ommadawn (album), 320
"One After 909," 130
One for the Road (album), 318
One World (album), 324
Orban
    de-esser, 190, 241, 270
    equalizer, 190, 247, 273, 279, 314
    Parasound stereo parametric equalizer, 276
Optimists, The (film), 214
Orchestral Manoeuvres in the Dark, 238, 289
Oriole Records, 221, 222, 242
Ortofon
    cutting head, 95
    lathe, 116, 255
Osbourne, Ozzy, 299
Osibisa, 284
Otari, 113
    tape machines. *See* tape machines
Outlaws, The, 136, 147
Owen, Frank, 150, 151, 304, 322

Packabeats, The, 134, 136, 147
Padgham, Hugh, 5, 7, 13, 101, 108, 113, 115, 204, 205, 296
Page, Jimmy, 63, 78, 159, 263, 285, 303

Painton faders, 102, 109
Palin, Michael, 241
Palmer, Robert, 324
Pandora Time Line, 62, 270
PanScan autopanner, 299
"Paperback Writer," 38
Paranoid (album), 234
Parker, Chris, 16, 32
Parlophone Records, 6, 36, 55
Parsons, Alan, 16, 27, 28, 36, 84, 214
Pathway Studio, 266–268
Paul, Les, 9, 97, 113
Pearl microphones. *See* microphones
Pearson, Johnny, 120
Peckham, George, 96, 259, 260
Peer/Southern Music, 235
Pender, Ron, 258
Pendleton, Harold, 238, 241
Perfect Timing (album), 288
Perkins, Alan, 75, 305, 306, 315, 316, 321
Perkins, Carl, 218
"Perpetual Change," 117
Pettinger, Russel, 155
Pharo, Roger, 239, 241
Phase 4, 68
phasing, 13, 81, 94, 96, 116, 171, 172, 175, 254, 271
Philips, 13, 41, 69, 70, 71, 72, 73, 74, 87, 254
    film projectors, 214
    tape machines. *See* tape machines
Philips Records, 69, 70, 71, 89, 254
Philips Studio, 69–74, 80, 87, 89
Phillips, Sam, 33
Phonogram, 72, 290
    analog delay line, 74
    compressors/limiters, 74
    "Magnetic Audio Delay Wheel," 74, 254
    mixing boards. *See* mixing boards
Phonogram Records, 70, 71, 73, 254, 290
Physical Graffiti (album), 318
Pilot, 214
Pinder, Mike, 43, 63
Pinewood Film Studios, 214, 311
Pink Floyd, 1, 11, 16, 27, 28, 39, 66, 117, 229, 232, 238, 244, 250, 261, 288, 289
Pitney, Gene, 234
Plant, Robert, 169, 282, 303
Platt, Tony, 266
Please Please Me (book), 3, 5, 14
Plugge, Leonard, 88, 89
Police, The, 1, 47, 198, 204, 205, 218, 219, 268, 294
Polygram, 43
Porter, Barry, 179, 183, 192
"Power to the People," 259
Pressure Drop (album), 324
Preston, Denis, 87, 89, 99, 100, 101, 102, 103, 106, 145
Pretenders, The, 238, 247, 248

Price, Bill, 7, 43, 48, 49, 50, 54, 55, 61, 62, 66, 195, 198, 202, 213, 214, 215, 216, 217, 246, 247
Prickett, Ray, 75, 77, 78, 79, 80, 83, 89, 96, 145, 314, 315
"Private Life," 247
Procol Harum, 112, 175, 209, 219, 238, 278
Pultec
    EQP-1A, 62, 85, 167, 189, 234
    EQP-1A3, 62
    equalizers, 7, 22, 48, 92, 95, 106, 130, 143, 167, 222, 225, 237, 241, 243, 263, 273, 314
    HLF-3C, 167
    MEQ-5, 85
Punter, John, 43, 196, 198, 211, 213
"Purple Haze," 231
Putnam, Bill, 73
Pye, 41, 85, 157, 305, 314, 318
    compressor, 85, 115, 167, 250
    limiter, 167
    TVT limiter, 252
Pye Mobile, 270, 305, 307, 314–316, 319, 320
Pye Records, 41, 75, 76, 78, 91
Pye Studios, 75–86, 268, 273, 277, 278, 304, 306, 312, 314, 318
Pythons, The (book), 241

quad. *See* quadraphonic
Quad
    22 preamplifier, 137
    amplifiers. *See* amplifiers
Quad Eight
    mixing boards. *See* mixing boards
    spring reverb, 292
quadraphonic, 27, 52, 54, 59, 73, 81, 93, 111, 247, 249, 250, 251, 270, 277, 282
Quadrophenia (album), 278, 316, 318
Quatro, Suzi, 229, 286
Queen, 1, 11, 179, 192, 247, 271, 272, 284, 298, 322, 328
Queen's Hall, 15, 303

Radford amplifiers. *See* amplifiers
Radiators, 292
Radio Antilles, 201
Radio Luxembourg, 89, 90, 145, 226, 227
Rafferty, Gerry, 276, 301
"Rain," 38
Raindirk mixing boards. *See* mixing boards
RAK Mobile, 286, 325–326, 327
RAK Music Management, 285
RAK Publishing, 285
RAK Records, 285, 286
RAK Studios, 285–289
Ramone, Phil, 2
Ramport Studio, 261, 262, 277–278, 296, 297, 316
Raw Power (album), 226
RayRik Studios, 237, 254
RCA Corporation, 5, 7, 59

35mm magnetic recorders, 131
amplifiers. *See* amplifiers
    LM1/322 preamplifier, 136
microphones. *See* microphones
    Orthophonic preamplifier/filter, 136
RCA Studio B (Nashville), 2
RCA Studios (Hollywood), 3
RCA Victor, 68
Rebis
    limiters, 292
    mixing boards. *See* mixing boards
    parametric equalizers, 296
Recording Studio Design (book), 307, 314, 319
Regent Sound Studios, 149, 233, 234, 235, 236
Repsch, John, 138, 144, 146
Reslosound microphones. *See* microphones
Revolver (album), 4, 130
Revox tape machines. *See* tape machines
RGM Sound, 133
Richard, Cliff, 3, 16, 227
Richards, John, 121
Richards, Keith, 2, 4, 154, 307, 308, 309
Richards, Ron, 195
"Ride a White Swan," 182
Ridge Farm Studio, 298–299
Rivera, Jake, 267
Robinson, Dave, 267
Robinson, Eric, 89, 98
Rockfield Studios, 268, 280
Roger Mayer gates, 277
Rolling Stones, the, 1, 2, 3, 20, 42, 43, 66, 67, 89, 119, 150,
    152, 158, 166, 174, 175, 192, 227, 231, 234, 238,
    262, 277, 298, 307, 314
Rolling Stones Mobile, 13, 262, 305, 307–314, 318, 321, 322
Rolling Stones Rock and Roll Circus (television show), 305
Ronnie Lane Mobile, 278, 316–318
Ronnie Scott's, 306
Ronson, Mick, 187, 274
Ross-Trevor, Mike, 222, 223, 224, 225
Rotten, Johnny, 246
Roundhouse Theatre, 282, 283, 284
Roundhouse Studio, 282–284
Rowe, Dick, 55, 57
Roxy Music, 202
Royal Albert Hall, 108, 201, 258, 303, 309
RPG diffusors, 276
Rubber Soul (album), 12, 27
Rubettes, the, 300
Rutles, The (album), 253
Rye, Arthur, 236
Ryemuse, 236–238

Sabotage (album), 250
Sagatone amplifier. *See* amplifiers
Sage, Barry, 322, 324
Sanders, Colin, 297

Sarm, 265, 278–279
Sarm East. *See* Sarm
Sarm West, 265, 279
Savage, Mike, 43, 54
Savage, The, 81, 268
"Savoy Truffle," 179
Sawmills, 280–282
Saxons, the, 144
Sayer, Leo, 120, 192
Scamp rack. *See* ADR
Scary Monsters (album), 292
Schnee, Bill, 274
Schoeps microphones. *See* microphones
Schulze, Klaus, 264
Scorpio Sound, 272–274
Scott, Andy, 228
Scott, Ken, 16, 23, 27, 179, 184
Screaming Lord Sutch, 135
Scully, Larry, 133
Scully tape machines. *See* tape machines
"Season of the Witch," 285
"See Emily Play," 244
Sennheiser
    dummy head, 279
    microphones. *See* microphones
Sex Pistols, the, 1, 235, 238, 245, 246, 247
Sgt. Pepper (film), 206
Sgt. Pepper's Lonely Hearts Club Band (album), 36, 39, 64,
    234, 307
Shakespeare in Love (film), 120
Shearer, Ken, 13, 201, 202, 258
Sheer Heart Attack (album), 247
Sheffield, Barry, 177, 183, 186
Sheffield, Norman, 177, 178, 180, 182, 183, 185, 186, 187,
    188, 189, 191, 192, 193
Shelton, Louie, 210
Shepperton Film Studios, 43, 192, 311
Shrieve, Michael, 264, 265
Shure microphones. *See* microphones
Siddle, Dave, 119, 120, 121, 122, 124, 127, 128, 131,
    231, 232
Silver, Peter, 228
Simon, Paul, 2, 235
Simon Sound Services disc cutter, 143
Sinclair, David, 278
Sinclair, Jill, 279
Sinclair, John, 278
Slade, 131, 169, 290
Slade, Dick, 191
Slaughter, Keith, 16, 195, 198, 201, 299, 300
Slea, Mike, 122
Small Faces, The, 98, 172, 238, 284, 316
Smith, John, 257, 258, 259, 260
Smith, Mike, 54, 104, 105
Smith, Norman, 8, 16, 29, 31
Smith, Peter, 89, 328

Smiths, The, 294, 299
"Smoke on the Water," 311, 314
Solid Bond Studios, 70, 73, 261
Solid State Logic. *See* SSL
"Someone Saved My Life Tonight," 241
Sonet Records, 282
Songs from the Wood (album), 250
Sony microphones. *See* microphones
Sound and Recording Mobiles. *See* Sarm
Sound Man (book), 3, 156, 170, 171
"Sound of Silence, The," 235
Sound Techniques, 124, 127, 130, 182, 222, 241, 242, 243,
    244, 245, 281
    mixing boards. *See* mixing boards
Sound Techniques Studios, 6, 119, 222, 241–245, 280
Soundcraft mixing boards. *See* mixing boards
Southern Music. *See* Peer/Southern Music
Sparks (band), 291, 292
Spector, Phil, 2, 71, 113, 234
Spectrasonics compressor, 115
Spedding, Chris, 326
Speight, Bernard, 35
Spot Productions, 237, 238
Spot Productions Studios. *See* Spot Productions
Spot Studios. *See* Spot Productions
Springfield, Dusty, 69, 235
"Sprinkling of Clouds, A," 271
Squire, Chris, 117
SSL, 297
    mixing boards. *See* mixing boards
Stagg, Allen, 25, 89, 90, 91, 95, 97
"Stairway to Heaven," 263
Star Sound, 226–229
Starr, Ringo, 218, 261
Startling Studios, 261
State Records, 300
Status Quo, 70, 75, 81, 86, 98, 276
Stavrou, Mike, 198, 210, 211, 212, 213, 218
Stax Studios, 4, 7, 281
STC microphones. *See* microphones
Stealers Wheel, 261
STEED (Single Tape Echo / Echo Delay), 35, 36
Steve Miller Band, the, 263
Stewart, Ian, 262, 307, 308, 309, 310
Stewart, Rod, 250, 316
Sticklen, Derek, 80
Sticky Fingers (album), 174, 175, 308, 314
Stiff Records, 267
Stigwood, Robert, 236
Stock/Aitken/Waterman, 240
Stockhausen, Karlheinz, 199
Stone, Mike, 179, 278
Stone Alone (book), 309
Stoned (book), 234
Storyk, John, 276
Straight Shooter (album), 318

Strawberry Studios, 261
"Stuck in the Middle with You," 261
Studer, 6, 9
    amplifiers. *See* amplifiers
    tape machines. *See* tape machines
"Substitute," 155
Sullivan, Peter, 195
"Sultans of Swing," 268
Summerhayes, Tim, 287, 288, 326
"Sun God," 144
Sun Studios, 33
Sunset Sound Studios, 154, 243, 274
"Sunshine Superman," 285
Supertramp, 179, 191, 238, 274, 278
Survival Projects panner, 279
Sweet, The, 228, 229, 289
Sweet Sixteens, 213
Swettenham, Dick, 13, 93, 149, 151, 158, 159, 160, 161, 167,
    169, 171, 175, 262, 292, 307
"Sympathy for the Devil," 154

T. Rex, 5, 8, 41, 182, 212, 273
TAD speaker components, 291
Tales from Topographic Oceans (album), 250
Talmy, Shel, 91, 233, 268
Tamla Motown. *See* Motown
Tannoy monitors. *See* monitors
tape machines
    3M M23, 24, 27, 28, 159, 163, 209, 231, 305, 307, 315
    3M M56, 10, 56, 113, 163, 186, 208, 215, 216, 313
    3M M79, 56, 113, 163, 208, 247, 249, 273, 277, 278,
        281, 313, 322, 325
    Ampex 300, 139, 222, 236
    Ampex 350, 82, 235
    Ampex 351, 82, 139, 164
    Ampex 354, 55, 82, 139
    Ampex A300, 55, 56, 82, 105, 109, 112
    Ampex A350, 162
    Ampex AG300, 94, 163, 253
    Ampex AG330, 163
    Ampex AG-350, 82
    Ampex AG-440, 94, 112, 113, 185, 246, 254, 313
    Ampex AG-440C, 270
    Ampex AGB-440B, 247
    Ampex ATR-100, 254, 299
    Ampex ATR-102, 94, 210, 296
    Ampex ATR-104, 296
    Ampex ATR-124, 322
    Ampex MM1000, 55, 82, 83, 239, 247, 254
    Ampex MM1100, 73, 270, 272, 306, 315, 322
    Ampex MM1200, 94, 322
    Ampex MR-70, 82, 185, 186
    Ampex PR10, 139, 237
    EMI BTR1, 92, 94
    EMI BTR2, 26, 34, 35, 36, 48, 54, 56, 57, 94, 139,
        144, 163, 221

EMI BTR3, 26
EMI TR50, 104, 105, 139
EMI TR51, 104, 105, 138, 139, 304
EMI TR90, 48, 54, 56, 82, 105, 222, 226
Ferrograph Studio 8, 209
Grundig, 304
Leevers-Rich, 237, 238, 239, 254
Lyrec TR4, 112
Lyrec TR16, 138
Lyrec TR16-S, 138, 139
Lyrec TR532, 287, 288, 291
Magnetophon, 9, 221
MCI JH-16, 114, 115, 209, 276
MCI JH-24, 114, 240, 276, 299, 301
MCI JH-100, 240, 276
MCI JH-114, 241
MCI JH-120, 240, 241
MCI JH-140, 240
Nagra, 314, 316
Otari MTR-90, 274, 294
Philips, 56, 112, 127, 236, 263
Philips 3302 (cassette), 154
Philips EL3501, 73, 164
Philips Pro/50, 73
Philips Pro/51, 163, 254
Philips Pro/75, 73
Revox A77, 164, 267, 276, 291
Revox B77, 267
Scully 100, 113
Scully 270, 113
Scully 280, 55, 113
Scully 280B, 113
Scully 284-8, 55, 82, 105, 112, 114
Studer A62, 127, 209
Studer A80, 28, 29, 55, 74, 83, 94, 105, 114, 127, 187,
   209, 223, 225, 228, 232, 238, 240, 244, 247, 249,
   254, 272, 276, 278, 279, 282, 284, 288, 289, 290,
   291, 315, 316, 317, 322, 328
Studer A80 Mk II, 273
Studer A80R, 209
Studer A800, 296, 297
Studer B62, 127, 164, 186, 229, 272, 290, 291, 326
Studer B67, 113, 164, 287, 291
Studer C37, 55, 187, 249
Studer J37, 26, 27, 28, 33, 34, 55, 56, 171, 209, 223,
   234, 249
Tascam, 321
TEAC TD-102, 235
Telefunken, 273, 293
Telefunken 15A, 299
Telefunken M10, 26
Telefunken M15, 105, 296
Telefunken T9u, 26
Tolana, 163
Vortexion WVB, 138, 139
Wollensak, 314

Tascam, 113
   tape machines. *See* tape machines
Taylor, Mick, 309
Taylor, Roger, 271
TEAC tape machine. *See* tape machines
Telefunken, 60
   microphones. *See* microphones
   mixing boards. *See* mixing boards
   tape machines. *See* tape machines
   V72 preamp, 79
Teletronix
   LA-2A leveling amplifier, 61, 85, 188, 234, 241, 279
   LA-3A compressor, 188, 189, 296
"Telstar," 133, 144, 147
Ten Years After, 68, 238, 250, 309
Thames Television, 272
Them, 57
Thick as a Brick (album), 250
Thin Lizzy, 68, 119, 192, 278, 291, 292, 299, 301
Thomas, Chris, 202, 209, 246, 247
Thompson, Danny, 324
Thompson, Gordon, 3, 14
Thompson, Mike, 245
Thompson, Paul, 202
Thompson, Robin, 245
Three Imaginary Boys (album), 250
Threshold Studios, 43, 44, 270
"Tiger Feet," 286
Time and a Word (album), 118, 280
Timms, John, 75, 77, 78, 84, 86, 120, 121, 122, 124,
   127, 224
Timperley, John, 89, 151, 236, 237, 251, 252
Tin Pan Alley, 233
Tin Pan Alley Studios, 233–235
Tiros Electronics mixing boards. *See* mixing boards
"To Sir with Love," 285
"Tobacco Road," 285
Toft, Malcolm, 179, 184, 186, 187, 189
Tolana tape machine. *See* tape machines
Tomlinson, Eric, 89, 94, 121, 122, 149
Tommy (album), 89, 95, 98
Top of the Pops (albums), 237
Top of the Pops (television show), 237, 298
Tornados, the, 133, 137, 147
"Totem Pole," 146
Townhouse, The, 7, 13, 151, 205, 262, 269, 271, 272, 278, 283,
   294–298, 321
Townsend, Ken, 13, 16, 20, 33, 34, 35, 39, 66
Townshend, Pete, 77, 97, 110, 156, 262, 277, 316
Toyashima, Sam, 297
TPA Studios. *See* Tin Pan Alley Studios
Traffic, 262
Trans Am, 238
TRIAD. *See* Trident Audio Developments
Trident Audio Developments, 192, 276
   CB9066 parametric equalizer, 190, 279

Trident Audio Developments (*continueed*)
     CB9146 FET compressor, 190
     mixing boards. *See* mixing boards
Trident Audio Productions, 191
Trident Studios, 4, 5, 6, 10, 12, 13, 27, 107, 112, 114,
          177–193, 225, 227, 243, 245, 248, 252, 276, 278
Trident Tape Services, 191
Trilion Video, 192
Triumph Records, 100
Troggs, The, 158
Trojan Records, 255
Tsangarides, Chris, 251
Tubular Bells (album), 269, 322
Turner amplifiers. *See* amplifiers
Twickenham Film Studios, 291
Two Weeks Last Summer (album), 270

U2, 226
Ultravox, 70, 238, 288
United Western Studios, 274
Unitrack, 127
Universal Audio
     175/175B compressor, 189
     176 compressor, 189
UREI
     1176 limiter, 63, 85, 103, 106, 130, 167, 188, 189, 212,
          213, 225, 228, 240, 250, 263, 270, 272, 279, 289,
          291, 293, 296, 322
     1176N limiter, 276, 288
     Little Dipper notch filter, 270, 279
     monitors. *See* monitors
Uriah Heep, 284
"Us and Them," 27
Utopia Records, 290
Utopia Studios, 289–290

Valley People, 292
Vangelis, 241
Varnals, Derek, 43, 44, 45, 46, 47, 49, 50, 51, 52, 53, 54, 55,
          57, 58, 60, 61, 62, 63, 64, 67
Veale, Eddie, 13, 108, 111, 241, 265, 279, 282, 292, 311
Vernon, Mike, 275, 276
Vernon, Richard, 275, 276
"Video Killed the Radio Star," 289, 298
"Vienna," 238, 288
Vienna (album), 288
Vince, Peter, 16, 21
Virgin Group, the, 151, 175, 268, 270, 271, 272, 278, 294, 297
Virgin Records, 262, 268, 269, 272, 278, 298, 319, 320
Virgin Studios Group, the, 298
Visconti, Tony, 5, 7, 8, 11, 12, 114, 181, 182, 185, 186, 187,
          189, 190, 240, 279, 290, 291, 292
Vixen (album), 212

Waddington, Tony, 300
Wainman, Phil, 289, 290

Wake, Roger, 70, 72, 73, 74
Wakeman, Rick, 191, 318
Walker, Nigel, 198, 204
Wall of Sound, 10, 71
Wallace, Roy, 44, 49, 65, 66
Walsall Timing Developments mixing board. *See* mixing
          boards
War Child (album), 250
Warner Brothers, 232
Waterman, Pete, 240, 268
Watkins, Charlie, 144
Watts, Charlie, 3, 154, 309
Watts, Pete "Overend," 115
Wayne, Jeff, 118
"We Will Rock You," 247
"Wear Your Love Like Heaven," 226
Wegg, Trisha, 286, 288
Weinreich, Dennis, 274
Welcome to the Pleasuredome (album), 279
Weller, Paul, 70, 261
WEM Fifth Man, 144
Wembley Stadium, 119, 120
Wessex Studios, 245–248, 294
Western Electric. *See* Westrex
Westlake Audio, 43, 78, 270, 271, 290
Westrex, 107, 108, 115, 116, 117, 161
     compressors, 85, 235, 279
     limiters, 306
     microphones. *See* microphones
"What You Need," 247
Whetstone, Andy, 108, 109, 111
Whetstone, Guy, 107
White, Simon, 239
White Album (*The Beatles*) (album), 10, 12, 27, 39, 179
White Bicycles (book), 1, 242, 244
"White Elephant" speaker. *See* monitors/EMI RLS 10
"White Riot," 226
White room equalizer, 284
"Whiter Shade of Pale, A," 112, 175
Whitfield Street Studios, 221–226
Who, The, 1, 2, 74, 77, 89, 95, 98, 107, 110, 118, 131, 155,
          166, 175, 177, 223, 226, 231, 237, 238, 261, 277,
          297, 301, 305, 306, 311, 316, 318, 322
Who Are You (album), 278
Who Sell Out, The (album), 231
"Whole Lotta Love," 159
"Wild Horses," 174
Wilkinson, Kenneth, 41, 43, 51, 65, 66
Williams, Pip, 288
Williams, Trevor Osmond, 15
Williamson, Robin, 244
Wilson, BJ, 209
"Wind Cries Mary, The," 231
Wings, 169, 217, 326
Winstanley, Alan, 268
Winwood, Muff, 261

Winwood, Steve, 157, 261, 264, 265, 324
Witchseason Productions, 244
Wollensak tape machine. *See* tape machines
Wonder, Stevie, 198, 218, 219
"Won't Get Fooled Again," 166
Wood, John, 6, 13, 222, 241, 242, 243, 244, 245
Wood, Phillip, 238, 239
Wood, Ronnie, 316
Woolworth's, 15, 41, 221
Worrell, Ken, 283
Wright, Lawrence, 233
Write Me a Love Song, Charlie (album), 260
Wyman, Bill, 4, 309

Yamaha, 274
    amplifiers. *See* amplifiers
    monitors. *See* monitors
Yamashta, Stomu, 264
Yardbirds, the, 107, 114, 118, 158, 231, 238
"Yellow Submarine," 4, 20

Yellow Submarine (album), 130, 232
Yellow Submarine (film), 130
Yes, 1, 107, 111, 116, 117, 118, 238, 279, 280, 284, 298, 299, 322
Yes Album, The (album), 117
You (album), 271
"You Don't Have to Say You Love Me," 71, 74
"You Really Got Me," 75, 91, 98
"You Sexy Thing," 286
Young, Geoff, 108, 118
"Young Americans," 240
"Young, Gifted and Black," 255
"Your Mother Should Know," 253
Yu, Joseph, 151, 304

Zabriskie Point (album), 117
Zimbler, Robert, 121, 122, 127, 231
Zodiac Studios, 290
Zomba Records, 250
ZTT Records, 265, 279